WITHDRAWAL

Innovations in Mobile Educational Technologies and Applications

David Parsons
Massey University, New Zealand

Managing Director:	Lindsay Johnston
Editorial Director:	Joel Gamon
Book Production Manager:	Jennifer Romanchak
Publishing Systems Analyst:	Adrienne Freeland
Development Editor:	Development Editor
Assistant Acquisitions Editor:	Kayla Wolfe
Typesetter:	Henry Ulrich
Cover Design:	Nick Newcomer

Published in the United States of America by
Information Science Reference (an imprint of IGI Global)
701 E. Chocolate Avenue
Hershey PA 17033
Tel: 717-533-8845
Fax: 717-533-8661
E-mail: cust@igi-global.com
Web site: http://www.igi-global.com

Library of Congress Cataloging-in-Publication Data

Innovations in mobile educational technologies and applications / David Parsons, editor.
     p. cm.
  Includes bibliographical references and index.
  Summary: "This book presents a collection of knowledge on the developments and approaches of mobile educational technology, bringing together points of view from both technological and pedagogical practices"--Provided by publisher.
   ISBN 978-1-4666-2139-8 (hardcover) -- ISBN 978-1-4666-2140-4 (ebook) -- ISBN 978-1-4666-2141-1 (print & perpetual access) 1. Educational technology. 2. Mobile computing. I. Parsons, David, 1959 Oct. 13-
   LB1028.3.I525 2013
   371.33--dc23
                                        2012019286

British Cataloguing in Publication Data
A Cataloguing in Publication record for this book is available from the British Library.

The views expressed in this book are those of the authors, but not necessarily of the publisher.

Table of Contents

Section 1
Mobile Learning Research Directions

Section 2
Mobile Learning Design Solutions and Theoretical Frameworks

Section 3
Mobile Learning Solution Development

Section 4
Evaluating Mobile Learning Interventions

Detailed Table of Contents

Section 1
Mobile Learning Research Directions

Mobile learning is perhaps nine or ten years old. This *thought piece,* based on my keynote at IADIS Mobile Learning 2010 in Oporto, looks back at those years to ask if we started in the right place and went in the right direction, and if we have gone as far as we can go. In earlier articles (Traxler, 2007) we have, perhaps uncritically, summarised the achievements of the mobile learning community during this time. The community has demonstrated that it can take learning to individuals, communities and countries that were previously too remote for other educational initiatives. The community has also shown that it can enhance and enrich the concept and activity of learning, beyond earlier conceptions, with learning experiences that are more personalised, authentic, situated and context-aware than ever before. The community has shown that it can challenge and extend existing theories of learning and finally the community has often made the claim that mobile learning increases motivation, especially amongst learners who would normally be considered distant, disengaged or disenfranchised. This piece in effect asks whether these achievements have been as straightforward and as unproblematic as they seemed at first sight.

In this paper, the authors present a survey of published research in mobile learning. The authors investigate 114 papers from mLearn 2005, 2007, and 2008, and classify them according to two dimensions: research method and research purpose. Research methods and purposes are important parts of how research is conducted. Opinions and approaches toward research differ greatly. The classified papers are evenly distributed among the research methods investigated, with one exception, there are few in basic research. In terms of research purpose, papers that describe research are well represented but there is a lack of papers targeting evaluation. Papers recounting both basic research and research evaluation are imperative, as they help a research field to mature and researchers to avoid repeating known pitfalls. This maturity, in turn, leads to better scalability and sustainability for future research efforts in the mobile learning community.

Chapter 3

As mobile devices become ubiquitous, it is necessary to analyze if and how these devices can be used for learning. This systematic review is part of a larger review that analyzed 21 mobile learning research studies published from 2005-present. Eleven studies that focused specifically on student learning outcomes and processes are summarized in this review in order to better understand the direction of mobile learning in mainstream education. Overall, studies were found to be positive and indicated several benefits of using mobile devices for learning including an increase in achievement, productivity, engagement, and motivation. This paper also highlights recommendations for future research and practice in the field of mobile learning, specifically focusing on the way personal mobile device ownership may influence learning both inside and outside the classroom.

Mobile learning is gaining attention in Europe. Researchers are examining both pedagogical and technical issues regarding mobilized content delivery; however, little is known about current learners' thoughts toward mobile learning. In this article, based on an empirical research study, the authors show what learners think about mobile learning and related learning technologies. Data consisting of 300 learners' thoughts and experiences in connection with mobile learning (living in five different European countries) have been gathered and analysed. Results indicate that current positive attitudes toward mobile learning may be negatively influenced by experience, if previous patterns with other learning technologies are repeated.

Section 2
Mobile Learning Design Solutions and Theoretical Frameworks

This article questions the design of mobile learning activities that lead students to spend time focusing on the mobile devices at the expense of interacting with other students or exploring the environment. This problem is approached from an interaction design perspective, designing and analysing geometry-learning activities. The authors present six guidelines for designing mobile learning activities, where mobile devices support rather than distract students from contents and contexts relevant to the learning goals. The guidelines are developed through video analysis of groups of middle school students doing learning activities outdoors and evaluated using the task model. The guidelines suggest that students (1) assume roles based on a different functionality of each device, (2) use devices as contextual tools, that the activities, (3) include physical interaction with the environment, (4) let teachers assume roles, (5) encourage face-to-face communication, and (6) introduce students to the mobile devices.

Marcus Winter, University of Brighton, UK
Lyn Pemberton, University of Brighton, UK

Recent research has identified excessive device focus as a serious problem in collaborative mobile learning as it undermines key ideas of learners engaging with their co-learners in context-rich authentic settings. Various recommendations have been formulated to address device focus in the design of mobile learning technology and pedagogy and foster students' engagement with both their peers and their environment. This paper describes how some of these recommendations have been implemented and extended in the design of Invisible Buildings, a mobile collaborative game-based activity for schoolchildren. It reports the results of an empirical evaluation of the learning experience with primary school children, focusing on students' engagement with their social and physical context during learning activities, and providing insights into their behaviour and strategies with respect to device sharing. Findings broadly confirm the effectiveness of the implemented measures and show good student acceptance of the tools employed and the overall learning experience.

Elizabeth FitzGerald, University of Nottingham, UK
Mike Sharples, University of Nottingham, UK
Robert Jones, University of Nottingham, UK
Gary Priestnall, University of Nottingham, UK

A consistent finding of research into mobile learning guides and outdoor learning games has been the valueof audio as a medium of communication. This paper discusses the value of location-based and movementsensitive audio for learning. Three types of audio learning experience are distinguished, based primarily upon differing levels of narrative cohesion: audio vignettes, movement-based guides and mobile narratives. An analysis of projects in these three areas has resulted in the formulation of guidelines for the design of audio experiences. A case study of a novel audio experience, called 'A Chaotic Encounter,' delivers an adaptive story based on the pattern of movements of the user.

Andrew Middleton, Sheffield Hallam University, UK

This paper challenges the dominant perception evident in the literature that mobile podcasting is primarily a medium for knowledge transmission. It describes why and how mobile audio learning can be facilitative, active and integrated, and how it can involve diverse voices, including those of students, in ways that usefully disrupt didactic pedagogy. Audio is described as an active learning environment, capable of supporting connectionto the real world around education in which students are able to act as autonomous learner-gatherers. The paper responds to concerns raised by Ciussi, Rosner, and Augier (2009) that some students are disinterested in podcasting and uses a scenario-based design methodology (Carroll, 2000) to describe and evaluate six innovative applications. It concludes that mobile audio can be understood as an active medium capable of richly and meaningfully engaging learners.

The advent of podcasting offers opportunities for students to learn while performing another activity. While podcasting is advocated by many as helping to learn anywhere and anytime, research indicates that it is not so easy for people to do two things at the same time. Two experiments were set up to examine the effect of performing a secondary task while learning with an iPod. In the experimental groups, the participants had to combine a learning task (listening to an educational podcast) with a secondary task (walking or jogging). The control group only had to perform a learning task. Afterwards, all the participants had to complete a learning test. In the first study, there were no significant differences between the learning performances of students of the different conditions. In the second study, the students who were sitting down outperformed the students who were moving while studying.

Chapter 10

With growing interest in mobile learning to address the educational requirements of a generation of students who have grown up with digital technology, and given the widespread adoption of mobile devices by indigenous people and in developing countries, there is a need for improved practice and better theoretical understanding of m-learning. This could be achieved through a more accessible body of knowledge of m-learning principles, teaching strategies and case-studies. This paper proposes the establishment of an online portal to influence and support good m-learning practice. An m-learning portal, incorporating a range of online, Web 2.0 and mobile technologies, would foster collaboration between researchers and educators and inform emerging national and international approaches using mobile technologies at all levels of the education sector and across all disciplines.

Section 3
Mobile Learning Solution Development

Chapter 11

Printed and digital learning materials are usually developed separately. Therefore, little notice has been given to the possibilities of combining the two. This study introduces a new concept that combines printed and digital materials. A user-centric approach was chosen to develop a "hybrid book", a combination of a traditional schoolbook and a mobile phone. Learning materials were combined into one entity by enabling access to the digital material through images in the book. The user groups of interest were 11- and 12-year-old pupils, their teachers, and parents. The concept was tested with materials for English as a foreign language (EFL). After a human-centred design process, the final application was given to one class for actual use and evaluation for a period of three weeks. Many potential benefits of using mobile phones for learning purposes were recognized, as they facilitated utilization of the digital content both inside and outside the classroom.

This research was motivated by previous work using mobile phones to support science teaching and learning in a variety of ways. This paper explores in detail how mobile phone cameras can support science teaching and learning during the planning, implementing, and evaluation stages of a lesson. A case study of a science lesson carried out in a school in Sri Lanka is described. The methodological approach of this study is qualitative and data were collected using observations, informal interviews and field notes. The results show that mobile phone cameras support the teacher in a range of ways during lesson planning, lesson implementation, and evaluating learning. Furthermore, the camera function of mobile phones was reported by teachers and students as enhancing the effectiveness of student learning, providing more opportunities for students' active participation, increasing interactions and collaborative learning opportunities.

Chapter 13

Mobile technology opens up opportunities for collaborative learning in otherwise remote contexts outside the classroom. A successful realization of these opportunities relies, however, on mobile learning activities providing adequate collaboration structures. This article presents an empirical study aimed at examining the role played by mobile devices, teachers and task structures as a means for collaborative learning in geometry. The study focused on the analysis of the nature of collaboration that unfolded when students measured areas outdoors in the field. The analysis of the mobile learning activity was conducted from an Activity theory perspective. The findings obtained indicate that the collaboration observed may be impaired if: 1) the functionalities needed for collaborative problem-solving are asymmetrically distributed on a number of mobile devices; 2) task-related information is not accessible to all learners; 3) the task structure is not sufficiently complex; 4) teacher scaffolding is too readily available; and 5) necessary collaborative skills are not developed.

Section 4
Evaluating Mobile Learning Interventions

Chapter 14

Thomas Cochrane, Unitec, New Zealand

This paper provides a comparative analysis of five mlearning case studies involving 4 years of action research mlearning projects. The projects investigated the potential of mobile web 2.0 tools to facilitate social constructivist learning environments across multiple learning contexts. Highlighted are the design framework, identified critical success factors, and implementation strategy developed from the thirteen mlearning projects undertaken between 2007 and 2009, with an analysis of the eight 2009 projects and their subsequent adaptation in 2010. The projects illustrate the impact of mlearning supported by sustained interaction via communities of practice facilitating pedagogical shifts from teacher-directed to student-generated content and student-generated contexts.

Chapter 15

Agnes Kukulska-Hulme, The Open University, UK

John Pettit, The Open University, UK

Linda Bradley, Chalmers University of Technology, Sweden

Ana A. Carvalho, University of Minho, Portugal

Anthony Herrington, Curtin University, Australia

David Kennedy, University of Hong Kong, Hong Kong

Aisha Walker, University of Leeds, UK

The paper reports on research concerned with learners' uses of mobile technologies based on an international survey that targeted students registered in selected master's and doctoral programmes in Australia, Hong Kong, Portugal, Sweden, and the United Kingdom. The survey findings were enriched by local knowledge, as the authors administered questionnaires in their own countries. The research gives an account of uses of handheld devices by students from departments of education, educational technology, engineering, and information technology in the domains of learning, work, social interaction and entertainment. The paper illuminates learners' choices in the midst of evolving social practices, and challenges the common preconception that mobile devices are not suitable for academic study. In today's global education marketplace, educators must know the technology habits and expectations of their students, including those from other countries. Knowing about students' previous practices and the techno-cultural setting they come from can help institutions determine what mobile applications are most appropriate to support learning.

Chapter 16

Susan Gwee, Nanyang Technological University, Singapore

Yam San Chee, Nanyang Technological University, Singapore

Ek Ming Tan, Nanyang Technological University, Singapore

This paper investigates whether there are gender differences in gameplay time and learning outcomes in a social studies mobile game-based curriculum. Seventeen boys and 24 girls from a ninth-grade class in Singapore used a mobile learning game Statecraft X to enact governorship in the game world. The data suggest that boys spent significantly more time playing Statecraft X than girls. However, there were no significant gender differences in their scores in an essay question assessing their learning about governorship in terms of criteria of relevance of content, perspective, and personal voice. There was also no significant correlation between gameplay time and relevance of content, perspective, and personal voice scores. Thus, higher engagement in gameplay alone does not necessarily lead to higher-order learning outcomes. This paper discusses the factors giving rise to these results.

E-learning has been promoted as a key component of improving educational access and opportunity internationally, but for disenfranchised learners, many forms of e-learning are just as alien as the educational systems they have rejected. M-learning utilises technologies, activities and social systems that are integrated into many people's lives, including those who have had limited access to, or rejected, formal education systems. This paper discusses projects conducted in Northern Australia that explored a range of e-tools to support indigenous students' engagement and recognition of their knowledge and contexts. Mobile learning tools emerged as the preferred way to learn throughout the project. This approach challenges educational institutions to connect to students' lives and contexts. This paper shows how participants utilised m-learning to demonstrate their diverse knowledge systems, the decisions they made about representing knowledge though m-learning, and the implications for trainers and assessors.

This research explores the relationship between e-learning and m-learning by investigating distance education students' use of a learning management system, "Interact," for virtual team work. The paper explores their experience of online collaborative group assignments in the subject "Information Management in Organisations." International and local students were grouped. Each group undertook a case study project to propose solutions for identified problems in their chosen organisations. Students developed their assignment in wikis and used various tools for communication and document storage. An anonymous web-based survey was conducted after students completed the group assessment. The results reflected a wide range of factors including technology use, working with students from a different country, and challenges they faced completing group assessment online. Their feedback on their e-learning experience indicated the need for m-learning to address their concerns. The findings indicate a need for m-learning to support e-learning further, which could significantly improve the facilitation of online collaborative group assignments.

Chapter 19

This paper describes an investigation which was carried out to determine if mobile learning can be used to help high school students improve their performance in mathematics. The investigation was driven by the need to develop innovative learning solutions to eradicate the problem of low pass rates in mathematics in the Caribbean. A mobile learning application called MobileMath was developed targeting a subset of the mathematics curriculum. MobileMath offers the learner different learning strategies, game-based learning, and personalization. Two of the evaluation studies conducted are described in this paper. The first study focused on students using mobile learning on their own, while the second study explored the effects of teacher support while using mobile learning. A t-test analysis shows that there was a significant improvement in performanceby students in both evaluation studies. The paper also compares the students' performance with actual usage of the mobile learning application.

Chapter 20

Claire Bradley, London Metropolitan University, UK
Debbie Holley, Anglia Ruskin University, UK

This paper reports on empirical research conducted to find out about higher education students' mobile phone ownership, and the ways in which they are using their mobiles for learning. A survey with a group of first-year students has been followed up by an in-depth study, in which three students were lent Flip Video Camcorders to capture their mobile learning activities and were interviewed to discover more about their practice. The video footage and interview data have been compiled into three rich case studies which help us to better understand students' practice and attitudes towards mobile learning. The paper focuses on the survey data and the three case studies, which were analysed using grounded theory. The outcomes of this research can inform the work of educators seeking to design effective mobile learning activities that build on existing student practice and extend mobile learning within the blend of learning activities that we offer students.

Preface

This volume draws together all the articles published by the *International Journal of Mobile and Blended Learning* in its third year of publication (2011). I very much welcome the opportunity to bring these articles to the attention of a wider audience than those who currently subscribe to the journal. Being able to bring them together into a single volume also gives me an opportunity, in this preface, to reflect on broader themes than those covered in the editorials of the individual issues, and to present a more coherent view of the current state of the art in mobile and blended learning.

During 2011, the journal made significant progress in raising its profile in the international research community. The number of indices in which it was listed increased to eleven, including Cabell's Directory and DBLP. In addition, the journal's presence was extended through more informal channels, including new dedicated pages on both Wikipedia and Facebook. The journal's relationship with the International Association for Mobile Learning (IAmLearn) also continued to develop. Forging links with relevant research forums is a fundamental part of the journal's mission and is mutually beneficial. The publication of the journal, and the series of books (this one included) that are based upon it, is about much more than just publishing a few papers. The *International Journal of Mobile and Blended Learning* is the embodiment of a global research community, strongly supported by its professional association, conference committees and contributors. Its increasing popularity and status is a reflection of the commitment and quality of that community. As you read the chapters in this book, you cannot fail to be impressed by the maturity and breadth of current mobile and blended learning research.

Central to the journal's mission of engagement with the mobile and blended learning community is an ongoing relationship with international conference events in the field. Special issues that contain the best work from these conferences are a regular (and essential) feature of the journal. Therefore the next section of this chapter reviews the main conferences that have provided much of the material for this book. This is followed by a discussion of some general concepts in design research methodologies that may help us to frame the various research themes embodied in this volume. This is followed by a brief introduction to each of the chapters, grouped into their appropriate research themes, in order to guide the reader through the remainder of this book.

MOBILE AND BLENDED LEARNING: A GLOBAL RESEARCH COMMUNITY IN MOTION

Mobile and blended learning research is truly a cosmopolitan endeavor. The main international mobile learning conferences attract contributors from all over the world, from both developed and developing countries, from across the continents, providing a rich and varied set of contexts in which mobile and blended learning are applied. This volume contains contributions from Australia, Belgium, Finland, Hong Kong, Hungary, New Zealand, Portugal, Singapore, Sri Lanka, Sweden, the United Kingdom, the United States and the West Indies. In fact in its first 3 years of publication, the journal has published work from authors in 24 different countries. This kind of mix serves to underline the international appeal of mobile and blended learning research, and gives us the opportunity to learn from differing global perspectives. As time goes on we also see increasing synergies in the research themes that appear in books, journals and conference proceedings within the field. Some of these core themes are reflected in the structure of this volume.

2011 was an unusual year for the journal in that the leading mobile learning conferences, the World Conference on Mobile and Contextual Learning (mLearn) and IADIS (International Association for Development of the Information Society) Mobile Learning, played a greater than usual role in providing the papers for the journal, with three out of four issues being special conference editions. The nature of these primary sources explains why this particular collection is primarily about research into mobile learning, rather than blended learning, though one or two chapters also encompass aspects of blended learning.

With pleasing symmetry, we began the year with a special issue from mLearn 2009, and closed it with a special issue from mLearn 2010. In addition, issue two contained revised and extended versions of the best papers from the IADIS Mobile Learning conference 2009. Given the emphasis on these conferences reflected in this book, it would seem appropriate to begin this introductory chapter with a brief retrospective on these important events in the mobile learning calendar.

THE WORLD CONFERENCE ON MOBILE AND CONTEXTUAL LEARNING (mLEARN)

The World Conference on Mobile and Contextual Learning (mLearn) is the world's longest running mobile learning conference, and is also the conference of the International Association for Mobile Learning, which was founded in 2007. The conference itself, however, has been running since 2002. mLearn is a truly global event, and past conferences have been held in Birmingham (UK), London (UK), Rome (Italy), Cape Town (South Africa), Banff (Canada), Melbourne (Australia), Telford (UK), Orlando (USA), Valetta (Malta), Beijing (China), and Helsinki (Finland). The first special edition of the *International Journal of Mobile and Blended Learning* to contain papers from mLearn was published following the 2008 conference, in its first year of publication (2009). These papers also appeared in Parsons (2011).

The 8th World Conference on Mobile and Contextual Learning, which was held in Orlando, Florida, in 2009, was a bellwether event. It marked the first time that the international mobile learning community gathered in the United States and began development of partnering opportunities that leverage the longer history of research initiatives in Europe and other geographies with the learning technologies that the U.S. has been introducing at a rapid pace. The chapters which emerged from this conference reflect on some of the key concerns of the mobile learning researchers who attended mLearn 2009. These research topics will no doubt continue to spur new ideas and new relationships that can help us advance the state of the art in mobile and blended learning. To that end several chapters stand out as extremely relevant. These include the focus of our past and future research efforts, how students across the world are using mobile devices for learning in practice, how m-learning can empower disenfranchised learners, how we can increase our levels of collaboration in mobile learning, and how experience with mobile learning may impact on learners' perceptions about its value. A common theme among these chapters is that we can, and should, learn from the past, from both our failures and our successes, in order to fully achieve the potentials of mobile learning.

The 9th World Conference on Mobile and Contextual Learning, which was held in Malta in 2010, was characterized by projects and research primarily centered on the user. In a world in which people are spending an average of 20 hours per week using digital representations of themselves (Bailenson & Blascovich, 2011) primarily networked through social connections in a web of ties, (Christakis & Fowler, 2011), mobile technology becomes the essence of communication. People want to be connected anytime, anywhere, to share their thoughts and information, in a myriad of data-exchange mechanisms and processes. Whereas a couple of decades ago, the only access to information which people had was the media, which was controlled or owned by a specific person or organization, nowadays there is an overload of information controlled by *everyone*. This information now belongs to everyone because it is a product of everyone. "Crowdsourcing," a term coined by Howe (2006), implies that everyone is now a producer and consumer of information; everyone has become a teacher and a learner in his/her own way. That is one of the primary reasons why mobile learning is such a fundamental field of study in today's changing world. The paradigm of learning has shifted and even though some categories of society might be resisting this change, the reality of today's world is that we are indeed building our own learning networks using the just-in-time approach. Learning is triggered by need in the context of our everyday life activities. The chapters here from mLearn 2010 highlight the importance of context and design vis-à-vis the user, in adapting technology to education and the learner and not vice versa. This research domain captured in the mLearn series of conferences is exciting because the ubiquity of the technology has indeed made ventures possible which a few years ago would have been considered futuristic. At this point in time, the main limitation to creating a world which presents fewer barriers to a global mobile Education system is, ultimately, our imagination.

THE IADIS MOBILE LEARNING CONFERENCE

IADIS Mobile Learning, which has been running since 2005, has a more European focus than mLearn with regard to its location, and has so far been run in Qawra (Malta), Dublin, (Ireland), Lisbon (Portugal), Algarve (Portugal), Barcelona (Spain), Porto (Portugal), Avila (Spain) and Berlin (Germany).

The chapters included here are from the second special issue of IJMBL to include revised and extended papers from this conference, the second volume having included papers from the 2009 conference (see also Parsons, 2011). The 2010 IADIS Mobile Learning Conference theme was "Mobile Learning, a Retrospective Outlook." Its aim was to provide a framework to debate, examine, and analyze the most relevant research topics in the area of mobile learning over the preceding five years with a view to providing an outlook for the research agenda and challenges for the future. In particular, among other topics, the scientific committee sought contributions which expounded and contributed to the current understanding of mobile learning in relation to: the relevance of context, location and learner mobility; the tensions between personal informal learning and traditional classroom education; the design of mobile learning activities and the integration of mobile devices in the broader educational scene; and the phenomenon of user generated content versus content delivery and its implications for learning.

The chapters in this book from the various conference proceedings do not appear here grouped based on their original publication venues. Rather, they have been re-contextualised within a broader view of the research cycle, as described in the next section.

MOBILE LEARNING RESEARCH AND SYSTEMS DESIGN METHODOLOGIES

Research is a practical activity requiring the exercise of judgement in context; it is not a matter of simply following methodological rules (Hammersley & Atkinson, 1994, p. 23).

In any edited book of research, a useful role of an editor is to try to contextualize the various contributions in terms of their research methodologies, and how they might be regarded as different perspectives on a core scholarly endeavor. All research contexts have their own favored set of methods, which together crystallize into a methodology suitable for that field of study. Some fields tend toward the quantitative and empirical, some to the qualitative and exploratory. Others are so broad that they require many different types of approach to try to explain the processes that go on within them. Of course a methodology may embrace a wide spectrum of individual research methods, and there is no right or wrong method to bring to a field of study. Nevertheless, the nature of the phenomena under investigation will tend to make us lean towards a particular set of methods that we regard as being the most suitable for revealing the realities underlying our research interests. Mobile and blended learning is in essence an interdisciplinary field, embracing theories of teaching and learning, and information systems development. In many cases, mobile learning research implies a design science process, with a development research model, since it is generally associated with the use in context of an information technology artifact. Within this process, there are many methods that may be brought to bear in identifying requirements, designing and implementing solutions and evaluating their success (or otherwise).

In order to provide some narrative structure to this book, I have categorised the various articles in an order that I feel relates to the various concerns of the mobile learning research lifecycle. Of course, as discussed above, there is no single lifecycle to research, and the field of mobile and blended learning is one that encompasses a wealth of concerns and methods, both quantitative and qualitative, empirical and interpretative. As Hammersley & Atkinson point out (1994, p. 23) "research is a practical activity requiring the exercise of judgment in context; it is not a matter of simply following methodological rules". In all the work presented here, however, there is the concept of an underlying information system applied to a learning context. This chapter therefore takes a common view of mobile leaning research models as being rooted in development research. De Villiers (2012) provides a simple model that synthesises the work of other authors (Figure 1). This conceptual model summarises the key aspects of research work that involves some kind of contextualised artefact, as mobile or blended learning applications will be. Starting with the analysis of a given problem, the model moves through a design based on a theoretical framework, and solution development, to evaluation and testing. As in the general assumptions of design research, this is an iterative cycle of analysis, reflection and refinement (Vaishnavi & Kuechler, 2007). Importantly, the outcome from such research has two products. One is the immediate solution that has been implemented. The other is the general design principles that can be derived from reflections on the research process. These distance outcomes can then inform future research efforts. Of course not all the chapters in this book directly relate to the creation and testing of a prototype solution (though many of them do). Nevertheless, each one contributes in some way to at least one part of this cycle. For example the chapters that review the literature to identify areas for future work provide us with support for the problem analysis stage. Chapters that refer to using pre-existing mobile learning tools provide us with interventions that are evaluated and tested, leading to both immediate and distance outcomes. Others focus on theoretical frameworks than can guide us in designing mobile learning solutions. All of these approaches therefore make an important contribution to the overall cycle of development research in mobile learning that we can all contribute to, and all benefit from.

The primary structuring of this chapter takes its lead from the model in Figure 1. First, there are four chapters that address mobile learning research directions (problem analysis) by looking at published research, or exploratory surveys, and identifying various themes and possible areas for further analysis. This is followed by six chapters addressing aspects of mobile learning design solutions (based on theoretical frameworks), following through the logic that once a useful area of research has been identified, then it is necessary to design a suitable activity to provide a context for evaluation. This is followed by a section on mobile learning solution development, exploring tools and infrastructure for mobile learning, containing three chapters. This sequence is based on the assumption that once a mobile learning innovation has been designed, it has to be implemented and put into practice. Finally, the book concludes with seven chapters on evaluating mobile learning interventions, covering various case studies and activities, which encapsulate aspects of evaluating mobile learning innovations (their immediate and distance outcomes). These chapters relate to aspects of mobile learning primarily from the end-users perspective, since once a mobile learning system is in place it becomes an artefact for use in the end-users context.

It is not sufficient, however, to consider the role of mobile and blended learning research models purely from a constructionist perspective. Each of our research projects takes place in a broader context that includes not only material artefacts but social structures and individual experiences. Mingers (2001), developing Habermas's theory of communicative action, described the three worlds relevant to research methods; The Material World, Our Social World and My Personal World (Figure 2). In the words of George Harrison "I'm living in the material world…met my friends all in the material world…to the

Figure 1. Development research model (from De Villiers 2012)

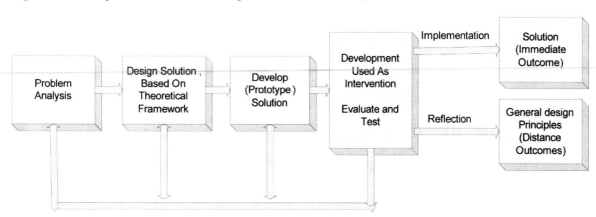

Refinement of problem solution methods

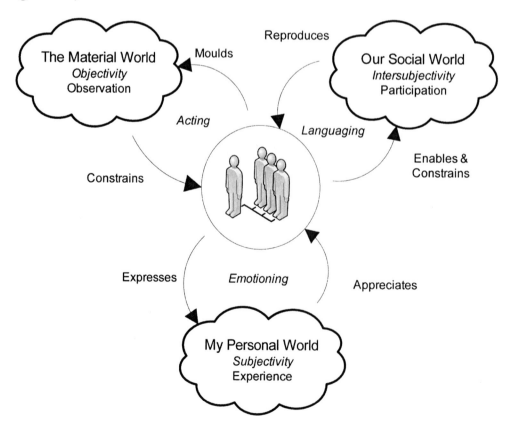

Spiritual Sky" (George Harrison – Living in the Material World (1973)). The material, the social and the personal are on a continuum.

The mobile learning researcher works in the material world. Teaching and learning are, after all, rooted in practical real world processes that involve physical locations and artefacts. In addition, however, teaching and learning are inherently social activities. Though mobile learning is sometimes characterised in a simplistic manner as *anytime anywhere* learning, with an emphasis on solitary activities like reading course material on a bus, in practice it is much more than that. Much technology enhanced learning takes place in a social world, including participation with other learners. Further, there is a personal dimension to the learning experience, where emotions have an important role to play. As you read through the chapters in this book, you will see that some chapters focus strongly on one of these three worlds, while others broadly encompass them all. Of course none of these worlds operates in isolation, so while we may, for example, focus strongly on the learner's social world (as Wallace does in her chapter on disenfranchised learners), this impacts strongly on their personal world, and the material world artefacts and environments that are being used in, and surround, the learning experience. Thus the three worlds view of research is an important reminder of the complexity, but also the richness, of working in a research field like mobile and blended learning.

Figure 2. Three worlds relevant to research methods – Developed from work by Habermas (adapted from Mingers 2001)

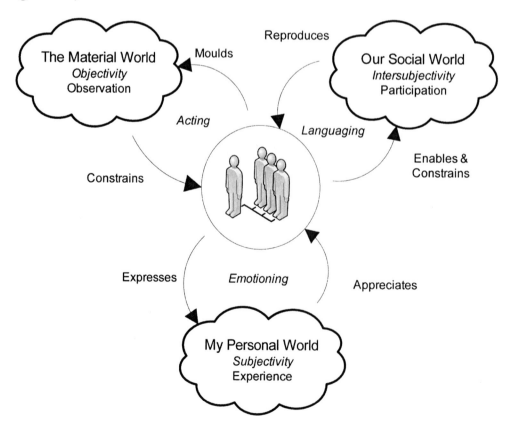

MOBILE LEARNING RESEARCH DIRECTIONS

This section of the book includes four chapters that, in various ways, consider the future direction of mobile learning research. In order to do so they begin by looking back, either in terms of reviewing the past achievements of mobile learning, by looking at past literature and identifying fruitful themes for the future, or by considering what future learners might want and need from mobile learning. The first of these chapters, John Traxler's "Mobile Learning: Starting in the Right Place, Going in the Right Direction?" looks back over the past ten years of research in the field and questions whether we started in the right place, have gone the right direction, and gone as far as we can. The retrospective journey Traxler proposes is landmarked by five achievements in mobile learning: 1. Enhancing Learning; 2. Reaching Out; 3. Theory Building; 4. Motivation; and 5. Community. His outlook is guided by four challenges: 1. Scale and Generality: Transferability and Relevance; 2. Sustainability; 3. Embedding; and 4. Evidence and Evaluation.

In "A Survey of Research Methods and Purposes in Mobile Learning," Anna Wingkvist and Morgan Ericsson provide a comprehensive survey of papers from past mLearn conferences. They conclude that we may be failing to engage enough in basic research, and also in evaluation. Such insights may help us to address this particular imbalance in the future (it should be noted that the original version of this paper won the best paper award at the conference.)

In "Mobile Technology and Student Learning: What Does Current Research Reveal?" Pamela Pollara and Kelly Kee Broussard review in detail eleven papers selected from a much broader set of candidates, in order to answer the question in their paper's title. They selected the papers for analysis by applying a set of selection criteria including recency, device type, methodology, and formal learning context. Among other things, the authors acknowledge that the United States has not in the past been a leader in mobile learning research, though of course activity in this area has increased enormously in recent years. Given the vast amount of published research, any such review must be taken within the context of its scope. The sources used were primarily the ERIC and EdLitLib (AACE) databases, with additional studies found through Google Scholar, Academia.edu, and Webfeat. A single review of this kind is, therefore, not going to provide a complete overview if taken in isolation. However the role of such reviews is to complement other perspectives such as Wingkvist and Ericsson's. Thus while these two reviews may, when viewed alone, have an individual perspective, together with others they can begin to give us an overall picture of mobile learning research, helping us to understand what we have already achieved as a research community, and where we should focus our future efforts. Pollara and Broussard conclude that "it is critical that education embraces this new technology and develops pedagogies to support and enhance learning with the use of these devices."

In their chapter "Empirical Research on Learners' Thoughts About the Impact of Mobile Technology on Learning," Gábor Kismihók and Réka Vas sound a warning based on international survey data that suggests that current positive attitudes towards mLearning may be disappointed by actual experience, if the past results of eLearning experiences are repeated (incidentally Gábor received an Honorable Mention for the Best Student Paper Award at the conference.) As mobile learning researchers and practitioners, we should take heed of this warning and ensure that we do not repeat the mistakes of the past.

These retrospective chapters provide a raft of problem analysis from past research, and together identify a number of potential challenges that researchers might choose to address.

MOBILE LEARNING DESIGN SOLUTIONS AND THEORETICAL FRAMEWORKS

According to Figure 1, the next stage after problem analysis is to design solutions based on theoretical frameworks. This section of the book comprises six chapters that provide design focused commentaries on mobile learning. Although they also to some extent embrace the subsequent phases of the development research model, they are grouped here based on their primary interest in exploring design characteristics and frameworks. Two themes in particular stand out in this section: device focus and the role of audio.

In "Mobile Devices as Support Rather than Distraction for Mobile Learners: Evaluating Guidelines for Design," Johan Eliasson, Teresa Pargman, Jalal Nouri, Daniel Spikol, and Robert Ramberg address the design of mobile learning activities that effectively encompass all three worlds of research methods, but examine in detail the social world, as students work with peers, both enabled and constrained by their learning environment. In particular, the authors question designs which lead learners to focus on mobile devices at the expense of interacting with their peers or with the outdoor environment, and which may be counterproductive when a situated learning approach is desired. The paper presents two design iterations of a geometry learning activity and their results in terms of: 1. students' visual focus on devices, and 2. heuristics for designing mobile learning activities which balance the learners focus between mobile devices and the learning tasks. The retrospective examination of mobile learning in this article illustrates the achievement in enhancing learning by leveraging the advantages of the context, peer-interaction and situated learning. The outlook is provided by the five design heuristics that can help students balance their focus between the device and the learning task.

In "Unearthing Invisible Buildings: Device Focus and Device Sharing in a Collaborative Mobile Learning Activity," Marcus Winter and Lyn Pemberton also address the issue of excessive device focus as a problem in collaborative mobile learning, which may undermine learner engagement with co-learners in context-rich authentic settings. Various recommendations have been formulated to address device focus in the design of mobile learning technology and pedagogy and foster students' engagement with both their peers and their environment. This chapter describes how some of these recommendations have been implemented and extended in the design of Invisible Buildings, a mobile augmented reality collaborative game-based activity for schoolchildren, in which mobile devices are embedded in simulated tools for investigating a buried virtual Roman villa. It reports the results of an empirical evaluation of the learning experience with primary school children, focusing on students' engagement with their social and physical context during learning activities, and providing insights into their behaviour and strategies with respect to device sharing. Findings broadly confirm the effectiveness of the implemented measures and show good student acceptance of the tools employed and the overall learning experience.

In "Guidelines for the Design of Location-Based Audio for Mobile Learning," Elizabeth FitzGerald, Mike Sharples, Robert Jones, and Gary Priestnall address the value of audio as a medium of communication. This chapter discusses three types of audio learning experience; audio vignettes, movement-based guides and mobile narratives. The authors provide some guidelines for the design of audio experiences, and provide a case study of a novel audio experience called "A Chaotic Encounter," which delivers an adaptive story based on the pattern of movements of the user. Unlike the previous chapters, this contribution focuses more on the emotioning of the individual user experience.

Like the previous chapter, Andrew Middleton's "Audio Active: Discovering Mobile Learner-Gatherers from Across the Formal-Informal Continuum" addresses the role of audio in mobile learning. His work contests the perception that podcasting is primarily a medium for knowledge transmission. His argument echoes the words of McLuhan and Fiore, in their classic 1967 text "The Medium is the Massage (sic)", that the use of this tool as an amplifier of the lecturer's voice is a way of looking "at the present through the rear-view mirror". In his chapter, Middleton presents six mobile audio learning scenarios: audio personal development planning, audio notes, previsit, field trip commentary, user voices and *pocketables*, which were elaborated during a workshop involving 70 participants at a Podcasting for Pedagogic Purposes Special Interest Group, applying a scenario-based design method. The retrospective analysis of this chapter is critical of the use of podcasting to date, contesting that teaching using recorded lectures is not an appropriate way to facilitate mobile learning. Its outlook proposes scenarios in which mobile audio should be used to involve the learners' voices to usefully disrupt didactic pedagogy. We might see this design approach as attempting to bridge the personal and social worlds of learning, to bring podcasting from only personal consumption to a shared social construction.

The next chapter in this section, "Listening to an Educational Podcast While Walking or Jogging: Can Students Really Multitask?" by Joke Coens, Ellen Degryse, Marie-Paul Senecaut, Jorge Cottyn, and Geraldine Clarebout, again looks at the role of audio. This work develops a theme explored earlier by Doolittle (2009), who described some experiments on the impact of navigational distraction when listening to podcasts while mobile. The chapter explores some wider aspects of distraction, and concludes that there can be many different factors that can impact on a student's capability for addressing two tasks simultaneously, including levels of fatigue, motivation and physical fitness. The authors conclude that "Our results so far suggest that many factors must be considered when answering the question 'Can students really multitask?'" This question has important implications for the design of mobile learning solutions, in particular from the perspective of the personal world.

Finally, in "Advancing Collaboration between M-Learning Researchers and Practitioners through an Online Portal and Web 2.0 Technologies," Laurel Evelyn Dyson and Andrew Litchfield highlight the opportunities for collaboration in mobile learning research and deployment using portal technology. They propose the design for an online knowledge base (or *mPortal*) for researchers and educators to develop and share mLearning best practices, strategies, and case studies. This work focuses very much on the social world of participation, enabling us to learn from and collaborate with each other in mobile and blended learning systems design.

MOBILE LEARNING SOLUTION DEVELOPMENT

This section leads on naturally from the previous one, and covers similar ground, but the chapters here provide more emphasis on the implementation issues of mobile learning solutions.

The first chapter in this section, "Involving the End-Users in the Development of Language Learning Material," is by Anu Seisto, Maija Federley, Timo Kuula, Janne Paavilainen, and Sami Vihavainen. In their contribution, the authors present the *Hybrid book*, which combines the traditional schoolbook and the mobile phone and provides access to digital material through images on the printed page. The article describes the design of the hybrid book through a user-centric approach involving students, their teachers, and parents. Seisto and colleagues design with the users, bearing both context and medium in mind. For example they differentiate between activities to be completed at school from those at home, and make use of audio delivered through the mobile phone. This study also presents the evaluation of an English as a Foreign Language hybrid book conducted with 25 pupils over three weeks. This chapter reflects on the need for further research into alternative formats of books, to take advantage of the new opportunities that the physical world of technology opens up to us.

"Identifying the Potential of Mobile Phone Cameras in Science Teaching and Learning: A Case Study Undertaken in Sri Lanka," by Saku Ekanayake and Jocelyn Wishart, presents a study designed to use camera phones in the three stages of a lesson: planning, implementation and evaluation; to support students' learning as well as teachers' teaching. This qualitative study examines a science lesson designed by a group of 18 teachers and implemented in a school with the direct participation of four of the 18 teacher-designers. This chapter builds on the extensive work conducted in the field on contextual, collaborative science learning which uses mobile devices to capture and transfer data. Its contribution lies in the use of camera phones throughout all the stages in science learning outlined by Shulman (1987) and by focusing on how mobile technologies also have an important role to play in supporting teaching. Thus this study enriches our understanding of how (returning to the themes in Traxler's chapter) mobile learning both enhances learning and reaches out, and also addresses the challenge of embedding mobility in learning activities.

In "Exploring the Challenges of Supporting Collaborative Mobile Learning" Jalal Nouri, Teresa Cerratto-Pargman, Johan Eliasson, and Robert Ramberg address task structure in mobile learning by analysing a collaborative activity taking place outdoors, addressing the subject of geometry. The study focuses on the nature of collaboration between students out in the field from an Activity Theory perspective. This chapter suggests that collaboration observed may be impaired by uneven distribution of functionality on different mobile devices, lack of task related information being available, or the task being too simple. Additional factors are providing too much teacher scaffolding and not specifically developing collaborative skills.

EVALUATING MOBILE LEARNING INTERVENTIONS

Perhaps unsurprisingly, this final section is the largest in the book, since it addresses the evaluation of mobile learning interventions. Of course a number of the previous chapters have also included evaluation, but the work in this section is primarily, or exclusively, about the evaluation phase of various projects, in some cases looking across multiple projects in a single chapter. In a number of cases, the learning tools being used were not created by the authors, so the focus was not on design and development, but on the evaluation of an intervention using third party tools. Some of these chapters highlight the socially constructed worlds of institution, gender and culture, while others focus on the individual experience.

The first chapter in this section is "Reflections on 4 Years of mLearning Implementation (2007-2010)" by Thomas Cochrane, which may usefully be read in the context of the author's "Transforming Pedagogy Using Mobile Web 2.0" (Cochrane & Bateman, 2009). It is good to have the opportunity to read this reflective piece of work that summarizes Cochrane's extensive activities in practical mobile learning projects over the last few years, which have covered a broad range of interventions, but consistently looking at constructivist learning. This chapter reviews the outcomes from multiple projects, and concludes that the "keys to mlearning sustainability are an institutional cultural and strategy shift as well as a lecturer and student ontological shift in relation to learning and teaching."

In "Mature Students Using Mobile Devices in Life and Learning" Agnes Kukulska-Hulme, John Pettit, Linda Bradley, Ana Carvalho, Anthony Herrington, David Kennedy, and Aisha Walker analyze the traditional boundaries between work and life as well as formal and informal learning environments and contexts. In order to assess the extent to which mobile technology has aided the goal of *anytime, anyplace* learning, thus rendering those traditional barriers less distinct, the authors polled an international sample of adult learners to determine the context and scope of actual use of personal mobile technologies as well as the social, psychological, and cultural factors that influence actual use. By giving voice to authentic experiences from learners across the globe, the authors provide some important questions from the personal world of research. One of these is whether there is the possibility that increasing use of mobile devices in universities may disadvantage some students.

In "The Role of Gender in Mobile Game-Based Learning," Susan Gwee, Yam San Chee, and Ek Ming Tan investigate whether there are gender differences in gameplay time and learning outcomes, in the context of in a social studies mobile game-based curriculum. Their research suggests that boys spend significantly more time playing such games than girls. However, there were no significant gender differences in assessment of their learning about the topic. There was also no significant correlation between gameplay time and relevance of content, perspective, and personal voice scores. The authors conclude that higher engagement in gameplay alone does not necessarily lead to higher-order learning outcomes.

In "Empowered Learner Identity through M-Learning: Representations of Disenfranchised Students' Perspectives" Ruth Wallace presents a case study on the use of mobile technologies to empower disenfranchised learners from Indigenous populations in Northern Australia. Wallace discusses how these mobile learning initiatives have been shown to engage with learners' lives and contexts. Learners responded well to the use of technology as a medium for authentic, situated digital storytelling that reflected their personal and cultural knowledge and experience. Beyond the original case study, this research has broader implications for engaging and empowering learners who exist outside the reach of mainstream formal education due to economic or cultural factors. This chapter is particularly strongly rooted in the social world of the learner.

Addressing similar themes of the learner's role in social learning, but from a perspective of learners who are often distant from each other, is Lisa Soon's chapter "E-Learning and M-Learning: Challenges and Barriers in Distance Education Group Assignment Collaboration." This chapter approaches the blending of e-learning and m-learning, and takes as its starting point some analyses of student experiences in distance education using e-learning tools, and reflects on the opportunities for overcoming some of their difficulties by using mobile technologies. The context of the study included students who were both geographically and culturally distant, with on line communication for collaborative work made more problematic by differences in time zones, as well as personal circumstances. With practical teaching issues in mind, Soon outlines a "Framework of Student Requirements in Online Group Work in Distance Education." Part of this framework is a component embodying personal and portable learning. From a practical perspective, the pervasiveness of mobile technology can perhaps provide some benefits in enabling students to communicate even when not in front of a desk top computer. In addressing the deeper concerns of intercultural communication, as also addressed by Botha et al. (2009), the potential of mobile learning tools to address Soon's concerns about "social and cultural issues associated with the use of mobile technology in learning" has been recognized. The task now is to leverage these tools to address the practical problems of international distance learning.

Vani Kalloo and Permanand Mohan's chapter "An Investigation into Mobile Learning for High School Mathematics" may be juxtaposed with Daher (2010). Both articles address the teaching of mathematics using mobile Java applications. However whereas Daher's paper focused on the learning community aspects of school students using these tools, Kalloo and Mohan focus more on measuring learning outcomes. In particular they look at the context of use of the mobile learning application, and consider the impact of teacher support in how students might benefit from mobile learning. In looking at their own research data, they conclude that "more students from the teacher supported group showed an improvement in performance. This data implies that the teacher support was a complementary component but not required in mobile learning. " A further conclusion was that the game based elements of the mobile learning application proved the most popular with students, having implications for future development of the application, with a greater focus on game based learning.

In "Empirical Research into Students' Mobile Phones and their Use for Learning," Claire Bradley and Debbie Holley research higher education students' mobile phone ownership, and the ways in which they are using their mobiles for learning. In their study, students were lent Flip Video Camcorders to capture their mobile learning activities and were interviewed to discover more about their practice. Three case studies from the work help us to better understand students' practice and attitudes towards mobile learning. The outcomes of this research can inform the work of educators seeking to design effective mobile learning activities that build on existing student practice and extend mobile learning within the blend of learning activities that we offer students.

CONCLUSION: IMMEDIATE AND DISTANCE OUTCOMES

In the framework adopted for this chapter, the gradual refinement of problem solution methods leads to both implementation and reflection, the latter leading to the distance outcomes of general design principles. Further, these principles are made manifest within the three overlapping worlds of research methods, where we observe, participate in and experience innovative and inventive new ways of learning with mobile technology.

Some distinctive themes have emerged from the contributions to this book. For example there is significant work on the nature of excessive device focus in mobile learning activities, and the various roles that audio can play in the learning experience. There is also extensive work on the impact of learners' expectations, contexts, tool use, and distribution. In many chapters the complex interplay is revealed between the material world, where learning systems are deployed, the social world in which learning takes place, which may be isolated social or distributed, and the personal world that may itself be divided in complex ways between concurrent concerns.

Many of the chapters in this book report on the immediate outcomes of specific research activities. One of the valuable roles of a collection like this is that we can bring together this rich collection of outcomes and reflect on them to consider the distance outcomes that will take us into the future of mobile and blended learning. As you read this book I therefore hope you will gain insights into your own world of knowledge and understanding that will enhance your mobile and blended learning experiences, whether that be as a designer, an implementer, an evaluator, a teacher, or a learner.

David Parsons
Massey University, New Zealand

REFERENCES

Bailenson, J., & Blascovich, J. (2011). Virtual Reality and social networks will be a powerful combination: Avatars will make social networks seductive. *IEEE Spectrum: Inside Technology*. Retrieved June 10, 2012, from http://spectrum.ieee.org/telecom/internet/virtual-reality-and-social-networks-will-be-a-powerful-combination

Botha, A., Vosloo, S., Kuner, J., & van den Berg, M. (2009). Improving cross-cultural awareness and communication through mobile technologies. *International Journal of Mobile and Blended Learning, 1*(2), 39–53.

Christakis, N., & Fowler, J. (2011). *Connected: The amazing power of social networks and how they shape our lives*. London, UK: Harper Collins.

Cochrane, T., & Bateman, R. (2009). Transforming pedagogy using mobile Web 2.0. *International Journal of Mobile and Blended Learning, 1*(4), 56–83.

Daher, W. (2010). Mathematics learning community flourishes in the cellular phone environment. *International Journal of Mobile and Blended Learning, 2*(2), 1–17.

De Villiers, M. R. (2012). Models for interpretive information system research. In More, M., Gelman, O., Steenkamp, A., & Raisinghami, L. (Eds.), *Research methodologies, innovations and philosophies in software systems engineering and information systems*. Hershey, PA: IGI Global.

Doolittle, P. (2009). iPods as mobile multimedia learning environments. In H. Ryu & D. Parsons (Eds.), *Innovative mobile learning: Techniques and technologies*. Hershey, PA: IGI Global.

Hammersley, M., & Atkinson, P. (1994). *Ethnography: Principles in practice* (2nd ed.). Routledge.

Howe, J. (2006). The rise of crowdsourcing. *WIRED Magazine, 14*. Retrieved June 10, 2012, from http://www.wired.com/wired/archive/14.06/crowds.html

McLuhan, M., & Fiore, Q. with Agel, J. (1967). *The medium is the massage: An inventory of effects*. New York, NY: Random House.

Mingers, J. (2001). Combining IS research methods: Towards a pluralist methodology. *Information Systems Research, 12*(3), 240–259.

Parsons, D. (2011). *Combining e-learning and m-learning: New applications of blended educational resources*. Hershey, PA: IGI-Global.

Shulman, L. S. (1987). Knowledge and teaching: Foundations of the new reform. *Harvard Educational Review, 57*(1), 1–22.

Vaishnavi, V., & Kuechler, W. (2007). *Design science research methods and patterns: Innovating information and communication technology*. Boston, MA: Auerbach Publications.

Acknowledgment

I am indebted to David Metcalf, Inmaculada Arnedillo-Sánchez, Matthew Montebello, Vanessa Camilleri and Alexiei Dingli, whose guest editorials for the special editions of the journal for the mLearn and IADIS Mobile Learning conferences were invaluable sources for the writing of the book's preface.

Section 1
Mobile Learning Research Directions

Chapter 1
Mobile Learning:
Starting in the Right Place, Going in the Right Direction?

John Traxler
University of Wolverhampton, UK

1. INTRODUCTION

Mobile learning is perhaps nine or ten years old. This *thought piece,* based on my keynote at IADIS Mobile Learning 2010 in Oporto, looks back at those years to ask if we started in the right place and went in the right direction, and if we have gone as far as we can go. In earlier articles (Traxler, 2007) we have, perhaps uncritically, summarised the achievements of the mobile learning community during this time. The community has demonstrated that it can take learning to individuals, communities and countries that were previously too remote for other educational initiatives. The community has also shown that it can enhance and enrich the concept and activity of learning, beyond earlier conceptions, with learning experiences that are more personalised, authentic, situated and context-aware than ever before. The community has shown that it can challenge and extend existing theories of learning and finally the community has often made the claim that mobile learning increases motivation, especially amongst learners who would normally be considered dis-

DOI: 10.4018/978-1-4666-2139-8.ch001

tant, disengaged or disenfranchised. This piece in effect asks whether these achievements have been as straightforward and as unproblematic as they seemed at first sight.

2. THE FIRST ACHIEVEMENT: ENHANCING LEARNING

The mobile learning community has demonstrated that it can enhance, extend and enrich the concept and activity of learning itself, including aspects of

- *Contingent mobile learning* and teaching, where learners can react and respond to their environment and their changing experiences, where learning and teaching are no longer *hard-wired*. Learners may, for example, gather and process fieldwork data *in situ* in real-time on geography field trips and then follow these up with further investigations based on their own hunches or curiosity. Likewise, teachers may change their teaching in response to the changing affordances of the environment and their learners, for example using pico-projectors and improvised interactive whiteboards in the field (Traxler & Griffiths, 2009) or personal response systems with groups of learners (Draper & Brown, 2004)
- *Situated learning*, where learning takes place in surroundings that make learning meaningful, for example learning religion studies whilst visiting temples, mosques, churches and synagogues, learning fish biodiversity at sea or learning language in the community (Burke, 2010; Pfeiffer, 2009, Comas-Quinn, 2009)
- *Authentic learning*, where learning tasks are meaningfully related to immediate learning goals, for example basic literacy or numeracy in work-based learning on the job, in for example hospitals or game parks

(Kneebone & Brenton, 2005; de Crom & de Jager, 2005)
- *Context-aware learning*, where learning is informed by the history, surroundings and environment of the learner, for example learning in botanical gardens, museums or heritage sights (Lonsdale et al., 2004; Brown, 2010). Until recently this has been episodic and isolated but the increased functionality of mainstream retail devices opens up enormous possibilities for developing more intelligence and using more history behind the learner experience; and *augmented reality mobile learning*, where learning builds on local context supplemented by an extra audio or video overlay (Smith, 2009)
- *Personalised learning*, where learning is customised for the preferences and abilities of individual learners or groups of learners (Kukulska-Hulme & Traxler, 2005; Yau & Joy, 2006)
- Learning based on *user-generated contexts* (Cook, 2010), a more recent concept that conflates aspects of context-aware, augmented reality and personalized mobile learning.
- *Game-based learning*, now increasingly mobile (Facer et al., 2004; Giles, 2009; Kato et al., 2008; Pulman, 2008)
- *Assessment* aligned to the affordances of mobile technologies, for example with physiotherapy students (Dearnley et al., 2008)

These achievements have usually been focused on pedagogy and technology, and have often been part of the *research economy*, that part of higher education separate from mainstream teaching and learning where researchers, developers and innovators bid for funds, implement projects, write papers and move on. Consequently, most of this research and development has been proof-of-concept, project-based, fixed-term and small-scale with little consideration of how to embed, sustain or scale up. Sometimes these achievements have been technology-driven, in the sense that specific technological innovations coming to market have been deployed in academic settings to demonstrate technical feasibility and pedagogic possibility. Sometimes, especially in the early days, they have been miniature but portable e-learning where mobile technologies have been used to re-enact approaches and solutions found in conventional e-learning, porting some e-learning technology such as an e-portfolio or a VLE onto mobile technologies (Ramsden, 2005), an understandable and cautious approach that existing e-learning players to extend their expertise and content incrementally. Sometimes they have used mobile technologies in class-room settings to support static collaborative learning perhaps connected to other classroom technologies, personal response systems and graphing calculators for example, again a technical enhancement to an existing pedagogy. Nowadays the community has a greater collective experience to build on and a clearer mobile learning identity.

There is however another perspective on the usually benign depiction of innovative mobile learning. There are several analyses that portray e-learning as a major component of the industrialization of learning (Peters & Keegan, 1994), part of the necessary industrialisation that accompanied the *massification* and *commodification* of education in the closing decades of the last century (Teichler, 1999, Wilmott, 1995). If one accepts these analyses then much of that industrialization was fairly simple Fordism, applying machines to take over the manufacturing of educational capital (Amin, 1994). This puts mobile learning within universities and perhaps colleges and schools in an uncomfortable position. Is mobile learning part of a transition from manufacturing educational capital *just-in-case* to manufacturing it *just-in-time*, a transition from simple educational production lines towards flexible manufacturing (Eaton & Schmitt, 1994), and are *user generated contexts*

merely part of the *consumerisation* of education, enabling the education system to use mass customisation (Da Silveira et al., 2001, Gilmore & Pine, 1997) to reach the *long-tail* (Brown & Adler, 2008; Brynjolfsson & Smith, 2006) of learners' preferences and needs?

3. THE SECOND ACHIEVEMENT: REACHING OUT

The mobile learning community has also demonstrated that it can take learning to individuals, communities and countries that were previously too remote or sparse, economically, socially or geographically, for other external educational initiatives to reach. This has included addressing

- *Geographical or spatial distance*, for example reaching into deeply rural areas. This is becoming educationally richer as networks drive out greater bandwidth and coverage but is however still held back by shortage of more modern handsets and support.
- *Sparsity*, connecting thinly spread and perhaps nomadic learners to create viable communities of learners, sometimes held back lack of experience in supporting communities of distance learners and sometimes by the ways that the most widespread network tariffs restrict access to services.
- *Infrastructural or technical barriers*, for example, areas of in South Asia or sub Saharan Africa, supporting those communities lacking mains electricity, secure clean buildings or land-line connectivity
- *Social exclusion*, for example reaching students unfamiliar with and lacking confidence in formal learning, for example the homeless, gypsies, marginal groups, those not-in-education-employment-or-training (NEETs) (Attewell & Savill-Smith, 2004), lower socio-cultural groups (Unterfrauner

et al., 2010), non-traditional students (Traxler & Riordan, 2004)

- *Physiological or cognitive differences*, for example supporting learning opportunities for the hearing impaired or people with dyslexia (Rainger, 2005)
- *Private learning*, for example helping chaperoned or secluded women and girls in some cultures to access informal and social learning.
- *Dead-time*, small bursts of otherwise unused time, such as waiting in lifts, cafes, buses, queues, sometimes used as an example of 'bite-sized' learning. Although possibly educationally limited, mobile phones will always be carried by learners whereas books or laptops might not be. Podcasts (Dale, 2007; Gorra et al., 2009) have similar affordances.
- *Work-based learning* and mobile training/performance support (Nikoi, 2007) where the technologies used to improve the flexibility, responsiveness, productivity and efficiency of mobile workers by delivering information and support just-in-time and in context for their immediate priorities, sometimes also used to improve supervision or oversight, for example first-response paramedics or roving repair and maintenance personnel (Gayeski, 2002). The perceptions of extending the working day, of deskilling and of surveillance are significant issues. (Attwell & Costa, 2008)
- *Mobile content*, specifically m-libraries, (Needham & Ally, 2008) has, like work-based mobile learning and games-based mobile learning, been a recent addition to mainstream mobile learning.

This is of course essentially a deficit model. Mobile technologies and mobile learning are used to address perceived deficiencies in other delivery mechanisms. Implicitly the mobile technologies are treated as just dumb conduits and dumb receptacles through which learning is stored and transported. Technology however always has some ideology and thus pedagogy embedded in it; there is not a neutral technology (Bates, 1995; Roberts, 2002; Ananny & Winters, 2007). This includes mobile technologies. These technologies insert the pedagogies of *outsiders* into communities and cultures that of course already have their own learning. This may however be the learning of a culture that is fragile in the face of technology enhanced learning from the outside. This is true of geographically remote, sparse or nomadic communities in the developing world but it may also be true of gypsy communities, ethnic minorities and other marginal groups in our own societies.

One example, from rural Kenya, shows the contrast between a mobile learning system based on social constructivism (Traxler, 2007b) and the local pedagogy, dubbed *instructivist*, actually enacted in class-room practice (Pontefract & Hardman, 2005).

Implicit in much of this activity has been the notion that mobile technologies and mobile learning can reduce *digital divides*. This is an interesting and important but problematic proposition for several reasons (Traxler, 2008). The phrase *digital divide* refers to the access, ownership and distribution of ICT technologies and devices. It is however not a monolithic and undifferentiated concept. The very different properties and affordances and the very different distribution of different ICTs means it can only be a simplification. The distribution, ownership and access of some ICTs, such as plasma screens, TV or PC, are not even similar to those of others, such as mobile phones or games consoles. The same is true of software technologies such large-scale databases and of infrastructure such as bandwidth, mobile apps and *cloud computing*. In the case of learning technologies, there is an additional divide, that between individuals and communities on the one hand and institutions and organisations on the other. So unlike any other ICT, mobile technology does not repeat, reinforce or replicate existing digital divides.

There is however not a straightforward relationship. Whilst mobile phones offer institutions and governments the means to deliver learning and attack digital divides in ways that different from other ICTs, they do so under changed conditions. Mobile phones give learners ownership, agency and control of their learning in ways that PCs and plasma screens do not and are a rather different instrument of social policy.

Furthermore, with mobile devices, learners no longer need to engage with information and discussion at the expense of *real life* as they would with most other ICTs but can do so as part of *real life* as they move about the world, using their own personal devices to connect them to other people and ideas of their own choosing, perhaps using their own devices to generate and produce content and conversation as well as store and consume them. This must be changing how people relate to technology and learning, and to the institutions and governments that control them. The personal, cultural, and social implications of this hinge on the essential difference between desktop ICTs and mobile technologies. Interacting with other ICTs takes place in a bubble, in dedicated times and places where the learner has their back to the rest of the world for a substantial and a probably premeditated episode. Interacting with mobile technologies is different and woven into all the times and places of learners' lives.

There is however also a risk that mobile technologies used to deliver learning act as either Trojan horses or *cargo cults* (Lindstrom, 1993; Worsley, 1957), either vehicles for some extra and unwelcome cultural or social baggage or conversely empty vessels laden only with extra and inappropriate expectations. This is true of any technology enhanced learning. What makes mobile learning more potent and more worrying than desktop e-learning tethered within buildings and institutions is the extent to which mobile technologies pervade so much of so many societies, a kind of educational fifth column in our midst?

4. THE THIRD ACHIEVEMENT: THEORY BUILDING

The mobile learning research community has also challenged and extended theories of learning in extensions to Laurillard's (2007) own 'conversational framework' and engaged with wider theories, 'activity theory' (Engestrom, 1987) and 'wildfire learning' (Engestrom, 2009), and Beddall-Hill and Raper (2010) engaging with 'actor network theory'. There have also been significant achievements in developing theories of mobile learning native to the mobile learning research community itself (Sharples et al., 2007)

These advances cannot however be seen in isolation. One factor is of course that much mobile learning research and development has an historical relationship to e-learning, to the perceived agenda, achievements, direction, inadequacies and failings of e-learning (Holmes & Gardner, 2006), and so draws on a similar ancestry in psychology, perhaps cognitive psychology, in computing, perhaps artificial intelligence, and in education, usually in schools. This delineates in advance the likely look-and-feel of much mobile learning theory and mobile learning research. There is now a greater but not systematic engagement with social sciences, for example in the work of the London Mobile Learning Group (Bachmair et al., 2009; Pachler, 2010). Other disciplines, information systems, development studies or anthropology perhaps, might also have contributions to make and these too would enrich theory building within the mobile learning research community.

Looking at the activities of the community other issues become apparent.

An informal panel took place at mLearn2009 in Orlando, Florida, that tried to tease out different regional conceptions of mobile learning around the world, ranging, at the risk of caricature, from informal contextual mobile learning in Europe to *drill-and-kill* corporate and military mobile training in America to mobile service delivery in Southern Africa. This reveals the breadth of the community in terms of its definitions of itself. On the other hand the activities for example of the distance education community (see for example, Distance Education, Volume 31, Issue 2 August 2010) reveal how much mobile learning may be taking place elsewhere unacknowledged. It is also now likely that much practitioner activity takes place un-documented and is only informally or locally evaluated. There also seems to be a growing lack of communication and connection between the practitioner community, and the policy and vendor communities, and the research community; developments in practice are increasingly driven by public understanding and policy-maker understanding of the affordances of the technologies rather than the evidence of educational researchers.

This begs questions about whether theory building should be *top-down*, based on axioms and truths from *pure* science, or *bottom-up*, looking across instances and evidence from practice. There have been several attempts at the latter (Frohberg et al., 2009) but they always raise methodological problems, principally the risks of being circular and self-referential.

Something else that must be factored implicitly into theory building is motivation. Does mobile learning research generate knowledge for knowledge's sake or, like parts of the ICTD community, does it have an explicitly pro-poor agenda (Heeks, 2008). To put it another way, is mobile learning research like astronomical research or medical research? Are there consequences in terms of defining the mobile learning research agenda and building mobile learning theories?

5. THE FOURTH ACHIEVEMENT: MOTIVATION

A further claim is made, most often in funding proposals, that learning with mobile devices increases learners' enthusiasm and motivation (there is considerable impressionistic *soft* evidence for this claim) and consequently retention and pro-gression, key educational performance indicators, are improved (a very dubious proposition, that assumes motivation is a key determinant of attendance). There are however also some remarks in research literature (Jones et al., 2007). This is probably something everyone in the mobile learning community would like to believe but is unlikely to be a universal truth; it is more likely to be a myth that has flourish in the spaces would there should have been evidence.

6. THE FIFTH ACHIEVEMENT: COMMUNITY

Finally we ought to recognise that there are now several substantial national programmes and initiatives, and that the community now supports an international professional association, several peer-reviewed academic journals and a range of national and international conferences, ranging from those for practitioners and policy-makers to those for researchers.

Since 2001, mobile learning has matured and consolidated. The community now has a peer-reviewed academic journal, the International Journal of Mobile and Blended Learning (http://igi-global.com/ijmbl) and a professional research body, the International Association for Mobile Learning http://www.iamlearn.org/). It also has several prestigious international conferences such as IADIS Mobile Learning and mLearn (Traxler et al., 2008). There are some key emerging working texts (Kukulska-Hulme & Traxler, 2005; Metcalf, 2006; JISC, 2005, Ally 2009; Herrington et al., 2009) and emerging guidelines for practitioners (Vavoula et al., 2004). Mobile learning has gained clarity about the significant issues (Sharples, 2006), a more sharply defined research agenda (Arnedillo-Sánchez et al., 2007) and an awareness of the need for ethical guidelines and frameworks (Lally et al., 2010; Traxler & Bridges, 2004). Within the UK specifically, there has been considerable public sector investment, £4m - £5m per annum for three years to date in the vocational sector in the MoLeNET programme (Attewell et al., 2010) for example, and large-scale projects in the primary schools of Bristol and Wolverhampton (http://www.learning2go.org/).

7. THE CHALLENGES

There are a variety of challenges still to be addressed. These are mostly in the periphery of the community, understandably beyond the core of technology and pedagogy, especially when one considers the genesis of much mobile learning in pilots and trials. These challenges include:

7.1. Scale and Generality: Transferability and Relevance

The community is still a long way from developing an understanding of how specific successful pilots, projects and trials can be scaled up, partly because it is never clear characteristics were responsible for that success and which were merely coincidental, local or contingent. A similar problem applies to replicating a success. Understanding how to abstract or generalise is a challenge across social interventions (Lee & Baskerville, 2003). Part of the problem may occur at the project design phase when decisions about where to site interventions or how to samples from them may not have led to optimal results; there are always pay-offs between possible generality (getting a result with the widest relevance) and specificity (getting a result that is as trustworthy as possible).

7.2. Sustainability

The sustainability of pilots and trials is their capacity to reach balance between costs on the one hand and building human, economic and social capital on the other. In countries of *big* government, such as UK, Singapore or Sweden, there is an assumption that evidence impacts and influences policy and that this then unlocks public funds. This places the onus of researchers, developers and innovators to think very carefully about evaluation and dissemination. In other countries, those of *small* government and those of bad government, the sustainability of pilots and trials depends on some complex but haphazard interplay between free markets, public bodies and social enterprises. In South Africa, often the test bed for these issues, the Meraka Institute is exploring 'Living Labs', such as the one at Sekhukhune (Schaffers et al., 2007), to develop suitable strategies that will take innovations in technology enhanced learning from the controlled environment of the school into the uncontrolled environment of the community.

In many parts of the *developing* world however, national educational priorities are quite stark, concentrating on child literacy, primary teacher training and little else. Project proposals do not always have an exit strategy or a convincing business model, and researchers and innovators may in any case not be the best people to develop them.

7.3. Embedding

The integration of mobile learning with other technology enhanced learning systems and with institutional and organisational processes has not been a high priority. Much of the focus of mobile learning has been outside formal learning anyway. Funders, researchers and developers have often prioritised the project, the innovation and the external audience rather than the environment of the host institution and the internal audience. There are also perhaps cultural and psychological differences between innovators at the edge of institutions and mainstream teachers, regulators and administrators at the core of institutions - Rogers 2003 is the obvious starting point for any investigation of innovation, personality and organisations.

7.4. Evidence and Evaluation

The mobile learning community needs to demonstrate greater relevance, significance and impact. Sadly, researchers and developers have not always had the time, resources and expertise (Traxler & Kukulska-Hulme, 2006) to generate rigorous, credible and appropriate evidence. The evaluation of mobile learning has been inherently more challenging than the evaluation of e-learning because the context and the environment act as confounding variables, attenuating the signal-to-noise ratio, whilst methods are potentially epistemologically inappropriate (Buscher & Urry, 2009). The 'Hawthorne effect' is undoubtedly often at work (Mayo, 1933) in pilots and trials managed by visionaries and innovators whilst short-term projects do not always have time for technology to stabilise and novelty to wear off. Evaluations can focus inappropriately on 'hard' objective outcomes (Dewson et al., 2002) because of the political climate in which funding bodies operate. Furthermore projects, for ease of experimental design and deployment, have until recently invariably used project devices not learner devices. Outcomes may be good but not transferable to any financially sustainable model based on learner devices. Fixed-term projects are also likely to employ enthusiastic innovative teaching staff alongside, not within, the compulsory curriculum, specifically the assessed curriculum, thus undermining the credibility or transferability of outcomes to the core curriculum with mainstream teachers.

8. THE WIDER CHALLENGES

The development of mobile learning has often been driven by pedagogic necessity, technological innovation, funding opportunity; it has come out of particular regions, institutions and disciplines, and sometimes out of the perceived inadequacies of conventional e-learning. These historical factors have shaped mobile learning but they have limited it and now challenge it too.

Mobile learning can be characterised as a specific enterprise within education systems. Mobile devices are near-universal and their impact brings near-universal connectedness to people, data, content and media. There are subtle but pervasive transformations of jobs, work and the economy, of our sense of time, space and place, of ethics and politics, of knowing and learning, and of community and identity. Finally, there is the possibility that these transformations challenge education systems and hence challenge mobile learning.

REFERENCES

Ally, M. (2009). *Mobile learning: Transforming the delivery of education and training.* Athabasca, AB, Canada: Athabasca University Press.

Amin, A. (1994). Models, fantasies and phantoms of transition. *Post-Fordism. Reading (Sunderland)*, 1–39.

Ananny, M., & Winters, N. (2007). Designing for development: Understanding the one laptop per child in its historical context. In *Proceedings of the IEEE/ACM International Conference on Information and Communication Technologies and Development*, Bangalore, India (pp. 1-12).

Arnedillo-Sánchez, I., Sharples, M., & Vavoula, G. (Eds.). (2007). *Beyond mobile learning workshop.* Dublin, Ireland: Trinity College Dublin Press.

Attewell, J., & Savill-Smith, C. (2004). *Learning with mobile devices.* London, UK: LSN.

Attewell, J., Savill-Smith, C., Douch, R., & Parker, P. (2010). *Modernising education and training - mobilising technology for learning.* London, UK: LSN.

Attwell, G., & Costa, C. (2008). *Integrating personal learning and working environments.* Retrieved from http://www.pontydysgu.org/wp-content/uploads/2008/11/workandlearning.pdf

Bachmair, B., Pachler, N., & Cook, J. (2009). Mobile phones as cultural resources for learning – an analysis of mobile expertise, structures and emerging cultural practices. *MedienPädagogik, 29,* 1–29.

Bates, A. W. (1995). *Technology, open learning and distance education: Routledge studies in distance education.* London, UK: Routledge.

Beddall-Hill, N., & Raper, J. (2010). Mobile devices as 'boundary objects' on field trips. *Journal of the Research Center for Educational Technology, 6*(1).

Brown, E. (Ed.). (2010). Education in the wild: Contextual and location-based mobile learning in action. In F. Fischer, L. Hofmann, & S. Schulz (Eds.), *D3.1: A report from the STELLAR Alpine Rendez-Vous workshop series.* Nottingham, UK: University of Nottingham.

Brown, J. S., & Adler, R. P. (2008). Minds on fire: Open education, the long tail, and learning 2.0. *EDUCAUSE Review, 43*(1), 16.

Brown, T. H. (2005). Beyond constructivism: Exploring future learning paradigms. *Education Today, 2.*

Brynjolfsson, E., Hu, Y., & Smith, M. D. (2006). From niches to riches: Anatomy of the long tail. *Sloan Management Review, 47*(4).

Burke, D. (2010). Using mobile devices to enhance fieldwork. In Law, P., & Wankel, C. (Eds.), *Streaming media in higher education.* London, UK: Streaming Media.

Buscher, M., & Urry, J. (2009). Mobile methods and the empirical. *European Journal of Social Theory, 12*(1), 99–116. doi:10.1177/1368431008099642

Comas-Quinn, A., Mardomingo, R., & Valentine, C. (2009). Mobile blogs in language learning: Making the most of informal and situated learning opportunities. *ReCALL, 21*(1), 96–112. doi:10.1017/S0958344009000032

Cook, J. (2010). Mobile phones as mediating tools within augmented contexts for development. *International Journal of Mobile and Blended Learning, 2*(3), 1–12. doi:10.4018/jmbl.2010070101

Da Silveira, G., Borenstein, D., & Fogliatto, F. S. (2001). Mass customization: Literature review and research directions. *International Journal of Production Economics, 72*(1), 1–13. doi:10.1016/S0925-5273(00)00079-7

Dale, C. (2007). Strategies for using podcasting to support student learning. *Journal of Hospitality, Leisure, Sport and Tourism Education, 6,* 49–57. doi:10.3794/johlste.61.155

de Crom, E. P., & de Jager, A. (2005). The "ME"-learning experience: PDA technology and e-learning in ecotourism at the Tshwane University of Technology (TUT). In *Proceedings of the MLEARN Conference,* Cape Town, South Africa.

Dearnley, C. J., Haigh, J., & Fairhall, J. (2008). Using mobile technologies for assessment and learning in practice settings: A case study. *Nurse Education in Practice, 8*(3), 197–204. doi:10.1016/j.nepr.2007.07.003

Dewson, S., Eccles, J., Tackey, N. D., & Jackson, A. (2002). *Measuring soft outcomes and distance travelled: A review of current practice.* London, UK: Department for Business Innovation & Skills.

Draper, S. W., & Brown, M. I. (2004). Increasing interactivity in lectures using an electronic voting system. *Journal of Computer Assisted Learning, 20*(2), 81–94. doi:10.1111/j.1365-2729.2004.00074.x

Eaton, B. C., & Schmitt, N. (1994). Flexible manufacturing and market structure. *The American Economic Review, 84*(4), 875–888.

Engeström, Y. (1987). *Learning by expanding: An activity-theoretical approach to developmental research.* Helsinki: Orienta-Konsultit.

Engeström, Y. (2009). Wildfire activities: New patterns of mobility and learning. *International Journal of Mobile and Blended Learning, 1*(2). doi:10.4018/jmbl.2009040101

Facer, K., Joiner, R., Stanton, D., Reidt, J., Hull, R., & Kirk, D. (2004). Savannah: Mobile gaming and learning? *Journal of Computer Assisted Learning, 20,* 399–409. doi:10.1111/j.1365-2729.2004.00105.x

Frohberg, D., Göth, C., & Schwabe, G. (2009). Mobile learning projects – a critical analysis of the state of the art. *Journal of Computer Assisted Learning, 25*(4), 307–331. doi:10.1111/j.1365-2729.2009.00315.x

Gayeski, D. (2002). *Learning unplugged - using mobile technologies for organizational and performance improvement.* New York, NY: American Management Association.

Giles, J. (2009). *Physios recommend a healthy dose of gaming.* Retrieved from http://www.new-scientist.com/article/mg20227145.700-physios-recommend-a-healthy-dose-of-gaming.html

Gilmore, J. H., & Pine, B. J. (1997). The four faces of mass customization. *Harvard Business Review, 75*(1), 91.

Gorra, A., Sheridan-Ross, J., & Finlay, J. (2009, April 22-24). Podcasting - an evaluation of two case studies from the UK. In *Proceedings of the 5th International Conference on Multimedia and Information and Communication Technologies in Education,* Lisbon, Portugal.

Heeks, R. (2008). ICT4D 2.0: The next phase of applying ICT for international development. *Computer, 41*(6), 26–33. doi:10.1109/MC.2008.192

Herrington, J., Herrington, A., Mantei, J., Olney, I. W., & Ferry, B. (2009). *New technologies, new pedagogies: Mobile learning in higher education.* Retrieved from http://ro.uow.edu.au/edupapers/91

Holmes, B., & Gardner, J. (2006). *e-Learning: Concepts and practice* (pp. 35-42). London, UK: Sage.

JISC. (2005). *Innovative practice with e-learning: A good practice guide to embedding mobile and wireless technologies into everyday practice.* Bristol, UK: Joint Information Services Committee.

Jones, A., Issroff, K., & Scanlon, E. (2007). Affective factors in learning with mobile devices. In Sharples, M. (Ed.), *Big issues in mobile learning* (pp. 17–22). Nottingham, UK: University of Nottingham.

Kato, P. M., Cole, S. W., Bradlyn, A. S., & Pollock, B. H. (2008). A video game improves behavioral outcomes in adolescents and young adults with cancer: A randomized trial. *Pediatrics, 122*(2), 305–317. doi:10.1542/peds.2007-3134

Kneebone, R., & Brenton, H. (2005). Training perioperative specialist practitioners. In Kukulska-Hulme, A., & Traxler, J. (Eds.), *Mobile learning: A handbook for educators and trainers.* London, UK: Routledge.

Kukulska-Hulme, A., & Traxler, J. (2005, April). Making the case for personalization through mobile learning. In *Proceedings of CAL,* Bristol, UK.

Kukulska-Hulme, A., & Traxler, J. (2005). *Mobile learning: A handbook for educators and trainers.* London, UK: Routledge.

Lally, V., Sharples, M., Bertram, N., Masters, S., Norton, B., & Tracy, F. (2010). *Researching the ethical dimensions of mobile, ubiquitous, and immersive technology enhanced learning (MUI-TEL) in informal settings: A thematic review and dialogue*. London, UK: University of Glasgow.

Laurillard, D. (2007). Pedagogic forms of mobile learning: Framing research questions. In Pachler, N. (Ed.), *Mobile learning - towards a research agenda* (pp. 153–177). London, UK: Institute of Education.

Lee, A. S., & Baskerville, R. L. (2003). Generalizing generalizability in information systems research. *Information Systems Research, 14*(3), 221–243. doi:10.1287/isre.14.3.221.16560

Lindstrom, L. (1953). *Cargo cult: Strange stories of desire from Melanesia and beyond*. Honolulu, HI: University of Hawaii Press.

Lonsdale, P., Barber, C., Sharples, M., Byrne, W., Arvanitis, T., Brundell, P., et al. (2004). Context awareness for mobilearn: Creating an engaging learning experience in an art museum. In *Proceedings of the World Conference on Mobile Learning*, Rome, Italy.

Mayo, E. (1933). *The human problems of an industrial civilization*. New York, NY: Macmillan.

Metcalf, D. S. (2006). *mLearning: Mobile learning and performance in the palm of your hand*. Amherst, MA: HRD Press.

Needham, G., & Ally, M. (Eds.). (2008). *M-libraries: Libraries on the move to provide virtual access*. London, UK: Facet Books.

Nikoi, S. (2007). *Literature review on work-based mobile learning*. Retrieved from http://wolf.lec.ac.uk/file.php/1/Literature_Reviews/LITERATURE_REVIEW_ON_WORKBASED_MOBIL_LEARNING_1.pdf

Pachler, N. (2010). The socio-cultural ecological approach to mobile learning: An overview. In Bachmair, B. (Ed.), *Medienbildung in neuen Kulturräumen: Die deutschsprachige und britische Diskussion* (pp. 155–169). Wiesbaden, Germany: VS Verlag für Sozialwissenschaften.

Peters, O., & Keegan, D. (1994). *Otto Peters on distance education: The industrialization of teaching and learning*. London, UK: Routledge.

Pfeiffer, V. D. I., Gemballa, S., Jarodzka, H., Scheiter, K., & Gerjets, P. (2009). Situated learning in the mobile age: Mobile devices on a field trip to the sea. *International Journal of Research in Learning Technology, 17*(3), 187–199. doi:10.1080/09687760903247666

Pontefract, C., & Hardman, F. (2005). The discourse of classroom interaction in Kenyan primary schools. *Comparative Education, 41*(1), 87–106. doi:10.1080/03050060500073264

Pulman, A. (2008). *Mobile assistance – the Nintendo DS Lite as an assistive tool for health and social care students*. Retrieved from http://www.swap.ac.uk/docs/casestudies/pulman.pdf Rainger, P. (2005). Accessibility and mobile learning. In A. Kukulska-Hulme & J. Traxler (Eds.), *Mobile learning: A handbook for educators and trainers*. London, UK: Routledge.

Ramsden, A. (2005). Evaluating a PDA for delivering VLE functionality. In Kukulska-Hulme, A., & Traxler, J. (Eds.), *Mobile learning: A handbook for educators and trainers*. London, UK: Routledge.

Roberts, G. (2002, March 26-28). Complexity, uncertainty and autonomy: The politics of networked learning. In *Proceedings of the 3rd International Conference on Networked Learning*, Sheffield, UK.

Rogers, E. (2003). *Diffusion of innovations*. New York, NY: Free Press.

Schaffers, H., Cordoba, M. G., Hongisto, P., Kallai, T., Merz, C., & van Rensburg, J. (2007). Exploring business models for open innovation in rural living labs. In *Proceedings of the 13th International Conference on Concurrent Enterprising* (pp. 49-56).

Sharples, M. (Ed.). (2006). *Big issues in mobile learning*. Nottingham, UK: Kaleidoscope Network of Excellence.

Sharples, M., Taylor, J., & Vavoula, G. (2007). A theory of learning for the mobile age. In Andrews, R., & Haythornthwaite, C. (Eds.), *The Sage handbook of e-learning research* (pp. 221–247). London, UK: Sage.

Smith, C. (2009). *The unit of construction + the multiple point of view = the evolution of form: Electronic visualisation and the arts*. London, UK: British Computer Society.

Teichler, U. (1999). Massification: A challenge for institutions of higher education. *Tertiary Education and Management, 4*(1).

Traxler, J. (2007a). Defining, discussing and evaluating mobile education. *International Review of Research in Open and Distance Learning, 8*(2).

Traxler, J. (2007b). IS4DEV – IS development & development issues. In Barry, C., Lang, M., Wojtkowski, W., Wojtkowski, G., Wrycza, S., & Zupancic, J. (Eds.), *The inter-networked world: ISD theory, practice, and education*. New York, NY: Springer.

Traxler, J. (2008) Mobility, modernity, development. In *Proceedings of the 1ˢᵗ International Conference on M4D Mobile Communication for Development*, Karlstadt, Germany.

Traxler, J. (2008). Modernity, mobility and the digital divides. In *Proceedings of the International Conference on Research in Learning Technology*.

Traxler, J. (2009). Mobile learning evaluation: The challenge of mobile societies. In Vavoula, G., Pachler, N., & Kukulska-Hulme, A. (Eds.), *Researching mobile learning: Frameworks, methods and research designs* (pp. 151–165). London, UK: Peter Lang.

Traxler, J. (2010, June 21-22). Mobile people, mobile societies, mobile cultures not just mobile learning. In *Proceedings of the ICA Mobiles Preconference*, Singapore.

Traxler, J. (2010). Students and mobile devices. *International Journal of Research in Learning Technology*.

Traxler, J. (2010). Sustaining mobile learning and its institutions. *International Journal of Mobile and Blended Learning, 2*(4), 129–138. doi:10.4018/jmbl.2010100105

Traxler, J., & Bridges, N. (2004, June). Mobile learning—the ethical and legal challenges. In *Proceedings of the MLEARN Conference on Mobile Learning Anytime Everywhere*, Bracciano, Italy (pp. 203-208).

Traxler, J., & Griffiths, L. (2009). IWB4D – interactive whiteboards for development. In *Proceedings of the International Conference on Information and Communication Technologies and Development*, Doha, Qatar (p. 488).

Traxler, J., & Kukulska-Hulme, A. (2006). The evaluation of next generation learning technologies: The case of mobile learning. In *Proceedings of the International Conference on Research in Learning Technology*, Oxford, UK.

Traxler, J., & Riordan, B. (2004). Using PDAs to support computing students. In *Proceedings of the Annual ICS Subject Centre Conference*, Belfast, UK.

Traxler, J., Riordan, B., & Dennett, C. (2008). The bridge from text to context. In *Proceedings of the MLEARN Conference*, Wolverhampton, UK.

Unterfrauner, E., Marschalek, I., & Fabian, C. (2010). Mobile learning with marginalized young people. In *Proceedings of the IADIS International Conference on Mobile Learning* (pp. 28-35).

Vavoula, G. N., Lefrere, P., O'Malley, C., Sharples, M., & Taylor, J. (2004). Producing guidelines for learning, teaching and tutoring in a mobile environment. In *Proceedings of the 2nd IEEE International Workshop on Wireless and Mobile Technologies in Education* (pp. 173-176).

Willmott, H. (1995). Managing the academics: Commodification and control in the development of university education in the UK. *Human Relations*, *48*(9), 993–1028. doi:10.1177/001872679504800902

Worsley, P. (1957). *The trumpet shall sound: A study of "cargo" cults in Melanesia*. London, UK: MacGibbon & Kee.

Yau, J., & Joy, M. (2006). Context-aware and adaptive learning schedule for mobile learning. In *Proceedings of the International Workshop on Mobile and Ubiquitous Learning and the International Conference on Computers in Education* (p. 31).

This work was previously published in the International Journal of Mobile and Blended Learning, Volume 3, Issue 2, edited by David Parsons, pp 57-67, copyright 2011 by IGI Publishing (an imprint of IGI Global).

Chapter 2
A Survey of Research Methods and Purposes in Mobile Learning

Anna Wingkvist
Linnaeus University, Sweden

Morgan Ericsson
Uppsala University, Sweden

ABSTRACT

In this paper, the authors present a survey of published research in mobile learning. The authors investigate 114 papers from mLearn 2005, 2007, and 2008, and classify them according to two dimensions: research method and research purpose. Research methods and purposes are important parts of how research is conducted. Opinions and approaches toward research differ greatly. The classified papers are evenly distributed among the research methods investigated, with one exception, there are few in basic research. In terms of research purpose, papers that describe research are well represented but there is a lack of papers targeting evaluation. Papers recounting both basic research and research evaluation are imperative, as they help a research field to mature and researchers to avoid repeating known pitfalls. This maturity, in turn, leads to better scalability and sustainability for future research efforts in the mobile learning community.

INTRODUCTION

Naismith et al., (2004) defines mobile learning as mobile technology that supports learning across locations, or learning that takes advantage of the opportunities offered by portable technologies.

There has been a rapid growth in research, development, and deployment of mobile learning in recent years (Taylor et al., 2006). According to Kukulska-Hulme et al., (2009), this rapid growth has led to a number of significant activities in schools, workplaces, museums, cities, and rural

DOI: 10.4018/978-1-4666-2139-8.ch002

areas around the world. There are, however, a number of issues identified that need further attention (Sharples et al., 2008). Research conducted into mobile learning is often small-scale and has seldom been developed into learning aids that are in wide use; hence we are faced with limitations of both scale and sustainability (Keegan, 2005). The field is compelled to evolve and find common ground in order to develop comprehensive principles and realistic visions, moving beyond specific implementations and branded technologies (Cobcroft et al., 2006). In addition, Traxler and Kukulska-Hulme (2005) conclude that few previous studies have been based on sound theory.

Mobile learning is still considered a young research field. The first research publications appeared in the late 1990s and the first international conference, the World Conference on Mobile Learning (shortened to 'mLearn'), was held in 2001. Vavoula and Sharples (2009) state that many of the influences on mobile learning research, and in turn frameworks, methods, and tools, have been borrowed from other research fields such as Technology-Enhanced Learning and Mobile Human-Computer Interaction. Influences from research fields such as Computer Supported Collaborative Work and E-learning can also be seen. Many researchers active in the field of mobile learning have backgrounds in Computer Science, Information Systems, and Media Technology. The body of researchers includes both academics and professionals (e.g., educators and software developers.)

A young research field is often highly opportunistic and technology driven. A primary focus is set on producing solutions and less attention is given to research methods and the execution of the scientific process. As mobile learning matures it is necessary to examine how this line of research is being conducted. At the same time we need to understand the impact of the technology and comprehend the knowledge that is produced. This introduces challenges to all aspects of mobile learning research. Vavoula and Sharples (2009)

state that as the understanding of mobile learning deepens, the "borrowed" frameworks, methods, and tools might no longer be adequate and need to be processed and evolved. They in turn propose a framework built on holistic and systematic evaluation divided into three levels of granularity (micro, meso, and macro) to guide data collection. Vavoula and Sharples (2009) also note that mixed methods are increasingly present in the design of evaluation for mobile learning. This can also be seen in terms of how the entire research process is conducted. Realizing and consciously being aware of the spectrum of research methods will, in the long term, allow us to influence the future direction of the research done in the field of mobile learning.

Emphasis on research methods and research purposes is important as these decide how research results are used and interpreted. Making methods and purposes explicit is also important because they help a research community to be built and allow this community to formally share results. Publications produced with explicit and sound method and purpose are outlets for knowledge transfer. For instance, Traxler (2007) specifies that the significant challenges for research in mobile learning lies in scalability and sustainability, and therefore frameworks, methods, and tools need to respond to these challenges. Hence, it is necessary to have a thorough understanding of the fit between the approach chosen and the goal of the research. Wingkvist and Ericsson (2009) suggest careful scaling according to pre-set specifications to increase the sustainability of research initiatives in mobile learning.

Discussing research methods and purposes is an integral and intricate part of scientific conduct. Initiators of this discussion were Wynekoop and Conger (1990), followed by Kjeldskov and Graham (2003), and later Jensen and Skov (2005). The classification schema presented within these papers demonstrates a usable and straightforward approach to enhance the discussion of research methods. In order to survey methods and purposes, the World Conference on Mobile Learning (mLearn) was selected as the data source for the publications accredited to mobile learning. The mLearn conference represents current practice conducted within mobile learning and highlights how research is carried out.

The rest of this paper is organized as follows; this introduction is followed by a presentation of eight well-established research methods and four research purposes. These provide the two dimensions of our survey, allowing us to review and discuss the results. We then present the classification and an interpretation of the results, and end the paper with our conclusions.

RESEARCH METHODS

In this section we present the eight research methods, including their strengths, weaknesses, and primary use in mobile learning research. The research methods are extracted from Wynekoop and Conger (1990) with supplementary input from references on research methods prominent in Information Systems (due to the first author's background and main area of expertise). The methods considered are case studies, field studies, action research, experiment studies, survey research, applied research, basic research, and normative research. Research methods often overlap, so we emphasize the defining characteristics of each of the methods to show the classification of existing papers. The eight research methods are environment dependent, artificial, or environment independent (Benbasat, 1985). The first three methods, case studies, field studies, and action research are used in a natural (real) setting and are environment dependent, while experiments are carried out in a somewhat artificial setting. The remaining four (survey, applied, basic, and normative research) are all environment independent (but not artificial). This categorization of the eight methods is summarized in Table 1.

Case Studies

Case studies, according to Yin (2003), are an example of an empirical enquiry that investigates a contemporary phenomenon within its real life context, especially when the boundaries between phenomenon and context are not evident. From the researcher's perspective the boundary from the phenomena is distinct as the researcher is a passive and independent outsider. Case studies are often intensive evaluations of small scale entities such as groups, organizations, individuals, systems, or tools. In general the data is collected by a combination of qualitative and quantitative methods such as observations, interviews, and questionnaires, with limited experimental or statistical control imposed. This often results in a complicated analysis, as data collected in a natural setting are by default very rich and sometimes conflicting or incoherent. On the other hand, case studies are particularly well suited for research focusing on describing and explaining a specific phenomenon and for developing hypothesis or theory. However, case studies can be very time consuming and the findings hard to generalize. In mobile learning, case studies could be used to provide rich data explaining phenomena involving the use of mobile devices in a specific context.

Field Studies

Field studies are characterized by taking place in a natural setting, allowing the researcher a flexible stance in respect to variables, the degree of and manipulation of the same. However, as control increases over variables the pragmatism decreases. Using a range of qualitative and quantitative approaches, data are often collected through observations and interviews, supporting the study of complex situated interactions and processes as addressed by Klein and Myers (1999). The phenomena are placed in a social and cultural context. The advantage is the corpus of data, realistically extracted and in a relatively short time period. The disadvantages are unknown biases, extensive data

Table 1. Summary of research methods (adapted from Wynekoop and Conger, 1990)

	Method	Strengths	Weaknesses	Use
Environment dependent setting	Case studies	Process understanding Demonstrate Causality Natural setting Rich data	Costly, time demanding Limited generalizability No experimental control	Descriptions Explanations Generating hypothesis
	Field studies	Natural setting Independent variables manipulation Replicable	Difficult data collection Unknown sample bias No experimental control No guarantee of independent variable variation	Studying current practice Evaluating new practice Post hoc study of processes and outcomes in practice Generating hypothesis
	Action research	First hand experience Applying theory to practice Close relationship with subjects	Ethics consideration Researcher bias Time demanding Unknown generalizability	Generating hypothesis/theory Testing theories/hypothesis
Artificial setting	Experiment studies	Control of variables Replicable	Limited realism Unknown generalizability	Controlled experiments Testing theory/product
Environment independent setting	Survey research	Relatively easy, low cost Can reduce sample bias	Context insensitive No variable manipulation	Collecting data from large samples Providing statistic picture Developing hypothesis Testing relationships between factors Descriptive data collection
	Applied research	The goal is a product which may be evaluated	Solution constrained May need further design to make product general	Product development Goal-oriented hypothesis testing Testing hypothesis/concepts
	Basic research	No restrictions on solutions Solve new problems	Costly, time demanding May produce no solution Solution may not match known problems	Building theory Solving new problems
	Normative research	Insight into firsthand experience Basis for other forms of research	Opinions may influence outcome	Descriptions of practice Building frameworks Informing and teaching concepts

collection, and having no guarantee that the data are representative. In relation to mobile learning, field studies could be applied in current practice for either informing design or understanding the mobility of users, evaluating design or theory by conducting research in a realistic setting.

Action Research

Action research is particularly suited to application in an actual and natural setting; to study social and cultural phenomena. According to Baskerville and Myers (2004) the researcher actively participates in solving a problem while at the same time evaluating the results and making a knowledge contribution at large. For example, action research

allows the introduction, transformation, evaluation, and extraction of theories. The advantage of being engaged in the activity is that it facilitates first-hand understanding and supports the learning process for all those involved. However, the disadvantage is that it can be very time consuming, and since the researcher takes part in the phenomena studied, retaining a critical stance can be hard. Even though the outcome is attached uniquely to the research conducted, it does offer a degree of external validity since others can interpret the theoretical contribution made. Nevertheless it can still be difficult to generalize upon. In relation to mobile learning, action research provides the perfect opportunity for a researcher to jointly collaborate with the "team".

Experiment Studies

Experiment studies are characterized by the researcher's ability to control dependent variables, often by creating an artificial setting or situation. Being able to do this can be prohibitively difficult or even impossible and a researcher often resorts to quasi-experiment studies as presented by Denscombe (1998). These quasi-experiments usually take place in uncontrolled environments, variables from undetected sources are neither measured nor held constant, and these may produce misleading correlations between variables under study. Data can be collected depending on the style of the subsequent analysis desired. The major advantages of experiment studies are the opportunity to focus on specific phenomena of interest and a large degree of control in terms of manipulation of variables before and during the study through, for example, assignment of test subjects and exposure to different treatment variables. Also, well-designed and executed experiment studies are highly replicable and facilitate data collection. Disadvantages include limited connection to the real world and an unknown level of generalizability of the results outside of the specific setting. In mobile learning research, experiment studies are suitable for evaluating design ideas, specific products, or theories about design and user interaction in controlled environments with little or no interference from the outside world.

Survey Research

Survey research provides information from a defined population and the data, which is gathered directly through, for example, interviews, literature reviews and questionnaires, is assumed to be independent to the environment as stated by Fowler (2002). In essence, data from survey research is collected without the researcher's intervention or stake other than the gathering of data and the presentation of the same. Data is most often analyzed quantitatively, but data from interview surveys can also be analyzed qualitatively. The advantages of surveys are that they facilitate large amounts of data to be gathered with relatively little effort, supporting broad generalization of results. Also a high level of control regarding sample subjects makes reduction of bias possible thus increasing validity. However, a disadvantage is that they suffer from providing only snapshots of studied phenomena and rely heavily on the subjective views of respondents. In respect to mobile learning, survey research could, for example, facilitate general information being gathered about user needs and requirements, or of a phenomenon, and from this help us to develop an understanding of the current situation.

Applied Research

Applied research is similar to prototyping and based on a trial-and-error practice relying on the expertise and reasoning of the researcher's capabilities through intuition, experience, deduction, and induction. The outcome is known in terms of requirements, but not the method of obtaining the same as mentioned by Järvinen (2004). In line with this goal orientation, the advantage is that some kind of result is produced, which can in turn be evaluated against the pre-set goal. The disadvantages are that the initial goal may be very limited and not generalizable, and that appropriate solutions for accomplishing the desired outcome may not be produced at all. Applied research is relevant for mobile learning in relation to design and implementation of systems, interfaces and techniques, which meet certain requirements for performance, user interaction, user satisfaction, etc.

Basic Research

Basic research allows the researcher to study well-known problems to which methods or possible solutions are yet to be identified. The aim is to find out what is part of reality and often the researcher is concerned with the development of a new theory (Järvinen, 2004). The approach is also trial-and-error based, riding on the competence of the researcher. The advantage is the directness of the research that is facilitated by the open choice of approaches and time, allowing a high level of creativity in the search for methods. The down side is that it can be very time consuming and there is no guarantee that a solution will eventually be produced. In relation to mobile learning, basic research may be applied to the development of theoretical frameworks for understanding fundamental principles, for example issues related to mobility or for identifying new problems related to learning while users are on the move.

Normative Research

Normative research is less rigorous in terms of research method per se, though usually addresses interesting phenomena from a pragmatic standpoint. This is done in order to stimulate and indicate directions for future research and, for example, covers writings of application descriptions, idea, concept, and suggestion development (Tolvanen, 1996). The narratives often seem intuitively correct but are not based on theory or research rigorously conducted, and are presented according to the style of a practitioner, i.e., giving a subjective view and focus on what worked in that particular situation. The advantage is that this kind of writing is more straightforward and often perceived as easier to formulate than presenting complex theoretical contributions. Drawbacks consist of limited theoretical foundation, weak methodological reflection, and low generalizability. However, such research that reaches the stage of publication often provides well-prepared arguments with considerable backing from other sources. For mobile learning, the papers describing general statements or designs, and procedures that worked well or did not prove successful, are representative.

RESEARCH PURPOSES

In this section the research purpose is defined as the second dimension of the survey. The purpose of a research effort is closely linked to the research method used and vice versa, so these two notions make an excellent pair when attempting to classify mobile learning papers. The definitions of the four research purposes are inspired by Wynekoop and Conger (1990), although a slight refinement was made. The original categories were: Understanding/Describing, Engineering, Re-engineering, and Evaluating. We divided Understanding/Describing into two categories and merged Engineering and Re-engineering into one category called Developing. These changes were done first to differentiate between Understanding and Describing in order to sharpen the categorization with respect to these concepts, and secondly to merge the other two because mobile learning applications and frameworks have not been around long enough to fully use the categorization of re-engineering. As a result of this refinement the categories for research purposes are: Describing, Developing, Understanding, and Evaluating. These four research purposes are explained and defined here:

1. **Describing:** Writings that describe the unit under study, such as features of the portrayed environment, the technical implementation, often represented in models at a low level of abstraction. Describing papers provide knowledge about the research in a straightforward manner with emphasis on actual results.

2. **Developing:** Writings that define frameworks, be it technical or theoretical, and emphasis on development and the presentation of solutions. A typical example is when the aim is to develop a new conceptual model or a prototype, i.e., papers that basically provide first hand knowledge in uncharted territory.

3. **Understanding:** Writings that seek to understand and make sense of conducted

research, while trying to bridge the result into a theoretical frame, often presenting new constructs based on identifying and enhancing theory. These papers provide knowledge of a wider theoretical setting, often found in research that is in the process of rethinking something.

4. **Evaluating:** Writings that evaluate the usefulness, benefits and shortcomings of the research, while hopefully giving pointers to other researchers. These papers can be seen as evaluating methods and purposes in practice and reflecting upon these, i.e., provide knowledge about lessons learned, which can give others a head start or at least the possibility to avoid pitfalls.

These four categories of purpose along with the research methods are used in the next section as a basis for classifying mobile learning research papers from three World Conferences on Mobile Learning, mLearn 2005, mLearn 2007, and mLearn 2008.

CLASSIFICATION OF MOBILE LEARNING RESEARCH

The proceedings of mLearn 2005 (van der Merwe & Brown, 2005), mLearn 2007 (Norman & Pearce, 2007) and mLearn 2008 (Traxler et al., 2008) were selected to get a picture of current practice in mobile learning. The proceedings of mLearn 2006 was omitted in this survey since it is neither available electronically nor in printed form.

Traxler (2007) notes that the mobile learning community was, at the time relevant to this survey, visible mainly through dedicated international conferences, of which mLearn is one of the main series, rather than through any journals (the International Journal of Mobile and Blended Learning was first published in Q1, 2009.) The mLearn conference series is renowned for including contributions from academics as well as prac-

titioners. All 114 full papers from mLearn2005, mLearn 2007 and 2008 have been classified in this paper. The papers are numbered in the order they are printed in the conference proceedings with the first paper from mLearn 2005 as paper #1, the first paper from mLearn 2007 as paper #39, and the first paper from mLearn 2008 as paper #77 (cf. Appendix). The data set as defined by Robson (2002) is the set of papers from mLearn 2005, 2007, and 2008, which provides a solid and adequately representative basis for this survey. Each paper was peer reviewed, which indicated that the published papers are of good quality and of importance to the community. 114 such papers is a relevant and sufficiently large sample from which to draw conclusions.

Initially the first author reviewed all papers. Each paper was read thoroughly with a particular focus on identifying the purpose of the presented research as well as the method applied to accomplish the research. Many papers can be classified as having a number of purposes or methods, but the most coherent and dominant from each category were selected to classify the paper according to the two dimensions, respectively. Moreover, an international Master's student repeated the same classification process. The results of the two classifications were compared and a final decision was made for each paper. This decision was then discussed and corroborated by the second author, who now also read all the papers. The complete survey result of the 114 papers is presented in Table 2, including the total share of each category as a percentage (%).

Table 2 shows that the most commonly used method within mobile learning research is the case study, with 22% (25 out of 114) of the papers. The second most common method is normative research, which 25% (28 out of 76 papers) used. Applied research and survey research are also commonly used; the former was used by 17% of the papers while the latter was used by 12%. In respect to the less generally used methods, field studies and experiment studies are more common,

Table 2. Classification of mobile learning research papers

	Case studies	Field studies	Action research	Experiment studies	Survey research	Basic research	Applied research	Normative research	Total (%)
Describing	7, 10, 24, 27, 39, 41, 44, 49, 60, 67, 70, 75, 78, 83, 88, 104, 108	21, 32, 40, 50, 66, 77, 97	8, 17, 87, 92, 109	6, 9, 23, 26, 54, 55, 65, 69, 111	12, 25, 34, 46, 76, 79, 91, 114		1, 3, 14, 35, 36, 43, 53, 62, 72, 94	11, 19, 30, 42, 47, 57, 61, 63, 71	57.02%
Developing	4, 29, 48	20, 95		51	107	5	37, 45, 58, 59, 64, 74, 84, 98	2, 13, 16, 18, 22, 28, 52, 56, 81, 82, 89, 90, 106	25.44%
Understanding	38, 93, 96, 105, 112	85	102		80, 86, 101, 103	73		15, 31, 33, 110, 113	14.91%
Evaluating					100		68	99	2.63%
Total (in %)	21.92%	8.77%	4.39%	8.77%	12.28%	1.76%	16.67%	24.56%	100.00%

with 9%, respectively, while action research was used by only 4% of the papers. Only two papers were classified as basic research. The classification shows that environmental independent research (survey, basic, applied, and normative research) dominates and was used by 55% of the papers. 36% used environment dependent methods (case studies, field studies, and action research) and focus on studying real use in a natural setting. 9% of the papers use an artificial setting (experiment studies). In environmental independent research, normative research was the most common method, followed by applied research (44% and 30% respectively.) Case study dominated the environment dependent methods and was used by 61% of the papers. By definition, 100% of the artificial research used experiment research.

In Figure 1 the papers are first divided by environment and secondly by method to show the number and percentage that cover each category. The most common purpose of the research was to describe the study (Describing), with 57% (65 of 114). This was followed by Developing and Understanding, 25% (29 of 114) and 15% (17

of 114), respectively. Only 3% (3 of 114) of the papers had Evaluating as their research purpose. Research with the purpose of *describing* most commonly used case study as the research method. This was used by 26% of the describing papers. The rest of the describing papers were almost equally distributed among experiment, survey, applied, and normative research (14%, 12%, 15%, and 14% respectively), while 7% of the papers used action research. The papers with a purpose of *developing* usually used applied or normative research, and 73% (i.e., 28% and 45% each) of all the developing papers used either of those two methods. 10% of the papers used case studies and 7% used field studies. The remaining 10% were equally divided between experiment study, basic research and survey research. The *understanding* papers were most commonly either case studies or normative research (30% each). 24% of the understanding papers used survey research. The remaining papers used field studies, action research, or basic research (6% each). The three *evaluating* papers were divided into using survey research, applied research, and normative research.

Figure 1. Papers divided by environment (left) and method (right) in percentage

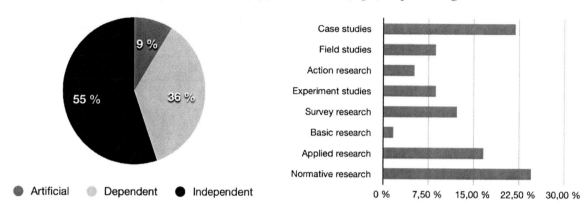

The case study research method was most commonly used for the purpose of describing. 68% of the case study papers fall within this category. Similar results hold for field studies, action research, and experiment studies, where 70%, 83%, and 90% of the use of these methods is done with the purpose of describing. Applied and survey research are generally used for two purposes each, with applied research most commonly used for either describing or developing, with 53% and 42% respectively, while survey research is often used for either describing (57%) or understanding (29%). Normative research is done for the purpose of developing, describing or understanding (32%, 46%, and 18% respectively).

Within mobile learning there is a tendency towards research in an independent environment aiming at describing and developing. In the environmental dependent category, case study dominates with 41% (17 papers) and for all the 41 papers in that whole category, 29 papers have the purpose of describing. Understanding (and presenting theoretical frameworks) is the focus of seven papers (17%), which limits the body of knowledge for mobile learning. Of the 19 papers of applied research, 42% have the purpose of developing and understanding. Of the ten papers in the experiment category, 90% use this method for describing purposes. Of the ten papers that

report field studies, seven papers use this method for describing purposes, while two papers use it for developing. The last paper uses experiment research for an understanding purpose. Applied and normative research is most commonly used for describing or developing. In the case of applied research, 52% of the papers utilizing this method are describing, while 42% are developing. In the case of normative research, 32% are describing, while 46% are developing. The two papers that used basic research used it for developing and understanding.

DISCUSSION

This section presents an analysis of the results of the classification presented in the previous section. Generally, the research conducted is either close to one situation in particular, gathering empirical data, or on a normative level presenting ways to utilize the essence of mobile learning in an abstract sense. These two represent opposite ends of the spectrum given method choice and purpose and out of the 114 papers considered in this survey, 79 papers fall into either of these (69%). This suggests a need for a broader scope in terms of the methods and purposes of mobile learning research to help the field to mature and also help other researchers to avoid repeating known pitfalls. This maturity, in turn, will lead to better scalability and sustainability for future research efforts in the mobile learning community.

Mobile learning is evidently an interdisciplinary field with ties to, for example, Computer Science, something that might explain the emphasis on applied research and data gathering. Methods used in related fields, e.g., Information Systems and Software Engineering are also noticeable within mobile learning, for example in action research, case studies, and field studies. A difference compared to these related disciplines is how few papers are found in artificial environments and experiment studies in this review. From the 114 papers, only ten presented some kind of experiment studies. In some related fields, experiments are more common, for example Kjeldskov and Graham (2003) show that experiment studies are the second most common research method used in Mobile Human-Computer Interaction. This divergence may be a result of the difficulty of emulating aspects of mobile learning, such as mobility and the dynamics of context changes in an experimental setting. Field study, on the other hand, offers an ideal opportunity for the study of rich real-world cases. Mobile learning is applicable and well understood in a natural and environment dependent setting. The use of research methods such as case study and action research aids and strengthens the result when studies are conducted. Mobile learning researchers could learn from other disciplines that have struggled with the study of similar phenomena often depending on the degree of involvement from the researcher. Experimental studies and the use of control groups are subsequently essential.

The prevalence of gathering empirical data and the research that is conducted to describe a phenomenon shows a strong connection to real-world cases. Much of the research conducted is done to describe how the real world works and is often presented as the result of a small-scale study where a population used mobile learning technology. This data is presented, not interpreted,

and offered as a description of the process. At the other end of the spectrum there is the normative research that is also done with the purpose to describe and develop. Many of the papers that fall into this category present either a description of a current situation or a future situation describing what may happen or how something should be developed. These papers are based on some evidence and are generally visionary. Between these two, basic research and evaluating research would be expected, but have not been found. Of the papers reviewed, 5 fall into either of these categories, none in both.

There is a distinct lack of evaluation and basic research among the papers reviewed. The one paper we found in basic research is mirrored in the survey of Jensen and Skov (2005) that also only found one such paper in relation to their field (Children's Technology Design). Many of the papers include an attempt at reflection. This is often not the main purpose and almost always leads to the evaluation from an end-user perspective. There is little reflection by revisiting results, or evaluation of the effort compared to other efforts. This is a problem. In a similar manner, much of the research is done to describe, not understand or evaluate. This may indicate a lack of maturity and a lack of clear definitions. There is still a need to describe how it works in order to define it. There is a need to bridge the gap between descriptive small-scale research and normative visionary research, by evaluating and trying to understand. This is where knowledge is produced and theories are formed.

One reason for the lack of evaluating and basic research might be the speed with which mobile technologies are developed and improved upon. A generation of mobile devices is short-lived, which may result in many technical aspects being lost when a new generation is introduced or many studies feeling outdated and old, which in turn may affect evaluations and reflections. This may direct us towards simply stating facts or presenting visionary plans. However, without proper focus on the research process, including methods and purposes, it is hard for research in mobile learning to transfer already obtained knowledge as the starting point for new efforts.

One way to describe the papers reviewed is to consider some of them as standing on the frontiers looking into the future and others working hard to keep up with current development. A challenge for mobile learning research would be to stop, turn around, and reflect over the results once again. This is the way to reach the visionary future, which is predicted by looking ahead and avoiding already known pitfalls. Also, a head start is given if research is built upon previous research instead of the wheel being reinvented every time a new mobile learning initiative gets under way.

Given this review it must be stated that research methods and a classification of research according to defined methods is not an exact science. Some definitions can be considered vague or even overlapping with other methods. To make issues even more complicated, few papers contain a discussion of the exact methods used, so in many cases it is down to a judgment call. With the overlapping and vague methods it was sometimes hard to pick one, and only one, method. For example, is a study conducted in a natural setting but with all variables fixed a field study or an experiment?

Further along these lines, it should be acknowledged that the survey presented in this paper has some limitations. It can for example be questioned if the research papers presented at a conference, although marketed central to the field, is really representative of the research and activities that are conducted within the field. Furthermore, it is not always easy to compress the research to fit the page limitations or topics of interest at a conference. Notwithstanding these constraints, the conference series selected for this review provides papers from a wide range of researchers and research projects. The authors read each paper several times, and carefully discussed the method and the purpose before it was classified. The purposes and methods matrix, as classifica-

tion tool, has been used for a number of similar reviews. Further, the results of the classification in this paper show a clear trend that is difficult to attribute to vague method definitions. Based on these observations, the authors of this paper are confident that the research conducted is of value, even with the limitations placed on it.

CONCLUSION

Research methods and research purposes are an integral and intricate part of how people conduct research. In this paper we present a two dimensional matrix where we compare research methods and research purposes from 114 papers. The first dimension consists of eight research methods: case study, field study, action research, experiment, survey, applied research, basic research, and normative research. The second dimension consists of four research purposes: Describing, Developing, Understanding, and Evaluating. The 114 papers we investigated represent a broad selection within current practices in mobile learning.

Our classification shows an even distribution in respect to research methods, with only basic research being under-represented. In terms of research purposes, describing is the most frequent, and is used within more than half of the papers, followed by one-fourth of developing papers, and one-seventh understanding. Evaluating, on the other hand, is represented only within about one-fortieth of the total number of papers we have investigated. Our survey reveals that there is a clear lack of papers utilizing basic research in terms of research method and evaluating as a research purpose. This indicates a void that could be filled with publications specifying lessons that were learned, describing benefits as well as shortcoming of research already conducted.

In a young and evolving research field it is necessary to try new research methods, which in turn can greatly improve the diversity of the research published. Mobile learning is an excellent example of an evolving field where researchers apply various methods to solve their problems. Our survey shows exactly that, and our findings further present a number of opportunities for future research. We suggest that researchers revisit and evaluate their research methods. This can lead to evolution and presentation of new frameworks, methods, and tools. This holistic approach and systematic description is important not only for method and purpose in research but also for improving the overall system development process that mobile learning research is faced with.

ACKNOWLEDGMENT

The authors would like to take this opportunity to thank fellow colleagues Marcelo Milrad, Anita Mirijamdotter, and international master's student Lusia Erldorfer for their feedback and contribution to this paper.

REFERENCES

Baskerville, R., & Myers, M. (2004). Special issue on action research in information systems: Making IS research relevant to practice. *Management Information Systems Quarterly, 28*(3), 329–335.

Benbasat, I. (1985). An analysis of research methodologies. In MacFarlan, F. (Ed.), *The Information System Research Challenge* (pp. 47–85). Boston, MA: Harvard Business School Press.

Cobcroft, R., Towers, S., Smith, J., & Bruns, A. (2006). Mobile learning in review: Opportunities and challenges for learners, teachers, and institutions. In *Proceedings of the Online Learning and Teaching (OLT) Conference 2006* (pp. 21-30).

Denscombe, M. (1998). *The good research guide for small scale social research projects* (1st ed.). Buckingham, UK: Open University Press.

Fowler, F. (2002). *Survey research methods* (3rd ed.). Thousand Oaks, CA: Sage.

Järvinen, P. (2004). *On research methods*. Tampere, Finland: Juvenes-Print.

Jensen, J., & Skov, M. (2005). A review of research methods in children's technology design. In *Proceedings of the 2005 Conference on Interaction Design and Children* (pp. 80-87).

Keegan, D. (2005). The incorporation of mobile learning into mainstream education and training. In *Proceedings of mLearn 2005: 4th World Conference on Mobile Learning.*

Kjeldskov, J., & Graham, C. (2003). A review of mobile HCI research methods. In *Proceedings of Mobile HCI 2003: 5th International Symposium on Mobile Human-Computer Interaction.*

Klein, H., & Myers, M. (1999). A set of principles for conducting and evaluating interpretive field studies in information systems. *Management Information Systems Quarterly, 23*(1), 67–93. doi:10.2307/249410

Kukulska-Hulme, A., Sharples, M., Milrad, M., Arnedillo-Sánchez, I., & Vavoula, G. (2009). Innovation in mobile learning: An European perspective. *International Journal of Mobile and Blended Learning, 1*(1), 12–35.

Naismith, L., Lonsdale, P., Vavoula, G., & Sharples, M. (2004). *Literature review in mobile technologies and learning*. Bristol, UK: NESTA FutureLab.

Norman, A., & Pearce, J. (Eds.). (2007). Making the Connections. In *Proceedings of mLearn 2007: 6th World Conference on Mobile Learning*, Melbourne, VIC, Australia.

Robson, C. (2007). *Real World Research: A Resource for Social Scientists and Practitioner-Researchers*. Oxford, UK: Blackwell Publishing.

Sharples, M., Milrad, M., Arnedillo-Sánchez, I., & Vavoula, G. (2008). Mobile learning: Small devices, big issues . In Balacheff, N., Ludvigsen, S., de Jong, T., Lazonder, A., Barnes, S., & Montandon, L. (Eds.), *Technology Enhanced Learning: Principles and Products*. Berlin, Germany: Springer.

Taylor, J., Sharples, M., O'Malley, C., Vavoula, G., & Waycott, J. (2006). Towards a task model for mobile learning: A dialectical approach. *International Journal of Learning Technology*, *2*(2-3), 138–158. doi:10.1504/IJLT.2006.010616

Tolvanen, J., Rossi, M., & Liu, H. (1996). Method engineering: Current research directions and implications for future research. In S. Brinkkemper, K. Lyytinen, & R. Welke (Eds.) *Proceedings of IFIP TC8, WG8.1/8.2: Working Conference on Method Engineering*. London, UK: Chapman & Hall.

Traxler, J. (2007). Defining, discussing, and evaluating mobile learning: The moving finger writes and having writ… . *International Review of Research in Open and Distance Learning*, *8*(2), 1–12.

Traxler, J. (2007). Flux within change. In *Proceedings of mLearn 2007: 6th World Conference on Mobile Learning*.

Traxler, J., & Kukulska-Hulme, A. (2005) Evaluating mobile learning: Reflections on current practice. In *Proceedings of mLearn 2005: 4th World Conference on Mobile Learning*.

Traxler, J., Riordan, B., & Dennett, C. (Eds.). (2008). The Bridge from Text to Context. In *Proceedings of mLearn 2008: 7th World Conference on Mobile Learning*.

van der Merwe, H., & Brown, T. (Eds.). (2005). Mobile Technology: The Future of Learning in Your Hands. In *Proceedings of mLearn 2005: 4th World Conference on Mobile Learning*.

Vavoula, G., & Sharples, M. (2009). Meeting the challenge in evaluating mobile learning: A 3-level evaluation framework. *International Journal of Mobile and Blended Learning*, *1*(2), 54–75.

Wingkvist, A., & Ericsson, M. (2009). Addressing sustainability for research initiatives in mobile learning through scalability. In *Proceedings of the IASTED International Conference, Web-based Education (WBE 2009)*.

Wynekoop, J., & Conger, S. (1990). A review of computer aided software engineering research methods. In *Proceedings of IFIP TC8, WG 8.2: Working Conference on The Information Systems Research Arena of The 90's*, Copenhagen, Denmark.

Yin, R. (2003). *Case study research, design and methods* (3rd ed.). Thousand Oaks, CA: Sage.

APPENDIX: FULL PAPERS

mLearn 2005

1. Ally, M. et al., *An Intelligent Agent for Adapting and Delivering Electronic Course Materials to Mobile Learners*
2. Angarita, M. et al., *Edugaming PCs and QUICKPDA eBooks: A New Model for Surpassing Fragmentation in Mobile eHealth*
3. Arias, R. & Pasch, G., *XML saves the day: Porting a Rich-Media Collection to a Mobile Platform in Three Weeks Flat*
4. Attewell, J., *From Research and Development to Mobile Learning Tools for Education and Training Providers and their Learners*
5. Barker, A. et al., *A Proposed Theoretical Model for mLearning Adoption in Developing Countries*
6. Bradley, C. et al., *Adult Multimedia Learning with PDAs –The User Experience*
7. Burke, M. et al., *Utilizing Wireless Learning Pocket-PCs to Promote Collaboration in Field-based Courses*
8. Corlett, D. et al., *Interactive Logbook: a Mobile Portfolio and Personal Development Planning Tool*
9. de Crom, N. & de Jager, A., *The "ME"-Learning Experience: PDA Technology and eLearning in EcoTourism at TUT*
10. Divitini, M. & Marken, E., *Blending Mobile and Ambient Technologies to Support Mobility in Practice Based Education: the Case of Teacher Education*
11. Edwards, R., *Your Learners are Increasingly Mobile, is Your Learning?*
12. Facer, K. et al., *Challenges and Opportunities: Making Mobile Learning a Reality in Schools*
13. Feisst, M. et al., *Adaptive Heterogeneous Learning Systems*
14. Katz, H. & Worsham, S., *Steaming mLearning Objects via Data Resolution*
15. Keegan, D., *The Incorporation of Mobile Learning into Mainstream Education and Training*
16. Landers, P., *Meta Learning: Experiences from the Inclusion of mLearning in a standards-Based and Corporate-Wide Learning Content Management Framework*
17. Laouris, Y. & Anastasiou, H., *The Introduction of IT in the lives of Children as a service to Global peace: Experience from a Nation-Wide Experiment Introducing IT in the Lives of Children: Fifteen Years Later*
18. Laouris, Y. & Eteokleous, N., *We need an Educationally Relevant Definiton of Mobile Learning*
19. Louw, W., *Taking the Distance Out of Distance Education through the means of mLearning*
20. Leach, J. et al., *4D Technologies: Appropriating Handheld Computers to Serve the Needs of Teachers and Learners in Rural African Settings*
21. Matilla, P. & Fordell, T., *MOOP – Using mLearning Environment in Primary Schools*
22. McMillan, J., *Seven Reasons Why mLearning Doesn't Work*
23. Naismith, L. et al., *Evaluation of CAERUS: a Centex Aware Mobile Guide*
24. Ng'ambi, D., *Mobile Dynamic Frequently Asked Questions (m-DFAQ) for Students and Learning Support*
25. Nonyongo, E., *Effectiveness of SMS Communication Between University and Students*

26. Pemberton, L. & Fallahkhair, L., *Design Issues for Dual Device Learning: Interactive Television and Mobile Learning*
27. Ragus, M. et al., *The Australian Mobile Learning Network: Australian Innovations*
28. Sharples, M. et al., *Towards a Theory of Mobile Learning*
29. Silander, P. & Rytkönen, A., *An Intelligent Mobile Tutoring Tool Enabling Individualszation of Students' Learning Process*
30. Smyth, G., *Wireless Technologies Bridging the Digital Divide in Education*
31. Stead, G., *Moving Mobile into the Mainstream*
32. Swan, K. et al., *Teaching and Learning with Mobile Computing Devises: Closing the Gap*
33. Traxler, J. & Kukulska, A., *Evaluating Mobile Learning: Reflections on Current Practice*
34. Treadwell, I., *The Usability of PDAs for Assessment of Practical Performance*
35. Veith, P. & Pawlowski, J., *Conception and Development of Reusable and Modular Mobile Content*
36. Wentzel, P., *Mobile Learning in the Netherlands: Real-time Database Access in an Educational Fieldwork Setting*
37. West, P. et al., *Content Exposure of Slide Show Presentations for Selective Download and Annotation via Mobile Devices*
38. Wishart, J. et al., *Using Personal Digital Assistants (PDAs) with Internet Access to Support Initial Teacher Training in the UK*

mLearn 2007

39. Ally, M. et al., *Use of Mobile Learning Technology to Train ESL Adults*
40. Arrigo, M. et al., *A Collaborative Mlearning Environment*
41. Bressler, D. & Kahr-Hoejland, A., *Learning Informal Science with the Aid of Mobile Phones: A Comparison of two Case Studies*
42. Cochrane, T., *Mobile Blogging: A Guide for Educators*
43. Cochrane, T., *Moving Mobile Mainstream: Using Communities of Practice to Develop Educational Technology Literacy in Tertiary Academics*
44. Cooney G. & Keogh, K., *Use of Mobile Phones for Language Learning and Assessment for Learning, A Pilot Project*
45. Elson, B. et al., *Blueprint for an Adaptive Training - Virtual Learning Environment (Adapt-VLE) for the Training of Dentists*
46. Goerke, V. & Oliver, B., *Defining the Handheld Computer for a First Year University Student: Is it a 'Handy' Accessory or an Essential Learning Tool?*
47. Green J., *Using Mobile Technologies for Open and Distance Learning Community Development*
48. Gregson, J., *M-Learning: The First Piece in the Distance Learning Jigsaw?*
49. Hartnell-Young, E., *Making the Connections: Theory and Practice of Mobile Learning in Schools*
50. Hawkins, G. et al., *21st Century Assessment for 21st Century Learners*
51. Hwang, W. et al., *A Study on Ubiquitous Computer Supported Collaborative Learning with Hybrid Mobile Discussion Forum*
52. Kolesnikova, S., *Learning Resource Authoring Techniques in Mobile Platform*
53. Kukulska-Hulme, A., *Self-Service Education: Smartphones as a Catalyst for Informal Collective and Individual Learning*

54. Lefoe, G., *New Technologies, New Pedagogies: Using Scenarios for Staff Development with Mobile Technologies*
55. Madia, M., *Selection Interviews using Mobile Technology*
56. Mann, S and Reimann, P., *Mobile Technology as a Mediating Tool for Learning in the Convergences from Technology, Collaboration and Curriculum Perspectives*
57. Matthee, M. & Liebenberg, J., *Mathematics on the Move: Supporting Mathematics Learners Through Mobile Technology in South Africa*
58. Mittal, A. et al., *Content-Based Network Resource Allocation for* Mobile Engineering Laboratory Applications
59. Mittal, A. & Gupta, C., *A Novel Remote Laboratory Control and Evaluation Framework*
60. Nalder, G. et al., *Self-Organising M-Learning Communities: A Case-Study*
61. Ng, W. & Nicholas, H., *Ubiquitous Learning With Handheld* Computers in Schools
62. Nussbaum, M. et al., *Comparative Study of Peer Learning Mediated by Interconnected PCs and PDAs*
63. Kress, G. & Pachler, N., *Thinking About the 'M-' in Mobile Learning*
64. Pande, A. et al., *Contemporary Environments of Learning and the Dilemma of the School Network Aware Efficient Resource Allocation for Mobile-Learning Video Systems*
65. Petrova, K., *Student Revising for a Test using SMS*
66. Shao, Y. et al., *Designing a Mobile Group Blog to Support Cultural Learning*
67. Song, Y. & Fox, R., *Educational Affordances of Handheld Devices: Undergraduate Student Perceptions*
68. Sharples, M. et al., *An Evaluation of MyArtSpace: A Mobile Learning Service for School Museum Trips*
69. So, S., *A Study On the Acceptance of Mobile Phones for Teaching and Learning With Pre Service Teachers*
70. Stewart, K., *Mobile Learning – Designing the Learning Context*
71. Taylor, C., *Hunting Mobile Literacies: Listening To the Experiences of Students*
72. Thompson, K. & Stewart, K., *The Mobile Jigsaw – A Collaborative Learning Strategy for Mlearning about the Environment*
73. Traxler, J., *Flux Within Change*
74. Jianhua, W. & Jing, L., *Research of Device Adapting Based On MAS in Field of Mobile Learning*
75. Clark, S. et al., *Short Podcasts: The Impact On Learning and Teaching*
76. Anarki, F., *Assessment of Mlearning A Case Study: Assumption University of Thailand*

mLearn 2008

77. Anastopoulou, A. et al., *Learning 21st Century Science in Context with Mobile Technologies*
78. Arrigo, M. et al., *Some Considerations on a Mobile Learning Experience in a Secondary School*
79. Attewell, J., *Towards Sustainable Large Scale Implementation of Mobile Learning: the Mobile Learning Network (MoLeNET)*
80. Bird, P. & Stubbs, M., *A Bridge too far? – Embedding Mobile Learning in UK Higher Education*
81. Botha, A. et al., *MobilED: A Tool by Any Other Name...*

82. Botha, A. & Ford, M., *"Digital Life Skills" for the Young and Mobile "Digital Citizens"*
83. Botha, A. et al., *Improving Cross-cultural Awareness and Communication through Mobile Technologies*
84. Byrne, P., *A Mobile Computer Supported Collaborative Learning Tool for Digital Narrative Production*
85. Canova Calori, I. & Divitini, M., *Reflections on the Role of Technology in City-wide Collaborative Learning*
86. Chen, W. et al., *Mobile VLE vs. Mobile PLE: How Informal is Mobile Learning?*
87. Cochrane, T., *Designing Mobile Learning Environments: Mobile Trials at Unitec 2008*
88. Collins, T. et al., *Supporting Location-based Inquiry Learning Across School, Field and Home Contexts*
89. Cook, J. et al., *Appropriation of Mobile Phones for Learning*
90. Ngoc Do, K. & Bouzeghoub, A., *A Situation Based Metadata for Describing Pervasive Learning Objects*
91. Drummond, S., *Turning Point: Transferring Data via Bluetooth® Technology*
92. Drummond, S., *Digital Mini Film Festival: a Framework for Mobile Learning*
93. Eicker, S. & Matthee, M., *Obstacles and Challenges Encountered in South African Secondary School Mobile Learning Environments*
94. Fotouhi-Ghazvini. F., *The MOBO City: A Mobile Game Package for Technical Language Learning*
95. Göth, C. & Schwabe, G., *Designing Tasks for Engaging Mobile Learning*
96. Hartnell-Young, E., *Mobile Phones for Learning in Mainstream Schooling: Resistance and Change*
97. Kenny, R. et al., *The Feasibility of Using Mobile Devices in Nursing Practice Education*
98. Kristoffersen, S., *Learning for life: Implementing a Medication Management Module to Support Learning Among Adolescent Diabetics*
99. Kukulska-Hulme, A. & Bull, S., *Theoretical Perspectives on Mobile Language Learning Diaries and Noticing for Learners,*

Teachers and Researchers

100. Laine, T. & Joy, M., *Survey on Context-Aware Pervasive Learning Environments*
101. Minocha, S. & Booth, N., *Podcasting and Learning Experiences: User-centred Requirements Gathering*
102. Nikoi, S. & Edirisingha, P., *Accounted Learning: A WoLF-oriented Approach to Mobile learning*
103. O´Neill, L. & Loftus, M., *Best Practices for mobilizing Educational Media in Higher Education*
104. Passey, D., *The Role of Mobile Technologies in Moving 'Digital Natives' to 'Learning Natives'*
105. Pettit, J. & Kukulska-Hulme, A., *Do Smart Devices Make Smart Learners*
106. Pham-Nguyen, C. et al., *Pervasive Learning System Based on a Scenario Model Integrating Web Service Retrieval and Orchestration*
107. Pimmer, C. & Gröhbiel, U., *Mobile Learning in corporate settings Results from an Expert Survey*
108. Pulman, A., *The Nintendo DS as an Assistive Technology Tool for Health and Social Care Students*
109. Savill-Smith, C., *Introducing Mobile Learning into Further Education (the Mobile Learning NETwork, MoLeNET programme) – Large-scale Research and Evaluation*
110. Sprake, J., *Designing Participant-Generated Context into Guided Tours*

111. Tschirhart, C. et al., *Language Learning 'On the Go'*
112. van den Berg, M et al., *MobilED: A Step Backwards to Look Ahead*
113. Vavoula, G. & Sharples, M., *Challenges in Evaluating Mobile Learning*
114. Woodgate, D. et al., *Mobile Learning in Context: School Science Data Collection as Legitimate Peripheral Participation*

This work was previously published in the International Journal of Mobile and Blended Learning, Volume 3, Issue 1, edited by David Parsons, pp 1-17, copyright 2011 by IGI Publishing (an imprint of IGI Global).

Chapter 3
Mobile Technology and Student Learning:
What Does Current Research Reveal?

Pamela Pollara
Louisiana State University, USA

Kelly Kee Broussard
Louisiana State University, USA

ABSTRACT

As mobile devices become ubiquitous, it is necessary to analyze if and how these devices can be used for learning. This systematic review is part of a larger review that analyzed 21 mobile learning research studies published from 2005-present. Eleven studies that focused specifically on student learning outcomes and processes are summarized in this review in order to better understand the direction of mobile learning in mainstream education. Overall, studies were found to be positive and indicated several benefits of using mobile devices for learning including an increase in achievement, productivity, engagement, and motivation. This paper also highlights recommendations for future research and practice in the field of mobile learning, specifically focusing on the way personal mobile device ownership may influence learning both inside and outside the classroom.

INTRODUCTION

Technology in today's modern society is constantly evolving at a rapid pace. Tech savvy consumers are demanding access to information and instantaneous communication on portable devices to keep up with a growing mobile society. Users are performing various tasks on their mobile devices including those related to work, play, communication, and socialization. This extreme growth in the capabilities of mobile technology in combination with increasing affordability has led to the

DOI: 10.4018/978-1-4666-2139-8.ch003

acknowledgement of a ubiquitous learning tool by various researchers and educators in both K-12 and higher education. Though since its inception much work has been done to define mobile learning and discuss specific challenges of pedagogy, the majority of primary studies have flourished in the last five years due to the transformation of mobile learning from a subsidiary of e-learning (i.e. mobile e-learning) to its own field (Traxler, 2009). As non-traditional methods of education become more prevalent and thus, informal and flexible learning environments become necessary for students in an ever-connected society, research of m-learning will play a significant role in determining if institutions can support 21st century needs (Fetaji, 2008).

Background and Prior Reviews

Because m-learning research is still in its infancy, the amount of available primary research studies is still, relative to other fields of study like e-learning, small. Most literature reviews and conceptual papers seek to establish a foundation for m-learning, develop theory, or focus on design. Specifically, prior reviews and papers have focused on the type of m-learning projects being done (Fetaji, 2008), the nature of research questions (Ali & Irvine, 2009), and the type of activities that can be supported with mobile technologies (Naismith et al., 2004).

Yet, there are still many questions to consider about mobile learning research. While the topics summarized in other reviews have undoubtedly added to the field, there is a lack of research that specifically focuses on student learning outcomes and processes.

Purpose

The goal of this review is to enable researchers to identify current research practices in order to understand the current direction of mobile learning and further research in this growing field.

This systematic literature review will summarize, evaluate, and explain the research applicable to understanding learning outcomes and results of recent mobile learning studies.

This review is part of a larger systematic review that examined three research questions: 1) What type of m-learning research is currently being done? 2) What are the student learning outcomes and processes? 3) What are student perceptions of m-learning?

The results in this paper focus specifically on the second research question. Eleven studies out of the 21 reviewed examined learning in some way. Thus, we analyze these in this paper in order to understand the type of learning that is being done with mobile technologies and the outcomes and benefits of those processes. Researchers paid particular attention to the type of technology used, the interaction that the technology was used to support, type of learning task, benefits of the intervention, the outcome measured, and the results of the study. Recommendations for further research have been made based on an analysis of the studies and the suggestions provided in studies included in this review.

METHODS

Inclusion and Exclusion Criteria

Studies that examined attitudes and achievement associated with mobile learning in a variety of different contexts were selected for this literature review. For the purpose of this study, we used Ally's (2009) definition of m-learning which describes m-learning as the process of using a mobile device to access and study learning materials to communicate with fellow students, instructors or institution (Ally, 2009; Ali & Irvine, 2009). Although there are a plethora of mobile devices that can be considered, we limited our review to personal mobile devices, specifically PDA's, mobile phones, and mp3 players, used for either formal or informal learning or as part of practical work experience or practicum. It should be noted that while we have recently seen a convergence of these devices into one multi-functional device (i.e. smartphones), some of the research was done prior to this convergence. Thus, we label the device as it was referred to in the original study. We specifically selected the mobile phone, mp3 player, and the PDA for investigation because these are the devices that most smartphones can now all function as. These devices are also personally owned and able to be used by students for learning. This "personalization" factor, which is related to ownership, has been linked to intrinsic and extrinsic motivation, which may lead to positive learning outcomes and enable the growth of mobile learning in education (Sharples, 2006; Yordanvova, 2007). We have excluded studies that use handheld devices (i.e. student response clickers) that cannot be used independently outside of a classroom. These devices often function by using software located on a central computer usually belonging to the instructor and have no function outside of that setting. After selecting and analyzing seven initial studies, inclusion criteria were focused to include only studies that answered our research questions listed above.

While much of the prior literature focused on mobile learning theory and its validity as a means to learn, we sought to explore the most recent studies (2005-present) and address questions that would examine the viability of mobile learning within mainstream education. While in most cases it was not common that the characteristics we were looking to summarize were always clearly defined, any study that did not address one of our three research questions was immediately eliminated.

We also examined methodology. We included both experimental and non-experimental studies, but we excluded studies in which particular software was developed for a specific device or environment only. We felt as if the direction of mobile learning is moving toward applications that can be used on a variety of mobile device

platforms and vast number of users. Therefore, studies that tended to be too restrictive in this way were excluded. Few large-scale studies exist, so we did not exclude any studies based on sample size. We did, however, take into consideration the validity and quality of the design. Studies that did not provide substantial information about research design or methodology were excluded from the review.

Finally, in order to examine the use of mobile learning at all levels of education; we included studies where participants were K-12 students, undergraduates, or graduate students. We did not include any studies that examined self-directed mobile learning, although this should be of interest for future research.

Search Strategies

Based on the framework for developing literature reviews (Hart, 1999; Petticrew & Roberts, 2006); our search was completed in two phases. The first phase was an initial search that yielded an abundance of reviews. During this phase the direction of the review was focused and inclusion and exclusion criteria were determined based on results and correspondence to research questions related to our investigation of prior literature reviews. Seven studies were explored in-depth in order to focus and limit the scope of the review. During the second phase, we began selecting articles from the initial search after inclusion and exclusion criteria had been firmly established. A subsequent search was also performed during this stage for articles that clearly aligned with our refined criteria.

Throughout the search process ERIC and EdLitLib (AACE) databases were primarily used to locate appropriate studies, although additional studies were found through Google Scholar, Academia.edu and Webfeat. We limited the search to articles published after 2005 because of the advances in technology and the ubiquitous nature of mobile devices that has grown exponentially

Table 1. Summary of characteristics (n=11)

Participants		N			Research Design		Technology Used in the Study				Study Results	
K-12	University	<50	>50	?	Experimental study	Survey-driven study	Mobile phones	PDA	mp3 players	Other/Combination/not specified	Positive Results	Mixed Results/Not clear
3	8	6	4	1	3	8	5	3	1	2	11	0

in the last five years. The following keywords were used in the search: "m-learning;" "mobile learning;" "mobile learning and education;" "mobile devices and education;" and "m-learning and education." We did not focus on a specific device or learning environment (we found that including the search terms "mobile phone" or "PDA" was too limiting). As stated previously, the initial search provided a plethora of results, however many were not relevant. Researchers scanned abstracts for appropriateness and found 219 articles to be specifically focused on mobile learning according to our operational definition. After examining the articles further and applying our inclusion and exclusion criteria, 21 primary studies were found to meet all of our criteria. Eleven of those studies examined student learning outcomes and identified benefits associated with the mobile learning intervention.

Study Features Coding and Analyses

A variety of study features were coded during the research process to ensure the validity of the studies and their applicability to the research question regarding student learning. We chose criteria that would enable us to determine what specific kinds of mobile learning interventions produced positive results in either attitude, achievement, or engagement in mobile learning. We coded the mobile device used (referred to in our table as "technology used") and the type of interaction the technology supported (student-student, student-content, student-instructor) to determine how all participants in educational processes are

using m-learning. Learning tasks were coded to show a variety of different uses for m-learning, which is associated with a growth in the field and an increase in acceptance and use. Prior research indicates that six types of learning activities could be utilized with mobile learning (Naismith et al., 2004). Thus, we also chose to analyze the type of learning task associated within each study. All studies were found to have either behaviorist or constructivist tasks.

Two researchers conducted the searches and coded the studies selected for inclusion in the systematic review (Table 1). Some studies were dually coded to ensure validity of the coding strategies. All coding was discussed in detail in team meetings over Skype and through wiki discussion and collaboration.

RESULTS

Eleven of the initial 21 studies analyzed were found to pertain specifically to student learning outcomes and processes (Table 2). Eight of the studies regarding benefits of student learning outcomes and processes were survey-driven studies while only three were experimental studies. Most of these studies were designed to measure only the attitudes (n=6) students had about m-learning rather than only student achievement (n=2) because of the implementation of m-learning. However, researchers did present findings related to student learning even if this was not the intended focus. Three studies were designed to measure both attitudes and achievement.

Table 2. Benefits of student learning outcomes and processes (n=11)

Author (year)	Technology used	What type of interaction was the technology used to support	Learning task	Behaviorist or constructivist task	Benefits identified in the study	Outcome measured	Results/Conclusion
Al-Fahad (2009)	Mobile phone	Student/content, student/instructor	Not defined	Not defined	Students became active learners, not passive learners	Attitude	Positive
Cavus & Uzunboylu (2009)	Mobile phone	Student/instructor, student/student	Individual projects, group discussion, assessment	Constructivist	Links critical thinking skills with mobile learning and predicts that critical thinking skills increase when students are engaged in mobile learning, creativity also improved after the study	Attitude	Positive
Guenter et al (2008)	PDAs	Student/content, Student/student	Group projects, group discussion	Constructivist	Multi-modal and multi-sensory experiences, high level of collaboration, control over learning process	Attitude	Positive
Hsu, Wang, & Comac (2008)	Mobile phone, telephone	Student/content, student/instructor	Individual projects, assessment, practice	Constructivist	Increased understanding of content	Achievement, Attitude, Engagement	Positive
Manair (2007)	Mobile phone, PDA	Student/content	Individualized learning of content	Behaviorist	Possibility of learning to occur on mobile devices	Attitude	Positive
McConatha, Praul, Lynch (2008)	Web enabled mobile phones	Student/content	Individual learning of content, review	Behaviorist	Students who use the technology scored higher than those who used traditional methods of study	Achievement	Positive
Rogers, Et al (2010)	LillyPad mobile learning application on PDAs	Student/content, Student/student	Group projects, group discussion	Constructivist	Generated excitement and interest, collaborative learning	Attitude, Engagement	Positive
Shih, et al (2010)	hyperbook and hyperpen	Student/content	Individualized learning of content	Behaviorist	Students were willing to access supplemental materials, enriched learning experience, students took pleasure in learning	Achievement	Positive
Wang, et al (2009)	Mobile phone (text messages)	Student/content, Student/student, student/instructor	Teacher directed lecture, group discussion, assessment	Behaviorist	Change from passive learners to active learners	Achievement, attitude, engagement	Positive
Williams & Bearman (2008)	Mp3 players, iPods specifically	Student/content, student/instructor	Teacher directed lecture	Behaviorist	Better utilization of study time, review materials better, reinforce materials/topics, enjoyed portability	Attitude, Engagement	Positive
Wyatt, et al (2010)	PDA	Student/content, student/instructor, student/student	Individualized learning of content, group projects, assessment, individual projects	Behaviorist & constructivist	Enhanced collaborative learning process	Achievement, Attitude	Positive

A slight majority of the learning tasks performed by the research subjects were behaviorist tasks (n= 5) while the rest were deemed to be constructivist (n= 4). Only the tasks in one study could be classified as both behaviorist and constructivist. The learning tasks used in the studies varied by study with some studies using a combination of tasks. We were able to identify tasks facilitating the individualized learning of content (n= 5), group projects/discussion (n= 5), assessment (n= 4), and teacher directed lecture (n= 2) through the use of the m-learning technology tool.

The type of student interaction the technology was most commonly used for was the interaction between student and content (n=10). Interaction between student and instructor (n=6) and interaction between students (n=5) was also supported by these technologies. By far the most common m-learning technology tool tested was the mobile phone (n=5) and PDA (n= 3). One study analyzed both the mobile phone and PDA as it related to a difference in screen size (Manair, 2007). Mobile phones were used primarily for their data connectivity to send and receive SMS (text) messages and access information via the Internet. One study used an mp3 player for podcasting purposes.

Benefits were identified by all studies included in the review. One study by Williams & Bearman (2008) found students "reported benefits in using the podcasts to better understand and/or review lecture concepts" (p. 7). Several studies indicated an increase in achievement among students (McConatha et al., 2008; Shih et al., 2010; Wyatt et al., 2010; Hsu et al., 2008; Williams & Bearman, 2008). McConatha et al. (2008) found that "students…using web-enabled cell phones to assist in their review of test materials outscored the students who used more traditional means (handouts and review lectures) to practice and review materials" (p. 5). More productive study time and better access to materials are benefits of m-learning identified in these studies.

Al-Fahad (2009), Wang et al. (2009), and Rogers et al. (2010) all reported that students became more excited about the learning process and became more engaged active learners rather than passive learners. These students became the drivers in their own education, taking pleasure in guiding their own learning process. The enhancement of student collaboration was evident in studies by both Guenter et al. (2008) and Wyatt et al. (2010). Students not only worked together more effectively in some cases, they were excited to work in these groups according to the Lillypad environmental study conducted by Rogers et al. (2010).

CONCLUSION AND DISCUSSION

Key Findings

Mobile learning research is certainly gaining momentum. The recent availability of solid research studies indicates that a strong base is currently being built for m-learning research methodology. Almost all of the studies analyzed in this review have utilized strong and focused research questions, significant sample sizes, detailed surveys, and acknowledgement of possible limitations. Many of the studies utilized one-group pre-and post-tests or surveys. In most cases, as is common with educational research, researchers found that they were limited by available populations and the type of methodology that could be employed. Although often difficult to accomplish, there is still a need to engage in more quantitative experimental mobile learning research (Ali & Irvine, 2009). We believe that this type of research is crucial to the development of a research base that will promote the success of m-learning endeavors in classrooms around the world and give validity to a new kind of learning that may not seem adequate yet to many educators.

The list of m-learning devices was extremely broad in prior literature (Fetaji, 2008). The reviewed articles, however, suggest that the most pervasive form of m-learning technology is the mobile phone. Mobile phones and PDAs were most often the m-learning technology of choice for researchers (Guenter et al., 2008; Hsu et al., 2008; Al-Fahad, 2009; Rogers et al., 2010; Wyatt et al., 2010; Wang et al., 2009; Cavus & Uzunboylu, 2009; Manair, 2007). The use of mobile phones in research studies is not surprising when strong evidence suggests that most learners already own mobile phones that can be used with many m-learning applications and that increasingly multi-functional mobile phones are eliminating the needs for multiple devices. (Bottentuit & Coutinho, 2008).

Evidence of the potential benefit to student learning was identified by several studies that support student learning through the use of m-learning (Guenter et al., 2008; Manair, 2007; Shih et al., 2010; Wyatt et al., 2010; Hsu et al., 2008; Al-Fahad, 2009; Williams & Bearman, 2008; Rogers et al., 2010; Wang et al., 2009; Cavus & Uzunboylu, 2009). This facet of m-learning was generally cited as a possibility for future research in prior literature, but is becoming a more often studied feature of m-learning (Fetaji, 2008; Traxler 2009; Najimi & Lee, 2009). Both attitude and achievement were examined with regard to benefits to student learning. In addition, several studies noticed an increase in achievement among students (Shih et al., 2010; Wyatt et al., 2010; Hsu et al., 2008; Williams & Bearman, 2008).

As more valid studies continue to be conducted with proper methodology combined with tested pedagogical practice, it is logical that these results could unearth solid evidence to support m-learning as a viable learning tool.

Recommendations for Future Research

We found that the majority of the research on mobile learning is being conducted outside of the United States and we predict a larger sample would have similar results. While, m-learning studies and practice are still rare in the US, the European Union has already established a training program that seeks to move from distance and e-learning to m-learning, which they refer to as "the environment of tomorrow" (Fetaji, 2008). Thus, our first recommendation would be to establish a similar initiative in the United States. The Horizon Report, 2011, which has been published in collaboration with the New Media Consortium and the Educause Learning Initiative, provides an overview of six emerging technologies or practices that they predict will be adopted by mainstream education within the next four to five years. They predicted that in one year or less, mobile computing, m-learning, will become more commonly adopted in the classroom. Thus, further research will become even more critical (Levine et al., 2010). The establishment of an initiative to research m-learning and inform the practice of educators will only work to ensure the success of m-learning in the United States.

The speed at which mobile technology is increasing is becoming problematic for research. In fact, since the most of the studies analyzed here have been done, mobile technology has advanced so much that the analysis of different types of devices is becoming obsolete. Most phones are now multifunctional and capable of performing the tasks of most computers, PDA's, and mp3 players. Thus, we believe that research should be focused on personal mobile devices. It seems unnecessary to devote time and resources to procurement of devices when most learners already own devices that support many m-learning opportunities. We believe that research should continue to be devoted to developing practical applications that could be used on a variety of mobile device platforms. We predict students are already using their personal mobile devices for informal learning as they use them in almost every other aspect of their lives. And, the results of this study suggest that they would also like to use them in more formal educational settings. Thus, it is necessary that researchers and teachers explore new ways and best practices to incorporate mobile devices as learning tools both inside and outside the classroom.

The literature reveals a focus on attitudinal studies, which while necessary for establishing that the learner is comfortable with the device and is motivated to use it, shows little about its affect on learning. However, now that studies have shown learner acceptance and motivation, research should be devoted to understanding if the use of a mobile device or mobile application for educational purposes can lead to an increase in skills, comprehension, and knowledge.

While research has begun to examine theories of mobile learning, we found that many studies lacked connection to a theoretical framework (Traxler, 2009). An increase in theory work would certainly benefit the increase of researchers studying mobile learning.

Recommendations for Practice

Traxler (2009) points to evidence of the maturation of m-learning's separate and unique identity from other types of learning citing the emergence of a theoretical framework, the launch of international journals, and development of pilot studies and learning initiatives globally. Certainly the studies cited in this systematic review further substantiate his claims that m-learning has value and the potential to positively affect learning in a variety of contexts. Although most researchers would consider m-learning to still be in its infancy and perhaps claim that there is not enough research to substantiate a research-based practice initiative in K-12 or higher education, the results cannot be ignored in the studies that have been done. The vast majority of the studies reviewed here have yielded positive results in both achievement and attitude.

The need for ubiquitous learning opportunities is immediate. And, it seems as if education is falling behind. Businesses and entrepreneurs seeking to meet the needs of a population that more frequently requires anytime, anywhere

access are currently meeting these learning needs. If education is to have any place in this niche, we must acknowledge that the research must constantly evolve with the technology. Of course this may be problematic because of the fast-paced development of mobile devices and the time commitment that accompanies a sound research project. However, the benefit of mobile learning, as highlighted in this review, is that the technology, the device, is personal. And, because personal mobile device ownership is universal, it is critical that education embraces this new technology and develops pedagogies to support and enhance learning with the use of these devices. As capabilities continue to increase, the demand for instant communication and access to learning materials will rise and modern education must meet that challenge.

REFERENCES

Al-Fahad, F. N. (2009). *Students' attitudes and perceptions towards the effectiveness of mobile learning in King Saud University*. Saudi Arabia: Turkish Online Journal of Educational Technology.

Ali, R., & Irvine, V. (2009). Current m-learning research: A review of key literature. In *Proceedings of the World Conference on E-Learning in Corporate, Government, Healthcare, and Higher Education* (pp. 2353-2359).

Ally, M. (Ed.). (2009). *Mobile learning: Transforming the delivery of education and training*. Athabasca, AB, Canada: Athabasca University Press.

Bottentuit, J. B., Jr., & Coutinho, C. (2008). The use of mobile technologies in higher education in Portugal: An exploratory survey. In *Proceedings of the World Conference on E-Learning in Corporate, Government, Healthcare, and Higher Education* (pp. 2102-2107).

Cavus, N., & Uzunboylu, H. (2009). Improving critical thinking skills in mobile learning. *Procedia Social and Behavioral Sciences, 1*(1), 434–438. doi:10.1016/j.sbspro.2009.01.078

Davis, F. D. (1989). Perceived usefulness, perceived ease of use, and user acceptance of information technology. *Management Information Systems Quarterly, 13*(3), 319–340. doi:10.2307/249008

Fetaji, M. (2008). Literature review of m-learning issues, m-learning projects and technologies. In *Proceedings of the World Conference on E-Learning in Corporate, Government, Healthcare, and Higher Education* (pp. 348-353).

Guenther, S., Winkler, T., Ilgner, K., & Herczeg, M. (2008). Mobile learning with moles: A case study for enriching cognitive learning by collaborative learning in real world contexts. In *Proceedings of the World Conference on Educational Multimedia, Hypermedia and Telecommunications* (pp. 374-380).

Hart, C. (1999). *Doing a literature review: Releasing the social science research imagination.* London, UK: Sage.

Holzinger, A., Nischelwitzer, A., & Meisenberger, M. (2005) Mobile phones as a challenge for mlearning. In *Proceedings of the IEEE International Conference on Pervasive Computing and Communications* (pp. 307-311).

Hsu, H., Wang, S., & Comac, L. (2008). Using audioblogs to assist English-language learning: an investigation into student perception. *Computer Assisted Language Learning, 21*(2), 181–198. doi:10.1080/09588220801943775

Johnson, L., Levine, A., Smith, R., & Stone, S. (2011). *The 2011 Horizon Report.* Austin, TX: The New Media Consortium.

Kukulska-Hulme, A., Traxler, J., & Pettit, J. (2007). Designed and user-generated activity in the mobile age. *Journal of Learning Design, 2*(1), 52–65.

Maniar, N. (2007). M-learning to teach university students. In *Proceedings of the World Conference on Educational Multimedia, Hypermedia and Telecommunications* (pp. 881-887).

McConatha, D., Praul, M., & Lynch, M. J. (2008). Mobile learning in higher education: An empirical assessment of a new educational tool. *Educational Technology, 7*(3), 15–21.

Naismith, L., Lonsdale, P., Vavoula, G., & Sharples, M. (2004). *Literature review in mobile technologies and learning.* London, UK: NESTA Futurelab Series.

Najimi, A., & Lee, J. (2009). Why and how mobile learning can make a difference in the K-16 classroom? In *Proceedings of the Society for Information Technology & Teacher Education International Conference* (pp. 2903-2910).

Petticrew, M., & Roberts, H. (2006). *Systematic reviews in the social sciences: A practical guide.* Oxford, UK: Blackwell. doi:10.1002/9780470754887

Rogers, Y., Connelly, K., Hazlewood, W., & Tedesco, L. (2010). Enhancing learning: A study of how mobile devices can facilitate sense making. *Personal and Ubiquitous Computing, 14*(2), 111–124. doi:10.1007/s00779-009-0250-7

Sharples, M. (2006). *Big issues in mobile learning.* Nottingham, UK: Kaleidoscope Research.

Shih, K., Chen, H., Chang, C., & Kao, T. (2010). The development and implementation of scaffolding-based self-regulated learning system for e/m-learning. *Journal of Educational Technology & Society, 13*(1), 80–93.

Traxler, J. (2009). Learning in a mobile age. *International Journal of Mobile and Blended Learning, 1*(1), 1–12. doi:10.4018/jmbl.2009010101

Wang, M., Shen, R., Novak, D., & Pan, X. (2009). The impact of mobile learning on students' learning behaviours and performance: Report from a large blended classroom. *British Journal of Educational Technology, 40*(4), 673–695. doi:10.1111/j.1467-8535.2008.00846.x

Williams, B., & Bearman, M. (2008). Podcasting lectures: The next silver bullet? *Journal of Emergency Primary Health Care, 6*(3), 1–14.

Wyatt, T. H., Krauskopf, P. B., Gaylord, N. M., Ward, A., Huffstutler-Hawkins, S., & Goodwin, L. (2010). Cooperative m-learning with nurse practitioner students. *Nursing Education Perspectives, 31*(2), 109–112.

Yordanova, K. (2007). Mobile learning and integration of advanced technologies in education. In *Proceedings of the International Conference on Computer Systems and Technologies* (pp. 1-5).

This work was previously published in the International Journal of Mobile and Blended Learning, Volume 3, Issue 3, edited by David Parsons, pp 34-42, copyright 2011 by IGI Publishing (an imprint of IGI Global).

Chapter 4
Empirical Research on Learners' Thoughts About the Impact of Mobile Technology on Learning

Gábor Kismihók
Corvinus University of Budapest, Hungary

Réka Vas
Corvinus University of Budapest, Hungary

ABSTRACT

Mobile learning is gaining attention in Europe. Researchers are examining both pedagogical and technical issues regarding mobilized content delivery; however, little is known about current learners' thoughts toward mobile learning. In this article, based on an empirical research study, the authors show what learners think about mobile learning and related learning technologies. Data consisting of 300 learners' thoughts and experiences in connection with mobile learning (living in five different European countries) have been gathered and analysed. Results indicate that current positive attitudes toward mobile learning may be negatively influenced by experience, if previous patterns with other learning technologies are repeated.

INTRODUCTION

The Department of Information Systems at Corvinus University of Budapest has been actively researching and adopting mobile learning for many years (Kismihók & Vas, 2009; Kismihók, 2007; Vas, Kovács, & Kismihók, 2009). This work started with pilot content development in the early 2000s (Dye, Jones, & Kismihók, 2006). Since then, mobile educational services have been incorporated into the mainstream educational activities of the Department, thus more and more attention has been focused on learners' perceptions of this novel technology. With funding from the European

DOI: 10.4018/978-1-4666-2139-8.ch004

Commissions' Lifelong Learning Programme, a quantitative research study has been carried out in order to learn more about educators' and learners' perceptions of mobilized educational services.

Structure of this Article

First the framework of our empirical study is presented, regarding learners' attitudes towards using mobile technology in education. Then we describe of the research design and the various statistical analyses that were performed on the data collected. Finally we conclude with further challenges and research directions.

LEARNERS' ATTITUDES TOWARDS MOBILE LEARNING

Research Context

IMPACT was an EU Lifelong Learning project ended in 2008, which aimed to discover empirically how technology enhanced learning changed the way we teach and learn (Agrusti et al., 2008; Krämer, 2007). Within this study a complete work-package has been dedicated to mobile technology and mobile learning, questioning whether it is still in its infancy or has managed to make a step forward towards being an everyday routine. We were also interested in what learners think about mobile learning. Nevertheless the ultimate goal of the project was to provide a set of variables that help instructors to understand the implications of various technologies on their students and also to provide research-based principles for how instructors should use technology in their teaching. Furthermore, a more pragmatic outcome was to get information for planning a technology supported educational service portfolio at the Department of Information Systems at the Corvinus University of Budapest.

The idea of assessing learners' perspectives about educational technology being used in

education is not novel. In the field of technology supported learning, comparing eLearning to face to face education has been done several times in the past. Researchers measured topics like student's satisfaction (Johnson, Aragon, Shaik, & Palma-Rivas, 2000), effectiveness of on-line education (Sargeant et al., 2004; Solimeno, Mebane, Tomai, & Francescato, 2008), investigated students' conceptions about learning through online discussions (Ellis, Goodyear, Prosser, & O'Hara, 2006) and also learning outcomes (Herman & Banister, 2007). In general these studies concluded that there is no significant difference between on-line and face-to face studies, when it comes to learning outcomes (Solimeno et al., 2008).

Nevertheless, mobile learning is still rarely investigated from this comparative point of view. Some work has been done on examining the user acceptance of mobile devices in education (Huang, Lin, & Chuang, 2007), but most researchers have concentrated on trialing various mobile learning applications and collecting student feedback about them, for example a pilot study in Finland for supervising trainee teachers using mobile devices (Seppälä & Alamäki, 2003). Collecting thoughts about mobile learning is also included in articles summarising various pilot researches, trying to give a perspective of the fields for other researchers and practitioners (Cobcroft, Towers, Smith, & Bruns, 2006; Corbeil & Valdes-Corbeil, 2007; Sharples, 2006). This practice was reflected by Traxler and Kukulska-Hulme, suggesting the development of "good" mobile learning evaluation, which leaves the frames of single application validation processes behind (Traxler & Kukulska-Hulme, 2005). Later Traxler went further, to address the necessity of developing evaluation methods which are also reliable on a bigger scale (Traxler, 2007). He articulated that important features of mobile learning (that it is personal, contextual, and situated) make such evaluation very difficult.

It is clear that there is a lack of research on the actual general impact of mobile technology on learning. Therefore our research was attempting to target this issue and collect primary data about learners' general views on mobile learning in five European countries. The methodology employed in the IMPACT project was based on the "Identifying and implementing educational practices supported by rigorous evidence" framework (U.S. Department of Education, Institute of Education Sciences, 2003). In this case the framework has been used for setting up a combination of blended quantitative techniques (questionnaire with general learning questions, in combination with specific questions and questions on educational background of respondents). This questionnaire was utilised by a quantitative analysis (in-depth statistical analyses) using inductive statistics and randomized controlled trials with survey sampling. The purpose of sampling is the accomplishment of efficiency, representation, and minimal disruption. Using inductive statistics was necessary as only weak agreements exist on the meaning of variables. The data was gathered and analysed throughout 2007-2008. The final data analysis was performed in late 2008. Descriptive statistical analyses presented in this article were produced with SPSS 15.0, for the cluster analysis we used SPSS 16.0.

Research Hypotheses

As it was mentioned before, the main idea of this research was to investigate learners' thoughts towards mobile technology in education. In order to reach this goal the following domain specific hypothesis had been made:

- There is no significant difference in the judgment of people with or without experience in mobile learning that the use of mobile technology can enhance the general quality of learning.
- It is generally accepted that the use of mobile learning in education is beneficial for

improving the communication between students and educators.
- Incorporating mobile learning into educational activities adds additional value for the learning programmes provided by higher educational institutions.

Questionnaire

The designed questionnaire consists of three sections:

- **Section 1:** Personal information including social indicators like gender, age, profession, or education as judgments depends on such indicators.
- **Section 2:** Experiences with technology-enhanced learning, and
- **Section 3:** Questions related to mobile learning experiences.

For testing perceptions, thoughts and opinions about the impact of technology on learning, it was decided to use intensity questions in order to measure the strength of a respondent's feeling or attitude on questionnaire items in Sections 2 and 3. We allowed answers uniformly on five-part (Lickert – type) scale ranging from a high degree of agreement to complete disagreement. The "questions" were in the form of statements that were either definitely favourable or definitely unfavourable toward the matter under consideration. The answers were recorded as numerical values ranging from one to five. The highest value showed the most favourable attitude toward the subject of a particular question. The weights were not shown on the actual questionnaire and, therefore, were not seen by the respondents. The odd number of possible answers was chosen so that respondents who were neither pro nor contra could express their uncertainty about a particular item in the questionnaire.

Main and Control Groups

The main (intervention) group, which was selected on the basis of their personal experience with mobile learning, comprised 150 respondents from the Department of Information Systems at the Corvinus University of Budapest, Hungary and from Ericsson Education, Ireland. (These organisations have already incorporated mobile learning into their teaching portfolio.)

The control group was also composed of about 150 respondents (however a few question responses were missing from the sample, as the results show), from four of our project partners, namely Roma Tre University (Italy), Plovdiv University (PU, Bulgaria), Distance Education International (DEI, Ireland) and Fernuniversitat Hagen (FeU, Germany).

In both groups, experience with technology-enhanced learning was expected to vary.

Main Group

At Corvinus University of Budapest learners involved in mobile learning related courses were asked to fill out an online questionnaire. The original questionnaire was translated into Hungarian in order to increase comprehension and avoid possible misinterpretations of items by non-native English learners. An informative message was sent via e-mail, which was designed to briefly inform the respondents on:

- Purpose of the project,
- Responsible organizer,
- Guaranteed anonymity,
- Link to the questionnaire.

Within Ericsson Education Ireland, questionnaires were distributed to groups who were engaged with mobile learning during their corporate training. The majority of the respondents were primarily from the categories of management and training consultants. All data was sent and responded to in electronic format.

Control Groups

The control group was composed of 150 respondents from Roma Tre, DEI, FeU and PU. Before the submission, the questionnaire was translated into the appropriate language of each partner. Each partner chose the appropriate manner to submit the questionnaires to their respondents.

In Bulgaria the lecturers at University of Plovdiv handed out printed copies of the Bulgarian version of the questionnaire to randomly selected learners. After the students had completed their questionnaires, they were collected and the data was compiled in an Excel spreadsheet that was used to perform the data analysis.

The people who filled in the questionnaires under the direction of Distance Education International (DEI) were students at Dublin Institute of Arts and Digital Technology (IADT), Ireland. The questionnaires were administered to the respondents in a classroom situation in an evening course and filled out in the presence of the teacher.

In Italy the data was gathered among postgraduate students enrolled in Roma Tre University. The groups were chosen in order to represent this particular tier of learners. The questionnaires were administered before classes, giving the respondents sufficient time to answer. Data were then converted into electronic format.

Descriptive Statistics

Differences Between Main and Control Groups

The total sample size of the study was 300 (N=300), which was equally distributed between two groups: the main (intervention) group with 150 and the control group also with 150 samples. This kind of sampling was made to meet the requirements of the United States Department of Education's 'Identifying and implementing educational practices supported by rigorous evidence'. Specifically, effort has been made to comply with one of the fundamental stipulations: "*A rough rule of thumb is that a sample size of at least 300 students (150 in the intervention group and 150 in the control group) is needed to obtain a finding of statistical significance for an intervention that is effective"* (U.S. Department of Education, Institute of Education Sciences, 2003, p. 15).

Cross-tabulation has been carried out in order to identify the main differences between the groups regarding the research questions. In the following section we describe the significant results of this comparison.

Personal Issues

The main group contained 99 male and 51 female respondents, whereas the control group was comprised of 59 male and 89 female participants (2 respondents didn't answer this question). The difference is assumed to be a consequence of the different backgrounds of the various source groups in the study.

Regarding their occupations, the main group was more heterogeneous. Apart from the unemployed group, all other categories were represented with a significant number of replies. On the control group side the picture was simpler; most of the respondents were students (99 out of 149. One respondent did not answer this question).

The high proportion of student answers in the control group was visible by educational categories as well. The majority of people in the control group had only high school matriculation and most of them were still studying. The main group was more mature (105 respondents out of 150 had some kind of degree from a higher educational institution).

Impact of ICT on Learning

Regarding the Impact of ICT on learning the analysis was only significant in connection with a limited number of factors. We introduce here three questions, which best describe the contrast between the two groups.

An interesting and significant result of the comparison was that people who were engaged

in mobile learning before were more negative regarding the intensity of communication in online education compared to traditional face-to-face education. However, while most of the respondents in both groups disagreed with the statement visible in Figure 1, there was a remarkable amount of positive answers in the control group (44 out of 150 agreed) and also relatively high, very negative feedback from the main group (27 out of 149 answers strongly disagreed).

The negativity of the main group was also visible in stating whether the impact of technology on learning is beneficial or not (Figure 2). Just like in the previous case, here the control group was more optimistic than the main group, with relatively low uncertainty in both groups. 64 respondents in the main group disagreed with this statement at some level, compared to 27 negative answers in the control group, while 56 agreed in the main group (against 97 in the control group).

A less critical response seems evident towards educational games. Nevertheless here there is still some uncertainty. As Figure 3 demonstrates, the majority of the individuals were positive in both groups with a small but notable positive bias in the control group (93 in the main and 111 in the control group respectively), but the number of uncertain answers were almost twice as many in the main group (43 in opposition to 22). It also has to be stated that the significance value of the Pearson Chi-square test was just above the 0,05 limit (0,056).

Mobile Learning

An interesting but not significant change in the judgment of the main group appears in the items connected to mobile learning. Here with a 0,072 significance level (with a 0,05 cut off value) the main group was more positive than the control group (Figure 4 and Figure 5). 74 out of 142 of those, who already used a mobile learning related service, said that mobile learning is something that they could recommend to someone else (control group: 55/150). However the number of uncertain

Figure 1. Contacts between teachers and students

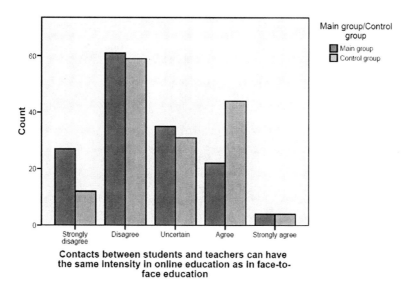

answers was also high in both groups: 44 in the main and 55 in the control group.

One possible reason for being positive about mobile learning is that the majority of the main group also thought that mobile devices in general increase access to education and training. 85 out of 150 gave positive answers to this question. It should also be mentioned that there is a certain relationship between this item and the previous one, as the Spearman – rho correlation coefficient shows a more than moderate connection with a value of 0,606.

This positive relationship did not appear for the statement associated with mobile communication (Figure 6). Here the critical tendency of the main group is quite strongly represented again.

Figure 2. Impact of technology on learning is beneficial

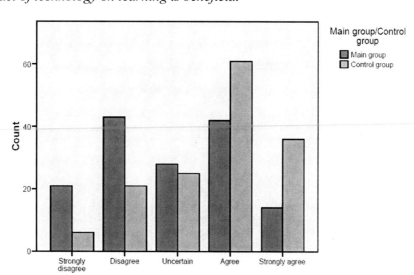

Figure 3. Educational games

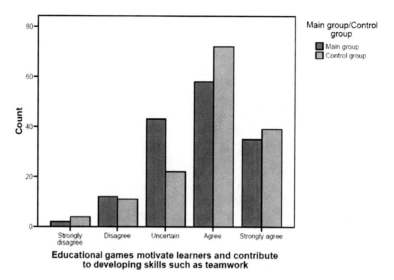

Educational games motivate learners and contribute
to developing skills such as teamwork

The same number of people (44) disagreed or were uncertain regarding the communicational benefits of mobile technology in education. This is a surprising result, as the main function of a mobile phone is the communication itself! However, from the questionnaire, researchers could not find out what kind of mobile services the respondents from the main group used, as there are several portable services available where the centre of attention is not communication, but on the mobility of learners.

The control group was also more positive regarding the importance of the general availability of mobile phones in education. As can be seen in Figure 7, respondents in the main group were more pessimistic (56/149) or uncertain (44/149), while 76 respondents in the control group were positive about this issue.

Figure 4. Proposing mobile learning

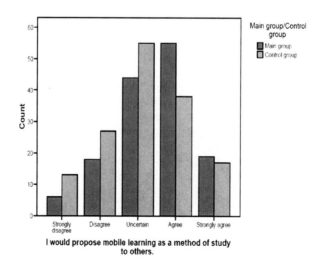

I would propose mobile learning as a method of study
to others.

Figure 5. Access to education

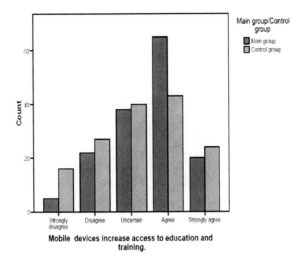

There was a general agreement about the statement regarding whether possessing a mobile phone is sufficient to undertake an academic or a professional educational program or not (Figure 8). Both groups rejected this idea (125/149 in the main group and 110/150 in the control group), but as with previous statements, the main group had a more negative attitude with a high number of 'strongly disagree' responses (89).

Other Influences: T-Test

The t-test applied to our two sample groups allows us to compare the mean values within the outcomes of both groups. Figure 9 presents these values. In general, there are no big differences in the mean values between the main and the control group, but some items still differ significantly. For the question '*The opinion that the impact of technology on learning is beneficial is correct*' the mean values were 2,9 in the focus and 3,67 in the

Figure 6. Communication

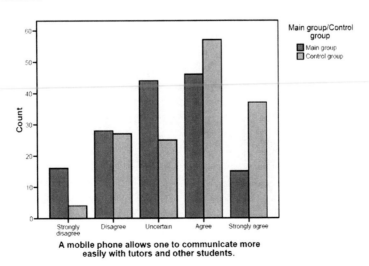

Figure 7. Availability of mobile phones

control group showing again the control group's positive attitude towards technology.

Cluster Analysis

In order to enhance our understanding of the responses, it is logical to create certain clusters within the focus and control group. K-Means Cluster analysis was selected for this purpose as this procedure tries to identify reasonably homogeneous groups based on our variables (Füstös, Kovács, Meszéna, & Simonné Mosolygó, 2004). Distances between clusters were computed using simple Euclidean distance. There was no need for standardisation, as all items included in the cluster analysis were ordinal and Lickert-scale based variables. For this investigation we decided to create three clusters with iteration and repeated

Figure 8. Undertaking a professional study only with a mobile phone

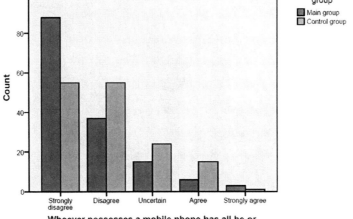

Figure 9. T-test results

Group Statistics

	Main group/Control group	N	Mean	Std. Deviation	Std. Error Mean
Thanks to technology, the problems of access to learning for students with disabilities have been resolved	Main group	147	3,41	,866	,071
	Control group	150	3,61	,962	,079
Contacts between students and teachers can have the same intensity in online education as in face-to-face education	Main group	149	2,43	1,035	,085
	Control group	150	2,79	1,038	,085
Online communication allows increased amounts of communication between teachers and students when compared with other forms of education	Main group	150	3,15	1,019	,083
	Control group	150	3,44	1,020	,083
The opinion that the impact of technology on learning is beneficial is correct	Main group	148	2,90	1,233	,101
	Control group	149	3,67	1,112	,091
From my personal study experience I find that the impact of technology on learning is valuable	Main group	150	4,15	,862	,070
	Control group	150	4,05	,854	,070
Information and communications technology has usually been used to encourage us to be active participants in learning	Main group	149	3,40	1,013	,083
	Control group	149	3,71	,816	,067
Information and communications technology has been used to support the development of higher level thinking skills such as synthesis and problem solving	Main group	145	3,46	,928	,077
	Control group	149	3,63	,903	,074
Information and communications technology has been used to support more individualized learning programmes tailored to our own individual needs	Main group	147	3,56	,915	,075
	Control group	150	3,69	,898	,073
Learning is enhanced when text and pictures are integrated in a multimedia environment	Main group	150	4,19	,888	,072
	Control group	150	4,05	,947	,077
Educational games motivate learners and contribute to developing skills such as teamwork	Main group	150	3,75	,950	,078
	Control group	148	3,89	,973	,080
I would propose mobile learning as a method of study to others.	Main group	142	3,44	1,014	,085
	Control group	150	3,13	1,107	,090
A mobile phone allows one to communicate more easily with tutors and other students.	Main group	149	3,11	1,152	,094
	Control group	150	3,64	1,119	,091
Mobile devices increase access to education and training.	Main group	150	3,49	1,008	,082
	Control group	150	3,21	1,224	,100
The fact that a mobile phone is a generally available device is important for education.	Main group	149	2,85	1,137	,093
	Control group	150	3,27	1,175	,096
Whoever possesses a mobile phone has all he or she needs for undertaking academic or professional study.	Main group	149	1,65	,958	,078
	Control group	150	2,01	,997	,081

this analysis twice. We have verified the existence of these groups for the items measuring the impact of ICT in general (Item 7-16) and also for items related to mobile learning (Item 17-21). We anticipated seeing that the previous results and the described attitudes towards the various educational technologies were based on the heterogeneity of the groups. We also considered that the experience of several classification approaches in the field of technology enhanced learning and innovation adoption (Kozma, 2003; Peng, Tsai, & Wu, 2006; Valenta, Therriault, Dieter, & Mrtek, 2001) must be taken into consideration before the identification of our clusters.

Valenta and her colleagues (2001) examined the clusters of opinions held by students, with respect to technology and its application to education, across two populations: traditional college undergraduate students and adult learners (non-traditional graduate students). They identified 3 groups of students: (1) Most important to *Time and Structure in Learning group* was that web-based education provides flexible time management. (2) Among those in the *Social Interaction in Learning group* the primary objective was the potential for a discussion with as few participants as possible, which results in fewer subtleties in teaching with web-based education. Enrichment from other perspectives and potential interference with work were also ranked important in this group. (3) For the members of the *Convenience in Learning group* the emphasis was on the fact that web-based education lets them work at home and saves travel time. In this research the authors have not examined mobile technology aspects. It also has to be taken into consideration that none of the participants in this research had any experience with online coursework or had previously taken a web-based course. However in two of the identified clusters students are positive concerning the impact of technology on education and only the members of the Social Interaction in Learning group have reservations about the positive effects of technology on education.

The study of Kozma (2003) looks at how classrooms worldwide are using technology to change the practices of teachers and students. He examined the findings from 174 case studies of innovative pedagogical practices using technology from 28 participating countries. As part of the research Kozma also performed a cluster analysis to examine how classroom practices were used together within cases and seven meaningful patterns of classroom practice were identified. In this research the authors have not examined the opinion of students and teachers about the impact of technology, but the cluster analysis clearly reveals that some groups are keen to use the latest technological innovations in education, while others are more careful and need a certain period of time to adopt new technology. In this research users that are skeptical concerning the impacts of technology on education were not identified.

Peng and his colleagues (2006) investigated university students' attitudes and self-efficacy and explored the role of their perceptions towards the Internet. They identified 4 clusters of university students. These are: (1) *Technology*, (2) *Tool*, (3) *Toy* and (4) *Tour*. They found that learners who perceived the Internet as a tour or a toy, in general, exhibited attitudes that were more positive (concerning technology supported learning) and their sense of communicative self-efficacy was better than learners who simply perceived the Internet as technology or tool.

It is also worth noting Rogers' categories of innovation adoption (Rogers, 2003). Rogers suggests a total of five clusters of adopters in order to standardize the usage of adopter categories in diffusion research. The categories of adopters are: (1) *Innovators*, who are the first individuals to adopt an innovation and are willing to take risks. (2) The *Early adopters*, the second group of individuals who adopt an innovation. These individuals have the highest degree of opinion leadership among the other adopter categories.

(3) Individuals in the *Early majority* category adopt an innovation after a varying degree of time. This time for adoption is significantly longer than the innovators or early adopters. (4) Members of the *Late majority* category will implement an innovation after the average members of the society. These individuals have a high degree of skepticism concerning innovations. (5) *Laggards* are the last to adopt an innovation and typically tend to be focused on "traditions". The initial assumption of our cluster analysis was that the interviewees should be grouped according to their attitude towards technology. Accordingly, Rogers' classification is a good starting point in identifying the clusters of active participants in virtual learning environments. At the same time our calculations did not underpin the definition of five clusters, only the formation of three groups was justified.

Considering the classification approaches described above (Kozma, 2003; Peng et al., 2006; Valenta et al., 2001), also the cited innovation adoption model (Rogers, 2003) and considering our own practices in the past (Vas, Kismihók, Kő, Szabó, & Bíró, 2007), we decided to set up three technical categories for classifying active participants in virtual learning environments.

- **Technology Pioneers:** These are the pioneers, who make use of the most recent technology in their studies. Among those people in this cluster, we found that the impact of technology on learning is quite valuable (at this question the final cluster center was 4 on a five point scale both in the main and control groups). Members of the Technology Pioneers cluster also strongly believe that contacts between students and teachers can have the same intensity in online education as in face-to-face education (here the final cluster centers were also 4 compared to only 2,43/2,79 in the main and control groups). These learners usually possess the latest technology in their palm, they are motivated to try and use new, innovative electronic services in education. ICT encourages the members of this cluster to actively participate in learning (with a value of 4 in both cluster centers compared to only 3,40/3,71 mean group values), supports the development of higher level thinking skills (also 4 in both groups, compared to 3,46/3,63) and of more individualized learning programmes (final cluster centers were 4 again, compared to 3,56/3,69 in the main and control groups). These learners are sometimes well ahead of their tutors, when it comes to knowing and handling technology. They believe that multimedia environments enhance learning experience and educational games motivate learners (4/4 compared to 3,75/3,89). However, when we take a look at the figures connected to mobile learning questions the dividing line between the main and the control group appears. The members of the main group have reservations about the impact of mobile technology in education, therefore the cluster center of the main group underperforms the control group's values. For instance, members of this cluster agree that mobile devices increase the access to education, but this agreement is significantly stronger in the control group (the cluster center values are: 4 in the main and 5 in the control group). Pioneers in both groups do not agree with the statement that *"whoever possesses a mobile phone has all he or she needs for undertaking academic or professional study"*. (The cluster center values are: 2 in the main group and 3 in the control group, compared to 1,65/2,01 group mean values.)

- **Technology Adopters:** Members of this group have reasonable skills for adopting and incorporating information technology into their educational activities. Among those in this cluster ICT usually encour-

ages them to actively participate in learning (at this question both cluster centers were 3 compared to 3,40/3,71 in the main and control groups). At the same time, this mean value is palpably lower than in the case of "Technology Pioneers" cluster (3 compared to 4). They are inclined to accept that ICT supports the development of higher level thinking skills (with a cluster center value 3 in the main group and 4 in the control group compared to 3,46/3,63) and of more individualized learning programmes (same cluster center values to the previous question, compared to 3,56/3,69), although this is not a strong belief. They usually follow the recommendations of the Pioneers and their tutors. They are confident in using technology, but technology is not their desire, they have - in general - a neutral approach. Just like the Pioneers, they also think that the impact of technology on learning is valuable (at this question both cluster centers were 4, compared to 4,15 and 4,05 mean values in the main and control groups). The members of this cluster are slightly positive concerning the role of technology in resolving the problems of access to learning for disabled students (3/4 cluster centers compared to 3,41/3,61). It must also be noted that the distance between the pioneers and the adopters in the control group is significantly lower than in the main group.

- **Technology Skeptics:** People affiliated to this group pick up technology slower and articulate a critical voice towards technology supported learning. Participants of this cluster do not believe that learning is enhanced when text and pictures are integrated in a multimedia environment (at this question cluster center values were 2/1 compared to 4,19/4,05 in the main and control groups) or that educational games motivate learners and contribute to developing skills such as teamwork (with cluster center values 3/1 compared to 3,75/3,89). They see the importance of ICT in education, but they think this phenomenon is overvalued. The members of the "Technology Skeptics" cluster accept to a certain degree – at least in the main group – that impact of technology on learning is beneficial (with cluster center values 3/1 compared to 4,15/4,05), but they do not admit that ICT can support the development of higher level thinking skills (cluster center values were 2/1 compared to 3,46/3,63 in the main and control groups) or more individualized learning programmes (with cluster center values 2/1 compared to 3,56/3,69).

Conclusions of Cluster Analysis

In this research we attempted to cluster participants in both the main and control groups. Nevertheless a possible bias of this approach is that the main group has already been engaged with mobile learning applications, suggesting that the number of technology pioneers is expected to be higher and the number technology skeptics is expected to be lower in that group respectively. We also separated the general ICT and the mobile learning sections for the investigation, in order to see whether group compositions are stable across different domains.

This analysis has been done with SPSS 16.0. After the cluster analysis was performed we checked the cluster centers of each group and based on this analysis we assigned the relevant categories (pioneers, adopters, skeptics) to each group. For this reason the order of the different clusters in the main and control group differ, but this has no impact on the validity of the results.

Main Group

In the main group the identified classes are the following:

- **Cluster 1:** Technology Pioneers,
- **Cluster 2:** Technology Adopters
- **Cluster 3:** Technology Skeptics

As is visible from Figures 10 and 11, there is a significant difference between the general ICT and the mobile learning related categorization. Regarding ICT, in general 80 respondents were classified as pioneer, 50 as adopter and only 10 as skeptical. This is not a surprise, as members of this group have enough experience in eLearning, they have been using and exploring the latest educational applications.

However it must also be emphasized that eLearning is not a new phenomenon. Web based learning and ICT usage on campus have been with us for the last 10-15 years, meaning that learners gained experience in computer based learning applications and developed substantial skills for computer literacy. But mobile learning is also new for this generation! Therefore it is striking to see how they approach this novel learning technology. Figure 11 shows the main group clusters in mobile learning: 43 pioneers, 57 adopters and 40 skeptics. It is clear that the number of skeptics grew four times bigger among the technologically experienced respondents.

Control Group

In the main group the identified classes are the following:

- **Cluster 1:** Technology Skeptics
- **Cluster 2:** Technology Adopters
- **Cluster 3:** Technology Pioneers

There is no wonder that the number of pioneers in this group is lacking behind the main group

Figure 10. Main group clusters regarding general ICT items

Number of Cases in each Cluster

Cluster	1	80,000
	2	50,000
	3	10,000
Valid		140,000
Missing		10,000

figures in the same domain. According to Figure 12, it counts 39 members, which is less than half compared to the main group. The number of skeptics is also small (13). Our interpretation is that the majority of learners in our current educational systems are adopting necessary technology for their studies as it is requested by their supervisors.

Hence, when we investigate control group divisions in the mobile learning domain, we see that the disparity between the control and the main group is slowly diminishing (see Figure 13). 38 pioneers, 59 adopters and 53 skeptics were identified, which is not an immense difference, if we also consider that there were 10 respondents in the main group, which we could not assign to any of these three clusters. It seems the general perception of unknown technology – here mobile technology – is brighter than the technology which is already in use.

In general we concluded that learners both in the main and control groups had a constructive attitude towards technology enhanced learning scenarios. Nevertheless, respondents were much more careful and critical with the new and emerging mobile learning, than with traditional eLearning. People already engaged with this technology became more vigilant with the adoption and became more critical as well. It is still a question though, whether this critical stance is due to the infancy or the limited suitability of mobile technology in education. This analysis can't answer this question.

Figure 11. Main group clusters regarding mobile learning items

Number of Cases in each Cluster

Cluster	1	43,000
	2	57,000
	3	40,000
Valid		140,000
Missing		10,000

Figure 12. Control group clusters general ICT items

Number of Cases in each Cluster

Cluster	1	13,000
	2	93,000
	3	39,000
Valid		145,000
Missing		5,000

Lessons Learned

Our analytical research in the field of mobile learning attempted to measure what learners think about this technology on a larger scale than many previous studies. A range of statistical analyses were applied on the collected data including descriptive statistics covering the whole population of respondents, t-tests comparing the main and control groups, non-parametric correlations, cross tabulation, variance analysis and K-means Cluster Analysis. The results of this analysis are two-fold. On the one hand a number of useful and significant data have been gathered and analysed, which describe the most important differences between traditional and mobile learners. As it is visible from the descriptive statistics and the cluster analysis there is a remarkable skepticism

towards mobile technology in education from the main group, which is balanced by the positive expectations of the control group.

On the other hand some of the analysis did not provide statistically significant results, therefore based on our observations it is not possible to say unequivocally that our main research ideas are either completely justified or groundless.

Still, regarding the first hypothesis, "*There is no significant difference in the judgement of people with or without experience in mobile learning that the use of mobile technology can enhance the general quality of learning.*" There is significant data available in this research, which shows that this might not be true! The abovementioned skepticism shows that people who are engaged with technology based learning are a bit more careful about articulating their expectations, es-

Figure 13. Control group clusters regarding mobile learning items

Number of Cases in each Cluster

Cluster	1	53,000
	2	59,000
	3	38,000
Valid		150,000
Missing		,000

pecially positive expectations towards technology in learning situations. This is also in line with previous research using a similar methodology in the field of eLearning (Johnson et al., 2000). There Johnson and his colleagues revealed that *"student satisfaction with their learning experience tends to be slightly more positive for students in a traditional course format although there is no difference in the quality of the learning that takes place"* (Johnson et al., 2000, p. 44).

Concerning our next research statement, *"It is generally accepted that the use of mobile learning in education is beneficial for improving the communication between students and educators."* It was generally accepted that communication has great importance in education and using mobile devices might have a positive impact on educational communication between learners and educators. However mobile learning as a category is quite broad, and there is no evidence that those participants in the main group were articulating their views, based on practicing education related communication on mobile devices and applications. This was one of the weaknesses of the questionnaire, which should be handled in future research.

Regarding the third question: *"Incorporating mobile learning into educational activities adds additional value for the learning programmes provided by higher educational institutions."* This research failed to gather significant evidence. There is no doubt that mobilised educational services were treated positively in both groups and there is also an affirmative support from both groups towards technology in education. But no evidence from this study offered verification of added value in learning programmes when integrating mobile learning in academic processes.

Whilst we cannot draw too many conclusions from some aspects of our study, we should at least be aware that experience with technology enhanced learning does not always appear to lead to an increase in positive attitudes towards it. On the contrary, it seems to lead to an increase in skepti-

cism. At the very least, as proponents of mobile and blended learning, we believe that addressing future investigations towards why this might be the case is essential. We believe that further exploration of the thoughts and attitudes of mobile learners with the support of further quantitative studies may help to improve the general level of mobile learning services. Furthermore, research like this helps us, as education providers, to try to ensure that we are not going to disappoint future learners with systems that do not meet their expectations of what technology can deliver.

ACKNOWLEDGMENT

This data collection and analysis was funded by the European Commission's IMPACT project (Project Nr.: IMPACT - IE/06/C/F/RF-81300).

REFERENCES

Agrusti, F., Keegan, D., Kismihók, G., Krämer, B. J., Mileva, N., & Schulte, D. (2008). *The Impact of New Technologies on Distance Learning Students*. Dublin, Ireland: Ericsson.

Cobcroft, R. S., Towers, S. J., Smith, J. E., & Bruns, A. (2006). Mobile learning in review: Opportunities and challenges for learners, teachers, and institutions. In *Proceedings of the Online Learning and Teaching (OLT) Conference 2006*, Brisbane, QLD, Australia. Retrieved from http://eprints.qut.edu.au/5399/

Corbeil, J. R., & Valdes-Corbeil, M. E. (2007). Are You Ready for Mobile Learning? *EDUCAUSE Quarterly, 30*(2), 51–58.

Dye, A., Jones, B., & Kismihók, G. (2006). *Mobile Learning: The Next Generation of Learning-Exploring Online Services in a Mobile Environment*. Paper presented at the EDEN Annual Conference 2006.

Ellis, R. A., Goodyear, P., Prosser, M., & O'Hara, A. (2006). How and what university students learn through online and face-to-face discussion: conceptions, intentions and approaches. *Journal of Computer Assisted Learning, 22*(4), 244–256. doi:10.1111/j.1365-2729.2006.00173.x

Füstös, L., Kovács, E., Meszéna, G., & Simonné Mosolygó, N. (2004). *Alakfelismerés.* Budapest, Hungary: Új Mandátum.

Herman, T., & Banister, S. (2007). Face-to-Face versus Online Coursework: A Comparison of Learning Outcomes and Costs. *Contemporary Issues in Technology & Teacher Education, 7*(4), 318–326.

Huang, J., Lin, Y., & Chuang, S. (2007). Elucidating user behavior of mobile learning: A perspective of the extended technology acceptance model. *The Electronic Library, 25*(5), 586–599. doi:10.1108/02640470710829569

Johnson, S. D., Aragon, S. R., Shaik, N., & Palma-Rivas, N. (2000). Comparative analysis of learner satisfaction and learning outcomes in online and face-to-face learning environments. *Journal of Interactive Learning Research, 11,* 29–49.

Kismihók, G. (2007). *Mobile Learning in Higher Education: The Corvinus case.* Paper presented at the Online Educa Berlin 2007 Conference, Berlin, Germany.

Kismihók, G., & Vas, R. (2009). Mobile Learning Research at the Corvinus University of Budapest. In A. Szűcs (Ed.), *Book of Abstracts: LOGOS Conference on Strengthening the Integration of ICT Research Effort.* Budapest, Hungary: EDEN.

Kozma, R. B. (2003). Technology and Classroom Practices: An International Study. *Journal of Research on Technology in Education, 36*(1), 1–14.

Krämer, B. J. (2007). *Data Analysis Report on the Impact of Technology on Learning in Open Universities and Distance Education.* Retrieved November 23, 2008, from http://deposit.fernuni-hagen.de/62/

Peng, H., Tsai, C., & Wu, Y. (2006). University students' self-efficacy and their attitudes toward the Internet: the role of students' perceptions of the Internet. *Educational Studies, 32*(1), 73–86. doi:10.1080/03055690500416025

Rogers, E. (2003). *Diffusion of Innovations* (5th ed.). New York, NY: Free Press.

Sargeant, J., Curran, V., Jarvis-Selinger, S., Ferrier, S., Allen, M., Kirby, F., & Ho, K. (2004). Interactive on-line continuing medical education: Physicians' perceptions and experiences. *The Journal of Continuing Education in the Health Professions, 24*(4), 227–236. doi:10.1002/chp.1340240406

Seppälä, P., & Alamäki, H. (2003). Mobile learning in teacher training. *Journal of Computer Assisted Learning, 19*(3), 330–335. doi:10.1046/j.0266-4909.2003.00034.x

Sharples, M. (Ed.). (2006). *Issues in Mobile Learning: Report of a workshop by the Kaleidoscope Network of Excellence Mobile Learning Initiative.* Nottingham, UK: Learning Sciences Research Institute, University of Nottingham.

Solimeno, A., Mebane, M. E., Tomai, M., & Francescato, D. (2008). The influence of students and teachers characteristics on the efficacy of face-to-face and computer supported collaborative learning. *Computers & Education, 51*(1), 109–128. doi:10.1016/j.compedu.2007.04.003

Traxler, J. (2007). Defining, Discussing, and Evaluating Mobile Learning: The moving finger writes and having writ.... *International Review of Research in Open and Distance Learning, 8*(2).

Traxler, J., & Kukulska-Hulme, A. (2005). Evaluating Mobile Learning: Reflections on Current Practice. In *Proceedings of mLearn 2005: Mobile technology: The future of learning in your hands*. Retrieved from http://oro.open.ac.uk/12819/

U.S. Department of Education, Institute of Education Sciences. (2003). *Identifying and implementing educational practices supported by rigorous evidence: A user friendly guide*. Washington, DC: Author. Retrieved from http://www.excelgov.org/evidence

Valenta, A., Therriault, D., Dieter, M., & Mrtek, R. (2001). Identifying Student Attitudes and Learning Styles in Distance Education. *JALN*, *5*(2), 111–127.

Vas, R., Kismihók, G., Kő, A., Szabó, I., & Bíró, M. (2007). Hungarian Experiences of Using an Ontology-based Adaptive Knowledge Evaluation Approach in Teaching Business Informatics in a Mobile Learning Environment. In *Proceedings of the Workshop on Cross-Media and Personalized Learning Applications on top of Digital Libraries*, Budapest, Hungary (pp. 47-64).

Vas, R., Kovács, B., & Kismihók, G. (2009). Ontology-based mobile learning and knowledge testing. *International Journal of Mobile Learning and Organisation*, *3*(2), 128–147. doi:10.1504/IJMLO.2009.024423

This work was previously published in the International Journal of Mobile and Blended Learning, Volume 3, Issue 1, edited by David Parsons, pp 73-88, copyright 2011 by IGI Publishing (an imprint of IGI Global).

Section 2
Mobile Learning Design Solutions and Theoretical Frameworks

Chapter 5
Mobile Devices as Support Rather than Distraction for Mobile Learners:
Evaluating Guidelines for Design

Johan Eliasson
Stockholm University, Sweden

Teresa Cerratto Pargman
Stockholm University, Sweden

Jalal Nouri
Stockholm University, Sweden

Daniel Spikol
Linnaeus University, Sweden

Robert Ramberg
Stockholm University, Sweden

ABSTRACT

This article questions the design of mobile learning activities that lead students to spend time focusing on the mobile devices at the expense of interacting with other students or exploring the environment. This problem is approached from an interaction design perspective, designing and analysing geometry-learning activities. The authors present six guidelines for designing mobile learning activities, where mobile devices support rather than distract students from contents and contexts relevant to the learning goals. The guidelines are developed through video analysis of groups of middle school students doing learning activities outdoors and evaluated using the task model. The guidelines suggest that students (1) assume roles based on a different functionality of each device, (2) use devices as contextual tools, that the activities, (3) include physical interaction with the environment, (4) let teachers assume roles, (5) encourage face-to-face communication, and (6) introduce students to the mobile devices.

DOI: 10.4018/978-1-4666-2139-8.ch005

INTRODUCTION

In formal learning activities outside the classroom, mobile devices are used, for example, in mathematical and scientific inquiry on field trips, for studying local history and for guidance on museum visits. In these kinds of activities, learners are mobile in the physical environment. The mobile devices are used for guiding students to places relevant for the learning goals or for exploring the environment by capturing aspects of it. Reasons for introducing mobile devices to learning outside the classroom may be that they enable new learning experiences in that the mobile devices can be used to support learning in authentic contexts, support peer collaboration and motivate learning (Wijers, Jonker, & Drijvers, 2010). However, the new technology might distract students from the new learning experiences (Figure 1). In viewing mobile learning activities outdoors from a socio-cultural perspective (Säljö, 1999, 2000), we consider a main visual focus on devices is a problem.

Against this background, we propose to investigate the following question: *how do we design formal mobile learning tasks and activities outside the classroom so that students can balance their focus between the mobile devices and the contents and contexts relevant to the learning goals?*

This article reports on the design and analysis of mobile geometry-learning activities in two it-erations (the two iterations have previously been reported on separately as the projects Geo Math (GeM) (Eliasson, Spikol, Cerratto Pargman, & Ramberg, 2010) and Math edUcation and pLayful LEarning (MULLE) (Eliasson, Nouri, Ramberg, & Cerratto Pargman, 2010)). This article contributes (1) an analysis of students' visual focus on devices and (2) guidelines for designing mobile learning activities allowing students to balance their focus between mobile devices and the learning tasks. The analysis of episodes of the activity observed were performed using the task model (Sharples, Taylor, & Vavoula, 2007). In comparison with other theoretical models, relevant to mobile learning research, the task model, we believe, is a powerful analytical tool that can be used to relate students' focus on devices to individual aspects in the design of the learning activities.

In this article, we argue that the question of balancing visual focus on devices with the learning goals given by the task is fundamental to pedagogies using mobile devices from a socio-cultural perspective (Säljö, 1999, 2000). Furthermore we suggest that balancing visual focus on devices with the learning goals given by the task needs to be taken into account from a design perspective. From a socio-cultural perspective there is a need to search for solutions on how the design of mobile learning activities can help students balance their visual focus between devices and the educational task at hand.

Figure 1. Two pairs of students focusing on mobile devices rather than the environment

RELATED WORK

A recent critical study on mobile learning research projects reports that roughly one third of these research projects strive to move learning away from the classroom to more natural environments (Frohberg, Göth, & Schwabe, 2009). As noted by these authors, the research projects they have studied consisted of field trials conducted with small groups of students, with the aim of facilitating collaborative learning. Some of these projects cited by Frohberg, Göth, and Schwabe (2009) introduced mobile devices to not only present information about tasks to users, but also to control the flow of the learning activity in detail. This type of design, we believe, is related to the underlying philosophy of device-centric approaches that lead small groups of learners to maintain a strong focus on devices and device interaction.

Some previous research reports point directly to the problem of students having difficulties focusing on anything other than the mobile devices. In the review by Frohberg, Göth, and Schwabe (2009) the authors noted that there is "very little work which discusses the placement of mobile tools as means of control" (p. 318) and that "[v]ery few Mobile Learning projects with physical context explicitly considered, positioned or focused the usage of mobile technology as instruments to gain transparency and steer flexible learning activities there." (Frohberg, Göth, & Schwabe, 2009, p. 318). On the other hand, there are projects where it has been observed that the participants of a study end up focusing on the device much more than intended. Cole and Stanton (2003) compare projects they have been involved in; KidStory, Hunting the Snark and Ambient Wood, and report that the children had problems focusing on anything else but the mobile device. Their analysis showed that the problem was that the device was displaying a continuous flow of information and their solution was to provide information only occasionally. Göth, Frohberg, and Schwabe (2006) report on a campus guide called the Mobile Game where: "In the current version of the MobileGame

the focus of the players is permanently on the device" (p. 159). They suggest the following five solutions: plan for discontinuous usage, plan focus switches, use technologies only if it brings added value, do not use animations if the application is in the background, and reduce features as much as possible. In a follow-up study Göth and Schwabe (2010) redesigned the automatic updates of screen contents to students manually pushing an update button. The change resulted in a marginal improvement in how much the students were distracted by the device. Additionally, in the project Caerus (Naismith, Sharples, & Ting, 2005) focus on the mobile tourist guide was reported to be a problem, with "a large amount of 'heads-down' interaction" (p. 58). Rethinking implementation and investigating both technical and non-technical navigational aids were the suggested solutions. The latest report we have found on strong focus on the device is a field trial of a mobile 3D reconstruction of a Cistercian Abbey (Cook, 2010), where students participating in the field trial stated that "having to look at the mobile devices was a distraction from engaging with the archaeology site itself" (p. 6).

This review of related research work suggests that mobile devices as distraction rather than support are a problem that is noted by other researchers. However, with one exception the solutions suggested are not elaborated. In the only exception, Göth, Frohberg, and Schwabe (2006), the evaluation of the follow-up study (Göth & Schwabe, 2010) resulted in only marginal improvements.

These findings are intriguing, especially because we believe one of the main arguments for introducing mobile devices to learning is to provide students with opportunities to learn things in situ, in the physical environment inside and outside the classroom. Furthermore, we think that perspectives such as the socio-cultural perspective on learning might have an important role to play in pedagogies introducing mobile devices with the objective of bringing students closer to tangible and authentic phenomena outdoors.

RESEARCH METHOD

We designed and implemented geometry-learning activities, by adopting design practices from design-based research (Design-Based Research Collective, 2003), where we followed design practices from co-design (Penuel, Roschelle, & Shechtman, 2007) in two design iterations. These design iterations involved working in iterative cycles together with teachers and other stakeholders taking part in the design of learning activities. Design-based research follows an iterative cycle of identifying, developing, building and evaluating similar to that of interaction design processes. We evaluated the designs of the learning activities through analysing two outdoor activities, each held with two groups of three students. The outdoor activities were designed together with other learning activities, both indoors and outdoors. The evaluation of visual focus on devices was performed with interaction analysis (Jordan & Henderson, 1995). The interaction analysis was used for the identification of episodes from the outdoor activities relevant to focus on devices. The task model suggested by Sharples, Taylor, and Vavoula (2007) was used for further analysing the individual episodes identified in the interaction analysis.

Expanding from previous work (Kurti, Spikol, & Milrad, 2008), we designed and evaluated geometry-learning activities in two iterations. The outcome of the first evaluation resulted in a set of design guidelines that were fed into the second iteration and refined in the second evaluation (Figure 2).

Design Methods

We held three co-design workshops together with teachers in the months before the field activities. In both iterations we designed tasks based on what mathematical concepts the students were currently working with. The outcome of these workshops led to a design of both the activity and the mobile devices.

The design team consisted of researchers from computer science, mathematics, human computer interaction and learning and practicing teachers from natural sciences and mathematics. The design activities included visits to potential outdoor settings, design of tasks and activities and development of ideas into sketches and paper prototypes together in the design team. The second design activity also involved reviewing the previous study with the design team. The goals of the team were to get the students away from the desk, to make mathematics more tangible and to provide opportunities for the students to collaborate, discuss, and solve mathematics problems outside the classroom. In particular, we were interested

Figure 2. Process of designing for balanced focus on mobile devices in two iterations

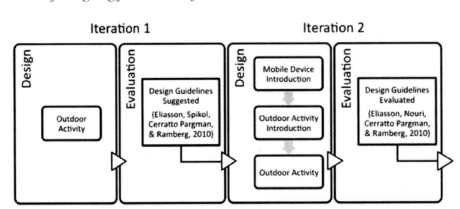

Figure 3. Clue device showing an animation of how to measure a rectangle by using a smaller cardboard square

in bringing the students outside the classroom for them to have the possibility of experiencing geometric concepts in-situ, in the physical environment. The mobile devices were designed to let students estimate answers, measure distances and calculate areas and reflect on their answers.

Design Changes Based on Suggested Guidelines

During the second iteration, we designed learning activities taking into account the design guidelines suggested earlier (Eliasson et al., 2010). One goal was thus to use different pedagogical activities to help the students get prepared for the outdoor activity. Therefore we aimed at designing a coherent set of activities serving one or more specific roles in the whole pedagogical structure. We also aimed at designing an outdoor activity building on lessons from the first design iteration.

In the second design we moved functionality from one device to another, thereby creating a 'task device' and 'clue device' (Figure 3). This was in line with a guideline from the first iteration

that suggested creating a different functionality for each device (Eliasson et al., 2010).

In the design of the first outdoor activity, the main device and the slave device were designed to work together as one measuring tool (Gil & Pettersson, 2010). In the second design, the tool functionality was the same.

During the first outdoor activity, the teachers did not have an assigned role but were allowed to intervene if they deemed it necessary. In the second design, the role of the teachers and the technical personnel were to intervene only if first approached by students. If they were asked a question, teachers and technical personnel were told to encourage the students to look for the answer themselves. If none of this worked, the teachers and technical personnel could answer questions and help out in finding solutions.

In the design of the first outdoor activity all communication within the groups was placed outside the devices. This was not changed for the second design.

During the preparation of the outdoor activity of the second design iteration, the students were given two introductory sessions. One session where they would familiarise themselves with the devices (an indoor activity) and another session where they would be introduced to the scenario for the outdoor activity, the interaction with the mobile application and familiarise themselves with the measuring capabilities of the devices (outdoor activity).

Learning Activities and Tasks

In the two iterations (Figure 2), learning activities on geometry were designed. The students worked with the concept of volume in the first design of the geometry-learning activity and in the second design iteration the students worked with the concept of area. In the first design the scenario was that the students played the role of architects planning for new buildings and the scenario for the second design was that an imaginary, almost extinct, species needed to be relocated from the local zoo to a field close to the school. The task for the students was to see to that the new enclosures for the animals had the right measurements.

In the learning activities the students worked in groups of three, where each group used two mobile devices. In both iterations we had two student groups participating in the field activities. Measuring large distances for calculating areas and volumes required the students to use our mobile software application, which measures the distance between two mobile devices using GPS. The reason for not using real tools for land surveying is that the mobile devices are more accessible to students and that they can be designed to have different functionalities. Apart from measuring, the mobile devices presented students with tasks based on where they were located and where they were in the task structure. The mobile devices were also used for submitting answers, displaying clues and providing feedback.

The outdoor activities had a similar task structure in both designs. In the second design the outdoor activities started when the students were handed the mobile devices. One of the mobile devices informed them to go to a small field nearby, where they were asked to guess the area of two small rectangles marked by plastic cones. The rectangles had different length and width, but were both 12 m². Each group had prepared one 1x1 meter cardboard square to measure the areas. After completing a task they would send the answer to receive a new task. When they had guessed and calculated the areas correctly they received a message on the task device to go to the big field. In the big field they were first asked to guess the area of the large rectangle (4000 m²) and then to measure the area. The student groups calculated the rectangle by measuring each side of it using the mobile devices and multiplying the two sides. The students' last task was to go to a third field to create their own rectangle with the area 4000 m². The field tasks had a progression from measuring small areas with the cardboard square, to measuring large areas with the mobile devices and finally to construct an area.

Data Collection

In the first iteration we used one close-up video camera for collecting data on interaction at the group level for one of the two groups. We also had two wide-angle video cameras for complementary angles when action occurred out of view of the close-up camera. No separate audio was used, but was instead collected from the video cameras' audio track. In the first iteration all 3 teachers were interviewed a number of times during the design process, both before and after the study. 4 of the 6 students were interviewed after the study. Additionally we collected data from worksheets (questionnaires) filled in by the students before and after the study, and that the researchers that were present in the field also filled in.

In the analysis of the first iteration we used the interviews and the worksheets (Spikol & Eliasson, 2010). For the analysis of the second iteration (Eliasson et al., 2010) we used all the video data from the close-up camera complemented by the wide-angle cameras only when needed for clarification, and with interviews and worksheets as a backdrop.

In the second iteration we added a second close-up camera for following the second group and collected audio from small microphones that each student wore. In the second iteration we did not interview the teachers, but interviewed all 6 students both before and after the study. No worksheet data were collected in the second iteration.

In the analysis of the second iteration (Eliasson et al., 2010) we used all the video data from the 2 close-up cameras, complemented by the wide-angle cameras and audio only when needed for clarification. The purpose of the interviews with the students was to enable an analysis of concept development, which relies on successful interaction in the outdoor activity.

Analysis Methods

We evaluated the formal learning activities through analysing the outdoor activities of the second iteration, each held with two groups of three students. The outdoor activities were set within the frame of other learning activities; both indoors and outdoors (Figure 2). The analysis of mobile devices in the foreground of interaction rests on interaction analysis (Jordan & Henderson, 1995) for the identification of relevant episodes and the task model (Sharples et al., 2007) for analysing individual episodes. The outcome of the first evaluation was a set of design guidelines (Eliasson et al., 2010) that were fed into the second iteration and refined in the second evaluation.

Interaction analysis is a method appropriate for our analysis because it combines video analysis, focuses on human interactions and is rooted in ethnography. This makes it appropriate for us because we want to analyse focus on devices primarily from video data. It also fits the evaluation of the first iteration, which was largely

open-ended, where an ethnographic approach to analysis helps identify problems in human interaction relevant for further research. Unlike critical incident analysis (Sharples, 1993; Vavoula & Sharples, 2009), interaction analysis provided us with an analytical focus on the whole activity.

Interaction Analysis

In the first evaluation, four people from our research group reviewed the 1.5 hour video from the outdoor learning activity, and the problem concerning balancing focus between devices and the environment was identified. The identification of the problem led us to form categories relevant to designing for balanced device focus. The categories were the basis for five guidelines for designing geometry-learning activities where mobile devices support rather than distract students from contents and contexts relevant to the learning goals.

In the second evaluation the goal was to analyse the outdoor learning activity in terms of students' focus on devices. Three people from our research group, who were also involved during the data collection in the field, were engaged in the interaction analysis. 2 x 1.5 hours of recorded video and audio material were analysed in searching for episodes where focus on devices was especially strong or where it was notable that focus on devices was absent. Each researcher took individual notes on episodes. Each episode from the video was kept to a maximum of five minutes. Audio sources were used as a complement when it was difficult to understand what the students were saying from just the audio track of the video film.

The individual notes were compared and put together into one single list of episodes relevant to visual focus on devices. The combined list had 57 relevant episodes. The list was then reduced to 17 episodes. The reduction of the number of episodes was based on where students' focus on devices was particularly strong or extraordinarily weak. The final list contained 17 episodes, which were distributed over 5 categories (see Analysis of Visual Focus on Devices). Two of the researchers crosschecked these remaining episodes to confirm the interpretation of them. The episodes were then analysed using the task model.

Task Model Analysis

The aim of the task model analysis was to get an understanding of how the individual components of the activity system constrain the mediation of learning by causing unwanted focus on devices. Simultaneously the analysis also aimed at describing how these components support the mediation of learning by decreasing or resolving unwanted focus on devices.

The task model offers a set of concepts that can be used to describe an activity as a whole and as a system built up of components and the relationships between these components. Sharples, Taylor, and Vavoula (2007) provide a structured task model presented as a triangle (Figure 4). The task model has the basic component structure of subject-object-context, with the components tool, control and communication mediating the interaction between the basic components. The actions, thoughts and the final learning outcome

are mediated as a result of the interactions between these components (Wertsch, 1991). The task model establishes a distinction between a technological and a semiotic layer. Figure 4 shows that the subject is seen as a learner in the technological layer and as a user in the semiotic layer. With this distinction the model presents one view for 'technology designers' and one view for 'learning theorists' (Taylor, Sharples, O'Malley, Vavoula, & Waycott, 2006). This is not a separation between the layers, instead the layers should be seen as forming a dialectic relationship where they can be moved together and apart, depending on what is to be emphasised in the analysis (ibid).

In the task model the structure of the activity consists of the following six components and their relations: 1-subject, 2-tool, 3-object, 4-control, 5-context and 6-communication (Figure 4). The last three (control, context and communication) correspond to rules, community and division of labor in the original activity system model (Engeström, 1987). Along with distributed cognition (Hutchins, 1995), the activity system model has a long tradition as a tool for analysis in the human-computer interaction (HCI) research field (Kaptelinin & Nardi, 2006). Advantages of using the task model before the activity system model are the two layers (i.e. technological and semi-

Figure 4. The task model, adapted from Sharples, Taylor, and Vavoula (2007)

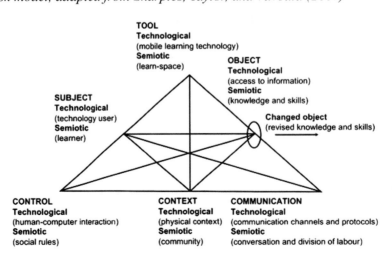

otic) and a more narrow scope of mobile learning activities. The task model also has the advantage of describing an activity as collaborative, object-oriented and tool-mediated, which are all important aspects of the mobile learning activities observed.

For each episode the task model allowed us to describe all aspects of the activity relevant for the subject to reach its goal (object). Because of the structure of the task model, each description of an episode also includes which of the components tool, control, context or communication contribute to the subject reaching its goal. By looking specifically at the technological layer, we could compare the components identified in the analysis with the support that was part of the design of the activity. From analysing each episode in this way, we were able to show if the students were relying on support that was part of the learning activity or if they had to rely on support not considered in the design of the learning activity.

For a few episodes we needed to go beyond the task model, describing mobile learning activities in broader sense than Sharples, Taylor, and Vavoula (2007). The reason was that both mobile and non-mobile tools are used in the activities we design. This view of how a mobile learning activity can be mediated is still in line with the activity system model (Engeström, 1987).

ANALYSIS OF VISUAL FOCUS ON DEVICES

We present the analysis of the episodes from the outdoor activity of the second iteration. In each episode the students' goals of finding information and reaching the learning goals are related to focus on devices. In the episodes, focus on devices is either present, but the students manage to resolve it by using tools provided through the design of the activity, as in Figure 5, or notably absent, as in Figure 6.

The 17 episodes are organised into five categories representing the types of focus on devices that occurred in the outdoor activity, namely: Mobile clue, Natural constraints, Teacher support, Reference to Introductory Activities and Between tasks.

We present one episode to represent each of the categories, where the first two episodes are presented in a graphical form including the analysis of each interrelation between every component playing a role in the task model analysis. The names of the participants are replaced with codes. S1 through S6 are students, where S1, S2 and S3 are in group 1 and S4, S5 and S6 are in group 2. The personal and possessive pronouns "she" and "her" are used for both sexes. T1 is a teacher and R1 is a technician.

Mobile Clue

14 minutes into the activity, group 1 searched for information on how to perform a measurement. The group turned their focus from the task device to the clue device for information. The clue showed a short animation on how the measurement could be done (Figure 3). Once they had watched the clue, they continued with the activity.

Focus on the mobile device occurs in this activity because the information the students need is on the clue device. As soon as they have watched the clue they no longer focus on the mobile device. Group 1 is aware of clues and has used them before in the introductory activity, which allows them to use the clue and then to shift focus and move on. The mobile interaction structures are the same throughout the outdoor activity and therefore they know what to expect.

The left triangle in Figure 5 shows the technological layer of the task model of how group 1 tries to find information on how to perform a measurement. They use a mobile clue, to get the information they need. On the technological layer the subject is group 1, the goal is to find information on how to measure and the tool is a mobile clue. The right triangle in Figure 5 shows the same episode described on the semiotic layer of the task model.

The 'technology designers' view interacts with the 'learning theorists' view in Figure 5. The two layers interact in each component so that the mobile interaction design is dependent on and has an effect on the activity rules and vice versa. Similarly there is an interaction between the mobile clue and the mobile representation.

Figure 5 shows how S1 is able to contextualise the mobile clue (labelled "1" in Figure 5) whereby the representation (2) is made available for internalisation (3). To be able to do this S1 who uses the task device must involve the group member S2 (4) who use the clue device (5). To involve S2, S1 must follow the rules of the activity (6), which are given by the mobile interaction design (7). Using their roles (8), given by the different functionality of each device (9), the group manages to find the information on how to measure (10). They can thereby learn how to measure (3) and shift focus from the clue device to continue to measure the area with the cardboard square.

The analysis shows that S1 is able to use the mobile clue because of the consistent design of mobile clues (mobile interaction design) and roles of students given by the task device and clue device (functionality of devices). The components in the technological layer are then interacting with the components in the semiotic layer enabling S1 to learn how to measure. In this episode, the two components on the technological layer *mobile*

interaction design and the *functionality of devices* are what resolve the focus on the clue device.

Natural Constraints

43 minutes into the activity S4 was trying place one of the cones on the field for their self-made rectangle. S4 tried one position and with the help of S5 made a measurement using the mobile devices for measuring. The measurement she received as feedback from the mobile device was too short, which made her move backwards to expand the side of the rectangle. When she reached the edge of the field she noticed this and had to tell the group members that they had to come up with an alternative strategy, which they eventually did and solved the problem that way.

The reason for not focusing on the mobile device in this activity was that S4 used the mobile device for measuring while focused on the natural constraints and the task restrictions. During the design of the activity, the rectangles that could fit into one specific field depended on the natural form of that field. As the activity was designed to use the constraints of the field, we believe this absent focus on devices can be referred to the design of the learning activity.

The left triangle in Figure 6 shows an instantiation of the task model similar to the task model. In this instantiation the technological layer in the task model is instead seen as a physical layer. In episodes where the mobile device is conceptualised as a tool the instantiation is identical to the

Figure 5. Technological (left) and semiotic (right) layer of group 1 using a clue

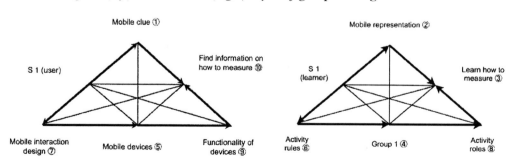

task model, but when other aspects of the activity are identified as tools the instantiation is similar but not identical to the task model.

The two triangles in Figure 6 show an episode where S4 tries to expand the self-made rectangle of group 2. When doing this she has to stay within the borders of the field. On the technological layer the subject is S4, the goal is to find limits for expanding the self-made rectangle and the tool is natural constraints. The right triangle in Figure 6 shows the same episode on the semiotic layer.

Figure 6 shows how S4 encounters the edge of the field as natural constraints (1), which lets her use the task restrictions (2) on the semiotic layer to learn how to expand the rectangle (3). To learn this S4 also needs help from S5 (4) to measure the increasing distance between their devices at each end of the expanding rectangle (5). The collaboration with S5 is mediated by the rules of the activity (6), which is dependent on the design of the activity (7). Mediating between S5 and the goal are the two roles (8) necessary to perform a measurement, which in turn are related to the layout of the field (9).

The analysis shows that S4 is able to use the natural constraints because of the *design of field activity* that sets the rules of the activity and the dimensions of the field (*field layout*), which calls for two different roles for the students to perform measurements using the devices.

Teacher Support

49 minutes into the activity S1 thought that she had locked one of the sides of the rectangle on her mobile device to 2 meters. She was hesitating because she thought that this meant that the final answer would be wrong. This was because the goal to create an area of 4000 m² and such a large area would not fit on the field when one side is set to 2 meters. S1 told T1 about her problem and T1 gave her the answer that nothing is locked until they send the final answer. With this S1 could continue measuring the way she was.

In this activity focus on the task device is present because of S1's current understanding of how a measurement is done. This focus on the device disappears when T1 confirms that nothing is set until they send in the final answer. The reason for this lies in the rules of the activity and the use of the teacher as a tool. The role of the teacher support was to step in when the students have no other way of solving a problem. In this activity T1 steps in when S1 is stuck and has no other option than to seek teacher support.

Reference to Introductory Activities

23 minutes into the activity group 2 finished measuring the areas on the small field and started searching for the big field where the task device told them to go. They searched for cones and when S6 asks where to go S5 explicitly refers to a picture of the meadow on the computer. What

Figure 6. Physical (left) and semiotic (right) layer of student 4 expanding the rectangle

she means by that is a picture of the meadow that was shown in the introductory activity. Thereby they can draw the conclusion that they are walking in the right direction.

The task model is used to analyse why the group does not focus on the mobile device in this episode. The reason for not focusing on the device in this activity is found to be that they can fall back on prior knowledge, this time knowledge they gained in the introductory activity. This episode shows how the introductory activity, and the whole pedagogical design leading up to the outdoor activity, served to bridge prior knowledge and skills.

Between Tasks

24 minutes into the activity group 1 finished measuring the areas on the small field and started walking towards the big field. Half way to the big field they put their mobile devices away and started discussing the sequence of subtasks on the small field.

Using the task model, the reason for not focusing on the mobile devices can be interpreted as that they knew what was expected from them. In this observed activity, they use the design of the activity as room for reflection. Group 1 finds room for reflection and uses verbal communication and their externalisation of ideas to create common understanding. In the video review after the outdoor activity the group explained why they put their mobile devices away in their pockets. They said that the reasons were that they received the instruction to go to the big field before leaving the small field and they knew where to go.

RESULTS: DESIGN GUIDELINES

In the second design iteration, the task model has been used to analyse what learning support was needed in the outdoor activity of the second design. The kinds of support needed were also compared to the support that was developed in a design process based on the guidelines from the first design iteration. This comparison resulted in six evaluated guidelines.

• Let students assume roles outside the classroom based on a different functionality of each device

We interpret that the mobile clue design was a success in terms of different functionality for the devices. In the mobile clue episode the students seamlessly move between devices without referring to their properties as mobile phones. In essence, the fact that each device has a well-defined functionality can help the students to balance focus on devices as they do not have to learn how to change the functionality on one of the devices. Instead they can assume roles related to the well-defined functionality of the devices.

As a side effect of having a separate clue device we could observe negotiation and coordination between the students. When the student holding the task device wanted to know about clues, the options available were to ask if there were new clues available and/or walk over to the clue device. We interpret this as the separation of functionality between devices can encourage collaboration between students if interdependence between the students is maintained.

• Let students use mobile devices as contextual tools for measuring, probing or capturing aspects of the physical environment

Our observations showed that both groups knew how to perform a measurement using the two devices, even the first time they received a task that involved this. When using the two devices as a measuring tool the students did not focus on the devices more than intended.

In the second design mobile devices were used for introducing tasks, providing feedback, and offering clues, apart from being used as a tool for measuring distance. Measuring distance was the only functionality that used the built-in sensors explicitly.

- Design for physical interaction with the environment

When the learning activities only require the students to interact with the mobile devices, the human-computer interaction is placed in the foreground, and the physical environment in the background. One simple way of including the physical environment is to design for physical interaction with the environment in the design of the activities.

- Let teachers assume roles

We interpret that throughout the outdoor activity the teacher support did contribute positively to students being able to continue the learning activity. For example in the episodes where students were seeking assistance (as in the episode beginning 49 minutes into the outdoor activity), the teacher support resolved the focus on devices. We also observed episodes where the teachers and the technical personnel intervened on their own initiative, despite that they thereby overstepped their assigned restrictive roles. The given instruction was to not intervene unless the students asked them questions. We argue that even more restrictive roles will not solve the problem of teachers wanting to help out. Instead we argue that teachers have to find their roles in relation to technology through the co-design process.

- Encourage face-to-face collaboration

We did not introduce any changes between the first and second designs. The implication to place all group communication outside the devices is still valid, when group members are within shouting distance of each other. When the distance between students is larger, phone calls are an alternative when the students are familiar with the interaction needed to place a call.

From the analysis we could see one more option on how to encourage face-to-face collaboration. There was one main reason for how group 1 could use the transition to the big field for reflection. The reason was that they knew where they were going and did not have to monitor the devices when going to the big field. From this episode we can see that focus on devices was absent between tasks. Providing space between tasks like this does not mean that the students will collaborate and communicate more, but at least this will give them the possibility to do so.

- Introduce unfamiliar aspects of the mobile devices and other learning support

In novel mobile learning activities the mobile devices, the software or the structure of the tasks may be unfamiliar to the students. When the mobile devices are guiding the activities there is a risk of a too strong focus on the devices. The evaluation of the second design points to the value of introducing the tools to the students prior to the mobile learning activity. With no introduction of the tools the students will need to appropriate the tools during the mobile learning activity, which leads to a strong focus on the device during this appropriation. A technical introduction and an introduction to the activity can lead to a sought for balance in focusing on the educational task at hand.

DISCUSSION AND FUTURE WORK

Mobile learning opens up contexts for field activities that need to be structured, with students in control. This requires that learning theorists and interaction designers develop mobile learning activities where students are able to balance their focus between mobile devices and learning tasks. In this context we analysed focus on devices and notably absent focus on devices in a mobile learning activity on geometry. The analysis showed that focus on devices could be reduced or resolved by support related either to the design of the mobile devices or to the design of the mobile learning activity. The results showed how the support identified could be related to the design guidelines. Based on the results, the guidelines can now be expressed as follows.

The mobile devices should:

- Let students assume roles
- Be used by students as contextual tools for measuring, probing or capturing

The mobile learning activities outside the classroom should:

- Be designed for physical interaction with the environment
- Let teachers assume roles
- Encourage face-to-face collaboration

The introductory activities should:

- Introduce unfamiliar aspects of the mobile devices and other learning support

When the focus on one device is too strong the goals of the socio-cultural perspective of learning may not be met because the context for learning is shifted away from the physical environment. With this said on the negative aspects of device focus, we note that it is not to be considered something only negative. Positive aspects of device focus could be when a group stands around a mobile device to establish common ground or when the digital context is used to enhance the physical through for example augmented reality. Orchestrating this kind of visual focus on devices into the learning scenario is a key factor for experiencing geometric concepts in the physical environment outdoors, with a situated learning perspective.

The contribution of this article is that it shows how to balance visual focus on devices in mobile learning activities on geometry. The results are very much in line with guidelines previously suggested in our iterative design effort. By using an analysis tool based on a well-established conceptual framework this article puts focus on devices in the context of the mobile learning activities. In this way the guidelines we present are based on the observed activities, in particular on aspects of the activities that were analysed to reduce or resolve focus on devices. The first set of guidelines (Eliasson et al., 2010) are also supported by Winter and Pemberton (2010), who used the guidelines for designing learning activities on archaeology. The limitations of this article are the small number of students participating and to what extent additional teachers in the outdoor and introductory activities match the real world problems.

The problem of balancing focus on devices is not unique to the kind of structured mobile learning activities we study. Instead we argue that focus on devices might be used to guide design for several types of activities where novel devices or device functionality is used. As with all new design there will be aspects of the devices and of the activities that are new to users, so balancing focus on devices will continue to be an issue we need to take into account.

In the next iteration of design we plan to use more standard mobile phones and software to address the problem of students not being used to the mobile devices. At the same time we might introduce a new context for balancing focus on devices when in future design iterations we want to make use of augmented reality in the field. For the next design cycle the goal is to keep learners active, where the technical devices are tools in the hands of intelligent users. This goal is in line with the ambitious aim for ubiquitous computing to create engaging experiences that provoke us to learn, understand, and reflect more upon our interactions with technologies and each other (Rogers, 2006).

REFERENCES

Cole, H., & Stanton, D. (2003). Designing mobile technologies to support co-present collaboration. *Personal and Ubiquitous Computing, 7*(6), 365–371. doi:10.1007/s00779-003-0249-4

Cook, J. (2010). Mobile phones as mediating tools within augmented contexts for development. *International Journal of Mobile and Blended Learning, 2*(3), 1–12. doi:10.4018/jmbl.2010070101

Design-Based-Research-Collective. (2003). Design-based research: An emerging paradigm for educational inquiry. *Educational Researcher, 32*(1), 5–8. doi:10.3102/0013189X032001005

Eliasson, J., Nouri, J., Ramberg, R., & Cerratto Pargman, T. (2010). *Design heuristics for balancing visual focus on devices in formal mobile learning activities*. Paper presented at the 9th International Conference on Mobile Learning.

Eliasson, J., Spikol, D., Cerratto Pargman, T., & Ramberg, R. (2010). Get the bees away from the hive: Balancing visual focus on devices in mobile learning. In *Proceedings of the IADIS International Conference Mobile Learning*.

Engeström, Y. (1987). *Learning by expanding: An activity-theoretical approach to developmental research*. Helsinki: Orienta-konsultit.

Frohberg, D., Göth, C., & Schwabe, G. (2009). Mobile learning projects - a critical analysis of the state of the art: Original article. *Journal of Computer Assisted Learning, 25*(4), 307–331. doi:10.1111/j.1365-2729.2009.00315.x

Gil, D., & Pettersson, O. (2010). Providing flexibility in learning activities systems by the use of multi-role mobile devices. In *Proceedings of the 6th IEEE International Conference on Wireless, Mobile, and Ubiquitous Technologies in Education* (pp. 166-170).

Göth, C., Frohberg, D., & Schwabe, G. (2006). The focus problem in mobile learning. In *Proceedings of the Fourth IEEE International Workshop on Wireless, Mobile and Ubiquitous Technology in Education* (pp. 153-160).

Göth, C., & Schwabe, G. (2010). Navigation support for mobile learning. In *Proceedings of the 43rd Hawaii International Conference on System Sciences* (pp. 1-10).

Jordan, B., & Henderson, A. (1995). Interaction analysis: Foundations and practice. *Journal of the Learning Sciences, 4*(1), 39–103. doi:10.1207/s15327809jls0401_2

Kaptelinin, V., & Nardi, B. A. (2006). *Acting with technology: Activity theory and interaction design*. Cambridge, MA: MIT Press.

Kurti, A., Spikol, D., & Milrad, M. (2008). Bridging outdoors and indoors educational activities in schools with the support of mobile and positioning technologies. *International Journal of Mobile Learning and Organization, 2*(2).

Naismith, L., Sharples, M., & Ting, J. (2005). Evaluation of CAERUS: A context aware mobile guide. In *Proceedings of the 4th World Conference on mLearning* (pp. 112-115).

Penuel, W. R., Roschelle, J., & Shechtman, N. (2007). Designing formative assessment software with teachers: An analysis of the co-design process. *Research and Practice in Technology Enhanced Learning, 2*(1), 51–74. doi:10.1142/S1793206807000300

Rogers, Y. (2006). Moving on from Weiser's vision of calm computing: Engaging UbiComp experiences. In P. Dourish & A. Friday (Eds.), *Proceedings of the 8th International Conference on Ubiquitous Computing* (LNCS 4209, pp. 404-421).

Säljö, R. (1999). Learning as the use of tools: A socio-cultural perspective on the human-technology link. In Littleton, K., & Light, P. (Eds.), *Learning with computers: Analysing productive interaction*. London, UK: Routledge.

Säljö, R. (2000). *Lärande i praktiken: Ett sociokulturellt perspektiv*. Stockholm, Sweden: Prisma.

Sharples, M. (1993). A study of breakdowns and repairs in a computer-mediated communication system. *Interacting with Computers, 5*(1), 61–77. doi:10.1016/0953-5438(93)90025-O

Sharples, M., Taylor, J., & Vavoula, G. (2007). A theory of learning for the mobile age. In Andrews, R., & Haythornthwaite, C. A. (Eds.), *The Sage handbook of e-learning research*. Thousand Oaks, CA: Sage.

Spikol, D., & Eliasson, J. (2010). Lessons from designing geometry learning activities that combine mobile and 3D tools. In *Proceedings of the 6th IEEE International Conference on Wireless, Mobile, and Ubiquitous Technologies in Education* (pp. 137-141).

Taylor, J., Sharples, M., O'Malley, C., Vavoula, G., & Waycott, J. (2006). Towards a task model for mobile learning a dialectical approach. *International Journal of Learning Technology, 2*(2-3), 138–158. doi:10.1504/IJLT.2006.010616

Vavoula, G., & Sharples, M. (2009). Meeting the challenges in evaluating mobile learning: A 3-level evaluation framework. *International Journal of Mobile and Blended Learning, 1*(2), 54–75. doi:10.4018/jmbl.2009040104

Wertsch, J. V. (1991). *Voices of the mind: A sociocultural approach to mediated action*. Cambridge, MA: Harvard University Press.

Wijers, M., Jonker, V., & Drijvers, P. (2010). MobileMath: Exploring mathematics outside the classroom. *ZDM*, 1-11.

Winter, M., & Pemberton, L. (2010). *Unearthing invisible buildings: Device focus and device sharing in a collaborative mobile learning activity*. Paper presented at the 9th International Conference on Mobile Learning.

This work was previously published in the International Journal of Mobile and Blended Learning, Volume 3, Issue 2, edited by David Parsons, pp 1-15, copyright 2011 by IGI Publishing (an imprint of IGI Global).

Chapter 6

Unearthing Invisible Buildings:
Device Focus and Device Sharing in a Collaborative Mobile Learning Activity

Marcus Winter
University of Brighton, UK

Lyn Pemberton
University of Brighton, UK

ABSTRACT

Recent research has identified excessive device focus as a serious problem in collaborative mobile learning as it undermines key ideas of learners engaging with their co-learners in context-rich authentic settings. Various recommendations have been formulated to address device focus in the design of mobile learning technology and pedagogy and foster students' engagement with both their peers and their environment. This paper describes how some of these recommendations have been implemented and extended in the design of Invisible Buildings, a mobile collaborative game-based activity for schoolchildren. It reports the results of an empirical evaluation of the learning experience with primary school children, focusing on students' engagement with their social and physical context during learning activities, and providing insights into their behaviour and strategies with respect to device sharing. Findings broadly confirm the effectiveness of the implemented measures and show good student acceptance of the tools employed and the overall learning experience.

INTRODUCTION

Over the last decade our understanding of mobile learning has shifted focus from mobile devices and technologies to learner mobility and the social practice it enables. A key concept in this new understanding is context, created by the learner in interaction with others, with their surroundings and with the tools they use (Kukulska-Hume et al., 2009). As learning processes are inextricably linked to, and located within, a particular context, learning in context-rich authentic settings can make the learning experience more relevant and meaningful for students and help to bridge the gap between theory and practice (Rogoff, 1982; Lave, 1988; Brown et al., 1989; Engeström, 1991). In

DOI: 10.4018/978-1-4666-2139-8.ch006

addition, the construction of new knowledge from concrete and detailed experience can help learners to gain a deep and multifaceted understanding, which in turn enables them to more easily transfer skills and knowledge to other problem domains (Spiro et al., 1988). Collaborative situated learning activities put additional emphasis on the social aspects of learning and require students to test ideas, processes and concepts with their peers, negotiate meaning, and in the process construct new knowledge relevant to their common task. Rooted in Vygotsky's (1978) and Bandura's (1977) ideas of learning through observation, communication and social interaction, the benefits of collaborative learning are now widely accepted.

Key to leveraging these manifold theoretical advantages of collaborative mobile learning is that students register, engage and interact with their environment and with their co-learners during the learning activity. Recent research, however, has pointed out that in many mobile learning projects where students share a mobile device to complete tasks collaboratively; their engagement with the environment and with each other is reduced significantly as they focus too much on the shared mobile device (Eliasson et al., 2010, 2011; Göth et al., 2006).

From an HCI perspective, where device focus and its underlying issues have been researched for some time (e.g., Satyanarayanan, 1996; Kristoffersen & Ljungberg, 1999), efforts to address the problem are generally aimed at reducing the cognitive load for users when interacting with the device. Earlier approaches in this context include *Minimal Attention User Interfaces* (Pascoe et al., 2000), which groups interaction tasks into interaction modes to reduce interface complexity, and sonically-enhanced user interfaces that balance visual interaction with acoustic feedback to reduce cognitive load (Brewster, 2002). More recent efforts include user interfaces that account for contextual information, such as enlarging touch targets when a user is walking (Kane et al., 2008), gestural input (Crossan et al., 2008, 2009) and

Around-Device Interaction (Kratz & Rohs, 2009) for simple actions that don't require fine-grained interaction, and tactile feedback for situations where interaction with graphical displays is not suitable (Hoggan et al., 2007).

Göth et al. (2006) proposed the development of a *mobile phone metaphor* (as opposed to a *small screen metaphor* derived from the desktop) for the design of situated mobile learning applications, which takes into account the specific use context, hardware characteristics and network requirements of mobile devices. Unlike desktop applications which claim the exclusive and uninterrupted focus of the user, the mobile phone metaphor accounts for discontinuous use by requesting the user's attention when necessary and then switching into the background automatically when the user's focus is no longer required. A detailed discussion of task switching in mobile situations and its demand on cognitive resources is offered in Oulasvirta et al. (2005).

From a pedagogical perspective, Eliasson et al. (2010) recently proposed addressing the problem of excessive device focus with a range of measures, including assigning learners dedicated roles that require negotiation and coordination in collaborative learning situations, conceptualising mobile devices as tools that support learners in completing activities (as opposed to controlling and structuring the activity) and integrating teachers and support staff into mobile activities to scaffold learning and keep learners focused on the task.

This paper describes how device focus and the related issue of device sharing among students were addressed in the design of *Invisible Buildings*, a mobile collaborative game-based activity for schoolchildren. It explains how some of the recommendations in Eliasson et al. (2010) were implemented and further extended in the project, and reports on the empirical evaluation of these measures with respect to device focus and device sharing in groups as well as usability, acceptance and overall user experience.

The following sections first give an overview of the Invisible Buildings project and then describe specific design aspects in the learning experience aiming to address the problems of device focus and device sharing. We explain how the learning experience was empirically evaluated with two classes of school children and conclude with a discussion of our findings and their validity.

1. INVISIBLE BUILDINGS

Invisible Buildings is a whole-day, cross-curricular learning experience for primary school children aged 9-10 years. It is based on the discovery and excavation of an imagined Roman Villa beneath the school grounds and links to a wide range of curriculum subjects including History, ICT, English and Mathematics.

Grounded in social-constructivist ideas of learning where students actively construct knowledge through active experimentation and interaction with their physical and social environment, the learning experience integrates mobile location-based games with complementary classroom-based activities. Alternating outdoor and indoor activities enables students to intermittently reflect on the purpose and meaning of their practical experience, which is seen as a necessary step in experiential learning (Kolb, 1984; Ackermann, 1996).

The learning experience is structured into three outdoor activities (Metal Detector, GeoPhys, Digger) in which students cooperate to uncover virtual objects and structures in the school grounds, and three indoor activities where pupils reflect on their outdoor experience, discuss the meaning and implications of found objects and prepare their next steps outdoors. Together, these activities form a chain of discovery, reasoning and further action (Figure 1) that ultimately leads them to uncover a virtual Roman Villa beneath their school grounds, a model of which they can then explore in the concluding indoor activity.

The learning experience includes custom-made mock-up tools derived from authentic archaeological practice, with integrated GPS-enabled smartphones running custom-made applications for each outdoor task. The applications have contrast-rich, graphical, single-purpose user interfaces requiring only minimal user interaction. They are driven primarily by the GPS data generated as students move around the school grounds.

In order to integrate outdoor and indoor activities, a related project website can be made available through the school's Virtual Learning Environment. Virtual objects found in the school grounds are submitted automatically and in real-time to the project website for subsequent whole-group discussions in the classroom. To reduce context switching costs for students between different activities and representations (Rogers et al., 2010) and provide a coherent overarching narrative in the learning experience, the same virtual objects and floor plan were used in the mobile applications and on the website.

In addition to the found virtual objects and uncovered floor plan of the Roman Villa, the website also holds background information and related resources, including an online catalogue of objects from different historical periods and a custom-made game. The online catalogue enables students to visually identify found objects and learn about their purpose and history, supporting teacher-led whole-class discussions. The custom-made game is played by students in the final indoor activity and involves placing the virtual fragments excavated in the last outdoor activity in the correct positions on the floor plan. Once all fragments are in place the game reveals an interactive 3D model of the Roman Villa.

The children's task-related activities are coordinated and motivated by a professional actor presenting himself to students as an archaeologist and introducing researchers and technology personnel as his helpers. Logistical aspects such as forming groups and teams and supervising students' ordered migration between classroom and

Figure 1. Chain of activities and reasoning leading to the discovery of a virtual Roman villa beneath the school grounds

Introduction

Using a Metal Detector, students find assorted virtual metal objects in the school
ground. Found objects are discussed with Archaeologist and sent automatically to   << outdoor
the related project website for the indoor activity.

indoor >>   Teacher-led whole-group discussions of found objects, projected to a whiteboard.
Students look up objects in a catalogue for information about them (e.g. stylus for
Roman wax tablet). Results point towards a Roman Villa!

Using a Geophysical H-Frame, students scan the school ground for subterranean
disturbances. They successively uncover a floor plan indicating the remains of a   << outdoor
Roman Villa. Floor plan is sent to project website for next indoor activity.

indoor >>   Teacher-led whole-group discussions of the floor plan, supported by expert
comments from Archaeologist. Students identify most promising locations to dig,
e.g. corners of the building and staircases which are more robust and likely to last.

Using a generic Digger, students dig at agreed positions to virtually unearth
fragments of the Villa's ruins. Found fragments are sent to project website for final   << outdoor
indoor activity.

indoor >>   Students play custom-made game on the project website where they place found
fragments of the Villa on the correct positions on the floor plan. Once all fragments
are in place, an interactive 3D model of the Roman Villa appears on screen.

Debriefing

school ground are covered by the teacher. In order to keep group sizes manageable and optimise use of the available equipment, classes are divided into two halves which alternate in completing outside / inside tasks. For outdoor activities, each group is then further divided into teams of four pupils each, who stay together for the whole day and collaborate in each learning activity.

2. DESIGN ASPECTS

Dedicated Roles

Eliasson et al. (2010) suggest using two or more mobile devices with different roles in a team, which implicitly assigns different roles to the students using them. The concept of roles in co-located collaboration resonates with Johnson and Johnson's (1994) ideas of cooperative learning and positive interdependence. It has been explored in the context of field trips (Hine et al., 2004) and pervasive gaming (Leichtenstern & André, 2009), where it was found to help structure interaction

and balance the level of activity among students (Leichtenstern & André, 2009). Contrary to Eliasson et al.'s (2010) recommendation, *Invisible Buildings* uses only one mobile device per team; however, it defines dedicated roles for team members in each task, which are explained to students in detail before they begin their outdoor activity (Table 1).

In order to give each team member an opportunity to control the main tool for the task and interact with the integrated smartphone, roles are swapped after a certain time when the archaeologist gives the agreed signal.

Auxiliary tools (Figure 2) were introduced for each supporting role to emancipate team members in relation to the main tool controller and accentuate their specific purpose in the task. These tools included an electronic stopwatch to measure time, a hooter to call the archaeologist for consultation when objects were found, a set of plastic cones to mark the locations of found objects and the Roman Villa's floor plan as it was uncovered and a notepad to take notes during the activity and make drawings of found objects.

Table 1. Roles in each team for the different tasks

Task 1: Metal Detector	
Controller	Control the tool, interact with mobile device
Stopwatch	Measure time
Hooter	Alert archaeologist when objects are found
Notes	Take notes, make drawings of found objects
Task 2: Geo Phys	
Controller	Control the tool, interact with mobile device
Cones	Put down cones to mark outlines of floor plan
Hooter	Alert archaeologist when wall / line is found
Notes	Take notes, make drawing of floor plan
Task 3: Dig	
Controller	Control the tool, interact with mobile device
Helper	Secure boring head in position (inside cone)
Helper	Push digger lever
Helper	Push digger lever

Based on research into conflicts and competition between children over shared resources in collaboration around a tabletop (Marshall et al., 2009), it was hoped that these auxiliary tools would reduce interference from students in supporting roles with the device controller, as they add weight to their roles and encourage independence.

Mobile Devices as Tools

In order to avoid students being pushed into a passive role by mobile applications that structure and control the flow of learning activities, Eliasson et al. (2010) suggest conceptualising mobile devices as tools and utilising their inbuilt sensors to complete activities. Tools in the form of

Figure 2. Auxiliary tools for supporting roles included a hooter to notify the Archaeologist and a clipboard for note-taking

dedicated sensors and probes, used independently or coupled to a mobile phone, or in the form of software applications utilising smartphone hardware such as a GPS receiver, magnetometer or digital compass, have been used successfully in a number of enquiry learning projects that teach science concepts through hands-on investigations (e.g., Rogers et al., 2004; Metcalf & Tinker, 2004; Klopfer & Squire, 2007; Vogel et al., 2010).

The idea of using mobiles as tools was further extended in Invisible Buildings by integrating the smartphones into physical mock-ups of tools used in authentic archaeological excavations. The integration of smartphones into larger physical tools is conceptually similar to a range of commercial products. For instance, Mobile Art Lab's Phone-Book (PhoneBook, 2010) embeds a smartphone into a physical children's book and thereby reduces the mobile device to an interactive image in the book that changes content when pages are turned. Another example, based on the Wii controller instead of a smartphone, is gaming peripherals which embed the controller into physical tools such as steering wheels, golf clubs or ping pong rackets, with similar ergonomic qualities to the real-world tool they represent. It was hoped that the integration of smartphones into mock-up tools would emphasise their task-specific purpose in each learning activity and create a more "life-like gaming experience" (Burrill, 2010) where attention is focused on using the physical tool in the task at hand instead of the smartphone.

Three different types of mock-up tools were provided, including a metal detector, geo-physical H-frame, and a generic digging instrument. For each tool the integrated mobile device ran a different application with a task-specific, graphical touch-screen interface designed to look like an authentic tool interface (Figure 3). The only screen-based user interaction required from students was to confirm found objects and successful digs in the Metal Detector and Digger applications. All other user input was in the form of location data generated by players roaming the school grounds

to detect virtual objects and structures. The smartphones' inbuilt network capabilities were used to transfer found virtual objects and underground structures to the related project website as they were found. Transfers were triggered automatically and required no user interaction. These measures aimed to reduce the smartphone to a mere user interface for the mock-up tool and thereby further enhance its credibility while deflecting attention from the smartphone itself.

In order to make the mock-up tools reusable and light enough for children to carry, they were composed of standard lightweight plastic waste water pipes, bends and couplings that could be easily re-configured into the next tool in-between the learning activities. The smartphones were strapped into a small open plastic box fixed to the tool handle in order to protect the device and reduce screen glare (Figure 4), a well-known problem in outdoor smartphone use (Luckin et al., 2005; Wobbrock, 2006).

Integrate Teachers and Support Staff

While most field studies involving technologically complex prototypes depend on researchers and technical support personnel being present on the scene, the role of these helpers and their impact on students' learning experience and behaviour is seldom reported on. Eliasson et al. (2010) recommend that teachers and technical personnel should be integrated into the learning experience as their involvement can scaffold students' learning and help them to stay focused on the task instead of the device. Accordingly, all adults involved in the *Invisible Buildings* project played a role in the learning activities. Teachers were responsible for logistical issues (e.g., dividing classes into two groups, supporting team formation in each group, supervising students leaving the classroom for outdoor activities and returning for indoor activities, etc.) and in addition provided technical and subject related support. Technical personnel and research staff provided technical support and

Figure 3. Metal detector application running on the mobile device embedded into the Metal detector tool

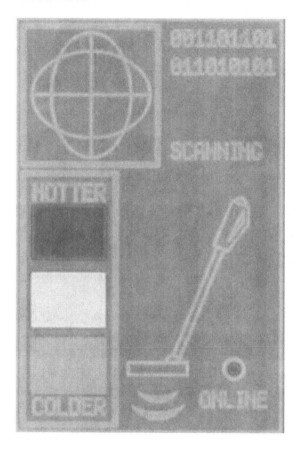

helped to keep students on task with guidance and encouragement.

In addition to the involvement of teachers and technical personnel, a professional actor was introduced to play the part of an Indiana Jones-style archaeologist. The archaeologist was responsible for coordinating operations, setting the scene for the day, appointing teachers and technology personnel as his helpers, constructing the narrative of the virtual dig as it unfolded, explaining the various outdoor activities and related tools and sharing his expert opinion on found objects and structures. Involved early on in the development process of the learning activity, the actor was familiar with the day's structure and had prepared himself for the role by watching episodes from a popular British television series where a team of specialists carry out an archaeological dig while the process is explained by a narrator in layman's terms. It was hoped that the involvement of the archaeologist would add authority and authenticity to the tools and practices employed in the learning activities and thereby further motivate students and keep them focused on completing their tasks.

Encouraging Face-to-Face Collaboration

Instead of building collaboration directly into the mobile application and thereby forcing students to collaborate through the device, Eliasson et al. (2010) recommend placing collaboration outside the mobile device as this increases face-to-face discussions between students. This point was addressed by using the mobile devices as tools only and leaving it to teachers, the archaeologist and students themselves to structure and control the learning experience. Face-to-face collaboration between students was expected when students negotiated directions and locations to probe and when they discussed the meaning of found objects. Indoors, students reflected on their outdoor experiences in teacher-led, whole-group discussions and collaboratively planned further outdoor action based on previous results and the outcomes of their discussions.

3. EVALUATION

Invisible Buildings was evaluated over two consecutive days with two mixed gender classes of primary school children aged 9 to 10 years. Overall, 53 children took part in the study.

The primary aims of the evaluation were to:

- Establish whether the implemented measures helped to mitigate device focus,
- Examine device sharing among students, and

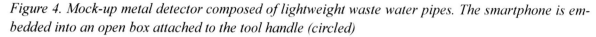

Figure 4. Mock-up metal detector composed of lightweight waste water pipes. The smartphone is embedded into an open box attached to the tool handle (circled)

- Assess the usability and acceptance of the mock-up tools.

The evaluation was carried out by usability experts from the Interactive Technologies Research Group at the University of Brighton.

Methodological Considerations

Due to the complex nature of device focus and device sharing in collaborative mobile learning situations it seems mandatory to investigate these problems in their natural setting and to employ qualitative methods that give a detailed and contextualised view of students' behaviour. As the learning activities implement several measures in combination, some of which depend on each other and directly bear on students' tasks, it was not possible to isolate variables and carry out a comparative study. Instead, the evaluation looked at the described condition only and recognises the relative and situated character of findings.

The main data collection tool in the evaluation was video, which provides rich and detailed views on the situation, records actual behaviour as opposed to professed behaviour, and allows for repeated reviewing of the same event during the analysis (Roschelle, 2000). The latter aspect was crucial for our qualitative analysis, which involved usability experts to identify and repeatedly review critical scenes related to device focus, device sharing and usability aspects.

In addition, a questionnaire was developed to collect students' views directly after each outdoor activity when their impressions were still fresh. Special care was taken with regard to the design of the questionnaire to ensure it was suitable for children of this age group (Barendregt et al., 2008). The main aim of the questionnaire was to survey the children's user experience of the outdoor learning activities and gather any other comments they would offer. The data could then be triangulated with video observations regarding usability, acceptance and user experience.

Ethical Considerations

With respect to the involvement of underage volunteers in the study, ethical issues were considered before and throughout the evaluation.

Based on Anderson's (1990) guidelines regarding volunteers in research projects and Burgess' (1989) discussion of ethics in educational research, specific considerations included collecting data anonymously and not making it available to third parties, informing pupils and their parents about the context and purpose of the study and pointing out to them that they could withdraw at any time without giving a reason. A consent form was distributed before the event, and pupils and their parents had an opportunity to discuss details with the supervising teacher.

Data Collection

First-Person Video Observation

In order to record interactions from the user's point of view and obtain a contextualised view of the device screen, the device controller in a selected team of students wore a head-mounted camera fixed on a baseball cap, together with a microphone attached to his/her outer clothing and a carrier belt holding a miniature video recorder and energy supply. As pupils swapped roles during the learning activities taking turns at controlling the mock-up tool and integrated smartphone, the camera cap, microphone and belt were transferred to the next student with the help of a researcher, so that the head-mounted camera always had a direct view on the mobile device and would record all user interactions.

Third-Person Video Observation

To complement the head-mounted camera view, one researcher accompanied the same group of pupils with a handheld video camera to record video material from a third-person perspective. In addition to documenting whole-group interaction and interaction between groups, the material gave a useful second perspective on critical situations, which helped researchers during the analysis to better understand these situations as a whole.

In order to enable researchers to understand the students' overall learning experience during the day, indoor activities were recorded with a static video camera in the classroom.

Questionnaires

A questionnaire was administered after each outdoor task when pupils returned to the classroom, to collect immediate feedback on the learning activity. The questionnaire asked students to rate the outdoor activity based on a set of eight qualities. Students were told to tick as many of these as they wanted. The categories and related pictograms were derived from the Problem Identification Picture Cards (PIPC) method developed by Barendregt et al. (2008) specifically for usability evaluations with children. While the original PIPC method uses cards for each category, which children throw into a box during game play, this setup seemed not practical for an outdoor setting. Instead, our questionnaire offered all categories on a single page using a familiar multiple choice layout with tick boxes. In addition, there was room at the bottom where pupils could further qualify their ratings and leave open comments.

Data Analysis

Video Analysis

The video material was evaluated by a panel of three usability experts, all of whom have a background in mobile HCI. It involved a data reduction step carried out by one panel member who had also been involved in the data collection, and several screening sessions with all panel members.

The data reduction included viewing the large amount of video data resulting from the first-person, third-person and indoor cameras and editing them into segments tightly covering each outdoor and indoor activity, while discarding any passages relating to setup, idle recording and equipment testing. The first-person and third-person video material was not combined into a single video stream, but instead kept independent for review on two monitors if synchronised viewing was required. Three complete outdoor activities from first- and third-person perspectives, lasting between 21 and 28 minutes each, were selected for review by the panel.

To prepare for the screening sessions, panel members had a preliminary discussion on device focus and device sharing in collaborative mobile learning situations, and on potential indicators relating to these aspects such as face-to-face discussion between students or verbal and gestural references to the landscape. All panel members had read the research reports by Goth et al. (2006) and Eliasson et al. (2010) relating to device focus and Marshall et al. (2009) relating to children's sharing of resources in co-located collaboration. With respect to usability, panel members agreed to focus particularly on the robustness and ergonomy of the mock-up tools. The discussion helped to focus and establish a common frame of reference for the analysis.

During the screening sessions, panel members used an emergent coding scheme informed by the preceding discussions to identify and annotate critical scenes in the video material. Notes were compared after each session, leading to discussions and repeated reviews of critical scenes to better understand the issues at hand. A total of 17 critical scenes were identified relating to:

- Learner independence in the team
- Collaboration and discussion
- Tools and roles
- Awareness of the environment
- Device control and device sharing
- Issues in handling the mock-up tools
- Equipment failure
- Credibility of mock-up tools and virtual content

Questionnaire Analysis

The analysis of PIPC ratings (Barendregt et al., 2008) for the learning activities involved aggregating and quantifying students' choices for each outdoor activity to identify any trends in the data (Table 2). Results for the category "Don't know/ understand" were ignored in the analysis as it was noticed during the data collection that instead of the intended meaning as "I am not sure how to rate the activity and/or did not understand it", some students interpreted it as a choice between "I don't know" and "I understand" and ticked the box to indicate that they understood the activity.

The data shows that students almost unanimously rated the outdoor activities as *Fun*, despite some students also selecting the categories *Scary*, *Difficult* and *Takes too long* for the same activities, indicating that they found the activity too advanced (i.e., more suitable for older students), too challenging or had a control problem where they perceived things as taking too long. An upward trend for more critical ratings can be recognised as the day progressed and students became more familiar with the mock-up tools and outdoor setting of the activities.

Open comments were analysed in a two-step emergent coding process, involving first data reduction and then data visualisation to identify common themes, as described in Miles and Huberman (1994). The vast majority of comments expressed students' enthusiasm for the learning activity (94%) and/or pointed out their favourite aspects (18%). A small number of comments offered suggestions on how the learning activity could be improved (3%), pointed out problems with the tools (4%) or expressed disappointment because they did not get a turn at operating the main tool (2%).

Table 2. Aggregated PIPC ratings based on 114 returned questionnaires

	Activity 1: Metal Detector	Activity 2: Geo Phys	Activity 3: Dig
Boring	0%	0%	5.5%
Fun	100%	95%	100%
Difficult	5%	10%	22%
Takes too long	2.5%	5%	16.5%
Childish	2.5%	2.5%	0%
Silly	0%	0%	0%
Scary	7.5%	7.5%	11%
Don't know/understand	-	-	-

4. FINDINGS AND DISCUSSION

Device Focus

The video analysis found many instances where students were seen standing or walking in a group to complete their role-specific tasks with only the device controller observing the mobile screen while students in supporting roles focused on their own auxiliary tools. This suggests that the assignment of specific roles in each task and the introduction of auxiliary tools supporting these roles helped divert pupils' focus away from the mobile device and towards their environment, team members and the current task at hand.

For the note-taking role in particular, which required prolonged interaction to make drawings of found objects, it was observed several times that the note-taker let the team move on while finishing a drawing before catching up, suggesting that the role and auxiliary tool fostered independence while working towards a common goal.

With respect to conceptualising smartphones as tools and integrating them into mock-ups of authentic archaeological equipment, it was observed that while the children tried to get a look at the device screen in key situations, e.g., when a virtual object was found, they usually focused on their own task and only helped to carry and operate the mock-up tool as required in Tasks 2 and 3 (Figure 5). Interestingly, students were clearly aware of the embedded smartphone but willingly accepted the mock-ups as functional tools, which was illustrated by the fact that they called them by their tool name ("Metal detector", "GeoFizz", "Digger") in normal operation but used phrases like "The mobile phone is broken" when there was a problem with the application.

The video material shows much face-to-face collaboration where students communicate with team members to coordinate their actions, discuss the line of action (e.g., in which direction to scan the ground), talk about found objects and their meaning or just express their excitement and enthusiasm. Students were also often seen to engage with their physical environment, for instance pointing out terrain features like small hills or dips and speculating whether these would be promising areas to scan with their equipment. In addition, there was regular communications with the teacher and archaeologist who helped to structure and control the activities by prompting tool swaps between students and telling them when to finish and return their tools. These observations seem to confirm the view that using mobile phones as tools and placing flow control and collaboration outside the device promote students' engagement with their peers and teachers and heighten their awareness of the environment.

The involvement of the archaeologist, teachers and technical personnel into the learning activity seemed to be pivotal in motivating students and keeping their focus on the task instead of the

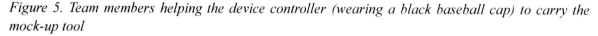

Figure 5. Team members helping the device controller (wearing a black baseball cap) to carry the mock-up tool

device. It was observed that alerting one of the involved adults, preferably the archaeologist, on each find and receiving affirmation and expert advice as to the found object's relevance and meaning seemed very important to pupils. Some pupils went to great lengths to attract the attention of the archaeologist when something was found, by calling and using the provided hooter for a long time, before either succeeding or eventually moving on without a consultation when the archaeologist or helpers were not available.

In the last outdoor activity, where no virtual objects or structures were to be found as students virtually "dug" at previously marked locations, and where consequently the teams had no regular and formalised consultations with the archaeologist or one of the present teachers or helpers, students were often observed to adopt a more playful attitude and to handle the equipment with less care. For instance, the two cases where the mock-up tool disintegrated during use were both observed in the third activity involving teams on their own while the adults were busy with other teams.

These observations clearly show that that the involvement of the archaeologist, teachers and tech personnel into the activities motivated students, helped to scaffold their learning and encouraged them to stay focused on the task. In addition, it ensured prompt support when equipment broke or malfunctioned, deflecting attention from technical problems and helping students to engage with subject-related problems.

Device Sharing

Despite the mitigating effects of the implemented measures on device focus, children were still observed in some cases to gather around the mobile device like "bees around the hive" (Morrison et al., 2009; Eliasson et al., 2010), especially when no immediate action was required from students in supporting roles and the task at hand depended heavily on visual feedback on the mobile screen.

While in these situations some team members continued to respect the main tool controller's prerogative to interact with the device and only

Figure 6. Team members pointing at the device screen

pointed their fingers at the screen (Figure 6), students used a range of strategies to gain or defend control of the device, including grabbing the tool, pushing their own hand towards the device (Figure 7), blocking the hands of others and pushing others' hands away from the tool (Figure 8). Children were also observed to exercise control by proxy, e.g., by resting a hand, often for extended periods, on the arm of the device controller (Figure 9), by tugging and/or pushing the controlling pupil or by putting one or more hands on other parts of the mock-up tool further away from where the mobile device was encased.

In some cases a communal control phenomenon was observed where four children locked shoulders or otherwise held each other tightly, and, looking down towards the embedded smartphone and/or the ground, moved as a single unit in small tentative steps, without it being obvious how decisions on direction and speed were formed.

Tool Usability and Acceptance

Some children were observed to indicate through gestures and verbal references that the mock-up tools were heavy to carry over longer periods, which was also mentioned twice in questionnaire

Figure 7. Team member pushing hand towards the device

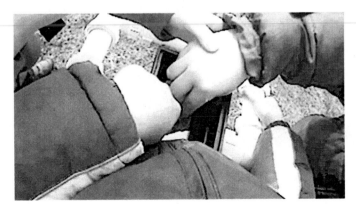

Figure 8. Device controller removing team member's hand

comments. However, these were isolated instances while overall the children seemed to have no serious problems handling the tools.

In terms of tool robustness, it was observed several times that the tool handle was not stiff enough and started bending under the weight of the rest of the tool (Metal Detector), that parts of the tool came off (Metal detector, Digger) and in two cases that the whole tool disintegrated (Digger) during use. However, these problems did not seem to suspend children's willing belief in the functionality and purpose of the tool, nor did they affect their resolve to complete the task at hand. Furthermore, in almost all instances these problems were promptly and easily fixed by the numerous helpers in attendance, without jeopardizing task completion or resulting in reprimands over pupils' sometimes rough handling of the equipment.

With respect to screen glare, the dark box in which the mobile device was embedded to minimise glare problems did not fulfill its purpose.

Figure 9. Control by proxy - team member resting hand on device controller's arm for extended period

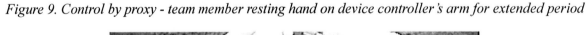

Children were often observed having difficulties reading the screen and trying to shield the device with cupped hands. The first-person video material confirms this problem as the device screen is often difficult to recognise due to reflections.

With respect to acceptability, the mock-up tools and overall learning experience were well received by students. Many episodes in the video material show students expressing their excitement and enthusiasm. A similar picture emerged from the large number of open comments in the questionnaires expressing students' exhilaration at handling the mock-up tools and being involved in such an exciting project. An upward trend, albeit at low levels, in more critical PIPC ratings as day progressed may however suggest that at least some of students' enthusiasm was related to the novelty of the experience.

5. CONCLUSION

Responding to recent research pointing out device focus as a "massive problem" (Göth et al., 2006) in mobile learning that is "seldom questioned or understood as a main research problem" (Eliasson et al., 2010), this paper has described how device focus and related issues like device sharing in collaborative mobile learning situations have been addressed in the *Invisible Buildings* project. Drawing on a set of recommendations formulated in Eliasson et al. (2010), which approach the problem of device focus on a conceptual and pedagogical level, the learning experience implemented measures that aimed to foster face-to-face collaboration between students and divert focus away from the mobile device towards the learners' physical and social context.

These measures included:

- Assigning students specific roles in outdoor activities and accentuating each role's importance and purpose in collaborative tasks with auxiliary tools

- Using smartphones as a set of tools for completing tasks instead of instruments for structuring and controlling tasks
- Embedding smartphones into larger mock-up tools derived from authentic archaeological practice to emphasise their task-specific purpose and heighten the game experience for students
- Promoting face-to-face collaboration through a requirement for team interaction and teacher-led group discussions instead of embedding collaborative features into the mobile applications
- Integrating teachers, tech personnel and an external subject expert into the learning activities to scaffold learning and keep students focused on the task.

The empirical evaluation of the project with two classes of primary school children suggests that these measures helped to mitigate device focus. While the study was not comparative and only evaluated the condition described here, it established that device focus was not a big problem in the project and that overall students showed a good degree of awareness of their physical environment, engagement with their peers and independence while working towards a common goal. They fulfilled their roles in collaborative activities, made use of the mock-up tools and auxiliary tools to complete tasks, communicated with team members in both task-related and social modes and engaged with the archaeologist, teachers and tech personnel to discuss the meaning of found objects and their wider implications in the context of the project.

In addition to evaluating the mobile learning experience with respect to device focus, the paper also took a closer look at the related problem of device sharing in collaborative mobile learning situations. While the measures mitigating device focus also reduced the need for device sharing, a range of behaviours and strategies employed by pupils to gain or defend device control were observed in key situations where all team members pushed towards the mobile device. Although these were less complex than children's conflicts and competition over shared resources around a tabletop (Marshall et al., 2009), there seem to be interesting similarities that transcend technological context and point towards non-technical approaches in the learning experience design.

While the large number of adults involved in delivering, supervising and monitoring the learning experience was a design decision consistent with the recommendations in Eliasson et al. (2010) and proved to be very effective in keeping students focused on the task at hand, it can also be seen as a methodological weakness in the overall evaluation of the learning experience: such a high adult-pupil ratio can potentially impact on validity due to the Hawthorn Effect (Turnock & Gibson, 2001) or "good bunny effect" (Robson, 2002), where the knowledge of being part of a research study and the presence of persons of authority can have a significant impact on the behaviour of participants. This must however be recognised as a common problem in the empirical evaluation of novel technologies involving unreliable equipment, as they require the presence of developers for ad-hoc technical support and researchers to collect data.

In summary, the experiences in the *Invisible Buildings* project seem to support the design recommendations in Eliasson et al. (2010) with respect to device focus in mobile learning and suggest they are equally applicable to the related problem of device sharing. Embedding smartphones into mock-up tools to heighten the experience and to emphasise their role as tools, introducing auxiliary tools that accentuate and support students' roles in collaborative tasks and introducing an external expert to add authenticity and authority to the learning experience, extended these recommendations conceptually and physically. These measures were well received by students who willingly accepted the mock-ups as functional tools, made use of auxiliary tools in supporting roles, eagerly consulted with the archaeologist and generally took part in both outdoor and indoor activities with great enthusiasm.

Some interesting aspects for future research into device focus and device sharing in collaborative mobile learning situations include the dynamics and communication between students gathering around a mobile device, potential positive aspects of this bee-hiving such as shared awareness among learners, and ways to leverage the phenomenon for specific learning goals. In a wider context, there remain many open questions relating to students' learning and to sustainability, both in terms of delivery of the learning experience and regarding students' enthusiasm for it.

ACKNOWLEDGMENT

We thank all the children and teachers at Sunnymede Primary School in Billericay, Essex, who took part in the evaluation. Invisible Buildings was developed by Locomatrix (2010) and the Essex Curriculum ICT Team with advice from the Interactive Technologies Research Group at the University of Brighton. The project was supported by the UK Technology Strategy Board with grant number AL018H.

REFERENCES

Ackermann, E. (1996). Perspective-taking and object construction: Two keys to learning. In Kafai, Y., & Resnick, M. (Eds.), *Constructionism in practice: Designing, thinking, and learning in a digital world*. Mahwah, NJ: Lawrence Erlbaum.

Anderson, G. (1990). *Fundamentals of educational research*. London, UK: Falmer Press.

Bandura, A. (1977). *Social learning theory*. New York, NY: General Learning Press.

Barendregt, W., Bekker, M., & Baauw, E. (2008). Development and evaluation of the problem identification picture cards method. *Cognition Technology and Work, 10*(2), 95–105. doi:10.1007/s10111-007-0066-z

Brewster, S. (2002). Overcoming the lack of screen space on mobile computers. *Personal and Ubiquitous Computing, 6*(3), 188–205. doi:10.1007/s007790200019

Brown, J. S., Collins, A., & Duguid, S. (1989). Situated cognition and the culture of learning. *Educational Researcher, 18*(1), 32–42.

Burgess, R. G. (Ed.). (1989). *The ethics of educational research*. New York, NY: Falmer Press.

Burrill, D. A. (2010). Wii will become silhouettes. *Television & New Media, 20*(10), 1–11.

Crossan, A., McGill, M., Brewster, S., & Murray-Smith, R. (2009). Head tilting for interaction in mobile contexts. In *Proceedings of the 11th International Conference on Human-Computer Interaction with Mobile Devices and Services* (p. 6).

Crossan, A., Williamson, J., Brewster, S., & Murray-Smith, R. (2008). Wrist rotation for interaction in mobile contexts. In *Proceedings of the 10th International Conference on Human Computer Interaction with Mobile Devices and Services* (pp. 435-438).

Eliasson, J., Pargman, T., Nouri, J., Spikol, D., & Ramberg, R. (2011). Mobile devices as support rather than distraction for mobile learners – Evaluating guidelines for design. *International Journal of Mobile and Blended Learning, 3*(2), 1–15.

Eliasson, J., Spikol, D., Pargman, T., & Ramberg, R. (2010). Get the bees away from the hive: Balancing visual focus on devices in mobile learning. In *Proceedings of the IADIS International Conference on Mobile Learning* (pp. 77-84).

Engeström, Y. (1991). Non scolae sed vitae discimus: Toward overcoming the encapsulation of school learning. *Learning and Instruction, 1*, 243–259. doi:10.1016/0959-4752(91)90006-T

Facer, K., Joiner, R., Stanton, D., Reid, J., Hull, R., & Kirk, D. (2004). Savannah: Mobile gaming and learning? *Journal of Computer Assisted Learning, 20*(6), 399–409. doi:10.1111/j.1365-2729.2004.00105.x

Göth, C., Frohberg, D., & Schwabe, G. (2006). The focus problem in mobile learning. In *Proceedings of Fourth IEEE International Workshop on Wireless, Mobile and Ubiquitous Technology in Education* (pp. 153-160).

Hine, N., Rentoul, R., & Spechty, M. (2004). Collaboration and roles in remote field trips. In Attewell, J., & Saville-Smith, C. (Eds.), *Learning with mobile devices: A book of papers* (pp. 69–72). London, UK: Learning and Skills Development Agency.

Hoggan, E., Anwar, S., & Brewster, S. (2007). Mobile multi-actuator tactile displays. In I. Oakley & S. Brewster (Eds.), *Proceedings of the Second International Conference on Haptic and Audio Interaction Design* (LNCS 4813, pp. 22-33).

Kane, S. K., Wobbrock, J. O., & Smith, I. E. (2008). Getting off the treadmill: Evaluating walking user interfaces for mobile devices in public spaces. In *Proceedings of the 10th International Conference on Human Computer Interaction with Mobile Devices and Services* (pp. 109-118).

Klopfer, E., & Squire, K. (2007). Environmental detectives - the development of an augmented reality platform for environmental simulations. *Educational Technology Research and Development, 56*(2), 203–228. doi:10.1007/s11423-007-9037-6

Kolb, D. A. (1984). *Experiential learning: Experience as the source of learning and development*. Upper Saddle River, NJ: Prentice Hall.

Kratz, S., & Rohs, M. (2009). HoverFlow: Expanding the design space of around-device interaction. In *Proceedings of the 11th International Conference on Human-Computer Interaction with Mobile Devices and Services* (p. 4).

Kristoffersen, S., & Ljundberg, F. (1999). "Making place" to make IT work: Empirical explorations of HCI for mobile CSCW. In *Proceedings of the International ACM SIGGROUP Conference on Supporting Group Work* (pp. 276-285).

Kukulska-Hulme, A., Sharples, M., & Milrad, M., Arnedillo- Sánchez, I., & Vavoula, G. (2009). Innovation in mobile learning: A European perspective. *International Journal of Mobile and Blended Learning*, *1*(1), 13–35. doi:10.4018/jmbl.2009010102

Lave, J. (1988). *Cognition in practice: Mind, mathematics, and culture in everyday life*. Cambridge, UK: Cambridge University Press. doi:10.1017/CBO9780511609268

Leichtenstern, K., & André, E. (2009). Studying multi-user settings for pervasive games. In *Proceedings of the 11th International Conference on Human-Computer Interaction with Mobile Devices and Services* (p. 25).

Locomatrix. (2010). *Locomatrix homepage*. Retrieved from http://locomatrix.com

Luckin, R., du Boulay, B., Smith, H., Underwood, J., Fitzpatrick, G., & Holmberg, J. (2005). Using mobile technology to create flexible learning contexts. *Journal of Interactive Media in Education*, (22): 1–21.

Lumsden, J., Kondratova, I., & Langton, N. (2006). Bringing a construction site into the lab: A context-relevant lab based evaluation of a multimodal mobile application. In *Proceedings of the 1st International Workshop on Multimodal and Pervasive Services* (pp. 62-68).

Marshall, P., Fleck, R., & Harris, A. Rick, J., Hornecker, E., Rogers, Y. et al. (2009). Fighting for control: Children's embodied interactions when using physical and digital representations. In *Proceedings of the 27th International Conference on Human Factors in Computing Systems: Enhancing Reality* (pp. 2149-2152).

Metcalf, S. J., & Tinker, R. F. (2004). Probeware and handhelds in elementary and middle school science. *Journal of Science Education and Technology*, *13*(1), 43–49. doi:10.1023/B:JOST.0000019637.22473.02

Miles, M. B., & Huberman, A. M. (1984). *Qualitative data analysis*. Newbury Park, CA: Sage.

Morrison, A., Oulasvirta, A., Peltonen, P., Lemmelä, S., Jacucci, G., Reitmayr, G., et al. (2009). Like bees around the hive: A comparative study of a mobile augmented reality map. In *Proceedings of the International Conference on Human Factors in Computing Systems: Enhancing Reality* (pp. 1889-1898).

Oulasvirta, A., Tamminen, S., & Roto, V. (2005). Interaction in 4-second bursts: The fragmented nature of attentional resources in mobile HCI. In *Proceedings of the SIGCHI Conference on Human Factors in Computing Systems* (pp. 919-928).

Pascoe, J., Ryan, N., & Morse, D. (2000). Using while moving: HCI issues in fieldwork environments. *ACM Transactions on Computer-Human Interaction*, *7*, 417–437. doi:10.1145/355324.355329

PhoneBook. (2010). *PhoneBook at mobile art lab*. Retrieved from http://www.mobileart.jp/phonebook_en.html

Price, K., Lin, M., Feng, J., Goldman, R., Sears, A., & Jacko, J. (2004). Data entry on the move: An examination of nomadic speech-based text entry. In C. Stary & C. Stephanidis (Eds.), *Proceedings of the 8th ERCIM Workshop on User Interfaces for All* (LNCS 3196, pp. 460-471).

Robson, C. (2002). *Real world research* (2nd ed.). Oxford, UK: Blackwell.

Rogers, Y., Connelly, K., Hazlewood, W., & Tedesco, L. (2010). Enhancing learning: A study of how mobile devices can facilitate sensemaking. *Personal and Ubiquitous Computing, 14*(2), 111–124. doi:10.1007/s00779-009-0250-7

Rogers, Y., Price, S., Fitzpatrick, G., Fleck, R., Harris, E., Smith, H., et al. (2004). Ambient wood: Designing new forms of digital augmentation for learning outdoors. In *Proceedings of the Conference on Interaction Design and Children: Building a Community* (pp. 3-10).

Rogoff, B. (1982). Integrating context and cognitive development. In Lamb, M. E., & Brown, A. L. (Eds.), *Advances in developmental psychology* (*Vol. 2*). Mahwah, NJ: Lawrence Erlbaum.

Roschelle, J. (2000). Choosing and using video equipment for data collection. In Lesh, R. (Ed.), *Handbook of research data design in mathematics and science education*. Mahwah, NJ: Lawrence Erlbaum.

Satyanarayanan, M. (1996). Fundamental challenges in mobile computing. In *Proceedings of the Fifteenth Annual ACM Symposium on Principles of Distributed Computing* (pp. 1-7).

Spiro, R. J., Coulson, R. L., Feltovich, P. J., & Anderson, D. (1988). Cognitive flexibility theory: Advanced knowledge acquisition in ill-structured domains. In *Proceedings of the 10th Annual Conference of the Cognitive Science Society* (pp. 375-383).

Turnock, C., & Gibson, V. (2001). Validity in action research: A discussion on theoretical and practice issues encountered whilst using observation to collect data. *Journal of Advanced Nursing, 36*(3), 471–477. doi:10.1046/j.1365-2648.2001.01995.x

Vogel, B., Spikol, D., Kurti, A., & Milrad, M. (2010). Integrating mobile, web and sensory technologies to support inquiry-based science learning. In *Proceedings of the 6th IEEE International Conference on Wireless, Mobile, and Ubiquitous Technologies in Education* (pp. 65-72).

Vygotsky, L. S. (1978). *Mind in society*. Cambridge, MA: Harvard University Press.

Wobbrock, J. (2006). The future of mobile device research in HCI. In *Proceedings of the Workshop on Next Generation of Human-Computer Interaction* (pp. 131-134).

This work was previously published in the International Journal of Mobile and Blended Learning, Volume 3, Issue 4, edited by David Parsons, pp 1-18, copyright 2011 by IGI Publishing (an imprint of IGI Global).

Chapter 7
Guidelines for the Design of Location-Based Audio for Mobile Learning

Elizabeth FitzGerald
University of Nottingham, UK

Robert Jones
University of Nottingham, UK

Mike Sharples
University of Nottingham, UK

Gary Priestnall
University of Nottingham, UK

ABSTRACT

A consistent finding of research into mobile learning guides and outdoor learning games has been the value of audio as a medium of communication. This paper discusses the value of location-based and movement-sensitive audio for learning. Three types of audio learning experience are distinguished, based primarily upon differing levels of narrative cohesion: audio vignettes, movement-based guides and mobile narratives. An analysis of projects in these three areas has resulted in the formulation of guidelines for the design of audio experiences. A case study of a novel audio experience, called 'A Chaotic Encounter,' delivers an adaptive story based on the pattern of movements of the user.

INTRODUCTION

A consistent finding of research into mobile learning guides and outdoor learning games has been the value of audio as a medium of communication (see e.g., Bhaskar & Govindarajulu, 2010; Naismith, Sharples, & Ting, 2005; Schwabe & Goth, 2005). This complements earlier findings from studies of distance learning which showed that students like being informed by the voice of their educator, listening to interviews or debates, hearing from experts and being encouraged with a reassuring audio message (Durbridge, 1984). The difficulty with audio as an instructional medium is that it can be hard to concentrate on a voice for long periods, it is difficult to retain de-contextualised audio information for later reflection (Laurillard, 2002) and some topics can be explained more effectively through pictures or graphics (McConnell & Sharples, 1983; Minocha & Booth, 2008).

DOI: 10.4018/978-1-4666-2139-8.ch007

This indicates two, diverging, opportunities to exploit audio as a medium for mobile learning: in podcasts, where the audio is de-contextualised and may need to be supplemented by graphics, images or video to explain or illustrate a topic; and in location-based guides, where the physical surroundings complement the audio commentary. The focus of this paper is on the latter, with a broad scope of audio experiences that include guides, games and stories, either matched to location by position-sensing technology such as GPS, or that respond to the physical movement of the user.

The initial challenges for designers of location-based mobile learning are to:

- Ensure that the learner is at the right place and looking in the right direction, so that the sound and the view are matched,
- Minimise the need for learners to interact with the device, so that that they have a 'heads up' continual flow of visual information rather than frequently shifting gaze between the scenery and the screen.

Physical movement around the environment can provide an effective method of interaction (Bristow, Baber, Cross, & Woolley, 2002). Contextualised information can be adapted to the user's preferences and profile, their route, their current position and orientation and how long they have been at the current position. Thus a person's movement and position can provide means of interacting with a combination of the physical surroundings and audio educational material, without the need to gaze at a screen or press buttons.

This paper provides an overview of the use of audio for location-based encounters. It provides a classification of types of verbal audio and examples of their implementation in mobile learning systems, followed by guidelines for the effective use of audio, drawn from the examples. We then present a case study called 'A Chaotic Encounter', as an example of a novel approach that combines movement-based guides with mobile narratives (i.e., an adaptive narrative). We report an evaluation with ten users along with suggestions for future work.

TYPES OF AUDIO EXPERIENCE

Audio has been used effectively in many location-based experiences, including mobile gaming (Drewes, Mynatt, & Gandy, 2000; Lyons, Gandy, & Starner, 2000); tourism (Aoki et al., 2002; Naismith et al., 2005); educational visits (O'Hara et al., 2007; Vavoula, Sharples, Rudman, Meek, & Lonsdale, 2009) and theatrical events (e.g., Hotter than Hell, http://www.aerial.fm/docs/projects. php?id=101:0:0:0), or a combination of these activities (Rowland et al., 2009; Schnädelbach et al., 2008).

Audio can give directions, for example to tell the user to follow a path until a particular landmark is reached, or to orientate them so they are facing a specific feature of the landscape or museum exhibit. It can engage the user in a task-based activity, particularly in educational scenarios, where students are asked to make notes or take measurements and observations relating to their immediate environment. It can also provide information about an object or scene, function as a story-telling device, or create ambient sounds relevant to the environment such as birdsong or machinery. These can instil a more authentic atmosphere than bare instruction and make the experience more realistic and engaging, as demonstrated in Ambient Wood, a playful learning experience, where children explored and reflected upon a physical environment that had been augmented with an assortment of digital abstractions (such as an unusual slurping sound, to represent a massively amplified recording of a butterfly sucking nectar) (Rogers et al., 2004).

In this paper, we concentrate on the use of spoken audio rather than non-verbal audio. We propose three broad classes of movement-based audio experiences:

- *Audio vignettes*, where the user's movement into a location triggers audio, but there is no adaptivity based on previous movement;
- *Movement-based guides*, where the aim is to adapt information to objects or surroundings, and the interaction and adaptivity may be informed by the user's previous movements;
- *Mobile narratives*, where an audio narrative is performed based on a sequence of user movements.

These three forms of audio guide have some common properties and requirements (e.g., audio as the main means of delivery), some differences (e.g., whether the audio should be independent of previous location, adaptive to it, or cumulative), and some dependencies on the particular design goal (e.g., whether, and how, the users should be explicitly informed of the relation between their movement and the audio). In particular, we have drawn upon existing research to explore the issue of narrative dependency and the ordering of audio segments as presented to the end user. These three categories start with the lowest level of dependency upon other audio segments (audio vignettes), and work along a continuum until a high level of dependency is seen (mobile narrative) and correct ordering of the media becomes critical to the experience of the user (Figure 1).

Narrative – the organisation of content into meaningful plots and stories – is a particularly useful tool in constructionist learning (Sims, 2003) and recent work by Yiannoutsou and Avouris (2010) suggests that different structures of narrative can have a wide range of different affordances for learning, arguing that "the kinds of narratives suitable for [playful learning] need to be studied extensively" (p. 155). Our paper aims to contribute to this area by presenting a model of how the organisation of content can contribute towards the learning design of a performative audio experience.

AUDIO VIGNETTES

We classify audio vignettes as short pieces of audio triggered by movement from the user. However, there is no history of where the user has been, and hence no adaptivity based on previous movement. Thus, users engage with chunks of audio that are independent of each other and of their relative locations. Depending on the design, it could be possible to interact with some, all, or none of the audio segments in a particular place or sub-area, with either the computer or the user choosing which aspects of the place to engage with. Missing out some vignettes should not necessarily disadvantage the user since the information in each should be self-contained, although there might be

Figure 1. Increasing level of dependency and ordering of audio chunks for each type of audio experience

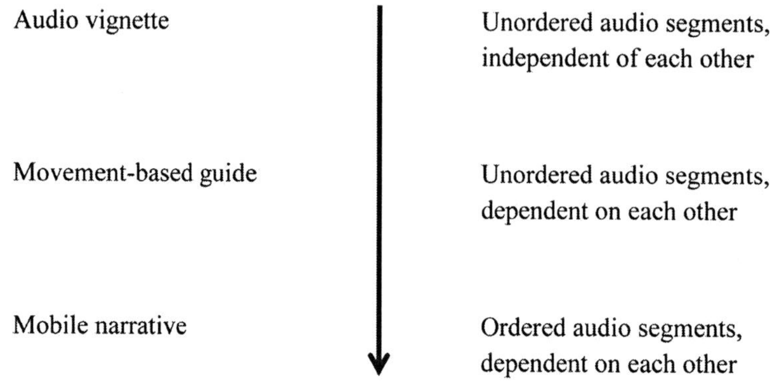

Audio vignette	Unordered audio segments, independent of each other
Movement-based guide	Unordered audio segments, dependent on each other
Mobile narrative	Ordered audio segments, dependent on each other

added value if related vignettes are played within a short space of time (e.g., audio descriptions of information relating to archaeological exhibits found at the same geographical location or with a common theme).

Examples include work by Bederson (1995), who created non-linear browsing for museum exhibits: a piece of audio was attached to each artwork and this was activated based on the proximity of the user. Since this was a non-linear system, users could approach any exhibit in any order; they could re-visit them or choose to skip over any that they were not interested in. Rozier et al. (2000) attempted to take this further, by allowing users to overlay their own audio recordings onto existing 'audio imprints' that were already present in their immediate environment.

The 'Riot! 1831' project (Reid, Hull, Cater, & Clayton, 2005) provides an excellent example of audio vignettes. This was an interactive play created using mScape (http://www.hpl.hp.com/downloads/mediascape/), based around the riots which engulfed the Queens Square area of Bristol in 1831. Participants were given PDAs running the mScape client; they were then free to explore Queens Square on their own. GPS positioning on the device monitored the user's position and the area was divided into regions. When the GPS reported that the user had entered one of these regions, it triggered a short audio vignette depicting events of the riot which occurred in that place. These were not sequenced in any way, so users could freely wander between regions (and vignettes) in any way they chose. Evaluations of 'Riot! 1831' report a positive experience for most users, however some feedback indicated that there seemed to be no overarching narrative and it could be difficult at times to get a more holistic overview (Reid et al., 2005). The authors also encountered problems with the GPS signal often being adversely affected by buildings or weather conditions. When this occurred, they intervened to stop participants from using the system and encouraged them to return later.

Issues relating to the effectiveness of audio vignettes in outdoor locations have been explored through the 'Augmenting the Visitor Experience' project (Priestnall, Brown, Sharples, & Polmear, 2009). Here, groups of students were asked to develop their own mScape for an area of the English Lake District, which would act as a free roaming visitor guide to some of the hidden cultural and geographical aspects of the landscape around them. Pre-recorded audio vignettes describing vistas from specific locations were made available, along with audio descriptions of points of interest and miscellany relating to areas with more indeterminate boundaries. An important aspect of the most recent occurrence of the field project was to encourage students to record their own audio using mp3 voice recorders. These audio vignettes were associated with trigger regions defined by the students, which could be varying size, shape and position. The effectiveness of audio was then tested in the field, using video diaries created by the students as one mechanism for gathering evidence. Findings revealed difficulties experienced by the users in associating standalone audio vignettes with the corresponding landscape features. A particular challenge posed by outdoor environments is that there are often many separate features of interest in a scene, and in natural environments they may not be visually distinct from one another, causing ambiguity in identification. Figure 2 shows a typical scene on a geography fieldtrip where aspects of the landscape are described by an expert guide. The figure shows examples of features relevant to the history of the physical landscape, which often requires the use of specialist geographic terms combined with physically 'pointing things out', to convey the message.

As with 'Riot! 1831' there were issues with GPS reliability, but also more subtle influences on the user experience, resulting from audio not being delivered at the locations intended. The positional wander of the GPS devices could cause audio to be delivered too early, before the object of interest was in view, or indeed too late, after it had been visited. There were also instances of trigger zones being missed completely due to GPS wander or inaccuracies in their placement on the map.

The audio vignette is an important category of audio guide and one that has proved popular at many tourist attractions and museums, with the user normally required to indicate each location through button presses, which removes ambiguities related to position. Its popularity is due in part to the relative ease of authoring and delivering the vignettes, where each audio segment can be offered on its own, with no need to predict or respond to the route taken by the visitor. It also allows freedom of movement by the user, with no compulsion to follow a prescribed path.

MOVEMENT-BASED GUIDES

In a movement-based guide, the user's movement within and between locations, as well as changes to physical posture, orientation and gaze can all provide means of interaction and opportunities for adapting the content and delivery of educational material. In a museum or gallery, the layout of rooms and exhibits is designed as a structured information space, so any physical movement around the rooms is also a traversal between concepts. This can be used to advantage in a mobile guide. Consider a person standing in front of a painting in a gallery. A context-aware guide could adapt its content and presentation to take account of the person's route to that location ("you seem to be interested in pre-Raphaelite paintings"), their current location ("the portrait here is also by Rossetti"), their orientation and gaze ("if you turn further to your right you can see a similar painting by Burne-Jones"), and the time they have been at the current location ("now look more closely at the folds of the dress"). Similar concepts can be applied in outdoor settings, which although not designed deliberately for educational purposes, can have structure, coherence and continuity that can be exploited by a movement-based guide. For example, a rural landscape can reveal contrasts in agricultural use, or changing rock formations along a pathway.

Figure 2. The challenge of replicating the role of a human field guide, in this case illustrating some aspects of the formation of the physical landscape around Derwent Water, Cumbria, UK

Figure 3. CAGE guide, with ultrasonic transmitters on the radiator ledges, and the receiver attached to the handheld device. The audio could be delivered through a speaker or earpiece.

The CAGE system was a prototype movement-based guide designed for a city art gallery (Rudman, Sharples, Vavoula, Lonsdale, & Meek, 2008). The location of the user was determined automatically by an ultrasonic positioning system that was accurate to about 10cm (Figure 3). The user received audio that continually adapted to: the nearest painting (as determined by the ultrasound positioning system); the length of time at a painting (the system assumed that the longer a person stayed at one place, the more they were interested in that painting); and the previous time at the position (the content was only repeated on request).

CAGE was evaluated through a comparison with a traditional printed guide. In general, the location-based delivery of content worked well and people liked using the technology. The adaptivity matched users' expectations, and feedback indicated that they found the presentations appropriate and useful. The evaluation found no significant differences between the handheld guide and printed sheet as sources of information, which is not surprising since they contained similar content. A particular success was one painting where the users were given increasing level of information the longer they stayed, encouraging them to look more closely into details of the imagery. This also worked with groups, who shared the audio commentary. One group of participants spent over three minutes pointing out details to each other and discussing what they were hearing. Other pairs of visitors talked about what they were seeing, prompted by the information from the guide.

Although the CAGE evaluation indicates success in customising the delivery of content based on the route, position and time at the current location, it was less successful in enabling users to make links between exhibits in different locations or in encouraging them to break their linear movement along the gallery. Further research is needed into how people's physical movement can be used as the basis for a coherent sequence of instruction or guidance.

A difficulty of movement-based guides lies in authoring the content so that it adapts to the user's activity. This is a well-recognised problem for intelligent tutoring systems and partial solutions range from the labour-intensive task of creating different content for typical routes, to implementing a computational model of the learner's interest and activity linked to automated generation of audio content (Gustafsson, Bichard, Brunnberg, Juhlin, & Combetto, 2006). The design of adaptive tutoring systems, based on computational models of learner activity and inferences as to the learner's cognitive state, is an active area of research, with recent work exploring how such models can be presented to the learner to promote reflection (see e.g., Bull & McEvoy, 2003).

MOBILE NARRATIVES

In a mobile narrative, an audio narrative is performed that is based on the sequence of movements carried out by the user. Hence, the audio heard by a user will depend upon where the user goes to, and has come from. For example, one would expect a mobile narrative to integrate aspects of location that the user has already visited, but not those that they have not.

It differs from a movement-based guide in having a strong story-telling component and a level of dependency upon the previous audio segment. It may present different perspectives, so that an event or a place is told by different characters, presenting multiple interpretations that can prove fascinating to a user (Lim & Aylett, 2007; Tozzi, 2000). These different perspectives can also provide a deeper learning experience than having a single narrative, since users can critically analyse the viewpoints and make their own conclusions, compared to having a single stream of information provided to them. It could also be more engaging than individual audio vignettes, since different aspects of the mobile narratives form part of a larger story, thus creating a broader background upon which these narratives are set (Roden, Parberry, & Ducrest, 2007).

An example of how this has been created is the 'Mobile Narrative' framework, developed to facilitate the delivery of context-sensitive stories on the iPhone platform (Wiesner, Foth, & Bilandzic, 2009). The framework allows an author to create a textual story, divided into multiple chapters. Certain chapters can then be restricted so that the end user can only read that chapter at a specific time or location, as monitored by the phone's internal clock and GPS receiver. Those reading the stories were often irritated by this imposed inaccessibility, regarding it as arbitrary and resenting their loss of control while writers were concerned that these limitations reduced accessibility. This project has only so far been developed in textual format and not in spoken audio, however it highlights the potential pitfalls of forcing users to access content only at specific times or that meet certain criteria, thus reducing and limiting their interactivity with the narrative.

In contrast, 'History Unwired' was a freely-usable mobile narrative (in terms of cost to the user and lack of time restrictions) created as a walking tour around part of the lesser-visited yet culturally-rich areas of Venice. It was delivered over location-aware PDAs and mobile phones, to over 200 users, as an alternative to the mass tourism offerings provided elsewhere (Epstein & Vergani, 2006). It followed the personal stories of five local Venetians, who had been interviewed to provide folkloric commentaries on the area in which they lived. Location sensing was provided via Bluetooth due to intermittent GPS coverage in the streets of Venice. Initial user evaluations suggest that the authenticity of the storytellers was very well-received, with some users even meeting one or two of the characters in person. The narrative also provided opportunities to 'open up' parts of the city whilst also respecting the privacy of the residents ('closed' areas).

GUIDELINES FOR EFFECTIVE AUDIO EXPERIENCES

Based on the above examples and the design experience of the authors, the following design guidelines are proposed for the creation of effective audio experiences. These are offered as initial suggestions to the mobile learning community and further work is needed to test and refine the guidelines. The guidelines are categorised under several headings: interactivity; narration; trails/navigation; technical issues; and sensitivity to the local environment.

Interactivity

- An audio experience should be interactive: in the examples given above, the ability of the user to interact with and potentially influence the story (or at least have some control over it) appears to add significant value to the experience. See Miller (2008) for a fuller discussion of the value of interactivity.

- This interaction should be dependent on the user's movements. A history or trail of where the user has been can enable the delivery of an enhanced experience and can avoid repetition, as in the CAGE project. For further discussion see also Davis et al. (2006) and Ballagas and Walz (2007).

- Under some circumstances, the precise dynamic by which movement affects the narrative could be obscured from the user (providing there is sufficient justification in doing so). This allows the narrative to provide 'ambient informatics' (Greenfield, 2006) regarding the user's movements – the experience is enhanced by allowing the user to gain this information subtly. This is exemplified by 'I Seek The Nerves Under Your Skin', an adaptive poem in which the user had constantly to accelerate in order to continue hearing the poem. The ongoing narrative provided subtle information about the speed of the runner (Marshall, 2009). Gaver et al. (2003) also note that such ambiguity allows the designer to raise questions about a user's behaviour without having to necessarily answer them and can additionally compensate for the inaccuracies of sensors. However this takes away control from the user, which is generally not a desirable course of action, either from an educational or design perspective and so the benefits in doing so must be clear and far outweigh the disadvantages to the user. A better option might be to provide this as an alternative experience rather than the only one available.

Narration

- It is preferable for the narrative at all times to remain coherent and flowing, so that the user does not get 'lost' in the different audio offerings. It is necessary to strike a balance between user choice and narrative cohesion (Ryan, 2001).
- Reducing the reliance on visual material can make an audio experience more engaging and promote curiosity in the user (Sprake, 2006). To that end, the delivery should employ audio alone whenever it can tell a compelling story or complement the visual surroundings. There is an established precedent for this in the examples of audiobooks and audio guides, which allow people to listen without impeding their routine patterns of movement. The content should therefore be able to respond to these patterns without necessarily affecting them. However, users can also be encouraged to experiment with new and unusual styles of movement in order to gain a different narrative experience, as shown by Marshall (2009).

Trails/Navigation

- It cannot be assumed that users will follow the path proposed by the guide. The evaluation of the CAGE system indicated that it is difficult to persuade people to deviate from a typical route, so it may be better to adapt rather than persuade.

Technical Issues

- The audio should adapt to the failings of sensor technology in order to avoid having to abandon the experience when sensors stop functioning, as was the case for 'Riot! 1831' but was overcome by using Bluetooth in 'History Unwired'.
- Where the precise location of the audio in relation to features in the landscape is important, then the shape and extent of the 'trigger' regions should be designed to allow for fluctuations in calculated position caused by inaccuracies and 'wander' in the GPS data (Benford et al., 2003).

Sensitivity to the Local Environment

- Even when GPS positioning can be assumed to be accurate, there remains the issue of the 'geographic relevance' of audio, particularly when it is important that the user associates that audio with specific features in the landscape. Evidence from field exercises (Priestnall et al., 2009) is that users commonly fail to associate the audio description with the landscape, by looking in the wrong direction. This suggests that designers should understand the geographical reference points and landmarks that may be important in a particular environment, and incorporate them into the audio descriptions where possible
- Sensitivity to local surroundings is especially important when the audio experience takes place in an outdoor location. In History Unwired, sensitivity to local humour, privacy, art and culture was instilled from an early stage in the design of the experience. At the same time, there was a delicate balance to be maintained, so that the

tour was not sensationalistic or voyeuristic (Epstein & Vergani, 2006).

- Safety is a critical factor to take into account. Both Paterson et al. (2010) and Llewellyn-Jones (2007) highlight that immersive experiences, particularly those involving audio, can distract users from their immediate surroundings and so might not take due care and attention when encountering hazards such as traffic or uneven surfaces. Users should be made aware of this issue before engaging with such an experience.

CASE STUDY: A CHAOTIC ENCOUNTER

In this section, we present an example of a relatively unexplored category, that combines movement-based guides with mobile narratives (an adaptive narrative), drawing upon the aforementioned guidelines. Users of *A Chaotic Encounter* are provided with a small PocketPC featuring a GPS sensor, touchscreen and a headphone jack. This system, created using mScape (Stenton et al., 2007), delivers an entertaining audio story, based on Nottingham folktales, which adapts its content to reflect the listener's movement patterns. Its design was informed by the guidelines described above, with particular reference to narrative structure and movement-based interaction. Specifically, it aimed to investigate whether users preferred to explicitly steer the story's development manually, or have the plot automatically adapt itself according to their movements.

The narrative is structured around the tree-branch model outlined in Phelps (1998), as this provides the linearity necessary for an enjoyable story (Paay et al., 2008). The story is divided into three levels, each of which corresponds to the classic story structure of Exposition-Climax-Denouement defined by Freytag (1895).

At each level, there are one or more 'acts': short audio segments which perform the function of that level – for example, all of the acts at the Climax level depict the characters encountering a problem that must be solved, while those at the Denouement level present the solution of that problem and the story's conclusion. Each act can branch to one of three acts on the next level: these three all fulfill the same story-advancing function necessary for their level but differ in their content. Each has a 'Chaos Rating' representing the predictability of their content: a Low Chaos act features few characters and is relatively mundane, while a High Chaos act has many characters and is more surreal. A Medium Chaos act sits between these two extremes of the bland and fantastic. Thus, as the listener progresses from one level to the next, they have a range of Chaos Levels to choose from but will always experience a traditionally linear story.

The mechanism which determines this choice is hidden from the user. The system constantly records the user's speed and direction of movement during each act and then, at the end of the act, draws on this record to determine the appropriate Chaos Level to progress to. This calculation is based on the number and extent of the recorded changes: if these values are low (that is, if the user maintains a constant speed and direction) then a Low Chaos act is selected whereas if they are high (if the user often changes speed and direction, moving erratically) then a High Chaos act is delivered instead. Once this decision has been made and enacted, the movement records are erased so that the process can begin anew during the next act. The whole decision-making process takes place quickly enough so as to appear seamless to the user: one act instantly segues into the next so that the listener is left with the impression that they are hearing one continuous audio narrative when, in fact, it is composed of several segments corresponding to specific branches in the narrative tree (Figure 4). It is only with multiple uses that they might come to realise that it is interactive at all, or that their movements have an effect.

The system is designed such that, after initial activation, the screen is unused and the device can be left in a pocket throughout playback. However, should GPS reception become unavailable for a prolonged time while the story is playing, the system provides brief audio and visual messages warning them that this has occurred and to move away from potential sources of interference. The user can also avoid GPS altogether: when the system is activated, it allows them to choose between 'automatic' and 'manual' settings. Automatic mode uses the GPS system described above, while manual mode does not rely on sensors at all: rather than measuring the listener's movements, at the end of each act it pauses playback and presents, via the touchscreen, an interface for manually choosing the Chaos Level of the next act, which begins playing once the choice is made. This method sacrifices the device's ability to match story to motion and therefore provide ambient feedback to the user about their movements - however, it does provide much improved reliability by removing the dependency on GPS.

User trials were conducted with a group of ten participants, three of whom agreed to be interviewed and complete a questionnaire about their experience. Users were selected on the criterion that they regularly listen to a portable audio device while making routine journeys. They each tested the system individually, and were initially informed that the system relied on GPS technology to measure movement but were not told how or why this was this case. Instead, they were briefed to initially listen to the story in automatic mode at least twice, while walking through the city. Following this, they were encouraged to try manual mode. Finally, they were debriefed and given the questionnaire assessing the extent to which they felt their movements had an effect on the narrative, whether they became more conscious of their movements, how much

Figure 4. Narrative structure in a chaotic encounter

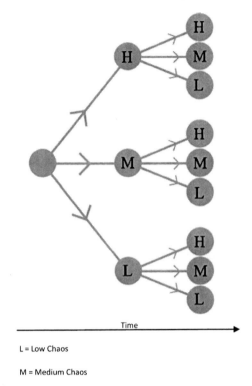

L = Low Chaos

M = Medium Chaos

they engaged with the story and their opinions on the two modes of operation.

The questionnaire consisted of open-ended questions that asked participants to compare the manual mode and the automatic mode and also included a basic usability assessment of the experience. User responses to the design were mixed: all agreed that they had enjoyed hearing the story, demonstrating the value of adhering to classic dramatic story structure; on their second listen, some reported feeling confused and unable to understand what they were meant to be doing differently, while others responded positively and quickly began experimenting with different movement styles. However, it was possible to resolve the difficulties experienced by those who did not understand how to interact with the system by providing a more detailed explanation of the method by which movement influenced the story. Following this, these users successfully replayed the story – some of them several times. One user reported that although they enjoyed exploring the relationship between movement and story, they ultimately chose to use manual mode to provide precise control and prevent repetition. This suggests that ambiguity can be a potential resource in effective design, but can risk alienating users and must be carefully managed.

Nevertheless, the participants generally agreed that the manual mode, driven by explicit choice, was less enjoyable as it regularly interrupted the story to demand that they interact with the screen. This demonstrates Ryan's claim that explicit interactivity threatens immersion by forcing the user to step out of the fictional world (Ryan, 2001). However, in some cases the intermittent availability of GPS caused incorrect recording of movement, leaving the user being presented with the same story multiple times. This demonstrates the need to find an alternative to GPS that provides more reliable movement sensing, as well as a method that does not rely on movement sensing but also does not require constant user input. The former could be solved by the use of accelerometers, which are more reliable and sensitive than GPS (Slyper & Hodgins, 2008). The latter could use a randomiser to determine story progression when movement data is unavailable – this would strip the experience of its ambient reflectivity, but would not break immersion. This method could also store details of the previous story path taken and avoid it in future, to prevent accidental repetition.

While this project was focused on exploring the potential for using movement as a resource for providing ambient flexibility in otherwise rigidly ordered audio content, the work here also suggests potential areas in which such a system could be employed. In particular, two opportunities for learning are evident: firstly, since interaction with alternate story paths can increase replay value (Schell, 2008), users are more likely to retain memories of the audio content as they are exposed to it several times (Ausubel, 2000). While the research questionnaire, in line with the aims

of the project, did not specifically address learning outcomes, participant feedback nevertheless indicated that users had understood and retained the content of the folk story presented to them.

The second learning application is in human geography. A system such as *A Chaotic Encounter* can address the need identified by McDonough (1994) to make people's everyday movements a subject of study by those same people. By focusing an individual's attention on their patterns of movement, this system could provide a stimulating starting-point for discussions on the relationship of a person to the public space they inhabit, and the role of technology in mediating this. Other applications with a learning component could include tourism, in which stories and/or mythology relating to the history or geography of an area could be used as the basis of the plot. Alternatively it could be used as an unconventional means of promoting exercise, to encourage its listeners to change acceleration in their speed of movement, in order to hear different narratives.

CONCLUSION AND FUTURE WORK

We have presented an overview of how verbal audio can be used effectively by users as they physically move around their environment. We described three categories of how this can be achieved: through *audio vignettes*; *movement-based guides*; and *mobile narratives*. From case studies from these categories, we distilled some guidelines for the design of audio for engaging location-based experiences. These guidelines have yet to be tested fully but they are offered here as a starting point for future work and for discussion by the mobile learning community.

We have also presented *A Chaotic Encounter*, an example of an adaptive narrative, that provided users with differing narratives depending on their movements (described here as the amount of user 'chaos' that the system reacts to). Preliminary user trials, although not extensive, have indicated a mixed reaction by users. However it has highlighted an important aspect of the work, namely the immersive experience of the story based upon the location of the user. Despite the limitations of using GPS technology to track movement patterns, users of *A Chaotic Encounter* reported that it was a mostly entertaining experience. All users found the concept of movement-based narratives novel and enjoyable, and agreed that a branching narrative structure was exciting and inspired curiosity. This demonstrates that it is possible to introduce interactivity to a narrative without rendering it incoherent, that such interactivity is seen as highly valuable when it provides subtle information on user behaviours, and that audio is a very good medium through which to deliver such narratives as it requires minimum interruption.

Future work will explore how audio guides can be used to augment a sense of place through a combination of guidance and narrative storytelling and also building on previous work carried out by Walker into cinematic narratives (Walker, 2004). Further research is needed into the cognitive and social aspects of audio guiding, including how words and phrases are interpreted in relation to location, how people gain a 'sense of place' from spoken commentary, and ways to engage groups of visitors in a shared narrative. By drawing on literary-linguistic theories, we aim to investigate how the story content of an audio narrative can be structured and composed in order to achieve its desired effect – be this entertainment or education.

ACKNOWLEDGMENT

Robert Jones' studentship is supported by the Horizon Doctoral Training Centre at the University of Nottingham (RCUK Grant No. EP/G037574/1). This work was part funded by the RCUK's Horizon Digital Economy Research Hub grant, EP/G065802/1.

REFERENCES

Aoki, P. M., Grinter, R. E., Hurst, A., Szymanski, M. H., Thornton, J. D., & Woodruff, A. (2002). Sotto voce: Exploring the interplay of conversation and mobile audio spaces. In *Proceedings of the SIGCHI Conference on Human Factors in Computing Systems*, Minneapolis, MN.

Ausubel, D. P. (2000). *The acquisition and retention of knowledge: A cognitive view*. New York, NY: Springer.

Ballagas, R., & Walz, S. (2007). REXplorer: Using player-centered iterative design techniques for pervasive game development. In Magerkurth, C., & Röcker, C. (Eds.), *Pervasive gaming applications - A reader for pervasive gaming research*. Aachen, Germany: Shaker Verlag.

Bederson, B. B. (1995). Audio augmented reality: A prototype automated tour guide. In *Proceedings of the Conference on Human Factors in Computing Systems*, Denver, CO (pp. 210-211).

Benford, S., Anastasi, R., Flintham, M., Drozd, A., Crabtree, A., & Greenhalgh, C. (2003). Coping with uncertainty in a location-based game. *IEEE Pervasive Computing / IEEE Computer Society [and] IEEE Communications Society, 2*(3), 34–41. doi:10.1109/MPRV.2003.1228525

Bhaskar, N., & Govindarajulu, P. (2010). Advanced and effective learning in context aware and adaptive mobile learning scenarios. *International Journal of Interactive Mobile Technologies, 4*(1), 9–13.

Bristow, H. W., Baber, C., Cross, J., & Woolley, S. (2002). Evaluating contextual information for wearable computing. In *Proceedings of the 6th IEEE international Symposium on Wearable Computers*, Seattle, WA (pp. 179-185).

Bull, S., & McEvoy, A. T. (2003). An intelligent learning environment with an open learner model for the Desktop PC and Pocket PC. In Hoppe, U., Verdejo, F., & Kay, J. (Eds.), *Artificial intelligence in education* (pp. 389–391). Amsterdam, The Netherlands: IOS Press.

Davis, S. B., Moar, M., Jacobs, R., Watkins, M., Riddoch, C., & Cooke, K. (2006). Ere Be Dragons: Heartfelt gaming. *Digital Creativity, 17*(3), 157–162. doi:10.1080/14626260600882430

Drewes, T. M., Mynatt, E. D., & Gandy, M. (2000). Sleuth: An audio experience. In *Proceedings of the International Conference on Auditory Display*, Atlanta, GA (pp. 1-6).

Durbridge, N. (1984). Media in course design, No. 9, audio cassettes. In Bates, A. W. (Ed.), *The role of technology in distance education* (pp. 99–108). Kent, UK: Croom Helm.

Epstein, M., & Vergani, S. (2006). *History unwired: Mobile narrative in historic cities.* Paper presented at the Working Conference on Advanced Visual Interfaces, Venezia, Italy.

Freytag, G. (1895). *Technique of the drama: An exposition of dramatic composition and art.* Chicago, IL: S. C. Griggs & Company.

Gaver, W., Beaver, J., & Benford, S. (2003). Ambiguity as a resource for design. In *Proceedings of the SIGCHI conference on Human Factors in Computing Systems*, Ft. Lauderdale, FL (pp. 233-240).

Greenfield, A. (2006). *Everyware: The dawning age of ubiquitous computing.* Berkeley, CA: New Riders.

Gustafsson, A., Bichard, J., Brunnberg, L., Juhlin, O., & Combetto, M. (2006). Believable environments: Generating interactive storytelling in vast location-based pervasive games. In *Proceedings of the ACM SIGCHI International Conference on Advances in Computer Entertainment Technology*, Hollywood, CA.

Laurillard, D. (2002). *Rethinking university teaching: A framework for the effective use of learning technologies* (2nd ed.). London, UK: Routledge. doi:10.4324/9780203304846

Lim, M. Y., & Aylett, R. (2007). Narrative construction in a mobile tour guide. In M. Cavazza & S. Donikian (Eds.), *Proceedings of the 4th International Conference on Virtual Storytelling: Using Virtual Reality Technologies for Storytelling*, Saint-Malo, France (LNCS 4871, pp. 51-62).

Llewellyn-Jones, C. (2007). The value of location-based games for learning [Electronic Version]. In *Proceedings of the IAS Workshop Three: What do Mobile Technologies do Best?* Retrieved from http://www.bristol.ac.uk/education/research/networks/mobile/events/iaswshop3notes/games-forlearning.pdf

Lyons, K., Gandy, M., & Starner, T. (2000). Guided by voices: An audio augmented reality system. In *Proceedings of the International Conference on Auditory Display*, Atlanta, GA (pp. 57-62).

Marshall, J. (2009). I seek the nerves under your skin. In *Proceedings of the Seventh ACM Conference on Creativity and Cognition*, Berkeley, CA (pp. 477-478).

McConnell, D., & Sharples, M. (1983). Distance teaching by CYCLOPS: An educational evaluation of the Open University's telewriting system. *British Journal of Educational Technology, 14*(2), 109–126. doi:10.1111/j.1467-8535.1983.tb00454.x

McDonough, T. F. (1994). Situationist space. *October, 67*, 59-77.

Miller, C. (2008). *Digital storytelling: A creator's guide to interactive entertainment.* Berkeley, CA: New Riders.

Minocha, S., & Booth, N. M. (2008). Podcasting and learning experience: User-centred requirements gathering. In *Proceedings of the mLearn Conference on the Bridge from Text to Context*, Wolverhampton, UK.

Naismith, L., Sharples, M., & Ting, J. (2005). Evaluation of CAERUS: A context aware mobile guide. In *Proceedings of the 4th World Conference on mLearning*, Cape Town, South Africa.

O'Hara, K., Kindberg, T., Glancy, M., Baptista, L., Sukumaran, B., Kahana, G., & Rowbotham, J. (2007). Collecting and sharing location-based content on mobile phones in a zoo visitor experience. *Computer Supported Cooperative Work, 16*, 11–44. doi:10.1007/s10606-007-9039-2

Paay, J., Kjeldskov, J., Christensen, A., Ibsen, A., Jensen, D., Nielsen, G., & Vutborg, R. (2008). Location-based storytelling in the urban environment. In *Proceedings of the 20th Australasian Conference on Computer-Human Interaction on Designing for Habitus and Habitat*, Cairns, Australia (pp. 122-129).

Paterson, N., Naliuka, K., Jensen, S. K., Carrigy, T., Haahr, M., & Conway, F. (2010). Design, implementation and evaluation of audio for a location aware augmented reality game. In *Proceedings of the 3rd International Conference on Fun and Games*, Leuven, Belgium (pp. 149-156).

Phelps, K. (1998). *Story shapes for digital media.* Retrieved from http://www.glasswings.com.au/modern/shapes

Priestnall, G., Brown, E., Sharples, M., & Polmear, G. (2009). A student-led comparison of techniques for augmenting the field experience. In *Proceedings of the mLearn Conference*, Orlando, FL (pp. 195-198).

Reid, J., Hull, R., Cater, K., & Clayton, B. (2005). Riot! 1831: The design of a location based audio drama. In *Proceedings of the 3rd UK-UbiNet Workshop*, Bath, UK.

Roden, T. E., Parberry, I., & Ducrest, D. (2007). Toward mobile entertainment: A paradigm for narrative-based audio only games. *Science of Computer Programming, 67*(1), 76–90. doi:10.1016/j.scico.2006.07.004

Rogers, Y., Price, S., Fitzpatrick, G., Fleck, R., Harris, E., Smith, H., et al. (2004). Ambient wood: Designing new forms of digital augmentation for learning outdoors. In *Proceedings of the Conference on Interaction Design and Children: Building a Community*, Baltimore, MD (pp. 3-10).

Rowland, D., Flintham, M., Oppermann, L., Marshall, J., Chamberlain, A., Koleva, B., et al. (2009). Ubikequitous computing: Designing interactive experiences for cyclists. In *Proceedings of the 11th International Conference on Human-Computer Interaction with Mobile Devices and Services*, Bonn, Germany (p. 21).

Rozier, J., Karahalios, K., & Donath, J. (2000). Hear & there: An augmented reality system of linked audio. In *Proceedings of the International Conference on Auditory Display*, Atlanta, GA (pp. 63-67).

Rudman, P. D., Sharples, M., Vavoula, G. N., Lonsdale, P., & Meek, J. (2008). Cross-context learning. In Tallon, L., & Walker, K. (Eds.), *Digital technologies and the museum experience: Handheld guides and other media* (pp. 147–166). Lanham, MD: Alta Mira Press.

Ryan, M.-L. (2001). *Narrative as virtual reality: Immersion and interactivity in literature and electronic media.* Baltimore, MD: Johns Hopkins University Press.

Schell, J. (2008). *The art of game design.* San Francisco, CA: Morgan Kaufmann.

Schnädelbach, H., Egglestone, S. R., Reeves, S., Benford, S., Walker, B., & Wright, M. (2008). Performing thrill: Designing telemetry systems and spectator interfaces for amusement rides. In *Proceedings of the Twenty-Sixth Annual SIGCHI Conference on Human Factors in Computing Systems*, Florence, Italy (pp. 1167-1176).

Schwabe, G., & Goth, C. (2005). Mobile learning with a mobile game: Design and motivational effects. *Journal of Computer Assisted Learning, 21*(3), 204–216. doi:10.1111/j.1365-2729.2005.00128.x

Sims, K. (2003). *Paul Ricoeur.* London, UK: Routledge.

Slyper, R., & Hodgins, J. (2008). Action capture with accelerometers. In *Proceedings of the ACM SIGGRAPH/Eurographics Symposium on Computer Animation*, Dublin, Ireland (pp. 193-199).

Sprake, J. (2006). Accidental tours and illegal tour guides: Taking the textbook out of the tour. In Naripea, E., Sarapik, V., & Tomberg, J. (Eds.), *Place and location: Studies in environmental aesthetics and semiotics* (pp. 195–214). Tallinn, Estonia: Estonian Academy of Arts.

Stenton, S. P., Hull, R., Goddi, P. M., Reid, J. E., Clayton, B. J., Melamed, T. J., & Wee, S. (2007). Mediascapes: Context-aware multimedia experiences. *IEEE MultiMedia, 14*, 98–105. doi:10.1109/MMUL.2007.52

Tozzi, V. (2000). Past reality and multiple interpretations in historical investigation. *Studies of Social Political Thought, 2*, 41–57.

Vavoula, G., Sharples, M., Rudman, P., Meek, J., & Lonsdale, P. (2009). Myartspace: Design and evaluation of support for learning with multimedia phones between classrooms and museums. *Computers & Education, 53*(2), 286–299. doi:10.1016/j.compedu.2009.02.007

Walker, K. (2004). Learning on location with cinematic narratives. In *Proceedings of the 1st ACM Workshop on Story Representation, Mechanism and Context*, New York, NY (pp. 55-58).

Wiesner, K., Foth, M., & Bilandzic, M. (2009). Unleashing creative writers: Situated engagement with mobile narratives. In *Proceedings of the 21st Annual Conference of the Australian Computer-Human Interaction Special Interest Group: Design: Open 24/7*, Melbourne, Australia (pp. 373-376).

Yiannoutsou, N., & Avouris, N. (2010). Reflections on use of location-based playful narratives for learning. In *Proceedings of the IADIS International Conference on Mobile Learning*, Porto, Portugal (pp. 149-156).

This work was previously published in the International Journal of Mobile and Blended Learning, Volume 3, Issue 4, edited by David Parsons, pp 1-18, copyright 2011 by IGI Publishing (an imprint of IGI Global).

Chapter 8
Audio Active:
Discovering Mobile Learner-Gatherers from Across the Formal-Informal Continuum

Andrew Middleton
Sheffield Hallam University, UK

ABSTRACT

This paper challenges the dominant perception evident in the literature that mobile podcasting is primarily a medium for knowledge transmission. It describes why and how mobile audio learning can be facilitative, active and integrated, and how it can involve diverse voices, including those of students, in ways that usefully disrupt didactic pedagogy. Audio is described as an active learning environment, capable of supporting connection to the real world around education in which students are able to act as autonomous learner-gatherers. The paper responds to concerns raised by Ciussi, Rosner, and Augier (2009) that some students are disinterested in podcasting and uses a scenario-based design methodology (Carroll, 2000) to describe and evaluate six innovative applications. It concludes that mobile audio can be understood as an active medium capable of richly and meaningfully engaging learners.

INTRODUCTION

Ciussi, Rosner, and Augier (2009) in their study of students' interest in using podcasting on their mobile devices identify two myths in the literature: firstly, those students who have grown up with the Internet are uncomfortable with, or unaware of, podcasting; secondly, that the much vaunted idea of "'learning anytime anywhere' is...something of a myth" (Ciussi, Rosner, & Augier, 2009, p. 95). Importantly, they question whether these findings would be true in situations where podcasts are integrated into an active, learner-centred pedagogy. Building upon this, this paper presents a view of

DOI: 10.4018/978-1-4666-2139-8.ch008

mobile educational audio that is designed to be learner-centred, active and integrated, and challenges approaches to educational podcasting that see it as a technical extension to existing learning environments, suited to information transmission.

This paper describes the use of educational audio in terms of its capacity to change modes of engagement across the formal-informal learning continuum, especially in ways that heighten activity, authenticity and learner-centredness. Ciussi et al. (2009) suggest that knowledge construction and knowledge sharing offer two contexts for effective learning with mobile audio. This suggestion is explored using a scenario-based design methodology (Carroll, 2000), a method that allows the curriculum designer to imagine, describe and evaluate pedagogy.

BACKGROUND

General academic access to digital audio production is relatively recent. Its use, therefore, should promote innovation, especially in addressing the needs and expectations of learners in the Digital Age, and society in general. Areas of audio innovation include the user-generation of content, the growing appreciation of mobile learning and exploration of less formal methods of learner engagement. These ideas are explored here to provide background to the evaluation of a set of six mobile audio scenarios.

Looking Back to the Future

Consideration of audio and podcasting by learners, teachers and their institutions is inevitably obscured by previous experiences of education. McLuhan and Fiore (1967, pp. 74-75) describe this problem with evaluating the potential of technology as looking "at the present through the rear-view mirror"; recognising that it can be difficult to think creatively beyond the paradigm that we know and expect.

'Dead-time learning' (Learn Out Loud, 2005) is a concept that seems to make sense to those interested in understanding the potential of educational audio: learning can be delivered at times that would otherwise be unproductive to the commuting or otherwise displaced student through the introduction of mobile technology. It recognises the complex student demographics of the twenty first century and the busy lives that many students lead as they work and study. However, Middleton (2009) discusses how filling these cognitive voids with knowledge delivered in the form of recorded lectures via podcast feeds is at odds with the drive for learner-centred pedagogy in the higher education sector.

There are other problems with this 'common sense' view of podcasting. Firstly, amongst the minority of students that understand the idea of podcasting subscription, most use a PC rather than a portable MP3 player to listen to media (Atkinson, Buntine, & McCrohan, 2007; Evans, 2008; Lane, 2006; Lee & Chan, 2007; Malan, 2007; Morganteen, 2006; Walls, Kucsera, Walker, Acee, & McVaugh, 2010). Furthermore, Rothwell (2008) and Sutton-Brady, Scott, Taylor, Carabetta, and Clark (2009) specifically highlight students' preference for listening in the informal setting of home. Secondly, though some commentators such as Cebeci and Tekdal (2006) have highlighted the benefits of listening and learning on the move anywhere or anytime, Salmon and Nie (2008) have noticed how students find it difficult to concentrate whilst mobile. Bell, Cockburn, Wingkvist, and Green (2007) show some frustration with the limited vision for how educational podcasting can be used and suggest several ideas of their own including audio announcements, FAQs, hands-free instruction, and feedback to students, as well as involving people from beyond the classroom to reinforce material.

Several authors, including Parsons, Reddy, Wood, and Senior (2009) and Copley (2007), have noted the limited value of recorded lectures as a teaching method. The value of the lecture itself is also regularly challenged as being anachronous in the age of technology-enhanced learning (Benvenuto, 2002; Mayes & de Frietas, 2004) and as being a factor, for example, in the depersonalisation of learning resulting from the massification of education (Bryson & Hand, 2007). Conversely, Mayes, and de Frietas (2004) caution that any use of e-learning needs to be clear about the added value of the 'e'. Similarly, therefore, it is important to understand the value of the 'm' in the case of m-learning.

A further problem with the view that gaps in the daily lives of students can be filled with supplementary listening material is that it misses the idea that audio can be integral, and not just supplementary, by making use of active voices rather than passive ears.

Kukulska-Hulme and Traxler (2005, p. 2) hint at the range of applications for audio by listing mobile learning's attributes as being "spontaneous, personal, informal, contextual, portable, ubiquitous, and pervasive." Lee and Chan (2007) add to this by pointing out, in the context of podcasting, that "it adds yet another modality of learning" (p. 216), signalling that education should seek to innovate with it pedagogically.

To summarise, there is scope to reconsider how audio is used beyond the traditional temporal and spatial situations of higher education where its use is facilitative, active and integral, and where it may involve the voices of learners as much as their capacity to listen. Mobility in this paper, therefore, describes a disrupted and active learning environment that supports connection to the real world, formally and informally.

Addressing Student Diversity Creatively

Bradwell (2009) describes how today's student profile is diverse and universities must avoid inadvertently excluding them. Instead, universities must find ways to be inclusive, accommodating the wider demands of their diverse student body. The idea of the typical student is gone and with it expectations that student engagement will be predictable and regular: These days all students are exceptional. This difference brings many challenges to teaching and learning, including a need to address student isolation, which can lead to student drop out when feelings of pressure and lack of support become overwhelming (Boulos, Maramba, & Wheeler, 2006).

Diversity can also result in pragmatic, content-centric curriculum design and an approach to delivery that is discordant with the escalation of connectedness experienced by students through social networking (Oblinger & Oblinger, 2005; SPIRE, 2007). For example, with reference to the recording and distribution of lectures, it appears that podcasting can deliver learning to everyone irrespective of their ability to be located together in time and place. Such methods, however, offer passive experiences that are especially disappointing and outmoded in the Digital Age of Web 2.0 when the 'net gen' learner is likely to be expecting more interactivity in and beyond the formal curriculum (Conole, de Laat, Dillon, & Darby, 2008).

The Digital Age of Work

A need to consider mobile technology creatively is not only driven by demographic and technical change, but by the imperative of a digitally driven society. In the UK, the *Learning Literacies in the Digital Age* report (JISC, 2009) highlights how the nature of work, learning and knowledge is changing, as is the texture of social life and literacy practices. It suggests education needs to address this change to ensure that the UK economy is not hampered by "a lack of high-level skills and a dearth of future capacity... The future demands skilled, digitally-aware learners with the capacity to participate in learning throughout their life, using technologies of their own choosing" (JISC, 2009, p. 1).

Disruptive Technology

The wise use of technology may help to ensure students have a rich experience of learning. SPIRE's review of Web 2.0 technologies (SPIRE, 2007) indicates how it can support both a personally accommodating and socially active student experience, even when it is asynchronous and remote by necessity. Conole et al. (2008) ask whether institutions are matching the array of technologies that students are using every day and, importantly, whether they are observing, and consequently designing around, how those technologies inform the daily lives of students. They argue that student use of technology is now pervasive, personalised, niche adaptive, organised, transferable, redefined in terms of time and space boundaries, characterised by changed working patterns, and integrated.

This offers a useful context for educational audio designers and suggests more attention is paid to what students do in order to understand how audio can bring benefits that match student's life-wide behaviour.

Education should manage its disruption through innovative development. Digital technologies have proven to be disruptive in many sectors including the newspaper, publishing and music industries. According to Anderson and Elloumi (2004) they also need to be understood as disruptive to education. Disruption is often reported as being problematic, yet disruptiveness has two sides to it: one that undermines the status quo and one that drives innovation through disequilibrium. Being open and creative, therefore, is critical; something that practically and culturally is not easy for large organisations like universities (Tosey, 2006). Education needs to find simple and effective ways of innovating pedagogically, with benefits that are transparent to all involved.

The Producers

The literature on podcasting, discussed in Middleton (2009), is split between the idea of educational podcasting as a teaching space and as a learning space. Learner-production is just one way in which podcasting can be used in a learner-centred curriculum. Cobcroft, Towers, Smith, and Bruns (2006, p. 5) discuss how learners can be "empowered to undertake user-led education" by using audio to involve their "peers and communities within and beyond the classroom."

Pervasive Voices: Recognising Formal, Semi-Formal and Informal Spaces and Experience

Picking up on Conole et al.'s (2008) keywords, voices are pervasive, personal, niche adaptive, organised, transferable, active in different ways according to time and space, adaptable to changing working patterns and, potentially, easy to integrate. As learners, teachers, experts and publics, our voices and behaviours innately adapt to context. When students in an Audio Notes project were given MP3 recorders and asked to use them in any way that they would find useful to aid their learning, it emerged that they discovered and captured useful learning voices in many varied situations (Nortcliffe & Middleton, 2009a). Most of these situations did not directly connect with a formal view of university education, being categorised as,

- **Formal:** notes from the planned curriculum;
- **Semi-formal:** unplanned notes from the formal curriculum; and,
- **Informal:** notes from beyond the formal curriculum. (*ibid*)

These student initiated applications ranged from the recording of formal events such as lectures and feedback tutorials at one extreme, through semi-formal incidents such as corridor conversations with tutors and peers to clarify understanding, to informal self-initiated recordings such as "idea catching" and impromptu, opportunistic discussions with people not directly involved with their course.

Chan, Lee, and McLoughlin (2006, p. 112) invert the mobile podcasting opportunity from one that provides another channel for pushing content to the learner to one that can liberate "learners from the tyranny of the screen... so learning can coincide with other activities, rather than replacing them." Rather than supplementarity, this suggests coincidence, complementarity and augmentation, with benefits to be found in authentic situations and contrasting with the idea of deadtime learning through the transmission of knowledge. Supplementarity appears frequently in the literature on podcasting (Bell et al., 2007), whereas complementarity and augmentation would suggest more integration. This holistic, experiential view of university learning resonates with Jackson's concept of *the life-wide curriculum* and his notion of *complete education*, which seeks to embrace personal development, accredited and non-accredited academic learning, real-world application and diverse influences in a student's life, on and off campus (Jackson, 2008). However, he describes the difficulty in extrapolating the learning from complex and immersive learner experiences. Audio, and other recording media, may have a role to play in this extrapolation and delayed replay of intensive and immersive experience, wherever it happens.

Audio Visions

In 2005 Gardner Campbell created a rich and colourful vision for podcasting (Campbell, 2005) which explained how audio was pervasive, accessible and timely. Bull (2005, p. 343) similarly described a world where "the new technology of MP3 players gives users unprecedented power of control over their experience of time and space." But both authors describe a control that is primarily concerned with what will be listened to: what knowledge or entertainment is *received*. Five years later, Campbell's vision of a ubiquitous audio-enhanced curriculum is still a long way off for most; students are not listening to podcast lectures *en masse*, even if the advent of Apple's iTunes U (McKinney, Dyck, & Luber, 2009) implies that they should be.

As the Audio Notes project introduced above demonstrated, digital audio is a flexible, personal and socially unifying medium. It is a connective medium that recognises learning as a dynamic, continuously affected process and which is able to capture and asynchronously convey the knowledgeable and enquiring voices that are the essence of learning, irrespective of location or device. In some cases this can be facilitative and provocative: if the opportunity to record had not existed would the conversation ever have happened? De Jong, Specht, and Koper (2008) also recognise the provocative value of mobile technologies and Sharples (2002, p. 509) describes mobile technology as an "environment in which conversational learning takes place," an idea that is developed in 2005 when Sharples asks, how can education itself be transformed by mobile technologies? In terms of MP3 recorders and players, this notion of conversational mediation is particularly useful.

Audio can now be understood as interventionary from a pedagogic design perspective; as a medium that enables connectivity, orientation, motivation, personal and social challenge, and learner reflection. It fits well, therefore, with the needs of the Digital Age learner, but what does audio enhanced learning look like in a mobile context?

SCENARIO-BASED DESIGN: THE GENERATION, SHARING AND EVALUATION OF IDEAS

Wali, Winters, and Oliver (2008, p. 56) propose that,

future studies look at mobile learning in terms of learning activities taking place across contexts (both physical and social), placing more emphasis on the relationship between learning activities and social context, which has been shown to affect and be affected by learning practices.

This view informs this paper which presents and discusses a set of scenarios for the mobile use of educational digital audio.

Scenario-Based Design

Ciussi et al. (2009) describe a familiar dilemma in evaluating new and emerging technologies for learning: that they can't be understood until they have been used, yet they can't be used until they have been understood. They found that many students did not understand podcasting and it must be assumed that for early academic adopters there is a similar level of unfamiliarity. This is compounded by Rogers' *Diffusion of Innovation* theory (Rogers, 1962) which highlights why even good ideas find resistance. Not only are some individuals more reticent than others by nature, but adoption will be governed by different states of readiness. Those categorised as Innovators and Early Adopters may be prepared to take more risk to find benefits, while the Late Adopters and Laggards will wait for sound evidence. Even then they may continue to resist change. Those using the technology will attempt to mitigate the risk, and this in turn may affect the success of the innovation. It is difficult, therefore, to evidence value in anything that is different and new.

Potential therefore needs to be communicated through what Conole et al. (2008) call 'mediating artefacts'. Case studies, for example, are widely used in education to provide accounts of practice. However, as Cohen, Manion, and Morrison (2001) point out, case study methodology is typically of limited use: case studies report on particular, unique instances of action, and generalising from these is difficult. Bassey (1999), however, describes how case study storytelling techniques can be used to elicit understanding. This idea connects to practice in the discipline of Human Computer Interface design where scenario-based design is used by Computer Scientists to evaluate interface usability before systems are built (Carroll, 2000). He explains that scenarios provide a useful mechanism to evoke and co-ordinate collaborative reflection on designs because "scenarios are at once concrete and flexible" (Carroll, 2000, p. 43). Scenarios also provide mechanisms for looking at imagined interactivity in detail, even whilst ideas and understanding are still emerging. Carroll (2000) explains that scenarios aid communication amongst stakeholders, thereby making design activities more accessible. To be effective, scenarios should have the following characteristics: setting, actors, goals or objectives and actions and events (Potts, 1995).

Mwanza and Engeström (2003) have applied this method to evaluate technology-enhanced pedagogy using story-like descriptions to envision current and future relationships between subjects involved in teaching and learning activities. Milrad (2006) used scenario-based design with groups of workshop participants to evaluate ideas for mobile learning. Scenario-based design and the resultant scenarios, therefore, provide a way to quickly and safely investigate and mitigate the risks of using emerging technologies and to evaluate their pedagogic potential, countering the difficulties facing academic innovation outlined earlier.

Scenarios, therefore, are a useful tool for imagining, demonstrating and evaluating diverse possible digital audio applications.

SIX MOBILE AUDIO LEARNING SCENARIOS

The scenarios discussed here were selected to represent a variety of ideas and starting points relevant to the theme of mobile audio-enhanced learning and have been reviewed against some of the main tenets arising from the literature already discussed. The six ideas originated in a creativity workshop run by the author involving 70 participants at a meeting of the Podcasting for Pedagogic Purposes Special Interest Group. 176 scenarios for educational podcasting were generated through a facilitated creative process involving academics, learning technologists and educational developers.

The aim of the workshop was to reveal new ways of using audio to enhance learning. Working collaboratively, participants were asked to respond imaginatively to an array of words that had been extracted from the literature on educational podcasting, e-learning and learning technology. Working in pairs, they were randomly assigned three words as the basis for a 'wacky' title. Using the title as a creative trigger, and using word association techniques, each pair were asked to write a description that explained the title and educational value of the approach. Useful scenarios therefore emerged by justifying the title. Later, the titles were used as the basis for other creative conversations that resulted in further ideas. The method took people from positions of comfort and preconception in a safe, collaborative activity to new, less constrained positions. Subsequently the scenarios were typed up, put online for review and then developed into succinct descriptions which have been reviewed at other SIG events and used to seed further idea generation activities.

The six ideas that are discussed here are a subset of the various activities and are indicative of the many ways that students and academics have identified for using audio in a mobile learning context. All of the scenarios selected for discussion here have subsequently been tested and in some cases have been implemented at scale.

Scenarios

1. **a-PDP (audio Personal Development Planning):** The purpose of this method is to create a rich audio diary to support learner reflection and action planning. Each day, on the way home, a student uses an MP3 recorder or mobile phone memo tool to answer three questions: 1. What have I done today? 2. What have I learnt today? 3. What am I going to do about it? Having made the recording on leaving campus, the student begins the next day by playing back the previous recording. Periodically the student reviews and reflects upon their brief a-PDP entries, producing considered written summary statements.

2. **Audio notes:** There are many ways that students can use audio to make notes. One technique is to use a personal MP3 recorder or phone memo tool to summarise a seminar or lecture. This can be particularly useful when this is done co-operatively with other students. Other methods include recording personal ideas, decisions from group work meetings, dissertation supervision, lab notes, etc. Students can also use recording devices to gather feedback from tutors and peers.

3. **Previsit:** Students' engagement in their field trip or museum visit begins as they listen to briefing podcasts on the journey to their visit using materials produced by the tutor, the museum, or students who have been on visits previously.

4. **Field trip commentary:** Student groups on field trips are assigned the task of creating an audio report, perhaps on different themes, so that when they return to college they have a rich collection of material. The recordings can involve interviews with people they meet, observations about places and processes, the ambient sound of the location, discussions with experts and peers, and other information that would not otherwise be available to them. The gathering of data and

the making of the commentary provides a framework for enquiry during the trip whilst the expectation of its use motivates them.

5. **User voices:** Medical patient voices (or stories) are collected by academic staff, developers or students. They are used by Health students as a way to encounter patient stories vicariously through digital media. These stories inform various follow-on activities. A Client Voices podcast could use a similar approach in Business modules.

6. **Pocketables:** A 'pocketable' is an audio or video podcast that demonstrates a technique or process. Its purpose is to reduce anxiety prior to the initial performance of that process by the student. Audio, video, screencasts or machinima (films made in 3D Virtual Worlds and games) can all be used to produce such information. In situations where students have been involved in a simulated activity, recordings of their own commentary on their earlier performance can be used to make a direct connection to their learning, thus instilling confidence.

SIX MOBILE AUDIO SCENARIOS DISCUSSED

This selection of mobile audio learning scenarios confirm Ciussi et al.'s (2009) suggestion that the medium is capable of supporting both knowledge construction and knowledge sharing, but the scenarios also demonstrate how mobile audio can be used to mediate authentic and active learner engagement in and beyond formal learning spaces. The use of scenarios permits a review of the audio applications in terms of their capacity to: mediate learner engagement; promote learner activity; be integral to the student's learning experience; provide a platform for learner voices; support learner connection to the world beyond university; and situate the learner across the formal-informal learning continuum.

Mediating Learner Engagement

The Previsit technique, as with other types of preview techniques (Sutton-Brady et al., 2009), is an example of how audio can be used to orientate the learner. The documentary method in the Field Trip Commentary creates a recognisable documentary-like framework that mediates the collective student enquiry and provides a presentation environment. a-PDP is a simple tool that facilitates the capture and transference of learning across media and over time. The User Voices model shifts the focus from both the teacher and the learner to external voices whose presence mediates knowledge construction, whilst the Pocketables method reduces anxiety and instills learner confidence.

Promoting Learner Activity

All of the scenarios presented here put the learner as the central actor with the expectation that they will either act as gatherers of rich data or act in response to authentic situations. In the Field Trip Commentary scenario, for example, the students gather evidence in many forms because they are expected to create and share a documentary record of their investigations. The a-PDP method uses audio as a support for action planning, whilst the Pocketables methods reminds the learner of the techniques they must use.

Integration

Similarly, all of the scenarios present audio as being integral to learning and not as an end in itself. In the a-PDP method the student refers back to what has happened, reflects on what this means, and decides what they should do next because of this. The audio creates a bridge that takes the learner from one day to the next, and later supports a periodic review of their learning. The Audio Notes scenario describes various techniques including the production of audio summaries. Such summaries can, for example, be shared with peers, affecting the social nature of study. In the Previsit model the learner is engaged prior to arrival, thereby affecting the quality of their subsequent experience. In the Field Trip Commentary the richness of sound and voices aids ongoing connection with the initial experience; in the User Voices scenario the listener becomes personally engaged with the experience of the patients or clients and this is used to inform further practical or theoretic engagement. In the Pocketables scenario the learner is reminded of what they have done before, affecting what they do next. In all cases, the audio provides a particular richness and a different view of the subject.

A Platform for Learner Voices

Three of the scenarios are based around the use of student voices. A fourth, Pocketables, can be enhanced by using the learner's own voice. In the Previsit technique an adaptation of the idea would see students producing Previsit materials for next year's cohort. Similarly, the User Voices scenario could position the learners as digital story gatherers. This audio form offers a natural platform for learner presentation; it offers a clear framework for enquiry and reporting and almost demands performance. Performance, in the form of audio presentation, requires a degree of fluency and confidence on the part of the student and this heightens its learning value.

Real World Connection

All of the scenarios describe situations beyond the traditional classroom, with several connecting the learner to real world situations. The Pocketables scenario, for example, supports the learner as they prepare to act in an authentic situation. Empathy with patients and clients and exposure to real world situations can be enhanced by digital audio, as in the case of User Voices. Real world voices are evident in the User Voices and Previsit scenarios too.

Formal, Semi-Formal, and Informal Learning

The a-PDP idea and many of the applications for Audio Notes are simple devices for mediating learner reflection and follow-on activity at the learner's discretion. Ephemeral and incidental conversations that previously happened amongst friends over a cup of coffee can now be collected and reviewed as rich opportunities. Both a-PDP and Audio Notes mediate personal reflection, sometimes in a social context. The situation may not be new, but the use of the recorder allows the ephemeral to be captured. This can turn what was once informal and inconsequential into something that is highly valued. Audio's pervasive capacity can bring value to situations in which learning is immediate or still forming.

CONCLUSION

The use of scenarios enabled creative thinking in the generation and evaluation of ideas for how digital audio as a form of mobile learning can change modes of engagement in formal, semi-formal and informal learning situations. Scenarios are useful in communicating how innovation can happen, even when stakeholders are not in a position to fully understand the associated benefits and dangers of something because they have not been able to try it in reality; this helps to reduce the associated risk and raise stakeholder confidence. If the literature on educational podcasting has been preoccupied with lecturecasting and other transmissive methods, it may be indicative of how institutional investment in technical systems can deter technology-enhanced learning by sustaining a culture of technology-led thinking. The scenario-based design approach used in the workshops addressed this by facilitating collaborative idea generating conversations involving diverse technical and pedagogical areas of expertise.

The scenarios described here have demonstrated how mobile audio-enhanced learning can be spontaneous, personal, contextual, portable, ubiquitous and pervasive, and how it can help educators to rethink active and integrated modes of learner engagement, especially in terms of time and space boundaries. Such methods may be disruptive, and therefore challenging; nevertheless, media used simply, in ways similar to those described here, can help academics to make more use of diverse and rich situations. The ready access of the audio medium can be seen as facilitative and involving, rather than as something that dominates the learner's experience. Similarly, mobile audio can be understood as a communicative medium that enables greater connectivity with the world around education, thereby leading to more authentic engagement.

The recording of lectures for use in the learner's 'dead time' is a relatively weak approach to using digital audio in a mobile learning context. Instead it has been shown how audio can address the needs of today's students and their desire for a social, autonomous, active and interactive experience of learning. Many useful voices exist within the formal, semi-formal and informal environments, yet they remain largely untapped. This is likely to change as education recognises audio's potential as a dynamic medium capable of supporting enquiry and reflection amongst its diverse student body.

If Ciussi et al. (2009) have found that some students are unaware of, or uncomfortable with, podcasting it is, as they suggest, likely to have been hampered by the lack of meaningful integration of the media, and this is likely to be a result of the difficulty academia has had in imagining innovative pedagogy. The idea of learning 'anytime anywhere' by listening needs to be reassessed: it is not helpful to think of podcasting as a mobile relay platform for existing pedagogy; instead, audio-enhanced learning should be understood as a new opportunity that affords different ways of engaging the learner. Rather than seeing mobile devices as mechanisms for transmitting and amplifying the teacher's voice, scenario-based design has allowed us to imagine and concretise views of mobile audio as an active, authentic, social and learner-centred medium.

REFERENCES

Anderson, T., & Elloumi, F. (2004). Introduction. In Anderson, T., & Elloumi, F. (Eds.), *Theory and practice of online learning* (pp. 1–11). Athabasca, AB, Canada: Athabasca University Press.

Atkinson, L., Buntine, A., & McCrohan, R. (2007, September 4-6). Podcasting at RMIT University: Evaluating a faculty-based trial. In *Proceedings of the ALT 14th International Conference*, Nottingham, UK.

Bassey, M. (1999). *Case study research in educational settings: Doing qualitative research in educational settings*. Buckingham, UK: Open University Press.

Bell, T., Cockburn, A., Wingkvist, A., & Green, R. (2007). Podcasts as a supplement in tertiary education: An experiment with two computer science courses. In Parsons, D., & Ryu, H. (Eds.), *Proceedings of Mobile Learning Technologies and Applications* (pp. 70–77).

Benvenuto, M. (2002). Educational reform: Why the academy doesn't change. *Thought & Action*, *18*, 63–74.

Boulos, M., Maramba, I., & Wheeler, S. (2006). Wikis, blogs and podcasts: A new generation of web-based tools for virtual collaborative clinical practice and education. *BMC Medical Education*, *6*(41), 1–8.

Bradwell, P. (2009). *The edgeless university: Why higher education must embrace technology*. Retrieved from http://www.demos.co.uk/publications/the-edgeless-university

Bryson, C., & Hand, L. (2007). The role of engagement in inspiring teaching and learning. *Innovations in Education and Teaching International, 44*(4), 349–362. doi:10.1080/14703290701602748

Bull, M. (2005). No dead air! The iPod and the culture of mobile learning. *Leisure Studies, 24*(4), 343–355. doi:10.1080/0261436052000330447

Campbell, G. (2005). There's something in the air: Podcasting in education. *EDUCAUSE Review, 40*(6), 32–47.

Carroll, J. M. (2000). Five reasons for scenario-based design. *Interacting with Computers, 13*(1), 43–60. doi:10.1016/S0953-5438(00)00023-0

Cebeci, Z., & Tekdal, M. (2006). Using podcasts as audio learning objects. *Interdisciplinary Journal of Knowledge and Learning Objects, 2*, 47–57.

Chan, A., Lee, M. J., & McLoughlin, C. (2006). *Everyone's learning with podcasting: A Charles Sturt University experience.* Paper presented at the ASCILITE Conference of Who's learning? Whose technology? Sydney, Australia.

Ciussi, M., Rosner, G., & Augier, M. (2009). Engaging students with mobile technologies to support their formal and informal learning. *International Journal of Mobile and Blended Learning, 1*(4), 84–98. doi:10.4018/jmbl.2009090805

Cobcroft, R., Towers, S., Smith, J., & Bruns, A. (2006, September 26). *Mobile learning in review: Opportunities and challenges for learners, teachers, and institutions.* Paper presented at the Online Learning & Teaching Conference.

Cohen, L., Manion, L., & Morrison, K. (2001). *Research methods in education* (5th ed.). London, UK: Routledge.

Conole, G., de Laat, M., Dillon, T., & Darby, J. (2008). Disruptive technologies, pedagogical innovation: What's new? Findings from an in-depth study of students' use and perception of technology. *Computers & Education, 50*(2), 511–524. doi:10.1016/j.compedu.2007.09.009

Copley, J. (2007). Audio and video podcasts of lectures for campus-based students: Production and evaluation of student use. *Innovations in Education and Teaching International, 44*(4), 387–399. doi:10.1080/14703290701602805

De Jong, T., Specht, M., & Koper, R. (2008). Contextualized media for learning. *Journal of Educational Technology & Society, 11*(2), 41–53.

Evans, C. (2008). The effectiveness of m-learning in the form of podcast revision lectures in higher education. *Computers & Education, 50*(2), 491–498. doi:10.1016/j.compedu.2007.09.016

Jackson, N. J. (2008). *The life-wide curriculum concept: A means of developing a more complete educational experience?* Retrieved from http://lifewidecurriculum.pbwiki.com/A-more-complete-education

JISC. (2009). *Learning literacies in a digital age.* Retrieved from http://www.jisc.ac.uk/media/documents/publications/bpllidav1.pdf

Kukulska-Hulme, A., & Traxler, J. (2005). *Mobile learning: A handbook for educators and trainers.* Boca Raton, FL: Taylor & Francis.

Lane, C. (2006). *UW podcasting: Evaluation of year one.* Seattle, WA: University of Washington. Retrieved from http://www.washington.edu/lst/research_development/papers/2006/podcasting_year1.pdf

Learn Out Loud. (2005). *Dead time learning.* Retrieved from http://www.learnoutloud.com/content/blog/archives/2005/09/dead_time_learn.html

Lee, M., & Chan, A. (2007). Pervasive, lifestyle-integrated mobile learning for distance learners: An analysis and unexpected results from a podcasting study. *Journal of Open and Distance Learning, 22*(3), 201–218.

Malan, D. J. (2007). Podcasting computer science E-1. In *Proceedings of the 38th SIGCSE Technical Symposium on Computer Science Education*, Covington, KY (pp. 389-393).

Mayes, T., & de Freitas, S. (2004). *Stage 2: Review of e-learning theories, frameworks and models.* Retrieved from http://www.jisc.ac.uk/uploaded_documents/Stage%202%20Learning%20Models%20(Version%201).pdf

McKinney, D., Dyck, J. L., & Luber, E. S. (2009). iTunes University and the classroom: Can podcasts replace professors? *Computers & Education, 52*(3), 617–623. doi:10.1016/j.compedu.2008.11.004

McLuhan, M., & Fiore, Q. (1967). *The medium is the massage.* London, UK: Penguin Books.

Middleton, A. (2009). Beyond podcasting: Creative approaches to designing educational audio. *Journal of Research in Learning Technology, 17*(2), 143–155. doi:10.1080/09687760903033082

Milrad, M. (2006). How should learning activities using mobile technologies be designed to support innovative educational practices? In Sharples, M. (Ed.), *Big issues in mobile learning.* Nottingham, UK: Kaleidoscope Network of Excellence Mobile Learning Initiative.

Morganteen, J. (2006). *Casting around.* Museums Journal.

Mwanza, D., & Engeström, Y. (2003, November 7-11). Pedagogical adeptness in the design of e-learning environments: Experiences from the Lab@Future project. In *Proceedings of the World Conference on E-Learning in Corporate, Government, Healthcare, and Higher Education,* Phoenix, AZ.

Nortcliffe, A., & Middleton, A. (2009a, September 8-10). *Audio, autonomy and authenticity: Constructive comments and conversations captured by the learner.* Paper presented at the ALT Conference of In Dreams Begins Responsibility: Choice, Evidence, and Change, Manchester, UK.

Nortcliffe, A., & Middleton, A. (2009b, December 18). iGather: Learners as responsible audio collectors of tutor, peer and self-reflection. In *Proceedings of the National Conference of A Word in Your Ear,* Sheffield, UK.

Oblinger, D. G., & Oblinger, J. L. (2005). *Educating the net generation.* Washington, DC: EDUCAUSE.

Parsons, V., Reddy, P., Wood, J., & Senior, C. (2009). Educating an iPod generation: Undergraduate attitudes, experiences and understanding of vodcast and podcast use. *Learning, Media and Technology, 34*(3), 215–228. doi:10.1080/17439880903141497

Potts, C. (1995). Using schematic scenarios to understand user needs. In *Proceedings of the ACM Symposium on Designing Interactive Systems,* Ann Arbor, MI (pp. 247-256).

Rogers, E. M. (1962). *Diffusion of innovations.* New York, NY: Free Press.

Rothwell, L. (2008). Podcasts and collaborative learning. In Salmon, G., & Edirisingha, P. (Eds.), *Podcasting for learning in universities* (pp. 121–131). Buckingham, UK: Open University Press.

Salmon, G., & Nie, M. (2008). Doubling the life of iPods. In Salmon, G., & Edirisingha, P. (Eds.), *Podcasting for learning in universities* (pp. 1–11). Buckingham, UK: Open University Press.

Sharples, M. (2002). Disruptive devices: Mobile technology for conversational learning. *International Journal of Continuing Engineering Education and Lifelong Learning*, *12*(5-6), 504–520. doi:10.1504/IJCEELL.2002.002148

Sharples, M. (2005, April 28-30). Learning as conversation: Transforming education in the mobile age. In *Proceedings of Communications in the 21st Century: The Mobile Information Society Conference*, Budapest, Hungary.

SPIRE. (2007). *Results and analysis of the Web 2.0 services survey undertaken by the SPIRE project.* Retrieved from http://www.jisc.ac.uk/media/documents/programmes/digitalrepositories/spiresurvey.pdf

Sutton-Brady, C., Scott, K. M., Taylor, L., Carabetta, G., & Clark, S. (2009). The value of using short-format podcasts to enhance learning and teaching. *Journal of Research in Learning Technology*, *17*(3), 219–232. doi:10.1080/09687760903247609

Tosey, P. (2006). Interfering with interference. In Jackson, N., Oliver, M., Shaw, M., & Wisdom, J. (Eds.), *Developing creativity in higher education: An imaginative curriculum* (pp. 29–42). London, UK: Routledge.

Wali, E., Winters, N., & Oliver, M. (2008). Maintaining, changing and crossing contexts: An activity theoretic reinterpretation of mobile learning. *Journal of Research in Learning Technology*, *16*(1), 41–57. doi:10.1080/09687760701850190

Walls, S. M., Kucsera, J. V., Walker, J. D., Acee, T. W., & McVaugh, N. K. (2010). Podcasting in education: Are students as ready and eager as we think they are? *Computers & Education*, *54*, 371–378. doi:10.1016/j.compedu.2009.08.018

This work was previously published in the International Journal of Mobile and Blended Learning, Volume 3, Issue 2, edited by David Parsons, pp 31-42, copyright 2011 by IGI Publishing (an imprint of IGI Global).

Chapter 9
Listening to an Educational Podcast while Walking or Jogging:
Can Students Really Multitask?

Joke Coens
Katholieke Universiteit Leuven Kulak, Belgium

Ellen Degryse
Katholieke Universiteit Leuven Kulak, Belgium

Marie-Paul Senecaut
Katholieke Universiteit Leuven Kulak, Belgium

Jorge Cottyn
Katholieke Hogeschool Zuid-West-Vlaanderen, Belgium

Geraldine Clarebout
Katholieke Universiteit Leuven Kulak, Belgium

ABSTRACT

The advent of podcasting offers opportunities for students to learn while performing another activity. While podcasting is advocated by many as helping to learn anywhere and anytime, research indicates that it is not so easy for people to do two things at the same time. Two experiments were set up to examine the effect of performing a secondary task while learning with an iPod. In the experimental groups, the participants had to combine a learning task (listening to an educational podcast) with a secondary task (walking or jogging). The control group only had to perform a learning task. Afterwards, all the participants had to complete a learning test. In the first study, there were no significant differences between the learning performances of students of the different conditions. In the second study, the students who were sitting down outperformed the students who were moving while studying.

DOI: 10.4018/978-1-4666-2139-8.ch009

MOBILE LEARNING AND PODCASTING

Mobile devices and technologies such as iPods/MP3 players, mobile phones and laptops are popular and have become increasingly integrated into our daily lives (cf. the familiarity with technology of the 'Homo Zappiens' generation (Veen, 2009)). For example, in 2009, 91% of the Belgian population and 92% of the Dutch population used a mobile phone (Centraal Bureau voor de Statistiek, 2009; Federale Overheidsdienst Economie, 2009). Under the denominator 'mobile learning', the use of mobile technologies also penetrates education. Mobile devices are used to deliver content and/or to interact with classmates or the teacher, both within the classroom (cf. the notion of 1:1 (one-to-one) educational computing) and outside the classroom (mobile devices are used for example to support field trips and outdoor learning; (e.g., Chen, Kao, & Sheu, 2003, 2005; Pfeiffer, Gemballa, Jorodzka, Schieter, & Gerjets, 2009; Coens, Clarebout, & Reynvoet, 2009a.)

Podcasts are used for mobile learning. The term 'podcasting' is a derivative of the word 'broadcasting' and 'iPod' (the popular MP3 player from Apple Computer) (Meng, 2005). It refers to the distribution of audio/video files in digital format. These files can be downloaded to a desktop computer from the Internet and transferred to a portable media device such as an MP3 player. In recent years, podcasting has seen a significant growth in education. McGarr (2009) identified three broad types of educational use of podcasting. At the most basic level, podcasting is used to provide recordings of past lectures to students for the purposes of review and revision (substitutional use). This is the most common use of podcasting. Copley (2007) for example produced audio and video podcasts of his lectures and made them available to his students. The second most common use is in providing additional material (e.g., study guides, summary notes) to broaden and deepen students' understanding (supplementary use). Nathan and

Chan (2007) for example created podcasts in the form of discussions between the subject matter expert and a student. The third and least common use involves the creation of student generated podcasts (creative use). In a study of Frydenberg (2006) for example, students had to create their own podcasts based on the course material. In Wilson et al.'s study (2009), students used video iPods for the creation of dance performance.

One of the key benefits of podcasting (and in general of mobile learning) described in the literature is that podcasting has the ability to enhance flexibility and accessibility in learning (McGarr, 2009). Podcasting offers opportunities for education because it has the advantage of allowing learners to choose when and where they study (Evans, 2008). Learning materials can be accessed by the students in their own time and place; they are no longer bound to one place of study. They can learn anytime, anywhere and when it is convenient for them (Maag, 2006).

The increased flexibility relates to a specific feature of mobile learning in general, and podcasting in particular: students can learn while performing another activity (e.g., listening to an educational podcast while waiting for the bus, while driving a car or while doing the dishes; studying while being on the move). Students can become educational 'multitaskers'.

Can Students Really Multitask?

Multitasking

In daily life, people often (try to) do two things at once. They do their dishes while watching their children play, they drive a car while talking to the passenger (Hunton & Rose, 2005; Strayer & Johnston, 2001), and young people want to do homework while watching television (Pool, van der Voort, Beentjes, & Koolstra, 1999). Multitasking is a ubiquitous phenomenon. Studies have shown that up to 95% of the population reports multitasking each day and that large amounts of multitasking are occurring across all generations (Carrier, Cheever, Rosen, Benitez, & Chang, 2009; Kenyon, 2008; Salvucci & Taatgen, 2008). Students in particular are multitasking frequently (Foehr, 2006; Jeong & Fishbein, 2007).

Veen (2009) describes a view on the actual generation of children and youth, the 'Homo Zappiens' generation. Characteristic to this view is the assumption that teens possess multitasking skills. It is assumed that youngsters and children of this generation are frequent multitaskers. For example, youngsters do their homework while listening to their iPod and chatting on the internet.

Educational Multitasking

Research reveals that students value the flexibility offered by mobile learning. Evans (2008) found that 79% of the participants in his study agreed or strongly agreed with the statement "I think it is important to be able to listen to podcasts where and when I want". Research also reveals that students do undertake other activities while learning with a mobile device; students are educational multitaskers. Copley (2007) produced audio and video podcasts and made them available to his students. At the end of the semester, the students completed an online survey. The results of the survey suggested that 13% of the students listened to the audio podcasts while doing other things (e.g., 'on a bus', 'packing before Christmas holidays', 'while on the Internet' (Copley, 2007, p. 391)). Higginbotham (2006) reports on a similar survey study whereby podcasting was used to deliver course lecture materials to students. Thirty-four percent of the participants indicated that they accessed instructional materials using their portable media player while involved in other activities. Additionally, 67% of the students said that they would do that in the future. Finally, Evans (2008) found that 25% of the participants in his study indicated that they listened to an educational podcast while traveling.

Can Students Really Multitask?

Although people often believe that they can successfully combine two tasks, studies have found otherwise. Research reveals that it is not so evident for people to do two things at the same time and to divide their attention between multiple tasks ('divided attention'). For example, when people drive a car while using a cell-phone, they respond significantly slower to traffic signals (Strayer & Johnston, 2001).

Kirschner and Karpinski (2010) are critical of the concept of the 'Homo Zappiens' generation (Veen, 2009) and the assumption that children and teens of this generation have acquired specific multitasking skills. Are these children and teens really able to multitask effectively, efficiently and without loss to the main task?

In psychology, dual tasking and multitasking are examined. Dual-task interference has been found with a wide range of tasks, including very easy ones (Lien, Ruthruff, & Johnston, 2006). There are several general theories about the explanation for human performance in divided attention conditions, which are very diverse (Eysenck & Keane, 2005; Styles, 2006). A summary is given below.

In general, a distinction is made between two types of attention models: structural models and capacity models. Structural models assume that dual task performances are often limited because of structural limitations of the information processing system. The structure of the system does not allow for multiple tasks to be processed at the same time because there is only one processing channel. Capacity models assume that dual task performances are often limited because the information processing system possesses a finite amount of capacity or resources that can be used.

Structural models assume a central bottleneck (central bottleneck model (cf. Luria & Meiran, 2005; Pashler, 1984, 1998) and assume that the brain acts like a serial processor (Lien et al., 2006). The basic assumption is that certain critical mental operations are carried out only sequentially and that central mental processing takes place for only one task at a time (which causes response delays, because the secondary task central processing is delayed until the first task central processing has finished (Lien et al., 2006)). When two tasks require such a critical mental operation to be performed at the same time, a bottleneck arises and the tasks interfere. Many experiments are concerned with discovering the exact location of that bottleneck (Styles, 2006). Pashler (1994) for example assumes that there is a bottleneck in response selection.

Bottleneck models are mainly used to interpret the results of dual task studies involving pairs of simple speeded tasks, whereby participants have to execute two responses as rapidly as possible (e.g. responding to a tone by pressing a key as soon as possible) (Pashler, 1994; Wickens, 2002). The tasks involve a simple stimulus-response mapping and it usually takes less than a second to carry them out. When more continuous and complex tasks are examined, capacity theories are mostly used to interpret the results.

Limited capacity theories assume that there is some central processor in the brain which has limited capacity or resources. These resources can be used to perform activities or tasks. A well-known capacity theory is the theory of Kahneman (1973). The basic prediction of Kahneman's model is that two tasks can be performed together without loss of efficiency when the total quantity of required resources to perform both tasks does not exceed the quantity of available resources (Vandierendonck, 2006). A tradeoff occurs when there are insufficient resources available to perform both tasks (Pew & Mavor, 1998).

Where the theory of Kahneman assumes one single quantity of resources, other models (e.g., Navon & Gopher, 1979; Wickens, 1980, 2002) assume different sets of resources for different kinds of activities. Different tasks require different resources (Pew & Mavor, 1998). The processing system consists of multiple resources and two activities interfere when they appeal to the same set of resources.

Wickens (2002) for example describes a 4-dimensional multiple resources model. The model consists of four dimensions, each having two levels. The assumption is that two tasks that both demand the same level of a given dimension will interfere more with each other than two tasks that demand separate levels on that dimension. The four dimensions of the model are processing stages (perceptual and cognitive activities versus the selection and execution of responses), perceptual modalities (auditory versus visually), visual channels (focal vision versus ambient vision) and processing codes (spatial processes versus categorical (usually linguistic or verbal) processes). The assumption is that there will be greater interference between two tasks to the extent that they share processing stages, perceptual modalities, visual channels and processing codes.

In addition, divided attention studies whereby participants have to perform two tasks simultaneously under various conditions provide evidence that several factors determine the dual task performances of people. Evidence can be found that both learner characteristics, for example age (Bherer et al., 2005; Verhaeghen, Steitz, Sliwinski, & Cerella, 2003; Voelcker-Rehage, Stronge, & Alberts, 2006), training (Hunton & Rose, 2005; Van Selst, Ruthruff, & Johnston, 1999), working memory capacity (Doolittle & Mariano, 2008), task prioritization (Schaefer, Krampe, Lindenberger, & Baltes, 2008; Verghese et al., 2007) and task characteristics, for example the kind of task (Cherng, Liang, Hwang, & Chen, 2007; Clarebout, Coens, & Elen, 2008) and difficulty of the task (Cherng et al., 2007; Pool et al., 1999; Voelcker-Rehage et al., 2006) determine the ability of people to perform two tasks at the same time.

The Case of Mobile Learning

Within the context of mobile learning research there is little attention to the multitasking issue (Coens et al., 2009a). It seems that although it is recognized that the use of mobile devices offers opportunities for students to study where and whenever they want, actually only minimal research has been done on the learning effect of learning/studying with a mobile device while performing another (some exceptions: Clarebout et al., 2008; Coens, Clarebout, & Reynvoet, 2009b; Coens, Reynvoet, & Clarebout, 2011; Doolittle & Mariano, 2008, Doolittle et al., 2009). This is a gap within the domain of mobile learning research and there is need for research on what are the consequences of this multitasking for learning. This is particularly important because it is reasonable to suspect that the currency of handheld-use in daily life may enable greater (educational) multitasking because of the possibility of spatial and temporal co-presence of two or more activities (Kenyon, 2008).

Doolittle and Mariano (2008) report on an experiment whereby participants had to study with a mobile device while performing a secondary task (walking). The goal of the experiment was to evaluate the effects of learning in a stationary versus mobile learning condition. They compared the learning performances of students in a mobile context (students watched an instructional video about historical inquiry on an iPod while walking in a hallway) and students in a stationary context (students watched an instructional video on an iPod while sitting in a chair at a desk). They found that students in the stationary condition performed significantly better on a post-test (recall test and transfer test) than students in the mobile condition. Doolittle and Mariano explain this effect in terms of divided attention: when attention is divided during the learning phase of a task (e.g., students must attend to two stimuli: to the video and to the walking path), performance declines.

The iPod studies of Clarebout et al. (2008) also reveal that it is not so easy to study with a mobile device while performing an additional task. Students who studies video material from an iPod while sitting at a desk scored significantly better on a post test than students who studied the same video material from an iPod while riding on an exercise bike.

The effect of performing a secondary task on learning is less explicit in the iPod studies of Coens et al. (2009b, 2011). Two similar studies were set up. Students of the control group had to study from an iPod while sitting at a desk. Participants of the experimental groups were asked to perform a secondary task (screwing together nuts and bolts) while studying from an iPod. Furthermore, students of the different experimental conditions received different instructions related to the importance of the learning task and the nut and bolt task ("doing both tasks as well as possible", "learning score is important" or "nut and bolt score is important"). The effect of the conditions on the learning task was rather limited. Only one significant effect was found (and only in one of the studies) and it was limited to a difference between students of the control group (who did not have to combine the learning with another task) and students who focused on the nut and bolt task while learning.

The above studies reveal that, prior to providing course material on a mobile device; the question should be raised about what mental investment students have to make to learn material from a mobile device while performing an additional task.

The main aim of the studies reported here is to address the effect of multitasking on mobile learning in general and podcasting in particular. Two experiments were set up to examine the effect of performing a secondary task (walking or jogging) while listening to an educational podcast. This paper examines what the consequences are of multitasking for learning.

Method

Participants

In study 1, the participants were 36 first year Physical Education bachelor students from a Belgian university college (academic year 2009-2010). Twenty-five male and 11 female students, on average 18.81 years old (SD = 1.09), participated voluntarily. The majority of the participants had their own MP3 player (25 students possessed an MP3 player, 11 students did not possess an MP3 player).

In study 2, 75 secondary education students participated (school year 2009-2010). Twenty-eight were male, 47 were female. They were on average 15.05 years old (SD = 0.73). Participation in the study was obligatory. The majority of the participants had their own MP3 player (51 students possessed an MP3 player, 24 students did not possess an MP3 player).

Instruments

- **Learning material:** In both studies, an educational podcast was used (auditory information). The podcast was played on an iPod. In study 1, the podcast was part of the physiology course and the topic of the podcast was cytology and histology. The provision of the podcast replaced the traditional face-to-face lecture. All students were invited to participate in the experiment on voluntary basis. The podcast took four minutes; students had to play the lesson twice. In study 2, the topic of the podcast was dyspraxia. In this study, the content was not part of a specific course. Students were obliged to participate in the experiment, which took place during a physical education class. The podcast took 11 minutes and 40 seconds; students had to listen to the lesson once.

- **Prior knowledge test and learning test study :** Both the prior knowledge test (to be completed before the learning event) and the learning test (to be completed after the learning event) consisted of three multiple choice questions and two fill-in-the-blanks exercises. Different questions were used but the difficulty of both tests was the same. The maximum score that students could get on each test was 6. The tests were marked by the researcher using an answer key prepared by the subject teacher.

- **Prior knowledge test and learning test study 2:** The prior knowledge test (to be completed before the learning event) consisted of two questions. Students had to indicate (1) whether they already knew anything about dyspraxia (a lot, a bit or no prior knowledge) and (2) what exactly they already knew (open question). The learning test (to be completed after the learning event) consisted of 15 questions (11 multiple choice questions and four fill-in-th-blanks exercises). The maximum score that students could get on the test was 20. The tests were marked by the researcher using an answer key. This answer key was prepared by the researcher.

Procedure

In both studies, participants were randomly divided into three groups. Students of the first group listened to the podcast while they were sitting down. Students of the second group were asked to walk while listening. Students of the third group had to jog at a moderate pace while listening (in study 1, heart rate monitors were used for the students who had to combine learning and jogging). Students were asked to concentrate on the podcast and it was indicated that they would receive a test about the learning material.

The outline of both studies was identical. First, students had to complete a general survey about their age, their use of mobile devices in daily life etc. Second, students had to complete the prior knowledge test. Then, they listened to the educational podcast, whether or not combined with the walking or the jogging. Finally, after a short break of five minutes in which students could recover, students completed the learning test. In study 2, students had to complete a Sudoku puzzle during the break.

Analyses

ANOVA's were performed with the condition (sitting, walking, jogging) as the independent variable and the learning performances of the students as the dependent variable. For study 1, the difference between the score on the learning test and the score on the prior knowledge test was used. This difference score is an indication of the progress the students made. For study 2, the score on the learning test was used instead of the difference score because none of the students had indicated that they already knew something about dyspraxia.

Results

Study 1

The descriptives (Table 1) show that students who were sitting down while listening to the podcast learned the most. Students who where jogging while learning learned the least. However, the

differences between the learning performances of students of the different conditions (sitting, walking, jogging) are not significant; $F(2,33) = 1.603$; $p = .217$; $\eta^2 = .089$.

Study 2

The descriptives (Table 2) show that students who were sitting down while listening to the podcast learned the most. Students who were walking learned the least. A marginally significant effect was found of the condition (sitting, walking, jogging) on the learning scores; $F(2,72) = 3.073$; $p = .052$; $\eta^2 = .079$. The post-hoc test reveals that students who studied while sitting down outperformed the students who studied while walking; LSD; $p = .025$. Similarly, students who studied while sitting down outperformed the students who studied while jogging; LSD; $p = .054$.

CONCLUSION AND DISCUSSION

Two studies were presented where some of the participants were asked to walk or to jog while listening to an educational podcast. Both studies reveal different results. In study 1, no significant differences were found between the learning performances of students in the stationary condition, the learning performances of students in the walking condition and the learning performances of students in the jogging condition. In study 2, the learning outcomes of the participants in the different conditions differed significantly. Students

Table 1. Descriptives learning performances (difference score learning test and prior knowledge test) – study 1

	n	M	SD
Sitting	12	2.71	1.88
Walking	12	2.29	2.53
Jogging	12	1.17	2.09
Total	36	2.06	2.22

Table 2. Descriptives learning performances (score on the learning test) – study 2

	n	M	SD
Sitting	25	12.08	3.02
Walking	25	10.02	3.31
Jogging	25	10.32	3.19
Total	75	10.81	3.26

who studied while sitting down outperformed the students who studied while moving.

The results of both presented studies are not univocal. In a certain way, they are a reflection of the different research results found in the field of educational multitasking so far. Some studies reveal clear significant effects of multitasking (learning with a mobile device while doing something else) on the learning performances of students (e.g., Doolittle & Mariano, 2008), other studies do not (e.g., Coens et al., 2009b, 2011).

The different results of study 1 and study 2 could be caused by the different podcasts that were used. In study 1, the podcast took four minutes and students had to listen twice. In study 2, the podcast took almost 12 minutes and students had to listen only once. The different results of both studies could be an indication that mobile learning is more suitable for situations in which small chunks of content have to be learned.

Another explaining factor for the different results of both studies could be that the students participating in study 1 were more motivated to study the material than the students participating in study 2. First, the content that was used in study 1 was part of the physiology course. It was also part of the exam syllabus. This could have caused all participants to try to perform well on the learning task. The content that was used in study 2 was not part of a specific course and it made no part of an exam syllabus. This could have caused students to be less focused on the learning task and more amenable to distracting factors like the walking or jogging. Second, students participated in study 1 on voluntary basis. They participated because they wanted to. In study 2, students were obligated to participate. Possibly, they were less motivated to perform well than the students participating in study 1.

There are a lot of factors that could be important and that could have an influence on the ability of a person to multitask while learning. One variable that could play a part is already revealed. Coens et al. (2009b, 2011) found that the variable 'perception of importance' plays a part and is important. In the studies of Coens et al. (2009b, 2011) it was assumed that it is unlikely that within a real context, a person will perceive both tasks as equally important. For example, when someone is listening to an educational podcast while driving, it is assumed that that person will give top priority to the driving task, because he/she wants to avoid having an accident. Coens et al. (2009b, 2011) found that students performed worse on a learning test only if they focus on the secondary task instead of the learning task while multitasking. Within the context of the reported studies, students had to focus on the learning task. This could explain the results of the first reported study: no significant differences were found. All students concentrated their attention on the learning task, which made part of the exam syllabus.

In a lot of divided attention studies, participants have to perform two tasks together under various conditions. Such studies provide evidence that several factors determine the dual task performances of people. Both learner characteristics and task characteristics play a part. In the context of combining a motor task and a cognitive task for example, the extent to which the motor task is fatiguing seems to be a determining factor. In general, it is more difficult to combine a fatiguing motor task with a cognitive task than combining a non-fatiguing motor task with a cognitive task (Lorist, Kernell, Meijman, & Zijdewind, 2002; Zijdewind, van Duinen, Zielman, & Lorist, 2006). Possibly, the walking and jogging task were more fatiguing for the students participating in study 2, which could explain the different research results. Students participating in study 2 had to walk or jog for a longer time period than students participating in study 1 (respectively 8 minutes versus 11 minutes and 40 seconds). Furthermore, students participating in study 1 were bachelor students in physical education. They were used to physical efforts. The students participating in study 2 were not.

Further research is needed that clearly shows when students are capable of addressing two tasks simultaneously in an efficient and effective way. Our results so far suggest that many factors must be considered when answering the question "Can students really multitask?"

REFERENCES

Bherer, L., Kramer, A. F., Peterson, M. S., Colcombe, S., Erickson, K., & Becic, E. (2005). Training effects on dual-task performance: Are there age-related differences in plasticity of attentional control? *Psychology and Aging, 20,* 695–709. doi:10.1037/0882-7974.20.4.695

Carrier, L. M., Cheever, N. A., Rosen, L. D., Benitez, S., & Chang, J. (2009). Multitasking across generations: Multitasking choices and difficulty ratings in three generations of Americans. *Computers in Human Behavior, 25,* 483–489. doi:10.1016/j.chb.2008.10.012

Centraal Bureau voor de Statistiek. (2009). *De digitale economie 2009.* Retrieved from http://www.cbs.nl/NR/rdonlyres/E87BCAE8-8F0E-4F43-90FE-B44F3D513E8A/0/2009p34pub.pdf

Chen, Y. S., Kao, T. C., & Sheu, J. P. (2003). A mobile learning system for scaffolding bird watching learning. *Journal of Computer Assisted Learning, 19,* 347–359. doi:10.1046/j.0266-4909.2003.00036.x

Chen, Y. S., Kao, T. C., & Sheu, J. P. (2005). Realizing outdoor independent learning with a butterfly-watching mobile learning system. *Journal of Educational Computing Research, 33,* 395–417. doi:10.2190/0PAB-HRN9-PJ9K-DY0C

Cherng, R., Liang, L., Hwang, I., & Chen, J. (2007). The effect of a concurrent task on the walking performance of preschool children. *Gait & Posture, 26,* 231–237. doi:10.1016/j.gaitpost.2006.09.004

Clarebout, G., Coens, J., & Elen, J. (2008). The use of ipods in education: The case of multitasking. In Zumbach, J., Schwartz, N., Seufert, T., & Kester, L. (Eds.), *Beyond knowledge: The legacy of competence* (pp. 75–82). New York, NY: Springer. doi:10.1007/978-1-4020-8827-8_11

Coens, J., Clarebout, G., & Reynvoet, B. (2009a, May). *Mobile learning: een stand van zaken.* Poster presented at the Onderwijsresearchdagen, Leuven, Begium.

Coens, J., Clarebout, G., & Reynvoet, B. (2009b, August). *Mobile learning viewed from the perspective of multitasking.* Poster presented at the Earli Biennal Conference, Amsterdam, The Netherlands.

Coens, J., Reynvoet, B., & Clarebout, G. (2011). Mobile learning. Can students really multitask? *Journal of Educational Multimedia and Hypermedia, 20*(1), 5–20.

Copley, J. (2007). Audio and video podcasts of lectures for campus-based students: Production and evaluation of student use. *Innovations in Education and Teaching International, 44,* 387–399. doi:10.1080/14703290701602805

Doolittle, P. E., Lusk, D., Byrd, C., & Mariano, G. (2009). iPods as mobile multimedia learning environments: Individual differences and instructional design. In H. Ryu & D. Parsons (Eds.) *Innovative mobile learning: Techniques and technologies.* Hershey, PA: IGI Global.

Doolittle, P. E., & Mariano, G. J. (2008). Working memory capacity and mobile multimedia learning environments: Individual differences in learning while mobile. *Journal of Educational Multimedia and Hypermedia, 17*, 511–530.

Evans, C. (2008). The effectiveness of m-learning in the form of podcast revision lectures in higher education. *Computers & Education, 50*, 491–498. doi:10.1016/j.compedu.2007.09.016

Eysenck, M. W., & Keane, M. T. (2005). *Cognitive psychology: A student's handbook*. Hove, UK: Psychology Press.

Federale Overheidsdienst Economie. (2009). *ICT-indicatoren bij huishoudens en individuen 2005-2009*. Retrieved from http://statbel.fgov.be/nl/modules/publications/statistiques/arbeidsmarkt_levensomstandigheden/ict_indicatoren_bij_huishoudens_individuen_2005_2009.jsp

Foehr, U. G. (2006). *Media multitasking among American youth: Prevalence, predictors and pairings*. Menlo Park, CA: The Henry J. Kaiser Family Foundation.

Frydenberg, M. (2008). Principles and pedagogy: The two Ps of podcasting in the information technology classroom. *Information Systems Education Journal, 6*(6).

Higginbotham, D. (2006). An assessment of undergraduate student's mobility skills and needs in curriculum delivery. In *Proceedings of the 29th Annual Conference of the AECT*, Dallas, TX (pp. 98-115).

Hunton, J., & Rose, J. M. (2005). Cellular telephones and driving performance: The effects of attentional demands on motor vehicle crash risks. *Risk Analysis, 25*, 855–866. doi:10.1111/j.1539-6924.2005.00637.x

Jeong, S., & Fishbein, M. (2007). Predictors of multitasking with media: Media factors and audience factors. *Media Psychology, 10*, 364–384. doi:10.1080/15213260701532948

Kahneman, D. (1973). *Attention and effort*. Upper Saddle River, NJ: Prentice Hall.

Kenyon, S. (2008). Internet use and time use: The importance of multitasking. *Time & Society, 17*, 283–318. doi:10.1177/0961463X08093426

Kirschner, P. A., & Karpinski, A. C. (2010). Facebook® and academic performance. *Computers in Human Behavior, 26*(6), 1237–1245. doi:10.1016/j.chb.2010.03.024

Lien, M., Ruthruff, E., & Johnston, J. C. (2006). Attentional limitations in doing two tasks at once. *Current Directions in Psychological Science, 15*, 89–93. doi:10.1111/j.0963-7214.2006.00413.x

Lorist, M. M., Kernell, D., Meijman, T. F., & Zijdewind, I. (2002). Motor fatigue and cognitive task performance in humans. *The Journal of Physiology*, 313–319. doi:10.1113/jphysiol.2002.027938

Luria, R., & Meiran, N. (2005). Increased control demand results in serial processing. Evidence from dual-task performance. *Psychological Science, 16*, 833–840. doi:10.1111/j.1467-9280.2005.01622.x

Maag, M. (2006). iPod, uPod? An emerging mobile learning tool in nursing education and students' satisfaction. In *Proceedings of the 23rd Annual Conference of the Australasian Society for Computers in Learning in Tertiary Education Who's Learning? Whose Technology?* Sydney, Australia (pp. 483-492).

McGarr, O. (2009). A review of podcasting in higher education. *Australian Journal of Educational Technology, 25*(3), 309–321.

Meng, P. (2005). *Podcasting & vodcasting: A white paper. Definitions, discussions & implications*. Columbia, MO: University of Missouri.

Nathan, P., & Chan, A. (2007). Engaging undergraduates with podcasting in a business project. In *Proceedings of the ASCILITE ICT Conference: Providing Choices for Learners and Learning*.

Navon, D., & Gopher, D. (1979). On the economy of the human information processing system. *Psychological Review*, *86*, 214–255. doi:10.1037/0033-295X.86.3.214

Pashler, H. (1984). Processing stages in overlapping tasks: Evidence for a central bottleneck. *Journal of Experimental Psychology. Human Perception and Performance*, *10*, 358–377. doi:10.1037/0096-1523.10.3.358

Pashler, H. (1994). Dual-task interference in simple tasks: Data and theory. *Psychological Bulletin*, *116*, 220–244. doi:10.1037/0033-2909.116.2.220

Pashler, H. (1998). *The psychology of attention*. Cambridge, MA: MIT Press.

Pew, R. W., & Mavor, A. S. (1998). *Modeling human and organizational behavior: Application to military simulations*. Washington, DC: National Academy Press.

Pfeiffer, V. D. I., Gemballa, S., Jarodzka, H., Scheiter, K., & Gerjets, P. (2009). Situated learning in the mobile age: Mobile devices on a field trip to the sea. *ALT-J Research in Learning Technology*, *17*(3), 187–199. doi:10.1080/09687760903247666

Pool, M. M., van der Voort, T. H. A., Beentjes, J. W. J., & Koolstra, C. M. (1999). De invloed van achtergrondtelevisie op de uitvoering van gemakkelijke en moeilijke huiswerktaken. *Pedagogische Studiën*, *76*, 350–360.

Salvucci, D. D., & Taatgen, N. A. (2008). Threaded cognition: An integrated theory of concurrent multitasking. *Psychological Review*, *115*, 101–130. doi:10.1037/0033-295X.115.1.101

Schaefer, S., Krampe, R. T., Lindenberger, U., & Baltes, P. B. (2008). Age differences between children and young adults in the dynamics of dual-task prioritization: Body (balance) versus mind (memory). *Developmental Psychology*, *44*(3), 747–757. doi:10.1037/0012-1649.44.3.747

Strayer, D. L., & Johnston, W. A. (2001). Driven to distraction: Dual-task studies of simulated driving and conversing on a cellular telephone. *Psychological Science*, *12*, 462–466. doi:10.1111/1467-9280.00386

Styles, E. A. (2006). *The psychology of attention*. Hove, UK: Psychology Press.

Van Selst, M., Ruthruff, E., & Johnston, J. C. (1999). Can practice eliminate the psychological refractory period effect? *Journal of Experimental Psychology. Human Perception and Performance*, *25*, 1268–1283. doi:10.1037/0096-1523.25.5.1268

Vandierendonck, A. (2006). *Aandacht & geheugen*. Gent, Belgium: Academia Press.

Veen, W. (2009). *Homo Zappiens. Opgroeien, leven en werken in een nieuw tijdperk*. Amsterdam, The Netherlands: Pearson Education.

Verghese, J., Kuslansky, G., Holtzer, R., Katz, M., Xue, X., Buschke, H., & Pahor, M. (2007). Walking while talking: Effect of task prioritization in the elderly. *Archives of Physical Medicine and Rehabilitation*, *88*, 50–53. doi:10.1016/j.apmr.2006.10.007

Verhaeghen, P., Steitz, D. W., Sliwinski, M. J., & Cerella, J. (2003). Aging and dual-task performance: A meta-analysis. *Psychology and Aging*, *18*, 443–460. doi:10.1037/0882-7974.18.3.443

Voelcker-Rehage, C., Stronge, A. J., & Alberts, J. L. (2006). Age-related differences in working memory and force control under dual-task conditions. *Aging. Neuropsychology and Cognition*, *13*, 366–384. doi:10.1080/138255890969339

Wickens, C. D. (1980). The structure of attentional resources. In Nickerson, R. (Ed.), *Attention and performance VIII* (pp. 239–257). Mahwah, NJ: Lawrence Erlbaum.

Wickens, C. D. (2002). Multiple resources and performance prediction. *Theoretical Issues in Ergonomics Science*, 3(2), 159–177. doi:10.1080/14639220210123806

Wilson, D., Andrews, B., & Dale, C. (2009). Choreo:pod: Dance and the iPod towards blended learning. *International Journal of Mobile and Blended Learning*, 1(1), 49–60. doi:10.4018/jmbl.2009010104

Zijdewind, I., van Duinen, H., Zielman, R., & Lorist, M. M. (2006). Interaction between force production and cognitive performance in humans. *Clinical Neurophysiology*, 117, 660–667. doi:10.1016/j.clinph.2005.11.016

Chapter 10

Advancing Collaboration between M-Learning Researchers and Practitioners through an Online Portal and Web 2.0 Technologies

Laurel Evelyn Dyson
University of Technology Sydney, Australia

Andrew Litchfield
University of Technology Sydney, Australia

ABSTRACT

With growing interest in mobile learning to address the educational requirements of a generation of students who have grown up with digital technology, and given the widespread adoption of mobile devices by indigenous people and in developing countries, there is a need for improved practice and better theoretical understanding of m-learning. This could be achieved through a more accessible body of knowledge of m-learning principles, teaching strategies and case-studies. This paper proposes the establishment of an online portal to influence and support good m-learning practice. An m-learning portal, incorporating a range of online, Web 2.0 and mobile technologies, would foster collaboration between researchers and educators and inform emerging national and international approaches using mobile technologies at all levels of the education sector and across all disciplines.

INTRODUCTION

In the first decade of the twenty-first century, interest in m-learning – learning facilitated by mobile technologies – is emerging as the most important innovation in education (Guy, 2009; Kukulska-Hulme & Traxler, 2005). This has come about most obviously because of the availability of wireless technologies but also, in large measure, from a realization that there is a serious mismatch between traditional teaching methods and the current generation of learners. In addition, given

DOI: 10.4018/978-1-4666-2139-8.ch010

the widespread adoption of mobile technologies in disadvantaged communities, m-learning can play a vital role in re-engaging the disengaged and narrowing economic disparity between the developed and developing world.

M-learning has the potential to depart significantly from traditional, didactic teaching pedagogies and also from the e-learning practices that grew out of them in the 1990s. Since e-learning systems are good at mass delivery of content, they tended to perpetuate the old transmission model of education (Martin & Webb, 2001). Figure 1 is a French drawing from 1910 which presciently foretells technology-supported teaching in the year 2000: students sit passively downloading information that has been "digitized" in the teacher's book-mincer or "web server". The lack of expression on the students' faces indicates that little learning is happening. Today, inactive, didactic lectures,

and their online equivalent, remain the dominant modes of instruction at university.

As a "disruptive" new technology mobile devices have an interesting potential to support new learning and teaching practices. By contrast with both classroom teaching and e-learning, m-learning can be "spontaneous, personal, informal, contextual, portable, ubiquitous (available everywhere) and pervasive" (Kukulska-Hulme & Traxler, 2005, p. 2). M-learning supports constructivist and experiential pedagogies, and lends itself to student-centred learning, where learners create new knowledge and content for themselves (Cochrane, 2006; Litchfield, Dyson, Wright, Pradhan, & Courtille, 2010).

In this paper we explore how the existing knowledge and experiences of researchers and practitioners might be leveraged to spread understanding of m-learning further. Despite growing

Figure 1. Educational technology in the year 2000, as viewed in France in 1910 (From http://www. paleofuture.com/blog/2007/9/10/french-prints-show-the-year-2000-1910.html)

recognition of the advantages of m-learning, the use of mobile technology in education is not as widespread as it should be. M-learning is yet in an exploratory phase, with educators still working out how to do it, how to finance it, which subjects and groups of students might benefit most, and how to get academics on board (Dyson, Raban, Litchfield, & Lawrence, 2009). There remain many gaps in our understanding of m-learning, such as its practical implementation across a range of disciplines, its theoretical foundation, and how to deal with ethical issues. We firstly discuss how m-learning can revitalize the learning not only of the "digital natives" generation but also of previously disenfranchised groups of learners. We then present our proposal for an m-learning portal to serve as a catalyst and offer practical support for change in the educational sector.

M-Learning for Improving the Education of the Digital Natives Generation

The average university student of today has grown up with digital technology and has spent far more time playing video games, browsing the Internet, sending text messages and watching television than reading books. Prensky (2001), who dubbed these students "digital natives", noted their immersion in the digital world and their constant interaction with it. Despite his failure to take into account individual differences in students (Bennett, Maton & Kervin, 2008), we can certainly say that the vast majority of this generation has had unprecedented access to mobile and computer technologies. Student ownership of mobile phones in Australia, for example, is over 95%, with the most common uses being text messaging and telephoning (Kennedy, Judd, Churchward, Gray & Krause, 2008). As a result students generally display:

digital fluency and familiarity with new technologies never before imagined ... are the speakers of

the digital language of computers, mobile telephones, the Internet ... typically produce and share digital content ... such as blogs, digital images, digital audio or video files and SMS messages ... [possess] digital expectancy (Duncan-Howell & Lee, 2007, p. 223)

Studies in the literature demonstrate how mobile technology can enhance learning for this generation of students through a variety of educational applications, including improved interactivity in lectures, mobile-supported fieldwork and ubiquitous learning support (Litchfield, Dyson, Lawrence & Zmijewska, 2007).

M-Learning for Diversity

Universities serve an increasingly diverse student body. In many English-speaking countries there are large cohorts of international students, most of whom have English as a second language and whose special needs for learning in a new environment need to be better addressed. Mobile learning can meet the requirements of international and non-English speaking background students by allowing them to review lectures, messages and other content outside normal classroom hours, for example, through podcasting (Nataatmadja & Dyson, 2008).

Beyond the university sector, there has been a realization that m-learning can work with underprivileged groups in society. This has resulted from the almost ubiquitous adoption of mobile phones across all social strata and hence a widespread familiarity with the technologies and the forms of interaction which they promote:

For disenfranchised learners, many forms of e-learning are just as alien as the educational systems they have already rejected. M-learning utilizes technologies, activities and social systems that are already integrated into many people's lives, including those who have had limited access to or rejected formal education systems. (Wallace, 2009)

In Europe, interesting m-learning and training projects have been implemented in Romany communities, for refugees and recent immigrants, adult literacy and numeracy learners, and hard-to-reach workplace learners (Stead, 2005). "ComeIn" is a new European project aimed at providing access to learning activities via mobile phones for young, marginalized people who cannot be reached by conventional education (Marschalek, Unterfrauner & Fabian, 2009). In Australia, m-learning has been successfully demonstrated with young people with poor employment histories, records of incarceration or other backgrounds of disadvantage (Ragus et al., 2005).

Indigenous people, too, have adopted mobile phones and MP3 players at a far greater rate than fixed-line phones or personal computers. For example, mobile phone ownership amongst Aboriginal people surveyed in Alice Springs, was found to be 56% compared to 25% who had access to a home phone, while Maori people were identified as using their mobile phones more frequently than non-Indigenous New Zealanders (Tangentyere Council & Central Land Council, 2007; Te Puni Kokiri, 2010). As a result, the advantages of m-learning for this group are now starting to be recognized. In the context of Aboriginal Australia, mobile phone calls and text messages have effectively recruited and organized students for courses in financial literacy; the multimedia capabilities of mobile devices have been used to collect evidence of prior learning and current competence and build m-portfolios for adult learners; and children's mathematics has been improved via mobile phone applications (AED, 2007; Sinanan, 2008; Wallace, 2009). Podcasting is delivering courses in Maori language and mobile devices for literacy learning have been tested with Native American children in Latin America (Kim, 2009; Switalla, n.d.).

Similarly in developing countries, mobile phones have had a much greater impact than any other form of ICT, with mobile subscribers outnumbering fixed-line subscribers by seven to one (Srivastava, 2008). In these countries, m-learning has a profound potential to allow educational institutions and their students to bypass e-learning, with its dependency on computers and infrastructure, which are often unavailable, and move to a technology which is widespread, cost-effective and which people know how to use. M-learning in the developing world is currently limited, but growing. Traxler and Kukulska-Hulme (2005) report on two cases: the ZMQ Project in India, which uses m-learning materials to educate poor villagers about health issues; and the School Empowerment Programme in Kenya, which employs bulk SMS messaging for in-service training of primary school teachers and local support personnel. South Africa has been one of the most active developing countries with regards to m-learning, using it, amongst other things, to deliver literacy programs and support student learning with SMS (Ng'ambi, 2005; Vosloo, Walton & Deumert, 2009).

The Need for an M-Learning Portal

Despite the potential of m-learning to transform the way we deliver education, and despite many successful m-learning projects, there remain unresolved issues. Traxler (Kukulska-Hulme & Traxler, 2005, p. 70) sees m-learning as:

approaching a critical phase in its development when its advocates must address the twin issues of 'blending' with other forms of delivery – both traditional and electronic – and of devising sustainable, reliable, generalized and large-scale formats across whole departments and institutions.

The question, then, is how to scale up from the many small experimental projects that have been the focus of m-learning to date. One answer suggested by Prensky (2005, p. 1) is to facilitate the exchange of information by teachers already using mobile technology in interesting ways:

If our goal is to bring schools and classrooms into the 21st century before that century ends, we need to take advantage of the large amount of innovation *that is already going on* in many classrooms by allowing our teachers to share it.

The most obvious vehicle for sharing insights into m-learning is the Internet. Already there are various m-learning organizations and research groups which have established websites. Examples include the International Association for Mobile Learning (IAMLearn – http://mlearning. noe-kaleidoscope.org), Mobile Learning Network (MoLeNet – www.molenet.org.uk), London Mobile Learning Group (LMLG – www.london-mobilelearning.net), Handheld Learning (www.handheldlearning.co.uk) and anzMLearn (an Australasian m-learning group – http://research.it.uts.edu.au/tedd/anzmlearn).

Limitations to these websites are that links between them are poor, none is comprehensive and, with the exception of anzMLearn, most have a European focus and generally ignore what is happening in the greater part of the world. The sites tend to promote the work of their own organizations and contributions are mainly by members. Resources provided by some websites are not sufficiently comprehensive or detailed to be very useful. Furthermore, many important issues in m-learning, such as achieving sustainability and cost effectiveness, the needs of diverse groups of learners and applications of m-learning for developing countries, are often overlooked. A major problem with most of the existing m-learning websites is that they shy away from full collaboration by falling into what Feenberg and Bakardjieva (2004, p.1) define as a "consumption" model rather than being true online communities: items are disseminated like an online library in which "Users scarcely talk to each other … and never see or sense each other's presence."

To remedy this situation, the authors propose the establishment of a truly international, collaborative m-learning portal freely accessible through the Internet. Portals – websites which offer an entry point to a range of services and resources collected into one convenient, online location – have long been used effectively in business (Hazra, 2002). In the education field, portals have most often been employed to provide access to digital libraries (Impagliazzo, Cassel & Knox, 2002). The proposed portal would provide a single, centralized location for collaboration in m-learning, with comprehensive links to existing m-learning resources and webpages. This would foster good practice in m-learning, provide professional development for teachers in this emerging field, and lead to a renewal of teaching methods to suit the needs of today's students.

The emergence of Web 2.0 technologies provides an excellent opportunity to make the m-learning portal truly collaborative. Beginning as tools largely for popular, mass communication on the Web, blogs, wikis, photo- and video-sharing technologies, and other social media are now being incorporated into some institutional frameworks to encourage greater public involvement, a two-way dialogue and a sense of community (Russo, Watkins, Kelly & Chan, 2007). The Internet user is no longer positioned as a mere consumer of content, but as a dynamic participant, shaking off the passivity of what McLuhan (1962) called the "Gutenberg heritage". Web 2.0 is about "moving beyond content delivery to personal publishing, ease of use, interactivity, collaboration, sharing and customisation" (Cochrane, 2006, p. 144). The incorporation of these tools will enable the m-learning portal to engage in many-to-many communication with the m-learning community rather than the top-down, one-to-many approach that dominates most current educational websites. This conversation will result in the co-creation of knowledge about m-learning by its practitioners and its dissemination to those who have not yet begun this journey. The reliability and authoritativeness of this body of knowledge will be supported through online discussions, peer review and interactive critical debate.

Underlying Principles

Three important foci of the m-learning portal include:

- The need to develop good quality learning experiences for students which involve active learning since we learn by doing.
- The need to ensure that m-learning is inclusive of all learners. To maximize global learning outcomes, the portal will investigate issues of learner cultural diversity in the context of increasing internationalization and globalization of education and the increased need for an educated and flexible workforce. Faced with a diversity of populations and needs, the notions of multiculturality and interculturality are becoming key aspects of curriculum design and change (Germain-Rutherford & Kerr, 2008).
- The importance of containing costs so that universities are able to move from short-term pilot projects to the full implementation of m-learning into mainstream courses over the long-term. Cost has been identified as a major, but not insurmountable hurdle, to greater sustainability in m-learning (Dyson et al., 2009).

Objectives of the M-Learning Portal

The m-learning portal's main, global m-learning objective is to:

1. Influence and support the design, development, implementation and evaluation of m-learning professional development and effective curriculum and program integration for educators. This includes a focus on enhancing active learning using sustainable and cost-effective strategies for culturally diverse learners.

In a co-ordinated approach, this m-learning outcome could be achieved through the following:

2. Develop an online body of knowledge of m-learning principles, teaching strategies and case studies for enhancing active experiential learning by encouraging sharing and collaboration between members of the m-learning community of researchers and practitioners.
3. Share insights and strategies for achieving sustainability in m-learning through the use of cost-effective strategies such as the utilization of students' own mobile devices and existing university wireless networks.
4. Investigate m-learning curriculum design that addresses learners' cultural diversity and equity issues.
5. Actively promote effective m-learning activities which meet the needs of Indigenous communities for education, cultural renewal and the removal of disadvantage.
6. Foster the collaboration and exchange between educators in the developed world and in developing countries to work towards greater equality of opportunity internationally.
7. Promote curriculum renewal through the collection of m-learning resources which focus on the effective development of graduate attributes as well as major issues of current concern, such as environmental and health education.
8. Offer a vehicle for effective professional development activities, mentoring, peer support, and promote professional development events focusing on m-learning.

Components of the M-Learning Portal

Components of the portal, accessible either from a computer or mobile device, are shown in Figure 2.

Figure 2. Components of the m-learning portal

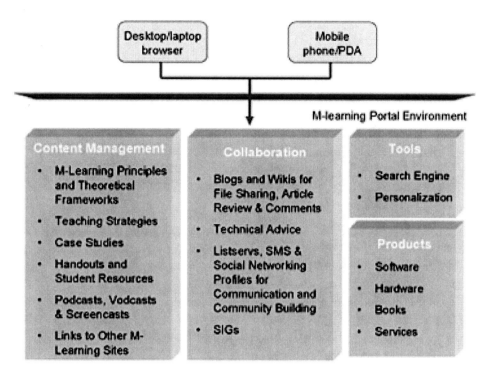

Components include:

Content Management:

- M-learning principles and theoretical frameworks, aimed at developing a more rigorous theoretical underpinning of m-learning than has existed to date.
- Effective m-learning teaching strategies.
- Case studies organized according to commonly accepted areas of m-learning (e.g., interactive classroom systems, podcasting, mobile-supported fieldwork, workplace training using mobile devices), and according to areas of importance, specified above, such as sustainability, cultural diversity in the student body, Indigenous learning, environmental studies, etc.
- Handouts, mobile files and other practical resources for students provided by participating educators.

- Podcasts, vodcasts and screencasts for teacher professional development or for provision to students.
- Links to a wide range of existing m-learning websites and online articles.

Collaboration:

- A variety of Web 2.0 tools to support collaborative work, feedback and comment, sharing of documents or technical tips.
- Communication tools, including email, text messaging, twitter and a presence on social network sites.
- Specific areas of m-learning, as detailed under case studies above, would be supported by Special Interest Groups (SIGs), each with their own blog, wiki, etc.

Tools:

- An insite search engine to allow rapid location of desired information and resources.
- An optional personalization and log-on function, whereby a registered user can enrol in their topics of interest, allowing articles and special-interest group blogs to be presented to them without searching.

Products:

- Online sale and advertizing of a range of products and services to provide the income to help make the m-learning portal sustainable.

CONCLUSION

The extraordinary growth in ownership of mobile devices in all nations presents a wonderful opportunity to improve global educational outcomes right across the world by enhancing active learning through the appropriate use of mobile technology. The availability of relatively low-cost mobile devices, such as mobile phones, PDAs, iPods, iPads and e-readers, has created new global access and learning opportunities. This can improve the quality of learning both in formal academic locations but also in economically and socially marginalized communities and in the developing world.

The proposed m-learning portal would support innovation and promote m-learning's more widespread adoption. It would do this by increasing the visibility of those already working in this area and by diffusing the outcomes of their investigations. By providing a vehicle for sharing insights and the lessons of experience, it would overcome the reluctance of some to try this new educational technology, giving much needed support and encouragement, and removing some of the complexity that is always a hurdle in the adoption of new ways of teaching and learning. The authors envisage that the m-learning portal will be a catalyst for change, developing new pedagogies relevant to our students' learning needs and advancing education into the twenty-first century.

REFERENCES

Aboriginal Economic Development (AED). (2007). Improving mathematics with mobile phones. *AED E-News, 3*.

Bennett, S., Maton, K., & Kervin, L. (2008). The 'digital natives' debate: A critical review of the evidence. *British Journal of Educational Technology, 39*(5), 775–786. doi:10.1111/j.1467-8535.2007.00793.x

Cochrane, T. (2006). Learning with wireless mobile devices and social software. In. *Proceedings of ASCILITE, 06,* 143–146.

Duncan-Howell, J., & Lee, K.-T. (2007). M-learning: Finding a place for mobile technologies within tertiary educational settings. In *Proceedings of ASCILITE 2007,* Singapore (pp. 223-232).

Dyson, L. E., Raban, R., Litchfield, A., & Lawrence, E. (2009). Addressing the cost barriers to mobile learning in higher education. *International Journal of Mobile Learning and Organization, 3*(4), 381–398. doi:10.1504/IJMLO.2009.027455

Feenberg, A., & Bakardjieva, M. (2004). Consumers or citizens? The online community debate. In Feenberg, A., & Barney, D. D. (Eds.), *Community in the Digital Age: Philosophy and practice* (pp. 1–30). Lanham, MD: Rowman & Littlefield.

Germain-Rutherford, A., & Kerr, B. (2008). An inclusive approach to online learning environments: Models and resources. *Turkish Online Journal of Distance Education, 9*(2), 64–85.

Guy, R. (Ed.). (2009). *The evolution of mobile teaching and learning.* Santa Rosa, CA: Informing Science Press.

Hazra, T. K. (2002). Building enterprise portals: Principles to practice. In. *Proceedings of ICSE, 02, 623–633*.

Impagliazzo, J., Cassel, L. N., & Knox, D. L. (2002). Using Citidel as a portal for CS education. *Journal of Computing Sciences in Colleges, 17*(6), 161–163.

Kennedy, G. E., Judd, T. S., Churchward, A., Gray, K., & Krause, K.-L. (2008). First year students' experiences with technology: Are they really digital natives? *Australasian Journal of Educational Technology, 24*(1), 108–122.

Kim, P. H. (2009). Action research approach on mobile learning design for the underserved. *Educational Technology Research and Development, 57*, 415–435. doi:10.1007/s11423-008-9109-2

Kukulska-Hulme, A., & Traxler, J. (Eds.). (2005). *Mobile learning: A handbook for educators and trainers*. London, UK: Routledge.

Litchfield, A., Dyson, L. E., Lawrence, E., & Zmijewska, A. (2007). Directions for m-learning research to enhance active learning. In *Proceedings of ASCILITE 2007*, Singapore (pp. 587-596).

Litchfield, A., Dyson, L. E., Wright, M., Pradhan, S., & Courtille, B. (2010, July 5-7). Student produced vodcasts as active meta-cognitive learning. In *Proceedings of the 10th IEEE International Conference on Advanced Learning Technologies*, Sousse, Tunisia (pp. 560-564).

Marschalek, I., Unterfrauner, E., & Fabian, C. M. (2009). Mobile learning activities to reach out for young marginalised people. In Metcalf, D., Hamilton, A., & Graffeo, C. (Eds.), *Proceedings of mLearn 2009* (p. 222). Orlando, FL: University of Central Florida.

Martin, E., & Webb, D. (2001). Is e-learning good learning? In Brook, B., & Gilding, A. (Eds.), *The ethics and equity of e-learning in higher education* (pp. 49–60). Melbourne, VIC, Australia: Victoria University.

McLuhan, M. (1962). *The Gutenberg galaxy: The making of typographic man*. London, UK: Routledge & Kegan Paul.

Nataatmadja, I., & Dyson, L. E. (2008). The role of podcasts in students' learning. *International Journal of Interactive Mobile Technologies, 2*(3), 17–21.

Ng'ambi, D. (2005). Mobile dynamic frequently asked questions (DFAQ) for student and learning support. In *Proceedings of the 4th World Conference on mLearning (mLearn 2005)*, South Africa, Cape Town (pp. 1-8).

Prensky, M. (2001). Digital natives, digital immigrants. *Horizon, 9*(5), 1–6. doi:10.1108/10748120110424816

Prensky, M. (2005). *If we share, we're halfway there*. Retrieved September 20, 2010, from http://www.marcprensky.com/writing/Prensky-If_We_Share.pdf

Ragus, M., Meredith, S., Dacey, D., Richter, C., Paterson, A., & Hayes, A. (2005). The Australian mobile learning network: Australian innovations. In *Proceedings of mLearn 2005* (pp. 1-21). Retrieved September 20, 2010, from http://www.mlearn.org.za/papers-full.html

Richardson, J., & Lenarcic, J. (2007, June 4-6). E-inclusion through text messaging: The emergence of an administrative ecology within an university student population via the use of a mobile academic information delivery system. In *Proceedings of the 20th Bled eConference*, Bled, Slovenia (pp. 1-9).

Russo, A., Watkins, J., Kelly, L., & Chan, S. (2006). How will social media affect museum communication? In *Proceedings of NODEM* (pp. 1-8).

Sinanan, J. (2008, December 8-12). Social tools and social capital: Reading mobile phone usage in rural Indigenous communities. In *Proceedings of OzCHI* (pp. 267-270).

Srivastava, L. (2008). The mobile makes its mark. In Katz, J. E. (Ed.), *Handbook of mobile communication studies* (pp. 15–27). Cambridge, MA: MIT Press.

Stead, G. (2005). Moving mobile into the mainstream. In *Proceedings of mLearn 2005* (pp. 1-9). Retrieved September 20, 2010, from http://www.mlearn.org.za/papers-full.html

Switalla, L. (n.d.). *Does the use of a podcast facilitate feedback/reflection to improve the pronunciation of Maori language*. Retrieved September 20, 2010, from http://www.scribd.com/doc/22622018/Maori-Language-Podcasting

Tangentyere Council & Central Land Council. (2007). *Ingerrekenhe antirrkweme: Mobile phone use among low income Aboriginal people, a Central Australian snapshot*. Alice Springs, NT, Australia: Author.

Te Puni Kokiri (Ministry of Maori Development). (2010). *Te reo paho: Use of broadcasting and e-media, Maori language and culture*. Retrieved September 20, 2010, from http://indigenouspeoplesissues.com/attachments/4722_Maori-Media-Factsheet2010.pdf

Traxler, J., & Kukulska-Hulme, A. (2005). *Mobile learning in developing countries*. Vancouver, BC, Canada: Commonwealth of Learning. Retrieved September 20, 2010, from http://www.col.org/SiteCollectionDocuments/KS2005_mlearn.pdf

Vosloo, S., Walton, M., & Deumert, A. (2009). m4Lit: A teen m-novel project in South Africa. In D. Metcalf, A. Hamilton & C. Graffeo (Eds.), *Proceedings of mLearn 2009* (pp. 207-211). Orlando, FL: University of Central Florida.

Wallace, R. (2009). Empowered learner identity through m-learning: Representations of disenfranchised students' perspectives. In Metcalf, D., Hamilton, A., & Graffeo, C. (Eds.), *Proceedings of mLearn 2009* (pp. 13–17). Orlando, FL: University of Central Florida.

Section 3
Mobile Learning Solution Development

Chapter 11
Involving the End–Users in the Development of Language Learning Material

Anu Seisto
VTT Technical Research Centre of Finland, Finland

Timo Kuula
VTT Technical Research Centre of Finland, Finland

Maija Federley
VTT Technical Research Centre of Finland, Finland

Janne Paavilainen
University of Tampere, Finland

Sami Vihavainen
Helsinki Institute for Information Technology, Finland

ABSTRACT

Printed and digital learning materials are usually developed separately. Therefore, little notice has been given to the possibilities of combining the two. This study introduces a new concept that combines printed and digital materials. A user-centric approach was chosen to develop a "hybrid book", a combination of a traditional schoolbook and a mobile phone. Learning materials were combined into one entity by enabling access to the digital material through images in the book. The user groups of interest were 11- and 12-year-old pupils, their teachers, and parents. The concept was tested with materials for English as a foreign language (EFL). After a human-centred design process, the final application was given to one class for actual use and evaluation for a period of three weeks. Many potential benefits of using mobile phones for learning purposes were recognized, as they facilitated utilization of the digital content both inside and outside the classroom.

DOI: 10.4018/978-1-4666-2139-8.ch011

INTRODUCTION

New digital media applications are continuously being developed and brought into use in educational contexts. In the case of language learning, interesting studies have recently been reported, for example an application that uses mobile phones to improve pronunciation (Ally & Tin, 2009).

A number of projects related to mobile learning have found that mobile technologies can support different parts of the learning experience and interweave into the learners' personal knowledge, interests, and learning needs (Kukulska-Hulme, Sharples, Milrad, Arnedillo-Sánchez, & Vavoula, 2009). Experiments have shown that the opportunity to study whenever and wherever has generally increased the motivation to study (Leino, Turunen, Ahonen, & Levonen, 2002). New technology offers children and adults the opportunity to communicate with teachers and fellow learners around the world, interact with rich learning resources and simulated environments, call on information and knowledge when they are needed to solve problems and satisfy curiosity, and create "personal learning narratives" through an extended process of capturing and organizing a situated activity (Sharples, 2000).

So far, books and other printed material are rarely taken into consideration in digital applications. The role of books in the school environment is still strong, even indisputable, in the foreseeable future. More convenient ways of merging the essential digital content, such as listening tasks, into everyday studies are needed (Seisto, Federley, Aarnisalo, & Oittinen, 2009). During the course of this study, we have become aware of the fact that printed learning material and digital material for elementary school children are often developed separately. Digital material is seldom used regularly, as it cannot be assumed that every child has access to a computer at home, and the number of computers at schools is limited. There

is therefore a clear need for a combined development of printed and digital material as well as an easy way to access digital material. The field we believe will gain the most obvious benefits from using printed and digital media side by side is language studies. A few additional features are needed for a printed schoolbook with which it is possible to communicate and that will adapt to proper level of knowledge. This has been the starting point for our study.

We aimed at game-like solutions for elementary school English education. Games or game-like features have great potential to enhance learning. This is because they have the ability to motivate and engage people (Bogost, 2007). People have an intrinsic curiosity (Malone, 1980) that makes them want to try to master challenges.

This paper describes the development process of a hybrid school book, in which a traditional printed school book and a mobile phone were combined into one entity. The study was based on a human-centered design approach in which the elementary school pupils and teachers, as well as the parents of the children, were used as informants. Our goal was to find out how the hybrid book would function in everyday use, where it would be used, and what kinds of benefits the use of the hybrid book could bring compared with traditional printed schoolbooks. The process consisted of four separate phases that were carried out in an iterative manner, all of them aiming at the same goal but from a different viewpoint. As human-centered design had a key role in the development process, attention was especially paid to using technology in a way that would be meaningful and easy for the main focus groups, the pupils and the teachers. Pedagogical aspects were included in each phase through interviews with the teachers and learning material publishers. This paper summarizes the main results of the whole development process.

DIDACTICAL AND PEDAGOGICAL FRAMEWORK

The design of the hybrid book was based on the didactics of English as a foreign language (EFL) and experience on teaching EFL. The involved teachers, some of them also authors of EFL school books, presented their views of important elements (including learning of vocabulary and grammatical rules), which formed the framework for the design process. Differentiation of pupils based on their performance, grammar exercises and listening exercises were key elements of the framework.

When placed within a broader pedagogical framework, a socio-cultural perspective on learning partly guided the design process. From this perspective the social and cultural nature of learning is emphasized (Lund, 2003), and, especially from Activity Theory's viewpoint, learning is mediated by tools that support the learners in their goals of transforming their knowledge (Traxler, 2009). Mobile phones as tools can be seen as culturally new but important artifacts, which are interwoven into the everyday lives of the students, and thus are part of their social interaction and informal learning. Printed school books on the other hand represent culturally familiar tools in the school environment. More generally, the theory behind mobile learning is largely presented from socio-cultural approach as well (Sharples, 2005; Traxler, 2009).

METHODOLOGY

Design Process

The basis of our study was human-centered design that is a standardized "approach to interactive systems development that aims to make systems usable and useful by focusing on the users, their needs and requirements, and by applying human factors/ergonomics, and usability knowledge and techniques" (International Organization for Standardization, 2010). The standard determines four activities that should be repeated iteratively until the designed system meets the user requirements:

1. Understand and specify the use context
2. Specify the user requirements
3. Produce design solutions to meet the user requirements
4. Evaluate the designs against the requirements

The user evaluations are an essential part of the design process (Kuutti, 2003). The users should be involved in the design process at the very early stages of the project, usually when the initial concept for the product or system is being formulated. The primary stakeholders for evaluating the design of the hybrid book in this study were determined as pupils, teachers and parents.

We aimed for a final hybrid application that would be well suited to its actual use from the teacher's viewpoint and, at the same time, be interesting to the children. In order to be able to effectively incorporate the feedback from the users in the design of the concept, information from the user groups was gathered at four different development phases, as illustrated in Figure 1. In the first phase we gathered information from the teachers about their attitudes towards the use of a hybrid book, including the mobile phone, as well as ideas for potential mobile tasks that would be useful in learning a foreign language (Seisto et al., 2009). Secondly, the pupils and teachers evaluated comic strip scenarios that represented different game-like tasks for the hybrid learning material (Paavilainen, Saarenpää, Seisto, & Federley, 2009). We had also considered several different technologies for combining printed and digital material and these were demonstrated and evaluated in the third phase (Kuula, Vihavainen, & Seisto, 2009). Finally, a field study was carried out with a class of 25 pupils who used the hybrid books in their studies. All four development phases were carried out as separate iteration

Figure 1. Development phases included in the design of the hybrid book

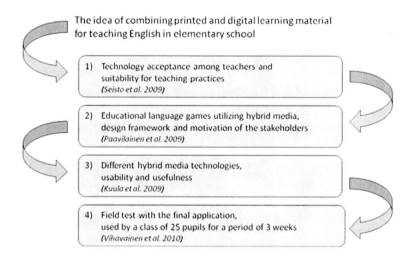

rounds comprising the four activities as defined in the standard ISO 9241-210:2010 (International Organization for Standardization, 2010).

Data Gathering and Analysis

Rather than relying solely on literature and our own preferences, we recruited the intended end-users - teachers and pupils - as informants for our study. The opinions of the parents of the pupils were taken into account from the viewpoint of acceptance of combining mobile phones with printed school material. Pedagogical aspects were discussed with teachers and learning material publishers.

The research material gathered in this study is mainly based on qualitative interviews. In the final phase (phase 4 in Figure 1) a mix of qualitative (interviews and personal diaries) and quantitative (questionnaires, logs) methods was used to capture subjective views of the system and data on the interaction with the exercises. In qualitative research, the object is examined as comprehensively as possible. The purpose is to reveal the facts rather than to verify the existing statements (Hirsjärvi, Remes, & Sajavaara, 2007). The aim of qualitative research is not to produce a statistical generalisation (Tuomi & Sarajärvi, 2002) but to understand the phenomenon being studied and to see it from the subject's point of view (Järvenpää & Kosonen, 1999). The interviews were carried out as theme interviews. This method is suitable when there is a defined field about which researchers want to gain more knowledge, and completely new aspects are expected to appear (Hirsjärvi & Hurme, 2000). The main emphasis is on learning about the practices and needs of the interviewee based on his or her individual experience. The themes of the interviews were prepared in advance, and a number of questions were defined, but during the interviews, free discussion and new thoughts were encouraged. The course of the interviews was allowed to vary, depending on the interests of the interviewee, and the remarks and observations made during the interview. The adults were interviewed individually and the children in pairs.

The interviews consisted of questions about the interviewees' demographics, their relationship with the school environment, prior experience of information technology, user experience of the mobile phone during the study, and user experience on the hybrid media system as a part of the learning experience. The questionnaire in the final phase of the study contained questions on the user's experience of the tested system. The questionnaire was a modification of the one used by Brooke (1996). All the pupils filled in the questionnaire after the intervention phase. In the final phase each pupil was also given a personal diary in which he or she was able to make notes on whether he or she used the system in or outside school and what kind of positive and negative experiences he or she had with the system.

The interviews were recorded and notes were made during the interviews. Approximately 34 hours of recorded interview data were gathered. The interviews were analyzed by the project group based on the audio files and the notes with the exception of the final phase in which questionnaires and diaries were also used to complement the qualitative research material.

INVOLVING CHILDREN IN THE DEVELOPMENT PROCESS

The initiative to involve the pupils in the development process was well received by all related groups: the teachers, the school principals, the parents and the children. The mobile tasks were reviewed and accepted in advance by a professional learning material publisher. The hybrid book enriched the existing learning material instead of replacing it, and thus no great risks with respect to learning outcomes were assumed to appear.

The children who were recruited to evaluate the prototypes for the study were 11 to 12 years old. Children of this age are able to verbalize their thoughts clearly and are used to discussing with adults. Furthermore, the themes of the interviews were in no way personal, nor did they include any subject that would be confusing or difficult for the children to discuss. It was therefore possible to conduct the interviews in a similar way to that used for adult interviewees, as outlined in the previous section. The following steps were followed, however, to take into consideration the young age of the interviewees:

- Pilot interviews were carried out with children who were familiar with the research group. The purpose was to check, in advance, the adequacy of the prototype testing procedure and questions for the age group.
- The parents of the children were informed of the study well in advance and given a careful explanation of what was being studied and how the results would be presented. The parents were asked for written permission to allow their children to participate in the study.
- At the beginning of the interviews, the researchers explicitly introduced the goal of the interview and the role of the interviewees, emphasizing that there were no right or wrong answers, that the English skills of the children were not being assessed, and that the insights of the children, as real end-users, were essential to the study (Höysniemi, 2005).
- Prototypes of the concepts or comic strip scenarios were presented as the basis for the discussions (Druin, 1999).
- The children were interviewed in pairs to establish a more relaxed atmosphere (Höysniemi, 2004).
- The interviews were not videotaped, as this has been noted to be uncomfortable for many young interviewees (Druin, 1999).
- In order to encourage the children to speak in their own words and discuss freely, open questions were used (as in any interview).
- The researchers paid special attention to allowing the children to formulate the answers without rushing or interrupting them.

The interviews were mostly carried out during school hours, which helped the researchers to motivate the children to contribute. The children regarded the testing of prototypes and interviews as a nice change from schoolwork. This made it even more important, however, to critically evaluate the interview data during the analysis. There is an obvious risk that the children do not criticize as easily as they give positive feedback, partly because they wish to use the electronic devices in schools more frequently, and partly because they do not want to be "unfriendly" to the interviewer.

TECHNOLOGY ACCEPTANCE

As the approach presented in this study involved a hybrid solution that combined the printed book with digital learning materials, it was also important to consider the user experience and acceptance of new technology in everyday schoolwork. One of the most demanding aspects of product development is to make sure that the product is what users really want and need (Faulkner, 2000). Users' attitudes to a certain product can be studied with the notion of user experience, which combines both task- and non-task-oriented aspects of product use. Already in 1973, Katz, Blumler, and Gurevitch (1973) presented the idea that the pleasure connected to the use of any media depends on the content, exposure to media per se, and the social context of the media use.

One of the most widely used technology acceptance theories is the Technology Acceptance Model (TAM). TAM predicts user acceptance of any technology in terms of two factors (Davis, Bagozzi, & Warshaw, 1989):

- **Perceived usefulness:** the degree to which a user believes that using the system will enhance his or her performance.
- **Perceived ease of use:** the degree to which the user believes that using the system will be effortless.

Research by Davis et al. (1989) indicates that although ease of use is clearly important, the usefulness of the system is even more important and it should not be overlooked. Users may be willing to tolerate a difficult interface in order to access functionality that is very important, while no amount of ease of use will compensate for a system that does not perform a useful task. Huang, Lin, and Chuang (2007) have extended TAM to explain and predict the acceptance of mobile learning. Their study investigated future acceptance of emerging m-learning technology rather than its current use. To understand the user perception of m-learning, Huang et al. (2007) integrated two individual, external variables into the proposed model: perceived enjoyment and perceived mobility. Perceived enjoyment denotes the extent to which an individual finds the interaction with m-learning intrinsically enjoyable or interesting. Perceived enjoyment is seen as an example of intrinsic motivation and has been found to influence user acceptance significantly. The perceived mobility value denotes user awareness of the mobility value of m-learning: mobility brings the ability to guide and support users in new learning situations when and where necessary.

RESULTS

Game-Like Features for the Hybrid Book

According to Markovíc, Petrovic, Kitti, and Edegger (2007), positive experiences aid penetration of learned material into long-term memory. Games can offer these positive learning experiences to students as they can provide meaningful tasks that students like to pursue. Technology is often also a motivating factor and makes students enthusiastic, at least in the beginning. If the benefit of using technology is easy to see, both students and teachers usually like trying out new technical devices. Using technology and games in schools can still, however, be challenging because they need to be easy to incorporate into the curriculum and should not demand too much effort from the teacher.

Figure 2. Example of a comic strip scenario used for user interviews on game-like features in the hybrid book

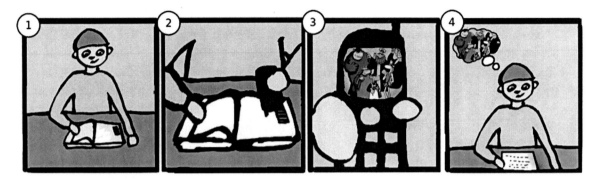

In this study, the game concepts were used as a tool for differentiation and motivational factors. Emphasis was also put on how to take into account the difference between the class and home environments when carrying out the learning tasks. Differentiation, in the form of adaptive levels of difficulty of games, gives more freedom to the student and provides an optimal learning curve for any given play sessions. In language education, the class setting favors social communication, verbal interaction, and listening comprehension tasks. The home environment is suited to reading and writing, or other tasks for which social interaction is not necessary.

A total of six comic strip scenarios were designed and shown to the informants who then commented on and discussed them with the interviewer. The scenarios were designed to address specific issues that would be clear in the use of educational games in both class and home environments. The purpose of these scenarios was to bring the designers and end-users closer together by offering a springboard that could be used in discussions and ideation. An example of a scenario is presented in Figure 2. This particular scenario represented a situation in which a pupil was studying a grammar issue from his English book. He could access extra learning material as a video clip on his mobile phone by using the phone to read a barcode printed on the book. In

the exam the next day he did very well as he could easily recall the video clip and the grammar issue taught in it. The methodology and detailed results have been reported by Paavilainen et al. (2009).

Overall, all the scenarios received positive feedback. The pupils not only paid attention to the game-like elements and entertainment value in the scenarios but were also concerned about their own learning and ways to improve it. The boys thought the best tasks at school were crossword puzzles, word finding and math problems. They were also interested in seeing more complex games that modeled real life in some way. These kinds of games would also be played at home. Computer and mobile devices were very familiar to the boys, and new technology was considered very exciting. The girls thought that games in general were interesting from an educational point of view and that all the scenarios were exciting, as they were so different from the current reality. Like the boys, the girls enjoyed the crossword puzzle tasks most. They were also keen to use new technology in the school environment, but one pair stated that there should not be too many gadgets at school as this would leave too little time for actual learning. This was an interesting point of view that underlines the idea that new technology can be interpreted as something that is only fun, not as something that can be educational.

Figure 3. Launching a task with a mobile phone from the page of a book

All interviewed teachers thought that using game-like activities during the classes would be a good thing. There should also still be enough room for traditional schoolwork however. In general, the games should make the pupils think, not force them to react mechanically to a certain stimulus. Computer and mobile technology is already used in schools but in a limited fashion. The pupils have little time to use computers during the week, but the use of mobile phones is more frequent. Mobile phones are used as calculators in math classes, and sometimes the pupils copy their homework assignments from the whiteboard by taking a photograph with their mobile phones. The teachers thought it was burdensome to check the students' work and that technology could help with that. Educational games must have some kind of evaluative aspects so the teachers can monitor the pupils' advancements. Simplicity and clarity were considered the most important aspects of an educational game, so that the teachers would also understand them easily.

CHOICE OF DIGITAL CONTENT

From the viewpoint of the final application, it was important to take into account the mobility and ease of use of the hybrid book anywhere and anytime. Based on the feedback obtained from teachers and pupils, the mobile tasks that we chose to implement in the field test were crossword puzzles, grammar exercises with differentiative features, and listening tasks.

As the crossword was one of the task types the children found particularly interesting, it was an obvious choice for the final hybrid book. As our aim was to combine printed and digital learning materials, however, the crossword contained words from the specific chapter of the book that was being studied, and the hints were in the form of audio files. After launching a task from a page of the book with a mobile phone (Figure 3), the child would first listen to the hint from the mobile phone and then write the word into the crossword.

In the grammar exercises, we demonstrated the possibility of differentiating between the tasks by simply giving the pupil an easier multiple-choice task than the previous one if he or she answered wrong and a more complicated task if he or she answered right. The grammar exercise was also based on the specific chapter of the book that was being studied in class.

Finally, the listening exercises were included in order to combine the possibility of reading the text from the book and listening to the text with the mobile phone at the same time, regardless of the time and place. With this task, we also wanted to make listening to the language easier, and thus more frequent than currently, for the pupils. Listening exercises are already available to pupils, but to use them at home requires extra effort. At school, everyone listens to a CD that the teacher plays. Making them available through the hybrid book made the exercises easier to access and increased their usefulness, as the pupils could listen to the chapters at their own pace. The pupils were very fond of the songs in their English books and the songs were therefore included in the hybrid book.

Demonstrations of the tasks were presented to a group of pupils, teachers, and parents prior to the actual classroom test, and some minor modifications were made. When the tasks had been finalized and access from the images in the book to the digital material had been implemented, the children in the class that took part in the three-week test period were already very eager to start.

"WHEN DO WE GET THE PHONES?!"

In the earlier phases of the project, valuable input from the different interest groups to the development of the hybrid learning material was gathered in interviews with short demonstrations of the prototypes. These short tests provided excellent information on the needs of the teachers and pupils for language learning, and guided the research to use technology for applications relevant to the users. In order to improve the reliability of the developed concept, however, a user study was set up with hybrid learning material in a real environment. The field trial also allowed the actual users to create new ideas for using mobile phones in language learning more freely. A class from Hämeenlinnan Yhteiskoulu (Hämeenlinna Elementary School) agreed to use the hybrid learning material prototype for three weeks. The pupils are in the 6th grade of elementary school (11-12 years old) and they are in their fourth year of studying English. There are 25 pupils in the class: 11 girls and 14 boys. They have two English lessons per week.

The pupils and the teacher were provided with Nokia E71-smartphones equipped with a 3.2 megapixel camera, a 2.4" display, and flat-rate data plans for access to the Internet. The applications and settings of the phones were pre-installed so that they would be as easy to use as possible for the tasks. The mobile phone tasks (described in

the previous paragraph) were developed for two chapters of the normal English study book. An image recognition application created at the VTT was used to link the digital material and the book. When the user opens the image recognition application on the mobile phone and takes a photo of the page of the printed book, a web site with the digital content relating to those pages of the book is opened.

During the trial, the pupils kept diaries on how often and where they used the hybrid schoolbook and made other remarks about their observations. At the end of the trial, the diaries were collected, each pupil answered a questionnaire, and eight pupils were interviewed. The teacher and four parents were also interviewed.

The children were very eager in the beginning and felt that they were privileged, as they were the only pupils in the school that were allowed to use mobile phones in the classroom and for homework. Naturally, the excitement settled somewhat during the test period, and the amount of time that the children spent doing English exercises "just for fun" decreased. The time frame of the user study is too short for a reliable evaluation of any actual long-term effects on learning, such as the effect of enhanced opportunities to listen to the vocabulary and texts in the chapters. These kinds of exercises seemed to motivate many of the children however. As reasons for their improved motivation the children generally mentioned an interest in using the new technology and more engaging lessons with variable exercises.

All the pupils said that they would like to use mobile phones frequently for studying. None of them thought that the use of the mobile tasks was laborious. The use of the application and the new phone was quite easy for the children, as only one third of the pupils said that they had to learn some or many new things before they could start on the hybrid book. Most of the children realized that mobile tasks could not replace all of the other learning materials however. The following motivations were mentioned: "Half with a book, half with a mobile would be good, in case, for example, the battery runs out," and "The book has more diverse exercises." The thought of a school without any printed books was confusing for most of the pupils.

Parents' attitudes to using mobile phones for learning were mostly positive. The idea of using modern technology more effectively in learning materials was appreciated, and it was considered important that schools should not be too distant from the leisure time and everyday media environment of the children. Some of the parents brought up concerns of potential expense and inequality if the acquisition of a smart phone for a child would be required for learning purposes.

The teacher valued the hybrid learning material, which made the variation of routines easier. The children have different learning styles, preferences, and needs for which the teachers want to have a variety of solutions to adjust their teaching to these differences. The concept of a hybrid book enables differentiation in a convenient way. It was also easier to allow the pupils to proceed at their own pace, even in the classroom. For example, the teacher usually played a text from a CD to the whole class. Using the mobile phones and headphones for listening resulted in less distractions, and every pupil could pause and rewind the audio file whenever he or she needed to. The teacher also appreciated the features of the application that made it easier to check if the pupils had done their homework and how they had performed.

Furthermore, the teacher came up with some of her own ideas for using the mobile phone. In some cases, the pupils would send text messages after completing English tasks. The pupils could also record spoken language in the form of small plays and deliver these files to the teacher for extra credit. After the trial, the pupils also suggested ideas for further development, such as mobile chat and pronunciation exercises.

DISCUSSION

Advantages of the Hybrid Book

Based on the interviews during this study, it is clear that the role of printed learning material at elementary school level is still very strong. The society around us, however, is becoming increasingly digitized, and children are becoming very talented users of different digital devices already before they start school. It is thus also clear that the schools, learning materials, and teaching have to follow the development that is taking place around them and include new technological solutions in their everyday work. The prerequisite for these solutions, however, is that they have to work well; they have to be easy to use and fit in with the everyday practices of the teachers and pupils.

As mentioned by Grenman (2010), books have indisputable strengths that currently cannot be attained through any other media. Books are fixed and, although the inability to modify their content can be seen as a disadvantage in the learning process, it is often also a strength. The same information can be found in the same place as it was before, making revision easier. In unexpected situations, such as power failures, it is still possible to rely on at least the book to work. It is obvious, however, that printed information cannot be easily updated and in some subjects, schoolbooks become outdated quickly. Some subjects benefit from the more illustrative approach that can be achieved with computers. With books alone, there is no instant feedback and there is therefore often a long delay before there is a chance to rethink and correct possible errors.

Combining schoolbooks with mobile phones may be one possible way to use the strengths of both printed and electronic learning materials and to provide a solution that is easy to adapt to everyday practices. Mobile phones would enable features that are otherwise impossible for books. Based on the experience of the field test, the teacher mentioned that it was easier to allow the pupils to proceed at their own pace with the hybrid schoolbook than without it, even in the classroom.

INVOLVING THE USERS IN THE DEVELOPMENT PROCESS

According to the socio-cultural perspective of learning, a school subject, such as English language, is a historical, cultural, and social construction (Lund, 2003). This should be taken into consideration when introducing new technology relating to a specific subject in schools. Teachers are particularly important, however, in the sense that it is through their practices that learners are apprenticed to exploit technologies as part of the overall learning environment. Teachers' encounters with ICT, and the way they integrate ICT into their work, constitute a complex and multi-faceted phenomenon (Lund, 2003). In the case of this research, the printed book served as a historically and culturally familiar artifact, whereas the mobile phone was a new tool in the school environment. The teacher was thus able to combine the familiar and the new – the "easy" with the "complex". Recent discussion on ICT use in Finnish schools has pointed out the reluctance of Finnish teachers to adopt ICT practices in everyday use. We started the development process by studying teachers' attitudes towards the hybrid book concept on the basis of the Technology Acceptance Model (TAM) for mobile learning by Huang et al. (2007). The results were encouraging as the most essential TAM criteria, perceived usefulness, ease of use, enjoyment and mobility, were fulfilled. The general opinion of the teachers was that the hybrid book device was fun to use and fairly good grades were given in the evaluation (average 8.1 on a scale from 4 to 10). Many of the teachers had some difficulties with the small screen of the mobile phone and in browsing with it. However, after 10 minutes of practicing to use the test phone, the teachers thought that the hybrid book was nice and exciting. Based on our experiences,

the teachers appeared highly motivated and had a positive attitude towards using the hybrid book. This may be explained partly by the combination of "old" and "new", so that instead of aiming at a big technology leap, we aimed for small steps towards more frequent use of new technology. The digital material was also divided into sections that were appropriate for the chapters of the book, which made it easier for the teacher to incorporate them into her teaching.

The inclusion of the teacher in the design process from the very beginning proved valuable. The teacher was able to interweave the use of the hybrid book into her current teaching practices, culture, and curriculum. The teacher also provided the research group with valuable information on didactics relating to EFL, which helped with the design of the mobile phone tasks. At the very early stages of the design process, the educational framework, based largely on socio-constructivist and socio-cultural theories, (including ideas of, for example, problem-based and collaborative learning) was introduced to the teacher. The idea of enhancing collaboration with the help of technology was seen as important. This is an obvious challenge and possibility for future research.

The adoption of new technology also generates negotiations between multiple stakeholders and, in this case, the parents were also interviewed in addition to the pupils and teachers. We saw that it is essential to involve these three user-groups in the process in order to create a useful concept. The social network that was involved could be seen as even broader, however, and included, for example, curriculum writers and other policy makers. In further research of the subject and the introduction of hybrid technology into schools, the whole community with its rules and division of labor should be recognized even more extensively (Engeström, 1987).

Another issue that should be considered in further research is related to the costs of elementary education. In Finland, free elementary school is an important value. The use of mobile technology must therefore not incur direct costs to the users. This was emphasized by both the interviewed teachers and parents. As the use of mobile Internet becomes more common, the number of flat-rate data plans and Wi-Fi hotspots will also increase strongly, thereby offering affordable use of digital learning materials over the Internet. The use of the hybrid book would not require a considerable investment in the school infrastructure either. Nonetheless, the optimum solution to the expense of using the hybrid book needs to be sought, at the latest, in the production phase.

CONCLUSION

The starting point of the project was to combine printed and digital learning material in order to enrich and enhance the learning experience and introduce the created concept to users in elementary schools. Our experience of the project indicates that the mobile hybrid book is a suitable learning tool for elementary education. The motivation of teachers and pupils was high, and the attitudes of parents supported the use of the hybrid book. The printed book is probably no longer enough, but it has not yet disappeared from schools. The idea of combining the two worlds of printed and digital material was well received.

The mobility of the hybrid book allows pupils to study anywhere and at anytime. Pupils are able to carry out English tasks on the move, for example, listening to a chapter from the book on the bus. The hybrid book also motivates pupils to study because it is interesting to use, and all the relevant content, printed or digital, can be accessed through one compilation, thereby forming a consistent entity. The hybrid book allows self-study in a meaningful way. It can offer new kinds of tasks and instant feedback from exercises. In addition, the hybrid book supports effortless differentiated teaching: supplementary material can be incorporated into the book as links instead of the teacher collecting it on a case-by-case basis.

From the teachers' point of view, the integration of printed and digital learning materials lowers the threshold for using digital learning materials, as they are clearly part of the study book and support the current curriculum. This would allow mobile learning to become an everyday activity in schools instead of a rare experiment. Moreover, it appeared that the free use of new devices in studies also inspired the pupils and the teacher to innovate new ways for technology-assisted language learning and to create their own content. Interestingly, the hybrid book thus seems to support both traditional practices and a renewal of language education.

In conclusion, our project verified the high potential of the mobile hybrid book in schoolwork. A longer test period is required, however, to gain more in-depth knowledge of the actual impact on the learning outcome. A sustainable business model should also be developed for the product.

ACKNOWLEDGMENT

M-real, Myllykoski, Stora Enso, UPM-Kymmene, and TEKES are acknowledged for funding this research.

REFERENCES

Ally, M., & Tin, T. (2009). Mobile phone to improve English pronunciation. In *Proceedings of the 8th World Conference on Mobile and Contextual Learning*, Orlando, FL (pp. 171-173).

Bogost, I. (2007). *Persuasive games: The expressive power of videogames*. Cambridge, MA: MIT Press.

Brooke, J. (1996). SUS: A quick and dirty usability scale. In Jordan, P. W., Thomas, B., Weerdmeester, B. A., & McClelland, I. L. (Eds.), *Usability evaluation in industry* (pp. 189–194). Boca Raton, FL: Taylor & Francis.

Davis, F. D., Bagozzi, R. P., & Warshaw, P. R. (1989). User acceptance of computer technology: A comparison of two theoretical models. *Management Science, 35*(8), 982–1003. doi:10.1287/mnsc.35.8.982

Druin, A. (1999). Cooperative inquiry: Developing new technologies for children with children. In *Proceedings of the ACM CHI Human Factors in Computing Systems Conference*, Pittsburgh, PA (pp. 592-599).

Engeström, Y. (1987). *Learning by expanding: An activity-theoretical approach to developmental research.* Helsinki, Finland: Orienta-Konsultit Oy.

Faulkner, X. (2000). *Usability engineering.* London, UK: Palgrave.

Grenman, K. (2010). *The future of printed school books.* Espoo, Finland: VTT Technical Research Centre of Finland.

Hirsjärvi, S., & Hurme, H. (2000). *Tutkimushaastattelu: Teemahaastattelun teoria ja käytäntö.* Helsinki, Finland: Yliopistopaino.

Hirsjärvi, S., Remes, P., & Sajavaara, P. (2007). *Tutki ja kirjoita.* Helsinki, Finland: Kustannusosakeyhtiö Tammi.

Höysniemi, J. (2005). Käytettävyystestaus lasten kanssa . In Ovaska, S., Aula, A., & Majaranta, P. (Eds.), *Käytettävyystutkimuksen menetelmät* (pp. 259–282). Tampere, Finland: Tampere University Press.

Höysniemi, J., Hämäläinen, P., & Turkki, L. (2004). Wizard of Oz prototyping of computer vision based action games for children. In *Proceedings of the International Conference on Interaction Design and Children* (pp. 27-34).

Huang, J.-H., Lin, Y.-R., & Chuang, S.-T. (2007). Elucidating user behavior of mobile learning: A perspective of the extended technology acceptance model. *The Electronic Library, 25*(5), 586–599. doi:10.1108/02640470710829569

International Organization for Standardization. (2010). *ISO 9241-210:2010: Ergonomics of human-system interaction – Part 210: Human-centred design for interactive systems.* Retrieved from http://www.iso.org/iso/catalogue_detail.htm?csnumber=52075

Järvenpää, E., & Kosonen, K. (1999). *Johdatus tutkimusmenetelmiin ja tutkimuksen tekemiseen.* Espoo, Finland: Helsinki University of Technology.

Katz, E., Blumler, J. G., & Gurevitch, M. (1973). Uses and gratifications research. *Public Opinion Quarterly, 37*(4), 509–523. doi:10.1086/268109

Kukulska-Hulme, A., Sharples, M., Milrad, M., Arnedillo-Sánchez, I., & Vavoula, G. (2009). Innovation in mobile learning: A European perspective. *International Journal of Mobile and Blended Learning, 1*(1), 13–35. doi:10.4018/jmbl.2009010102

Kuula, T., Vihavainen, S., & Seisto, A. (2009, October). *Playful learning with hybrid school books.* Poster presented at the MindTrek Conference, Tampere, Finland.

Kuutti, W. (2003). *Käytettävyys, suunnittelu ja arviointi.* Helsinki, Finland: Talentum Media Oy.

Leino, M., Turunen, H., Ahonen, M., & Levonen, J. (2002). Mobiililaitteet oppimisen ja opetuksen tukena. In P. Seppälä (Ed.), *Mobiili opiskelu: Joustavasti liikkeessä* (pp. 47-58). Helsinki, Finland: Helsingin yliopisto, Opetusteknologiakeskus.

160

Lund, A. (2003). *The teacher as interface. Teachers of EFL in ICT-rich environments: Beliefs, practices, appropriation*. Unpublished doctoral dissertation, University of Oslo, Norway.

Malone, T. W. (1980). What makes things fun to learn? Heuristics for designing instructional computer games. In *Proceedings of the 3rd ACM SIGSMALL Symposium and the First SIGPC Symposium on Small Systems* (pp.162-169).

Marković, F., Petrovic, O., Kitti, C., & Edegger, B. (2007). Pervasive learning games: A comparative study. *New Review of Hypermedia and Multimedia, 13*(2), 93–116. doi:10.1080/13614560701712873

Paavilainen, J., Saarenpää, H., Seisto, A., & Federley, M. (2009). Creating a design framework for educational language games utilizing hybrid media. In *Proceedings of CGAMES USA 14th International Conference on Computer Games*, Wolverhampton, UK (pp. 81-89).

Seisto, A., Federley, M., Aarnisalo, S., & Oittinen, P. (2009). Hybrid media application for language studies in elementary school. In *Proceedings of IADIS International Conference on Mobile Learning*, Barcelona, Spain.

Sharples, M. (2000). The design of personal mobile technologies for lifelong learning. *Computers & Education, 34*(3-4), 177–193. doi:10.1016/S0360-1315(99)00044-5

Sharples, M. (2005). Learning as conversation: Transforming education in the mobile age. In *Proceedings of the Conference on Seeing, Understanding, Learning in the Mobile Age*, Budapest, Hungary (pp. 147-152).

Traxler, J. (2009). Learning in a mobile age. *International Journal of Mobile and Blended Learning, 1*(1), 1–12. doi:10.4018/jmbl.2009010101

Tuomi, J., & Sarajärvi, A. (2002). *Laadullinen tutkimus ja sisällönanalyysi*. Helsinki, Finland: Kustannusosakeyhtiö Tammi.

Vihavainen, S., Kuula, T., & Federley, M. (2010). Cross-use of smart phones and printed books in primary school education. In *Proceedings of the 12th International Conference on Human Computer Interaction with Mobile Devices and Services*, Lisbon, Portugal (pp. 279-282).

This work was previously published in the International Journal of Mobile and Blended Learning, Volume 3, Issue 2, edited by David Parsons, pp 43-56, copyright 2011 by IGI Publishing (an imprint of IGI Global).

Chapter 12

Identifying the Potential of Mobile Phone Cameras in Science Teaching and Learning:
A Case Study Undertaken in Sri Lanka

Sakunthala Ekanayake
University of Bristol, UK

Jocelyn Wishart
University of Bristol, UK

ABSTRACT

This research was motivated by previous work using mobile phones to support science teaching and learning in a variety of ways. This paper explores in detail how mobile phone cameras can support science teaching and learning during the planning, implementing, and evaluation stages of a lesson. A case study of a science lesson carried out in a school in Sri Lanka is described. The methodological approach of this study is qualitative and data were collected using observations, informal interviews and field notes. The results show that mobile phone cameras support the teacher in a range of ways during lesson planning, lesson implementation, and evaluating learning. Furthermore, the camera function of mobile phones was reported by teachers and students as enhancing the effectiveness of student learning, providing more opportunities for students' active participation, increasing interactions and collaborative learning opportunities.

INTRODUCTION

Studies have been carried out worldwide to investigate the use of mobile phones for a range of different teaching and learning processes. It is now recognised that the mobile phone can add new dimensions to the teaching and learning process because it possesses a wide range of attributes such as its spontaneous, personal, informal, contextual, portable, ubiquitous and pervasive nature and its functions that include talk, text, still camera, video, radio, and internet (Kukulska-Hulme, 2005).

DOI: 10.4018/978-1-4666-2139-8.ch012

One of the most important features in the mobile learning environment (Parsons et al., 2007) is mobility itself which creates exciting opportunities for new forms of learning to emerge, these can change the nature of the physical relationship between teacher, learner and the object of learning (Laurillard, 2007). Mobility demolishes the need to tie particular learning activities to particular places or particular times (Traxler, 2010). The freedom of mobility offers opportunities for the learner to learn autonomously (MacCallum & Kinshuk, 2006). It also provides opportunities to obtain learning experiences outside the teacher-managed context (Naismith et al., 2004) by expanding learning beyond the four walls of the classroom, thus allowing interactions in the real world and bringing new interactions back into the classroom (van't Hooft & Swan, 2007). In an increasingly fast-paced world where the ability to communicate electronically is increasing, the portability of mobile devices facilitates learning, irrespective of the time of day and the location of the learner (Cooney et al., 2007). Scanlon et al. (2005) note that the mobility and portability of the mobile phone have the potential for making positive changes for accessing information and enhancing interaction in science learning. In terms of the functions of mobile phones, Marriott (2005) considers present-day mobile phones to be complete multimedia centres that combine the capabilities of the still camera, video camera, personal organiser, and a web browser into one single device. These functions could further add a new dimension to science teaching and learning which contains content and scientific processes that are currently viewed as difficult to teach (Taber, 2005; Wellington, 2004; Barton, 2004) by enhancing communication and interactions between teacher and students and amongst students, and enabling collaboration in practical activities or field work. Students are known to be interested in the use of mobile phones for learning as they could assist with communication, create more collaboration and enable creativity (Botha et al., 2009). How-

ever, the success of adopting mobile phones in a lesson depends on the teacher's preparedness to adopt the mobile technologies (Kukulska-Hulme et al., 2009). In this article we are focusing on the potential of using the mobile phone camera in science teaching and learning in school settings.

Theoretical Context

Webb and Cox (2004) claim that Shulman's (1987) model provides a useful description of the processes that teachers engage in when they are planning, teaching and evaluating their technology enhanced lessons. Shulman (1987) notes that, in general, teaching is initiated by some form of 'text'; a textbook, a syllabus, or an actual piece of material that the teacher or students wish to understand. Then the teacher adds variety and nuances (examples, simulations, dialogues, demonstrations) into what is to be taught to students so as to develop and expand the subject content and a range of other attributes a student should possess for learning (Shulman, 1987). The process of changing the 'text' to the outcome (new comprehension by both the teacher and the student) goes through six processes, namely: comprehension, transformation, instruction, evaluation, reflection and new comprehensions. These processes impose a challenge to the teacher whereby his or her pedagogical reasoning and actions are tested throughout the planning, implementation and evaluation cycle and become vital.

Understanding of student learning is an important aspect of the pedagogy of teaching. There are a number of studies reported in the recent research literature suggesting theories underpinning mobile learning. For example, Naismith et al. (2004) categorise the learning activities associated with mobile technologies around seven main learning theories or areas of behaviourist, constructivist, situated, collaborative, informal and lifelong learning and learning and teaching support in their "Literature Review in Mobile Technologies and Learning" written for Futurelab,

UK. Of these Wishart (2007) considers that the constructivist approach to learning is the theoretical approach most relevant to mobile learning. In addition, Sharples (2003) claims that mobile learning devices also assist conversational learning by offering opportunities for the construction of conversations with oneself, between learners, between teacher and learner, and with the world.

Examples of Previous Research Using Mobile Phone Cameras with School Children

Recent research literature provides evidence on the use of mobile phone and Personal Digital Assistant (PDA) cameras in school science lessons. For example, Hartnell-Young and Heym (2008) noted the value of using the mobile phone's camera to ensure the validity of a scientific experiment during a secondary level science lesson in the UK. In this study, students used mobile phone cameras as a collaborative activity to capture evidence during experiments into plant growth. The images that were taken during their experiments helped students to accurately record physical observations. Further, the authors mentioned that both teachers and students valued the chance to review the images as the students were able to look at the gradual biological change over a period of time. Earlier, Chen et al. (2004) reported on a study on the use of PDA cameras for nature learning where different kinds of butterflies in Taiwan were identified using a butterfly-watching system (a database of different butterfly species in the region with content-based image retrieval and an online nature journal). The students visited the butterfly farm where the networking system was set up, used their PDAs to take photographs of the butterflies they observed and then to query the database which would return possible matches for the species. The students decided which match was the best and the database would verify their

selection based on image content similarity. The students then made the final decision, which was recorded using their PDA together with their notes of the entire experience.

Mobile phone cameras have also been trialled successfully in other subject areas. Sharples et al. (2007) report a study termed MyArtSpace, which addressed the importance of connection between preparation prior to a school museum visit, the visit itself and follow-up in the classroom. The day prior to the museum visit, the teacher introduced the lesson and gave out worksheets that students would follow in the museum. During the museum visit, students were loaned a mobile phone, which could access a web-based client. The students, in pairs, used this to take images and send them to the MyArtSpace website. Later, back in the classroom, they prepared PowerPoint presentations using the images and created online galleries on the MyArtSpace website. According to the findings of this study, this activity met teachers' and students' expectations, supported curriculum topics in literacy and media studies, enhanced student engagement and bridged the gap between the museum and the classroom learning.

Hartnell-Young (2007) reports a study that used mobile phones with Short Message Service (SMS), still camera and Global Positioning System (GPS) functions for communication between pupils in the classroom and a group of pupils following a teacher designed hill trail activity. In this study, the pupils also used a combination of mobile phone and web based technology. The team on the hill trail, who had a GPS receiver with their phone, took pictures of the terrain and sent them to the website set up for this activity. The home team at school monitored the arrival of the new images on the website and checked whether the hilly terrain team was on track by comparing the map on the screen with the location of the picture. The researchers reported that the conversation between the two groups of students, facilitated by the images sent by the students in the hill trail, supported learning through bridging the gap between the outside world and the classroom.

Even though the research studies described here discuss the potential of mobile phone cameras in science teaching and learning, they only consider the lesson implementation stage identified by Shulman (1987). However, it is worthwhile to explore how the camera function supports the teacher during the planning, implementing and evaluation stages of a lesson. Therefore, in this research, we focused on how mobile phone cameras support science teaching and learning during these three stages of a lesson. The research itself was carried out in Sri Lanka.

This paper is structured as follows: first, we examine the existing situation in Sri Lanka in terms of using mobile phones in Sri Lankan schools. Then an overview of the methods used for data collection and analysis is provided. Thirdly, findings are outlined and discussed in relation to the literature. Finally, conclusions are drawn, limitations of the study are highlighted and future work in this area is suggested.

Background to the Study

Even though it was found from the literature survey that the use of mobile phone cameras could enhance science teaching and learning, mobile phones are normally not permitted in schools. This is recognized as one of the main barriers to the widespread use of mobile phones in science teaching and learning. Thus, before carrying out this study, the authors analyzed the possible barriers to the implementation of mobile phone based lessons in Sri Lanka guided by the steps given in Hartnell-Young and Heym (2008) on 'how schools can introduce mobile phones for learning'. The teachers', principals' and educationalists' fears of the possible risk of class disruption by permitting students to bring their mobile phones to the classroom (recently mobile phones have been banned in Sri Lankan schools) was overcome

by organizing a loaned set of mobile phones to be considered as belonging to the school. For this study, the mobile phones were loaned by a national mobile phone company. Sri Lankan teachers' and students' competence in using mobile phone cameras was first investigated. A survey of 152 teachers from the Central Province of Sri Lanka, selected using a stratified sample to represent the range of schools there, revealed that the mobile phone camera function is hardly used for classroom teaching and learning. In contrast, Power and Thomas (2006) reported that over 90% of primary school literacy and science teachers in South Africa's Eastern Cape Province and in Cairo, Egypt had used mobile phone cameras to take photos and share them with others (pupils and others) as part of their professional practice.

As the teachers were not at all familiar with the use of mobile phones for teaching, hands-on training opportunities were provided. Then two professional workshops (planning for and reviewing mobile phone use in teaching respectively) and structured using an approach based on Shulman's (1987) findings on different aspects of teachers' pedagogy, were carried out. A group of 20 teachers was purposefully selected from their survey results for further interviews and workshop participation. The workshops were conducted partly to provide continuing professional development for teachers and partly as the first author's PhD research to find out how teachers viewed the different attributes and functions of the mobile phone that could be used in Sri Lankan classrooms for science teaching and learning.

Data were collected using the aforementioned survey, interviews, and observations recorded during the professional development workshops and are used to discuss teachers' attitudes to and perceptions about their competencies of using mobile phones for teaching and learning. Further data collected from observation of subsequent lessons in the classroom were examined to identify the potential and evidence for using mobile phone cameras in science teaching and learning

Figure 1. Teachers' perceptions of their competency in using mobile phone cameras

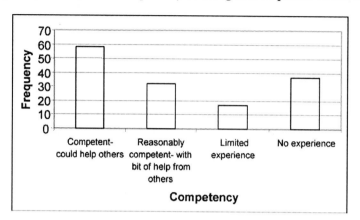

in Sri Lanka. The study reported in this paper is based on a detailed analysis of planning, teaching and evaluation that occurred during one of these lessons, one that focused on student use of mobile phone cameras. Prior to the participation of teachers and students in this study the researchers obtained permission officially from the Director of Education office (Central Province, Sri Lanka). Similarly, before participating in interviews and lesson observations consent forms were signed by all the relevant parties.

It was quickly identified that teachers recognized the potential of mobile phone camera for teaching and learning. For example, 143 out of the 152 teachers originally surveyed agreed with the statement 'I believe images/photographs facilitate science teaching and learning as they can bring information from the outside world to the classroom'. Further the teachers' competence in using mobile cameras, obtained from the survey and shown in Figure 1, indicated that, whilst teachers were unfamiliar with the use of the mobile phone for teaching activities, introducing the use of mobile phone camera to classroom teaching would be feasible.

From the survey, it was found that the teachers recognised the potential of using a camera in teaching and learning. However, only 9% of teachers had used a digital camera in their science teaching and learning. This may be due to the lack of availability of digital cameras in schools as the survey results showed that the availability of cameras in schools was only 3.9%. However, the high penetration of mobile phones in Sri Lanka (Figure 2) and high use by youngsters (first author's observation) suggest that students are well acquainted with mobile phone use. The teacher's ability to use the camera function of the mobile phone, students' ability to use mobile phones, and the availability of cheap phones suggested that it was worth exploring the use of the mobile phone camera for teaching and learning science in Sri Lanka.

METHODOLOGY

The methodological approach of this study is purely qualitative and carried out as a case study, which is used to investigate in detail the possible use of mobile phone cameras for science teaching and learning, in a sample science lesson. The lesson was designed during the professional development workshop described earlier and implemented in a Sri Lankan school. Eighteen teachers from different schools (of the Central Province) with varying levels of experience participated in the workshop. Of the 18 teachers, four directly contributed to this particular lesson development while the others provided critical input to refine the lesson. More

Figure 2. Mobile phone use as a percentage of 2008 estimated population Sources: Squares (Samarajiva, 2008), Diamonds (Telecoms, 2009)

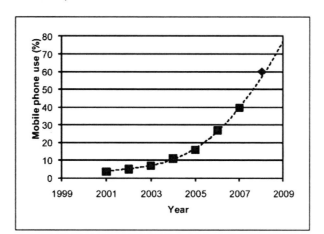

details on the workshop (planning and reviewing) can be found in Yatigammana Ekanayake (2009). One week after the planning workshop, the lesson was implemented with forty students in a girls' school. Prior to the lesson, all the students in the class were informed about the proposed research and their consent for video recording the lesson was obtained.

Even though the mobile phone is recognized as a ubiquitous device, which can support autonomous learning, a group activity had to be selected for this study mainly due to insufficient numbers of loaned mobile phones However, this provided opportunities for collaboration over the range of new learning activities offered by the use of the mobile phone cameras. This paper reports the observations made during the design and implementation stages of the lesson, the views of students selected at opportunity after the lesson and the teacher's views, which were collected during the second post-lesson professional development workshop.

The topic of the selected lesson was 'Investigating the mutual relationships between organisms and the environment - analysing the environment biologically' taken from the grade 11 science curriculum in Sri Lanka. The time duration of the lesson was 80 minutes. The lesson was implemented according to the following structure planned during the initial workshop.

- **Engagement:** First, the teacher asked two simple questions to test students' prior knowledge. Then a Photostory, which described the organisation levels of an ecosystem, was shown. This was to link the lesson with what the students had already learnt in the previous grades. After that, the teacher gave a briefing on the concepts of individual, population, community and ecosystem using the example pictures from the Photostory.

- **Lesson development:** There were four groups of students. Different roles, such as group leader, assistant leader, developer, assistant developers, writers and assistant writers were assigned to each member of the group. Each group was provided with two mobile phones and was assigned a specific location in the school garden. A file containing a worksheet and instructions was given to the group leaders. The teacher gave a briefing on the activity and reminded the groups of the responsibilities and role of each player and asked that the worksheet be completed during the allocated time period. Further, students were asked to capture five pictures to support their activity using the mobile phone camera. As groups, the students visited the four assigned places and were actively engaged in taking images and completing the worksheet while referring the pictures they captured (Figure 3).

After the allocated time students came back to the classroom and each group sent the 5 images taken from their assigned places to the teacher's computer using Bluetooth. Then each group presented their findings based on the worksheet while displaying to the class the pictures that they sent to the teacher's computer. After each presentation, the teacher gave a briefing reiterating the main points.

- **Evaluation:** Based on their completed worksheets and presentations the teacher assessed the students' learning in their groups.

Data Collection

The data for the above case study was collected using observations, interviews and field notes.

Observation was the main data collection method, which was used to gather students' and teacher's voices and activities as both video and audio data. Further, field notes were taken while acting as participant observer. Informal interviews were conducted with five students selected at random to probe more deeply about the lesson.

Data Analysis

The collected data was analysed using thematic analysis techniques with the support of NVivo8 qualitative data analysis software. First, field notes were transcribed and uploaded. Then the video and audio files were also uploaded, transcribed, and translated. After reading the transcribed field notes, viewing video files and listening to audio files a set of codes were derived and 'free nodes' were developed to represent these codes. The free nodes were planning, implementation, evaluation, participation, interactions, and achievement of goals. Next, using these 'free nodes', the transcribed files were sliced into meaningful segments. All the text segments in each free node were read again and the salient and common themes were identified. The two most salient themes were, 'mobile phone camera supported the teaching' and 'mobile phone camera supported student learning'.

Figure 3. Students engaged with the activity

FINDINGS AND DISCUSSION

The use of mobile phone cameras for the selected lesson supported both teaching and learning processes. From the two themes identified, the support of mobile phones for teaching will be discussed first and then the support for learning will be discussed.

The Mobile Phone Camera Supported Teaching

According to Shulman (1987) what the teacher does in the teaching process is to add different flavors to some form of text to develop students' knowledge, skill and attitudes. In this particular study, in a variation on the flavours described by Shulman (1987), the teacher used mobile phones during each of the three lesson stages.

Planning Stage of the Lesson

Good planning is essential for the success of a lesson (Parkinson, 2004). During the post lesson Reviewing Workshop the teacher reported using the mobile phone camera for two purposes during the planning stage of this lesson. One was to create a Photostory including images that represented the organisation levels of an ecosystem. He captured some images from the school garden and uploaded them to his computer to create the Photostory. In this instance the teacher used the mobile phone camera to represent the relevant scientific concept in an alternative way so as to make the desired representation for the students (Shulman, 1987).

The second purpose was using these images to create PowerPoint slides in order to assign the four locations of the school garden for the planned outdoor activities previously discussed. Each slide included three pictures (Figure 4) that were taken from one location of the school garden using the teacher's mobile phone camera. During the lesson implementation, the teacher asked the students to identify the location by viewing the slide and by asking questions. The use of these images clearly evoked an interest, even curiosity among the students.

These two observations revealed that the camera function of the mobile phone supported the teacher's pedagogical actions during lesson planning.

Lesson Implementation

During the lesson implementation we noticed that mobile phone camera supported the teacher in attracting students' attention towards the lesson which is crucial at the beginning of a lesson (Parkinson, 2005). The teacher did this by asking questions based on students' prior knowledge and while relating to students' familiar images included in the Photostory. The number of hands raised to answer the teacher's questions reflected the students' immediate engagement in the lesson.

After showing the Photostory and having a whole group discussion, the teacher integrated the mobile phone camera as a learning tool into the students' learning activity. As a consequence of this student centered instructional approach, the teacher could enhance students' active participation while providing them with opportunities to contribute to the lesson development. The teacher stated how his approach supported him to implement the lesson successfully as follows.

Actually, I have been teaching this lesson for five years. I have used the overhead projector and the multimedia projector to show photograph examples of different locations (captured by me or downloaded from the internet) based on my viewpoints. Sometimes these images are not familiar to students and therefore they were not fully engaged in the lesson. However, in this lesson students brought the images of mutual relationships from what they had observed, understood and experienced from the school environment. Therefore, it was easy to construct the lesson inside the classroom with active student participation.

Figure 4. Slide containing pictures from the same location in the school garden

Further, the teaching approach that was based on small group activities helped to make learning meaningful and effective by enhancing opportunities for student-student interactions and by increasing students' active participation. It is important to note that the teacher managed to plan the lesson this way due to the potential provided by the mobile phone camera.

Evaluation

Shulman (1987) proposed three aspects to the evaluation stage of teaching: checking for students' understanding during interactive teaching, testing student understanding at the end of lessons and evaluating one's own performance and adjusting for experience. Even though the teacher observed here did not use the mobile phone camera to check students' learning directly during interactive teaching, during the post lesson Review Workshop he explained the support of the mobile phone camera as he evaluated students' learning as follows:

During this lesson, I evaluate students learning as groups based on completed worksheet and group presentation. In terms of the group presentations, I considered the images they captured and sent to my computer. In this process, I considered the fact that the relevance of images reflects the students understanding of the concepts.

Mobile Phone Camera Supported Student Learning

In this lesson the teacher reported that students found more opportunities than usual in their science lessons to actively participate in their learning activity as the use of mobile phone cameras increased the range of group activities, the number of conversations amongst the group members, with the teacher and with technological devices, and the number of roles available to be assigned to students (for example during the learning activity two roles as photographer and assistant photographer were added to the group roles).

Figure 5. Student collaboration during the activity

At the beginning of the learning activity, each group tried to clarify the tasks assigned to them by reading and discussing the worksheet given to the group leader. During this process, there were conversations with one another (Figure 5) including asking questions about the activities and about the images that they should take. The ones who had understood the activity gave better explanations. In these ways, the conversations supported everyone in understanding the task and starting the activity as a group.

Next, students tried to identify the relationships seen amongst living organisms and the environment in their assigned location to obtain the most relevant photographs and to gather information to complete the worksheet. This was done by examining the environment individually or in pairs as assigned by the respective group leader. Once a member found something, it was shown to other group members and discussed.

Whilst there were different roles assigned to group members in terms of their responsibilities regarding the mobile phone use, each member of the group supported (while fulfilling their own responsibilities) selecting the best possible observation (image or video) to capture using their group's mobile phones. A student stated that

We did not gather in one place. We went all over the location to which we were assigned and tried to obtain information to complete the worksheet as well as to capture photographs of good examples to show the mutual relationships between organisms and the environment. My role was assistant writer. However as discussed earlier, I also tried to find the required information not only to complete the worksheet but also to find good examples. For example, I found a spider and its web on a leaf. I showed it to the developer and helped to capture that.

Student interactions relating to this, such as suggesting better options (e.g., showing good leaves, asking to zoom and changing the orientation) or through actions (removing other branches that covered the object required to be captured) were observed. The following excerpt provides evidence for these interactions.

Student 1: *I found a spider web under this leaf*

Student 2: *Can you see a spider too?*

Student 3: *mm..difficult to see*

Figure 6. Students completing the worksheet after the outside activity

Student 4: *Let me see. Ah I got it. spider is more towards the edge of the leaf. Can you see now?*

Student 2: *Yes.. I 'll take a picture*

Student 3: *Can't you zoom more? Because if we can get this picture with the spider, the web and the part of the leaf that would be ideal*

Student 2: *Yes I agree.. good idea*

In addition, during the learning activities, there were conversations to share students' technical skills and knowledge. The following dialogue shows how one student shared her experience:

Student 1: *Please remember to save the picture*

Student 2: *Yes, I think I saved it*

Student 1: *Are you sure?*

Student 3: *Press back button. Then it will be automatically saved*

After collecting the information they came to the classroom and completed the worksheets while referring to the pictures they had already taken (Figure 6). During this activity, the sharing of ideas

as well as arguing on certain points and coming to an agreement were a common observation. While completing the worksheet, the developer and assistant developer selected the images to be sent to the teacher's computer. They showed these images to the group to confirm whether the selected images supported their findings. Here, selecting the most relevant five images was seen as a collaborative process where there were conversations among group members. The selected images were sent to the teacher's computer using Bluetooth. The mobile phone images appeared to be acting as a shared platform supporting opportunities for conversational learning as described by Sharples (2003).

After completing the writing task during the allocated time, the group leader and assistant group leader of each group presented their findings to the class. While they were presenting they displayed the pictures that were already sent to the teacher's computer (which was connected to the multimedia projector) to the rest of the class to support their findings. During an informal interview after the lesson, one student said that she could easily understand other groups' presentations as they displayed the images while they were presenting their findings. After each presentation, the teacher briefed the students on the important points of the lesson while referring to the images in the presentation. Thus this learning environment provided an effective and meaningful learning experience by expanding learning beyond the four walls of the classroom, enabling interactions in the real world and bringing these new interactions back into the classroom as proposed by van't Hooft and Swan (2007).

It was found that the mobile phone camera enhanced the effectiveness of students' learning in four further ways: promoting their observational skills, creating opportunities for conversational learning, revision and enabling authentic learning activities. Considering the development of students' observational skills, the students reported that using the mobile phones had widened the opportunities to develop these key science skills (Hartnell-Young & Heym, 2008). One student said that they had to use "a different eye" (the researchers understood this as meaning she has to be watchful and carefully examine) to observe the environment in the process of capturing images of relationships between the organisms and the environment. She also said that this led her "to see unknown, interesting and amazing things" that are found in the environment. When the teacher probed the student asking, "what unknown and amazing things you saw", she explained as follows:

There was a pond in our assigned location. We were carefully trying to see what was happening there and captured a number of photographs. We saw there were tadpoles. They were eating a plant. While we were trying to get a good image, I saw 'kaneiiyan' (type of a fish) have built their habitat by drilling a hole into a plant. It was amazing. I showed it to the others.

Another student who participated in the lesson said that their teacher's effort to use mobile phones to capture the outside world as saved pictures in the mobile phone was timely because they could use a new technology in science learning. This is similar to the findings of a study reported by Sharples et al. (2007) where the students captured images using mobile phone cameras during a museum visit and send them to a server for later use in the classroom.

Further, she mentioned that if mobile phones are not used, they have to imagine the things when the teacher was describing them. In addition to this, another student who participated in the same lesson mentioned that due to the use of the mobile phone camera to capture the relevant images (of relationships between the organism and environment) they could see the school garden from a different viewpoint.

The teacher who conducted the lesson reported that the teacher-student and student–student conversations had increased as a consequence of the images taken by the mobile phone cameras. For example when students were engaging in learning activities, the student-student conversations increased as they were trying to select the best picture for their learning activity. During the Review Workshop, the teacher reported his views on the students' collaboration as follows:

…and after coming to the classroom I mean when the students were completing the worksheet, they all worked together. Before completing each section of the worksheet, they shared their ideas and decided what to write. Then the writer wrote them on the worksheet. Further, two students were busy with selecting photographs to be sent to the teacher's computer. Before sending them, they obtained the opinions of other members to select the best photographs.

Two types of student-teacher conversations were observed when the students used the mobile phone cameras during their learning activity. One example was when sending the information (that students had) to the teacher's computer prior to their presentation. The other common conversation was when getting the teacher's help to solve the problems that the students had encountered when they were using mobile phones in learning activities. For example, two students contacted the teacher due to the problem of insufficient memory on their phone. However, this did not affect the learning activity, as the teacher was quick to delete some previously saved video files (which were not related to this activity). Thus the images taken from the mobile phone camera again created a shared platform or 'conversational learning space' as postulated by O'Malley et al. (2005) around which learning conversations were taking place among students in a group, between them and the mobile devices, between groups and between teacher and students. Sharples (2003) adds that a mobile learning device can assist conversational learning by integrating learning descriptions across different locations and by holding the results of learning actions for later retrieval and reflection. The students also noted this with one reporting that as they had used mobile phone cameras during their lesson they could easily help absentees to understand the lesson they had missed as the observations had been captured. One student noted:

The captured images and filled worksheet would be good learning resources for absentees. They could look at them and ask questions from fellow students who could easily explain these to them.

During one presentation, a student expressed her view on the use of mobile phone camera as:

Today our science lesson was different. We used the mobile phone camera to capture images of the mutual relationships between organisms and the environment and brought the samples from the school garden into the classroom. This was a different experience. We could see the relationships in the real world. We studied them; we discussed about them and captured the relevant images. After that we completed the worksheet, discussed, and shared our ideas while referring to the pictures and finally we presented our findings to the other groups.

Students had various ideas in favour of the teaching approach, especially on the use of the mobile phone camera. For example, one student stated that

The field activity and the capturing of photographs using the mobile phone camera were very useful. This is different to what we learn from books. We could go to different places, look at examples of different relationships between the organisms and the environment, and capture them using the mobile phone camera. This was a different experience in contrast to the other lessons where we had to imagine certain things that the teacher showed/explained and what is given in a book. The possibility offered by the captured images to examine them in the classroom helped us to learn the relationships more effectively.

CONCLUSION

The findings of this case study suggest that the camera function of mobile phones offers a range of possible benefits for science teaching and learning in schools where opportunities arise for students to visit nearby locations. The use of the mobile phone camera helped the teacher's pedagogical practices relating to lesson planning, implementation and in assessing the students learning. However, it was found that teacher needs to adopt additional pedagogical practices to successfully implement the lesson such as selecting locations for the outside activities that are 'fit to be taught' and to familiarize themselves with common issues such as keeping the phones charged and deleting unwanted images to free up memory.

The use of the mobile phone camera not only provided a rationale for students to go into the field and capture the relevant images but was also reported as encouraging student participation, collaboration and understanding of concepts. In the observed lesson there was evidence for increased conversations among students apparently due to the shared platform provided by the images taken from the mobile phone camera thus supporting Sharples (2003) theory as to the importance of conversational learning theory in understanding mobile learning. The images not only added new flavours to the learning activity but also provided additional opportunities for student participation. Indeed the teacher reported students actively participated in this lesson when compared to the previous year where a different teaching approach was used. Both the teacher and students welcomed this approach and many students expressed positive comments on this learning activity.

Despite the fact that Sri Lankan students and teachers are not using mobile phones in an educational context, the data presented here shows a positive perception on their usefulness and underlines their value as an educational tool to support the educational process. The high penetration of mobile phones, teachers' ability to use their different functions and their cost effectiveness when compared to a still camera, emphasize the fact that the mobile phone camera can be a good choice to be considered in the teaching and learning of science in Sri Lankan schools.

Our findings derive from the use of mobile phone cameras in one science lesson that was carried out in one Sri Lankan school. Clearly, they are limited in their further generalisation due to the investigation of just one lesson in one school. We suggest that further studies in this area be undertaken. Further research could broaden our understanding of mobile learning opportunities and add to the number and type of effective mobile phone based lesson examples from a range of schools. It would also be valuable to investigate the effectiveness of the use of the mobile phone cameras in this science lesson by comparing this lesson with same lesson conducted using a more traditional approach.

ACKNOWLEDGMENT

The authors wish to thank Dialog GSM Company of Sri Lanka who provided mobile phones for this study. Further, the authors would like to thank the University of Peradeniya, Sri Lanka for supporting this activity, the Principal and staff of Pushpadane College, Sri Lanka for providing facilities to conduct this study and the teachers who designed and implemented the study. Further, the first author would like to thank Mr. Mahes Salgado for reading an early draft of the paper.

REFERENCES

Barton, R. (2004). *Teaching secondary science with ICT*. Buckingham, UK: Open University Press.

Botha, A., Vosloo, S., Kuner, J., & Berg, M. (2009). Improving cross-cultural awareness and communication through mobile technologies. *International Journal of Mobile and Blended Learning, 1*(2), 39–53. doi:10.4018/jmbl.2009040103

Chen, Y. S., Kao, T. C., Yu, G. J., & Sheu, J. P. (2004, March 23-25). A mobile butterfly-watching learning system for supporting independent learning. In *Proceedings of the 2nd IEEE international workshop on wireless and mobile technologies in education,* JungLi, Taiwan (pp. 11-18).

Cooney, G. Learnosity, & Keogh, K. A. (2007). *Use of mobile phones for language learning and assessment for learning, a pilot project*. Paper presented at the mLearn Conference, Melbourne, Australia.

Hartnell-Young, E. (2007). *Making the connections: theory and practice of mobile learning in schools*. Paper presented at the mLearn Conference, Melbourne, Australia.

Hartnell-Young, E., & Heym, N. (2008). *How mobile phones help learning in secondary schools.* Nottingham, UK: Learning Sciences Research Institute.

Kukulska-Hulme, A. (2005). Introduction. In Kukulska-Hulme, A., & Traxler, J. (Eds.), *Mobile learning: A handbook for educators and trainers* (1st ed., pp. 1–6). London, UK: Routledge.

Kukulska-Hulme, A., Sharples, M., Milrad, M., Arnedillo-Sánchez, I., & Vavoula, G. (2009). Innovation in mobile learning: A European perspective. *International Journal of Mobile and Blended Learning, 1*(1), 13–35. doi:10.4018/jmbl.2009010102

Laurillard, D. (2007). *Pedagogical forms for mobile learning: Framing research questions.* London, UK: WLE Centre.

MacCallum, K., & Kinshuk, K. (2006). *Mobile technology in facilitating learning goals.* Paper presented at the mLearn Conference, Banff, AB, Canada.

Marriott, M. (2005, July 4). Use this phone to find a date. Or see video. Or even talk. *New York Times.*

Naismith, L., Lonsdale, P., Vavoula, G., & Sharples, M. (2004). *Literature review in mobile technologies and learning.* Bristol, UK: Futurelab Series.

O'Malley, C., Vavoula, G., Glew, J. P., Taylor, J., Sharples, M., & Lefrere, P. (2005). *Pedagogical methodologies and paradigms: Guidelines for learning/ teaching/ tutoring in a mobile environment.* Bristol, UK: Futurelab Series.

Parkinson, J. (2004). *Improving secondary science teaching.* London, UK: Routledge. doi:10.4324/9780203464328

Parkinson, J. (2005). *Reflective teaching of science* (pp. 11–18). New York, NY: Continuum.

Parsons, D., Ryu, H., & Cranshaw, M. (2007). A design requirements framework for mobile learning environments. *Journal of Computers, 2*(4), 1–8. doi:10.4304/jcp.2.4.1-8

Power, T., & Thomas, R. (2006, September 6-9). *mLearning: The classroom in your pocket?* Paper presented at the BERA, Warwick.

Samarajiva, R. (2008). *Mobile penetration in Sri Lanka.* Retrieved from http://www.lirneasia.net/wp-content/uploads/2007/09/telecenternation-alalliance101.ppt

Scanlon, E., Jones, A., & Waycott, J. (2005). Mobile technologies: Prospects for their use in learning in informal science settings. *Journal of Interactive Media in Education, 25.*

Sharples, M. (2003). Disruptive devices: Mobile technology for conversational learning. *International Journal of Continuing Engineering Education and Lifelong Learning, 12*(5-6), 504–520.

Sharples, M., Lonsdale, P., Meek, J., Rudman, P., & Vavoula, G. (2007). *An evaluation of myartspace: A mobile learning service for school museum trips.* Paper presented at the mLearn Conference, Melbourne, Australia.

Shulman, L. (1987). Knowledge and teaching. *Harvard Educational Review, 57,* 1–22.

Taber, K. S. (2005). Conceptual development. In Alsop, S., Bencze, L., & Pedretti, E. (Eds.), *Analysing exemplary science teaching* (pp. 127–136). Buckingham, UK: Open University Press.

Telecoms, S. L. (2009). Sri Lanka - telecoms, mobile, broadband and forecasts. Retrieved from http://www.marketresearch.com/product/display.asp?productid=2508373&g=1

Traxler, J. (2010). *Education and the impact of mobiles and mobility an introduction to mobiles in our societies. Berlin, Germany: Springer-Verlag. van't Hooft, M., & Swan, K. (2007). Ubiquitous computing in education: Invisible technology, visible impact*. Mahwah, NJ: Lawrence Erlbaum.

Webb, M., & Cox, M. (2004). A review of pedagogy related to information and communications technology. *Technology, Pedagogy and Education, 13*(3), 235–286. doi:10.1080/14759390400200183

Wellington, J. (2004). Multimedia in science teaching. In Barton, R. (Ed.), *Teaching secondary science with ICT* (pp. 87–102). Buckingham, UK: Open University Press.

Wishart, J. (2007). *The seven 'c's - no, eight - no nine 'c's of m-learning*. Paper presented at the Kaleidoscope Alpine Rendez-Vous, Villars, Switzerland.

Yatigammana Ekanayake, T. M. S. (2009). *Mobile phones for teaching and learning science*. Retrieved from http://www.schoolnet.lk/research/mobile_phones_for_teaching_learning_science/

This work was previously published in the International Journal of Mobile and Blended Learning, Volume 3, Issue 2, edited by David Parsons, pp 16-30, copyright 2011 by IGI Publishing (an imprint of IGI Global).

Chapter 13
Exploring the Challenges of Supporting Collaborative Mobile Learning

Jalal Nouri
Stockholm University, Sweden

Johan Eliasson
Stockholm University, Sweden

Teresa Cerratto-Pargman
Stockholm University, Sweden

Robert Ramberg
Stockholm University, Sweden

ABSTRACT

Mobile technology opens up opportunities for collaborative learning in otherwise remote contexts outside the classroom. A successful realization of these opportunities relies, however, on mobile learning activities providing adequate collaboration structures. This article presents an empirical study aimed at examining the role played by mobile devices, teachers and task structures as a means for collaborative learning in geometry. The study focused on the analysis of the nature of collaboration that unfolded when students measured areas outdoors in the field. The analysis of the mobile learning activity was conducted from an Activity theory perspective. The findings obtained indicate that the collaboration observed may be impaired if: 1) the functionalities needed for collaborative problem-solving are asymmetrically distributed on a number of mobile devices; 2) task-related information is not accessible to all learners; 3) the task structure is not sufficiently complex; 4) teacher scaffolding is too readily available; and 5) necessary collaborative skills are not developed.

INTRODUCTION

Over the past decades, a large number of studies have demonstrated that collaboration can benefit learning from various theoretical and methodological perspectives. In fact, findings from over 1200 research studies have consolidated and refined theories of collaborative learning (Johnson & Johnson, 2009). Against this background, a strong consensus is asserting the higher achievement effects of collaborative learning on individual cognitive development as compared to individual-

DOI: 10.4018/978-1-4666-2139-8.ch013

istic learning and traditional instructional methods (Johnson & Johnson, 1985, 2009: Slavin, 1996). Along with previous and ongoing research, collaborative learning has also increasingly gained momentum in educational systems (Johnson & Johnson, 2009).

As a pedagogical technique, collaborative learning can be considered as an effective strategy to promote student achievement, higher order thinking, argumentation and explanation skills, autonomy, interdependence, retention, problem-solving, self-regulation, and use of metacognitive strategies (Mevarech & Kramarski, 2003; Nichols, 1996; Roseth, Johnson, & Johnson, 2008).

Since the foundation of the field of Computer supported collaborative learning (CSCL), a substantial body of research has also provided evidence on the positive effects of introducing technology into collaborative learning tasks. Several large meta-analyses indicate that participants who collaborate making use of information technology show greater increases in motivation, elaboration, dialogue and debate, higher-order thinking, self-regulation, meta-cognitive processes, and divergent thinking (Dillenbourg, Järvelä, & Fisher, 2009; Tutty & Klein, 2008). Furthermore, some of the CSCL environments developed have been proved to promote higher order social interaction and better learning in terms of deep understandings (Lehtinen, 2003).

With the emergence of the research field of mobile learning, the relevance of collaborative learning has increased even more, and that not exclusively because mobile technology can enhance collaboration (Pachler, 2010), but also because teacher availability may be an issue outside the classroom in outdoor mobile learning activities. In contexts where students are many and the distances larger than they are in ordinary classrooms, reducing teacher availability, the importance of effective collaborative scaffolding increases.

As a result of acknowledging the value of collaborative learning, the conceptual debates about the opportunities and affordances of mobile technology for collaboration have been both frequent and discussed in considerable depth (e.g., Pachler et al., 2010; Sharples, 2006; Winters & Price, 2005). Mobile technology is often presented as a means of stretching the affordances of human communication and collaboration and has repeatedly been claimed to provide greater opportunities to promote collaborative learning (Pachler et al., 2010; Sharples, Taylor, & Vavoula, 2007).

In line with this, several studies have utilized the opportunities for collaborative learning with mobile technologies, for instance those aimed at children in primary school, such as *Treasure Hunt* and *Ambient Wood* (Rogers & Price, 2009). In particular, Zurita and Nussbaum (2004) and Huizenga et al. (2009) have presented findings demonstrating higher achievement scores using mobile technology for collaborative learning when compared to traditional learning activities. Other researchers have presented findings showing that collaborative mobile learning can support student's development of collaboration skills (Cortez et al., 2009; Sanchez et al., 2009), and increase student motivation and engagement (Facer et al., 2004; Schwabe & Göth, 2005). Common to these studies, and mobile learning studies in general, is a strong focus on evaluating the learning *outcomes* and the effects of collaboration, with few studies analyzing the mediating learning *processes* (Sharples, 2009).

While the discussions about the opportunities of mobile technology are rich, collaboration has rarely been the main focus of analysis. This can be seen in the relatively limited documented empirical understanding about how we best design support for collaborative mobile learning (Stanton, 2002). Simply put, little is still understood about how we support the *processes* of collaboration and how we design the conditions necessary for fostering and promoting effective collaboration in mobile learning situations.

Effective collaboration is rarely a spontaneous phenomenon but rather the result of orchestration and scaffolding of productive interactions (Cerratto-Pargman, 2003; Dillenbourg & Schneider, 1995; Järvelä, 2007). The challenge for mobile learning research is thus to structure support for collaboration in contexts that are likely to be more dynamic, and in contexts that can change the conditions for social interactions by constraining the possibility to share knowledge and information (Winters & Price, 2005).

To meet this challenge and to contribute to the empirical understanding of collaborative mobile learning, we design and evaluate a mobile learning activity. The learning activity is aimed at a group of primary school students using mobile technology with the objective to collaboratively practice the mathematical concept of area in outdoor settings. In this specific context, we ask the question: *how does the mobile technology, the non-classroom context, and the activity system as a whole, affect the collaboration of the students?* And how do designers support collaboration for learning with mobile technology? The questions were examined within the context of an exploratory study, aiming at investigating the challenges of orchestrating and facilitating collaboration in mobile learning contexts.

The article presents a theoretical overview of collaborative learning and an analysis of a mobile learning activity from an activity theory perspective. In the analysis, we describe how the collaboration of the group of students was affected both by the mobile technology and other components of the designed activity, such as task structures and teachers. The article is structured as follows. First we define what we mean by collaborative learning and give an extended theoretical background. In the following two sections we describe the setup for the empirical study and describe how we use activity theory as a conceptual tool for analyzing the empirical data. We end by presenting and discussing the results of the study and identify particular challenges in designing for collaborative mobile learning.

Reconsidering the Concept of Collaboration

Although the concept of collaborative learning has a long and rich tradition with roots in developmental psychology theories (cf. Lév Vygotsky's *Social Development Theory* and Jean Piaget's theory of cognitive development) and as a pedagogical technique has been strongly emphasized in the last 15 years, researchers in the field have not yet agreed upon a consensus definition of collaborative learning (Dillenbourg, 1999).

The lack of consensus on what collaborative learning really means is in part the result of various disciplinary divisions that have contributed to the loss of a red thread in the study of collaborative activities, since the activity of collaboration arises as a research problem and not as a disciplinary object. Various interpretations are associated with the term of 'collaboration'. Some researchers define collaboration in a broad sense meaning that collaboration entails any activity that two or more individuals perform together, while others define it more specifically, distinguishing different forms of interactions. Furthermore, the notions of collaboration and cooperation are often used as synonymous terms causing problematic ambiguities.

Indeed, we believe the distinction between cooperation and collaboration is today important to make in a learning situation. While cooperation is distinguished as work that can be split between peers, i.e., individual work on sub-tasks, collaboration is characterized with a low division of labor and to a greater extent tasks that are performed together (Dillenbourg, 1999). Rogalski (1994), for instance, suggested that one may distinguish between cooperation and collaboration in relation to how goals (immediate goals, mid-term goals, long term goals) are shared by the individuals from the beginning to the achievement of a group task. Collaborating, in her terms, means individuals who share immediate, mid-term and long term goals in the achievement of a common task.

The definition of collaborative learning we have chosen to adopt in our work is the following, presented by Roschelle and Teasley (1989): *"a coordinated, synchronous activity that is the result of a continued attempt to construct and maintain a shared conception of a problem"*. Roschelle and Teasley (1989) distinguished between cooperation and collaboration by defining cooperation, as opposed to the aforementioned definition of collaboration, as *"an activity where each person is responsible for a portion of the problem solving"*. Fundamentally, the concept of collaboration is in our view related to social interaction forms and knowledge construction processes that theories of collaborative learning put forward (Lehtinen, 2003).

Collaborative Learning: Theoretical Foundation

Contemporary theories on collaborative learning, which are mainly derived from Piaget's cognitive development theory and Vygotsky's socio-cultural theory, view collaboration, as opposed to the aforementioned view on cooperation, as a mutual engagement between peers that predominately perform the tasks together (i.e., low division of labor). The underlying presumption is that social and synchronous interactions such as conflict, explanation, negotiation, mutual regulation, and co-construction of knowledge are means for effective learning to happen (Dillenbourg, 1999; Johnson & Johnson, 1985; Slavin, 1996).

The contribution of Vygotsky is based on the general and fundamental view that learning is a social phenomenon, and that development starts in the interpersonal plane, where cultural artifacts, both technological and symbolic tools, are shared through social interactions, and then internalized by the individual into the intrapersonal plane. Cognitive development is from his perspective essentially described as an ongoing dialogue between the individual and society (Laister, 2001). In this line of reasoning, engagement in collaborative activities is assumed to allow individuals to master concepts, and tools in general, they cannot do individually. For instance, Vygotsky's concept of the Zone of Proximal Development (ZPD) has been a key concept for the understanding of mechanisms in collaborative learning (Lehtinen, 2003). The Zone of Proximal Development (ZPD) is defined as *"the distance between the actual developmental level as determined by independent problem solving and the level of potential development as determined through problem solving under adult guidance or in collaboration with more capable peers"* (Vygotsky, 1978, p. 86). Put differently, the proposed claim with empirical support is that collaboration with a more capable peer can result in higher levels of cognitive development and understanding than what can be achieved by the individual alone (Slavin, 1996).

For Vygotsky social interaction precedes development; consciousness and cognition is the end product of socialization and social behavior. Social interaction plays a fundamental role in the process of cognitive development. In contrast to Piaget's understanding of child development (in which development necessarily precedes learning), Vygotsky suggested social learning precedes development. He stated that "Every function in the child's cultural development appears twice: first, on the social level, and later, on the individual level; first, between people (interpsychological) and then inside the child (intrapsychological)" (Vygotsky, 1978).

Piaget's (1926) contribution on the other hand is based on the conception that social-arbitrary knowledge - language, values, rules, morality and symbol systems - can only be learned in interactions with others (Slavin, 1996). The interaction between peers is also important in logical-mathematical thought in disequilibrating the child's egocentric conceptualizations and in the provision of feedback to the child about the validity of logical constructions (Lehtinen, 2003). Essentially, for Piaget, action and interaction plays a crucial role in the development of rationality and logical thinking.

Informed by Neo-Piagetian theories of cognitive development, the concepts of socio-cognitive conflict and the coordination of points of view (centrations), have especially offered a basis for research on collaborative learning (Lehtinen, 2003). The mechanism of socio-cognitive conflict which is seen to promote learning, functions when students on different levels of cognitive development, or students with differing perspectives, engage in social interactions that elicit the discrepancy between the viewpoints of two peers to the conscious mind (Dillenbourg, 1999). The mechanism of social cognitive conflict or "shock of our thought coming in contact with others" (Piaget, 1928, p. 204) may create a state of disequilibrium within the peers resulting in the construction of new conceptual understandings, and there is a great deal of research on peer interaction that indicates that cognitive conflicts emerging from social interactions do facilitate cognitive performances (Lehtinen, 2003).

Conditions for Collaborative Learning

While the documented effects of collaborative learning are many, research on the subject has repeatedly demonstrated that effective collaborative learning does not happen spontaneously without orchestration and scaffolding of productive interactions (Dillenbourg & Schneider, 1995; Järvelä, 2007). In other words, successful and effective collaboration requires that necessarily conditions are met. The literature review presented in the present article resulted in the identification of the following factors that are necessary to take account of in collaborative learning situations.

According to Dillenbourg, Järvelä, and Fisher (2009), three main categories of interactions that facilitate collaborative learning have been identified, namely: *explanation, argumentation/ negotiation* and *mutual regulation*.

Explanation, it is now well documented that providing an explanation improves the knowledge

of both the explainer himself and of the less knowledgeable peer (Dillenbourg & Schneider, 1995). This effect is known as the self-explanation effect.

Argumentation and negotiation relates to Piaget's concept of cognitive conflict. Argumentations can lead to disagreements and the verbalization of divergent views, which can't be ignored and which force the students to negotiate solutions and construct new conceptual understandings (Dillenbourg, 1999; Dillenbourg & Schneider, 1995; Lehtinen, 2003).

Scaffolding and mutual support refer to the emotional and conceptual support students can give each other in their attempts to co-construct knowledge. Mutual support also entails regulation and monitoring of partners' learning activities (Dillenbourg, 1999; Dillenbourg & Schneider, 2005).

Besides these categories of interactions, other factors have been identified as influencing productive interactions and effective collaboration, namely: *size and composition of the group, nature and complexity of the task, group rewards* and *positive interdependence* (Collazos et al., 2002; Dillenbourg & Schneider, 1995; Roshelle et al., 2010; Slavin, 1996).

Johnson and Johnson (1991) and Slavin (1990) have for instance shown the benefits of *symmetric* and *interdependent interactions* in learning. In particular, Johnson and Johnson (1991) provide evidence that interdependent interaction structures the relation between pairs, having a positive impact on learners' cognitive and social development.

More specifically, Johnson and Johnson (1991) distinguished the following skills as necessary for the emergence of true collaboration in learning: 1) *Communication skills*: a group needs to know how to communicate; 2) *Management skills*: a group needs to know how to lead and manage a group; 3) *Learning conflict resolution*: the flexibility of a group is measured in its ability to manage and resolve conflicts. This implies sharing, knowledge exchange, analyzing, criticizing, evaluating, denying, inferring, deducing, synthesizing and integrating information that can be organized in strategies for resolution, mediation, and negotiation of conflicts. Controversy facilitates the development of skills for problem solving, decentration and stimulates critical thinking; and 4) *Knowing how to build and maintain a spirit of trust*: trust becomes essential for a working group. The team members better express their opinions, reactions, feelings, information in a reassuring atmosphere. Sharing ideas, resources, and the establishment of a mutual trust is more difficult to establish in an uncertain context.

The notion of *symmetry* has been further developed by Dillenbourg (1999) who postulated three various forms of symmetry that characterize collaborative learning, namely *symmetry of action*, i.e., the extent to which same range of actions is allowed to each agent; *symmetry of knowledge*, i.e., the extent to which agents possess the same level of knowledge/ level of development, where a slight knowledge asymmetry among peers is generally considered as suitable; and *symmetry of status*, which is the extent to which agents have similar status with respect to their community.

Pléty (1996), working in the field of mathematics suggested that collaborative learning requires both work on content, and on management of learners' interdependent relationships. He also pointed out that the teacher plays a fundamental role during learners' development of reasoning strategies and learners' development of strategies for action. According to Pléty, a collaborative approach to learning must be analyzed both in terms of learners' conceptual development related to the educational activity at hand and also in relation to learners' management and maintenance of relationships within the team.

If the aim for mobile learning activities is to increase and optimize the probability that efficient collaboration occurs, we believe that the aforementioned conditions must be scaffolded and taken into account by designers and developers of mobile technology and mobile learning activities.

RESEARCH METHOD

In approaching the research questions we designed and implemented the learning activities, by adopting design practices from design-based research (Design-Based Research Collective, 2003). In particular, we relied on co-design (Penuel, Roschelle, & Shechtman, 2007) for the design iterations. By design practices we refer to working in iterative cycles together with teachers in creating a sketch and later a prototype that can be tested and eventually deployed in schools. The Design-Based Research Collective (2003) discusses design research in education and states that "[t]he challenge for design-based research is in flexibly developing research trajectories that meet our dual goals of refining locally valuable innovations and developing more globally usable knowledge for the field" (p. 7). The Design-Based Research Collective (2003) argues that design-based research blends empirical education research with the theory-driven design of learning contexts. Design-based research has proven a suitable methodological approach for the field of mobile learning, since design-based research attempts to combine the intentional design of learning activities with the empirical exploration of our understanding of the contexts for these learning activities and how they interact with the individuals (Hoadley, 2004). Design-based research follows an iterative cycle of identifying, developing, building and evaluating similar to that of interaction design processes.

Study Setup

We held three co-design workshops together with teachers in the months before the field activities. In the two iterations we designed tasks based on what mathematical concepts the students were currently working with. The outcome of these workshops led to a design of both the activity and the mobile devices.

In the first iteration the design team consisted of researchers from computer science and mathematics and practicing mathematics teachers from three local schools. The design activities of the first iteration were to visit potential outdoor settings and develop ideas into sketches together in the design team. The goals of the team were to get the students away from the desk, to make mathematics more tangible and to provide opportunities for the students to collaborate, discuss, and solve mathematics problems outside the classroom. Towards the end of the first design iteration researchers from human-computer interaction joined the design team.

In the second iteration the team consisted of three researchers from human computer interaction and learning, two researchers from computer science and two practicing natural sciences and mathematics teachers from one local school. The following design activities were to visit potential outdoor settings, design tasks for the outdoors activities and to work with paper prototypes. As part of the Outdoor Activity Introduction we also tested the hi-fi prototypes.

The study, which was part of The MULLE research project (Math edUcation and pLayful LEarning), was held in Sweden in the autumn of 2009 and aimed at fifth-grade primary school students practicing the area concept, playfully, across indoor and outdoor contexts, collaboratively, and with concrete content and physical manipulatives, mainly drawing on a socio-cultural perspective of learning (Vygotsky, 1978; Säljö, 1999). The students worked in two groups of three students each. Each group performed four sub-activities: two indoor introductory activities, an outdoor field activity, and an indoor debriefing activity.

The first activity in the study was the *familiarization with the devices*. The activity aimed at giving the students hands-on experience with the mobile devices used in the outdoor activity. Each child was given four tasks to complete on each of the two types of mobile phones we used, the primary device with a 9-key keypad (Nokia

N95) and the secondary device with touch screen (Nokia XpressMusic 5800, Figure 1). By solving the tasks, we observed the students had (1) successfully used the keypad to navigate the phone and that they had (2) managed to navigate two instances of tabbed interfaces present in the standard phone software interface.

The second activity in the study was the *familiarization with the outdoor activity*. It took place five days before the outdoor activity. The aim was to let students come prepared to the outdoor activity with experience of how the devices operated in the field and with a representation of the tasks. First a short film from the pilot trial was presented to show the students what the field studies look like. Then we introduced the scenario.

The scenario for the outdoor activity consisted of an imaginary, almost extinct, species needed to be relocated from the local wild animal park. The task for the students was to see to that the new enclosures for the animals had the right measurements. Measuring large enclosures required the students to use the mobile software application prototyped by our team. The application measures the distance between two mobile devices using GPS. Apart from measuring, the primary device presented students with tasks based on where they were located and where they were in the task structure. The primary device was also used for submitting answers and providing feedback, while the secondary device displayed clues.

The two student groups of three students in each group received the mobile devices to be used outside the school. After a short introduction they were told to follow the instructions on the primary device. The primary device told them to go to a meadow on the other side of the woods. On entering the small field, the primary device signaled that they were in the right location.

In the small field, the groups were introduced to the first task and asked to guess the area of two small rectangles marked by plastic cones. The rectangles had different length and width

Figure 1. The 'primary device' and the 'secondary device'

but were both 12 m². Each group had prepared one 1x1 meters cardboard square to measure the areas. After a completed task they would send the answer to receive a new task. When they had guessed and calculated the areas correctly they received a message on the primary device to go to the big field for the second task.

Methodological Framework for the Analysis of Collaboration

Activity Theory, more specifically Engeström's activity system model, was chosen for the analysis of the collaborative interactions observed in the study.

Activity theory can be used in different ways and for different purposes, and there is no standard method for putting Activity Theory ideas into practice (Kaptelinin & Nardi, 2006). One of the most powerful and frequently invoked uses of activity theory is nonetheless as a lens or orienting device to structure analysis of socio-cultural learning (Barab et al., 2004). The framework emphasizes the concept of activity, which is understood as the subject's purposeful interaction with the world, as the fundamental unit of analysis, and offers a set of

concepts that can be used in order to conceptualize a model of activity systems (Kaptelinin & Nardi, 2006), and in particular collaborative activities (Engeström, 1987; Nezamirad et al., 2005).

Inspired by Vygotsky (1978) and Leontiev (1978/1981), Engeström's activity system model depicts the constitutive components of tool-mediated and collaborative activities. Firstly, we adopted Engeström's activity system model because it takes into account these components that we believe are at the core of the present mobile learning activity. Secondly, the notion of division of labor put forward in the model stresses the collaborative aspect and provides a means for making a distinction between cooperative and collaborative processes (Nezamirad et al., 2005). This distinction is important to make when analyzing collaborative learning (Roshelle & Teasley, 1989). Thirdly, the hierarchical structure and dynamic transformation between activities, actions and operations facilitate analyzing collaborative activities and cooperative processes within them (Nezamirad et al., 2005). These three aspects offered by the model were central for the present study.

Figure 2. The activity system model (Engeström, 1987)

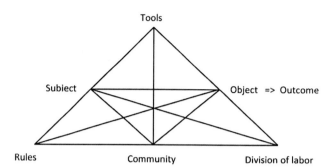

In the study here presented, we aimed to analyze the impact of the designed activity system on the collaboration of the participating learners. As such, Engeström's activity system model (Figure 2) has been used as a lens in order to highlight the components of the activity under analysis, components such as tools, rules and division of labor, which are assumed to mediate the activity and affect the collaboration. The analysis has been performed in three steps.

As a *first step*, the collected video data were mined for episodes where the collaboration of the students was weak. The episode selection criteria for weak collaboration were two-fold. Episodes were chosen by paying attention to: 1) low participation; and 2) poor communication conditions. For the low participation selection criteria, attention was focused on episodes in which group members were not at all, or to a minor extent, participating in the problem-solving, seen from both a conceptual and a physical/procedural level. As collaboration also requires good conditions for communication, attention was directed at episodes where the communication possibilities were constrained.

As a *second step* of the analysis procedure, questions were generated from the perspective of the components of Engeström's model. An example of such a question is: Can the tools used mediate this particular weak collaboration? In order to search for answers to these questions, the *third step* of the analysis comprised of going back to the collected data for further analysis, for instance, by directing the focus at the use of the tools and by paying attention to indicators of their possible influence on the collaboration.

The empirical data of this study were collected through audio- and video recordings. A microphone was attached to each child, and four researchers recorded the activities with cameras from both long and short distance. The total amount of video and audio data was approximately 6 hours.

RESULTS AND DISCUSSION

The intention behind the analysis was to investigate how the activity components affected the collaborative process. The results are presented through three representative episodes excerpted from the whole mobile learning activity observed. The first episode illustrated the activity engaged during the first task in which the task structure was an influential factor. The second episode described the impact of the mobile technology on learners' collaboration. The third episode described one of the group's collaborative efforts in the outdoor activity during all three tasks. Special emphasis was put on the influence of the teachers' interventions and absence of learners' collaborative skills. The analysis brought us to identify the following factors, namely: complexity of the task structure, the functions embedded in mobile technology, and the role of the teachers and learners' collaborative learning skills.

Figure 3. Activity model - task 1

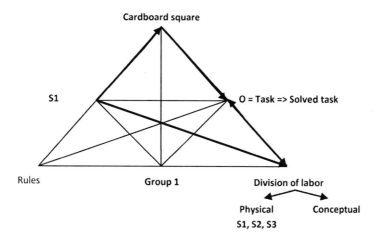

In the results section, the names of the participating students of group 1 are replaced with the codes S1, S2, S3, and for group 2, S4, S5, S6.

Complexity of the Task Structure

Considering at what level of complexity tasks for mobile learning activities are chosen and designed, we observed that it is fundamental to take account of what kind of division of labor the tasks bring into being in terms of student inclusion and exclusion in the learning processes. More specifically, questions like the following arise: how do we decompose complex tasks into subtasks and still promote positive interdependence? How do we support the specific categories of social interactions that successful collaboration requires (Dillenbourg, 1999) with mobile technology?

The observations of the first task performed revealed that the students had no significant difficulties solving it. Obstacles were certainly faced, but the problems and the students' conversations were to a large extent related to at times malfunctioning technology. From a conceptual learning perspective, we could observe that one of the students expressed a solution strategy. This strategy was subsequently executed with physical effort by the group members, primarily without negotiation and explicit reflection within the group. As such, the collaboration process during this part of the outdoor activity could be characterized as strong *cooperative* work on a physical/procedural level, and weaker, or non-existent, *collaborative* thinking on a conceptual level. Considering that the task was quite effortlessly completed, we think, in line with earlier research (Arvaja et al., 2000; Collazos et al., 2002) that a less complex task structure may have mediated a division of physical labor and have inhibited a need for discussions and collaboration on a conceptual level (Figure 3).

Consequently, serious attention has to be put on the design of the learning tasks, if (1) the ultimate learning objective for an activity is concept development and effective collaborative learning, which it was in this case, and (2) social interactions such as explanation, argumentation/negotiation, and mutual regulation, are assumed to facilitate the process of concept development (Dillenbourg, Järvelä, & Fisher, 2009; Johnson & Johnson, 1991: Slavin, 1990). Indeed, the tasks must be complex enough to simultaneously encourage interdependence and collaboration on both procedural and conceptual levels.

Figure 4. Activity model - task 2 and 3

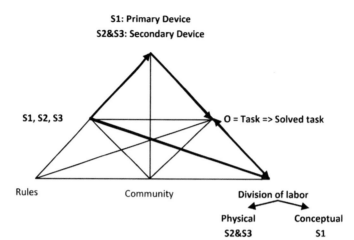

Functions Embedded in the Mobile Technology

The distribution of the devices and the functionalities offered had serious consequences for the collaboration observed. For instance, the last two tasks involved areas of rectangles of a much larger size than in the first task, which meant that larger distances and sides of the areas were to be measured. This required more use of the mobile devices and, in particular, the GPS distance measurement functionality. The measurements of the sides of the rectangles were performed as follows: one of the students placed herself at one of the ends of the sides with the primary device while the other two students placed themselves at the other end of the same rectangle side with the secondary device. With the primary device, the students could receive task instructions, send in and receive answers, obtain feedback, and start and redo measurements. The secondary device contained clues and its geographic coordinates were identified during the measurements. The distance between the two devices was further presented on the primary device.

During the last two tasks, we observed that the child with the primary device was the most dominating group member. S/he defined strategies,

did adjustments and directed the others through the tasks. This was the case in both participating groups. After an analysis of the last two tasks performed, we inferred that the tools used in the activity as well as their distribution structured a division of the students' labor on two levels, a conceptual and a physical/procedural level (Figure 4).

From a learning perspective, the student with the primary device in possession (S1) was to a large extent the only one working on a conceptual level and consequently she had more possibilities to learn on a conceptual level. By being the only one receiving the distance results on her device, while S2 and S3 were not in communication distance from her, she was also the one being most aware of the task progress, of eventual need for adjustments, choice of goals and actions or change of strategies. When adjustments were needed S1 signaled to the others what they should do and where they should go. S1 was connected to the learning process to a much higher degree than the others who, having only the secondary device in their possession, were in a sense obeying her instructions and carrying out the ordered physical labor and basic operations.

Collaboration on a conceptual level, and learning for all group members, was thus, among other factors, inhibited as a consequence of the large distances between the students, the restricted communication possibilities, and the unbalanced distribution of tools and tool functionalities. The result of this unbalance of learning interaction crystallized an undesirable asymmetry of action, knowledge and status (Dillenbourg, 1999) between the students observed, and a division of labor and interdependence characterized by what we understand as cooperation rather than collaboration (Rochelle & Teasley, 1989). Essentially, the design of the technology, i.e., the hierarchy attributed to the devices (primary and secondary device), did not afford a symmetric and interdependent interaction that enabled the learners to verbalize divergent views, negotiate solutions and construct new conceptual understandings, which is significant for collaborative learning to be beneficial for cognitive and social development (Johnson & Johnson, 1991; Slavin, 1990). Put differently, what we could not achieve was the participation of the students in what Roshelle and Teasley (1989) described as the "Joint Problem Space", consisting of agreed goals, actions, and descriptions of the current problem state.

One of the lessons learned from the study was that all functions needed for the conceptual and procedural learning processes should be made accessible for all of the participating students and distributed symmetrically if there are several devices. In addition, all students should have access to task-related information to be able to monitor the task progress.

Furthermore, if the outdoor task creates large distances between the learners, it is important to allow learners to use the communication capacity of the mobile devices. Communication at distance would enable them to maintain some degree of symmetrical knowledge, task awareness and a joint problem space, through sharing information, providing explanations, negotiating and adjusting goals and actions. Naturally, face-to-face interactions should be encouraged and supported to the extent possible.

Role of the Teachers and Learners' Collaborative Skills

While teachers certainly can play an important role in providing scaffolding and regulating collaborative processes in mobile learning activities (Nouri et al., 2010), for example by promoting the inclusion of excluded group members, in this study it became evident that teachers can hamper the collaboration as well. If teacher scaffolding is too readily available, or unequally distributed amongst group members, thus diminishing the need for collaborative scaffolding, the symmetry of action, knowledge, and status between the students can be affected negatively.

For instance, while the students of the first group were all engaged and active during the whole activity, two of the students in the second group (S5 and S6) became increasingly passive and unengaged as the activity progressed. In addition, we could observe that this group had more contact with the teachers than the first group, and that S4 in particular, which was the dominating child in group 2, received the most help. Moreover, we observed that S5 was insulted by S6 on several occasions when asking questions.

The reasons behind the fact that two of the students became increasingly passive could have been many. In either case, two possible contributing factors have been identified, namely: an increasing interdependency between some of the students and the teacher, and the lack of adequate collaborative skills. We believe that the exclusion of S5 and S6, to some extent, was enabled by the teachers constantly meeting the information needs of S4 instead of directing her to the group and thereby encourage collaborative problem-solving (Figure 5).

The insults on the other hand emphasized the lack of collaborative skills, i.e., the ability to maintain mutual trust and a reassuring atmosphere (Johnson & Johnson, 1991), and a lack of social- and collaboration rules, which we in this case as

Figure 5. Activity model – whole activity

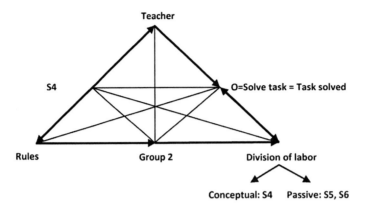

the designers of the activity did not provide. In addition, more attention should have been put on the formation of the groups, taking the individuals cognitive and knowledge levels into consideration.

CONCLUSION

It is claimed that mobile technology has the power to enhance collaboration (Pachler, 2010). It is also claimed that tools change the nature of learning (Kaptelinin & Nardi, 2006; Traxler, 2007), that new m-learning contexts can change the conditions for social interactions (Winters & Price, 2005), and that successful collaboration needs orchestration and scaffolding of productive interactions (Cerratto-Pargman, 2003; Dillenbourg & Schneider, 1995; Järvelä, 2007). The results of this study can confirm almost all of these claims except for the first one. Mobile technology may have, and we believe that it most likely does have, the capacity to promote collaboration within learning activities. However, the findings of this study indicate that the incorporation of mobile technology into a mobile geometry activity, if not designed properly, can strongly constrain the possibilities for collaboration and learning.

In this study, we observed that the hierarchy of functions embedded into the devices (primary and secondary device), and the asymmetrically distributed task-related information, influenced drastically the dynamics and quality of learning of the group of learners. The analysis made it evident that the distribution of devices and functionalities within them predetermined the roles of the students within each group, their division of labor, and thus the learning processes they had access to.

Thus, the findings of the study strongly indicate that it is fundamental, on the one hand, to carefully examine what type of learning and collaborative opportunities mobile technology will be able to open up so that collaborative mobile learning activities can be planned accordingly. On the other hand, it is crucial to negotiate with designers and developers the technical configuration of devices and functionality that predetermines the dynamics of learners' collaboration. Essentially, it is important that we ask ourselves how we empower the learners with the configuration and the distribution of the mobile technology and what that entails in terms of accessibility to essential learning processes.

Furthermore, we found that the design of the learning task and its structure, the role played by teachers, the absence of social rules and collaborative skills in the learning team, also constituted factors that have a great impact on collaborative interactions.

Curiously, all of these aspects have so far been overlooked in the field of mobile learning and are most definitely a subject for future work.

Regarding the use of Activity Theory and in particular the Activity System Model, we view the analysis tool as providing a good starting point for understanding the collaboration process in mobile learning activities. As a tool, and a lens, it was able to: 1) highlight relevant aspects of the activity, such as the tools and division of labor; 2) aid the generation of questions for further inquiry; and 3) provide concepts and a language that facilitated both the analysis and its presentation.

In conclusion, this study has shown that the success of collaborative learning depends to a great extent on the character of the resources at hand that mediate the interaction of students. This article has explored some of the challenges associated with collaboration in outdoor mobile learning activities. The complexity of the task and the functionality embedded in the mobile devices, as well as role of the teachers and learners' collaborative skills, were identified as main factors having a major impact on mobile collaborative learning activities. By empirically exploring contextual features of a mobile learning activity, and analyzing them in the light of theories of collaborative learning, our aim was to better understand how we can come closer to designing, orchestrating and aligning the mobile learning resources at hand so that the conditions for truly collaborative learning can be met.

ACKNOWLEDGMENT

We would like to thank the students and teachers participating from Rösjöskolan outside of Stockholm, Sweden, and the CeLeKT research group, Linnaeus University in Växjö, Sweden, for technical collaboration.

REFERENCES

Arvaja, M., Häkkinen, P., Eteläpelto, A., & Rasku-Puttonen, H. (2000). Collaborative processes during report writing of a science learning project: The nature of discourse as a function of task requirements. *European Journal of Psychology of Education*, *15*, 455–466. doi:10.1007/BF03172987

Barab, S., Evans, M. A., & Baek, E.-O. (2004). Activity theory as a lens for characterizing the participatory unit. In Jonassen, D. (Ed.), *Handbook for educational communications and technology* (pp. 199–214). Mahwah, NJ: Lawrence Erlbaum.

Cerratto Pargman, T. (2003). Collaborating with writing tools: An instrumental perspective on the problem of computer support for collaborative activities. *Interacting with Computers: The Interdisciplinary Journal of Human-Computer Interaction*, *15*, 737–757.

Collazos, C., Guerrero, L., Pino, J., & Ochoa, S. (2002). Evaluating collaborative learning processes. In J. M. Haake & J. A. Pino (Eds.), *Proceedings of the 8th International Workshop on Groupware*, La Serena, Chile (LNCS 2440, pp. 203-221).

Cortez, C., Nussbaum, M., Woywood, G., & Aravena, R. (2009). Learning to collaborate by collaborating: A face-to-face collaborative activity for measuring and learning basics about teamwork. *Journal of Computer Assisted Learning*, *25*(2), 126–142. doi:10.1111/j.1365-2729.2008.00298.x

Design-Based Research Collective. (2003). Design-based research: An emerging paradigm for educational inquiry. *Educational Researcher*, *32*(1), 5–8. doi:10.3102/0013189X032001005

Dillenbourg, P. (1999). What do you mean by collaborative learning? In Dillenbourg, P. (Ed.), *Collaborative-learning: Cognitive and computational approaches* (pp. 1–19). Oxford, UK: Elsevier.

Dillenbourg, P., Järvelä, S., & Fischer, F. (2009). The evolution of research in computer-supported collaborative learning: From design to orchestration. In Balacheff, N., Ludvigsen, S., de Jong, T., Lazonder, A., & Barnes, S. (Eds.), *Technology-enhanced learning*. New York, NY: Springer. doi:10.1007/978-1-4020-9827-7_1

Dillenbourg, P., & Schneider, D. (1995). Mediating the mechanisms which make collaborative learning sometimes effective. *International Journal of Educational Telecommunications, 1*(2-3), 131–146.

Engeström, Y. (1987). *Learning by expanding: An activity-theoretical approach to developmental research*. Helsinki, Finland: Orienta-Konultit.

Facer, K., Joiner, R., Stanton, D., Reid, J., Hull, R., & Kirk, D. (2004). Savannah: Mobile gaming and learning? *Journal of Computer Assisted Learning, 20*, 399–409. doi:10.1111/j.1365-2729.2004.00105.x

Hoadley, C. M. (2004). Methodological alignment in design-based research. *Educational Psychologist, 39*(4), 203–212. doi:10.1207/s15326985ep3904_2

Huizenga, J., Admiraal, W., Akkerman, S., & Dam, G. (2009). Mobile game-based learning in secondary education: Engagement, motivation and learning in a mobile city game. *Journal of Computer Assisted Learning, 25*(4), 332–344. doi:10.1111/j.1365-2729.2009.00316.x

Järväla, S., Laru, J., & Näykki, P. (2007). How people collaborate to learn in different contexts scaffolded by the mobile tools. In *Proceedings of the Beyond Mobile Learning Workshop*.

Johnson, D. W., & Johnson, R. T. (1985). The internal dynamics of cooperative learning groups. In Slavin, R., Sharan, S., Kagan, S., Hertz-Lazarowitz, R., Webb, C., & Schmuck, R. (Eds.), *Learning to cooperate, cooperating to learn* (pp. 103–124). New York, NY: Plenum.

Johnson, D. W., & Johnson, R. T. (1991). *Learning together and alone: Cooperative, competitive, and individualistic* (3rd ed.). Upper Saddle River, NJ: Prentice Hall.

Johnson, D. W., & Johnson, R. T. (2009). An educational psychology success story: Social interdependence theory and cooperative learning. *Educational Researcher, 38*, 365–379. doi:10.3102/0013189X09339057

Kaptelinin, V., & Nardi, B. (2006). *Acting with technology: Activity theory and interaction design*. Cambridge, MA: MIT Press.

Laister, J., & Koubek, A. (2001, September 26-28). 3rd generation learning platforms requirements and motivation for collaborative learning. In *Proceedings of the 4th International Workshop on Interactive Computer Aided Learning*.

Lehtinen, E. (2003). Computer supported collaborative learning: An approach to powerful learning environments. In De Corte, E., Verschaffel, L., Entwistle, N., & van Merriëboer, J. (Eds.), *Basic components and dimensions of powerful learning environments*. New York, NY: Pergamon Press.

Mevarech, Z. R., & Kramarski, B. (2003). The effects of metacognitive training versus worked-out examples on students' mathematical reasoning. *The British Journal of Educational Psychology, 73*, 449–471. doi:10.1348/000709903322591181

Nezamirad, K., Higgins, P., & Dunstall, S. (2005). Cognitive analysis of collaboration as an activity. In *Proceedings of the Annual Conference of the European Association of Cognitive Ergonomics* (pp. 131-38).

Nichols, J. D. (1996). The effects of cooperative learning on student achievement and motivation in a high school geometry class. *Contemporary Educational Psychology, 21*, 467–476. doi:10.1006/ceps.1996.0031

Nouri, J., Eliasson, J., Rutz, F., & Ramberg, R. (2010). Exploring mediums of pedagogical support in an across contexts mobile learning activity. In M. Wolpers, P. Kirschner, M. Scheffel, S. Lindstaedt, & V. Dimitrova (Eds.), *Proceedings of the International Conference Sustaining TEL: From Innovation to Learning and Practice* (LNCS 6383, pp. 414-419).

Pachler, N., Bachmair, B., Cook, J., & Kress, G. (2010). *Mobile learning: Structure, agency, practices*. New York, NY: Springer.

Penuel, W. R., Roschelle, J., & Shechtman, N. (2007). Designing formative assessment software with teachers: An analysis of the co-design process. *Research and Practice in Technology Enhanced Learning, 2*(1), 51–74. doi:10.1142/S1793206807000300

Piaget, J. (1928). *Judgment and reasoning in the child*. London, UK: Routledge & Kegan Paul. doi:10.4324/9780203207260

Pléty, R. (1996). *Cooperative learning*. Lyon, France: Presses Universitaires de Lyon.

Rogalski, J. (1994). Formation aux activites collectives. *Le Travail Humain, 54*(4), 425–443.

Rogers, Y., & Price, S. (2009). How mobile technologies are changing the way children learn. In Druin, A. (Ed.), *Mobile technology for children* (pp. 3–22). San Francisco, CA: Morgan Kaufmann. doi:10.1016/B978-0-12-374900-0.00001-6

Roschelle, J., Rafanan, K., Estrella, G., Nussbaum, M., & Claro, S. (2010). From handheld collaborative tool to effective classroom module: Embedding CSCL in a broader design framework. *Computers & Education, 55*, 1018–1026. doi:10.1016/j.compedu.2010.04.012

Roschelle, J., & Teasley, S. D. (1989). The construction of shared knowledge in collaborative problem solving. *Knowledge Creation Diffusion Utilization, 128*(3), 69–97.

Roseth, C. J., Johnson, D. W., & Johnson, R. T. (2008). Promoting early adolescents' achievement and peer relationships: The effects of cooperative, competitive, and individualistic goal structures. *Psychological Bulletin, 134*, 223–246. doi:10.1037/0033-2909.134.2.223

Säljö, R. (1999). Learning as the use of tools: A socio-cultural perspective on the human-technology link. In Littleton, K., & Light, P. (Eds.), *Learning with computers analysing productive interaction*. London, UK: Routledge.

Sanchez, J., Mendoza, C., & Salinas, A. (2009). Mobile serious games for collaborative problem solving. *Studies in Health Technology and Informatics, 144*, 193–197.

Schwabe, G., & Göth, C. (2005). Mobile learning with a mobile game: Design and motivational effects. *Journal of Computer Assisted Learning, 21*, 204. doi:10.1111/j.1365-2729.2005.00128.x

Sharples, M. (Ed.). (2006). *Big issues in mobile learning: Report of a workshop by the Kaleidoscope Network of Excellence Mobile Learning Initiative*. Nottingham, UK: LSRI, University of Nottingham.

Sharples, M., Taylor, J., & Vavoula, G. (2007). A theory of learning for the mobile age. In Andrews, R., & Haythornthwaite, C. (Eds.), *The handbook of e-learning research* (pp. 221–247). London, UK: Sage.

Slavin, R. E. (1990). Point-counterpoint: Ability grouping, cooperative learning and the gifted. *Journal for the Education of the Gifted, 14*(3), 3–8.

Slavin, R. E. (1996). Research on cooperative learning and achievement: What we know, what we need to know. *Contemporary Educational Psychology, 21*, 43–69. doi:10.1006/ceps.1996.0004

Stanton, D., & Neale, H. (2002). *Designing mobile technologies to support collaboration*. Retrieved from http://www.techkwondo.com/external/pdf/reports/2002-stanton-2.pdf

Traxler, J., Smith, T. F., & Waterman, M. S. (2007). Defining, discussing and evaluating mobile learning: The moving finger writes and having writ. *International Review of Research in Open and Distance Learning, 8*(2).

Tutty, J., & Klein, J. (2008). Computer-mediated instruction: A comparison of online and face-to-face collaboration. *Educational Technology Research and Development, 56*, 101–124. doi:10.1007/s11423-007-9050-9

Vygotsky, L. S. (1978). *Mind in society*. Cambridge, MA: Harvard University Press.

Winters, N., & Price, S. (2005). Mobile HCI and the learning context: An exploration. In *Proceedings of the International Workshop on Context in Mobile HCI*, Salzburg, Germany.

Zurita, G., & Nussbaum, M. (2004). A constructivist mobile learning environment supported by a wireless handheld network. *Journal of Computer Assisted Learning, 20*(4). doi:10.1111/j.1365-2729.2004.00089.x

This work was previously published in the International Journal of Mobile and Blended Learning, Volume 3, Issue 4, edited by David Parsons, pp 54-69, copyright 2011 by IGI Publishing (an imprint of IGI Global).

Section 4
Evaluating Mobile Learning Interventions

Chapter 14
Reflections on 4 Years of mLearning Implementation (2007–2010)

Thomas Cochrane
Unitec, New Zealand

ABSTRACT

This paper provides a comparative analysis of five mlearning case studies involving 4 years of action research mlearning projects. The projects investigated the potential of mobile web 2.0 tools to facilitate social constructivist learning environments across multiple learning contexts. Highlighted are the design framework, identified critical success factors, and implementation strategy developed from the thirteen mlearning projects undertaken between 2007 and 2009, with an analysis of the eight 2009 projects and their subsequent adaptation in 2010. The projects illustrate the impact of mlearning supported by sustained interaction via communities of practice facilitating pedagogical shifts from teacher-directed to student-generated content and student-generated contexts.

INTRODUCTION

The researcher has been primarily interested in transforming traditional teacher-directed pedagogy into social constructivist learning paradigms facilitated by mobile web 2.0. What began as an investigation of the affordances of web 2.0 in 2007 developed into three mobile web 2.0 proof of concept projects within the third year of the Bachelor of Product Design in 2008, the Diploma of Contemporary Music, and the Diploma of Landscape Design. These then quickly spread to projects within the first and second year of the Bachelor of Product Design programme in semester2 of 2008. The success of these projects led to the implementation of integrating mobile

DOI: 10.4018/978-1-4666-2139-8.ch014

web 2.0 technologies (based on an explicit social constructivist pedagogy) across all three years of the programme in 2009, and on wider scales into larger courses such as the Bachelor of Performing and Screen Arts, and the second year of the Bachelor of Architecture. Figure 1 illustrates the growth of the mlearning (wireless mobile devices or WMDs) projects at Unitec from 2006 to 2010, beginning with the two trial projects used to test the research instruments in 2006.

Mobile Web 2.0

MLearning (Mobile learning) technologies provide the ability to engage in learning conversations between students and lecturers, between student peers, students and subject experts, and students and authentic environments within any context. It is the potential for mobile learning to bridge pedagogically designed learning contexts (Laurillard, 2007), facilitate learner generated contexts, and content (both personal and collaborative), while providing personalisation and ubiquitous social connectedness, that sets it apart from more traditional learning environments such as fixed classrooms and computer labs. Non-wireless devices cannot bridge communication and share user generated content across multiple contexts with the ease and immediacy afforded by wireless mobile devices. Mobile learning, as defined in this paper, involves the use of wireless enabled mobile digital devices (Wireless Mobile Devices

Figure 1. Mlearning Projects 2006 to 2010

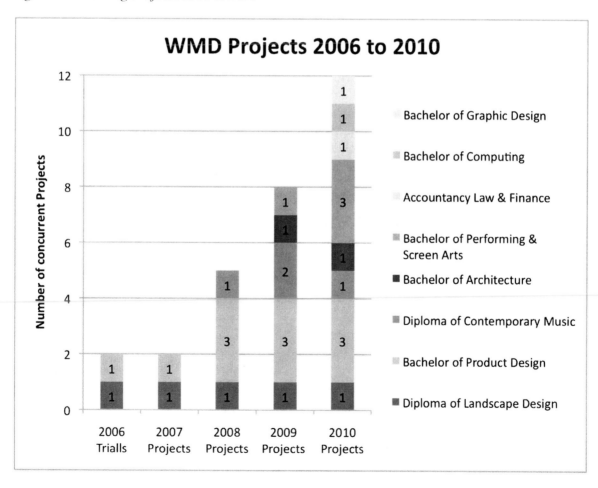

or WMD's) within and between pedagogically designed learning environments or contexts. Mobile Web 2.0 tools (web 2.0 services that are formatted for use with mobile devices) were used to enable student-generated content and student-generated contexts. Web 2.0 (O'Reilly, 2005), or 'social software' tools, share many synergies with social constructivist learning pedagogies. Many educators have harnessed web 2.0 tools for creating engaging student-centred learning environments. This appropriation of web 2.0 tools within a social constructivist pedagogy facilitates what has been termed "pedagogy 2.0" (McLoughlin & Lee, 2008a). From an activity theory perspective, WMD's are the tools that mediate a wide range of learning activities and facilitate collaborative learning environments (Uden, 2007).

Research Methodology

Participatory action research (McLoughlin & Lee, 2007; Wadsworth, 1998) was used as the methodology for this research, allowing the researcher to take on the key role of the 'technology steward' (Wenger, White, & Smith, 2009; Wenger, White, Smith, & Rowe, 2005) to guide the projects as well as receive and act upon direct participant feedback, reflection, critique and modification of the projects throughout the length of the research. The researcher has thus created an inter-related feedback loop between all of the mlearning projects across a variety of disciplines and contexts, channeling findings and reflections between each project.

The research questions were:

- What are the key factors in integrating Wireless Mobile Devices (WMDs) within tertiary education courses?
- What challenges/advantages to established pedagogies do these disruptive technologies present?
- To what extent can these WMDs be utilized to support learner interactivity, collaboration, communication, reflection and interest, and thus provide pedagogically rich learning environments that engage and motivate the learner?
- To what extent can WMDs be used to harness the potential of current and emerging social constructivist e-learning tools?

The research was qualitative, and was interested in bringing about positive change for the professional development of lecturers, and educational engagement of students within the researcher's institution. The data collection instruments were thus focused upon qualitative reflection and feedback from the participants. However a mix of quantitative survey questions were also used to provide multimode triangulation data (Sharples, 2009; Vavoula, Pachler, & Kukulska-Hulme, 2009) on the impact of the mlearning interventions on the participants' teaching and learning experiences. All of the data collection and guideline instruments were pre-tested and modified via two pre trials at Unitec during 2006, and updated as necessary during the subsequent projects.

The core data gathering tools used in this research consisted of:

1. Pre-project surveys of lecturers and students, to establish current practice, expertise and experience.
2. Post-project surveys and focus groups, to measure the impact of the wireless mobile computing environment, and identify emergent themes.
3. Lecturer and student reflections via their own blogs and eportfolios during the project, collated via RSS feeds. The research used the technologies that were an integral part of the projects, such as participant blog posts, peer blog comments, and VODCast reflections to capture data on the progression and impact of mobile web 2.0 on the participants' learning experience.

Implementation Model

The mobile web 2.0 projects implementation methodologies used a model of providing a common smartphone for the students within a course. The students and staff involved were encouraged to use the smartphones as if they owned them for the period of the trials. This approach was used to seed the concept and provide proof of concept results. Following the enthusiastic response from the students and lecturers involved in these trials, internal institutional funding was sought, and approved, for extending the initially small projects to larger-scale mlearning projects in 2009 involving the use of 250 smartphones, and 200 netbooks, followed by 450 smartphones and 400 netbooks in 2010. These larger scale projects were informed by the experiences of the previous projects and covered a wider range of courses and learning contexts. However, to create a sustainable model, the goal going forward into 2011 is to move to a student-owned model. As the cost of appropriate smartphones and 3G data costs drop, and with the rise of cost-effective netbooks and tablets such as the iPad student ownership of these devices is rising rapidly.

Pedagogical and Technical Support Model

A lot of mlearning and web 2.0 educational research has been put into the area of pedagogical integration, but there has been relatively little focus on the aspects of technological and pedagogical support, and little on the significant time frames required for teaching and learning reconceptualisations. The rapid development of mobile devices requires continual changes in technological and pedagogical support for mlearning. As a result, notwithstanding several notable exceptions (for example MoLeNET), most mlearning projects are short-term projects and tend not to look at the longitudinal impact of mlearning.

Two of the defining characteristics of the mlearning research reflected upon in this paper include:

1. The matching of the unique affordances of mobile web 2.0 with social constructivist pedagogy.
2. The explicit scaffolding of the required ontological shifts in pedagogical transformation via a structured and sustained intentional community of practice model over a significant period of time.

An intentional Community Of Practice model (Langelier, 2005) was used to guide and support the mlearning roll-out to achieve integration of the mobile web 2.0 technologies into lecturers' daily workflow and integration into course activities and assessment, establishing a collaborative learning environment. This comprised weekly professional development "technology sessions" (Community of Practice) with small groups of lecturers in a variety of departments facilitated by an appropriate 'technology steward' (Wenger et al., 2005). The same model was then used with the students and their lecturers in implementing mlearning within their courses. The concept of intentional communities of practice has found many applications, often forming juxtaposition between the organic nature of COPs and a specific foundational goal. For example, Head and Drakers (2005) argue for the use of intentional COPs to form the basis for a new approach to technology education. The concept of intentional communities of practice is similar to semi-formal learning communities (Kukulska-Hulme & Pettit, 2008) but was more longitudinal throughout the length of the mlearning projects described herein. The concept was foundational in developing a support strategy for the research. Intentional COPs formed the hub of the collaborative mlearning projects throughout the research, linking the researcher as the 'technology steward', the course lecturers,

Table 1. MLearning project design framework

Learning Practice	Mediating Circumstances		
Social Constructivism	Context	Technology	Agent
Lecturer Community of Practice	Lecturer professional development, pedagogical brainstorming	Face to face Scaffolded using LMS Smartphone Web 2.0 services	Lecturers as peers, with researcher as technology steward
Student and lecturer Community of Practice	Pedagogical integration and technical support	Face to face Scaffolded using LMS Smartphone Web 2.0 services	Students as peers, Lecturer as guide and pedagogical modeler, with the researcher as technology steward
Collaboration	Group projects	Social networking, Collaborative documents	Google Docs, student peers
Sharing	Peer commenting and critique	Web 2.0 media sites, eportfolio creation	RSS, student peers, lecturer
Student content creation	Student individual and group projects	Smartphone with camera and microphone, content uploaded to web 2.0 sites	Student and peers
Reflective	Journal of learning and processes, recording critical incidents	Web 2.0 hosted Blog	Personal appropriation, formative feedback from lecturer
Learning Context Bridging	Linking formal and informal learning	Smartphone used as communications tool and content capturing	Student interacting with context, peers, and lecturers

and the students as collaborative participants on each of the course projects.

Appropriating ideas from Herrington's mlearning implementation plan (Herrington, Herrington, Mantei, Olney, & Ferry, 2009), participants of each of the mlearning COPs were required to committ to the following:

Lecturers requirements for an mlearning roll-out:

1. Participation in a weekly Community Of Practice.
2. Personalised integration of mobile web 2.0 technologies.
3. Development of mlearning activities based on social constructivist pedagogy for students.
4. Implement at least a semester-long mlearning project with students.
5. Publish a research output based on the project.

Design Framework

The design framework for each of the projects is shown in Table 1. This framework was developed iteratively over the life of the research, which began in 2006 with two test projects that informed the practical implementation of the subsequent projects in 2007 to 2010. The framework table format is based loosely on that suggested by Sharples et al. (2009), emphasizing that the starting point of the design process is the learning practice and chosen pedagogical framework, which then informs the appropriate choice of mediating technologies.

To achieve an appropriate mlearning project design, the researcher typically worked with the volunteering lecturers from each department for six months before each project, brainstorming the application and integration of mobile web 2.0 into their courses. Google Docs was used to collaboratively create project outlines and assessment strategies that matched the design framework. Using a community of practice model for both the pre-project lecturer professional development, and the implementation of each project with the lecturers, the researcher and the course students created a basis from which other lecturers were then drawn in from the periphery of these project COPs and the subsequent spread of the projects as shown in Figure 1.

Critical Success Factors

Based on the experiences gathered from the thirteen mobile learning projects between 2007 to 2009 the researcher has identified six pedagogical critical success factors as emergent themes for mobile web 2.0 integration (Cochrane, 2010b). These success factors were identified across the mobile web 2.0 projects by evaluating the following:

- The level of student engagement and satisfaction achieved – as evidenced in evaluative surveys and focus group feedback.
- The level of moblogging (mobile blogging) achieved by students in the courses.
- Lecturer reflective feedback.
- The researcher's observations as a participant in the action research.
- Evaluation of each of the action research cycles (or projects).

Four of the critical success factors are similar to the list of nine characteristics of authentic learning (Herrington & Oliver, 2000) used as a basis for the Wollongong mlearning projects (Herrington et al., 2009) that led to the development of eleven design principles for mlearning. Other similar critical success factors have been identified by other researchers (Barker, Krull, & Mallinson, 2005; JISC, 2009). Each of the mlearning case studies described in this paper highlight the impact of combinations of these critical success factors.

1. The pedagogical integration of the technology into the course and assessment.
2. Lecturer modeling of the pedagogical use of the tools.
3. Creating a supportive learning community
4. Appropriate choice of mobile devices and web 2.0 social software.
5. Technological and pedagogical support.
6. Creating sustained interaction that facilitates the development of ontological shifts, both for the lecturers and the students.

In this paper the author evaluates in particular the impact of the sixth critical success factor across a variety of learning contexts by comparing the results of the eight 2009 mlearning projects and how these then informed the subsequent 2010 mlearning projects. The sixth critical success factor is expanded upon by the application of Luckin et al.'s (2008, 2010) concept of the Pedagogy-Andragogy-Heutagogy (PAH) continuum:

- Creating sustained interaction that facilitates the development of ontological shifts, both for the lecturers and the students. This involved:
  a. Staging and scaffolding the introduction of disruptive technologies by the establishment of an intentional community of practice supporting each project to reduce students' cognitive load and maximize the effectiveness of the zone of proximal development.
  b. Shifting lecturers from pedagogy to heutagogy – reconceptualising teaching and learning as proposed by Luckin et al. (2010) and McLoughlin and Lee (2010).
  c. Shifting students beyond their knowledge threshold – reconceptualising learning, and using the WMDs to engage students with "troublesome knowledge" (Land, Cousin, Meyer, & Davies, 2005).

Figure 3. Comparison of students' previous technology usage 2009

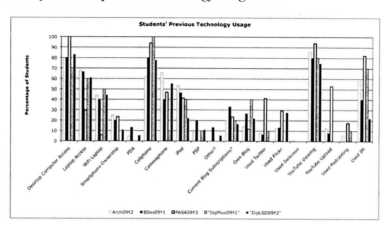

The various mlearning projects undertaken have illustrated that pedagogical integration of mlearning into a course/curriculum requires a paradigm shift on behalf of the lecturers involved, and this takes significant time. Hameed and Shah (2009) describe this process as a "cultural re-alignment". Many of the achieved mlearning scenarios were serendipitous rather than planned by the lecturers. Students also required significant time to gain the skills required to maximise the potential of new and emerging web 2.0 tools – as our pre-project surveys indicated (Figure 3), few students were already using these tools for their own content creation before the introduction of each project. Immersing students within a social constructivist pedagogical environment can be a new and challenging experience for the students, therefore implementation requires planned staging and scaffolding to support student learning (Cochrane, 2009).

Based upon these experiences, in order to achieve an explicit move to a social constructivist learning environment using mobile web 2.0 tools, a staged, and scaffolded approach was adopted (Table 2). This staged approach allows the bridging of the PAH (Pedagogy, Andragogy, Heutagogy) continuum (Luckin et al., 2008), and the embedding of mobile web 2.0 affordances that support each stage. Additionally, as the life-span

of mobile computing is generally shorter than that of desktop computing, a staged roll-out of WMD computing for students involved in three year long courses could be achieved to minimise the redundancy of the student-owned WMDs. Lecturer development is critical in facilitating the pedagogical focus of this roll-out. While this was the goal of each project, not all projects achieved this; reasons for this are discussed with respect to the critical success factors.

OVERVIEW OF THE 2009 MLEARNING PROJECTS

A wide variety of affordances of the WMDs were investigated throughout the various projects, some with more success than others. Experience and feedback from participants has shown that the focus should be on the affordances of WMDs that are most suitable for the small screens and slower text entry, as well as those affordances that are unique to WMDs (e.g. the built-in geotagging, media recording capabilities, and communications tools). In particular, it is the WMDs potential to bridge multiple learning contexts that facilitates rich interactions between formal and informal social constructivist learning environments. As Laurillard (2007) notes: "The intrinsic nature of

Table 2. A staged mobile web 2.0 implementation model

Stage	Web 2.0 Tools	MLearning Tools	Course Timeframe	PAH alignment
Level 1	Social Collaboration with peers and lecturer. Student generated content.	Use of student-owned netbook or mid-range smartphone, LMS and basic web2.0 sites	1 year Certificate programmes, or first year of longer programmes	Pedagogy (Lecturer directed)
Level 2	Social collaboration with peers and 'authentic environments'. Exploring context aware technologies.	Student-owned laptop and/or mid-range smartphone	Second year of two year or longer programmes	From Pedagogy to Andragogy (Student negotiated)
Level 3	Context Independent and bridging. Student generated contexts.	Student-owned laptop and/or high-end smartphone	Third year of programme	From Andragogy to Heutagogy (Student directed)

mobile technologies is to offer digitally-facilitated site-specific learning, which is motivating because of the degree of ownership and control" (p. 157). A concept map that has been developed during the research to graphically illustrate the links between multiple learning contexts, and a range of web 2.0 technologies that smartphones afford is shown in Figure 2. A mashup of several freely available web 2.0 tools was used rather than a single dedicated eportfolio platform, allowing for the integration of new web 2.0 tools as they became available. The smart phones were used to bridge multiple learning contexts (both the formal and informal learning contexts), providing constant connectivity with peers, lecturers, course content, and student's own online eportfolios, while enabling student creation of new context-aware media via the smart phones variety of recording, and content sharing affordances.

The following sections provide an overview of the 2009 projects.

Bachelor of Product Design mLearning Projects

All three years of the Bachelor of Product Design degree were included in the 2009 mlearning projects, allowing staging of the integration of mlearning and bridging the PAH continuum across the three years of the degree.

First Year Mobile Project

The first year project was designed to lay a foundation for the second and third year mobile web 2.0 projects to build upon in the rest of the course. The pedagogical focus was thus more teacher-directed (pedagogy). The first year project established students' eportfolios: integrating blogging, followed by moblogging (mobile blogging) into the course. This scaffolded the introduction of web 2.0 and mobile web 2.0 tools into the students' learning experience to facilitate the beginnings of their online eportfolio and introduction to the educational use of social networking for collaborative projects. The core assessment involved an online Blog/eportfolio documenting and showcasing students' design processes and forming the basis of the beginnings of a collaborative hub with their class peers. Students were supplied with a Dell mini9 3G netbook in semester one, and this was supplemented with the addition of a Nokia Xpressmusic 5800 smartphone at the end of semester one.

Second Year Mobile Project

The focus of the second year project was on a move from pedagogy to andragogy, building on the students' 2008 first year mobile web 2.0 experience, integrating moblogging, social networking, and student-generated content into the

Figure 2. Mobile Web 2.0 concept map

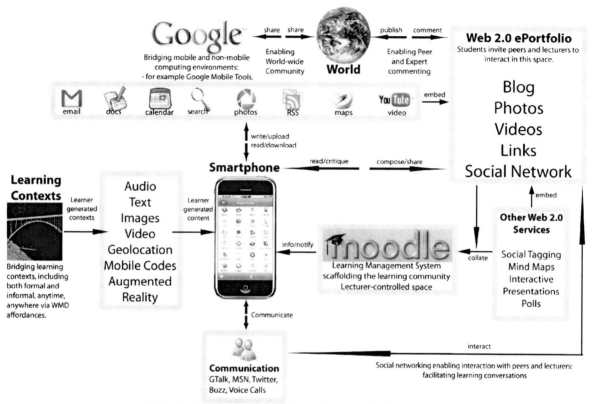

Mobile Web 2.0 Enabling Social Collaboration

course, facilitating more in-depth collaboration and peer critique. The majority of these students had established an online eportfolio in the previous 2008 mlearning project. The 2009 project utilised the Nokia Xpressmusic 5800 to facilitate an assessed online Blog/eportfolio documenting and showcase students' design processes, forming the basis of collaborative critique and show-casing with worldwide peers and potential employers or clients. Ning was used as a teacher-facilitated collaborative hub linking external stakeholders with the projects. Second semester projects focused on sharing and critiquing student design projects using Google Docs and Vox Group blogs, using the smartphone to capture and share project progress and presentations.

Third Year Mobile Project

The third year mlearning project focused upon the unique affordances of mobile web 2.0 to enable context-bridging learning environments that facilitated a move from Andragogy to student-generated projects and student-generated contexts (Heutagogy). Students and lecturers were supplied with Nokia N95 smartphones and upgraded to the Nokia N97 in Semester two. The third year course is based around a Studio Design model where students undertake three design projects throughout the year, one of which is substantial and developed by the students themselves, with the guidance of their lecturers. The project involved documenting the research and design of these products throughout the year, including working with a client company in small design teams. The first project was a collaborative project with Applied Trades and Landscape Design students. The mobile web 2.0 technologies were also used to establish a weekly 'nomadic' studio session with staff and students focusing on context bridging and full integration of moblogging into course projects. Students were required to maintain an online Blog/eportfolio documenting and showcasing their design processes while away from the face-to-face Design Studio, and forming the basis of a collaborative hub with worldwide peers and potential employers/clients. Additionally, communication and collaboration made use of instant messaging, microblogging, and reflective VODCasts during the 'nomadic' (beyond the classroom) studio session.

Diploma Landscape Design

In 2007 students used Nokia N80 smartphones to document and share their design for an exhibition garden at the annual Ellerslie Flowershow. The 2008 project integrated the use of smartphones for reporting a field-trip to Japan. The short-term nature of these projects and the wide-range of student experiences and capabilities in the increasingly mature and part-time student demographic of the course led to a rethink of the mobile web 2.0 integration in 2009, leading to a focus upon 3G enabled netbooks for creating student eportfolios. The participants were provided with Dell Mini9 netbooks for the duration of the course. The 2009 mlearning project was a collaborative project with UATI (Unitec Trades Department), Product Design and Landscape Design students. Students were required to create a reflective design process blog and eportfolio using Ning. The social networking features of Ning were also used to establish communication, collaboration, and sharing between the three groups of lecturers and students. This was followed in semester 2 with a group design project facilitated using a Ning social network, using Nokia Xpressmusic 5800 smartphones to document a client's pool design and build project.

Diploma of Contemporary Music

The 2009 mlearning project within the Diploma of Contemporary Music was informed by the lessons learnt from the initial 2008 project where student volunteers from across the programme and two course lecturers took part in an investigative project using iPod Touches and iPhones throughout the year. During 2008, no assessment tasks were directly related to the use of the iPhones or iPod Touch's, and this resulted in varying commitment to the project by the students. While all the participants regularly used the devices, there was limited use for directly course-related activities. This suggested that while the students appropriated the use of the tools into their personal and informal learning, they had not been convinced (neither modeled by the lecturers) of the potential for the iPhones and associated activities to be useful within their formal learning environment. It also suggested that students are more likely to respond to tasks for which they receive course credit. It became clear that the iPhone project needed to be embedded in a course, with clearly related assessment tasks, for the students to participate more fully in it. In particular 2009 projects were designed to investigate the use of MySpace, student created podcasts, and microblogging as authentic mobile learning environments within the context of music delivery, promotion and critique.

The 2009 project was explicitly linked to two courses, one within the second year of the Diploma of Contemporary Music, the other within the first year of the course with second year students as peer mentors. Thus the integration of mlearning was staged across the two years of the course, and the use of mobile web 2.0 tools were integrated into the course assessment. All students in the paper were issued with an iPhone 3G for use within the course throughout 2009, and were also encouraged to personalise the use of the iPhone into their daily routines. Internet access was available for free via the campus WiFi network, but students and lecturers were responsible for any voice and 3G data costs accrued. A compilation of student reflections as Vodcasts (Online video recordings) of the 2009 mlearning project is available on YouTube: http://nz.youtube.com/watch?v=0It5XUfvOj

1. The second year paper (5011) involved an investigation of the current and future uses of web 2.0 technologies in music production and distribution. Students used iPhones to record environmental sounds off campus and then included these sounds into an original recording project. Students were also required to create and maintain a MySpace presence for promoting their music. The iPhones were used to upload photos and videos and edit their MySpace blog. Thus the iPhones facilitated both learner-generated content (Bruns, 2007) and learner-generated contexts (Cook, Bradley, Lance, Smith, & Haynes, 2007; Luckin et al., 2008).
2. The first year paper (4006) involved recording and peer critique of student music practice sessions and performances.

Bachelor of Architecture

An architecture lecturer COP was formed during the second half of semester one 2009, facilitated by the researcher as the technology steward, to investigate the potential of mobile web 2.0 tools to enhance the course, and to familiarize the lecturers with these tools. The approach developed for the previous mlearning COPs and projects were used to guide the implementation of this COP. Following this lecturer COP a plan was developed for a student mlearning project in semester 2 of 2009. The 2009 project was the first mlearning project for Architecture, investigating the potential of mobile web 2.0 within the course to facilitate group work and helping to build a 'learning community' among the 115 second year students. The focus was on the combined Design Studio course for 2009 where students were spread across four studio spaces. The participants were provided with

Nokia Xpressmusic 5800 smartphones and Dell Mini9 netbooks for the duration of the course. Students created and shared their architectural designs using Photoshop and Archicad creating real and virtual presentations for 'crits' and included elements of mobile video streaming and models captured using the smartphone's camera. The project also investigated the use of location services (geotagging) and mobile code use in Architecture. However, as the key second year Design Studio lecturer refused to participate, there was no assessment attached to the mlearning project, and student involvement was completely voluntary. This limited the impact of the mlearning project.

Bachelor Performing and Screen Arts

This project focused upon an investigation of the potential of mobile web 2.0 technologies in the field of Film and Television within the Bachelor of Performing and Screen Arts (PASA). The PASA mlearning integration was focused on the context of the mlearning tools themselves as key new technologies that are becoming important in reinventing and democratizing the recording and distribution of film that will have significant impact on the industry. The tools themselves were thus the focus of learning as well as used to record students' learning journeys, thus acting as mediators (Uden, 2007) and bridges of external learning contexts (Vavoula, 2007). The participants were provided with Nokia Xpressmusic 5800 smartphones and Dell Mini9 netbooks for the duration of the course. Topics covered by the mlearning project included: mobile video streaming and sharing, collation and broadcasting mobile video using Livestream or UStream, creating an online identity, and associated business practices. The course lecturer created a Vox group, and all resources for the project were shared with the class via this group page (http://unutechsy309.groups.Vox.com/), including links to several Google Docs.

Film and TV major students investigated the current and future uses of web 2.0 technologies in performing arts film production and distribution. Students researched and reported on various technologies using a weekly podcast/vodcast that was peer critiqued by students on the course. Students experimented with live video streaming and collation of video using Livestream.com. The focus was upon students developing an understanding of the importance of a quality online profile and presence in the emerging crowd-source web 2.0 environment.

RESULTS

This section briefly provides indicative comparison and discussion of student feedback from the 2009 mlearning projects. The impact of the projects is drawn out further in the discussion section of the paper.

Example Student Feedback

A comparison of the five case studies in 2009 is useful to identify emergent themes. Figure 3 gives a comparative overview of the five groups of students' previous technology experience prior to the 2009 mlearning projects.

Most notably, the PASA students personal wireless laptop ownership was much lower than that of the other students. Previous to the 2009 mlearning project the Department of Performing and Screen Arts had no wifi coverage, and therefore little incentive for student laptop ownership. This appears to have been significant in the PASA students' personal appropriation of the netbooks and smartphones, which was much higher in general than that of the other student groups. The introduction of the flexibility of ubiquitous Internet connectivity afforded by the WMDs was greatly appreciated by the PASA students. Another difference with the PASA students to the other 2009 mlearning student groups was their level of

engagement with Twitter and YouTube content creation. The context of their studies being Film and Television made their engagement with YouTube contextually relevant, whereas their appropriation of Twitter appeared to be a convenient way of forming student learning and social community with the technology they had available (they all previously had cellphones of some sort). Figure 3 indicates that the majority of the students were previously consumers of web 2.0 content rather than producers. While cellphone ownership was almost ubiquitous, the group with the least previous experience of smartphone use were the Diploma of Contemporary Music students, who were in general from lower socio economic backgrounds than the rest of the students.

In comparison to the other student groups, the majority of the PASA students found the interface of the smartphone easy to use with little problems encountered. "It was so quick and easy and made me access my blog more often than I would have without it" (PASA student smartphone feedback). This may have been due to a more recent version of the smartphones' firmware being installed, or a difference in socially determined technology expectations between the groups. The researcher has observed that a strong vocal proponent or opponent tends to have significant influence over the student groups, particularly when lecturers are ambivalent.

Table 3 summarises the student end of project survey responses from each of the eight 2009 mlearning projects. Omitted questions from the table were demographic only. These results were explored further via the focus groups and discussions between the researcher and the course lecturers. In general the two groups (Bachelor of Product Design year 3, and Diploma of Contemporary Music year 2) where the most regular and sustained COP formation occurred during the projects responded with the most positive student feedback.

As Table 3 indicates, the introduction of mobile web 2.0 enhanced students' experience of group

Table 3. Comparative student satisfaction with mlearning projects 2009

End of project Survey Question	Percentage Student agreement/satisfaction with statement (strongly agree plus agree)							
	Arch Y2 (n=115)	BDes Y1 (n=15)	BDes Y2 (n=15)	BDes Y3 (n=8)	PASA Y3 (n=17)	DipMus Y1 (n=10)	DipMus Y2 (n=12)	DipLSD Y2 (n=15)
4. What has been your experience of group work facilitated by Blogs and RSS?	69%	60%	57%	80%	65%	100%	89%	67%
6. It was easy to use the smart-phone?	92%	20%	64%	100%	88%	75%	90%	73%
7. This mobile learning experience was fun.	88%	70%	55%	100%	88%	75%	90%	60%
8. Based on my experience during this trial, I would use a smart-phone in other courses	80%	50%	73%	100%	77%	88%	90%	67%
9. I would be willing to purchase my own smartphone?	62%	40%	73%	100%	88%	75%	100%	20%
11. In your opinion, does mobile learning increase the quality of learning?	62%	80%	73%	100%	53%	25%	100%	47%
12. Mobile blogging helped create a sense of community (group work)?	53%	60%	82%	80%	29%	38%	90%	67%
13. Accessing your course blog was easy using the mobile device?	52%	40%	46%	100%	71%	75%	78%	67%
14. Mobile learning increases access to education?	75%	50%	64%	100%	82%	38%	90%	73%
15. Communication and feedback from the course lecturer was made easier?	64%	70%	55%	80%	59%	38%	78%	67%
16. Mobile learning is convenient for communication with other students?	91%	90%	82%	80%	88%	88%	90%	67%

work, and the majority of the students enjoyed the mlearning project and valued the connectivity afforded by the WMDs. The PASA project returned the lowest satisfaction score for the facilitation of a learning community, due to the lack of regular weekly COP formation. A lack of regular formative feedback and engagement with the WMDs for communicating by the course lecturers in the first year Product Design and first year Diploma of Contemporary Music projects was noted by the students. In general, the PASA students were more excited about their mlearning experience than the other students, who had previously had alternative access to wireless connectivity via a significant number of these students owning wireless laptops and having wifi coverage of their learning spaces for longer than the PASA students. The first year Product Design and Diploma Landscape Design projects had the least focus upon the use of smartphones, as these projects focused upon establishing students' web 2.0 eportfolios as a first stage. While not all of the student responses were positive, in most cases the remaining responses were 'uncertain', with very few negative responses to the projects. Responses to focus group questioning of students indicated that they saw the potential positive impact of the mlearning projects on their courses, but in some cases either the choice of mobile device or a lack of continuing commitment to the projects by some course lecturers minimized this potential.

Students were asked to rate (on a scale of 1 least to 10 highest) a range of mobile affordances. Figure 4 indicates that there were not too many significant differences between the different student mlearning groups appropriation of these affordances of WMDs. The main differences being those that related specifically to each learning context – for example the Architecture students appreciated geotagging for building location, the PASA students enjoyed Twitter for social and learning community formation, and the Product Design students appropriated blogging as a form of learning community formation.

Students were also asked to rank the most important factors in their uptake of mobile devices as a result of their 2009 experiences. The results in Figure 5 indicate that there are features of WMDs that were generally important to most student groups future uptake, including: the cost of the device and data connectivity, wifi capability, the quality of the built-in camera, and the inclusion of a large screen for viewing content and web surfing.

DISCUSSION

Impact of the MLearning Case Studies

The fifteen mlearning projects represented within the five case studies covering 2007 to 2009 provide rich examples of practical pedagogical integration of mlearning within a variety of tertiary education courses. This section briefly summarizes the main lessons learnt from each case study, and how these informed the implementation of the subsequent 2010 mlearning projects.

Case Study 1: Diploma of Landscape Design 2007 to 2010

Beginning in 2007, the first mlearning project paved the way for the following projects, highlighting a range of technical and implementation issues that could be improved upon. The 2007 to 2008 mlearning projects emphasized the disruptive nature of mlearning, highlighted in earlier mlearning studies by Sharples (2001) and Stead (2006), illustrating the process of lecturer pedagogical reconceptualisation of teaching, and the process of student reconceptualisation of learning required as the second year of the course (Cochrane, 2009) moved from teacher-centred (pedagogy) to social constructivism (andragogy to heutagogy). The introduction of mobile web 2.0 facilitated a move along the Pedagogy-Andragogy-Heutagogy (PAH) continuum, as proposed by Luckin et al. (2010) and McLoughlin and Lee (2008a). The importance of a robust yet flexible technical and pedagogical support strategy was highlighted. The unique student profile (all the students were aged between 43 and 69) of the 2008 iteration of the Landscape Design mlearning project highlighted the importance of choosing appropriate WMDs for the needs of each unique student group, as the chosen smartphones were too complex for this demographic to appropriate. In response the 2009 Landscape Design mlearning project used netbooks to minimize the cognitive load for the students, identified as a common flaw of social constructivist learning by Kirschner et al. (2006), and highlighted the importance of learning community formation to be integrated into the course. However, the course lecturers have yet to go beyond a project level integration of mobile web 2.0 within the course, focusing upon specific projects within the second year of the course only, and thus missing the opportunity to stage and establish the initial integration of mlearning into the first year of the course and build upon this in the second year. The 2010 mlearning project therefore did not build significantly upon the previous mlearning

Figure 4. Comparison of 2009 Student perceptions of the most useful functions of WMDs

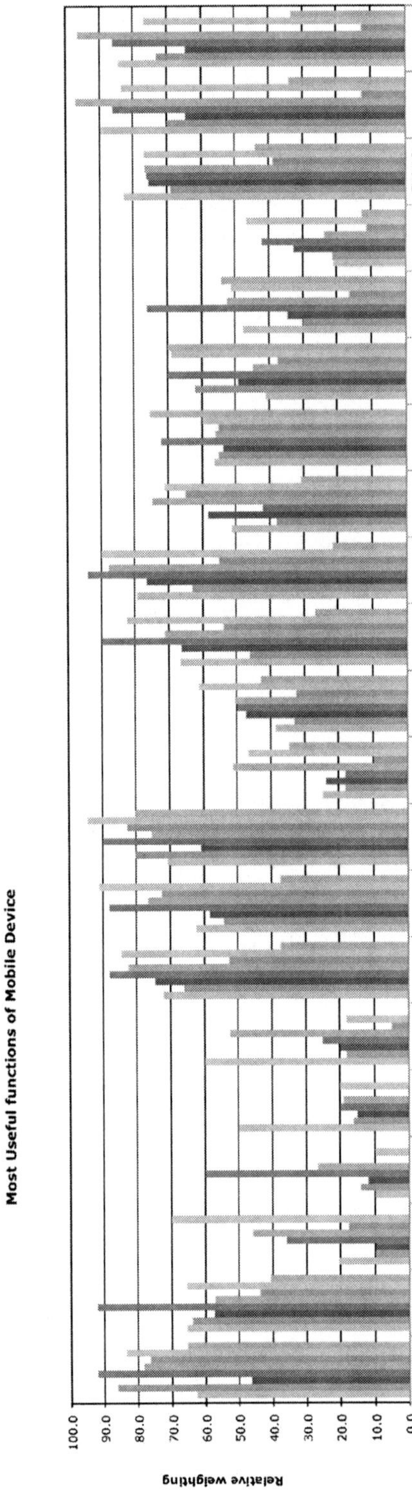

Most Useful functions of Mobile Device

	Email	IM	Twitter	QR Codes	Geotagging	Google Maps	Video	Audio	web browsing	doc editing	due reading	calendar	contacts/ address book	notes	online course access	blogging	file sharing	RSS subscriptions	Taking & uploading Photos	Txt	Phone Calls
Andi09Y2	62.7	65.4	20.3	10.0	50.0	60.0	72.0	62.3	70.7	24.7	38.5	66.5	79.2	51.2	56.2	41.0	47.5	20.8	82.7	89.7	84.2
BDes09Y1	86	64	10	14	16	18	68	54	80	18	33	46	63	38	55	52	30	21	69	70	73
BDes09Y2	46.4	57.3	10.0	12.0	15.0	20.0	74.5	58.2	69.9	23.6	47.3	66.4	76.4	58.2	53.6	49.1	34.5	32.7	75.5	64.5	64.5
BDes09Y3	92	92	36	60	20	25	88	88	90	18	50	90	94	42	72	70	76	42	76	86	86
PASA09Y3	78.2	57.1	45.9	26.5	18.8	52.4	82.4	76.5	75.3	51.2	50.6	71.2	87.6	74.7	55.9	44.7	52.4	23.5	76.5	97.1	96.5
DipMud09Y1	76.25	43.75	17.5	0	0	5	52.5	72.5	82.5	10	52.5	53.75	55	65	55	37.5	16.25	11.25	38.75	12.5	12.5
DipMud09Y2	83.3	65.6	70.0	10.0	20.0	18.0	84.4	91.1	92.4	46.7	61.1	82.2	90.0	71.1	60.0	68.9	51.1	46.7	76.7	83.3	76.7
DipLSD09Y2	65.3	40.7					37.3	37.3	80.0	34.7	42.7	26.7	21.3	39.7	75.3	70.0	54.0	12.7	44.0	34.0	33.3

Relative weighting: 100.0, 90.0, 80.0, 70.0, 60.0, 50.0, 40.0, 30.0, 20.0, 10.0, 0.0

Figure 5. Comparison of 2009 student perceptions of most important factors when choosing a WMD

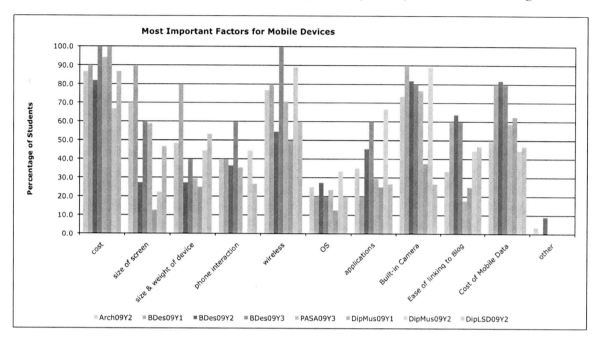

projects, but continued as a second-year project only. The Diploma Landscape Design mlearning projects have been characterized by short-term commitment to the development of a supporting community of practice by the course lecturers and a subsequent limited impact on the course overall.

Case Study 2: Bachelor of Product Design 2008 to 2010

The Product Design mlearning projects achieved significant progress in course integration, pedagogical reconceptualisation, and development of a staged and scaffolded implementation model for developing learning communities facilitated by intentional communities of practice across each year of the course. The case study illustrated the potential to stage and scaffold mlearning integration across all three years of a Bachelor level course, starting with establishing a learning community culture involving both the students and the lecturers and facilitation of a progression of teaching paradigms from pedagogy to heutagogy

(PAH)(Luckin et al., 2008) following the first year to third year of the course. The PAH continuum maps well with the progression of mobile web 2.0 course integration from web 2.0 appropriation in first year to student mobile facilitated content creation in second year, and finally the context aware and context bridging affordances of mlearning leveraged in the third year 'nomadic studio'. For some students the pedagogical approaches taken in the mobile web 2.0 projects were beyond their prior experience and comfort zones, requiring significant reconceptualisation on their roles as students (Chi & Hausmann, 2003). However, the researcher has observed that providing a regular COP facilitated by a technology steward, and finding an appropriate 'hook', such as showing how the technology can further a particular interest, or make a particular task easier, invariably breaks down any barriers. The first and second year Product Design mlearning projects demonstrated a commitment to a sustained community of practice involving the lecturers, the researcher, and the course students. However, the second year lecturer did not commit to a sustained COP, leading to a sporadic COP and limited impact on the course. The researcher observed that the sustained engagement of a supporting community of practice provided both a catalyst and a supportive environment facilitating participants' ontological shifts.

The 2010 Product Design mlearning projects built upon the staged implementation of mlearning into the course in 2009. A survey of 2010 first-year students indicated 80% owned a wifi laptop and cameraphone, therefore the 2010 project focused upon student-owned WMDs, and the remaining 20% of students were loaned netbooks and smartphones. However, while all second and third-year 2010 students owned their own wifi laptops, they were accustomed to institutionally-loaned smartphones from the 2008 to 2009 projects. A recommitment to a regular mlearning COP by the second year lecturers led to 2010 students using Nokia N97 smartphones, and at students' request, a third-year mlearning project using iPhones.

Case Study 3: Diploma of Contemporary Music 2008 to 2010

The Diploma of Contemporary Music mlearning project developed from an initial 2008 exploration of the potential of mlearning to engage students and enhance the course to an example of successful course integration and student adoption and appropriation of mlearning in 2009. During the 2008 first iteration of the mlearning project students and lecturers were enthusiastic and engaged by the tools, but skeptical as to the potential impact on the course and learning outcomes. The second 2009 iteration of the mlearning project integrated the mlearning tools into the course assessment leading to adoption and appropriation by the students beyond personal and social use, leveraging the learning context bridging (Vavoula, 2007) affordances of mobile web 2.0 for facilitating authentic (Herrington & Herrington, 2007)

course-related learning environments beyond the classroom. This was built upon in a 2010 project utilizing iPads within the second year of the course, although the integration of mlearning into the course was once again limited to one paper. The Contemporary Music lecturers have yet to fully realize the potential of fully integrating the use of mobile web 2.0 tools across the two years of the course. They have yet to conceptualise the benefits of mobile web 2.0 beyond specific 'projects'. A contributing factor to this is that all lecturers, with the exception of the director of the course are part-time lecturers. Therefore the Contemporary Music lecturers conceptualise themselves first as artists and performers rather than teachers, and invariably follow an apprenticeship (teacher-directed) model of teaching. The lecturers require release time for participating in the supporting COP where they can experiment with new forms of assessment afforded by the integration of mlearning into their courses. Thus the disruptive nature of mlearning that can facilitate a move from teacher-centered pedagogy to student-centered andragogy and even self-directed heutagogy has yet to be fully realized or appreciated within the Diploma. However, discussions with the researcher have shown that the dawning's of lecturer awareness of this potential are beginning to be visible, even though they are still skeptical. The process of lecturer ontological shift (Chi & Hausmann, 2003; Hameed & Shah, 2009) with regards to pedagogical reconceptualization is lengthened within a part-time lecturer environment.

Case Study 4: Bachelor of Architecture 2009 to 2010

The 2009 Architecture mlearning project was the widest scoped in terms of student numbers, encompassing the entire second year of the Bachelor of Architecture (115 students). However the project was a first implementation within the school, and formed an exploratory initiation into the potential of mlearning for both the lecturers and the students. This illustrates a consistent theme observed by the researcher in all of the 2007 to 2010 mlearning projects – the first implementation of an mlearning project breaks new ground, and while not necessarily producing significantly transformed pedagogy due to an initial lack of course integration, the first iteration creates the groundwork for the ontological shift required by the course lecturers to conceptualise the potential to integrate these new technologies into the course in subsequent iterations of the mlearning project. In 2009 key Architecture lecturers declined to be involved in the establishment of the initial lecturer investigative community of practice, leading to a lack of willingness to integrate the project into the course assessment. This case study therefore highlights the critical importance of lecturer participation in a supporting COP for professional development and subsequent course integration of the mlearning tools. This is the first significant step in the journey of ontological reconceptualisation of teaching by the lecturers, and the ontological reconception of learning by the students that the mobile web 2.0 projects have been explicitly designed to facilitate. As Laurillard (2007) emphasizes, the lecturer's input into the design of mlearning is critical.

In 2010 a smaller mlearning project was established with three Architecture lecturers and 25 students within an elective third-year course, with all of the participants committing to a weekly supporting COP throughout the duration of the course. This project utilized iPads and Android smartphones for geotagging student-generated content, and student-negotiated mlearning projects. These participants will then become 'technology-stewards' within the Bachelor of Architecture in 2011, seeding the integration of mlearning across the degree in 2011 and hopefully bringing in further Architecture lecturers from the periphery of this COP.

Case Study 5: Bachelor of Performing and Screen Arts 2009 to 2010

The Performing and Screen Arts mlearning project was one of the most complex of the mlearning implementations with regards to the use and exploration of the mobile technologies. The project was initially begun with the establishment of a lecturer COP investigating mlearning in semetser1 2009. However, the project's implementation suffered from the relatively short time the lecturers had for personally appropriating the mlearning tools themselves, and timetabling limitations led to a significant change in the community of practice support model used in semester2 of 2009, implemented over a compressed timeframe compared to the other projects. While not personally modeling (Herrington, Herrington, & Mantei, 2009; Herrington & Oliver, 2000) the use of the mobile web 2.0 tools to a high level, the course lecturers nevertheless created an atmosphere of high expectations of the students that created an energetic 'buzz' among them, facilitating experimentation and collaboration around the use of the tools. While there was a lack of course-focused community facilitated by the WMD implementation, there was a very high level of personal appropriation of the WMDs by the participating students. Students found the portability and ubiquitous connectivity of the smartphones empowering for both accessing course content and their social networks. This case study therefore highlighted the importance of the development of a regular supportive learning community, and the positive impact of high expectations from the lecturers on the participating students. The subsequent 2010 implementation of mlearning within the Bachelor of Performing and Screen Arts followed the model used within the Bachelor of Product Design, staging and scaffolding the integration of mlearning across all three years of the course, and thus creating a significant impact on the entire course. First year 2010 students were supplied with netbooks for eportfolio establishment, second year students were supplied with Nokia Xpressmusic smartphones enabling student-generated content, and third year students were supplied with Nokia N97 smartphones and investigated the content and contextual affordances of these devices.

Creating Sustained Engagement Facilitating Ontological Shifts

The case studies have shown that creating sustained engagement around the mlearning projects supported by communities of practice can facilitate ontological shifts among the participants. The mlearning projects identified two key issues around reconceptualising teaching and learning representing ontological shifts in the participants' understanding:

1. Shifting lecturers from pedagogy towards heutagogy, reconceptualising teaching as proposed by Luckin et al. (2008, 2010) and McLoughlin and Lee (2008b).

This was most clearly illustrated by the Bachelor of Product Design case study, where the integration of the mlearning projects facilitated a move from teacher-directed paper-based design portfolios and face-to-face studios to interactive online eportfolios and a flexible student-negotiated 'nomadic' studio that bridged multiple learning contexts.

2. Shifting students beyond their previous learning experiences, reconceptualising learning, and using the WMDs to engage students via a focus upon student-generated content and student-generated contexts.

This was illustrated by students in the Bachelor of Product Design 2009 mlearning case study where WMDs were utilized to facilitate bridging learning contexts beyond the face-to-face design studio. Another identified example was enhanc-

ing group work, as students often struggle when presented with collaborative group work. The integration of mobile web 2.0 into their courses provided tools to facilitate collaborative projects in innovative and engaging ways. For example this was illustrated by the SHaC09 collaborative mlearning project between the Diploma of Landscape Design and Bachelor of Product design students.

Both lecturers (as illustrated by the Diploma of Contemporary Music case study) and students can struggle with the introduction of social constructivist pedagogies that shift the participants along the PAH continuum. A key strategy developed through the action research cycles to facilitate a move along the PAH continuum was staging and scaffolding the curriculum integration of mobile web 2.0. Staging involves spreading the integration of mobile web 2.0 across the length of a course and aligning the unique affordances of WMDs to the level of pedagogy at each stage, while scaffolding involves providing the support required for students to meet these goals. Staging the introduction of disruptive technologies minimises students' learning load and scaffolding maximizes the effectiveness of the zone of proximal development, similarly to the process described by Attwell (2006, 2007). Thus beginning the introduction of web 2.0 integration into the first year of a course with a focus upon pedagogy and student-generated content will prepare students for the integration of the unique context-bridging affordances of WMDs facilitating a focus upon andragogy to heutagogy and student-generated contexts in subsequent years of their course, as outlined in Table 3.

Answering the Research Questions

This section briefly outlines the findings of the research discussed in this paper in relation to one of the research questions in particular.

What challenges/advantages to established pedagogies do these disruptive technologies present?

Mobile web 2.0 tools are disruptive technologies that democratize the learning environment, empowering students, and providing opportunities for social constructivist pedagogies. As theorized by Bruns (2007) and Laurillard (2007) and demonstrated by the research projects (for example within the Bachelor of Product Design, as reflected upon by Cochrane, Bateman, and Flitta (2009)) the ubiquitous connectivity of WMDs combined with the student content creation and sharing capabilities of web 2.0 shift the learning focus from teacher-directed to student-centred learning challenging instructivist pedagogies and providing a rich basis for flexible social constructivist pedagogies. Learning can then occur across multiple contexts, bridged by the ability of the WMDs to augment, capture, share and communicate learning experiences, as demonstrated by the SHaC09 mlearning project (Cochrane et al., 2009). This changes the role of the educator and the nature of learning for the students. These disruptions to the educators' and learners' conceptualizations of teaching and learning that are based on previous experiences require sustained engagement and expert modeling to reconceptualise, as the ontological shifts are come to terms with and the benefits realized. Technological and pedagogical support for these paradigm shifts is critical, as the case studies illustrated the critical role of establishing a supportive COP. The research extends the concepts of the Learner Generated Concepts group (Luckin et al., 2008, 2010) providing practical examples of how these disruptions facilitate appropriate shifts along the pedagogy (teacher-directed) to heutagogy (learner-directed) continuum. It was also found that good pedagogical design of contextual learning environments is essential and should include assessment integration and curriculum alignment for students to value the integration of mlearning activities.

CONCLUSION

Much has been learnt from the experiences of the fifteen mlearning projects from 2007 to 2009, with emergent themes explored herein. While an analysis of the subsequent projects in 2010 is outside the scope of this paper, a review of the 2009 projects reveal keys to mlearning sustainability are an institutional cultural and strategy shift as well as a lecturer and student ontological shift in relation to learning and teaching. Achieving this takes sustained engagement leading to significant learning activity and assessment redesign. Establishing collaborative intentional communities of practice is proposed as one approach to achieve this. The frameworks and models presented herein are beginning to achieve this at Unitec, transforming pedagogy and engaging students. Significant beneficial change has been achieved for the various participants and stakeholders involved in the research, including demonstrable transformation in pedagogical strategies and pedagogical reconception from participating lecturers, increased engagement and collaboration from participating students, and strategic input into the institutions new elearning strategy (Cochrane, 2010a). While requiring time-intensive input from the researcher, the outcomes have been very rewarding, with the development of a sense of trust and collaboration between all the participants, and between the researcher and the course lecturers in particular. Planning for a staged implementation of mlearning across the years of a course that also follows pedagogical development (from Pedagogy to Heutagogy) minimizes the cognitive load required of students and the level of pedagogical reconceptualisation for lecturers, maximizing the impact on the course and the student graduates. Course integration and authentic assessment that takes advantage of the unique affordances of WMDs is essential. Appropriate choice of WMDs can facilitate flexible learning spaces beyond fixed traditional computer laboratory spaces. A focus upon student-owned WMDs is also crucial for sustainability and will form the basis of future mlearning projects at Unitec. Allowing students to create personalisable learning spaces and use WMDs that they personally appropriate, leads to high engagement and the potential to create interactive collaborative learning environments.

REFERENCES

Attwell, G. (2006). The Wales-Wide Web. *Personal Learning Environments, 2006*, 11.

Attwell, G. (2007). The personal learning environments - the future of elearning? *eLearning Papers, 2*(1), 1-8.

Barker, A., Krull, G., & Mallinson, B. (2005). *A proposed theoretical model for m-learning adoption in developing countries.* Paper presented at the mLearn Conference.

Bruns, A. (2007, March 21-23). *Beyond difference: Reconfiguring education for the user-led age.* Paper presented at the ICE3: Ideas in Cyberspace Education: Digital Difference, Loch Lomond, Scotland.

Chi, M., & Hausmann, R. (2003). Do radical discoveries require ontological shifts? In Shavinina, L., & Sternberg, R. (Eds.), *International handbook on innovation* (*Vol. 3*, pp. 430–444). New York, NY: Elsevier Science. doi:10.1016/B978-008044198-6/50030-9

Cochrane, T. (2009). Mobilizing learning: Intentional disruption. Harnessing the potential of social software tools in higher education using wireless mobile devices. *International Journal of Mobile Learning and Organisation, 3*(4), 399–419. doi:10.1504/IJMLO.2009.027456

Cochrane, T. (2010a). Beyond the yellow brick road: Mobile web 2.0 informing a new institutional elearning strategy. *ALT-J Research in Learning Technology, 18*(3), 221–231. doi:10.1080/09687769.2010.529110

Cochrane, T. (2010b). Exploring mobile learning success factors. *ALT-J Research in Learning Technology, 18*(2), 133–148. doi:10.1080/0968 7769.2010.494718

Cochrane, T., Bateman, R., Cliffin, P., Gardner, J., Henderson, I., & Holloway, S. (2009, July 6-8). *Mobilizing learning: Mobile Web 2.0 scenarios in tertiary education.* Paper presented at the EDULEARN International Conference on Education and New Learning Technologies, Barcelona, Spain.

Cochrane, T., Bateman, R., & Flitta, I. (2009, April 22-24). *Integrating mobile Web 2.0 within tertiary education.* Paper presented at the m-ICTE Conference, Lisbon, Portugal.

Cook, J., Bradley, C., Lance, J., Smith, C., & Haynes, R. (2007). Generating learner contexts with mobile devices. In Pachler, N. (Ed.), *Mobile learning: Towards a research agenda* (pp. 55–73). London, UK: WLE Centre.

Hameed, K., & Shah, H. (2009, February 26-28). *Mobile learning in higher education: Adoption and discussion criteria.* Paper presented at the IADIS International Conference on Mobile Learning, Barcelona, Spain.

Head, G., & Dakers, J. (2005). Verillon's Trio and Wenger's Community: Learning in technology education. *International Journal of Technology and Design Education, 15*, 33–46. doi:10.1007/s10798-004-6194-3

Herrington, A., & Herrington, J. (2007). Authentic mobile learning in higher education. In *Proceedings of the AARE International Educational Research Conference*, Fremantle, Australia (pp. 1-9).

Herrington, A., Herrington, J., & Mantei, J. (2009). Design principles for mobile learning. In Herrington, J., Herrington, A., Mantei, J., Olney, I., & Ferry, B. (Eds.), *New technologies, new pedagogies: Mobile learning in higher education* (pp. 129–138). New South Wales, Australia: University of Wollongong.

Herrington, J., Herrington, A., Mantei, J., Olney, I., & Ferry, B. (Eds.). (2009). *New technologies, new pedagogies: Mobile learning in higher education*. New South Wales, Australia: University of Wollongong.

Herrington, J., & Oliver, R. (2000). An instructional design framework for authentic learning environments. *Educational Technology Research and Development*, 48(3), 23–48. doi:10.1007/BF02319856

JISC. (2009). *Higher education in a Web 2.0 world* Retrieved from http://www.jisc.ac.uk/publications/documents/heweb2.aspx

Kirschner, P., Sweller, J., & Clark, R. (2006). Why minimal guidance during instruction does not work: An analysis of the failure of constructivist, discovery, problem-based, experiential, and inquiry-based teaching. *Educational Psychologist*, 4(2), 75–86. doi:10.1207/s15326985ep4102_1

Kukulska-Hulme, A., & Pettit, J. (2008). Semiformal learning communities for professional development in mobile learning. *Journal of Computing in Higher Education*, 20(2), 35–47. doi:10.1007/s12528-008-9006-z

Land, R., Cousin, G., Meyer, J., & Davies, P. (2005). Threshold concepts and troublesome knowledge (3)*: Implications for course design and evaluation. In Rust, C. (Ed.), *Improving student learning diversity and inclusivity* (pp. 53–64). Oxford, UK: Oxford Centre for Staff and Learning Development.

Langelier, L. (2005). *Working, learning and collaborating in a network: Guide to the implementation and leadership of intentional communities of practice*. Quebec City, QC, Canada: CEFIRO (Recherche et Études de cas collection).

Laurillard, D. (2007). Pedagogcal forms of mobile learning: Framing research questions. In Pachler, N. (Ed.), *Mobile learning: Towards a research agenda* (pp. 33–54). London, UK: WLE Centre.

Luckin, R., Clark, W., Garnett, F., Whitworth, A., Akass, J., Cook, J., et al. (2008). *Learner generated contexts: A framework to support the effective use of technology to support learning*. Retrieved from http://api.ning.com/files/Ij6j7ucsB9vgb11pKPH-U6LKMGQQkR-YDVnxruI9tBGf1Q-eSYUDv-Mil6uWqX4F1jYA1PUkZRXvbxhnxuHusyL-1lRXVrBKnO/LGCOpenContextModelning.doc

Luckin, R., Clark, W., Garnett, F., Whitworth, A., Akass, J., & Cook, J. (2010). Learner-generated contexts: A framework to support the effective use of technology for learning. In Lee, M., & McLoughlin, C. (Eds.), *Web 2.0-based e-learning: Applying social informatics for tertiary teaching* (pp. 70–84). Hershey, PA: IGI Global. doi:10.4018/978-1-60566-294-7.ch004

McLoughlin, C., & Lee, M. (2007). Social software and participatory learning: Pedagogical choices with technology affordances in the Web 2.0 era. In *Proceedings of the ASCILITE ICT Conference: Providing Choices for Learners and Learning* (pp. 664-675).

McLoughlin, C., & Lee, M. (2008a). Future learning landscapes: Transforming pedagogy through social software. *Innovate: Journal of Online Education, 4*(5), 7.

McLoughlin, C., & Lee, M. (2008b). Mapping the digital terrain: New media and social software as catalysts for pedagogical change. In *Proceedings of the ASCILITE Conference*, Melbourne, Australia (pp. 641-652).

McLoughlin, C., & Lee, M. (2010). Pedagogy 2.0: Critical challenges and responses to Web 2.0 and social software in tertiary teaching. In Lee, M., & McLoughlin, C. (Eds.), *Web 2.0-based e-learning: Applying social informatics for tertiary teaching* (pp. 46–69). Hershey, PA: IGI Global.

O'Reilly, T. (2005). *What is Web 2.0: Design patterns and business models for the next generation of software*. Retrieved from http://www.oreillynet.com/pub/a/oreilly/tim/news/2005/09/30/what-is-web-20.html

Sharples, M. (2001). Disruptive devices: Mobile technology for conversational learning. *International Journal of Continuing Education and Lifelong Learning, 12*(5-6), 504–520.

Sharples, M. (2009). Methods for evaluating mobile learning. In Vavoula, G., Pachler, N., & Kukulska-Hulme, A. (Eds.), *Researching mobile learning* (pp. 17–39). Bern, Switzerland: Peter Lang.

Sharples, M., Crook, C., Jones, I., Kay, D., Chowcat, I., & Balmer, K. (2009). *CAPITAL year one final report*. Nottingham, UK: University of Nottingham.

Stead, G. (2006). Mobile technologies: Transforming the future of learning. In Pinder, A. (Ed.), *Emerging technologies for learning (Vol. 2006*, pp. 6–15). Coventry, UK: British Educational Communications and Technology Agency.

Uden, L. (2007). Activity theory for designing mobile learning. *International Journal of Mobile Learning and Organisation, 1*(1), 81–102. doi:10.1504/IJMLO.2007.011190

Vavoula, G. (2007). *Learning bridges: A role for mobile technologies in education*. Paper presented at the M-Learning Symposium, London, UK.

Vavoula, G., Pachler, N., & Kukulska-Hulme, A. (Eds.). (2009). *Researching mobile learning*. Bern, Switzerland: Peter Lang.

Wadsworth, Y. (1998). *What is participatory action research?* Retrieved from http://www.scu.edu.au/schools/gcm/ar/ari/p-ywadsworth98.html

Wenger, E., White, N., & Smith, J. (2009). *Digital habitats: Stewarding technology for communities*. Portland, OR: CPsquare.

Wenger, E., White, N., Smith, J., & Rowe, K. (2005). Technology for communities. In Langelier, L. (Ed.), *Working, learning and collaborating in a network: Guide to the implementation and leadership of intentional communities of practice* (pp. 71–94). Quebec City, QC, Canada: CEFIRO.

This work was previously published in the International Journal of Mobile and Blended Learning, Volume 3, Issue 3, edited by David Parsons, pp 1-22, copyright 2011 by IGI Publishing (an imprint of IGI Global).

Chapter 15
Mature Students using Mobile Devices in Life and Learning

Agnes Kukulska-Hulme
The Open University, UK

Ana A. Carvalho
University of Minho, Portugal

John Pettit
The Open University, UK

Anthony Herrington
Curtin University, Australia

Linda Bradley
Chalmers University of Technology, Sweden

David Kennedy
University of Hong Kong, Hong Kong

Aisha Walker
University of Leeds, UK

ABSTRACT

The paper reports on research concerned with learners' uses of mobile technologies based on an international survey that targeted students registered in selected master's and doctoral programmes in Australia, Hong Kong, Portugal, Sweden, and the United Kingdom. The survey findings were enriched by local knowledge, as the authors administered questionnaires in their own countries. The research gives an account of uses of handheld devices by students from departments of education, educational technology, engineering, and information technology in the domains of learning, work, social interaction and entertainment. The paper illuminates learners' choices in the midst of evolving social practices, and challenges the common preconception that mobile devices are not suitable for academic study. In today's global education marketplace, educators must know the technology habits and expectations of their students, including those from other countries. Knowing about students' previous practices and the techno-cultural setting they come from can help institutions determine what mobile applications are most appropriate to support learning.

DOI: 10.4018/978-1-4666-2139-8.ch015

INTRODUCTION

Recent reflection on technology-enhanced learning and teaching suggests a key design principle, that "Learners can be active makers and shapers of their own learning. They should be supported in using technologies of their own choice where appropriate" (JISC, 2009, p. 51). Learners might choose technologies that are familiar to them and that they have used successfully in the past. This could include mobile devices, although for many people such a choice would be a departure from their usual practice of using mobile phones and other portable devices for personal and social reasons, rather than learning. That is why the circumstances in which learners decide to use a mobile device, for learning and for other aspects of their lives, are worth investigating.

It has been shown that an everyday tool such as the mobile phone will not necessarily be readily adopted for learning; a variety of barriers to adoption continue to be identified, such as ergonomic, pedagogical, psychological and environmental factors and the issue of cost (Stockwell, 2008). At the same time, it is clear that some barriers are local, temporary and may be overcome. For example, since mobile device users are driving the proliferation of free Wi-Fi hotspots in parts of the world (Bradford, 2010), cost issues could become less of a barrier, and we can speculate that more widespread adoption by students and teachers is likely to follow. Furthermore, the increasing availability of free or inexpensive 'apps' (applications) for mobile phones is also spreading the message that the phone can be used as a convenient and powerful tool for learning.

Due to the rapidly changing landscape of technology use, there is a continual need to understand learner practices and their technology adoption, including any new barriers and enablers that can be identified. In an age when "communities are jumping across technologies" as needs and trends evolve (Wenger, 2010), educators and researchers also have to stay informed about how learners use personal technologies as members of communities that may be social, work-related or educational. Communities and networks facilitated by technology are, in turn, the means by which various technologies are promulgated and adopted; for example, when social network sites add real-time communications features such as instant messaging (Christakis & Fowler, 2009).

Our research is situated within emerging research on the 'learner's perspective' on e-learning and mobile learning, in the context of increasing learner autonomy, personal choice of tools and learning spaces, and decreasing institutional control. It also contributes to debates engendered by the idea that education must change in response to a new generation of learners. Typically the 'new generation' is understood as comprising those born in the period since the early 1980s, variously referred to as the Net generation (Tapscott, 1998, 2008), Digital Natives (Prensky, 2001, 2009) and Millennials (Oblinger & Oblinger, 2005), whose expectations in respect of technology use are claimed to be significantly different from the generations that preceded it. Jones, Ramanau, Cross and Healing (2010) have critiqued the 'new generation' arguments, concluding that "overall there is growing theoretical and empirical evidence that casts doubt on the idea that there is a defined new generation of young people with common characteristics related to their exposure to digital technologies and networked communication throughout their lives" (p. 6). Instead, their research points to the existence of a number of notable 'minorities' within the generation, such as "a large minority who make use of the Internet to download or upload materials and a smaller minority who contribute to blogs and wikis or engage with virtual worlds" (p. 21). Within their sample of First Year university students in the UK, almost all students owned a mobile phone; an mp3-device or other digital music player was commonly owned as well, but the use of these portable devices was not explored in any detail. Conole, de Laat, Dillon and Darby (2008) found that students made use of mobile phones frequently to phone and text each other, particularly when they had assignment queries.

We consider that learners who use handheld mobile devices (e.g., their phones and mp3-players) to support their learning constitute a minority at the present time. We agree that their age seems less important than their position as early adopters and instigators of change through their influence among their peers and through their networks. Nevertheless, age has a bearing on behaviour in terms of learners' experience and the ability to reflect on that experience. We decided to focus our investigations on more mature learners, that is, those who are at the point of completing their Higher Education, in particular those studying at master's or doctoral level in the fields of education, educational technology, engineering and information technology. Our assumption was that students registered on such programmes would be particularly strong in their capacity to reflect on their learning and to point the way to future practices that others might in time adopt. We wanted to invite them to volunteer their opinions, personal accounts, and information about how they use their mobile devices. A previous survey and interviews have been conducted with this target student population in the United Kingdom, demonstrating that it is possible to collect valuable data (Pettit & Kukulska-Hulme, 2007; Kukulska-Hulme & Pettit, 2009).

RESEARCH OBJECTIVES

In this section we discuss the objectives of our international survey by online questionnaire, which focused on students registered on selected master's and doctoral programmes in Australia, Hong Kong, Portugal, Sweden and the United Kingdom. The sample was purposive, targeting mostly older, 'mature' students, enrolled in study programmes at the authors' home institutions at the time of data collection. Some recent gradu-

ates were also invited to participate. The overall aim of the research was to give an account of everyday uses and more unusual deployments of portable technologies by the students, in relation to four areas:

- Learning
- Social interaction
- Entertainment
- Work

The widespread use of information and communication technologies in many contemporary societies means that it is increasingly difficult to draw boundaries between these four activities in people's lives, since there is interplay between them (Kukulska-Hulme & Pettit, 2009). We wanted to remain open to the possibility that the use of mobile technology in some or all of these areas might help contextualize how the technology is used in learning. We acknowledge that 'learning' is not an unambiguous term; increasingly, online social interaction is an explicit aspect of many courses, and some activity reported under the rubric of 'social interaction' may also relate to learning.

The research sought to identify how various mobile devices are used, on an individual basis and as part of communities, and to uncover emerging practices. The following key research questions guided the study:

- How do mature students make use of different types of mobile device in relation to learning, social interaction, entertainment and work?
- Does mobile device use support mature students in being part of communities and groups?
- Which are the most and least frequent uses of mobile devices?
- What are the perceived innovative aspects and disadvantages of mobile devices in relation to learning?

In addition to capturing accounts of experience, we were interested in gathering data that might challenge the still widespread opinion amongst educators that mobile devices are of little use for academic study. Activities such as web browsing, reading e-news, article reading, book reading and note taking are valued in the academic world but often considered implausible on handheld devices. Furthermore, we were interested in how mobile devices support informal and community learning. In short, we set out to investigate learner-driven practice with mobile technologies, any innovation arising from that practice, and the interface between formal and informal learning. The survey is a step forward in what is a long-term research commitment to understanding and interpreting evolving practice in learner-driven mobile learning.

The fast-changing technological landscape means that the interpretation of what counts as a 'mobile device' is constantly changing. The survey specified that we were not asking about the use of tablets and laptops. Since the survey was developed, other devices including notebook computers and ebook readers have become popular, making it even more difficult to draw boundaries between 'handheld learning', 'laptop learning' and 'desktop learning'. Our survey avoided confusion by asking questions about use of specific types of device, giving examples where it was deemed necessary (e.g. "Have you used a PDA, e.g. Palm, HP iPAQ, iPod Touch?").

Our research is concerned with mature students' experiences in the five countries where the survey was conducted; furthermore, we are able to highlight some differences that became apparent, which will enable educators to have more informed conversations with their students about their mobile learning practices, and will enable researchers to design further investigations of those apparent differences. We have used our own contextual knowledge as researchers living in these countries to assist with interpretation; in that sense, our research is international and local.

The survey findings were therefore enriched by local knowledge of social, economic or political factors which may have an impact on user choices.

The value of this research is expressed not only in the actual findings but additionally in that the findings constitute a good basis for conversations that can ensue between educators and learners. Students do not always realise the potential of new tools and this is an aspect where educators can help (Trinder, Guiller, Margaryan, Littlejohn & Nicol, 2008). Furthermore, given today's global education marketplace, it is necessary for educators to get to know the expectations of their international students, as distinct from their domestic cohort. Knowing something about their previous practices with mobile devices and the techno-cultural setting they come from, can help determine the most appropriate use of mobile technology.

The paper first presents some background information about the target students and their localities. This is followed by details of the questionnaire and our research findings. Finally, we discuss the findings and offer some reflections and conclusions.

PARTICIPANTS

The target student groups in Australia, Portugal, Sweden, Hong Kong and the United Kingdom were given information about the research and invited to complete the online questionnaire in their own time on a voluntary basis. Responses were anonymous, but respondents could provide their name and email address if they were willing to be contacted for follow-up research.

Australia

Participants were from the University of Wollongong, a regional Australian university. The mobile learning questionnaire targeted students enrolled in the one-year Masters by coursework degree in specialist areas which include: Adult

Education, Higher Education and Vocational Education; Educational Leadership; Information and Communication Technologies in Education and Training; Language and Literacy; Physical and Health Education; Special Education; and Teaching English to Speakers of Other Languages. Most students in the programme were Australian citizens (76%) with the remaining coming from 17 countries including Canada, PR China, Saudi Arabia, New Zealand, UK, India, Japan, Malaysia, Indonesia, and USA. Educational leadership was the most popular major studied (25%) followed by Adult Education (11%) and Language and Literacy (10%). The students came from a wide range of educational professions predominantly teachers and trainers from across the school and tertiary sectors.

Portugal

Participants from the University of Minho, Portugal, were registered students on the university's Masters in Education (Educational Technology), a programme developed by the Department of Curriculum and Educational Technology, at the Institute of Education and Psychology. Students on this programme are typically experienced practitioners working in the education sector, mainly teachers; most of the students are Portuguese but some are Brazilians. All participated in face-to-face sessions weekly. A virtual learning environment was used to access materials and sometimes to engage in discussion or group work. Podcasts were used to give students feedback about their assignments or group presentation.

Sweden

The participants were master's students in Computer Science and Mechanical Engineering at Chalmers University of Technology, Gothenburg, within programmes such as software engineering, interaction design, applied mechanics and production development. There are only campus-based

courses at Chalmers and no distance based ones. However, in 2008, 547 Masters students out of 1523 were international students. Higher education in Sweden is free of charge (although this may change in the future), which is a contributing factor to the high number of students from abroad. Also, the requirement that master's courses should be taught in English means that many international students choose Sweden.

Hong Kong

Participants from Hong Kong University were a mixture of full and part-time Masters of Science students (Information Technology in Education), a programme that had been running successfully for more than five years. The majority of students in this programme are primary or secondary teachers, however, the diversity of intake had broadened considerably to include individuals that work in publishing, banking and adult education training environments. The programme of study is undertaken in blended mode with face-to-face and online classes. Students enjoy free wireless access at the university and in numerous public locations around Hong Kong.

United Kingdom 1

The Leeds University group consisted of postgraduate students. The participants were all studying on MA programmes in Education, so the majority of them were teachers or lecturers, with a few other education professionals such as librarians and people working in educational management. Participants were not asked to identify their programme of study but from the 22 who gave their names, 13 were on the MA ICT in Education. Of these, 9 were distance students. The materials for some modules on the MA ICT in Education include podcasts which students may listen to online/on computer or may download to mobile devices -- although Walker (2009) shows that relatively few students transfer the podcasts to mobile mp3 players. At the time of this study, none of the other MA programmes at Leeds included podcasts or other materials intended for use on mobiles.

United Kingdom 2

Participants from The Open University were registered students and alumni of the university's Masters in Online and Distance Education (MA-ODE), a global-intake programme developed by the Institute of Educational Technology. Students and alumni of this programme are typically experienced practitioners working in the education sector; some are British nationals temporarily working overseas. All participate in the programme through online distance education, using a virtual learning environment to access materials and engage in discussion or group work. There is no requirement for them to meet face-to-face. Some of the students/alumni in this group are likely to have been involved in an MAODE special project in which they were given a PDA to use for learning during 2001.

INTERNATIONAL SURVEY

The International Survey was conducted between May 2008 and April 2009 by means of an extensive online questionnaire (see Appendix), adapted from one used previously for our study in 2005 (Kukulska-Hulme & Pettit, 2006, 2009). The questionnaire comprised a mix of closed and open questions in five sections. It enabled the capture of qualitative and quantitative data on the use of various mobile devices in diverse spheres of activity; the workings of communities and groups; frequency of specific actions; and reflections on benefits and disadvantages:

- **Section 1. About yourself:** Respondents gave information about their age, gender,

country where they spend most/all of their time, and job/profession
- **Section 2. The use of mobile devices – now or in the past:** For each device used (mobile phone, smartphone, PDA, mp3/mp4 player), respondents were asked to "give one or more examples in detail" to show how they used it for learning, for social interaction, for entertainment/quizzes/games, and for work/teaching (note: many target students and alumni worked in teaching)
- **Section 3. Being part of groups and communities:** The questionnaire explained that groups/communities could be formal or informal. Respondents were asked to describe the purposes of the groups they are part of, which devices they used, the benefits of being part of the group and to say whether they could be in this group if they did not use a mobile device.
- **Section 4. Specific uses for mobile devices:** Twenty-seven specific uses were listed (browsing websites, reading an e-book, listening to podcasts, taking photos, etc.). For each use, frequency had to be selected from 7 possible responses ranging from 'several times a day' to 'never'.
- **Section 5. Mobile devices for learning: what's special, what's a problem?** Respondents were asked to say what they consider to be new and innovative about their use of mobile devices for learning, and what is the single biggest problem or disadvantage that mobile devices bring them in relation to their learning.

The open questions enabled participants to write a response in their own terms. These questions were included so as to avoid the limitations of pre-set categories of response when the main objective was to capture accounts of experience that could be said to constitute "site-specific case

Table 1. Respondents to the survey

Country where survey was administered	Responses	% respondents from other countries*	Age range of respondents*	Female	Male
Australia	67	22%	3% < 25 33% 25–34 27% 35–44 30% 45–54 7% 55–64	78%	22%
Hong Kong	23	26%	9% < 25 57% 25–34 35% 35–44	70%	30%
Portugal	28	0%	61% 25–34 32% 35–44 7% 45–54	64%	36%
Sweden	66	14%	48% < 25 44% 25–34 6% 35–44 2% 45–54	20%	80%
UK (Leeds University)	38	53%	11% < 25 39% 25–34 34% 35–44 16% 45–54	68%	32%
UK (The Open University)	48	45%	4% 25–34 34% 35–44 42% 45–54 19% 55–64 2% 65 and over	54%	46%
TOTAL	270				

* Percentages have been rounded

studies" where rich and personal data is of prime importance (Cohen, Manion & Morrison, 2000, pp. 247-248). A constraint was that respondents were requested to write in English; judging from their responses, this was not a problem for the majority, but we cannot rule out some difficulty in self-expression.

Student participation in the research was voluntary and unconnected to study progress or assessment. A total of 270 students completed the questionnaire. Response rates were not recorded, as our research was deliberately based on volunteer samples. With the exception of Sweden, there were larger numbers of female respondents (Table 1). The students surveyed in Sweden were from programmes where there are large numbers of male students.

Whilst our survey was deployed in five different countries, the students who responded sometimes indicated that they spent "most or all of their time" in another country. The Australian group included 4 students from Japan and 11 from other countries; the Hong Kong group had 5 students from China and one from the US; the group from Sweden included 9 spending most or all of their time outside Sweden. Over half of the UK (Leeds University) group were from outside the UK, and nearly half of the UK (Open University) group were from outside the UK (one person did not reply to this question). Only the students in Portugal spent most or all of their time in that country. We note that these student profiles reflect the increasingly international mix among those studying at master's and doctoral levels globally.

Table 3. Examples of mobile phone/ smartphone use, for four categories of activity

	...for learning	*... for social interaction*	*... for entertainment/ quizzes/games*	*... for work/teaching*
Australia	Have the Bureau of Metereology as an application on the phone to check weather systems and fronts.	To contact friends and family as we do not have a land line, so all calls are on my mobile.	Play games, use iphone applications – yahtzee, dice games etc., music and audio books	As majority of my work involves being on the road, used as a communication tool.
Hong Kong	Use the dictionary to learn English. Get the group members together to prepare for the presentation.	Calls, messages, sending images. Check friends on Facebook. Windows Live Messenger.	May take photo or video all the time if you got a big memory card. Reading novels. Watch YouTube videos.	Mark down important points when came to mind. Take photos for records of site inspection.
Portugal	To interact with my group mates. To take photos. To know some events that are going to happen.	Sms and call to friends, and sms to a micro blog web site (Twitter). As a camera video and as a tom tom.	Sometimes I enter some contests and therefore use my mobile to answer the quizzes.	My students listen [to] podcasts in their cellphones, take pictures and make films for discussion…
Sweden	I use the calendar to structure my studies. Adding reminders to myself. Listen to educative radio shows.	To call abroad using Skype out number. Videophone calls to friends, family and work mates.	Reading news on internet. Built-in games on my phone, but got bored quite soon.	Help me remember stuff that I'm supposed to do. Sometimes I buy bus tickets with the mobile.
UK - Leeds	I have used the recorder to record memos to myself when I have ideas for research, essays etc. Translating from English into Arabic.	To call friends to arrange a meeting, but not to 'talk about life'. To plan things.	Sometimes when I'm waiting for an appointment, I tend to use the phone to play.	Video camera for recording and taking photos which I later transferred into my computer to use as a teacher.
UK - OU	Kanji a day – learning Japanese and Chinese characters. I have used it to read the news. Listening to the radio.	I send texts and pictures to family and to the Moblog community. Taking photos and videos spontaneously.	Exchanging funny videos with friends. Discussion forums and sharing links.	Make records of worthwhile experiences. This is a personal device and I keep it entirely separate from my work.

We recognize there may be a number of factors influencing mobile device use, including age of respondents, gender, nature of the program being studied, infrastructure and tariffs in the country concerned, and cultural practices.

Data from each of the five participating countries were stored in separate databases. The quantitative data were subjected to a descriptive statistical analysis, whilst the qualitative data were analyzed manually for each question in the survey, enabling us to examine use examples in detail. We extracted actual examples of use (see Table 3) and noted prominent cases where similar uses were mentioned by more than one respondent.

SURVEY FINDINGS

Presented below are salient findings from the survey, concentrating on characterizations of how various devices are used, what respondents say about the use of mobile devices as part of a group or community, key findings regarding specific uses, and finally, respondents' comments about positive and negative aspects of using mobile devices for learning.

How Mobile Devices Are Used

The questionnaire included a section on the use of mobile devices - now or in the past - where

Table 2. Devices used

	mobile phone	smartphone	PDA	mp3/mp4-player
Australia	91%	22%	15%	75%
Hong Kong	78%	35%	22%	65%
Portugal	86%	7%	7%	74%
Sweden	97%	11%	14%	80%
UK - Leeds	100%	19%	22%	62%
UK - OU	94%	25%	46% *	71%

* Includes students from the special project with PDAs, which may explain this relatively high percentage.

for each device used, respondents were asked to provide one or more examples. The data enabled us to answer the first research question: How do mature students make use of different types of mobile device in connection with learning, social interaction, entertainment and work?

First, we note that as could be expected, mobile phone use is shown to be near-universal, although there is minor variation across the groups (Table 2). The use of mp3 and mp4-players is also predictably high; the figures for use of smartphones and PDAs vary considerably across the groups.

The questionnaire data contains a rich array of 'use examples' for each of the four devices specified, under each of the four categories that respondents were asked to write about. If we set aside the most obvious examples, such as using the mobile phone to make calls or an mp3 player to listen to music, there is an abundance of use examples that illustrate the versatility of each device in the ways it can support a broad range of activity. Examples of reported mobile phone and smartphone uses across four categories are presented in Table 3, selected to show a broad range of uses (the examples are quoted verbatim). Overall we note that:

- There are receptive, productive and communicative uses
- Respondents are using mobile devices to capture ideas and experiences

- Mobile devices have a useful function as tools that remind the user about what she/he has to do
- Respondents make use of a range of applications for informal learning
- One function of games is to fill gaps in the day
- Some respondents appear to be drawing boundaries around disparate uses
- The mobile phone features as an alternative means of communication and to support physical mobility, e.g. as an alternative to having a land line or when work involves travelling

Overall in the 'learning' category of examples, the most prominent uses are contact with others, immediate access to information and answers, reading e-books, listening to podcasts, and scheduling. More unusual uses mentioned include creating an educational resource; use of vodcasts of educational and documentary TV shows; recording one's voice in preparing a presentation; recording something on an iPhone and replaying it on an iPod; taking photos of billboard advertisements and pictures in reference books; contacting experts in other fields; uploading notes to a blog. Facebook, Windows Live Messenger, MSN and Skype receive several mentions. Language learning is also a popular activity amongst respondents.

'Social interaction' examples contain references to keeping in contact with friends and

Table 4. Responses to the question, "Do you use a mobile device to be part of one or more groups or communities?" *

	No	Yes
Australia	61%	39%
Hong Kong	87%	13%
Portugal	86%	14%
Sweden	81%	19%
UK - Leeds	70%	30%
UK - OU	47%	53%

* Percentages have been rounded

family who are nearby or dispersed around the globe. Finding information, accessing sites such as YouTube, sending images, sharing playlists and exchanging music files with others are also reported, as well as contact during project work. Headphones attached to a mobile device are used to cut out unwanted social interaction during commuting or at work; dual headphones are used to listen together with others. Several respondents mention restricting their social use to contact with family and friends. Social interaction includes handing over your device to a friend so that they can browse through your pictures at their own pace.

The 'entertainment/quizzes/games' category shows productive activities such as making videos and taking photos, alongside listening, watching, reading and playing. 'Pre-installed' and 'default' games are often mentioned. Within 'work/teaching', mobile device use includes appointments, reminders, use in emergencies and on trips, as props in class, and to provide entertainment or materials for classes; there is also contact with students to offer tutoring or to discuss assessments. The quantity of data in all four categories precludes us from being able to list all reported uses.

The Use of Mobile Devices as Part of a Group or Community

The middle section of the questionnaire was designed to find out whether mobile device use supports respondents in being part of communities and groups, both formal and informal. It was explained that these communities and groups could relate "to friends, leisure, family, study, work, etc". If respondents stated that they use a mobile device to be part of one or more groups or communities (see Table 4), they were invited to give some details of their activities, which devices they used, and how they had benefitted from being part of the community/group. As seen in Table 4, there is considerable variation between the groups of respondents with regard to their reported use of mobile devices to be part of a community or group.

Apart from communication among family and friends, respondents refer to leisure and voluntary pursuits and keeping in touch with former colleagues by using mobile devices. The mobile phone/SMS and group texts, Skype, MSN, video meetings, GPS and micro blogging are key technologies. Tablets and laptops are mentioned in passing (even though they were supposed to be excluded from the survey), which possibly suggests that handheld devices may not always suffice. Social networking communities such as Facebook and identica.ca (a micro blogging community) are named in addition to traditional communities and friendship groups.

SMS plays an important role in alerting members of groups and communities and as a connection point between other technologies. For example, SMS is used to alert community members about an important email message which they might otherwise not see; Pager messages on the phone via SMS alert a volunteer that they are needed by their community; Members of a paragliding club report weather conditions via SMS to a central number and all members get the message forwarded on to them; A mobile phone is used by a teacher to redirect students to course-related resources.

Reported benefits of using mobile devices to be part of groups or communities include spontaneous communication, flexibility, speed, fun, support, experience sharing, intellectual stimulation and use of technology to cope with changing arrangements. The data from the UK-OU group are particularly rich in this regard; by contrast, the Hong Kong, Portugal and Sweden respondents were largely silent here.

Key Findings on Specific Uses for Mobile Devices

This section of the questionnaire was designed to elicit information about 27 distinct uses of mobile devices. This was a broad repertoire of possible uses, based on typical functionality of mobile devices such as web browser, video, camera, GPS, etc. (Trinder, 2005), and elaborated by the project team to include emerging activities such as video-sharing, micro-blogging and using location-based services. Respondents could also add other uses which were not listed. The aim was to find out which were the most and least frequent uses. We were also interested to identify the 'most intensive' uses, meaning that an activity was performed several times a day, as distinct from just once or twice a day. A subsidiary aim was to discover the extent to which respondents were using mobile devices for more academic activities such as reading academic papers or recording a seminar. The presented uses covered:

- Browsing, reading, viewing, listening;
- Accessing information and doing searches;
- Making and recording;
- Sharing (sending and posting);
- Playing a location-based game

This range is typical in taxonomies representing activities or tasks: assimilative, information handling, productive, communicative and experiential (e.g. used by Conole, 2007, who also includes 'adaptive' activity such as modelling or simulation). Uses that had some similarity were listed one after the other (e.g. reading an e-book, reading e-news, reading an academic paper; listening to music, listening to podcasts). Several were fairly specific, e.g. 'Sending a video clip from your mobile device to a video-sharing site'. Participants were asked to respond to each of the 27 uses, irrespective of mobile device employed, indicating the frequency of use on a 7-point scale (several times a day; once or twice a day; a few days a week; once a week; once a month; less than once a month; never).

The three most and least frequent uses, reported by each country, are shown in Tables 5 and 6. Table 5 distinguishes between 'most intensive uses' (defined as: several times a day) and 'most frequent uses' (once a week or more, i.e., an aggregation of the first four points on the scale, including several times a day).

The three most intensive uses are very clearly sending text messages, browsing websites and listening to music; reading e-news also makes an appearance (see Table 5). When it comes to the most frequent, but less intense uses, browsing websites is supplanted by taking photographs and using a mobile device to make notes. In the UK-OU group, 40% of respondents report listening to podcasts. (The relevant percentage for UK-Leeds is 39%, whereas it is considerably lower in Portugal 26%, Australia 26%, Hong Kong 22%, and Sweden 9%; however, it should be noted that we know some tutors provided podcasts as part of their study materials.)

Least frequent uses are those where the highest proportions of responses were 'never'; the responses here show that playing a location-based game was very infrequent, along with posting to a micro-blog, posting to your blog from your mobile device, sending a video clip from your mobile device to a video-sharing site, and (for the Hong Kong respondents) recording a formal interview.

Table 5. The most intensive and the most frequent uses*

	Most intensive uses (several times a day)	%	Most frequent uses (once a week or more)	%
Australia	1. Sending text-messages (SMS) 2. Browsing websites 3. Listening to music	33% 15% 12%	1. Sending text-messages (SMS) 2. Listening to music 3. Browsing websites	91% 58% 32%
Hong Kong	1. Sending text-messages (SMS) 2. Browsing websites =2. Listening to music 4. Reading e-news	30% 26% 26% 22%	1. Sending text-messages (SMS) 2. Taking a photograph 3. Listening to music	74% 61% 57%
Portugal	1. Sending text-messages (SMS) 2. Browsing websites 3. *[five uses come joint third]***	61% 18% 11%	1. Sending text-messages (SMS) 2. Using a mobile device to make notes 3. Taking a photograph	100% 75% 68%
Sweden	1. Sending text-messages (SMS) 2. Listening to music 3. Browsing websites	32% 15% 11%	1. Sending text-messages (SMS) 2. Listening to music 3. Taking a photograph	92% 62% 40%
UK Leeds	1. Sending text-messages (SMS) 2. Listening to music 3. Browsing websites	65% 18% 16%	1. Sending text-messages (SMS) 2. Listening to music 3. Using a mobile device to make notes	97% 61% 55%
UK OU	1. Sending text-messages (SMS) 2. Browsing websites =2. Listening to music 4. Reading e-news	29% 13% 13% 6%	1. Sending text-messages (SMS) 2. Listening to music 3. Listening to podcasts	67% 54% 40%

* Percentages have been rounded

** Joint third: Listening to music, Reading e-news, Taking a photograph, Using a mobile device to make notes, Using Google or another search engine.

Table 7 shows the frequency of reading e-books and academic papers. Respondents from Hong Kong report the highest frequency in relation to both uses. Along with reading books and papers, academic study may also involve doing interviews as part of research and attending seminars and presentations; frequencies of 'recording a formal interview e.g., as part of your research', and 'recording a seminar or other presentation by a speaker', were very low across all groups (0-6% reporting once a week or more).

Positive and Negative Aspects of Using Mobile Devices for Learning

Respondents were asked to write in their own words what they consider to be *new and innovative* about their experience of using mobile

Table 6. The least frequent uses*

Least frequent uses (never)	Aust	HK	Port	Swed	UK-L	UK-OU
Playing a location-based game	97%		86%	97%	97%	94%
Posting to a micro-blog	95%	91%	96%	97%	95%	89%
Posting to your blog from your mobile device	91%	83%	89%	95%	94%	
Sending a video clip from your mobile device to a video-sharing site				95%		87%
Recording a formal interview		78%				

* Percentages have been rounded

Table 7. Frequency of reading e-books and academic papers*

e-books	Australia	Hong Kong	Portugal	Sweden	UK Leeds	UK OU
Once a week or more	9%	43%	19%	8%	11%	10%
Academic papers	Australia	Hong Kong	Portugal	Sweden	UK Leeds	UK OU
Once a week or more	12%	35%	25%	11%	24%	21%

* Percentages have been rounded

devices for learning. Responses included well established advantages such as convenient access to information or to the Internet and the ability to contact people whenever needed. Specific new/innovative aspects noted by respondents included the following:

- Permanency of taking notes; paper is easily lost
- Multipurpose; you can take your work/entertainment with you
- Can combine a walk or run with listening to a podcast
- Podcasts give access to unique historical/scientific content
- Suits auditory learners
- Closer relationship between students and teacher
- Multimedia in one small device is a time-saver for teachers
- Instant documentation of whiteboard notes
- Taking photos of overhead slides
- Help with learning disabilities
- Alternative news source/ breaking news / immediate first hand reports
- Helps maintain a public diary with a community dimension
- Quick way to learn
- Gets you outdoors
- Field trips become more fruitful and challenging

There were also a few responses indicating that nothing was new ('same material, different format'). A further question asked about problems and disadvantages. Apart from expected answers

such as small screen size and issues of cost, which we do not report here, respondents mentioned various ergonomic, technical and social issues:

- Slow writing, difficulty scanning when reading
- Noisy environments, e.g. on public transport
- Restrictive environments, e.g. hospitals
- Can't connect mobile to projector
- Difficulty synchronizing several devices
- Poor sound quality
- Inequality of access
- Distracting, intrusive
- Feeling of 'physical togetherness' is missing
- Becoming dependent on the mobile

DISCUSSION AND REFLECTIONS

The study has delivered interesting first results into emerging use cases of mobile devices which can serve as a link to foster learning in formal and informal contexts. Mobile devices are shown to support informal and community learning. There are numerous reported benefits, particularly emphasized by the distance education students (UK – The Open University). While the predominant use for mobile devices is communication, it seems that other aspects of social interaction can benefit, such as the ability to share media between mobile devices directly or blended across other social networking technologies like Facebook.

Amongst the mature age students surveyed, receptive, productive and communicative uses are in evidence across learning, social, entertainment and workplace environments. The research confirms the global popularity of SMS, browsing websites, listening to music, taking photographs and making notes. It also highlights that reading e-news and listening to podcasts are relatively frequent activities among some students, and that article- and book-reading, once considered implausible on handheld devices, are popular among a minority.

Using mobile devices for entertainment and in the workplace highlights the importance of these technologies for users who themselves are mobile. Making productive use of downtime while travelling and keeping in contact with work colleagues has become part of daily life even though some clearly wish to retain a distinct work–life boundary. These activities are further enabled by the increasing availability of WiFi on different modes of commuter transport. The research provides good evidence of a contrast between claims that mobile learning can take place 'anytime, anywhere' and reported practice which often describes irregular usage dependent on a range of factors.

The data continue to show the main use for these devices involves communication through phone and text, and referencing information such as websites, readings and maps. What is interesting is that there appear to be many ways in which users are employing the technologies to generate products. Bruns (2005) coined the term 'produsers' to denote both of these approaches. Our survey shows that mobile devices are enabling users to create resources for teaching purposes, write blogs to keep their friends up to date with events, take and distribute photos and videos, and make and take notes and recordings.

Uses within specific countries suggest evolving social and cultural practices that may result from patterns of use among friends, family, colleagues and teachers. This research helps to identify uses of mobile devices that teachers and others can exploit to further unlock the potential for using these devices as cognitive tools to support learning (Herrington *et al.*, 2009). By considering apparent differences between learner practices in different countries, we enable researchers and teachers to become more sensitive to different circumstances facing students who are studying remotely or spending time away from their usual place of study, and can help educational practitioners designing learning for culturally diverse cohorts. As noted earlier, the student profiles in our survey reflect the increasingly international mix among those studying at master's and doctoral levels. We did not attempt to identify purely 'native' mature student samples and it can be argued that it would be futile and misrepresentative to do so, particularly in the programmes of study we were targeting. However a future large-scale and more comprehensive survey could attempt to make such distinctions.

Knowledge of national contexts in terms of technology proliferation, costs of connectivity or cultural imperatives can help to explain learner choices and behaviours (Katz & Aakhus, 2002). Thus the fact that in Hong Kong there are 11.5 million subscribers in a population of seven million people (OFTA, 2009), and there is free wireless access for students in many public locations in the city, can be regarded as helpful background knowledge. There has been an agreement developed between the major telecommunications player in Hong Kong (PCCW) and universities to provide free wireless access in over 7,900 wireless hotspots, and over 4700 registered Wi-Fi zones in public locations around Hong Kong. These locations include all universities, McDonald's, Starbucks, Pacific Place coffee shops and numerous other venues, including local ferry services. There is cheap internet access; bandwidth is inexpensive and 3G cards for notebook computers are becoming very common. Cost of access is therefore not likely to be seen as a problem. Similarly, in Sweden there is strong competition between mobile phone operators and the cost of buying a mobile phone, calling and texting is dropping. According to a report from the International Telecommunication Union (ITU, 2009), Sweden is among those countries that offer the most affordable ICT services globally. Contextualization of survey findings is an important challenge for future studies of mobile technology use especially if they are to be done on a large scale and involve many countries.

Looking back at our earlier studies in the UK (Pettit & Kukulska-Hulme, 2007; Kukulska-Hulme & Pettit, 2009), we notice that the present data shows a number of new practices among respondents, such as:

- Using 'apps' on the phone, including Facebook and MSN
- Using GPS to find places
- Watching movies, TV shows, vodcasts
- Listening to audio books, podcasts
- Being part of microblogging communities, e.g., Twitter
- Browsing websites
- Using location-based services, e.g. to find nearby taxis, banks, restaurants, etc.
- No longer having a land line

Current respondents also report feeling that paper is 'easily lost' and less reliable. Mobile device use is a fast-changing field that reflects rapid social changes as well as the increasing availability and smarter marketing of new devices. Anecdotally, our current respondents' "least frequent uses" reported in Table 6 – such as playing a location-based game, posting to a blog or micro-blog, and sending a video clip to a video-sharing site – are becoming more widespread, and we would expect these uses to figure more prominently in the future. On the other hand, several usability issues, especially difficulties interacting with a small screen, are still being reported.

In the time since this study was conducted smartphones have become cheaper and more common amongst students and a new generation

of 'slate' devices (e.g. Apple iPad ™) has come onto the market. References to Facebook, Skype, or microblogging in the data suggest that the device students are using qualifies as a smartphone. While there are no clear figures available from the data, it may be expected that the use of smart phones will increase as the market becomes dominated by these devices (see Gartner, 2010, who state that worldwide mobile phone sales grew 17 per cent in first quarter of 2010 and that smartphone sales in the first quarter of 2010 represent an increase of 48.7 per cent from the first quarter of 2009.) Several universities now offer 'apps' for smartphones using platforms such as Campus M (http://www.ombiel.com/campusm.html). Whilst mobile applications are fashionable they are not necessarily cheap and it is important that educators planning to develop apps understand how students perceive and use their mobile devices. Our findings indicate that institutions planning to offer mobile apps should build on the existing preferences of students for social communication, listening to audio, watching videos and reading short texts if the apps are successfully to enhance the learning experience.

It is interesting to compare our findings to those of Walls *et al.* (2010) who questioned the assumption that students are enthusiastic users of podcasts in their non-university lives and therefore keen for their university to start using them. They found that most students did not even know that podcasts existed but once the tutors started to offer podcasts then some students started subscribing to podcasts more widely. Unlike the Walls *et al.* study cohort, some of our students were already being provided with podcasts so that could account for the difference in the findings. However our findings do support the conclusion that when students are offered appropriate mobile resources then they will make use of them. Due to the high use of MP3/MP4 resources, teachers could consider using more podcasts and vodcasts as teaching materials. In previous studies about podcasts, the majority of students preferred to listen to podcasts on their laptop rather than using their MP3 player (Salomon *et al.*, 2007; Carvalho *et al.*, 2009). This preference may be due to an association of MP3 players with leisure rather than learning, a lack of broader adoption of mobile devices in education, or a reflection of an individual's everyday mobility and the places where they prefer to study.

CONCLUSION

Our research gives an international account of mobile device use from learners' perspectives, in relation to learning, social interaction, entertainment and work, with a view to helping researchers and educators incorporate the emerging learner practices into their plans for further research, development and designs for learning. We agree with Kennedy *et al.* (2008) that "an evidence-based understanding of students' technological experiences is vital in informing higher education policy and practice" (p. 109) since, as they point out, this will have implications for student access, equity and transition. We believe the insights gained from looking at learners' accounts of authentic experience are essential in improving understanding between learners and teachers as well as helping to shape future plans for the use of technology in education.

Whatever their age, learners constitute a pool of valuable experience and expertise in the use of mobile technologies. As a collective body, they own, or have access to, some of the latest mobile devices and applications. Pressures of study and assignment deadlines lead them to seek effective solutions to immediate needs on the go. If they are studying in different university departments, they are also in a good position to share experience freely across discipline boundaries, which is something that educators may find much more challenging to do.

Straub (2009) suggests that "the future of adoption research should focus not just on adoption and implementation of information technology in the formal organization but how individuals understand, adopt, and learn technology outside of the formal organization" (p. 646). We concur with this view, while also heeding his plea to avoid a 'proadoption bias', that is, the assumption that the goal is to disseminate information about innovations specifically so that they might be adopted by others (Rogers, 1995). Whilst some practices are worth adopting more widely, others may not merit it, but being better informed about evolving practices has to be a worthwhile goal.

The present investigation leads to various hypotheses for future research, including possible differences in communication choices depending on gender and age. Given the widespread use of SMS demonstrated in our study, we would advocate more research on how language use is adapted for texting (Hård, 2002; Baron, 2008). Furthermore, since the use of a mobile device represents a new technological means of reading books, articles and news, this might have an impact on how, and how much, students read, however further research would be needed.

The landscape of mobile devices has changed since our survey with some devices (standalone PDAs) becoming almost extinct and others (handheld GPS) endangered. The functionality of these devices has been incorporated into smart mobile phones and tablet devices. Not only are mobile devices becoming more affordable and thus more widely used, they also have enhanced connectivity using Wi-Fi. Our study has considered the broad use of mobile devices amongst students; the next research step should be to examine the specific applications that students use for learning, especially those produced by universities. How, where and when do students make use of these applications? In what ways do the applications contribute to the students' overall learning? If mobile applications become a significant part of a university's offering, does this disadvantage some students and, if so, how? Furthermore, as mobile devices become more widespread there will be new types of applications and probably substantial changes in practice which cannot necessarily be foreseen but which will also provide interesting directions for further research.

ACKNOWLEDGMENT

The authors would like to thank the students and alumni who completed the questionnaire for this study, from: Chalmers University of Technology, Hong Kong University, Leeds University, the University of Minho, The Open University and the University of Wollongong. They would also like to thank Donna Phillips from The Open University's Institute of Educational Technology who set up and administered the questionnaire.

REFERENCES

Baron, N. S. (2008). *Always On: Language in an Online and Mobile World*. Oxford, UK: Oxford University Press.

Bradford, K. T. (2010). *Mobile device users drive Wi-Fi hotspot proliferation*. Retrieved from http://blog.laptopmag.com/mobile-device-users-drive-wi-fi-hotspot-proliferation

Bruns, A. (2005). *'Anyone can edit': Understanding the produser*. Retrieved from http://snurb.info/index.php?q=node/286

Carvalho, A. A., Aguiar, C., Santos, H., Oliveira, L., Marques, A., & Maciel, R. (2009). Podcasts in Higher Education: Students and Teachers Perspectives. In Tatnall, A., & Jones, A. (Eds.), *Education and Technology for a Better World* (pp. 417–426). Berlin, Germany: Springer. doi:10.1007/978-3-642-03115-1_44

Christakis, N., & Fowler, J. (2009). *Connected – The Amazing Power of Social Networks and How they Shape Our Lives*. London, UK: Harper Press.

Cohen, L., Manion, L., & Morrison, K. (2000). *Research Methods in Education* (5th ed.). London, UK: RoutledgeFalmer. doi:10.4324/9780203224342

Conole, G. (2007). Describing learning activities: Tools and resources to guide practice. In Beetham, H., & Sharpe, R. (Eds.), *Rethinking Pedagogy for a Digital Age: Designing and delivering e-learning* (pp. 81–91). London, UK: Routledge.

Conole, G., de Laat, M., Dillon, T., & Darby, J. (2008). 'Disruptive technologies', 'pedagogical innovation': What's new? Findings from an in-depth study of students' use and perception of technology. *Computers & Education, 50*(2), 511–524. doi:10.1016/j.compedu.2007.09.009

Continental Research. (2008). *Continental Research: The Autumn 2008 Mobile Phone Report*. Retrieved from http://www.iabeurope.eu/

Gartner. (2010). *Gartner Says Worldwide Mobile Phone Sales Grew 17 Per Cent in First Quarter 2010*. Retrieved from http://www.gartner.com/it/page.jsp?id=1372013

Hård, Y. (2002). *Use and Adaptation of Written Language to the Conditions of Computer-Mediated Communication*. Retrieved from http://www.ling.gu.se/~ylvah/dokument/eng_diss_abstract.pdf

Herrington, J., Herrington, A., Mantei, J., Olney, I., & Ferry, B. (Eds.). (2009). *New technologies, new pedagogies: Mobile learning in higher education*. Wollongong, NSW, Australia: University of Wollongong.

ITU. (2009). *Measuring the Information Society: ICT Development Index. 2009 edition*. Retrieved from http://www.itu.int/ITU-D/ict/publications/idi/2009/index.html

JISC. (2009). *Effective Practice in a Digital Age: A guide to technology-enhanced learning and teaching.* Retrieved from http://www.jisc.ac.uk/publications/programmerelated/2009/effective-practicedigitalage.aspx

Jones, C. R., Ramanau, R., Cross, S., & Healing, G. (2010). Net generation or Digital Natives: Is there a distinct new generation entering university? *Computers & Education, 54*(3), 722–732. doi:10.1016/j.compedu.2009.09.022

Katz, J. E., & Aakhus, M. (2002). *Perpetual Contact: Mobile Communication, Private Talk, Public Performance.* Cambridge, UK: Cambridge University Press. doi:10.1017/CBO9780511489471

Kennedy, G. E., Judd, T. S., Churchward, A., Gray, K., & Krause, K.-L. (2008). First Year Students' Experiences with Technology: Are they really Digital Natives? *Australasian Journal of Educational Technology, 24*(1), 108–122.

Kukulska-Hulme, A., & Pettit, J. (2006, October 23-25). Practitioners as innovators: emergent practice in personal mobile teaching, learning, work and leisure. In *Proceedings of Mlearn '06: Mobile Learning Conference,* Banff, AB, Canada.

Kukulska-Hulme, A., & Pettit, J. (2009). Practitioners as innovators: Emergent practice in personal mobile teaching, learning, work and leisure . In Ally, M. (Ed.), *Mobile Learning: transforming the delivery of education and training* (pp. 135–155). Athabasca, AB, Canada: Athabasca University Press.

Oblinger, D. G., & Oblinger, J. L. (2005). *Educating the Net Generation.* Retrieved from http://www.educause.edu/educatingthenetgen

OFTA. (2009). *Key Telecommunications Statistics.* Hong Kong: Office of the Telecommunications Authority of Hong Kong. Retrieved from http://www.ofta.gov.hk/en/datastat/key_stat.html

Pettit, J., & Kukulska-Hulme, A. (2007). Going with the grain: mobile devices in practice. *Australasian Journal of Educational Technology, 23*(1), 17–33.

Prensky, M. (2001). Digital Natives, Digital Immigrants, Part 2. Do they Really Think Differently? *Horizon, 9*(6).

Prensky, M. (2009). H. Sapiens Digital: From Digital Immigrants and Digital Natives to Digital Wisdom. *Innovate, 5*(3).

PTS. (2009). *The Swedish Telecommunication Market – First half year 2009 – PTS –ER-2009: 29.* Retrieved from http://www.pts.se/en-gb/Documents/Reports/Telephony/2009/Svensk-telemarknad-forsta-halvaret-2009---PTS-ER-200929/

Rogers, E. M. (1995). *Diffusion of innovations* (4th ed.). New York, NY: Free Press.

Salmon, G., Nie, M., & Edirisingha, P. (2007). *Informal Mobile Podcasting and Learning Adaptation (IMPALA).* Leicester, UK: Beyond Distance Research Alliance, University of Leicester.

Stockwell, G. (2008). Investigating learner preparedness for and usage patterns of mobile learning. *ReCALL, 20*(3), 253–270. doi:10.1017/S0958344008000232

Straub, E. (2009). Understanding Technology Adoption: Theory and Future Directions for Informal Learning. *Review of Educational Research, 79,* 625–649. doi:10.3102/0034654308325896

Tapscott, D. (1998). *Growing up digital: The Rise of the Net Generation.* New York, NY: McGraw Hill.

Tapscott, D. (2008). *Grown Up Digital: How the Net Generation is Changing Your World.* New York, NY: McGraw Hill.

Trinder, J. (2005). Mobile technologies and systems . In Kukulska-Hulme, A., & Traxler, J. (Eds.), *Mobile learning: A handbook for educators and trainers* (pp. 7–24). London, UK: Routledge.

Trinder, K., Guiller, J., Margaryan, A., Littlejohn, A., & Nicol, D. (2008). *Learning from digital natives: bridging formal and informal learning.* Retrieved from http://www.heacademy.ac.uk/assets/York/documents/LDN%20Final%20Report.pdf

Walker, A. (2009). Confessions of a Reluctant Podcaster. In V. King, C. Broughan, L. Clouder, F. Deepwell, & A. Turner (Eds.), *Academic Futures* (pp. 209-222). Newcastle-upon-Tyne, UK: Cambridge Scholars Publishing.

Walls, S. M., Kucsera, J. V., Walker, J. D., Acee, T. W., McVaugh, N. K., & Robinson, D. H. (2010). Podcasting in education: Are students as ready and eager as we think they are? *Computers & Education, 54*(2), 371–378. doi:10.1016/j.compedu.2009.08.018

Wenger, E. (2010). SIKM community presentation online. Theme: Rethinking Ourselves (KM People) as Technology Stewards. Retrieved from. http://technologyforcommunities.com/

APPENDIX

Figure 1. Questionnaire

International Research Project: Your use of mobile devices

Dear Student or Alumna/ Alumnus,

Welcome to this online questionnaire about your use of mobile devices for learning, social interaction, entertainment and, if relevant to your situation, work/employment (e.g. teaching). If you have ever used a mobile/cellphone, PDA, iPod or other mobile device, we would like to gather your responses to the questions below. Your responses will provide valuable data to this international research project. We and the other researchers may quote extracts from your responses, in journal papers or other publications and reports, but **your words will always be anonymous.**

Please note that for this study we are not asking about your use of Tablets and laptops.

Many thanks for your time, and we hope you find the questionnaire interesting. You will be given early access to an online report or publication from the project, in order to inform you of the outcomes of the research.

Agnes Kukulska-Hulme & John Pettit
(on behalf of the international project team)
Institute of Educational Technology
The Open University, Milton Keynes, UK

First, please tell us something about yourself...

---

1. **Your age:**
   (Please select one only)

   ☐ Under 25

   ☐ 25-34

   ☐ 35-44

   ☐ 45-54

   ☐ 55-64

   ☐ 65 and over

---

2. **Female or male?**
   (Please select one only)

   ☐ Female

Figure 2. Questionnaire Continued

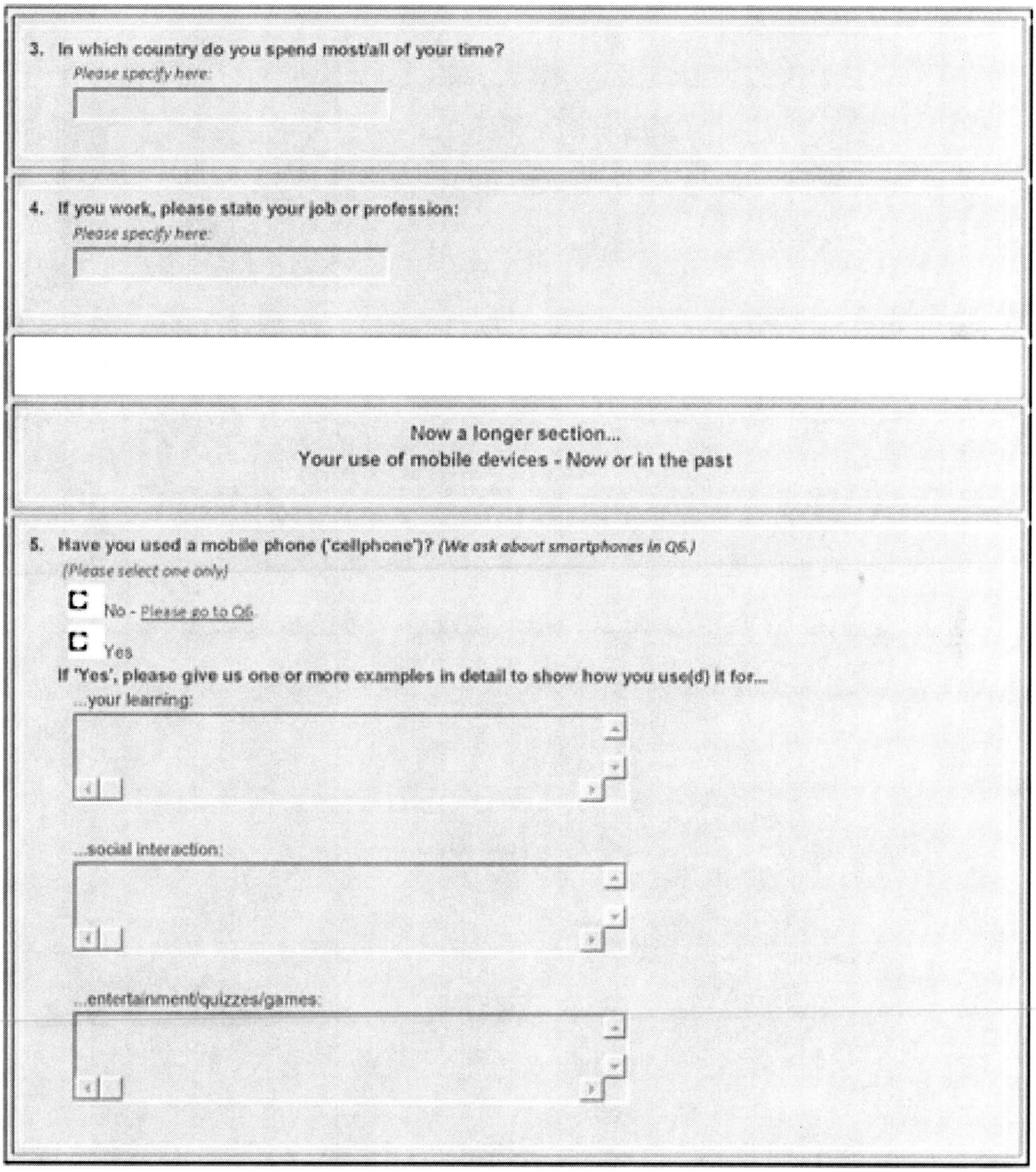

3. In which country do you spend most/all of your time?
Please specify here:

4. If you work, please state your job or profession:
Please specify here:

Now a longer section...
Your use of mobile devices - Now or in the past

5. Have you used a mobile phone ('cellphone')? *(We ask about smartphones in Q6.)*
(Please select one only)

☐ No - Please go to Q6

☐ Yes

If 'Yes', please give us one or more examples in detail to show how you use(d) it for....

...your learning:

...social interaction:

...entertainment/quizzes/games:

Figure 3. Questionnaire Continued

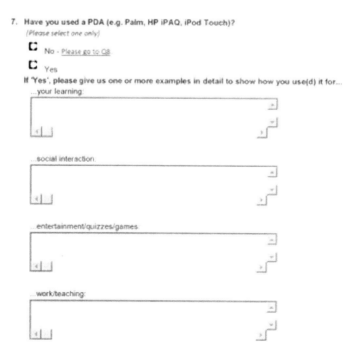

6. **Have you used a smartphone (i.e. mobile phone/PDA in one device, e.g. Blackberry, iPhone)?**
   (Please select one only)

   ☐ No - Please go to Q7.

   ☐ Yes

   If 'Yes', please give us one or more examples in detail to show how you use(d) it for...
   ...your learning:

   ...social interaction:

   ...entertainment/quizzes/games:

   ...work/teaching:

Figure 4. Questionnaire Continued

7. Have you used a PDA (e.g. Palm, HP iPAQ, iPod Touch)?
   (Please select one only)

   ☐ No - Please go to Q8

   ☐ Yes

   If 'Yes', please give us one or more examples in detail to show how you use(d) it for...
   ...your learning:

   ...social interaction:

   ...entertainment/quizzes/games:

   ...work/teaching:

Figure 5. Questionnaire Continued

8. Have you used an mp3-player or mp4-player (e.g. iPod)?

(Please select one only)

☐ No - Please go to Q9.

☐ Yes

If 'Yes', please give us one or more examples in detail to show how you use(d) it for...

...your learning:

...social interaction:

...entertainment/quizzes/games:

...work/teaching:

Figure 6. Questionnaire Continued

Being part of groups and communities

9. Do you use a mobile device to be part of one or more groups or communities? These can be formal or informal groups or communities, relating to friends, leisure, family, study, work etc.
   (Please select one only)

   ☐ No - Please go to Q12

   ☐ Yes

   If "Yes"...

   ...please tell us about the purposes of one such group or community:

   [text box]

   ...please also tell us which device(s) you use and explain how you use it/them:

   [text box]

10. What are the main benefits for you of being part of this group or community?
    Please specify here:

    [text box]

11. Could you be part of this group/community if you did not use a mobile device?
    (Please select one only)

    ☐ No

    ☐ Yes

Figure 7. Questionnaire Continued

Specific uses for mobile devices
(When you finish this section, you will have nearly completed the questionnaire)

12. Below are some things that you may have done 'with mobile devices' (phone, PDA, iPod etc
- but we
    are not asking about use of Tablets or laptops). For each activitiy, please select the button
that most
    accurately shows how often you do/did it. Or, if appropriate, select 'never'.

Browsing websites:
(Please select one only)

☐ Several times a day

☐ Once or twice a day

☐ A few days a week

☐ Once a week

☐ Once a month

☐ Less than once a month

☐ Never

Reading an e-book:
(Please select one only)

☐ Several times a day

☐ Once or twice a day

☐ A few days a week

☐ Once a week

☐ Once a month

☐ Less than once a month

☐ Never

Reading e-news:
(Please select one only)

☐ Several times a day

☐ Once or twice a day

☐ A few days a week

☐ Once a week

☐ Once a month

☐ Less than once a month

☐ Never

Figure 8. Questionnaire Continued

Reading an academic paper:
(Please select one only)

- Several times a day
- Once or twice a day
- A few days a week
- Once a week
- Once a month
- Less than once a month
- Never

Making a video clip:
(Please select one only)

- Several times a day
- Once or twice a day
- A few days a week
- Once a week
- Once a month
- Less than once a month
- Never

Viewing a video clip (one you or your friends have made):
(Please select one only)

- Several times a day
- Once or twice a day
- A few days a week
- Once a week
- Once a month
- Less than once a month
- Never

Figure 9. Questionnaire Continued

Viewing a video clip (from a site such as YouTube):
(Please select one only)

☐ Several times a day

☐ Once or twice a day

☐ A few days a week

☐ Once a week

☐ Once a month

☐ Less than once a month

☐ never

Sending a video clip from your mobile device to a video-sharing site:
(Please select one only)

☐ Several times a day

☐ Once or twice a day

☐ A few days a week

☐ Once a week

☐ Once a month

☐ Less than once a month

☐ Never

Posting to your blog from your mobile device:
(Please select one only)

☐ Several times a day

☐ Once or twice a day

☐ A few days a week

☐ Once a week

☐ Once a month

☐ Less than once a month

☐ Never

Figure 10. Questionnaire Continued

Posting to a micro-blog (e.g. Twitter, Jaiku, Pownce):
(Please select one only)

☐ Several times a day

☐ Once or twice a day

☐ A few days a week

☐ Once a week

☐ Once a month

☐ Less than once a month

☐ Never

Recording your own voice:
(Please select one only)

☐ Several times a day

☐ Once or twice a day

☐ A few days a week

☐ Once a week

☐ Once a month

☐ Less than once a month

☐ Never

Recording an informal conversation (e.g. friends talking):
(Please select one only)

☐ Several times a day

☐ Once or twice a day

☐ A few days a week

☐ Once a week

☐ Once a month

☐ Less than once a month

☐ Never

Figure 11. Questionnaire Continued

Recording a formal interview (e.g. as part of your research):
(Please select one only)

☐ Several times a day

☐ Once or twice a day

☐ A few days a week

☐ Once a week

☐ Once a month

☐ Less than once a month

☐ Never

Recording a seminar or other presentation by a speaker:
(Please select one only)

☐ Several times a day

☐ Once or twice a day

☐ A few days a week

☐ Once a week

☐ Once a month

☐ Less than once a month

☐ Never

Listening to music:
(Please select one only)

☐ Several times a day

☐ Once or twice a day

☐ A few days a week

☐ Once a week

☐ Once a month

☐ Less than once a month

☐ Never

Figure 12. Questionnaire Continued

Listening to podcasts:
(Please select one only)

☐ Several times a day

☐ Once or twice a day

☐ A few days a week

☐ Once a week

☐ Once a month

☐ Less than once a month

☐ Never

Accessing a social networking site (e.g. Facebook, MySpace, Bebo etc.):
(Please select one only)

☐ Several times a day

☐ Once or twice a day

☐ A few days a week

☐ Once a week

☐ Once a month

☐ Less than once a month

☐ Never

Taking a photograph:
(Please select one only)

☐ Several times a day

☐ Once or twice a day

☐ A few days a week

☐ Once a week

☐ Once a month

☐ Less than once a month

☐ Never

Figure 13. Questionnaire Continued

Sending a photograph from a mobile device to a photosharing or social networking site (e.g. Flickr,
Facebook, etc.):
(Please select one only)

☐ Several times a day

☐ Once or twice a day

☐ A few days a week

☐ Once a week

☐ Once a month

☐ Less than once a month

☐ Never

Sending a photograph from a mobile device direct to friends or family:
(Please select one only)

☐ Several times a day

☐ Once or twice a day

☐ A few days a week

☐ Once a week

☐ Once a month

☐ Less than once a month

☐ Never

Accessing a wiki (e.g. Wikipedia):
(Please select one only)

☐ Several times a day

☐ Once or twice a day

☐ A few days a week

☐ Once a week

☐ Once a month

☐ Less than once a month

☐ Never

Figure 14. Questionnaire Continued

Using Google (or another search engine):
(Please select one only)

☐ Several times a day

☐ Once or twice a day

☐ A few days a week

☐ Once a week

☐ Once a month

☐ Less than once a month

☐ Never

Sending text-messages (SMS):
(Please select one only)

☐ Several times a day

☐ Once or twice a day

☐ A few days a week

☐ Once a week

☐ Once a month

☐ Less than once a month

☐ Never

Using a mobile device to make notes:
(Please select one only)

☐ Several times a day

☐ Once or twice a day

☐ A few days a week

☐ Once a week

☐ Once a month

☐ Less than once a month

☐ Never

Figure 15. Questionnaire Continued

Using learning materials developed or adapted for mobile devices:
(Please select one only)

☐ Several times a day

☐ Once or twice a day

☐ A few days a week

☐ Once a week

☐ Once a month

☐ Less than once a month

☐ Never

Using a location-based service (e.g. to find nearby taxis, banks, restaurants etc.):
(Please select one only)

☐ Several times a day

☐ Once or twice a day

☐ A few days a week

☐ Once a week

☐ Once a month

☐ Less than once a month

☐ Never

Playing a location-based game (e.g. geocaching):
(Please select one only)

☐ Several times a day

☐ Once or twice a day

☐ A few days a week

☐ Once a week

☐ Once a month

☐ Less than once a month

☐ Never

Figure 16. Questionnaire Continued

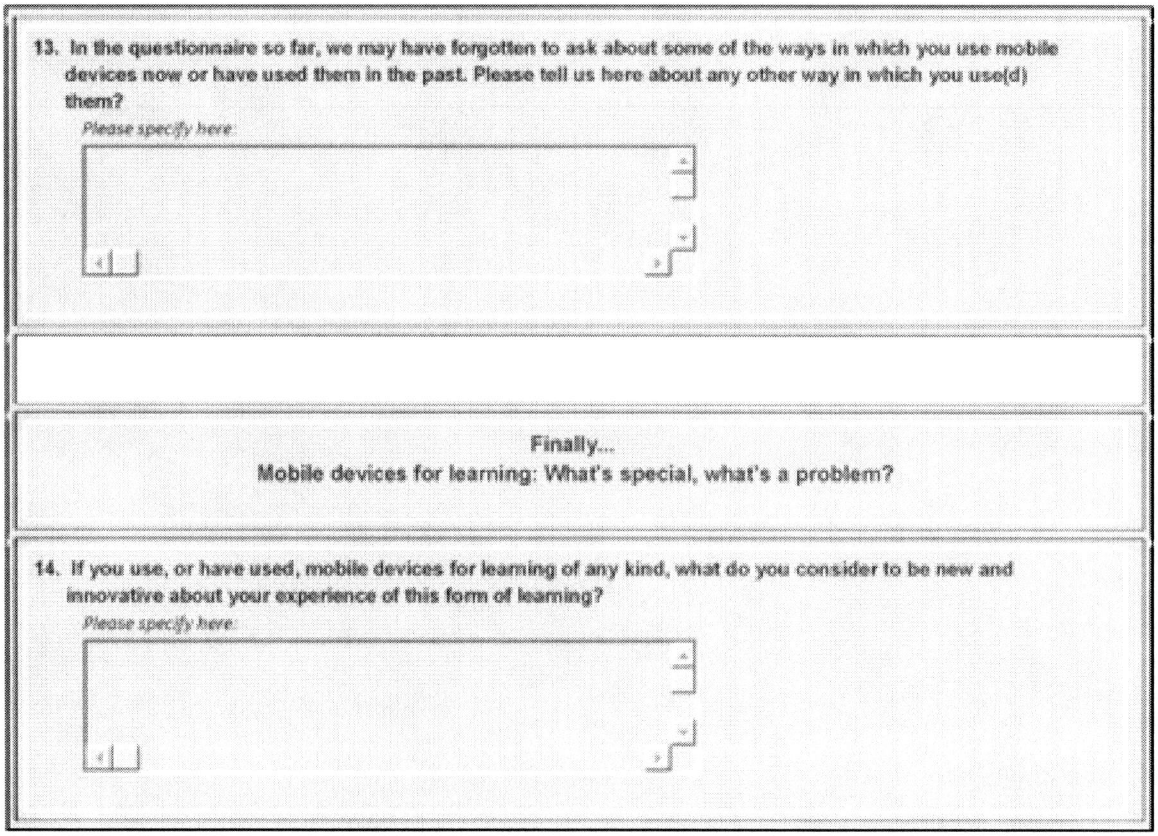

13. In the questionnaire so far, we may have forgotten to ask about some of the ways in which you use mobile devices now or have used them in the past. Please tell us here about any other way in which you use(d) them?

Please specify here:

Finally...
Mobile devices for learning: What's special, what's a problem?

---

14. If you use, or have used, mobile devices for learning of any kind, what do you consider to be new and innovative about your experience of this form of learning?

Please specify here:

Figure 17. Questionnaire Continued

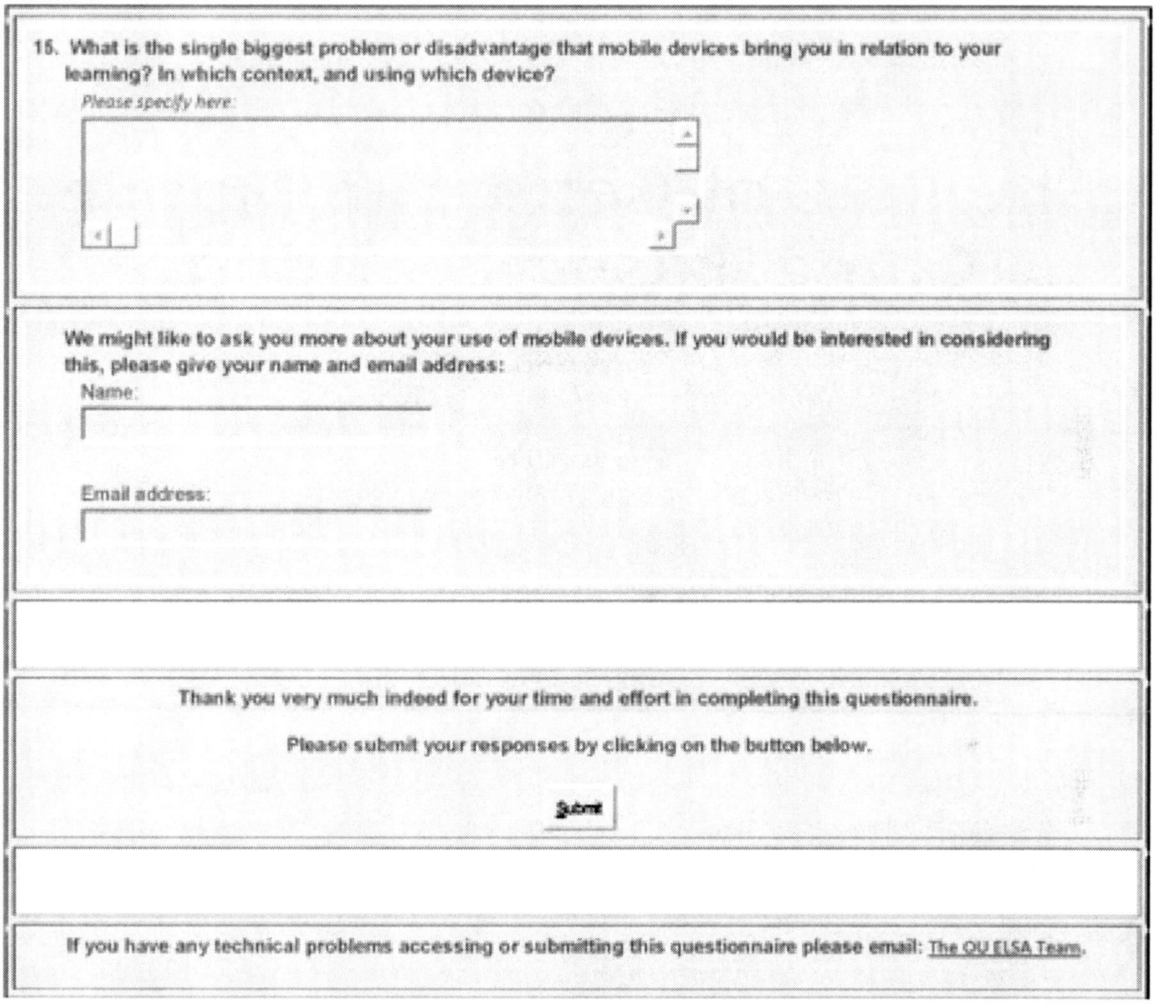

15. What is the single biggest problem or disadvantage that mobile devices bring you in relation to your learning? In which context, and using which device?

Please specify here:

We might like to ask you more about your use of mobile devices. If you would be interested in considering this, please give your name and email address:

Name:

Email address:

Thank you very much indeed for your time and effort in completing this questionnaire.

Please submit your responses by clicking on the button below.

Submit

If you have any technical problems accessing or submitting this questionnaire please email: The OU ELSA Team.

This work was previously published in the International Journal of Mobile and Blended Learning, Volume 3, Issue 4, edited by David Parsons, pp 19-37 copyright 2011 by IGI Publishing (an imprint of IGI Global).

Chapter 16
The Role of Gender in Mobile Game–Based Learning

Susan Gwee
Nanyang Technological University, Singapore

Yam San Chee
Nanyang Technological University, Singapore

Ek Ming Tan
Nanyang Technological University, Singapore

ABSTRACT

This paper investigates whether there are gender differences in gameplay time and learning outcomes in a social studies mobile game-based curriculum. Seventeen boys and 24 girls from a ninth-grade class in Singapore used a mobile learning game Statecraft X to enact governorship in the game world. The data suggest that boys spent significantly more time playing Statecraft X than girls. However, there were no significant gender differences in their scores in an essay question assessing their learning about governorship in terms of criteria of relevance of content, perspective, and personal voice. There was also no significant correlation between gameplay time and relevance of content, perspective, and personal voice scores. Thus, higher engagement in gameplay alone does not necessarily lead to higher-order learning outcomes. This paper discusses the factors giving rise to these results.

INTRODUCTION

Teenagers in the twenty-first century have the opportunity to engage in new digital literacy practices as they can now play digital games on mobile devices such as mobile phones and tablet devices. There are currently 5.3 billion mobile phone subscribers in the world (MobiThinking, 2011). In the United States, 23% of mobile users played games on the mobile phone; in Europe, 25%, and in Japan 16%. To explore the potential of out-of-school meaning-making practices of students, schools are looking into the inclusion of mobile digital games in the curriculum.

However, there are concerns about using digital games in the curriculum, one of which is

DOI: 10.4018/978-1-4666-2139-8.ch016

that gaming is established as a male activity and that males may have an unfair advantage in a game-based curriculum. Thus, the main objective of this paper is to examine whether indeed there is a relationship between mobile gameplay time and learning outcomes in a mobile game-centered social studies curriculum. We hypothesize that with more access to and control over a mobile device compared to traditional male-dominated gaming spaces; girls may play as often as boys and achieve similar learning outcomes.

Games and 21st Century Learning

Changes in society and economy in the developed countries require that young people are equipped with new skills that are consonant with a knowledge economy rather than an industrial one (Ananhiadou & Claro, 2009). These skills are often referred to as twenty-first century skills as they are more related to the needs of the economic and social models of this century. Wagner (2010) has identified seven survival skills for careers, college, and citizenship in the twenty-first century for American students. One of them is critical thinking and problem solving because the best companies want employees to be able to improve their products and processes or their services, or even create new ones. Thus, companies expect their employees to look at connections, to weigh evidence, to look at issues or problems in new ways, and to understand their interrelationships. Another skill is agility and adaptability because American workers need to adapt and be agile in daily lives due to changes in technology and the fast pace of work.

Twenty-first century learning is also the direction to which school reforms are directed in the United States (Alexander & Murphy, 2000; Lambert & McComb, 2000; Wagner, 2010) and in East Asia including Singapore (Koh & Luke, 2009). The United States administration stated that it would ensure that all students were trained to use technology to research, analyze, and communicate

in any discipline because of 21st century workplace demands (Obama & Biden, 2007). In Singapore, the emphasis is on the creation of a nationwide education and learning infrastructure so that students can learn on the go (Infocomm, 2009). Koh and Luke (2009) noted that there has been a move towards educational reform and innovation as a result of educational policies which encourage more critical and creative thinking practices in Singapore schools. Assessment reforms include the advent of alternative assessment methods such as Strategies for Active and Independent Learning (SAIL) and Science Practical Assessment (SPA).

Digital gameplay has been associated with gains in skills which are in line with twenty-first century skills required in the workplace. Good games confront players with problems, allowing them to make decisions after having critically thought through them by analyzing the information available and then evaluating the options given in the game space (Gee, 2003). Gee (2003) also noted that players in massively multiplayer games also often collaborate in teams, each using a different set of overlapping skills and sharing knowledge, skills, and values with others both in the game and outside. This results in the creation of distributed and dispersed knowledge within the community in ways that are consonant with the contemporary, high-tech, and cross-functional-team-centered workplace (Wenger, McDermott, & Snyder, 2002). Thus, Gee (2003) argued that game-based learning prepares students and workers better for the twenty-first-century workplace than traditional schools because it allows people to re-create themselves in new worlds, to enjoy themselves, and to engage in deep learning at the same time.

The Federation of American Scientists (2006) also recommends using video games in the classroom because these games integrate systems thinking, identified as a skill necessary in the twenty-first century. Video games enable students to learn higher-order thinking skills such as strategic thinking, interpretive analysis, problem solving, plan formulation and execution, and adaptation to rapid change (Federation of American Scientists, 2006, p. 3). Since digital games are systems, Walsh (2010) argued that students have to be reflective in the action of playing the game. In other words, before taking an action in the game, students have to think about the consequences of that action on the remainder of the game.

In summary, games create conditions in which learners can acquire twenty-first century skills. Indeed, in a second-order meta-analysis of the impact of technology on learning in elementary, secondary, and post-secondary institutions, Tamin, Bernard, Borokhovski, Abrami, and Schmid (2011) have also found that computer technology supporting instruction has a slightly but significantly higher average effect size than technology used for direct instruction. Tamin et al. (2011) concluded that one of technology's strengths seemed to be more of supporting students' efforts to achieve rather than acting as a tool for delivering content (p. 17). Mobile games, in particular, promote agility and adaptability as learners are able to access information frequently outside the classroom. Consequently, we think that mobile games do support student learning partly because of their mobile nature.

Gender and Gameplay

Traditionally, males have dominated game-based learning environments and gaming is established as a male activity (Bryce & Rutter, 2003). Previous research has shown that more males spend more time playing computer games than females (Bertozzi & Lee, 2007; Buchman & Funk, 1996; Chou & Tsai, 2007; Colwell & Payne, 2000; Green & McNeese, 2008; Lucas & Sherry, 2004; Solomonidou & Mitsaki, 2009; Winn & Heeter, 2009). Bertozzi and Lee (2007) reported that a survey of 263 adults from a small Midwestern town in the United States found that men spent 41.57 hours per week playing computer games compared to women who spent 30.54 hours per

week on the same activity. Similarly, Buchman and Funk (1996) also reported that for 900 American children surveyed from grades 4 to 8, the total length of computer gameplay time spent at home and in arcades for boys was about twice as long as that for girls.

However, compared to the American adults surveyed by Bertozzi and Lee (2007), the children spent a lot less time in computer gameplay. For example, the eighth-grade boys only spent 4.97 hours per week while the eighth-grade girls spent 2.52 hours per week in computer gameplay. Green and McNeese (2008) found in a survey of 6904 male and 7144 female American high school sophomores in public, Catholic, and other private schools in 2002 that being female was negatively associated with playing digital games on weekdays and weekends whereas being male was positively associated with weekday and weekend digital gameplay.

Lucas and Sherry (2004) also found that male students from two large Midwestern American universities were more likely to be play video games compared to female students. The female students played fewer hours or did not seek gameplay situations for social interaction due to their motivations for inclusion and affection. They also did not enjoy game-play situations involving mental rotation or competition because they felt that they had less control than in other interpersonal or play activities. In a more recent study, Winn and Heeter (2009) surveyed 276 American undergraduates aged 18 to 24 years from a large Midwestern university about their gaming practices in middle school, high school, and in university. Female undergraduates reported playing computer games an average of 2.85, 1.68, and 0.98 hours per week in middle school, high school, and in university respectively while male undergraduates reported spending 8.02, 7.67, and 5.30 hours per week playing computer games.

In the United Kingdom, Colwell and Payne (2000) found in a survey of 204 year eight male and female adolescents that boys played significantly more frequently than girls. Boys also played for a longer duration than girls. Similarly, Harris also found that in a survey of 328 year nine students from 50 secondary school students in the United Kingdom, more than twice the boys reported that they had a computer for their own use at home compared to girls and for a shared computer, more boys stated that they were the main user than girls. 71% of the boys were motivated to use the computer for playing games compared to 59% of the girls surveyed. A much higher percentage of boys used the computer most for games than girls. In addition, Marsh (2010) found that to promote learning, British educators tended to select internet sites that privilege boys' interests. Conversely, educators offered pre-school girls access to websites that did not correspond to their stated interests and preferences nor did they adopt technologies and digital literacy practices adopted by girls, such as dance mats and karaoke machines, in curriculum planning (Marsh, 2010).

In Taiwan, Chou and Tsai (2007) reported that in a survey of 535 high school students, boys spent more time playing computer game than girls. In Greece, Solomonidou and Mitsaki (2009) surveyed 296 people in Internet cafes and found that those aged between 15 and 22 used the Internet cafes most and that the majority of the users were men who went mostly to play individual or multiplayer computer games.

In Singapore, in a longitudinal survey of 2179 boys and 819 girls from grades 3, 4, 7, and 8 from 6 primary and 6 secondary schools, Gentile, Choo, Liau, Sim, Li, Fung, and Khoo (2011) reported that boys spent more time than girls playing digital games weekly over three time slots.

In summary, on both the international level and in Singapore, previous research has shown that digital gameplay is a pastime which is more popular with boys than with girls. Thus, there is the concern that girls will not perform as well as boys in a game-based learning environment as the former may spend less time in a game-based curriculum compared to the latter.

However, in her investigation of the learning effectiveness of an educational computer game for learning computer memory concepts in 88 16- to 17-year-old students in two Greek high schools, Papasterigou (2009) found that there were no significant differences in learning gains between boys and girls despite boys' prior greater involvement and experience with computer gaming. Since the students in her study played the computer game during specific lesson time slots, all boys and girls spent the same amount of time on gameplay. Thus, she did not investigate whether there were gender differences in the time spent in gameplay and whether time spent in gameplay had an impact on learning outcomes. Nor did her study involve a mobile game that may provide girls with more control over and access to computer games and therefore a more level playing field.

With the growth of the use of mobile devices in the work place and in schools (De Freitas & Griffiths, 2008; Facer, Joiner, Stanton, Reid, Hull, & Kirk, 2004; Klopfer, Perry, Squire, & Jan, 2005; Norris & Soloway, 2009; Pachler, Bachmair, & Cook, 2010; Petrova & Li, 2009; Sharples, 2006; Squire & Jan, 2007; Squire & Klopfer, 2007), it is now easier for games to be installed in mobile devices and males no longer have primary access to and control over public and domestic leisure spaces. Thus, girls may spend as much time playing games as boys if they have more access to and control over their game space.

We have thus selected *Statecraft X*, a strategy social studies mobile game application, because it redefines traditionally male-dominated gaming spaces. Installed on Apple iPhones, *Statecraft X* allows both boys and girls to have primary access to and control over public and domestic spaces. In the present study, girls played *Statecraft X* as often as they wanted to and where they wished to play as they were not constrained to a fixed time or space. The present study thus addressed the following research questions:

1. Are there gender differences in mobile gameplay time?
2. Are there gender differences in learning outcomes?
3. Is there a correlation between mobile gameplay time and learning outcomes?

METHODOLOGY

Participants

Seventeen boys and 24 girls participated in the present study which was the first intervention of three interventions in two schools in Singapore in 2010. They were from a high-ability ninth-grade class in a non-elite school. The students in this class are on the Express academic track where they will sit for the GCE 'O' Levels examination at the end of Grade 10. About the top 60% of each primary school cohort in Singapore fall into this category of students. Express students are expected to proceed to junior college and polytechnics after their 'O' Levels examinations. After finishing school at about 2 p.m., secondary school students usually either take part in school events, co-curricular activities, or do their homework.

The students were randomly assigned to two groups: Games 1 and 2. There were 21 students in Game 1 and 20 students in Game 2. Students in each game were assigned to four factions for gameplay: one all boys' faction (Dragon), one all girls' faction (Phoenix), and two mixed group factions (Griffin and Pegasus). One student was absent during the administration of the post-intervention survey.

The school management team chose two female social studies teachers to participate in the present study. The research team did not have any control over the choice of teachers. The lead teacher observed a four-day pilot study which took place in October 2009 in the same school so that she would be more confident of teaching a mobile game-based curriculum and so we would

have the opportunity to tailor the curriculum to the needs of the students together. In November 2009, these two teachers together with a male teacher participated in a two-day professional development workshop with the research team. They gave suggestions regarding the revision of the lesson plans, which were incorporated for the intervention study. During the intervention period from 18 January to 3 February 2010, the first author also had discussions with the two teachers regarding lesson plans. The teachers requested these meetings as they wanted to seek clarification about activities suggested in the lesson plans found in the mobile game-based curriculum.

Before the start of the study, we informed the two teachers and parents of students of the participating class that they were invited to participate in the present study and that their participation was voluntary. They were told of the purpose of the research, the procedure to be followed, the confidentiality of personal details and identities of the participants, the duration of the study, and the risks and benefits to participation.

Materials

Statecraft X is a social studies mobile game used in the present study. Hilmy and Loke (2009) designed the game based on principles of governance in the social studies curriculum for ninth-graders in Singapore. The four principles of governance found in Singapore's ninth-grade social studies textbook are:

1. Leadership is key;
2. Anticipate change and stay relevant;
3. Reward for work, and work for reward;
4. A stake for everyone, opportunities for all.

At the start of the six one-hour lessons, each student was loaned an Apple iPhone with *Statecraft X* installed in it. In this multi-player game, factions competed against one another to rule the fantasy kingdom of Velar. The back-story of the game is that King Topez of Velar passed away without leaving an heir, thus creating a power vacuum. Student governor-led political factions then had to look after their town people and try to take over the capital city.

The first game objective was for each faction to consolidate its power and position by winning the trust of the towns assigned to them at the beginning of the game, of neutral towns, and also of towns belonging to other factions. Second, all factions must collaborate to ensure that the kingdom of Velar survives attacks from neighboring kingdoms.

During the intervention period, the server triggered events involving the game world such as health epidemics, refugee influx, famine, and bandit attacks. Therefore, in addition to developing towns under their control, student governors had to cope with these events.

Besides *Statecraft X*, teacher-facilitated activities (e.g., whole class discussion and student presentation), online blogs, and forums supported the learning of the *Statecraft X* curriculum. In the classroom, students were situated in Bellalonia. The teachers role-played as the grand sages of Bellalonia while students role-played as governors of Bellalonia. Bellalonia allowed students to have an additional perspective of governance as this fictional world faces different problems from those of the game world and the real world. Students can also propose creative solutions to problems in Bellalonia and imagine different scenarios. This is not possible in the real and game worlds. Figure 1 situates the learner at the centre of the three worlds (Gwee, Chee, & Tan, 2010). To support in-class discussion and blogging activities on the Bellalonia web portal, the first and third authors created questions to guide students in reflecting on their governing practices in the game world of Velar, and on their knowledge of the real world so that they could solve problems in the fictional world of Bellalonia. The third author set up a web-portal situated in Bellalonia to provide a space for students to be informed of events happening in the game world of Velar and the fictional

world of Bellalonia, and for them to post their reflection blogs. Students could read additional materials from the real world on the web-portal. These readings provided students with additional perspectives of governance beyond *Statecraft X* and their textbook.

Procedure

All lessons were video-recorded. In the lead teacher's classroom, one video camera recorded the general classroom while one camera each was focused on three groups in the classroom. In the other teacher's classroom, one video camera recorded classroom activities. During the first lesson, students were loaned an Apple iPhone with *Statecraft X* installed in it. The game designer of *Statecraft X* taught students how to use the game through a tutorial session of learning how to manage towns, trade, move from town to town, and so on. Table 1 summarizes the sequence of in-class and out-of-class activities of the *Statecraft X* curriculum.

According to the following schedule that was worked out in consultation with the school, students could play during non-curriculum time: from 6 a.m. to 8 a.m. and from 2 p.m. to 10 p.m. on Mondays to Fridays, and from 6 a.m. to 11 p.m. on Saturdays. Sunday was set aside as a rest day, so no gameplay was allowed. Every hour, students were awarded twenty action points that they could use for various player actions.

The first author administered a post-intervention survey at the end of the last lesson to investigate the time spent on gameplay. She also administered an essay task a few days after the last intervention lesson during a regular social studies class in the morning. She asked students to complete the essay in 30 minutes. The essay instruction was:

Imagine that you are running for an election to be a member of parliament and that you have to formulate policies to convince the citizens of your country that you are the best candidate. Justify your proposed policies by using examples from what you have learnt, what you have read, and your personal experiences.

The first (Rater A, female) and third authors (Rater B, male) were the assessors of the essays. Both held graduate degrees, had at least eight years experience of teaching high school students in Singapore schools and were part of the *Statecraft X* research team. Rater A also had three years of experience in an improving teachers' assessment literacy project where she trained teachers to assess student work during assessment workshops based on a scoring guide and exemplars of student work. She also acted as an adjudicator during score resolution sessions when two teams of teachers gave different ratings to student work. Raters A and B assigned scores of levels 1 to 4 for the criteria of relevance of content, perspective, and voice to all 41 written scripts. Relevance refers to how relevant the policies proposed by a student were to the social and economic needs of the different segments of a country's population and whether the student had given examples from both traditional and non-traditional sources to support his or her policies. Perspective refers to whether a student

Table 1. Summary of activities

In-class activity	Out-of-class activity
Session 1: Game tutorial, whole class discussion	Gameplay, reflection blog
Session 2: Whole-class discussion, examination of four case studies in groups, student presentation	Gameplay, reflection blog, online forum, debate preparation
Session 3: Debate, whole-class discussion	Gameplay, reflection blog
Session 4: Whole-class discussion, group planning of individual writing assignment	Gameplay, reflection blog
Session 5: Writing of individual assignment	Preparation for presentation
Session 6: Presentation of final assignment, post-intervention survey	-
Session 7: Written essay	-

could give multiple perspectives to the proposed policies and integrate them or whether he or she could only give the textbook perspective. Voice refers to the personal voice used by a student and whether it matched the situation, how authentic the voice was, whether opinions were well-defined and detailed, whether he or she communicated strong

Figure 1. A play-between-worlds curriculum model

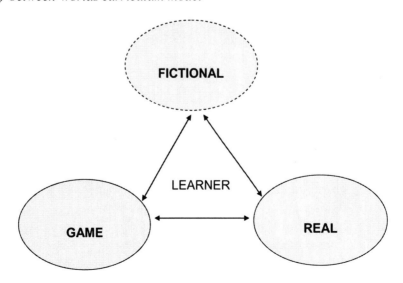

feelings and honest statements, and whether he or she showed that he or she cared for the topic.

Raters A and B then had a morning session of reviewing all scripts together to discuss a final score for each script. They used discussion to resolve discrepancies and to improve score accuracy as recommended by Johnson, Penny, Gordon, Shumate, and Fisher (2005). When there was a discrepancy, they compared the features of the student's script with the benchmark performance in the scoring guide together again and discussed why the student should be awarded a certain score. They considered any evidence that challenged the original scores and achieved a consensus score. They then assigned a final score or operational score for each criterion.

To learn more about their gameplay practices and their learning experiences, the first and third authors also interviewed seven girls and seven boys. Six students were interviewed immediately the last lesson of the *Statecraft* learning curriculum. The remaining eight were interviewed after classes the following day. The first and third authors told the students interviewed that their interviews were confidential and put them at ease before commencing the interviews. Each interview lasted about 30 to 40 minutes, and was audio- and video-recorded. A university-educated transcriber transcribed the interviews and the first author listened to the recorded interviews and checked all the transcripts.

Data Sources and Data Analysis

The data sources used in this paper were the post-intervention survey, the written speech, and the interview. The interview data will be used to discuss the findings of the present study. Table 2 summarizes the data sources, dependent measures, and analysis strategies used to answer the three research questions of this paper. Levene's test was used to test the assumption of equal variances. To address the first research question of whether there were gender differences in the amount of time

spent playing *Statecraft X* per week, a 2-tailed *t*-test was used on mobile gameplay time with gender as the independent variable.

To address the second question of whether there were gender differences in learning outcomes, a 2-tailed *t*-test was conducted on the dependent variables of relevance of content, perspective, and personal voice.

Inter-rater exact and adjacent agreement rates were also calculated for the variables of relevance, perspective, and voice. For the scoring of essays, most agencies and educational studies generally accept scores which are at least adjacent (e.g., Brennan, 1996; Penny, 2003).

To address the third question of whether there was a correlation between mobile gameplay time and learning outcomes, a 2-tailed non-parametric Spearman correlation test was run on the variable of time spent playing *Statecraft X* with the variables relevance, perspective, and voice, respectively.

RESULTS

Hours of Gameplay Time per Week

Levene's test showed that the assumption that variances were equal was not supported, $F = 5.86, p = .02$ (Table 3). Thus, we used the *t*-values which did not assume equal variances. Contrary to the hypothesis of the present study, the results indicate that boys ($M = 19.20, SD = 15.25$) spent significantly more time playing *Statecraft X* than girls ($M = 7.34, SD = 6.81$), $t = 2.92, p = .009, \alpha = .05$, 95% CI [3.36, 20.35]. The mean difference in gameplay time between boys and girls of 11.85 was high. A boxplot (Figure 2) shows the uneven distribution of gameplay time across boys and girls. Girls clustered towards the lower end of the distribution compared to boys. Indeed, 75% of the girls reported spending 10 hours or fewer hours per week playing *Statecraft X* compared to 31% of the boys. Except for one girl who reported spending 32 hours a week playing *Statecraft X*,

261

Table 2. Alignment of research questions, data sources, dependent measures, and analysis strategies

Research question	Data source	Dependent measure	Analysis strategy
Are there gender differences in game mobile play time?	Survey	Time spent per week in gameplay	2-tailed *t*-test
Are there gender differences in learning outcomes?	Written speech	Relevance score, perspective score, and voice score	2-tailed *t*-test
Is there a correlation between mobile gameplay time and learning outcomes?	Survey, written speech	Time spent per week in gameplay, relevance score, perspective score, and voice score	2-tailed non-parametric Spearman correlation test

Table 3. Levene's test for equal variances

	F	*p*
Gameplay Time	5.86	.02
Relevance	.91	.35
Perspective	.91	.34
Voice	.35	.56

the rest of the girls reported spending 15 or fewer hours a week in gameplay time. On the other hand, 63% of the boys reported spending more than 15 hours a week in gameplay time, including one boy who reported spending 62 hours a week playing *Statecraft X*.

Learning Outcomes

Before reporting on the data regarding the learning outcomes of boys and girls of the present study, we report the reliability data for exact and adjacent agreement for the different criteria of relevance, perspective, and voice of the essay task which were 92%, 100%, and 78% respectively.

See the Appendix for an example of a student's essay. Since Levene's test indicates that the variances for relevance, perspective, and voice can be assumed to be equal (Table 3), the *t*-values that we report in Table 4 reflect that. Consistent with the hypothesis of the present study, the results suggest that there were no significant differences in learning outcomes between boys and girls. This is the case for every criterion of the essay

task although the mean scores for boys for every criterion were slightly higher than those for girls. The greatest difference between boys and girls lies in the mean score for the criterion of voice, but the difference was not significant.

First, the relevance scores of boys ($M = 2.65$, $SD = 1.06$) and girls ($M = 2.58$, $SD = .83$) were not significantly different, $t(39) = .22$, $p = .83$, $\alpha = .05$. Second, the perspectives scores of boys ($M = 2.76$, $SD = .75$) and girls ($M = 2.58$, $SD = .83$) were also not significantly different, $t(39) = .72$, $p = .48$, $\alpha = .05$. Third, the differences between the voice scores of boys ($M = 3.65$, $SD = .61$) and girls ($M = 3.25$, $SD = .68$) were not statistically significant, $t(39) = 1.93$, $p = .06$, $\alpha = .05$.

Correlation between Gameplay Time and Learning Outcomes

The correlations between time spent playing *Statecraft X* and relevance, perspective, and voice were all non-significant. The results indicate that there were no significant associations between the time boys and girls spent playing *Statecraft X* and the learning outcomes of relevance, perspective, and voice. The Spearman correlation rank coefficients were -.08 ($p = .64$), -.10 ($p = .55$), and .19 ($p = .24$) for relevance, perspective, and voice, respectively. The first two correlations were negative while the last one was positive and the strongest among the three. That is, the results suggest that students who spent more time playing *Statecraft X* had lower relevance and perspective scores, but higher voice scores. There appeared to be a stronger association

Figure 2. Distribution of gameplay time across boys and girls

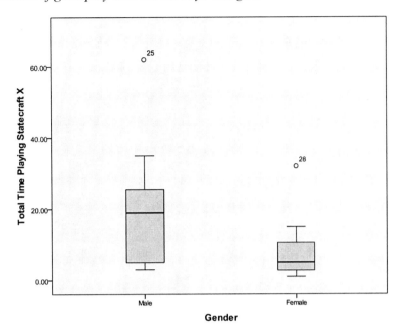

between gameplay time and voice scores although the association was still not significant.

In sum, the learning outcomes of students — relevance, perspective, and voice — did not have a statistically reliable relationship with gameplay time. In Figures 3, 4, and 5, scatter plots show that some students achieved relatively high scores on relevance, perspective, and voice of 3 and 4 despite having reported spending relatively little time in gameplay compared to other students in the present study.

DISCUSSION

The objectives of the present study were to investigate (1) whether there were gender differences in mobile gameplay time, (2) whether there were gender differences in learning outcomes, and (3) whether there was a significant correlation between mobile gameplay time and learning outcomes in ninth-grade students. Previous studies have not compared gender differences in mobile gameplay time where both males and females have

control over their gameplay time. To the best of our knowledge, the present study is also a first attempt to look at gameplay time and its effect on learning outcomes in a school. Consistent with previous studies (Bertozzi & Lee, 2007; Buchman & Funk, 1996; Chou & Tsai, 2007; Green & Mc-Neese, 2008; Lucas & Sherry, 2004; Solomonidou & Mitsaki, 2009; Winn & Heeter, 2009), we found that boys reported spending significantly more time playing *Statecraft X* than girls. We will now discuss the factors that could have contributed to significant gender differences in mobile gameplay time and to no significant gender differences in

Table 4. Gender differences in learning outcomes

	t	p	Mean Diff.	SE	95% CI	
					LL	UP
Relevance	.22	.83	.06	.29	-.53	.66
Perspective	.72	.48	.18	.25	-.33	.69
Voice	1.93	.06	.40	.21	-.02	.81

Note. CI = confidence interval; Diff = difference; LL = lower limit; SE; standard error; UP = upper limit.

Figure 3. Distribution of relevance scores and gameplay time

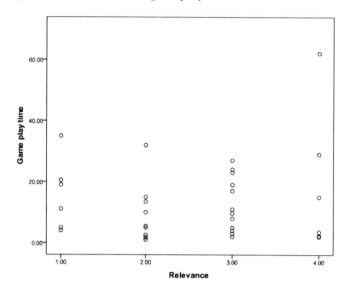

learning outcomes. We will also attempt to explain why there were no significant correlations between mobile gameplay time and the learning outcomes as measured by relevance, perspective, and voice scores for the essay task.

Game Design

One factor that might have contributed to gender differences in game play time was game design. *Statecraft X* might not have sufficiently appealed to girls due to the key nature of military actions in the game. As reported in Kafai (1994), girls in her study created games where there was little

Figure 4. Distribution of perspective scores and gameplay time

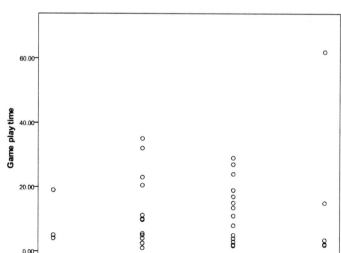

Figure 5. Distribution of voice scores and gameplay time

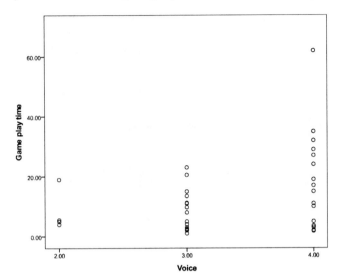

violence whereas the boys created games that were more combative in nature. In an earlier paper (Chee, Gwee, & Tan, 2011), we reported that the greatest difference in player actions between boys and girls was the category of military actions. Boys took about six times more military actions than girls. Another game design-related factor could be the objective of *Statecraft X*. During the first lesson, the game designer told the class that the objective of *Statecraft X* was to capture the capital city. However, Miller, Chaika, and Groppe (1996), who conducted focus group discussions with 30 adolescent females, noted that for the girls interviewed, winning was not a necessary objective although they like challenging activities. They found that girls preferred game design that included exploration, collaboration, challenge, vicarious adventures and activities, and sophisticated graphic and sound design. Thus, girls in the present study might have played *Statecraft X* less than boys due to game design.

In a subsequent intervention, the first author, a female researcher, advocated a change in the positioning of the game. The winning faction would be positioned as the faction that had the highest composite score of happiness, profit,

and population levels in the towns under their charge. With this shift, girls might engage in more gameplay. This change was instituted in a subsequent intervention but the investigation of this hypothesis is still pending.

Access to and Control Over Game Space

Given that each student had their own iPhone, each had equal access to and control over game space. However, boys still played *Statecraft X* more frequently than girls. Perhaps, consistent with the results of Lucas and Sherry (2004) teenage girls wanted some control over their daily lives and did not want gameplay to intrude too much into their daily lives at home which revolved around homework. Indeed, from the interviews conducted, six girls noted that they had a sense of control when they engaged in mobile game-based learning. One of them commented,

I have some control over my mobile as I give myself limited amount of time to play, and I also purposely, hurriedly use up my action points, so I will not feel inspired to play the game.

Another girl commented,

It didn't really interfere with my daily activities, even though I'm short of time. But I can take it as a break, something for me to do during my break when I stop studying. Yah, I have to relax my mind. So playing the game, some sort of keep me away from thinking of my homework, how to solve this question.

Yet another girl commented,

I think it's more than just a device for games. Example there's like, in the Internet. Then, it has the calendar, the notes all that. I think, for the current technology, all these are some called the basic for phone, but...I think it's not like what other advertisements say like, you can download lots of games to play, but I think...is...you can make it useful by, like, downloading learning videos, like things from the Internet, but, not too much because somehow this can also be something to distract you from your homework. So...yah. Make it more positive, than using it to, like, waste your time and not do your homework. And being too addicted to the phone games...like things you can do with that...yah. I think you shouldn't indulge yourself in, so much of that. Think should control your time.

In contrast, boys reported in their interviews that they were "addicted" to the game. They tended to keep checking the game every hour in case the people in their towns died, and they were quite "engrossed in the game."

Learning Outcomes

Consistent with Papasterigou's (2009) findings, this study found that there were no significant gender differences in the learning outcomes of a game-based curriculum. The non-significant gender differences in learning outcomes could be

due to the fact that a female researcher designed the lesson plans for the present study and another male researcher was also involved in the revision of the lesson plans. Moreover, having a curriculum model that goes beyond the game world into the fictional and real worlds might have allowed girls and boys who had little time for gameplay or who are novice gamers to still benefit from the *Statecraft X* curriculum. Although some students especially girls have less first-hand experience with *Statecraft X* gameplay, they might have gleaned insights from the blogs of their classmates and from class discussions and student presentations. Indeed, one girl commented,

I only use the blogsite to post my reflections. Then if I am like stuck at a certain question, I will read all my other classmates' blogs as reference and then, I will try to think of my own and type it...

According to the interview data, girls found blogs to be "very important," to "help them think more" and to help them "understand more about governing," They realized that they did not have certain strategies or made certain mistakes, overcoming problems and improving gameplay. They thought back of what they have done and what they could have done instead. One female student summed it by saying

It helped a lot, especially the reflection questions. Because we not only play, we not only think and suggest ways to play, we actually reflect on ourselves that how we played it, how do we feel about the game, and how do we manage to come up with ways to tackle our problems.

One girl commented that both blogs and discussions helped her:

Erm...because we did a lot of reflections in the blog and in the class discussions, so I can apply them into the final assignment ah.

Therefore, the reflection blogs might have served as paratexts (Consalvo, 2007). Paratexts, a concept which was first introduced by Gerard Genette in 1997 as the elements surrounding a text that contribute to its meaning, are defined as a system of media products which follow a digital game, such as guidebooks, commercials, previews, trading cards, and clothes (Walsh, 2010). In the present *Statecraft X* curriculum context, reflection blogs and discussion forums in the game portal are such paratexts as they support the game. The reflection blogs and discussion forums might have provided a platform on which the girls in the present study were able to reflect critically on their gaming experience. Indeed, although girls reported to have spent less time writing reflection blogs than boys, they reported spending more time reading reflection blogs and participating in the forum more than the boys. At the same time, they were able to produce texts read by other students who could use the information to reflect on their game and also to enhance their game strategies. The space occupied by the digital game paratexts is more fluid than the digital game itself and we think that this space mediated the game world and the learning outcomes found in the present study. This may have been especially the case for students who engaged less in gameplay, particularly the girls who participated in the present study. These girls may lack gaming capital which includes the ability to contextualize multiple objects, actions, combinations, and strategies possible during gameplay (Walsh, 2010). Indeed, girls in the present study reported spending an average of 1.3 hours a week playing video games other than *Statecraft X* while boys reported spending an average of 5.1 hours playing video games.

In contrast, boys found blogs to be an assignment to be submitted to the teacher and something not worth reading. One boy commented that "the only thing I think the blogs will actually help us is just the final assignment, that's all, to do the final assignment." Another boy commented, "Blog is like…very tiresome ah…like when I'm aching

from typing that those blog and maybe the others will be more torture because everybody's typing the same thing like that."

In summary, although the girls played *Statecraft X* less often than boys, they played enough to make meaning of the gameplay in terms of governance so that they were able to participate in the learning activities designed in the *Statecraft X* curriculum and to achieve desired learning outcomes. That is, even though a boy or a girl was not able to spend a lot of time in gameplay, he or she could still achieve good learning outcomes. It is also important to note that our earlier paper (Chee, Gwee, & Tan, 2011) showed that the same students who have participated in the *Statecraft X* mobile game-based curriculum had significant higher scores of relevance, perspective, and voice than those who were in the comparison group. Therefore, while waiting for game designers to create more gender-neutral games, educators can still use digital games in schools to foster learning.

Limitations of Present Study

The present study had certain limitations. First, the data concerning student gameplay time were based on self-reported survey data. There are issues with the accuracy and reliability of self-reported survey data. Second, the sample size was also small and may not generalizable. Third, the present study involved a short-term intervention in a high school. It would be interesting to investigate whether there would be long-term learning outcomes in school tests and examinations, and students' interest in social studies as a result of a social studies game-based curriculum. Another area for future research is to develop a web-based version of the *Statecraft X* game and to investigate gameplay time and learning outcomes in such a curriculum compared to a mobile version of the game. This will be a good comparison of a game played in fixed and mobile spaces and further illuminate the importance of access to and control over game space in game-based learning.

A male game designer also designed *Statecraft X* game initially. However, with input from female members of the *Statecraft* team, the game could be modified in such a way that both male and female preferences for gameplay are paid greater attention in future interventions.

CONCLUSION

The results of the study showed that the learning outcomes of a mobile game-based learning curriculum were not solely dependent on the hours students spent on gameplay. Although boys reported spending significantly more hours than girls in gameplay, the learning outcomes were also not significantly different between boys and girls. As shown in the present study, educational mobile games can contribute to learning in both male and female student populations even though girls may seem to be less engaged in gameplay than boys. The learning objectives of the curriculum, curriculum design, and learning materials may serve to breach the divide in game engagement and to provide gender equity in terms of learning outcomes. Future educational mobile games can also be produced with greater consideration of the preferences of girls in terms of game design. More gender-neutral mobile games that cater to male and female preferences may encourage girls to spend more time in gameplay and thus immerse themselves more in digital literacy practices which are desirable in the twenty-first century workplace. In this way, these games are less likely to suffer from gender. Educators who wish to use mobile games for learning could also consider designing a curriculum and curriculum materials to suit both boys and girls especially if the games were to favor either gender.

REFERENCES

Alexander, P., & Murphy, P. (2000). The research base for APA's learner-centered psychological principles. In Lambert, N., & McCombs, B. (Eds.), *How students learn* (pp. 25–60). Washington, DC: American Psychological Association.

Ananhiadou, K., & Claro, M. (2009). *21st century skills and competences for new millenium learners in OECD countries (No. 41)*. Paris, France: OECD.

Bertozzi, E., & Lee, S. (2007). Not just fun and games: Digital play, gender and attitudes towards technology. *Women's. Studies in Communications, 30*(2), 179–204.

Brennan, R. (1996). Generalizability of performance assessments. In Phillips, G. (Ed.), *Technical issues in large-scale performance assessment* (pp. 19–58). Washington, DC: National Center of Education.

Bryce, J., & Rutter, J. (2003). Gender dynamics and the social and spatial organization of computer gaming. *Leisure Studies, 22*, 1–15. doi:10.1080/02614360306571

Buchman, D., & Funk, J. (1996). Video and computer games in the '90s: Children's time commitment and game preference. *Children Today, 24*(1), 12–31.

Caftori, N., & Papryzcki, M. (1997). The design, evaluation and usage of educational software. *Technology and Teacher Education Manual, 1*, 23–27.

Chee, Y. S., Gwee, S., & Tan, E. M. (2011). Learning to become citizens by enacting governorship in the *Statecraft* curriculum: An evaluation of learning outcomes. *International Journal of Gaming and Computer-Mediated Simulations, 3*(1).

Chou, C., & Tsai, M.-J. (2007). Gender differences in Taiwan high school students' computer game playing. *Computers in Human Behavior, 23*(1), 812–824. doi:10.1016/j.chb.2004.11.011

Colwell, J., & Payne, J. (2000). Negative correlates of computer game play in adolescents. *The British Journal of Psychology, 91*, 295–310. doi:10.1348/000712600161844

Consalvo, M. (2007). *Cheating: Gaining advantage in videogames*. Cambridge, MA: MIT Press.

de Freitas, S., & Griffiths, M. (2008). The convergence of gaming practices with other media forms: What potential for learning? A review of the literature. *Learning, Media and Technology, 33*(1), 11–20. doi:10.1080/17439880701868796

Facer, K., Joiner, R., Stanton, D., Reid, J., Hull, R., & Kirk, D. (2004). Savannah: Mobile gaming and learning? *Journal of Computer Assisted Learning, 20*(6), 339–409. doi:10.1111/j.1365-2729.2004.00105.x

Federation of American Scientists. (2006). *Harnessing the power of video games for learning*. Retrieved from http://agamerseducation.wordpress.com/2005/10/25/harnessing-the-power-of-video-games-for-learning/

Gee, J. (2003). What video games have to teach us about learning and literacy. *ACM Computers in Entertainment, 1*(1), 1–4.

Genette, G. (1997). *Paratexts: Thresholds of interpretation*. Cambridge, UK: Cambridge University Press. doi:10.1017/CBO9780511549373

Green, M. E., & McNeese, M. N. (2008). Factors that predict digital play. *The Howard Journal of Communications, 19*(3), 258–272. doi:10.1080/10646170802218321

Gwee, S., Chee, Y. S., & Tan, E. M. (2010). Assessment of student outcomes of mobile game-base learning. In *Proceedings of the 18th International Conference on Computers in Education*, Putrajaya, Malaysia (pp. 412-416).

Hilmy, A. H., & Loke, S. K. (2009). *Design document for Statecraft X*. Unpublished manuscript, Singapore.

Johnson, R. L., Penny, J., Gordon, B., Shumate, S. R., & Fisher, S. P. (2005). Resolving score differences in the rating of writing samples: Does discussion improve the accuracy of scores? *Language Assessment Quarterly, 2*(2), 117–146. doi:10.1207/s15434311laq0202_2

Kafai, Y. B. (1994). *Minds in play: Computer design as a context for children's learning*. Mahwah, NJ: Lawrence Erlbaum.

Klopfer, E., Perry, J., Squire, K., & Jan, M.-F. (2005). Collaborative learning through augmented reality role playing. In *Proceedings of Computer Supported Collaborative Learning*, Taipei, Taiwan (pp. 316-320).

Koh, K., & Luke, A. (2009). Authentic and conventional assessment in Singapore schools: An empirical study of teacher assignments and student work. *Assessment in Education, 16*(3), 291–318. doi:10.1080/09695940903319703

Lambert, N., & McCombs, B. (2000). Introduction: Learner-centered schools and classrooms as a direction for school reform. In Lambert, N., & McCombs, B. (Eds.), *How students learn* (pp. 1–15). Washington, DC: American Psychological Association.

Lucas, K., & Sherry, J. L. (2004). Sex differences in video game play: A communication-based explanation. *Communication Research, 31*(5), 499–523. doi:10.1177/0093650204267930

Marsh, J. (2010). New literacies, old identities: Young girls' experiences of digital literacy at home and school. In C. Jackson, C. Paechter, & E. Renold (Eds.), *Girls and education 3-16: Continuing concerns, new agendas* (pp. 197-209). New York, NY: Open University Press.

Miller, L., Chaika, M., & Groppe, L. (1996). Girls' preferences in software design: Insights from a focus group. *Technology and Electronic Journal the 21ˢᵗ Century, 4*(2), 1-6.

MobiThinking. (2011). *Global mobile statistics: All quality mobile marketing research, mobile Web stats, subscribers, ad revenue, usage, trends.* Retrieved from http://mobithinking.com/mobile-marketing-tools/latest-mobile-stats

Norris, C., & Soloway, E. (2009). Leadership + Mobile technologies = Educational benefits: Cell phones in K12 are inevitable. *District Administration, 28.*

Obama, B., & Biden, J. (2007). *Reforming and strengthening America's schools for the 21st century.* Retrieved from http://www.timeandlearning.org/Obama%20Campaign%20Education%20Proposal.pdf

Pachler, N., Bachmair, B., & Cook, J. (2010). *Mobile learning: Structures, agency, practices.* New York, NY: Springer.

Papasterigou, M. (2009). Digital game-based learning in high school computer science education: Impact on educational effectiveness and student motivation. *Computers & Education, 52*(2), 1–12. doi:10.1016/j.compedu.2008.06.004

Penny, J. (2003). My life as a reader. *Assessing Writing, 8*(3), 192–215. doi:10.1016/j.asw.2003.08.001

Petrova, K., & Li, C. (2009). Evaluating mobile learning artefacts. In *Proceedings of the Ascilite Conference Same Places, Different Spaces,* Auckland, New Zealand (pp. 768-772).

Sharples, M. (2006). *Big issues in mobile learning: Report of a workshop by the Kaleidoscope Network of Excellence Mobile Learning Initiative.* Retrieved from http://www.lsri.nottingham.ac.uk/msh/Papers/BIG_ISSUES_REPORT_PUBLISHED.pdf

Solomonidou, C., & Mitsaki, A. (2009). Boys' and girls' computer activities and learning in internet café. *International Journal of Learning, 16*(11), 169–177.

Squire, K., & Jan, M.-F. (2007). Mad city mystery: Developing scientific argumentation skills with a place-based augmented reality game on handheld computers. *Journal of Science Education and Technology, 16*(1), 5–29. doi:10.1007/s10956-006-9037-z

Squire, K., & Klopfer, E. (2007). Augmented reality simulations on handheld computers. *Journal of the Learning Sciences, 16*(3), 371–413. doi:10.1080/10508400701413435

Tamin, R. M., Bernard, R. M., Borokhovski, E., Abrami, P. C., & Schmid, R. F. (2011). What forty years of research says about the impact of technology on learning: A second-order meta-analysis and validation study. *Review of Educational Research, 81*(1), 4–28. doi:10.3102/0034654310393361

Wagner, T. (2010). *Change leadership: A practical guide to transforming our schools.* New York, NY: Basic Books.

Walsh, C. (2010). Systems-based literacy practices: Digital games research, gameplay and design. *Australian Journal of Language and Literacy, 33*(1), 24–30.

Wenger, L., McDermott, R., & Synder, W. M. (2002). *Cultivating communities of practice.* Cambridge, MA: Harvard Business School Press.

Winn, J., & Heeter, C. (2009). Gaming, gender, and time: Who makes time to play. *Sex Roles, 61*(1), 1–13. doi:10.1007/s11199-009-9595-7

APPENDIX

An example of a student's essay:

All citizens will be given opportunities to enjoy the basic facilities like education, housing, and healthcare. To ensure the welfare of the citizens is well taken care of, the government will listen to their opinions and complaints. The government will not use violent approaches to solve any conflicts between countries, so that the citizens need not worry about the country having to go to war.

Heavy taxes will not be imposed. Subsidies will be given to needy families. Foreign talents will not be readily welcomed and introduced into the country, so that there will not be unnecessary competition between the people, and the citizens will not feel threatened by their presence, worrying that they will lose their place in the country.

The government will allow the citizens to have a say in decisions, and the view of the majority of the people will be considered. However, the view of the other people will not be neglected. Measures will be taken to ensure that all of the citizens will be satisfied with the government's decisions, and conflicts will not arise among the people.

This work was previously published in the International Journal of Mobile and Blended Learning, Volume 3, Issue 4, edited by David Parsons, pp 19-37, copyright 2011 by IGI Publishing (an imprint of IGI Global).

Chapter 17
Empowered Learner Identity through M-Learning:
Representations of Disenfranchised Students' Perspectives

Ruth Wallace
Charles Darwin University, Australia

ABSTRACT

E-learning has been promoted as a key component of improving educational access and opportunity internationally, but for disenfranchised learners, many forms of e-learning are just as alien as the educational systems they have rejected. M-learning utilises technologies, activities and social systems that are integrated into many people's lives, including those who have had limited access to, or rejected, formal education systems. This paper discusses projects conducted in Northern Australia that explored a range of e-tools to support indigenous students' engagement and recognition of their knowledge and contexts. Mobile learning tools emerged as the preferred way to learn throughout the project. This approach challenges educational institutions to connect to students' lives and contexts. This paper shows how participants utilised m-learning to demonstrate their diverse knowledge systems, the decisions they made about representing knowledge though m-learning, and the implications for trainers and assessors.

INTRODUCTION

E-learning ... offers the opportunities for different modes of interaction involving many more people from diverse cultural backgrounds. This involves a new set of literacies (Bowles, 2001, p. 102) *and relationships with learning and technolo-*gies. Approaches to learning that build on strong relationships with technologies increasingly utilise mobile technologies, and these mobile learning tools have been taken up by many disenfranchised learners and are located in their own contexts. An exploration of a project conducted with Indigenous learners in remote Northern Australian commu-

DOI: 10.4018/978-1-4666-2139-8.ch017

nities found that m-learning was a powerful tool in recognising knowledge and building people's confidence in themselves as learners. For many learners, m-learning has the potential to include a range of people previously disenfranchised from the education system as their ways of knowledge structures are not reflected in the mainstream system and lack of access to appropriate infrastructure is not recognised. This paper reports on an m-learning based approach that involved Indigenous people in the development of ways of learning that recognize learners' knowledge and skills, as well as the co-production of knowledge that address the skill and qualification gaps that need to be overcome to gain successful employment outcomes. This paper explores the constructs of mobile learning utilised and reflects on the outcomes of the project as a form of social learning that engages learners and their worlds.

Context

The role of e-learning in a knowledge economy is recognised in the European Union's approaches to lifelong *"e-learning that use e-learning for promoting digital literacy and thereby contribute to strengthening social cohesion and personal development and fostering intercultural dialogue"* (European Union, 2003).

In Australia, the intergovernmental Council of Australian Governments (2009) has established the need for a flexible vocational education system to increase access for, and engagement of, Indigenous people, and provide them with opportunities for engaging in the workforce through the Closing the Gap strategy. Within this agenda, "e-learning is not an end in itself but a means to the greater flexibility, responsiveness and long-term sustainability now required of the national training system" (Allen Consulting, 2010, p. 15). The potential of e-learning to improve educational and employment outcomes has been adopted in Australia and particularly by Indigenous learners ready for a positive learning

experience in the formal education system. The use of e-learning is, however, not unproblematic as there is differential access to computers and other technologies, Internet access, regular power supplies and appropriate materials.

Boyle and Wallace (2008) note that integrated e-learning developed with Indigenous people is more than understanding the technological or ICT resources but addressing organisational, systemic, pedagogic and cultural issues that challenge policy, educational institutions and systems, educators and educational brokers… (There is a) need to work with educational policy, institutions, trainers and brokers to re-imagine VET (Vocational Education and Training) in Indigenous contexts and then, together consider a new way to structure, fund and support remote Indigenous peoples' learning through e-learning.

As Christie (2004) notes, Aboriginal people have demonstrated a strong interest in communication through electronic media but the representations of Aboriginal people and knowledge need to be inclusive and avoid commodification and marginalisation of Aboriginal understandings and intent. Any examination of the potential of e-learning in improving educational and workforce outcomes of Indigenous learners, then, needs to consider the ways technologies and representations are flexible and inclusive of different ways of knowing and being represented in educational, workforce and local communities.

M-learning has been a key component of approaches that explore the potential of digital technologies to negotiate meaningful education and workforce development experiences. Mobile devices are characterised by the potential for making connection through spontaneous collaboration and communication, location focused information, being readily available, i.e., within sight, beaming information between devices and providing portable means of collecting and sharing audio and visual information (Kukulska-Hulme & Traxler, 2005). Mobile devices provide opportunities for a wider group of people to create and share new forms of information using multimedia forms for their own purposes. Some examples are collecting videos on a mobile phone, creating a digital story, responding to an automated bill by text message or a wedding invitation by MMS (Multimedia Messaging Service).

Any definition of m-learning in terms of hardware and software helps in recognising m-learning tools in daily life but is limited by the technology advances at the time of any publication. Pachler and Seipold (2009, p. 153) reject transmission and productivity based concepts of m-learning, noting that m-learning definitions are often reductive in nature and foreground the delivery of content to mobile devices in small micro-units…instead we see mobile learning as concerning the processes of coming to know, and of being able to operate successfully in and across, new and ever changing contexts and learning spaces with and through the use of mobile devices it may be more useful to describe m-learning in terms of its use and purpose. Mobile technologies are frequently connected to people's lives, and are used for people's own purposes for communication and connection beyond the educational. Jones, Issrof, Scanlon, et al. (2006) describe the motivational characteristics of m-learning as; the control learners have over learning for their own goals, ownership of the device and materials produced, and that they are fun to use, involve communication, learning-in-context and continuity between learning contexts. Naismith, Lonsdale, Vavoula, et al. (2004) note that m-learning relates to the following learning constructs; behaviourist, constructivist, situated, collaborative, informal/lifelong and support/co-ordination. Traxler (2009, p. 8) notes that mobile devices, systems and technologies also have a direct and pervasive impact on knowledge itself, and how it is generated, transmitted, owned, valued and consumed in our societies…For the era of mobile technology, we come to conceive of education as conservation in context, enabled by continual interaction through and with personal and mobile technology.

The potential for utilising m-learning to improve educational outcomes, then, is only realised by the degree to which m-learning is implemented in ways that support learners, trainers and policy makers to reconceptualise learners, their understandings of the world and to make connections to meaningful learning experiences.

THEORETICAL FRAMEWORK

Social Constructions of Learning and Engagement

Critical and social theorists have informed the development of understandings of the structures and processes that operate within society. Any educational structure or process is underpinned by an interpretation of the ways knowledge and behaviours are transferred and reproduced. The design of educational systems, and the tools that might be used, reflect the designers' critical perceptions of knowledge, agency, cultural and social practice. A consideration of learning and engagement in formal and informal learning experiences is informed by understanding the key concepts within the social order. Lave and Wenger (1991, pp. 50-51) in their description of a social theory of practice note the relational interdependency of agent and world, activity, meaning, cognition, learning and knowing. It emphasizes the inherently socially negotiated character of meaning and the interested, concerned character of thought action of persons-in-activity. This view also claims that learning, thinking and knowing are relations among people in activity in, with, and arising from the socially and culturally structured world. This world is socially constituted; objective forms and systems of activity, on the one hand, and agents' subjective and intersubjective understandings of them, on the other, mutually constitute both the world and its experienced form.

In an educational approach designed to work across cultures, social disenfranchisement and distance, it is valuable to be able to identify and take into consideration the ways that such approaches engage or exclude different perspectives and representations of knowledge.

A recognition of formal education approaches as socially contested recognises the ways power relations impact on learners' and teachers' experiences and helps us to understand the nature of engagement and disengagement. The alienation and disconnection of learners from formal education institutions and experiences has been explored by Smyth and Hattam (2005) and Te Riele (2003, pp. 148-150) who note the reasons for disengagement from formal education have related to the rigidity of school systems, negative relationships with teachers, not feeling accepted or supported and the lack of connection between the curriculum and students' own lives. Field (2005) argues that those who are most socially engaged demonstrate the values and attitudes related to demonstrating a sense of agency and being able to "exert control over key parts of one's life" (Field, 2005, p. 144). Those who are disengaged from formal education are disenfranchised from associated knowledge resources including a sense of efficacy as a learner at an individual and community level (Field, 2005).

For Bourdieu (1990), knowledge is socially constructed, mediated and open ended, developed through individual and collective action. A social theory of practice is used to understand the practices that inform social systems and institutions and impact on individuals and groups in society. Bourdieu in describing *habitus*, the socially constructed systems or principles that generate and organize practice and representations, explores the essentially socially negotiated nature of meaning. *Habitus* is historically produced, producing individual and group activities. Social practices can be understood in terms of the conditions under which they are generated and implemented, and the interrelationship between the social worlds that "*habitus* performs, while concealing it, in and through practice" (Bourdieu, 1990).

Berger and Luckman (2002, pp. 46-47) found that society and institutions are produced by people, people are socially produced and then experience the world they have created objectively and, with the transmission of that social world to the next generation, the whole process is enacted. They describe the ways that the institutions require legitimatisation and are justified. Institutions are understood in terms of the knowledge of their members, this knowledge institutionalizing members' behaviour and intersections. "Since this knowledge is socially objectivated *as* knowledge, that is, as a body of generally valid truths about reality, any radical deviance from the institutional order appears as a departure from reality" (Berger & Luckman, 2002, p. 49). Knowledge then, is fundamental to the functioning of society, ordering the world, the language to describe it, understanding and reproducing social reality (pp. 49-50).

Mobile Learning and Technologies

Gore (2001) recognises the importance of understanding the ways power relations operate at a micro level of pedagogical practice that function through surveillance, normalisation, exclusion and distribution. Understanding the social practices related to learning, the representations of knowledge systems and governance and their impact on learners, provides insight into the processes and institutions that operate and ways to proactively respond to the outcomes. This is particularly valuable in highlighting the invisible but transformative processes that impact on learning engagement and outcomes. The potential of examining m-learning as a social process is in understanding the ways that personal mobile devices connect to people's social lives and create effective and empowering learning experiences for disenfranchised learners.

The use of mobile technologies in learning environments has been integrated into formal educational contexts to enhance the communication of knowledge and development of ideas between learners, experts and their peers. "The mobile learning community has demonstrated that it can take learning to individuals, communities and countries that were previously too remote, socially or geographically, for other educational initiatives" (Traxler, 2008, p. 9). Access to mobile technologies and m-learning pedagogies can provide learners (including teachers) with meaningful, context driven ways to introduce and share their knowledge and worlds. The use of m-learning approaches presents people with opportunities to engage with a range of knowledge sets, constructs and contexts beyond those in formal or desk based educational settings. Through educational experiences, learners can use m-learning to make connections between learners' worlds, make unfamiliar contexts more accessible and create ways of interpreting knowledge that reflect different ways of knowing.

CASE STUDY

*Working from Our Strength*s – Recognising and building literacy through the training and assessment competencies, was designed to identify the best approaches to develop and present assessment material that showcased learners' abilities using e-learning. This project built on the work of Indigenous enterprise operators in remote communities across Northern Australia to develop effective strategies to ensure relevant, quality training and qualifications are implemented that support economic independence and knowledge management at a local and national level. Funded by the Department of Education, Science and Training, the project used e-learning tools and technologies to support Indigenous enterprise operators who needed targeted training and assessment for their staff.

The project explored a number of e-learning tools and examined their potential in accurately representing and recognising the knowledge that Indigenous people develop through their work. Previous paper based methods have not been effective because:

- Certificates and other paperwork provided to learners over a lifetime can be lost if people move or don't have adequate storage facilities at home or in their workplace
- Requiring assessment material be provided in English and in a written form excludes people who may speak English as an additional language, and have low levels of English written literacy
- They marginalise learners by focusing on those learners' weaknesses, rather than their strengths, and ignoring non-linear or alternative representations of people's knowledge and skills

The project considered e-learning approaches because:

- They showed people working and demonstrating their skills in their own work context
- They allowed people to demonstrate their skills visually and in their first language
- They were flexible and could accommodate different ways of knowing and representing knowledge.

This project was a chance to examine ways to ensure e-learning, including mobile technologies, could achieve these goals and also the limitations of these technologies. It involved established Indigenous tourism enterprise operators, and staff from a range of Indigenous businesses participated. Participants undertook recognition of prior learning (RPL) and current competence (RCC) processes that reflect the work undertaken in locally based enterprises and Aboriginal businesses using digital photographs, videos and stories, m-portfolios and web-based conferencing. Some examples of the approaches used were:

1. Working in pairs to take digital photographs of each other working, writing a set of critical reflection notes about the competencies and skills demonstrated throughout the session recorded.
2. Collecting a series of photographs and supporting documentation about the competencies they demonstrate at work. Learners used digital cameras and mobile phones to do this.
3. Making audio recordings of testimonials and advertisements about their work to be used in the resource, to report on the work outcomes and engage new clients
4. Making audio recording on mobile phones about their underpinning knowledge, why they worked in a specific way and how this demonstrated their knowledge of best practice in their context
5. Presenting the photographs and commentary as digital stories using Photostory and PowerPoint
6. Organising the information on a USB drive and e-portfolios

Through the 12 month life of the project, the participants explored a range of different electronic and mobile technologies and their potential for collecting evidence. Importantly each device, software and approach was presented as a possible way to show people's knowledge and skills. Participants were trained in using the devices and software but no approach for using the software for RPL was suggested as better than another. Participants had the opportunity to decide which technologies they could use for their own purpose, based on their experience and the information they wanted to share. After trialling the different approaches, the participants came together to share their ideas and to undertake a peer review.

After this peer review, the participants' individual portfolios were assessed by an external assessor.

The final product of the project outlined the process for developing a training plan with an Indigenous enterprise team, ways to use m-tools to collect evidence and examples of successful e-applications for RPL and training plans.

FINDINGS

While the project started by considering a range of e-learning approaches, m-learning strategies and resources were found to be most useful. The projects were based in remote Indigenous communities and were best managed by collecting and organising information with people, while they were involved in relevant work based and learning activities. In low ICT infrastructure and support environments, it was beneficial not to rely on complicated technology and use approaches that can work anywhere, anytime. M-learning approaches, such as using laptops and cameras were less intrusive and already, integrated into people's daily lives, even if they were not used regularly or to their full potential by participants. M-learning based evidence collection strategies ranged across making digital stories and audio files to collating images and texts from various sources. Once these were accepted by students as viable, people identified a broad range of ways to collect evidence. All of these approaches focussed on visual and audio representations of knowledge within the appropriate context.

Participants preferred simple, familiar and stable technologies that they could control and manipulate to their purpose. Of particular benefit were peer teams who collected evidence for each other in their own workplace contexts and then reflecting on the images and recordings before remixing the information to be presented to the assessor. As the learning and evidence collection strategies were a part of people's lives and accepted, different ways of thinking about what is involved in learning and what counts for assessment emerged. This encouraged people to focus on what they can do and how to document and communicate it so others could recognise those skills and competences. Learners also noted the feeling of empowerment they experienced by being involved in a learning process that included their worlds, worked from their own strengths in managing information and included more than text based ways of making connections. Assessors found alternative ways of recognising students' knowledge, strengths and potential points for connection around assessment.

Participants experimented with e-portfolios and finally decided to develop a folder system on their USB pens which had four folders that focussed on them and their learning, rather than an institution and another person's view of that person as a learner. The folders were 'my evidence', 'my units', 'my study plan' and 'my learning'. Learners used these to have a place to put all evidence as it was collected and then sort and allocate it to the various units being studied. It also helped when sharing useful information and exemplars as well as downloading information from the internet. By using a USB stick, participants kept complete control of their information until they chose to share it with peers, employers, colleagues, Aboriginal Liaison officer and finally the trainer and assessor.

It was important for learners that they could discuss the ways they used the m-learning tools and to refine their approach. Participants commented that they didn't know they were allowed to use audio files, bring pictures of themselves working and help each other to reflect on their strengths. Once they had seen different approaches, participants experimented with systems to manage and present portfolios on the web, USB pens and DVD-ROM. External assessors noted that they had a better understanding of participants' strengths by seeing them work in their workplace and activities that were used in the workplace.

The peer assessment process was valuable for learners to develop their e-portfolios and use of mobile technologies in their learning. Learners shared the work they had done and discussed its merits and applicability to the relevant competencies. Learners supported each other to use mobile technologies in ways that best showed their strengths. The next stage was a mock assessment where the assessor explicitly discussed the evidence, the use of technologies and the additional information or questions they would still like addressed before finalising the e-portfolio. By being able to see a variety of ways to collect that evidence and having that validated externally, learners were encouraged to refine and improve their e-portfolios. At this point learners were ready and proud to submit their e-portfolios for assessment. The assessor noted on the depth of information and that they had a clear idea of the learners' capacity in their own work.

The team developed approaches to learning, representing and creating knowledge, sharing ideas and assessing competence with Indigenous participants to better represent and reflect Indigenous people's existing and growing strengths and knowledge. This included the use of video, audio, digital stories, websites and m-portfolios. The potential use of the e-learning tools were not always expected and developed with participants as teams grew in confidence and knowledge about what was possible. The ownership of the final outcomes was shared, which was reflected in the accurate representations of Indigenous people. Appropriate representations sensitive to differences about their learning and use of e-learning generated a series of work across projects that was unexpected. This was most effective when Indigenous people were involved at every stage. Trust is the cornerstone of co-production and was the focus for developing strong relationships across people, groups and institutions. The critical mass of knowledge and resources was core in gaining external and agency support for project teams and their ideas.

The Indigenous people involved are proficient in a number of languages. M-learning tools provided an opportunity to record ideas and examples of their competence in their first language, reflect on the material while in situ and then translate that information, initially across languages, but also across cultures. The m-learning tools were useful for demonstrating alternative ways of interpreting a learning event and to demonstrate competence. This was useful not only for the learners, as they could assess their own skills and discuss what they meant by referring to images and recordings within the context, but also for off-site assessors who came to appreciate the learners and their context in a new way. This process helped to develop new relationships that focused on competence and strength rather than deficit notions of people or learning.

DISCUSSION

Learners are more than consumers, they are producers and teachers of knowledge and ideas as they relate to specific contexts (Gee, 2003). Learners are active interpreters of all learning, including m-learning, its use and potential. These interpretations relate to a sound understanding of the relevant context and relationship to people, places and knowledge systems. In an analysis of the ways Australian Aboriginal people produced resources in their own digital environments, Christie (2007, pp. 2-3) noted:

(Aboriginal) People use the digital resources in a social context as props or artefacts, in the same way that they would use nondigital resources like paintings, photos, diagrams, ceremonial objects, and of course the land itself and natural phenomena in talking about and representing themselves and their histories, and making agreements... the use of Aboriginal digital resources is serious business, making claims about ownership, about rights and responsibilities, and appropriate behaviour.

In these cases the ways that the resources are identified and validated, the way they are accessed and displayed and the ways assemblages are put together and used in context, is a crucial part of the knowledge production process, and negotiations over resources (Christie, 2007, pp. 2-3)

The preference for using mobile technologies in this project recognised the importance of Indigenous learners being able to work in ways that were connected to their daily practice and allowed the flexibility to represent ideas accurately. Participants used mobile technologies to ensure their representations of their own and local community knowledge was collected in context and in accordance with the ways that knowledge is understood culturally, in their community and in their enterprise. Digital knowledge systems and resources offered considerable opportunities to work in new ways. The mobile technologies used in the project are becoming increasingly intuitive in their use and accessible in remote areas. In fact mobile phones and cameras are widely available in remote areas and socially disadvantaged homes where computer based technologies are not readily available. Participants liked being able to collect information in their own workplace, using their own technology and being able to organise that information in a meaningful way. M-learning resources supported people to learn and demonstrate competence across language and knowledge systems as they could present their ideas in their first language (ensuring an accurate record) and then translate for the assessor. This was an improvement on attempting to record their ideas in an additional language and in writing, when the learner is more proficient in their first language and oral recording. The use of mobile technology in training was negotiated rather than mandated which meant that participants could reject or alter the use of technology to meet their priorities and abilities. This helped participants to accurately and fully record and share their ideas for assessment.

M-learning approaches extended and deepened the ways learners could explore, analyse and create knowledge in meaningful ways. M-learning provided a tool to record and organise information that articulated what was meaningful to learners and the power of the connection between people's lives and diverse forms of knowing and being. The use of m-learning led by Indigenous students and teachers led to representations of students' knowledge systems that challenged assessors to think differently about students' capacity, to focus on their strengths and the complexity of their knowledge and skills. This challenged assessors to move from a deficit perception of the participants that relied on proficiency in English written and oral language and knowledge of mainstream systems.

The integration of e-learning, including mobile learning, was also way for participants to accurately represent and share their own worlds while also exploring others in a safe environment. The peer review process was a way for learners to share and consider different ways of working and analyse the benefits or issues concerned.

The case studies demonstrated the need to develop straightforward, multilingual m-learning tools that will build the digital literacies of learners and trainers beyond the formal learning situation, and support the integration of m-learning into people's lives and lifelong learning experiences. This work has commenced with Aboriginal youth in the Northern Territory who are interested in extending their use of m-learning for their careers and engagement in a range of worlds. One of the most important challenges for trainers then is to hand over the power over m-learning experiences with the ownership of the m-learning tools. M-learning works when the mobile technology is a part of people's lives and they own its creation, manipulation and production into other forms. This also means adapting to different ways of representing and linking information; to other forms of knowledge, to the external world, to the local and global communities and to education. The ways that this knowledge is treated; the ways

it is assessed, recognised, legitimated and branded, has significant impact on disenfranchised learners' engagement in a range of learning experiences. Supporting the integration of learners' lives, as they see and interpret them, through the use of m-learning that includes many languages, images and voices, builds strong connections to disenfranchised learners' worlds and enables those learners to take the lead in their own learning journey.

The social nature of learning was evident in the use of e-learning and m-learning to enhance learning and engage learners. As Snyder and Prinsloo (2007) note, the relationships between digital literacy practices in different contexts are complex and differentiated by people's connections to local and global communities. The design and implementation of any mobile technology is developed in a complex social environment. Connecting the implementation and usage of any technology to people's culturally and socially determined lives and priorities is a central theme in educational design.

The impact of using m-learning tools was their role in developing empowered learner identities. Learners who are empowered are able to sustain their engagement in learning through challenges to their learning experiences, and how the learner identities on which they drew helped to address those challenges. For many learners the successful resolution of the contradictions between the learning recognised and imposed by local, peer, workplace and educational institutional communities is related strongly to individual's belief that they should have a role in education system. This did not mean being compliant; participants stated their role was to master and maintain their own integrity as a learner and community member and, for most, challenge the existing paradigm. This attitude tended to be more important in being successful than the strategy used. Supporting students' identity and participation are more than teaching a range of strategies; it was about resolving the nexus of membership that includes educational institutional community membership.

The learners, who had managed to continue engagement for a part of their programme, described their learner identity as it related to the institution and their own community. They had been able to negotiate strategies that worked for them to actively participate. This was optimised when students were able to make strong connections to their own purpose and understandings of the world. This was the power of m-learning, where learners had developed ways to negotiate how they saw themselves and how others saw them as competent learners in their own right and in relation to new knowledge.

CONCLUSION

The use of mobile technologies is not unproblematic. Clearly m-learning has considerable potential for improving the engagement of Indigenous learner but it is used within a social context. It can be inferred that m-learning is more than the incorporation of technologies, it is also about the ways those technologies are used, the ways knowledge is represented and the connections to learners' worlds. Participants were encouraged to use the technology as they saw fit to share their ideas. There was not a set way of sharing or presenting information. Through peer review participants explored the possibilities and connections to different socially determined ways of representing information. Technological and socially based approaches to m-learning that are designed to engage disenfranchised learners start from the learners' context, knowledge, skills and technology and develops ways to share and accommodate a range of perspectives and devices. They provide a forum to make it easier to share and collaborate, to work in diverse ways and then relate to the expectations of the assessment system.

Effective approaches to learning might best be exemplified in video gaming where as Gee (2003) notes, learners direct their learning, are able to repeat parts as often as they choose, learning

has consequences that are personal to the learner, learning is linked to a range of global and local communities, experimentation is encouraged, learning is highly customized and responsive and has inherent rewards. In this way learners are engaged in their own learning, act as co-producers of knowledge and building connections to their own and others' knowledge and skills as they see fit and when they are ready.

M-learning tools can be used to focus learning on exploring learner contexts, local and global knowledge. By recognising the diverse knowledge systems and contexts of a range of disenfranchised learners, such as youth, regional communities and small enterprise owners, there are opportunities to build bridges between their worlds and the formal education curriculum. These bridges provide points of connection and sharing, not for one to dominate or denigrate the other, rather to make connections to share ideas, build mutual understanding and extend possibilities for learning. M-learning approaches can be implemented to involve disenfranchised learners in positive learning experiences and active construction of knowledge and learner identities. Learners are able to work with and be assessed using material from their worlds as they relate to the worlds of work, community life and lifelong learning, to explore new possibilities and develop strong empowered learner identities. Any investment in m-learning then considers the technological, social and cultural implications in the development and implementation phases.

REFERENCES

Allen Consulting. (2010). *Strategic Review of the Australian Flexible Learning Framework (Framework) and its Oversight by the Flexible Learning Advisory Group: A Discussion Paper.* Retrieved from http://www.allenconsult.com.au/flexible_learning_review/downloads/flexible_learning_review_discussion_paper.pdf

Berger, P., & Luckman, T. (2002). The social construction of reality. In Calhoun, C., Gerteis, J., Moody, J., Pfaff, S., & Virk, I. (Eds.), *Contemporary Sociological Theory* (pp. 42–50). London, UK: Blackwell Publishing.

Bourdieu, P. (1990). *The Logic of Practice*. Stanford, CA: Stanford University Press.

Bowles, M. S. (2004). *Relearning to E-Learn: Strategies for electronic learning and knowledge*. Melbourne, Australia: Melbourne University Publishing.

Boyle, A., & Wallace, R. (2008). The role of e-learning in 'holistic' approaches to VET in remote Australian Indigenous contexts. In *Proceedings of the 2008 AVETRA Conference*, Adelaide, Australia.

Christie, M. (2004). *Aboriginal Knowledge on the Internet*. Retrieved from http://www.cdu.edu.au/centres/ik/pdf/AbKnowInternet.pdf

Christie, M. (2007). Fracturing the Skeleton of Principle: Australian Law, Aboriginal Law, and Digital Technology. *Learning Communities: International Journal of Learning in Social Contexts*.

Council of Australian Governments. (2009). *National Indigenous Reform Agreement (Clo9sing the Gap)*. Retrieved from http://www.coag.gov.au/coag_meeting_outcomes/2009-07-02/docs/NIRA_closing_the_gap.pdf

European Union. (2003). *Decision No 2318/EC of the European Parliament and of the Council, December 2003 adopting a multiannual programme (2004-2006) for the effective integration of information and communication technologies (ICT) in education and training systems in Europe (eLearning Programme)*. Retrieved from http://europa.eu/eur-lex/pri/en/oj/dat/2003/1_345/1_34520031231en00090016.pdf

Field, J. (2005). *Social Capital and Lifelong Learning*. Bristol, UK: The Policy Press.

Gee, J. P. (2003). *What Video Games Have To Teach Us About Learning and Literacy*. New York, NY: Palgrave Macmillan.

Gore, J. M. (2001). Disciplining Bodies: On the Continuity of Power Relations in Pedagogy. In Paechter, R. E. C., Harrison, R., & Twining, P. (Eds.), *Learning, Space and Identity*. London, UK: Paul Chapman Publishing.

Jones, A., Issroff, K., Scanlon, E., Clough, G., & McAndrew, P. (2006, July 14-16). Using mobile devices for learnings in Informal Settings: is it Motivating? In *Proceedings of IADIS International Conference on Mobile Learning*, Dublin, Ireland.

Kress, G., & Pachler, N. (2007). Thinking about the 'm' in m-learning. In Pachler, N. (Ed.), *Mobile learning: towards a research agenda*. London, UK: WLE Centre, IoE.

Kukulska-Hulme, A., & Traxler, J. (2005). Mobile teaching and learning. In Kukulska-Hulme, A., & Traxler, J. (Eds.), *Mobile Learning: A handbook for educators and trainers* (pp. 25–44). London, UK: Routledge.

Lave, J., & Wenger, E. (1991). *Situated Learning: Legitimate peripheral participation*. Cambridge, UK: Cambridge University Press.

Naismith, L., Lonsdale, P., Vavoula, G., & Sharples, M. (2004). *Literature Review in Mobile Technologies and Learning*. Bristol, UK: NESTA FutureLab.

Pachler, N., & Seipold, J. (2009). Harnessing mobile devices to connect learning in formal and informal settings: the role of digital narratives and discontinuous text production for narratives and discontinuous text production for meaning making. In *Proceedings of the 8th World Conference on Mobile and Contextual Learning*, Orlando, FL.

Smyth, J., Hattam, R., & Cannon, J. (2004). *Dropping Out, Drifting Off, Being Excluded: Becoming someone without school*. New York, NY: Peter Lang.

Snyder, I., & Prinsloo, M. (Eds.). (2007). The digital literacy practices of young people in marginal contexts. *Language & Education: An International Journal, 21*(3), 171-270.

Te Riele, K. (2003). *An Inclusive Learning Culture: Post-compulsory Education for a "Second Chance" Enriching Learning Cultures*. Paper presented at the 11th International Conference on Post-Compulsory Education and Training.

Traxler, J. (2008). From Text to Context. In *Proceedings of the mLearn 2008 Conference: The Bridge from Text to Context*.

Traxler, J. (2009). Learning in a Mobile Age. *International Journal of Mobile and Blended Learning, 1*(1), 1–12.

This work was previously published in the International Journal of Mobile and Blended Learning, Volume 3, Issue 1, edited by David Parsons, pp 53-63, copyright 2011 by IGI Publishing (an imprint of IGI Global).

Chapter 18
E–Learning and M–Learning:
Challenges and Barriers in Distance Education Group Assignment Collaboration

Lisa Soon
Central Queensland University, Australia

ABSTRACT

This research explores the relationship between e-learning and m-learning by investigating distance education students' use of a learning management system, "Interact," for virtual team work. The paper explores their experience of online collaborative group assignments in the subject "Information Management in Organisations." International and local students were grouped. Each group undertook a case study project to propose solutions for identified problems in their chosen organisations. Students developed their assignment in wikis and used various tools for communication and document storage. An anonymous web-based survey was conducted after students completed the group assessment. The results reflected a wide range of factors including technology use, working with students from a different country, and challenges they faced completing group assessment online. Their feedback on their e-learning experience indicated the need for m-learning to address their concerns. The findings indicate a need for m-learning to support e-learning further, which could significantly improve the facilitation of online collaborative group assignments.

INTRODUCTION

There is an advancement in teaching material delivery, with institutions moving away from students passively receiving print-based information such as paper materials from instructors to laser disks (or CD-ROMs) to web-based interactive learning. The School of Information Studies (SIS) at Charles Sturt University in Australia is the largest library education provider in Australia. It has been offering distance education for more than 30 years with no students enrolled in the face-to-face teaching mode. In the past, it adopted email and discussion forums to supplement print-based

DOI: 10.4018/978-1-4666-2139-8.ch018

information delivery. In recent years, in addition to the learning management system 'Interact' (also known as 'CSU Interact – Sakai'), popular technology and tools like Skype, GoogleDocs, podcasting, chat rooms, wikis, blogs, Facebook and Second Life have been employed to increase class member interaction and engagement in distance education.

This paper reports a group assignment conducted in the subject[1] "Information Management in Organisations" offered in the third year of an undergraduate program 'Bachelor of Library and Information Management' in the first semester, 2009. In this research, the learning experiences of distance education students in collaborating with other students in group assignments in the subject using e-learning technology were explored. E-learning here refers to the use of technology to support online learning and teaching. In particular, it discusses the use of wiki, chat room, group mail, announcement and common repositories in a private project site provided to each group in Interact. Students used e-learning technology for their group assignment communications interaction and collaboration work regardless of their geographical locations. Students communicated and collaborated with group members at pre-arranged dates and times wherever they were. The use of e-learning technology by distance education students was mandatory in their group assignment. The subject coordinator set up the learning environment with all tools made available in Interact where the students used the tools for communication, collaboration, interaction and participation in assignment development online. In preparing the learning environment with group work in mind, group assignment activities and the required use of Interact tools were carefully considered, pre-determined, and constantly monitored throughout the delivery of the subject. This was to ensure that students could reap the benefits of collaborative learning, hone team work skills and develop technological skills.

Many students opted for distance education in order to do their studies at times of their convenience. They wanted to plan their assignment tasks at a flexible time to fit into their normal routine and commitments. The results indicate that doing group work using e-learning technology purely from a home or office desk top computer could restrict their physical whereabouts, where the Internet access and computer use are restricted to fixed locations. Having considered the student learning needs, group assignment collaboration requirements and the technology to be put in alignment with the purposes of online group assignment, this research proposes a framework of learner requirements in online group work in distance education. It also discusses how the use of supporting portable m-learning devices such as iPhone, palm top and netbook could address learning needs and reduce some of the physical location restrictions.

This article adopts the following structure. The literature review section discusses e-learning and m-learning. It also explores the use of e-learning technology in distance education and highlights a gap in research. A methodology section follows to explain the case study method used in this research. The data collection techniques employed was a web-based survey and classroom observation. The results and discussion section explains the analysis of the results in this research. It also discusses the student experience in their use of e-learning technology in their group work such as their satisfaction with technology, the technology they actually used in their group work, challenges they faced in the online environment, and the possibility of m-learning. A conceptual model developed is based on the findings of this research to propose changes in online group work in distance education. The last section concludes this article. In adopting e-technology, this research stresses the importance of considering mobile devices to support personal and mobile learning (or m-learning).

LITERATURE REVIEW

E-learning refers to computer-enhanced learning and deals with both the technology and associated methodologies in learning using networked and multimedia technology (Lipshitz & Parsons, 2008). Titrade, El Baaboua, Sion, and Mihalcescu (2009) describe technology-supported education and learning as the instructions given through digital computer technology. Duncan-Howell and Lee (2007) explain that m-learning generally implies that the learning is "personal and portable". Scholars like Chen, Kao, and Shen (2003), Sharples, Taylo,r and Vavoula (2005), Seppala and Alamaki (2003), and Motiwalla (2007) share the view that mobile learning allows one to break away from teaching that takes place in a classroom, moving to another location while communicating via networks. In this paper, m-learning is regarded as part of e-learning technology but with a clear difference to make learning portable and mobile with the use of mobile technology devices. Both e-learning and m-learning technologies, however, involve information and communication technology to facilitate learning. This research explores e-learning and its related student experience in order to recommend the opportunities and identify the challenges facing the implementation of m-learning.

Mixing technology-enhanced learner experience with more traditional learning experience has been seen as normal practice in the development of computer-assisted learning in higher education (Bliuc, Goodyear, & Ellis, 2007). In face-to-face learning and teaching, e-learning is used to complement the teaching delivery. However, the use of e-learning plays a much more critical role in facilitating learning and teaching in distance education. Papachristos et al. (2010) comment that the flexibility in distance education provides greater opportunities for individuals to study and educate themselves. Learners in face-to-face education can see and conveniently interact with their peers. In contrast, distance education learners do not usually see and interact with their peers unless it is under some form of instruction.

Further, literature suggests that distance learners require a great deal of interaction to overcome their feelings of isolation (O'Neil, Singh, & O'Donoghue, 2004). Beldarrain (2006) suggests that distance education courses should include interaction as the foundation of effective distance education practices.

Technology can achieve certain types of engagement and interactions that would not otherwise be possible in face-to-face dealings (Beldarrain, 2006). For successful virtual collaboration, social relations are as important as the project content and team expertise (Karpova, Correia, & Baran, 2009). E-learning technology can increase real-time collaboration between learners. E-learning technology has the potential to help distance students stay connected and therefore overcome their feelings of isolation. Despite the advantages brought about by e-learning technology, some scholars comment differently. Robey, Khoo, and Powers (2000) suggest that face to face communication is an important ingredient in making virtual teams more effective, especially when group members are from different countries or cultural backgrounds. Smith and Ferguson (2002) claim that with the benefits of technology come a number of disadvantages, including potential technology failures, the lack of face to face interaction and interpersonal cues, and from the instructor's viewpoint a great deal of time and effort is required in converting and/or creating new material specific to the online mode. Online group work collaboration is also effective in supporting problem-based learning as a pedagogy that uses project work to drive learning (Guthrie, 2010). To be successful in designing web-based learning or e-learning, Luminita (2010) suggests that the university should adapt itself to the current necessities of its students as well. E-learning and m-learning are both powered by technology to facilitate learning. However, although both use technology, m-learning has the added advantage of allowing m-learners to make one's learning "personal and portable" (Duncan-Howell & Lee, 2007, p. 224).

Dix et al. (2000) explore the location, mobility, population and device awareness of the interactive mobile system. They remark that the merging of computer and communication technologies allows the development of systems that provide immediate access to information with portable network devices. E-learning, if used by learners who have the additional device features of 'personal' and 'mobile', would turn e-learning into m-learning. Following this line of thought, Cucu, Christescu, and Christescu (2010) support the use of information technology in education by proposing four principles of education technology development. Their four principles are: 1) anytime and anywhere access, including mobile devices; 2) user-generated content; 3) assigning the users active roles in the use of technology; and 4) creating a relationship between natural activities and educational activities. The four principles should be applied to enhance user access to learning environments and information and allow m-learning to happen in addition to e-learning.

Having reviewed the extant research, what is not clear is how distance education students feel about their use of new technology, especially when there is an assessment requirement to use technology in group assignments. The key research questions addressed in this paper are "What challenges and barriers do distance education students encounter in the use of e-learning technology to support online group work in distance education?" and "Can the adoption of mobile technology through the use of mobile devices for learning help overcome their difficulties?"

METHODOLOGY

It was unclear how distance education students used technology, their learning experiences, challenges and barriers they faced in their group assignments in real life. To explore this new unfamiliar context, the case study research method was deemed most appropriate for the research context. In educational research, case study enables the exploration of unknown scenarios of learning and teaching activities (Merriam, 1998, 2002). This research adopts a qualitative case study approach. Case study is warranted as this is a real-world situation where the boundaries between the phenomenon and its context are not clear (Yin, 2003, p. 13). This research adopted a web-based survey and frequent class observations throughout the semester as data collection techniques. The observation data were collected and analysed using a qualitative interpretive approach. The web-based survey was administered via Survey Monkey. The web-based survey consisted of closed- and open-ended questions. Survey Monkey provided many types of statistical reports to help in further analysis. It also provides some statistical figures for discussions. However, the open-ended answers were manually analysed using a qualitative interpretive approach. While the web-based survey had answers provided by students to address each question, observation of peer communications and teacher-and-student interactions was employed in this research to allow a deeper understanding of learner experience. The two collection methods provided rich, in-depth data from different resources to enable triangulation.

Towards the end of the semester, all students were asked to complete the voluntary, anonymous online survey questionnaire immediately after the completion of the assignment. The link to the questionnaire was sent to students' email addresses. Student perceptions were sought on a wide range of factors related to their experiences of online group assessment, including working with technology, communication and working with students from different countries. The survey questionnaire (see the Appendix) consisted of 14 main closed and open-ended questions and 5 demographic questions.

Class observation was used to monitor all student communications, interactions and other related group assignment activities in all the project sites. Most of the student communication and interaction happened in group emails, forum discussions and chat rooms. Group emails involved both the student-to-student and student-to-lecturer emails generated in the class throughout the semester. Observation also included a constant monitoring of student activities and feedback over the use of Interact tools for group work collaboration in all the project sites. All student group assignment activities like uploading materials in a common resource repository, chat-room messages, group email messages, announcements, calendar activities and the use of wikis for the assignments over the semester were closely watched and monitored.

Ethical clearance was sought from the university ethics office about the collection of on-line survey and observation data in this research. Consents were obtained from the students after an email announcement (with a consent form attached) was sent to all students involved about the observation of their use of the learning management system, "Interact", for their group assignments. Before proceeding to start the online survey, a screen about the research information and consent appeared. It informed the participants that the participation was totally voluntary and they could simply withdraw at any point of time without any penalty. It explicitly stated that by clicking the start button to proceed with the online survey, a participant gave his/her informed consent to the participation.

Having obtained the data, they were used to produce concept maps. Key themes were formed after the concept mapping. They will be discussed in the case study section below under sub-headings. With the concept maps obtained from different sources, the data from the survey discussed above, and the observations undertaken through all the different activities, were crossed checked in a triangulation process. Triangulation is used to help validate the data (Stake, 1995;

2000). The information from other sources, as discussed in the paragraph above, was obtained from the main subject site and all related group project Interact sites and the "end of session online evaluation survey" were all used to cross-check the information obtained to derive validated truth. The level of satisfaction of students, concerns, comments, and feedback about the subject and the quality of teaching, the lecturer, communication, assessment, workload, etc. were part of the data collected for analysis.

CASE STUDY

The online learning environment created by using the university's learning management system called "Interact" was used as an official platform for group projects. Interact has a number of tools for communication and collaboration to support team work, including Wiki, Synchronous Chat, group mail, announcement and resources (multimedia repositories).

The primary case study involved 73 undergraduate students from all parts of Australia (a large continent with scattered distance education students) and around the world. Teams of four to five students were formed by the subject coordinator. Students were given access to the project site and encouraged to start team collaboration and communication with the tools provided. Some teams were formed by having international students grouped together with Australian students. Late enrolment students were placed into groups whose members had dropped out. The teams were largely randomly selected and members were unlikely to have knowledge of one another. The subject coordinator played a role of mediator and advisor in group work facilitation.

Each group was allocated a private group project site, including tools like chat room, group mail, announcement, repository and a wiki site. Groups were required to use the wiki to develop their assignments for marking. As an induction to the class, the subject coordinator sent an email to all students in the first week of the semester explaining the purpose and how to use each Interact tool for group work. All students were advised to press the help key '?' when using each tool to obtain tutorial information and explanation when in doubt. While Interact was mainly used, students were encouraged to use any other supporting technology such as Skype for voice chat and Google Docs for developing their assignments.

Although there were 73 students involved in group assignments, 51 students, or about 70% of the class, completed the questionnaire. The majority of students were females. The majority were under 30 years of age. Over 60% worked fulltime. Slightly over two-thirds of the students spoke English as their first language. A very high percentage of the class had broadband access to the Internet. Most students were Australians, some were from Hong Kong and a minority were from other countries.

RESULTS AND DISCUSSION

The class reported the use of 'Interact' and its tools (wiki, chat room, etc.) was a great challenge to use. Many students had not used Wikis before the group assignment. A majority of students described a need for more time for Wiki training before embarking on their required group assignments. According to the cohort of students who participated in this research, their experiences showed that the Wiki assignment was the greatest challenge to them. The following results are based on the student experiences revealed in the web-based survey and observations.

Satisfaction with Technology

18.4% of the class strongly agreed that benefits were provided by using online technology for group work. 49% of the class supported technology use but they prefer to do group work off-line (i.e. not using technology for group work or want to work face-to-face). Hence, 67.4% (i.e. 18.4%+49%) of them accepted the use of m-learning or e-learning technology in distance education assignments. Some (12.2%) were neutral. But there were also some, representing a small number (6.1%) of the students, who strongly preferred to work off-line rather than using e-learning technology where students were dispersed across different time-zones. Among the many reasons given about their objections were unstable technologies, different personalities, time difference, location differences (e.g. members come from various countries) and not all members were committed to group tasks. The mix of responses indicate that, while some (67.4%) embraced technology and enjoyed using it in learning and group assignments, some (20.4%) disliked the use of technology in learning, especially involving group assignments where their group members were far apart.

Over 66% of students reported that they learned and used the Wiki and other Interact tools during this study. To reflect on the most valuable aspects of the group assignment experience, many students agreed that learning new technological skills was the most valuable aspect of their group assignment experience. They were amazed with their ability to use technology to communicate and conduct group work together online. They saw the final group assignment produced on the Wiki as a very great achievement. Distance education students appreciated the opportunity presented by the collaborative online group assignment which enabled them to learn new skills. Many of them noted that all members utilized technology extensively. Amongst all the tools provided to them for use, the Chat room and Wiki were the most popular.

Overall, the survey respondents expressed high satisfaction with online technology, and this agreed with and reflected their preference for the use of e-learning technology rather than offline work.

After initial hesitation using wiki, I found it useful. It was nerve wracking having to put my own work 'out there' for other students to comment on but I ended up gaining confidence about my work and understanding of what was required.

This subject provided an opportunity for my first group assessment for the first time using a wiki. Although I feel I could have achieved a higher mark working individually, it has been very challenging and a valuable growth experience.

Technology Used

Groups used different types of technology for different tasks in the process of developing their assignments. Synchronous and asynchronous tools complemented each other. They served different needs and were employed at different stages of the collaboration, providing a higher degree of flexibility in the computer-mediated communication.

Wiki was the main collaborative tool used for developing the assignment. The lecturer provided some guidelines on how to use the Wiki before releasing the assignment specifications to students. Each member of the group placed his/her contributed work as a section or paragraph of text and figures or tables on the Wiki. All members had an equal right to edit, rearrange or reject the work of other members. One could simply make a comment on the work of other group members. An example is the linguistic aspect of revision done by native English speakers to the work from non English background group-mates. Wiki's history helped the instructor to monitor both the students' activity and their levels of contribution to the project and therefore made the assessment of individual members easier. Allowing the marker to assess individual contributions is a challenge for group members in group projects. The majority of students found Wiki useful in preparing the group assignment. Many students enjoyed the fact that Wiki allowed them to work on their group project at a time of their convenience.

Chat room was a popular synchronous communication tool. It allowed immediate feedback and real time discussions. Students used this tool to introduce themselves, to brainstorm ideas, to assign tasks and to make important decisions. The majority of students were satisfied with the chat room.

Students also used asynchronous communication tools like *group mail* and *announcement*. The announcement tool allowed group members to deliver general news, arrange meetings and generally highlight specific ideas or activities. Only 2 groups used this tool as alternative means were available for small group communication. Group mail was an internal email system to facilitate communication. It was heavily used by all 12 groups. The instructor was included in this system and received the emails from different groups. The closed nature of the email and inclusion of the instructor offered learners privacy as well as a greater sense of connectedness to their instructor. Most students found group mail useful.

'Resources' is a tool in Interact that allows a group to share and store documents or data. Both the learners and the instructor used resource folders to offer sample work, articles and other items not included as web links. Group members stored a variety of files that offered general support to their assignment case study. Most teams regarded 'resources' as an ideal place to deposit their drafts and store items locatable on the Internet for other team members to read or view later.

Challenges in the Online Environment

When asked about the most negative aspects of the group assignment experience, the student responses revealed them as: (1). Difficulty of arranging a chat time to suit everybody in the group (76.6%); (2). Being dependent on other people (68%); (3). The inequality of the contributions among members (55%); (4). Some members lacked the required skills (40%); and (5). Conflicts amongst the group members (19%). The second, third and fifth negative aspects are common problems in group assignments regardless of online or offline assignments.

Students generally highlighted some critical challenges they faced. The greatest challenge identified was the synchronous communication and time issue. Although 78% of participants found the chat room facility useful for synchronous communication with their group members, it was difficult to arrange a chat time to suit everybody in the group. This was identified as the major barrier for almost 80% of students. At the time of assignment, there was a one to four hour time difference between Australia and international students and among Australian students themselves. As most students were working, arranging a time for synchronous communication was a challenge. Many were not able to attend all chat sessions owing to schedule conflicts.

They indicated that some members exhibited a lack of required skills. It appeared that for about 40% of respondents this lack of required skills to work with technology was a negative aspect of group work. More than half of the participants had no prior Wiki work experience. Becoming familiar with the technology and learning how to use it at the same time were overwhelming for a number of students. Several students reported their initial frustration with the process of working online because they had to learn how to use the technology:

The Wiki was fine once you figured out how to use it and what all of the codes were, but that took a bit of learning.

On the whole, they felt the impact of the lack of face to face meetings using the current technology. As the Interact chat room allowed only instant messaging, there was no video conferencing. A few students commented that their dial-up Internet access sufficed only for instant messaging and

they could not afford broad-band technology for video conferencing chats. Analyzing responses to open ended questions in the survey revealed that the lack of face to face meetings was a barrier in effective communication among multicultural groups. Given the language differences between Australian and Asian students, a lack of nonverbal information and contextual cues between group members made the interaction and understanding more challenging:

It is hard to conduct meetings online as your meaning can be misunderstood. I believe it would be good to meet the people within your group and to have some meetings in person.

I think it would benefit the group to be able to meet and get to know one another which would help with understanding what each are saying about a particular subject.

communicating with someone online when I know nothing about them, and don't want to make any false assumptions, and apart from that communicating online as opposed to in person is always different no matter who you are.

To meet online, your meaning can be misunderstood.

Students had varying skill levels in using the technology and came from different cultural backgrounds. Despite the challenges, all groups (except one) completed their wiki assignments successfully.

The major problems and challenges include the lack of required skills in using technology, time-zone differences and lack of face-to-face meetings. Distance education allows flexibility in terms of time, in that students can choose to study whenever and wherever suits them. Online learning, however, provides a time benefit whereby learners have more time to think and compose responses than would have been available in a face to face classroom (Gabriel, 2004). However, it has its challenges when it comes to synchronous communication. One student reported that she chose to study in distance education mode in order to study during her convenient time, but the group assignment worked against that flexibility. She commented that as a distance student she was able to fit her studies around her work/family commitments. This was not possible with a group assignment which caused frustration and resentment, as it was difficult to fit into a mutual schedule and she often felt guilty if her participation was not possible.

To overcome these barriers it is suggested that groups use video chats as alternatives to face to face meetings. In addition, to facilitate communication among group members, there should be introductory sessions prior to group assessment when students can introduce each other to their group, talk about their professional backgrounds, interests, some personal information (e.g. hobbies) along with showing the group their pictures. To reduce the need for synchronous communication, the structure of group assessment should be as clear as possible with clearly divided tasks for each group member. Developing these strategies will make virtual collaboration in a learning environment a more satisfying experience for both students and instructors. On the whole, this section has addressed the challenges and barriers that distance education students encounter in the use of e-learning technology to support online group work in distance education.

Is Mobile Learning Possible?

In the light of student challenges and barriers based on the above, students need to be willing to embrace technology, have mobile technology device awareness and adopt/use the technology. The findings suggest that the basic acceptance and use of e-learning technology are of paramount importance in order to break through the e-learning technology and move onto m-learning. It is seen that only when a learner is 'technology-ready' will the learner consider the added mobility features by using mobile devices to allow 'personal' and 'portable' learning to happen. Mobile devices can support student group communication and collaboration by providing anywhere and anytime access if they can arrange a suitable group discussion or group work task time. The devices should be portable and handy for use. Mobile and wireless devices powered by wireless access protocols are added into the technological infrastructure for mobility to make e-learning act like a mobile system (Motiwalla, 2007; Chen, Kao, & Sheu, 2003; Seppala & Alamaki, 2003; Dix et al., 2000). The design and use of m-learning further support mobility in education providing international access to mobility of information and knowledge (Sharples et al, 2002, 2005). Nonetheless, students should be encouraged to use the mobile devices like smart phones, palmtops, netbooks, etc, that connect to the Internet and get online for group work anywhere and anytime they like. For example, a student who wanted to care for a sick elderly family member at a hospital, and would like to participate in online group discussion, could spend an hour of group work discussion virtually.

Creating and staying connected within a virtual collaboration work space in any time that suits any student according to one's needs are critical. M-learning will help if group members can adopt and use the mobile devices in learning. In a virtual learning environment, if e-learning technology is strongly recommended for use, higher education institutions should also recommend m-learning that supports mobility and portable learning to students. Nevertheless, while m-learning provides the benefits of portability, mobility and personal choices, mobile technology does not have the capacity to address social and cultural issues associated with learning.

A Framework of Learner Requirements in Online Group Work in Distance Education

Students actually enjoy learning the use of any new technology and get overjoyed after they find they have obtained a new ability to use technology, based on the observation results of this research. Figure 1 is developed using the analysis results in this study. Figure 1 on the whole shows that students must be instructed, made aware of, given a chance to learn and be persuaded into using e-learning or supporting m-learning technology (as affordable technology for learning) in an effective learning environment. In the middle of Figure 1, the circle represents a student's adoption and use of e-learning. The six boxes around the circle show the contributing factors to the successful adoption and use of technology for online group work by distance education students.

In Figure 1, 'Positive Teamwork Attitude (Group Work Commitment)' (box 1) makes it

clear that, for the purposes of group assignments, students should be informed of the required positive team work attitude expected from each student, instilling a sense of group work commitment in all online students. 'Technology Acceptance' (box 2) suggests that each student should be guided, learn, accept and know how to use technology based on the subject requirements. A subject outline which indicates clearly that students must use the Internet and e-learning for the purpose of the study indicates a clear technology acceptance. 'Technology for Learning' (box 3) explains that technology must be used by distance education students in order for the online group assignment collaboration to happen. Technology these days is affordable. In the subject outline, students must be informed of the needs for e-learning, the Internet, LMS or other technological use expected for the online group work for the purpose of the subject. 'Personal and Portable Learning (anytime & anywhere)' (box 4) shows that, as the students of the e-learning or m-learn-

Figure 1. A framework of student requirements in online group work in distance education

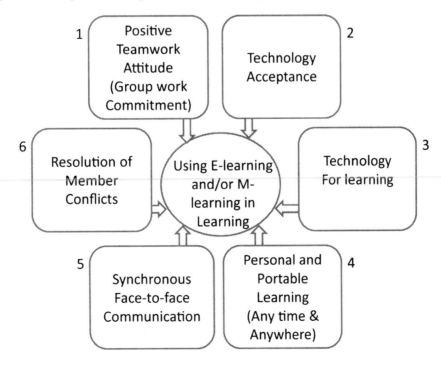

ing technology are seeking the convenience of study at a time flexible to them, they should try to identify and use the type of technological device that most benefits them with the suitable 'personal' and 'portable' learning features. 'Synchronous Face-to-face Communication' (box 5) explains that having the features of the e-learning environment, if the synchronous face-to-face communication is achieved, the m-learning device will 'add value' to students by allowing them to access the communication messages anytime anywhere to let them enjoy the 'personal' and 'portable' features of the technology for learning. 'Resolution of Member Conflict' (box 6) discusses that technology cannot replace real physical face-to-face interactions. Even in physical face-to-face interactions, member conflicts happen in group work. To use the technology effectively, the instructor or teacher must monitor and step in at any time to resolve member conflicts in the online group assignments (e.g. join the group in their chat room discussion).

All the six factors contribute to an effective learning environment and all six factors have their impact on the use of technology. It is proposed that educators should ensure that the six factors are used as a check list to assess what has been provided and established in a learning environment to ensure that e-learning and/or m-learning can be effectively used.

This section discusses the adoption of e-learning technology by also considering mobile devices to support personal and mobile learning. It establishes that mobile technology with the additional features of enabling personalisation and mobility has added value to e-learning by giving students more help in their learning experience.

CONCLUSION

Currently, more and more emerging technologies have allowed different things to happen in our lives. E-learning technology has allowed learn-

ing to take place on the web, whereas mobile technological devices further allow web-based learning to happen anywhere, anytime using many types of mobile devices. The findings from this paper have demonstrated that when distance education students are given an online group work assignment, they are able to learn and accept the use of e-learning for group work, despite their geographical distance and time zone challenges in meeting their group members. Being away from their face-to-face classrooms, they see their mobility in different geographical places and their ability to use the Internet for group work an enjoyable experience. In a distance education context, the use of mobile devices to access the same information and use collaboration tools such as in the e-learning computer or devices accessing the same information anytime and anywhere will give distance education students many more different advantages.

There are many benefits associated with using online collaborative group assessment in distance education. A student felt that even though he/she could achieve a higher mark by working individually, he/she enjoyed the valuable and challenging growth experience. One major benefit is to encourage mobile learning as distance students would then have many opportunities to collaborate with team members whenever and wherever they like. The challenge is that they need to learn how to use the appropriate mobile technology devices. An important outcome is that students need to know which and how mobile technology can help them perform group work in order to use it. These benefits are particularly important to a community of geographically distant students, in different time zones and keen to communicate, collaborate, interact and participate in their group work activities with the convenience to fit these activities into their lives using their mobile technology devices.

The results of the case study suggest that students are satisfied with the technology used in group work. If e-learning technology enables the groups to complete work collaboratively, the adoption and use of m-learning technology would have a much greater impact on enabling them to study conveniently, collaborate and participate in group work anywhere and anytime. As m-learning is powered by mobile technology with convenient and portable devices, students can give and take feedback and chat more freely in group work. Duncan-Howell and Lee (2007), however, caution that the use of m-learning tools themselves does not guarantee their potential being realized. There is a great need to encourage the adoption and use of m-learning devices. The most important challenge now is to ensure that educators have the ability to design and develop pedagogically sound opportunities and environments that enhance learning using m-learning technology.

This research presents a conceptual model which was developed based on a single case study which is a limitation of the research. The model will need to be extended or refined with more data collected from similar case studies. The paper is however certainly a good starting point for future research to investigate how more specifically the model illustrates how m-learning can help to make e-learning more feasible and useful. Further research effort will be needed to produce much deeper reflection on some issues discussed and their possible solutions. The findings show an acceptance of technology use in the compulsory distance education online group work assignments despite the earlier resistance to doing group work offline. Further research may explore how and what m-learning devices can be used to better enable distance education students to cope with work and studies. M-learning research may also investigate how to address social and cultural issues associated with the use of mobile technology in learning.

REFERENCES

Beldarrain, Y. (2006). Distance education trends: Integrating new technologies to foster student interaction and collaboration. *Distance Education*, 27(2), 139–153. doi:10.1080/01587910600789498

Bliuc, A.-M., Goodyear, P., & Ellis, R. A. (2007). Research focus and methodological choices in studies into students' experiences of blended learning in higher education. *The Internet and Higher Education*, 10(4), 231–244. doi:10.1016/j.iheduc.2007.08.001

Chen, Y. S., Kao, T. C., & Sheu, J. P. (2003). A mobile learning system for scaffolding bird watching learning. *Journal of Computer Assisted Learning*, (19): 347–359. doi:10.1046/j.0266-4909.2003.00036.x

Cucu, C., Cristescu, M.-P., & Cristescu, C.-I. (2010). Contributions to using IT in education: An educational video player. *Informatica Economica*, 14(2), 108–119.

Dix, A., Rodden, T., Davies, N., Trevor, J., Friday, A., & Palfreyman, K. (2000). Exploiting space and location as a design framework for interactive mobile systems. *ACM Transactions on Computer-Human Interaction*, 7(3), 285–321. doi:10.1145/355324.355325

Donnan, P. A. (2007). *Conducting assessment online: Educational developers perspectives*. New South Wales, Australia: University of Wollongong.

Duncan-Howell, J., & Lee, K. (2007). M-learning: Finding a place for mobile technologies within tertiary educational settings. In *Proceedings of the Ascilite Conference*, Singapore.

Gabriel, M. A. (2004). Learning together: Exploring group interactions online. *Journal of Distance Education*, 19(1), 54–72.

Garrison, D., & Vaughan, N. (2008). *Blended learning in higher education: Framework, principles, and guidelines*. New York, NY: John Wiley & Sons.

Gibson, J. J. (1977). The theory of affordances. In Shaw, R., & Bransford, J. (Eds.), *Perceiving, acting and knowing*. Mahwah, NJ: Lawrence Erlbaum.

Guthrie, C. (2010). Towards greater learner control: Web supported project-based learning. *Journal of Information Systems Education, 21*(1), 121–130.

Karpova, E., Correia, A.-P., & Baran, E. (2009). Learn to use and use to learn: Technology in virtual collaboration experience. *The Internet and Higher Education, 12*, 45–52. doi:10.1016/j.iheduc.2008.10.006

Lipshitz, A. R., & Parsons, S. P. (Eds.). (2008). *E-learning: 21st century issues and challenges*. New York, NY: Nova Science.

Luminița, Ș. (2010). Internet - a new way of training: Designing an e-learning platforms. *Young Economists Journal / Revista Tinerilor Economisti, 8*(14), 151-158.

McLoughlin, C., & Lee, M. J. W. (2007). Social software and participatory learning: Pedagogical choices with technology affordances in the Web 2.0 era. In *Proceedings of the Ascilite Conference*, Singapore.

Merriam, S. B. (1998). *Qualitative research and case study application in education*. San Francisco, CA: Jossey-Bass.

Merriam, S. B. (2002). Assessing and evaluating qualitative research. In Merriam, S. (Ed.), *Qualitative research in practice: Examples for discussion and analysis*. San Francisco, CA: Jossey-Bass.

Merriam, S. B. (2002). Introduction to qualitative research. In Merriam, S. (Ed.), *Qualitative research in practice: Examples for discussion and analysis*. San Francisco, CA: Jossey-Bass.

Motiwalla, L. F. (2007). Mobile learning: A framework and evaluation. *Journal of Computer Assisted Learning, 49*, 581–596.

O'Neil, K., Singh, G., & O'Donoghue, J. (2004). Implementing eLearning programs for higher education: A review of literature. *Journal of Information Technology Education, 3*(1), 313–323.

Papachristos, D., Alafodimos, N., Arvanitis, K., Vassilakis, K., Kalogiannakis, M., & Kikilias, P. (2010). An educational model for asynchronous e-learning: A case study in higher technology education. *International Journal of Advanced Corporate Learning, 3*(1), 32–36.

Robey, D., Khoo, H. M., & Powers, C. (2000). Situated learning in cross-functional virtual teams. *IEEE Transactions on Professional Communication: Technical Communication, 43*(1), 51–66. doi:10.1109/47.826416

Seppala, P., & Alamaki, H. (2003). Mobile learning in teacher training. *Journal of Computer Assisted Learning, 19*, 330–335. doi:10.1046/j.0266-4909.2003.00034.x

Sharples, M., Corlett, D., & Westmancott, O. (2002). The design and implementation of a mobile learning resource. *Personal and Ubiquitous Computing, 6*(3), 220–234. doi:10.1007/s007790200021

Sharples, M., Taylor, J., & Vavoula, G. (2005). Towards a theory of mobile learning. In *Proceedings of the mLearn 4th World Conference on mLearning*, Cape Town, South Africa.

Smith, G., & Ferguson, D. (2002). Teaching over the Web verses in the classroom: Differences in the instructor experience. *International Journal of Instructional Media, 29*(1), 61–67.

Stake, R. E. (1995). *The art of case study research*. Thousand Oaks, CA: Sage.

Stake, R. E. (2000). Case studies. In Denzin, N. K., & Lincoln, Y. S. (Eds.), *Handbook of qualitative research* (2nd ed.). Thousand Oaks, CA: Sage.

Suthers, D. D. (2005). Technology affordances for intersubjective learning: A thematic agenda for CSCL. In *Proceedings of the Conference on Computer Support for Collaborative Learning: Learning 2005: The Next 10 Years!* Taipei, Taiwan.

Titrade, C., El Baaboua, F., Sion, B., & Mihalcescu, C. (2009). E-learning. *Annals of the University of Oradea: Economic Science, 4*(1), 1066–1069.

Yin, R. K. (2003). *Case study research: Design and methods* (3rd ed., *Vol. 5*). Thousand Oaks, CA: Sage.

ENDNOTE

[1] A *subject* refers to an individual unit of study (usually one semester in length) that is worth a certain number of credit points. A series of subjects make up a *course*, such as Bachelor of Library and Information Management degree.

APPENDIX

Group Work Evaluation Survey

Section 1

1. What were the most valuable aspects of your group assignment experience?

    ☐ Working with students from a different country
    ☐ Gaining communication skills
    ☐ As a group you can achieve more –better quality
    ☐ Learning to work with Wiki and other Interact technologies
    ☐ Interactions with other students and overcoming feeling of isolation
    ☐ Learning from others and sharing ideas
    ☐ Learning to work in a group, which reflects real industry
    ☐ Other (please explain)

2. What were the negative aspects of this group assignment experience?

    ☐ Some members lack required skills
    ☐ Difficulty of arranging a chat time to suit everybody in the group
    ☐ The inequality in the contribution among members
    ☐ Being dependent on other people
    ☐ Conflicts
    ☐ Other (please explain)

3. What aspects of your group assignment experience could be improved?

4. This is the first time you have used wiki.

5. You would rather work alone than in any kind of group
    ○ Strongly agree   ○ Agree   ○ Don't know   ○ Disagree   ○ Strongly disagree

6. You would have preferred to do all the group work off-line rather than using online facilities
○ Strongly agree ○ Agree   ○ Don't know   ○ Disagree   ○ Strongly disagree

Any explanation?

7. All members of your group did a fair share of the work for this assignment
○ Strongly agree ○ Agree   ○ Don't know   ○ Disagree   ○ Strongly disagree

Any comment?

8. You found the Group Mail in Interact useful in communicating with the group members
○ Strongly agree   ○ Agree   ○ Not sure   ○ Disagree   ○ Strongly disagree   ○ Did not use

9. You found the announcement in Interact useful in communicating with group members
○ Strongly agree   ○ Agree   ○ Not sure   ○ Disagree   ○ Strongly disagree   ○ Did not use

10. You found the Chat in Interact useful for communicating with group members
○ Strongly agree   ○ Agree   ○ Not sure   ○ Disagree   ○ Strongly disagree   ○ Did not use

11. You found the group wiki useful in preparing the group assignment
○ Strongly agree   ○ Agree   ○ Not sure   ○ Disagree   ○ Strongly disagree   ○ Did not use

12. You found the group wiki easy to use
○ Strongly agree   ○ Agree   ○ Not sure   ○ Disagree   ○ Strongly disagree   ○ Did not use

13. Any additional comments or suggestions on using wiki in this assignment?

14. What is your feeling about working with students from a different country? Please explain why you liked or didn't like it.

Next

Group Work Evaluation Survey

Section 2

1. What is your gender? ○ Female   ○ Male
2. What was your age at your last birthday?
    ○ Under 25   ○ 26-30   ○ 31-35   ○ 36-40   ○ over 40
3. Is English your first (native) language? ○ Yes   ○ No
4. How many hours a week do you work in a paid employment?
    ○ I don't work   ○ less than 20 h/w   ○ 21-30 h/w   ○ Full time employment

    ☐ No internet access   ☐ I have dial-up internet   ☐ I have broadband (ADSL,
       at home   at home   Wireless) internet at home

    Others (please specify)

5. How is your internet access?

    [Prev] [Done]

This work was previously published in the International Journal of Mobile and Blended Learning, Volume 3, Issue 3, edited by David Parsons, pp 53-63, copyright 2011 by IGI Publishing (an imprint of IGI Global).

Chapter 19

An Investigation into Mobile Learning for High School Mathematics

Vani Kalloo
The University of the West Indies, Trinidad and Tobago

Permanand Mohan
The University of the West Indies, Trinidad and Tobago

ABSTRACT

This paper describes an investigation which was carried out to determine if mobile learning can be used to help high school students improve their performance in mathematics. The investigation was driven by the need to develop innovative learning solutions to eradicate the problem of low pass rates in mathematics in the Caribbean. A mobile learning application called MobileMath was developed targeting a subset of the mathematics curriculum. MobileMath offers the learner different learning strategies, game-based learning, and personalization. Two of the evaluation studies conducted are described in this paper. The first study focused on students using mobile learning on their own, while the second study explored the effects of teacher support while using mobile learning. A t-test analysis shows that there was a significant improvement in performance by students in both evaluation studies. The paper also compares the students' performance with actual usage of the mobile learning application.

INTRODUCTION

This paper presents a mobile learning investigation conducted in Trinidad and Tobago, which aimed to determine if mobile learning can assist students to improve their performance in mathematics. The investigation was driven by the need to develop innovative learning solutions to eradicate the problem of low pass rates in secondary school mathematics in the Caribbean. After reviewing the literature on learning technology for mathematics we designed and developed a mobile learning

DOI: 10.4018/978-1-4666-2139-8.ch019

Figure 1. CXC mathematics results for paper 1 and 2 Source: Caribexams 2004

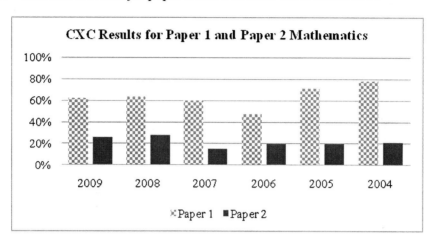

BACKGROUND

application with several features to appeal to the target students.

Next, we conducted several studies to evaluate the mobile learning application. Two of these studies are highlighted in this paper. In the first study, students were allowed to use the mobile learning application without teacher intervention. The objective of this first study was to determine if students would choose to use mobile learning without teacher intervention. In the second study, the students were encouraged to use the mobile learning application by a teacher. The objective of the second study was to determine if the students would use mobile learning more with teacher support and encouragement. The results of the first study are compared to that of the second study to understand the effects of teacher encouragement on student use of the mobile learning application.

The paper also discusses the effects of learning strategies deployed in the mobile learning application. These include games-based learning and personalization. Various statistical analyses are performed to show the results of the evaluation studies. The paper also discusses some of the challenges experienced in carrying out our research with mobile learning for mathematics. Finally, the paper concludes with some suggestions for future research.

This study was motivated by the problem of high failure rates in mathematics in the Caribbean. In the last six years the average pass rate of the Caribbean Examination Council (CXC) mathematics examination (an examination taken by most high school students in the English-speaking Caribbean) was 41%. This examination is made up of Paper 1 and Paper 2. Paper 1 is a multiple choice examination and Paper 2 is the more extensive examination requiring detailed answers and is thus a better indicator of high school mathematics proficiency. Figure 1 illustrates the percentage of students who passed Papers 1 and 2 in the last six years. It shows that for each year, the pass rate was much lower for Paper 2 than Paper 1. The average pass rate for Paper 2 is 22%.

This data reveals that, on average over the last six years, almost 80% of the students in the Caribbean failed Paper 2 of the CXC mathematics examination and 60% were awarded passing grades. This is convincing evidence that there is a need for innovative learning tools for mathematics in the Caribbean (Caribexams, 2004).

The mobile phone is one of the most ubiquitous technologies today. It is appealing to a large sector of the population, especially young people. It is also affordable and the infrastructure is widely available throughout the Caribbean. Almost every person in Trinidad and Tobago owns at least one mobile phone. As part of the research, a survey was conducted in Trinidad and Tobago with over 120 high school students between the ages of 11 to 18 years. It revealed that 83% of them own their own mobile phones.

Wagner (2005) identified several reasons why mobile technology is such a commonly used technology in recent times. Wagner points out that there are more wireless network services, customers are demanding better mobile experiences such as a rich Internet experience, and people connect anytime and anywhere more than ever before. Therefore, since mobile devices are so commonly used, this study hypothesized that mobile learning (learning that occurs with the aid of a portable device) could be a viable solution to the problem of high failure rates in mathematics.

In particular, the research set about to answer the following research questions. Can mobile learning assist students in improving their performance in mathematics? Can teacher support while using mobile learning impact on the use of the mobile application and ultimately performance? Will students require reminders to use the mobile application or will they be motivated to use it on their own? Can mobile learning motivate the students to practice mathematics skills? Will personalization make navigation and selection of the topics and features easier? Will personalization cause a significant difference in performance?

LITERATURE REVIEW

Mobile learning has been used widely for learning diverse subject areas by taking advantage of the many features of mobile devices. Duncan-Howell and Lee (2007) looked at the different types of mobile features that can be used for learning. These features include SMS, audio based learning, Java quizzes, learning modules, media collection via camera phones, online publishing, blogging using MMS, e-mail, web browsers, field trips using GPS positioning tools and concept maps via SMS.

The potential benefits of mobile learning have often been discussed in the literature. Naismith and Corlett (2006) concluded that mobile learning promotes positive learning outcomes such as motivation, engagement, personalization, collaboration, interactivity, and a sense of community. McFarlane, Roche, and Triggs (2007), Cook et al. (2007), Faux et al. (2006), Attewell (2005), and Perry (2003) reported that mobile learning had a significant motivational impact on learners. Jones et al. (2006) suggested reasons why mobile devices may be motivating. The learners have the freedom to choose their own goals, the ownership of the device can be motivating, learners can have fun with mobile learning, learners can communicate with their peers, and they can learn in context.

Mobile learning studies were first carried out in developed countries such as Europe, Asia and USA. However, in later years studies were conducted in some developing countries. Valk, Rashid, and Elder (2010) provides a review of various mobile learning studies conducted in developing countries. In particular, they looked at six m-learning projects carried out in the Philippines, Mongolia, Thailand and India. These studies mainly used SMS for learning and three of the studies stated that students improved their performances after using mobile learning.

One major problem identified in learning mathematics was that students thought learning mathematics was boring, causing them to lose interest. Games have proven to excite, motivate and maintain the players' attention. Games were included in our mobile learning application since it has been proven to be a valuable motivating strategy. A BBC report by Pratchett (2005) on gamers in the UK indicates that 92% of 11-15 year olds play games at least 3 times a week.

Figure 2 displays the results of a survey conducted in Trinidad and Tobago with over 120 high school students which revealed that 42% of the students play computer games at least once

Figure 2. How often students in Trinidad and Tobago play games

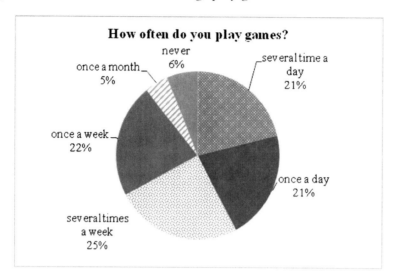

a day. It also illustrated that 89% of the students play computer games at least once a week. This data implies that students in Trinidad and Tobago play games frequently and justifies our decision to include games as a major feature of our mobile learning system.

Several studies have investigated the use of games for learning mathematics. Lin (2007) described a Pokémon learning game where the learning activities are embedded within the game. The player has to do addition and subtraction when buying monsters. Jonker and Wijers (2008) presented *Thinklets*, a set of mathematical e-learning games for problem solving. An evaluation was conducted with 600 Dutch children using *Thinklet*'s *Share Money*. The children found this game to be fun.

There have also been studies which investigated the use of games in mobile devices for learning mathematics. Vahey, Tatar, and Roschelle (2004) developed *NetCalc* for use in handheld computers. The activities were designed to teach graphing and distance-time relationships.

My Sports Pulse (2007) is an interactive educational game using SMS designed for learning the mathematics, science and technology principles inherent in sporting activities. Andrews and

Raynor (2008) described a pilot study for teaching mathematics with Tablet PCs for first year classes in engineering. The learners increased interactivity with peers and received immediate feedback on their problem-solving activities from the teachers.

Shin, Norris, and Soloway (2006) described a study where 50 participants had to solve problems on a Game Boy screen before it faded away. Students who played the game more than four times a week outperformed those who played only twice a week. Busa, Greenop, and Volsoo (2008) presented a project which created *Mathstermind*, an innovative mobile game that requires players to solve mathematical puzzles using simple arithmetic, inequalities, algebraic equations, and graphs. van't Hooft, Swan, and Bennett (2009) also looked at using mobile devices to learn mathematics in elementary schools. Eighteen students attended a class for 6 weeks and on the commute used a mathematics application. Findings indicated that they improved performance. Liebenberg (2008) described *MOBI*, a mobile learning application for learning mathematics in South Africa. *MOBI* allows students to listen to podcasts, view multimedia content, and chat with other students via instant messaging.

Some recent mobile learning projects are the *Dr. Math* project in South Africa (Conway-Smith, 2010) and the St Mary's City Schools Mobile Learning Technology (St Mary's, 2008). *Dr. Math* is a cell phone project in South Africa where students can get help from live mathematics tutors using a social networking tool for mobile phones. Third grade students in Ohio of the St Mary's City Schools Mobile Learning Technology used cell phones for learning in schools and at home. The cell phone contains software allowing students to do word processing, spreadsheets, concept maps and animation drawing. The experimental group increased their overall mathematics score by 3.36% in 18 weeks while the control group increased by 1.86%. Another ongoing study called Project *K-Nect* (2008) targets secondary at-risk ninth graders to focus on increasing their mathematics skills through mobile smartphones. Students communicate and collaborate with each other and have access to tutors outside of the school day to help them master mathematics skills and knowledge. A mobile learning study for mathematics called *MoMath* (2010) for learning mathematics in South Africa used MXit, a free instant messaging application. It provides learning through theory, exercises, tutoring, peer to peer support, competitions, tests and self assessments. The study shows that students used it on evenings, weekends and holidays. The usage of the mobile phones increased retention and motivation and there were improvements in the students' performance. Finally, Math4Mobile is a suite of mobile applications for learning graphs and can be used in classroom settings (Daher, 2010).

The studies mentioned above indicate that mobile learning can potentially improve students' performance in mathematics. In some of these studies the existing features of the mobile devices were used and in others studies mobile learning application were developed targeting mathematics to facilitate learning. Our approach goes further and creates mobile learning content specifically targeted for learning mathematics. The content is presented using various strategies.

DESIGN AND IMPLEMENTATION

The first author of this paper was previously a high school mathematics teacher. Her years of experience of teaching mathematics were utilized in designing the mobile learning application to target specific weaknesses which students are known to have. After reviewing current teaching methods, it was decided that the mobile learning application should not replace the teacher but be a complementary learning tool. Also, its aim was not to teach the students new topics but to help them improve their mathematics skills previously learned in school. Our mobile learning application is not tied to teaching in the classroom and gives students the freedom to use it anytime and at their own pace.

The main pedagogical principle that guided the design of the mobile learning application was to offer multiple strategies for learning mathematics. These strategies include text-based lessons, dynamic examples, tutorials, and quizzes. The application also featured games, collaboration, personalized recommendations, and user control. The use of multiple strategies gives the learner several choices for learning mathematics so each student could choose an activity which best suits his learning needs. The text-based lessons allowed the student to review the main mathematical concepts. The dynamic examples were intended to help the student understand how to solve mathematics problems on each topic. The tutorial gave the learner an opportunity to review topics and attempt solving a problem. The quiz was used to assess the learner and provided immediate feedback to the student. The games feature was designed to offer the learner a fun, interesting method of learning and practicing mathematics. Practicing mathematical skills has been identified as an important step in the process of learning mathematics.

In designing our mobile learning application, the design framework for mobile learning applications put forward by Parsons, Ryu, and Cranshaw (2007) was taken into consideration. Parsons, Ryu, and Cranshaw (2007) suggested that mobile learning should use the game metaphor, i.e., it should engage the learner, create excitement, and have rules, goals, objectives, immediate feedback, conflict, challenge, opposition, and competition. Kebritchi and Hirumi (2008) highlighted some recommendations given by game designers. They suggested that instructional support, hints, advice, and feedback are important. They also suggested that the instructional approach should be learner-centered and have a firm rationale. These recommendations were considered in the design of our mobile learning application.

Our mobile application is referred to as *MobileMath* and focuses on learning algebra. It targets topics in algebra such as *finding factors*, *manipulating directed numbers*, *simplification of algebraic terms*, *factorization*, and *solving of equations*. *MobileMath* offers a different *Lesson*, *Example*, *Tutorial*, *Quiz* and learning *Game* for each topic targeted. The *Lessons, Examples* and *Tutorials* are resources for reviewing important concepts taught in the classroom. Different *Lessons, Examples, Tutorials* and *Quizzes* are provided for each topic. For example there is a *Factors Lesson*, a *Directed Numbers Lesson*, a *Simplify Expressions Lesson*, a *Factorization Lesson* and a *Solve Equations Lesson*. The *Lesson* feature is a brief summary explaining the key concepts of the topic. It is not meant to teach a student the topic. It is meant to be a review or reminder of the topic that was previously taught by the teacher in the classroom.

The *Example*, shown in Figure 3, is a dynamic feature where the learner can change the numerical values in the worked example of a mathematics problem. The numbers in the boxes can be changed by the learner giving them some control. As the numbers change, the solution adjusts depending on the new numbers. This feature uses examples to help the student review the main concepts in algebra.

The *Tutorial* feature consists of three main parts. The first part is a summary of the topic followed by a correctly worked example of a

problem and finally a question for the student to try. The *Quiz* is a multiple choice assessment designed to determine if the learner fully understands the topic. The *Quiz* contains only ten questions to ensure that the student does not get bored and it provides immediate feedback.

The *Games* offered are games for practicing *Factors, Directed Numbers, Simplification of Expressions, Factorization* and *Solving Equations*. Figure 4 shows a screenshot of the *Factors* game and Figure 5 shows a screenshot of the *Directed Numbers* game. The main objective of the *Games* is to encourage students to practice algebraic skills. Games have been proven to draw and hold players attention, to keep them coming back for more and to create excitement and fun. The first game created was the *Bluetooth Game*. This game was a *Snakes and Ladders Game* where the student had to answer a question correctly in order to roll the dice and to move on the snakes and ladders board on the mobile screen. However, after further consideration and literature review it was decided that the game would be more effective if the mathematical content was part of the game as opposed to being separate as in the *Snakes and Ladders Games*. Lin (2007) has shown success in creating games with the content directly embedded in the games. It was apparent that the students would understand a skill best by having to use it in a game as opposed to playing a game and answering questions to play the game. This resulted in the creation of the other games.

The *Finding Factors* Game requires the student to choose a number from a moving conveyor belt and then enter a factor of the selected number. The *Directed Numbers* Game requires the player to roll a dice and move to one of the squares which is assigned a number value. The player then has to add the previous balance to the number he or she landed on and enter the new value. The *Simplification of Expression* Game requires the player to sort X-terms from the Y-terms as they drop in from the top of the screen. Then the

Figure 3. Example Feature

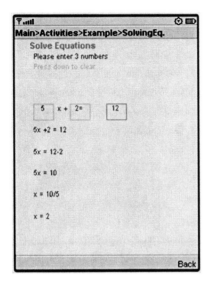

Figure 4. Factors Game

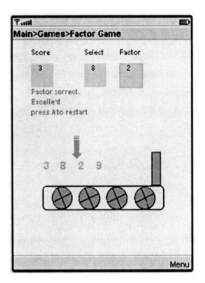

player needs to add this value to the ongoing X-terms or Y-terms value depending on which it is.

The *Factorization* Game requires the player to select two terms, a number term and an algebraic term from the set given. Then the player enters a common factor of these two terms. The *Solve Equation* Game is made up of several equations and a probable solution on each line. One column of the set is shuffled and the player has to put them back in the correct position. The final game is the *Solve Equation GPRS* Game where two players connect via GPRS to solve equations together. Since the game has GPRS access, the players can be in any location in order to play with each other. The number values used in all the game are randomly generated and as the game progresses, the level of difficulty increases.

The mobile application was created using J2ME. The main components of the system are a web server, a database, the mobile phones, Internet connectivity and a teacher to monitor students' progress. The server and the database were created using Apache Tomcat and MySQL respectively. The learning content was stored on the mobile phone and the usage data on each student was sent to the server to be stored in the

database. This data is used by the teacher to keep track of the students' progress. Most of the features of the mobile application could be used without the GPRS connection. Therefore any disruptions in the GPRS service did not hinder the usage of most of the features of the mobile application. The server is also used to facilitate a *Chat* feature enabling the students to communicate freely and a *GPRS game* which the students can play from any location.

Personalization was used to assist the learner in selecting the most suitable learning activity. There were five topics targeted and five features created for each of these topics resulting in a somewhat complex menu system. The learning activity was recommended depending on their knowledge level, ensuring that the student met the prerequisites in order to do that activity, and the time available for study. The personalization used in this study was client side personalization where the student's data was analyzed on the mobile device using decision rules created to determine the recommendations. The rules created were based on the mathematics curriculum, for instance if the student has completed and passed the quiz on the directed numbers only then the system should suggest the simplification of expressions topic, as directed numbers is a prerequisite for the simplification of expressions topic. The collaboration features were added to encourage the students to work together and eventually learn from each other.

MobileMath offers navigational personalization and attempts to determine if it helps the student navigate the menus. Depending on the student's previous knowledge and on their continuous use of the system, activities are recommended to the learner using traffic light coloured menu options shown in Figure 6 (Brusilovsky, Schwarz, & Weber, 1996). The system determines which activity the student should do next depending on the activities they have successfully completed. The green option is used to indicate the highly recommended activities. The red is used to indicate options which are not ready to be learned because the system recognizes that the learner did not complete the required prerequisites for these activities. The orange is used for the option between these two categories, meaning they are recommended but not as highly as the green options. Learners are not prevented from selecting any menu option, the colours are just used to recommend which activity the student should do next but she is free to select any option. If the student fails the *Quiz* or *Tutorial* frequently then the system determines that the student is having trouble and an alert message, shown in Figure 7, pops up to suggest that the student try a feature she has not used before. This mobile learning application was evaluated to determine the effects of mobile learning on the students.

EXPERIMENTAL DESIGN

After building the mobile application, three evaluation studies were conducted, each of three weeks' duration. The first study took place in June 2010, the second in August 2010, and the third in October 2010. The first and second studies aimed to find out if the mobile learning application would be used independently of classroom teaching. The third study aimed to find out the effect of mobile learning when used alongside classroom teaching. This paper focuses on the first and second studies which will now be referred to as Study 1 and Study 2. The third study is discussed elsewhere (Kalloo & Mohan, 2011). The target group of Study 1 and Study 2 were high school students between the ages of 12 and 18 years. They were taught algebra in their high schools in a previous term.

Study 1 consisted of 19 students who are collectively referred to as Group 1 and Study 2 consisted of 20 students who are collectively referred to as Group 2. The goal of Study 1 was to determine if the students would be motivated to use the mobile phones for learning mathematics on their own and if they did, to determine if they would improve their performance in mathematics. The goal of Study 2 was to determine if teacher support can encourage students to use mobile learning more often and for longer periods. It also set out to determine whether increased use of the *MobileMath* application would result in improved performance by the students.

At the beginning of both studies, the students were given a pre-test to evaluate their performance in algebra. Next, they were trained in using the *MobileMath* application. The students were all given a *Nokia 5130 Express Music* cellular phone pre-loaded with *MobileMath*. Each phone came with unlimited GPRS access, 150 post-paid calling minutes and 30 text messages. The students were left on their own to use the mobile phones for Study 1. Study 2 was different from Study 1 since it had the additional support from the teacher for using the mobile application. The teacher would monitor the student's incoming data and depending on their usage, the teacher sent the students personalized messages to encourage them to use the application. They were urged to use specific features or games. The teacher would also send simple questions that would probe them to use the application. The teacher met with the students

Figure 5. Directed Numbers Game

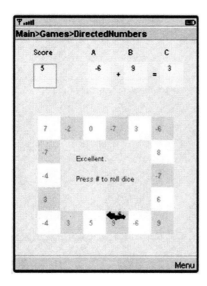

Figure 6. Coloured Menu

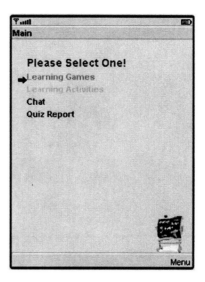

twice a week to encourage them to use the mobile application. At the end of both studies, a post-test was given. The results of the post-test were compared with the pre-test results to determine if there was any change in performance after the three week period. The students were also asked to fill out a questionnaire as part of the evaluation.

RESULTS

The pre-test and post-test scores of both groups were statistically analyzed. The mean value of the pre-test of Group 1 was 55.0658 and the mean value of the post-test was 63.4868, showing an increase in average performance. A 2-tailed significance t-test was performed on Group 1 scores, revealing a value of 0.025 which is less than 0.05. This implies that there is a significant difference between the pre-test scores and the post-test scores.

The mean value of the pre-test of Group 2 was 30.7, while the mean of the post-test was 40.85 showing an average increase in performance. The 2-tailed significance t-test value was 0.001 which is less than 0.05. This implies that there is a

significant difference between the pre-test scores and the post-test scores for Group 2.

Table 1 shows the data on usage of *MobileMath* and the performance of Group 1 and Group 2 on the pre-test and post-test. It shows that Group 1 acquired an average increase in performance of 8.8% and Group 2 attained an average increase in performance of 10.2%. The table shows that Group 2 used *MobileMath* longer and more times than Group 1. 12 out of 19 students showed improvements in performance from Group 1, while 19 out of the 20 students improved performance from Group 2, though some improvements were minimal.

Figure 8 shows the number of students of Group 1 and Group 2 who passed and those who failed the pre-test and post-test. It shows that for Group 1, the number of students who passed increased from 9 to 14 after using *MobileMath*. It shows that for Group 2, the number of students who passed increased from 2 to 7 after using *MobileMath*.

Table 2 shows the students' performance and usage of *MobileMath* and it compares the students whose performance was above average with those whose performance was below average. It shows

Figure 7. Alert Suggestion

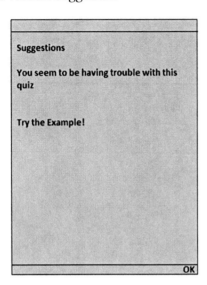

Table 1. Summary Data on Usage of MobileMath by Group 1 and 2

	Group 1	Group 2
Number of times *MobileMath* was used	514	861
Length of time *MobileMath* was used (hours)	14.4	58.5
Average Increase %	8.8	10.2
Average Pre-test %	55.2	30.6
Average Post-test %	64	40.8

that the students who performed above average for both groups used *MobileMath* longer and more often than the students who performed below average.

Table 3 compares the average the students' performance with the length of time *MobileMath* was used per topic for Group 1. The students who performed above average were compared with those who performed below average on each topic. The table shows that for *Factors, Directed Numbers, Simplification of Terms* and *Factorization*, the students who performed above average used the *MobileMath* application longer than those who performed below average.

Table 4 compares the students' performance and the length of time of using *MobileMath*, by topic, for Group 2. It shows that for *Directed Numbers, Simplification of Terms, Factorization* and *Solving Equations,* the students who performed above average used *MobileMath* longer than those who performed below average.

The usage data shows that *Games* were used the most by both groups and the *Tutorials* were used the second most. The data also shows that the *Quiz* and *Games* features were used the longest by both groups. All features were used more and for a longer period of time by Group 2 than Group 1.

Figure 9 shows the number of times in which *MobileMath* was used for each day of the three-week period by Group 2. Group 2 received teacher support. The bars, with the brick-styled pattern, represent the days when the students met the teacher. They met on the 29th, 30th of July, 5th, 6th, 12th, and 13th of August, 2010.

In the first week, the bar chart shows that the students used *MobileMath* the most on the two days they met with the teacher as compared to the rest of the week. In the second week, they used *MobileMath* the most on the second day after meeting the teacher. On the third week usage decreased quite a bit but they still used it the most on the second day after meeting the teacher.

Our research also investigates the impact of personalization on the students' performance. According to the data collected by the server, Groups 1 and 2 used the personalized recommendations 33% and 34% of the time, respectively. No correlation was found between the students' performance and use of the personalized recommendations. However, the questionnaire data reveals that 75% of the students agreed that the colours used to recommend learning activities were helpful.

The students were asked questions based on the alert messages, which made suggestions in the event that the students were having trouble with a feature such as failing the *Quiz* numerous times. Figure 10 highlights the students' response to the questions. It shows that 53% of the students received personalized recommendations and 97% of these students found the recommendation useful.

DISCUSSION

The t-test analysis revealed that there was a significant difference between the pre-test and the post-test scores for both Groups 1 and 2. The mean performances of Groups 1 and 2 improved from the pre-test to the post-test scores. Table 1 shows that Group 1 improved performance by 8.8% while Group 2 improved by 10.2%. This statistical data indicates that after using *MobileMath* Groups 1 and 2 improved their average performances. This is statistical evidence that *MobileMath* had a positive impact on the students' performance for Studies 1 and 2. This implies that mobile learning can be a tool to assist students in improving their mathematics performance.

Comparing these results to other mobile learning studies was a bit challenging as many studies lack detailed analysis of their results. The *MoMath* (2010) project mentioned in the literature review reported on their success by highlighting that 70% of usage of the mobile learning occurred outside of school hours. They further stated that it improved mathematics scores based on normal end-of-term tests. Some studies reported increases in performance in percentage terms; others simply stated that there were marginal increases; and,

there were yet others with inconclusive results (Valk, Rashid, & Elder, 2010). van't Hooft, Swan, and Bennett (2009) reported that their results indicated that students did improve. Valk, Rashid, and Elder (2010) pointed out that there is a lack of analysis of the findings of m-learning projects in the developing world. In agreement with Valk, Rashid, and Elder (2010), the literature reveals that for many similar studies there were no detailed reports of the analysis of the results. This paper gives a detailed analysis of the results of our research studies.

One of the research questions of this study was to determine if the students would choose to use mobile learning without encouragement from the teacher. The students of Study 1 were allowed to use the mobile learning application on their own without any coaxing. Even though they did not use the mobile learning as much as was expected they chose to use it on their own and improved their performance. Hence, Study 1 illustrates that the students were motivated enough to use the mobile learning on their own and as a result improved their performance.

The second research question of this study was to determine if the students would use the mobile learning application more if encouraged by

Figure 8. Number of students who passed the pre-test and post-test

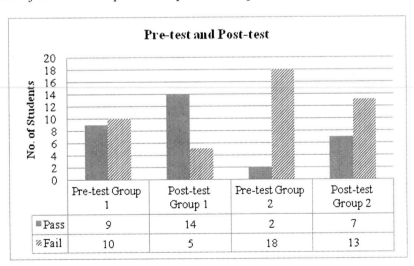

Table 2. Summary Data on Usage of MobileMath by Group 1 and 2

Average	Group	Increase or Decrease from pre-test to post-test	Duration of system use in minutes	Frequency of use of *MobileMath*
Above	1	25%	56.6	38.9
Below		-1%	39.2	20.2
Above	2	19%	221.6	46.2
Below		3%	137.8	40.5

Table 3. Comparison of performance increases and lengths of time by topic for Group 1

Group 1	Above Average		Below Average	
	Average Performance increase %	Average Length of Time	Average Performance increase %	Average Length of Time
Factors	36	14.1	0	8.2
Directed Numbers	12	4.5	-35	1.6
Simplify Terms	30	3.1	-6	3
Factorization	61	10.1	0	1.2
Solve Equation	23	0.5	-10	2.9

the teacher and if so, would they perform better. The students of Study 2 used *MobileMath* with teacher support and encouragement. Table 1 illustrates that Group 2 used mobile learning more and longer than Group 1. It illustrates that Group 2 used *MobileMath* 67% more times and 300% longer than Group 1. This evidence indicates that the students used the mobile learning application more with teacher encouragement. Figure 9 shows usage of *MobileMath* highlighting the days on which they received teacher support. It shows that the students used *MobileMath* more on the days

which they received teacher encouragement to use the system. This is further evidence that the teacher support encouraged the students to use the mobile learning more than if left on their own. However, when comparing their performances, Group 2 only improved performance slightly higher than Group 1 even though Group 2 used *MobileMath* much more than Group 1. Furthermore, 19 students of Group 2 improved performance after using *MobileMath* while 12 students of Group 1 improved. This can be attributed to that fact that Groups 1 and 2 started out the study at different

Table 4. Comparison of performance increases and lengths of time by topic for group 2

Group 2	Above Average		Below Average	
Topics	Average Performance Increase %	Average Length of Time	Average Performance Increase %	Average Length of Time
Factors	6.2	6.5	0.3	9
Directed Numbers	2.3	12.4	-1.1	8.5
Simplify Terms	6.3	13.7	0.4	8.3
Factorization	11.5	13.7	0	10.8
Solve Equation	5	4.7	-1.9	4.4

Figure 9. Number of Times Which MobileMath was Used Per Day by Group 2

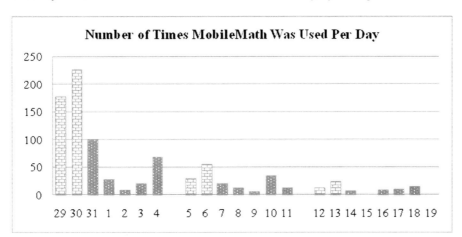

levels of mathematical proficiencies. The means of the pre-test for Groups 1 and 2 were 55.2 and 30.6 respectively. Therefore, since the groups' proficiencies were so different it is expected that they would improve performance at different rates. The data also suggests that *MobileMath* can potentially help students at different levels of mathematics proficiencies, so it can benefit students who may be failing mathematics or those who need to improve their grades.

Table 2 shows that the students who performed higher than average used *MobileMath* longer and more often than the students whose performance was below average. This data shows that the students who performed better used the mobile learning application more than other students. Tables 3 and 4 show the students' performance grouped by above and below average, and *Mobile-Math* usage categorized by topics. These tables illustrate that for 4 out of the 5 topics the students who performed above average used *MobileMath* longer. The data presented thus far implies that, for Group 1 and Group 2, there exists a correlation between the usage of *MobileMath* and the students' performance. Therefore, the more times students used *MobileMath* the more likely they were to improve performance.

The *Games*, *Tutorials* and the *Quizzes* were used the most. At least 65% of the students com-

mented that they enjoyed the *Game* feature the most. This data reveals that the *Games* should be the main focus of the mobile application since it was used so much and the students stated that they preferred it. The questionnaire data also revealed that at least 80% of the students found it useful to use mobile learning anytime and anywhere to study mathematics, the mobile learning activities helped them improve their skills, and that the activities on the mobile device were easy to use. This demonstrates that the majority of the students responded positively to mobile learning, implying that they would use it in the future for learning mathematics.

The server data illustrated that the personalized recommendations were not used as much as was expected. Figure 10 shows that most of the students who received the personalization alert messages found them useful. Therefore, the data demonstrates that the personalization was not used very much and there was no evidence that it had any impact on the students' performance. However, the students indicated that they thought the personalized hints were useful. The positive feedback from the students and past successes from other personalization studies suggest that personalization is still potentially beneficial to m-learning.

Figure 10. Responses to personalization questions

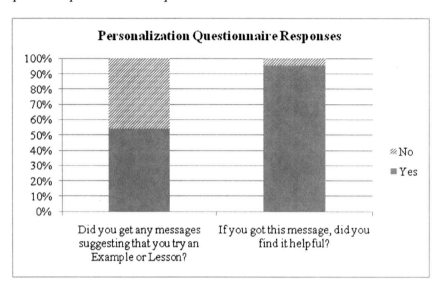

There were some concerns about loaning the mobile devices to the students. However after the three studies concluded, there was no significant damage done to the mobile devices. Therefore, our experience shows that when students are trusted with mobile devices most of them are likely to return the devices in good condition at the end of the evaluation. Thus, loaning mobile devices to students is not a major concern.

The results of the evaluation studies provide the answers to our research questions. The results show that students were able to improve their performance after using mobile learning. The results also revealed that teacher support resulted in the students using the mobile application more than without it. However, even if they used the application more often, this did not result in more improvements than the group without teacher support. The results prove that students do not need a reminder to use the application since they used it many without reminders. Analysis of usage data and students' responses to the questionnaire showed that mobile learning motivated the students. The students stated that the personalization was helpful; however, there was no correlation between use of the personalization features and the students' performance.

The major challenges encountered in our research centered on creating pedagogically useful learning content and activities for a constrained mobile device, the reliability and speed of the GPRS connection and finding students to participate in the evaluation studies since they could not be conducted in the schools. The issue of creating mobile content was solved by basing each feature on one small mathematics skill as opposed to an entire topic containing several skills. The delay in the GPRS connection resulted in the collaborative features not being used and therefore the students were unable to play the collaborative game. The problem of finding students to participate in the study was solved by advertising for students within the secondary schools.

CONTRIBUTION

This research developed a mobile learning application offering the learner a combination of multiple learning activities, personalized recommendations, and game-based learning for learning mathematics. The multiple learning activities provided the learner with several options for reviewing and practicing mathematics skills. The personalization guided the learner in choosing a suitable learning activity. The games offered a fun and engaging learning activity which encouraged and motivated the students to practice their mathematics skills. Each learning activity focused on one mathematics skill making it easier for the student to internalize each activity. The results of our research show that the features of the mobile learning application were successful in getting students to improve their mathematics performance.

CONCLUSION AND FUTURE RESEARCH

This paper presented an investigation into mobile learning to assist high school students in improving their performance in mathematics. The goal of this investigation was to find a possible solution which can contribute to solving the problem of high failure rates in mathematics in the Caribbean. Three evaluation studies were conducted where the students used mobile learning for the first time for three weeks. The results presented illustrate that the students significantly improved performance after using mobile learning for three weeks. The students responded positively on the questionnaire to using mobile learning. This implies that mobile learning can be used to assist students in improving their performance in mathematics.

The teacher supported group performed only slightly better than the group which had no intervention by the teacher. However they did use the application much more. In addition, more students from the teacher supported group showed an improvement in performance. This data implies that the teacher support was a complementary component but not required in mobile learning. In future studies, mobile learning should be supported by a teacher to ensure that the students sustain their motivation for using mobile learning. However, ideally the best solution would be to create a mobile learning system which can ignite motivation in the students without teacher intervention. Game-based learning can be further investigated as a means towards the creation of this ideal solution because games have the potential to motivate students. The *Games* feature of *MobileMath* was used the most and the students commented that they enjoyed it more than the other features. This implies that game-based learning is a promising area of future research for learning high school mathematics via mobile learning.

ACKNOWLEDGMENT

The authors acknowledge the support of the Campus Research and Publication Fund of the University of the West Indies and the Telecommunication Services of Trinidad and Tobago Foundation for their support in this project.

REFERENCES

Andrews, P., & Rayner, A. (2008, October 1-10). Using mobile technology to enhance the problem-solving abilities of students in key transitional courses in engineering, mathematics and science. In *Proceedings of the mLearn Conference: The Bridge from Text to Context*, Shropshire, UK.

Attewell, J. (2005). *Mobile technologies and learning: A technology update and m-learning project summary.* Retrieved from http://www.m-learning.org/docs/The%20m-learning%20project%20-%20technology%20update%20and%20project%20summary.pdf

Brusilovsky, P., Schwarz, E., & Weber, G. (1996). ELM-ART: An intelligent tutoring system on World Wide Web. In C. Frasson, G. Gauthier, & A. Lesgold (Eds.), *Proceedings of the Third International Conference on Intelligent Tutoring Systems* (LNCS 1086, pp. 261-269).

Busa, D., Greenop, K., & Volsoo, S. (2008, October 7-10). Guerrilla learning – developing highly enjoyable, deeply engaging and professional looking educational games for the mobile phone. In *Proceedings of the mLearn Conference: The Bridge from Text to Context*, Shropshire, UK.

Caribexams. (2004). *Caribbean Examination Council (CXC) mathematics pass rates assembled from data published by CXC annual school reports.* Retrieved from http://www.caribexams.org/m_pass_rates

Conway-Smith, E. (2010). *Teaching with cell phones.* Retrieved from http://www.globalpost.com/dispatch/education/100720/south-africa-teaching-cell-phones?page=0,0

Cook, J., Bradley, C., Lance, J., Smith, C., & Haynes, R. (2007). Generating learning contexts with mobile devices. In Pachler, N. (Ed.), *Mobile learning: Towards a research agenda* (pp. 55–74). London, UK: WLE Centre.

Daher, W. (2010). Mathematics learning community flourishes in the cellular phone environment. *International Journal of Mobile and Blended Learning*, 2(2), 1–17. doi:10.4018/jmbl.2010040101

Duncan-Howell, J., & Lee, K. T. (2007, December 2-5). M-learning: Finding a place for mobile technologies within tertiary educational settings. In *Proceedings of the Ascilite ICT Conference on Providing Choices for Learners and Learning*, Singapore (pp. 223-232).

Faux, F., McFarlane, A., Roche, N., & Facer, K. (2006). *Learning with handheld technologies: A handbook from Futurelab.* Bristol, UK: Futurelab.

Jones, A., Issroff, K., Scanlon, E., Clough, G., & McAndrew, P. (2006, July 14-16). Using mobile devices for learning in informal settings: Is it motivating? In *Proceedings of the IADIS International Conference on Mobile Learning*, Dublin, Ireland (pp. 251-255).

Jonker, V., & Wijers, M. (2008, June 23-28). Thinklets for mathematics education, re-using computer games characteristics in educational software. In *Proceedings of the 8th International Conference for the Learning Sciences*, Utrecht, The Netherlands (pp. 406-413).

Kalloo, V., & Mohan, P. (2011, July 6-8). Correlation between student performance and use of an mLearning application for high school mathematics. In *Proceedings of the Eleventh IEEE International Conference on Advanced Learning Technologies*, Athens, GA.

Kebritchi, M., & Hirumi, A. (2008). Examining the pedagogical foundations of modern educational computer games. *Computers & Education*, 5(4), 1729–1743. doi:10.1016/j.compedu.2008.05.004

Liebenberg, J. (2008, October 7-10). Mobile mathematics – lessons learnt. In *Proceedings of the mLearn Conference: The Bridge From Text To Context*, Shropshire, UK (p. 346).

Lin, Y. (2007, November 23-25). Integrating scenarios of video games into classroom instruction. In *Proceedings of the First IEEE International Symposium on Information Technologies and Applications in Education*, Kunming, China (pp. 593-596).

McFarlane, A., Roche, N., & Triggs, P. (2007). *Mobile learning: Research findings.* Retrieved from http://dera.ioe.ac.uk/1470/

MoMath. (2010). *Mobile learning for mathematics: Nokia project in South Africa.* Retrieved from http://www.symbiantweet.com/mobile-learning-for-mathematics-in-south-africa

My Sports Pulse. (2007). *My sports pulse game mechanics.* Retrieved from http://www.mysportspulse.com/index.php?option=com_content&task=view&id=80&Itemid=56

Naismith, L., & Corlett, D. (2006, October 22-25). Reflections on success: A retrospective of the mLearn conference series 2002-2005. In *Proceedings of the mLearn Conference*, Banff, AB, Canada.

Parsons, D., Ryu, H., & Cranshaw, M. (2007). A design requirements framework for mobile learning environments. *Journal of Computers, 2*(4), 1–8. doi:10.4304/jcp.2.4.1-8

Perry, D. (2003). *Handheld computers (PDAs) in schools.* Retrieved from http://www.tes.co.uk/teaching-resource/Handheld-computers-PDAs-in-schools-6072726/

Pratchett, R. (2005). *Gamers in the UK: Digital play, digital lifestyles.* Retrieved from http://open.bbc.co.uk/newmediaresearch/files/BBC_UK_Games_Research_2005.pdf

Project, K. -Nect. (2008). *Project K-Next homepage.* Retrieved from http://www.projectknect.org/Project%20K-Nect/Home.html

Shin, N., Norris, C., & Soloway, E. (2006, June 27-July 1). Effects of handheld games on students learning in mathematics. In *Proceedings of the 7th International Conference on Learning Sciences*, Bloomington, IN (pp. 702-708).

St Mary's. (2008). *St. Mary's City schools mobile learning technology.* Retrieved from http://www.smriders.net/Mobile_Learning/

Vahey, P., Tatar, D., & Roschelle, J. (2004, June 22-26). Leveraging handhelds to increase student learning: Engaging middle school students with the mathematics of change. In *Proceedings of the Sixth International Conference of the Learning Sciences on Embracing Diversity in Learning Science* (pp. 553-560).

Valk, J.-H., Rashid, A. T., & Elder, L. (2010). using mobile phones to improve educational outcomes: An analysis of evidence from Asia. *International Review of Research in Open and Distance Learning, 11*(1).

van't Hooft, M., Swan, K., & Bennett, J. (2009, March 27). Learning math while mobile: Creating opportunities for elementary math learning. In *Proceedings of the 3rd WLE Mobile Learning Symposium: Mobile Learning Cultures across Education, Work, and Leisure*, London, UK (pp. 65-68).

Wagner, E. D. (2005). Enabling mobile learning. *EDUCAUSE Review, 40*(3), 40–53.

This work was previously published in the International Journal of Mobile and Blended Learning, Volume 3, Issue 3, edited by David Parsons, pp 60-77, copyright 2011 by IGI Publishing (an imprint of IGI Global).

Chapter 20
Empirical Research into Students' Mobile Phones and their use for Learning

Claire Bradley
London Metropolitan University, UK

Debbie Holley
Anglia Ruskin University, UK

ABSTRACT

This paper reports on empirical research conducted to find out about higher education students' mobile phone ownership, and the ways in which they are using their mobiles for learning. A survey with a group of first-year students has been followed up by an in-depth study, in which three students were lent Flip Video Camcorders to capture their mobile learning activities and were interviewed to discover more about their practice. The video footage and interview data have been compiled into three rich case studies which help us to better understand students' practice and attitudes towards mobile learning. The paper focuses on the survey data and the three case studies, which were analysed using grounded theory. The outcomes of this research can inform the work of educators seeking to design effective mobile learning activities that build on existing student practice and extend mobile learning within the blend of learning activities that we offer students.

INTRODUCTION

It is now accepted that mobile devices have a number of important characteristics which make them attractive from an educational perspective, including increasing portability, functionality, multimedia convergence, ubiquity, personal ownership, social interactivity, context sensitivity, location awareness, connectivity and personalisation (Pachler et al., 2010). Much research has taken place documenting mlearning pilots and projects, and in developing theoretical frameworks

DOI: 10.4018/978-1-4666-2139-8.ch020

to scaffold mobile learning (e.g., Kukulska-Hulme et al., 2009; Laurillard, 2007).

Our research stems from the desire to be able to utilise the powerful mobile phones that students now have with them all the time - devices which they know how to use, and already use for a multitude of tasks in their everyday lives. We agree with Schuck et al. (2010) that, given the ubiquity of mobile devices, an imperative has arisen for educators in higher education to familiarise themselves with the affordances of mobile technologies for learning so that they are able to capitalise on their students' usage of these devices for effective learning (Schuck et al., 2010). Traxler (2010) also looks at the dreams and responsibilities inherent in universities in embracing students' own mobile devices, and in particular to unlock the dreams of agency, control, ownership and choice amongst students, but outlines a number of risks as well, and concludes that there are no simple solutions. Our approach is more pragmatic, believing that we first need an understanding of students' attitudes towards mobile learning and their uses of their mobiles for learning. Then we can begin to design effective mobile learning activities that will bring mobile phones into the blended learning arena, including them within learning scenarios, rather than excluding them. Such activities should utilise students' own technology, avoiding the need for the university to provide it and thus a whole set of operational issues (cost, training, support, adoption of use, etc.) which many earlier mobile learning initiatives experienced. There is however, a lack of research into how students are actually using their own phones for learning outside the formal classroom.

This paper presents findings from a project funded at London Metropolitan University (London Met) which has explored in depth how students are using their mobile phones to help with their learning. London Met is an inner-city University which encourages widening participation. As a result, the student body is diverse: there are many mature learners (many with children)

who are returning to education and international students who do not speak English as their first language. Most students also now work to fund their studies. Hence tutors are actively seeking strategies to engage learners both inside and outside the classroom within the blend of learning activities offered.

Context to the Study

To put this current work into perspective, the authors of this paper have been involved in a number of mobile learning initiatives and pilot projects at the university over the past few years, bringing mobile learning within the blend of learning activities used within the classroom. These include: a student mobile phone survey conducted over five years; lending mobile phones to masters level students to complete an out-of-classroom assignment, which included the provision of a phone-based checklist to remind them of their task; the provision of an online 'mediaBoard' for students to post images and discuss their groupwork in support of a field trip and assignment (Cook et al., 2006); the provision of study tips via SMS; the creation of learning objects for mobiles (Bradley et al., 2009); and the use of SMS messages in lectures to increase student participation and engagement (Bradley et al., 2010).

Much of our work aims to understand and improve the learning experience and help a diverse body of students to succeed at university. Evaluations and lessons learned from previous work have shown that students are motivated to use new technologies (and in particular mobile phones) for learning activities, and that carefully designed mobile learning activities can engage students to participate in them (Bradley et al., 2010; Bradley, Smith, & Cook, 2010). Once engaged within the learning process, they can be motivated to participate and stay engaged. We know from our student survey conducted over the last five years that all students now own a mobile phone, and that the phones they have are increasingly sophisticated (Bradley & Holley, 2010). It also tells us that students are open to the idea of anytime, anywhere learning, that enables them to schedule their own learning within their busy lives, whenever and wherever it is most appropriate.

Methodology

This project combines initial data from a student survey of mobile phone use for learning, with a small intimate study, where three students agreed to capture their daily 'life with a mobile phone' by using a Flip Video Camcorder. Whilst this could have been achieved through interviews, it was felt that a more creative method was needed to gain insights into their lived experiences. Therefore three students were loaned Flipcams for a month, and requested to film key points where they utilised their phones. The students were then invited along for an interview, and asked to share their films with the researcher. The researcher had not met the students before, and carried out a semi-structured interview to probe further into their practice and their rationale for doing it. For each student, notes taken from their interview and video footage were combined to provide a complete picture. This was then analysed using grounded theory (Strauss & Corbin, 1998), drawing on the available data to build up a picture of their practice and their views towards mobile learning. From this, a written case study for each of the three students was created. These cases provide three unique examples of student-initiated mobile learning, and offer insights into the functions of their mobiles as well as the types of learning activities that they use them for.

The methodology adopted falls within the 'mixed method' research approach, which is defined as, "empirical research that involves the collection and analysis of both qualitative and quantitative data" (Punch, 2009). For Johnson et al. (2008), this method is synonymous to a research paradigm, which they argue is a set of beliefs, values and assumptions that a community

of researchers has in common in regarding the nature and conduct of research. The emergence of a third paradigm is a contested area within the educational research community, with researchers such as Schwandt (as cited in Johnson et al., 2008) pointing out that in the so-called 'paradigm wars' it is "highly questionable whether such a distinction is any longer meaningful for helping us understand the purpose and means of human inquiry" (as cited in Johnson et al., 2008). Guba and Lincoln (2005) are rather more guarded in their acceptance that blending paradigms represents the best of both worlds. They comment, "the answer, from our perspective, has to be a cautious yes" (as cited in Johnson et al., 2008). Yet well-known authors introducing methodology texts talk of two paradigms (Kumar, 2011), and practice based texts (Campbell et al., 2009) highlight the subtleties of the two existing paradigms. For our study it was clear that we would be unable to follow our research interests with a single method, and despite the contentious issues raised by undertaking a mixed method study, we considered the questions raised by Punch (2009): what would it mean to combine the two approaches, and how would this be done?

Cresswell and Plano-Clark (2007) devised a four way classification of mixed methods research, one of which, the 'explanatory design' approach has been used in this study, where qualitative data helps to build upon initial quantitative results. Following Cresswell and Plano-Clark (2007), this study is sequential, in that the timing of data collection from the survey was collected and analysed before the student video diaries. In terms of weighting, we see an equal importance attached to both our data sets; and for the mix between the data sets, our second data set (i.e., our case students) were a subset of the quantitative study.

The research was conducted by a team of two: a researcher from the University's Learning Technology Research Institute (the first author), who conducted the survey, interviewed the students and analysed the data; and a lecturer in the Business

School (the second author), who facilitated the involvement of the students and helped with the study design and analysis of data. In accordance with university policy, before the project started permission was sought from the relevant ethics panel. All the students gave their consent to be involved in the project. Students completing the questionnaire were briefed about its aim when it was handed out. Students involved in the in-depth study were fully briefed about the project, and signed a consent form saying that they agreed that we could use all the material generated for our research and include it on the project website (this would include videos, photos and material from the interviews), and that they would return the Flip Cam at the end.

SURVEY RESULTS: STUDENT MOBILE PHONES AND THEIR USE

The first stage of the research was to conduct a survey with students to find out what mobile phones they have, what their attitudes are towards using them for learning, and what they actually use them for. We were interested in the experiences of first year, first semester students because these are the students most likely to drop out of their studies, and our previous work had indicated students engaging with mobile technologies were more engaged with their studies.

Developing a sense of belonging is a particular challenge for inner city universities with their diverse student body (Stuart, 2009). A short paper-based questionnaire was given to first-year students taking a core business module, "Studying Marketing and Operations". The results are presented in this section.

The students and Their Mobile Phones

74 students completed the questionnaire. All 74 students own a mobile phone. 73% of the students

were female, 28% male. Table 1 shows their age profile.

No students were aged over 35, and the majority 61% was 18-20, with another 33% aged 21-25 years. The gender and age characteristics reflect the average make-up of the module cohort, being predominantly female and in their late teens/early twenties (a significant number of fashion marketing students study this module).

63% of students have their phones on monthly contracts, and the other 37% use pay as you go (PAYG). Contracts usually provide inclusive call-time, SMS messages and data. The implication is that if students have these included within their monthly tariff, they will be less concerned about the costs incurred of using their phone (financial concerns are common amongst our students).

Table 2 shows how long students are likely to keep each handset. This provides a measure of how frequently new devices are acquired, each one generally having greater functionality than the previous one.

37% keep their phone for 12 months, but 35% like to keep their phone for "as long as possible". 27% keep a phone for 18 months (the current average length of a contract).

The range of handsets owned by the students is diverse: 72 students cited 37 phone models from 9 manufacturers (1 student had 2 handsets and several did not specify a precise model). 23 students owned 10 specified Nokia models; 14 owned 5 BlackBerry models; 14 owned 9 Sony Ericsson models; 9 owned 3 Samsung models; 6 owned 2 Apple iPhone models; 6 owned 5 LG models; and one student each owned an HTC, T-Mobile and a Vodaphone. About 80% of these handsets can be classified as Smart Phones (where this can be determined from the model information supplied,

Table 1. Age profile of students

Age range	18-20	21-25	25-30	30-35
% respondents	61%	33%	5%	1%

Table 2. Length of time that students keep a phone

Time period	6 months	12 months	18 months	As long as possible
% respondents	1%	37%	27%	35%

as some don't specify precisely what they have). Whilst there is not an industry standard definition of a Smart Phone, we have taken this to mean a high-end phone that includes web browsing and email. Figure 1 shows the phones that students own by make, with the number of Smart phones indicated.

These data are important, as they show the diverse range of phones that would have to be supported in any mobile learning initiatives.

The real indicator of what students can do with their phones is shown in Figure 2.

Colour screens are now standard for 97% of the students. The ability to be able to capture and generate content is also a possibility for a high proportion of students: 96% have a camera, 86%

can record video and 84% can record audio/voice. The ability to access data networks and share data is also becoming more commonplace: 80% of students can access the Internet from their mobiles, 50% can access WIFI, and 91% have Bluetooth, 46% 3G and 50% GPS. WIFI is important as it enables students to have free access to the Internet and other data sources where a freely-available WIFI network is available.

Students' Attitudes to Using Their Phones for Learning

Three questions were asked about their attitudes to using their mobile phones for learning and being contacted by the university. The responses to these questions are discussed in the "Discussion and Conclusion" section, as insights from the students interviewed have helped us better to understand the student viewpoint. Table 3 shows the responses to the question "How much is the ability to learn at any time and in any place important to you?" which was designed to find out

Figure 1. Phones owned by make

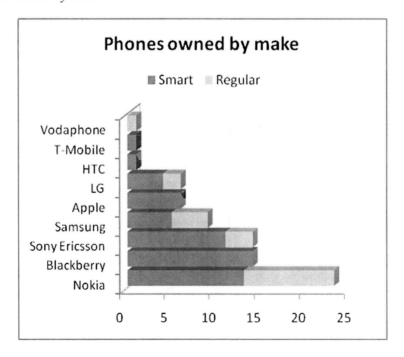

Figure 2. Features of students' mobile phones

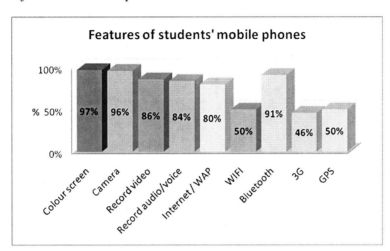

about their attitudes towards flexible learning, and therefore potentially mobile learning.

Adding the results at the positive and negative ends of the scale together (1 + 2 and 4 + 5) makes it easier to interpret the results. 56% think it is important to be able to learn at any time and in any place, 29% are unsure (choosing '3' in the middle), and 15% think it isn't important.

Table 4 explores the question "How useful would it be to access learning materials via your mobile?", as earlier research explored developing learning objects for mobiles.

59% think it would be useful to access learning materials from their mobile, 25% think it wouldn't be useful, and 16% are unsure.

Table 5 shows the responses to the question "How would you view the university contacting you via your mobile for learning purposes?" which aimed to find out how 'personal' students viewed their mobiles as being and whether such activities were seen to be intrusive.

Table 3. How much is the ability to learn at any time and in any place important to you

Extremely important	1	2	3	4	5	Not at all important
% respondents	30	26	29	7	8	

50% gave a positive view, 29% are unsure and 21% have a negative view, so student opinion is divided on this issue.

How Students Use Their Mobile Phones for Learning

The final question was "Do you currently use your mobile phone to help with your learning, and if so what do you use it for?"

22 students (29%) reported using their mobiles for learning, citing 34 different uses. These uses have been grouped into 7 categories in Table 6: conducting research/getting information, communicating, generating content/artefacts, using tools/ applications, organising, notetaking and "other".

The most common category of use was "conducting research and getting information", cited by 12 students. Of these, 10 involved using the Internet, and 2 simply cited "research", which probably meant using the Internet. Data from the last 3 years of our survey (since the question about mobile learning use was introduced) show that use of the Internet for research has increased the most, and has overtaken communication with this year's students (Bradley & Holley, 2010). The "communicating" category saw the next highest number of instances, with 6 uses: 4 used email

Table 4. How useful would it be to access learning materials via your mobile

Extremely useful	1	2	3	4	5	Not at all useful
% respondents	29	30	16	12	13	

Table 5. How would you view the university contacting you via your mobile for learning purposes

It would be a positive aspect	1	2	3	4	5	It would be a negative aspect
% respondents	26	24	29	10.5	10.5	

and 2 others used their mobiles to keep in contact with other students (one via Facebook). Interestingly, no students mentioned using text messaging. 4 students used their mobile for "generating content/artefacts", 3 for taking pictures or photos and 1 for voice recording. In the "using tools and applications" category, 3 used the calculator and 1 Microsoft Office. 3 students used their mobiles for organising their studying, citing using the organiser, checking exams and setting reminder alarms for meetings. One use was registered in the "notetaking" category. Four "other" uses were cited: accessing learning materials, presentations, record presentations and transport files.

CASE STUDIES OF STUDENT MOBILE PHONE USE FOR LEARNING

The second stage of the research was the in-depth study, for which the lecturer recruited three willing students to be involved: Sam, Shriya and Heidi (as the students gave their consent for their video and interview data to be used in our research and on the project website, their real names are retained for authenticity). Each of the three students took a different approach to filming a video diary. Sam filmed lots of short pieces, showing the types of activities he undertakes during a day, and he also interviewed other students on his course about what they do. Shriya filmed one long piece, about how she uses her mobile, and also filmed another student talking about and showing what he does. Heidi filmed herself on several occasions, talking about what she had recently used her mobile for, resulting in 3 clips (some were extra takes and were not used).

Case Study 1: Sam

Sam is a first-year student at London Met, studying Foundation art, media and design. He is male, between 18 and 20 years old, and has a BlackBerry Curve, which he has owned only for about 2 weeks (previously he had a Sony Ericsson which was a hand-me-down). He has his mobile on an 18-month contract, which gives him unlimited Internet access and a large amount of inclusive call time and a large number of texts. He has not been involved in any mobile learning activities during his first year at the university, saying, "If I have used it, it would have been something that I just wanted to do, not advised to do".

He uses his phone for the following learning activities:

- Setting reminders in the calendar and using the clock and alarm to help organise his studying and his schedule.
- Using the camera to capture images, notices and things to remember when he's at art galleries and exhibitions. These are mainly for reference so he can browse through them at his leisure, and he may go back and take higher quality photos with his camera to use in his course notebook or for coursework (he doesn't consider the camera on the BlackBerry to be of sufficient quality).
- Using the voice recording to record lectures if he thinks it will be important, so he can replay them later.
- Communicating with other students, mainly via phone calls as he has a lot of free call time. He also uses BlackBerry Messenger

Table 6. How students use their mobile phones to help with their learning

Category and mobile phone use	Total uses
Conducting research / getting information	12
	Internet (4 students)
	Google (3 students)
	Research (2 students)
	Researching on the Internet
	Accessing info pages
	Search information
Communicating	6
	Email (2 students)
	Saving emails
	To receive emails
	Contacting group assignment members
	Fashion Facebook group
Generating content / artefacts	4
	Take pictures/photos (2 students)
	Take pictures of artworks
	Voice recording
Using tools /applications	4
	Calculator (3 students)
	Microsoft Office
Organising	3
	Organiser
	Check my exams
	Putting reminder alarms for meetings
Notetaking	1
	Write notes
Other	4
	Accessing learning materials
	Presentations
	Record presentations
	Transport files (PDF, Word, Powerpoint …)

to communicate with other students with BlackBerrys, as this is free.
• Using the Internet and Google to look up necessary information.

His most common use is "probably the calendar, because that is really useful, because my organisational skills aren't very good, so it does help to have a little buzz when you need to do something".

He doesn't use his mobile for writing notes, apart from entering dates into the calendar to set reminders for things he needs to do: "I just write a brief line in the calendar saying I need to do this by that date." However, now he has a BlackBerry, he could see himself using it to take notes, because it has a full alphabetic keypad, unlike the limited keypad on his previous phone. "Yeah, I could definitely see myself using it for notes in the future." He doesn't use it at the moment because he's usually got pen and paper and it's easier to use them.

On a daily basis, he uses his phone most for calling people, as he has lots of inclusive minutes. He also uses BlackBerry Messenger, and plays games when he's sitting on a train or somewhere.

He uses his mobile to help with learning because it is "convenient". "Because it's convenient. I mean, I've got it in my pocket 24 hours a day, it's always there, and now I can use the Internet … it's just convenient." He uses his mobile for learning "when necessary" (he thinks that the ability to learn at any time and in any place is important). He probably engages in mobile learning once or twice a day on the days when he's at the university (about 3 or 4 days a week), and less on days where he's not there. Regarding the location of most of his mobile learning activities, he tends to carry out activities at gallery visits and exhibitions, during lectures for recording them or entering information such as dates and deadlines into the calendar, and at home for checking notifications of forthcoming deadlines, tasks, etc. to see what he has to do and bases his homework around the deadlines. He tends to drive into university, and therefore doesn't use his mobile whilst travelling.

He knows that many of his fellow students also use their mobiles for learning (he wasn't able to give a percentage), and said that the numbers were increasing because mobile technology and the phones that they have are becoming more sophisticated, saying you can do much more now than even last year. However, he acknowledged that people are different and how much they used their mobiles would depend on what phone they'd got. About half the students have a BlackBerry, partly because it's free to do BlackBerry to BlackBerry messaging and you can access Facebook

from it too. He also believes that mobile phones are no longer just for calling and texting, and have become a fashion accessory, and that everyone wants to have the latest phone. He reckons that he uses his phone more now than other students (because he's just got the new, more sophisticated one). He thinks that all the students in his course will have used their mobiles at least once during the year for learning purposes. One student, for example, listens to music on his phone when he draws to help him concentrate.

When asked if the university could do anything to make it easier to engage in mobile learning, he said maybe send reminder texts about deadlines, such as "Have you done the work? Do you need any help? If so, contact this number".

Case Study 2: Shriya

Shriya is a first-year international student from India, studying Event Management and Public Relations. She is female, aged between 18 and 20, and has a BlackBerry Curve which she has had for about 2 months. She uses "Pay as you go" and pays £5 per month for unlimited Internet access. She has not been involved in any mobile learning activities this year at the university, but she did experience mobile learning on a previous short course, "Photography and personal styling", at the London College of Fashion. During that, the tutor encouraged them to use their phones to take photographs and exchange ideas. Everyone was very enthusiastic to use their mobiles, and it was because of this course that she bought a good mobile phone (she wasn't interested in them previously because she didn't realise the benefits). She also realised that using mobile phones in such a situation had the power to "hook" you into the learning activities.

She bought a BlackBerry because it is equipped with all the Windows software. She has an Apple MacBook laptop, and finds it difficult to connect with some of the university systems (such as Webmail, the email system), whereas on her

BlackBerry she has no problems and can access anything she wants. She said, "I'm forced to use my phone as my main source of communication." She has started to use her BlackBerry for so much now that it has overtaken the use of her laptop.

Having the ability to learn at any time and in any place is important to her, and her BlackBerry facilitates this. She thinks it's extremely important to be able to access learning materials via her mobile. She believes that students are used to their phones and, because they can now do such things, it is important. She also has a positive attitude towards the university contacting her on her mobile for learning purposes. Sending messages to her mobile would be a faster process of communication, and she wouldn't object to what the university contacted her about, as long as it wasn't in the middle of the night.

She uses her phone for the following learning activities:

- To access email. Her email accounts forward to her mobile, so emails go straight to her phone, "so you don't need a laptop to sign in and it's best when you don't have access to the net".
- Communicate with classmates, via the BlackBerry Messenger (which is free amongst BlackBerry users) and chat, because these are free forms of communication for her. Using this she can chat, send files and pictures and share documents for free.
- To download materials from WebLearn (London Met's virtual learning environment).
- To access Facebook. One of her tutorial groups set up a Facebook group before Easter to facilitate the exchange of work and ideas for a group project. Over the Easter holidays, many of the students travelled abroad, and 3 of them were unable to fly back to the UK in time for the completion of the project because of the volcanic

ash cloud affecting European airspace. The group was therefore able to continue with the project, and those unable to be physically present at the university were able to participate through their participation in the Facebook group. What was started as a means of communicating turned into a "life saver" for these students.
- Access university systems, e.g., Webmail (the email system) and Evision (the student record system). As she can't access her university email from her laptop, her mobile has become the only means for accessing email now.
- She makes notes using the "Memopad" in which you can write quick notes and attach alarms to give reminders, which can also link through to the calendar. She also uses "Word to go" which is BlackBerry's cutdown version of Microsoft Word to write reports. She will start typing up notes in lectures, and then use these as the basis of her notes and reports. These files can then be emailed, or submitted as coursework.

Her most common daily use of her phone is for Facebook, followed by Messenger which she described as a "lifesaver". For learning, she uses it most for emailing tutors and writing reports.

She uses her phone for learning because it is easier, it is accessible (always connected to the Internet and other people), you can use it anywhere and everywhere, and you don't have to carry a heavy laptop around with you. She said, "It really helps you because it saves on time and money". She estimates using her phone for learning about 3-4 times a week, totaling about 20 hours.

She generally carries out her mobile learning activities in quiet places: in her room, in the park around the corner, but not in the library, because they don't allow the use of mobile phones (although a lot of students do use them). She doesn't like the concept of having to study in front of a computer, and her mobile therefore gives her more freedom to study where she wants to. Most of her learning activities are conducted in the evening, when she does most of her studying.

She didn't think that being involved in this project had encouraged her to use her mobile for learning any more than she currently does, because she was already using it a lot.

She thinks that the university could give students more encouragement to use their mobiles, for example, give interactive learning sessions on how they could use their mobiles for learning. She believes that using mobile phones can get students interested in the subject more, and they are fun and help to create enthusiasm for learning. This was her experience on the short course she attended which was mentioned earlier.

She says that many students are using their mobiles for learning. She lives in a student hostel, and has noticed that many now use their mobiles more than their laptops. There is Internet connection only on the ground floor, so you've got to go down there physically with your laptop, whereas with your mobile you can do it in your room. She commented that laptops are big and heavy, and that now a good mobile phone can cost the same as the cheapest laptop or netbook. Some students now don't actually buy a laptop because of this.

Case Study 3: Heidi

Heidi is a first-year international student from Estonia, studying Public Relations. She is female, and is aged between 18 and 20. She has a Sony Ericsson G502 which she has had for over a year, and uses 'pay as you go'. Her phone can access the Internet, but she doesn't do it because it is too expensive. She has a PC and Internet access at home and prefers to use this.

She thinks it is important to have the ability to be able to learn at any time and in any place, as it is "more convenient". For example, if you're waiting for someone you can check what you have to do for your coursework. She was undecided about being able to access learning materials on

her phone, mainly because she doesn't think her phone is able to access materials, but her response would be different if she had a more sophisticated phone. She thinks it would be extremely positive for the university to contact her via her mobile for learning purposes. For example, sending text messages would be good for notifications from the university about coursework deadlines or dates for presentations.

She uses her phone for the following learning activities:

- She makes notes and takes down thoughts for coursework by saving them as text messages. She finds this a more convenient way of making notes - for example, if she doesn't have a pen, or when on the tube where using her phone is easier than writing down notes in a notebook. She also uses text messages to remember things, such as room numbers for lectures and meetings and to make a note of page numbers in books that are interesting when she's reading on the tube. She often has 40-60 saved text messages on her phone.

- She sends text messages to communicate with other students. She prefers to use this method for communication because it's more convenient and it's cheaper.

- She also makes phone calls to communicate with others. She thinks this is a more convenient method of communication because you can say what you want to say faster, and it's also more effective, because people might not see the text. If she had a mobile with a contract or cheaper calls she would make calls more often rather than sending text messages.

- Taking pictures, for example of things she needs to remember, such as an equation for her Quantitative Analysis exam. She also takes pictures to use for her coursework, such as advertisements on the tube, or images she wants to keep that give her ideas.

- She often uses the calculator on her phone when she doesn't have a calculator with her (she's studying statistics as part of her course).
- At college in Estonia last year, she wrote notes in Notepad on her PC and then transferred these to her phone. She had forgotten that she used to do that and for some reason has not continued this practice.

On a daily basis she uses her phone most for texting, and then taking pictures of things. For learning, she uses her mobile most for making notes and texting other students. She uses her mobile for learning because "I know I have it on me always, and I can check it always. It's better than writing in a small calendar book for me". It makes it easier to get in touch with people and ask for advice, and makes it easier to write essays and coursework and keep up to date with what she needs to do. However, she doesn't like to set alarms and reminders on her phone as some students do, as she doesn't like her phone "beeping" all the time.

She thinks that other students use their mobiles mainly for texting and calling. One friend has an iPhone and uses it to access university systems, such as Webmail, Evision, etc. She commented that other students were "amazed" at her use of making notes as text messages (it's not a common practice). She believes that she uses her phone for learning activities about "more or less the same" as other students, probably using it every other day during the week in term time, which probably amounts to about an hour a week in total.

When asked where she tends to engage in mobile learning activities, she said "everywhere, actually" - for example, at university when she doesn't have a pen and needs to save some notes. She will engage in mobile learning when it is appropriate.

She felt that taking part in this research project has made her realise how much she does use her phone for studying, and found it interesting to

discover the different ways she uses it. She would probably use it more in the future if she had a phone that could access the Internet cheaply. If she had cheap or free Internet and a more sophisticated phone, she could see herself using it for accessing the Internet, for email, social networking, accessing Weblearn (the university's VLE) to check announcements and other university systems. For example, she was able to check her grades on her boyfriend's iPhone last semester.

She gave one example of how the university could make it easier for her to engage in mobile learning. She liked the idea of an application that would make it easy to access university systems (WebLearn, Evision, etc.), because the university is Internet-based. It would save time if you could access from a phone which you carry with you everywhere, and it would be a good opportunity for learning.

Each of these case studies illustrates a very different individual use of mobile learning. The common practices and key messages are discussed in the following section.

DISCUSSION AND CONCLUSION

Analysis of Findings

The student survey has provided useful background information about student mobile phone ownership and appropriation for learning. Whilst it focuses on students from one module, it does provide a snapshot of the reality within this group of students. The survey identified some key areas of interest; namely the flexibility offered by utilising the affordances of this technology; students' attitudes to the time and place of mobile learning; and finally their own learning activities.

The Flexibility Offered by a Mobile

Focusing on what the 3 students in the in-depth study have told us, we have an insight into why students think mobile learning is important, and where and when they engage with it. For Sam, using his phone for learning is "convenient", because it's there 24 hours a day (he sleeps with it next to him) and he has unlimited access to the Internet now. He uses his mobile for learning "when necessary", maybe once or twice a day on the days he's at university (about 3 or 4 a week). Activities tend to be located in-situ, at art galleries and exhibitions, during lectures (recording them or adding reminders) and at home for checking his schedule and what tasks he has to do. He said that any use of mobile learning was because "it would have been something that I just wanted to do, and not advised to do". Shriya uses her mobile for learning because it is easier, it is accessible (always connected to the Internet and other people), she can use it anywhere and everywhere, and prefers it because you don't have to carry a heavy laptop around with you, and you don't have to turn it on and log on to access emails. She believes that using her BlackBerry "saves on time and money". She was introduced to mobile learning on a previous course, where she was made aware of the benefits, seeing that using mobiles had the power to "hook" you into the learning activities. Heidi uses her mobile for learning because it's more convenient and it's easier: "I know I have it on me always, and I can check it always. It's better than writing in a small calendar book for me". She says it makes it easier to get in touch with people, ask for advice, write essays and coursework and keep up to date with what she needs to do. She engages in mobile learning when it is appropriate, and says she uses it "everywhere actually". Examples she gave were at university when she doesn't have a pen and needs to write some notes, on the tube if she sees a poster to capture for her coursework or for ideas, or take notes because it's easier than finding a pen and notebook. These findings link back to the affordances of mobile technologies suggested by Pachler et al. (2010).

Time and Place of Learning

There is evidence here that these students are changing their spaces for learning. Examples are Sam having his BlackBerry next to him 24/7 and using it wherever and whenever it is necessary, and Heidi multitasking on the move when she's out and about. Shriya generally carries out her mobile learning in quiet places, such as in her room or in the park around the corner, but not in the library (as they don't allow the use of mobiles). She doesn't like having to study in front of a computer, and using her mobile therefore gives her more freedom to study where she chooses to. This is in line with Traxler's view (2009) that mobile devices are reconfiguring the relationships between public and private spaces, which are being penetrated by mobile virtual spaces. The mobility of devices and the wider availability of data networks enable users to become more mobile, thus providing more freedom in where they choose to carry out activities.

Personal Study Activities

Our research shows that many students are actually using whatever mobile phones they have for a wide range of learning activities. Many of the learning activities cited by students in the survey are also carried out by the 3 students who participated in the in-depth study, who also contribute more detail about what they do and why they do it. Looking at the categories of use in which students are engaging in mobile learning, the following observations can be made.

The two categories with the greatest amount of use were "Conducting research/getting information" followed by "Communicating". However, it is evident that the ways in which students appropriate their mobiles in these areas depend to a large extent on the cost of Internet access and communication services (calls, text messages, etc.). For students involved in group projects (Shriya and Heidi), keeping in contact with other students was particularly important. Shriya uses "PAYG" on her BlackBerry but pays £5 a month for unlimited Internet access, and communicates mainly by email, BlackBerry Messenger, chat and Facebook. Using Messenger is free amongst BlackBerry users, and the other methods are covered by her monthly Internet payment. Heidi, on the other hand, uses mainly text messages to communicate because this is the cheapest method for her, and makes calls when that would be more effective. Sam encounters fewer barriers to cost, as he has a monthly contract which includes unlimited Internet access, and a large number of inclusive calls and texts, and tends to make calls to keep in touch with others, and also uses BlackBerry Messenger with other BlackBerry users. So, whilst the cost of communication and accessing the Internet is an issue for students, they are able to make use of the cheapest options to meet their needs.

Uses in the other categories are more likely to be influenced by what students are able to do with their devices and how they have taken the initiative to use what is available. Four students in the survey and all of our case students, use their mobiles for "Generating content/artefacts" in various ways. Taking photographs to include in coursework or a portfolio was one particular use, and used commonly by Sam and Heidi, and hinted at by Shriya (she talks about sharing pictures). Shriya also uses her mobile to write reports and coursework. Another student cited voice recording but didn't say what for. Four students mentioned that they used "Tools/applications" on their phones for learning. 3 said they used the calculator, as does Heidi for her Statistics module. One student said s/he used Office, and Shriya uses BlackBerry's version of this extensively for preparing reports and presentations. Using their mobiles to help with "Organising" their learning and their schedules was practised by 3 students in the survey and all of our case students to varying

degrees. Sam, who admitted that his organization skills aren't very good, uses the calendar and clock to set reminders and alarms to help organize his studying and schedule. Shriya attaches alarms to notes in Memopad, to help her remember deadlines. Heidi prefers to make reminders in the form of text messages, and doesn't like to set alarms and reminders on her phone because she doesn't want her phone "beeping" all the time. All 3 of our case students now rely on their mobile to some extent to organise their learning and maintain their learning schedules.

Notemaking is a particular theme identified by the case study students. Heidi takes notes in the form of text messages, which she saves to her phone to refer to later. She also uses the camera to take visual notes of images she needs to remember (such as an equation for an exam) or that give her ideas. Sam also uses his mobile to take visual notes of artwork in galleries to look at later or go back and capture more effectively with his camera, and to capture things he wants to remember, such as notices.

"Other" uses which don't fit into our categories include accessing learning materials, presentations, record presentations and transport files. Sam records lectures that he thinks will be important, and Shriya uses her phone to access university systems and download materials from WebLearn (the VLE).

Students are invariably appropriating their mobiles for learning according to their individual learning needs (e.g., to facilitate group projects, generate content for coursework or for portfolios, help organise their learning, remember things, and access university systems and the VLE), using the tools and services that they have available to them in their devices, and making use of what they prefer to use in their everyday practice. As Sam pointed out when asked if he was aware of how other students were making use of their phones for learning, "people are different" and individual student mobile phone use clearly reflects this, and to some extent it will also be dependent on the phones and types of contracts they have.

CONCLUSION

We can conclude that a wide range of mobile learning activities are being practiced and students are resourceful in the methods that they choose to carry them out, often unexpectedly, such as Heidi's use of capturing notes in the form of text messages. They also demonstrate a number of innovative uses for mobiles for learning, regardless of whether the mobile was a high specification 'Smart' phone or a basic model being run on a limited budget. For some students, their use of their mobile is overtaking and replacing the use of their laptop/PC. It is interesting that in the activities described in the three case studies, it is the students who are unlocking the dreams of agency, control, ownership and choice (Traxler, 2009), not the university.

Above all, this research helps us better to understand students' practices and attitudes towards mobile learning and therefore will help us more effectively to design mobile learning activities that build on existing student practice, and that can help to engage the students to participate in learning. It also provides an insight into the mobile phones that students have and what they can do with them, so we can design inclusive activities that a large number of students can potentially engage in, extending mobile learning within the blend of learning activities that we offer to students. It is surely time now for educators to work with their students to realise the affordances of the mobile phone for accessing learning at a time and place that takes into account the choices and needs of individual students.

All the data are included on the "Learning on the move" website, including the student videos and the case studies [www.londonmet.ac.uk/learningonthemove/index.html].

REFERENCES

Bradley, C., Haynes, R., Cook, J., Boyle, T., & Smith, C. (2009). Design and development of multimedia learning objects for mobile phones. In M. Ally (Ed.), *Mobile learning: Transforming the delivery of education and training*. Washington, DC: AU Press.

Bradley, C., & Holley, D. (2010, September 7-9). An analysis of first-year business students' mobile phones and their use for learning. In *Proceedings of the 17th ALT-C Conference on Into Something Rich and Strange: Making Sense of the Sea-Change*, Nottingham, UK (pp. 89-98).

Bradley, C., Smith, C., & Cook, J. (2010, December 1). Location and context sensitive mobile learning: The evaluation of an urban education tour. In *Proceedings of the MoLeNET Mobile Learning Conference*, London, UK.

Bradley, C., Weiss, M., Davies, C., & Holley, D. (2010, June 16-17). A little less conversation, a little more texting please - A blended learning model of using mobiles in the classroom. In *Proceedings of the 5th International Blended Learning Conference*.

Campbell, A., McNamara, O., & Gilroy, P. (2009). *Practitioner research and professional development in education*. London, UK: Sage.

Cook, J., Holley, D., Smith, C., Bradley, C., & Haynes, R. (2006, July 14-16). A blended m-learning design for supporting teamwork in formal and informal settings. In *Proceedings of the Conference on Mobile Learning.*

Cresswell, J. W., & Plano-Clark, V. (2007). *Designing and conducting mixed methods research.* Thousand Oaks, CA: Sage.

Johnson, R. B., Onwuegbuzie, A. J., & Turner, L. A. (2007). Towards a definition of mixed methods research. *Journal of Mixed Methods Research, 1*, 112. doi:10.1177/15586898062982 24doi:10.1177/1558689806298224

Kukulska-Hulme, A., Sharples, M., Milrad, M., Arnedillo-Sánchez, I., & Vavoula, G. (2009). Innovation in mobile learning: A European perspective. *International Journal of Mobile and Blended Learning, 1*(1), 13–35. doi:10.4018/jmbl.2009010102doi:10.4018/jmbl.2009010102

Kumar, R. (2011). *Research methodology.* London, UK: Sage.

Laurillard, D. (2007). Pedagogical forms of mobile learning: Framing research questions. In N. Pachler (Ed.), *Mobile learning: Towards a research agenda* (*Vol. 1*, pp. 33–54). London, UK: WLE Centre, Institute of Education.

Pachler, N., Bachmair, B., & Cook, J. (2010). *Mobile learning: Structures, agency, practices.* New York, NY: Springer.

Punch, K. F. (2009). *Introduction to research methods in education.* London, UK: Sage.

Schuck, S., Aubusson, P., Kearney, M., & Burden, K. (2010). Mobagogy – Mobile learning for a higher education community. In *Proceedings of the IADIS Mobile Learning Conference.*

Strauss, A., & Corbin, J. (1998). *Basics of qualitative research: Techniques and procedures for developing grounded theory.* Thousand Oaks, CA: Sage.

Stuart, M. (2009). *Student diversity, extra curricular activities and perceptions of graduate outcomes.* Retrieved from http://www.heacademy.ac.uk/resources/detail/publications/Stuart_Final

Traxler, J. (2009). Learning in a mobile age. *International Journal of Mobile and Blended Learning, 1*(1), 1–12. doi:10.4018/jmbl.2009010101doi:10.4018/jmbl.2009010101

Traxler, J. (2010). Students and mobile devices. *ALT-J. Research in Learning Technology, 18*(2), 149–160. doi:10.1080/09687769.2010.492847doi:10.1080/09687769.2010.492847

This work was previously published in the International Journal of Mobile and Blended Learning, Volume 3, Issue 4, edited by David Parsons, pp 38-53, copyright 2011 by IGI Publishing (an imprint of IGI Global).

Compilation of References

Aboriginal Economic Development (AED). (2007). Improving mathematics with mobile phones. *AED E-News, 3.*

Ackermann, E. (1996). Perspective-taking and object construction: Two keys to learning. In Kafai, Y., & Resnick, M. (Eds.), *Constructionism in practice: Designing, thinking, and learning in a digital world.* Mahwah, NJ: Lawrence Erlbaum.

Agrusti, F., Keegan, D., Kismihók, G., Krämer, B. J., Mileva, N., & Schulte, D. (2008). *The Impact of New Technologies on Distance Learning Students.* Dublin, Ireland: Ericsson.

Alexander, P., & Murphy, P. (2000). The research base for APA's learner-centered psychological principles. In Lambert, N., & McCombs, B. (Eds.), *How students learn* (pp. 25–60). Washington, DC: American Psychological Association.

Al-Fahad, F. N. (2009). *Students' attitudes and perceptions towards the effectiveness of mobile learning in King Saud University.* Saudi Arabia: Turkish Online Journal of Educational Technology.

Ali, R., & Irvine, V. (2009). Current m-learning research: A review of key literature. In *Proceedings of the World Conference on E-Learning in Corporate, Government, Healthcare, and Higher Education* (pp. 2353-2359).

Allen Consulting. (2010). *Strategic Review of the Australian Flexible Learning Framework (Framework) and its Oversight by the Flexible Learning Advisory Group: A Discussion Paper.* Retrieved from http://www.allenconsult.com.au/flexible_learning_review/downloads/flexible_learning_review_discussion_paper.pdf

Ally, M., & Tin, T. (2009). Mobile phone to improve English pronunciation. In *Proceedings of the 8th World Conference on Mobile and Contextual Learning,* Orlando, FL (pp. 171-173).

Ally, M. (2009). *Mobile learning: Transforming the delivery of education and training.* Athabasca, AB, Canada: Athabasca University Press.

Ally, M. (Ed.). (2009). *Mobile learning: Transforming the delivery of education and training.* Athabasca, AB, Canada: Athabasca University Press.

Amin, A. (1994). Models, fantasies and phantoms of transition. *Post-Fordism. Reading (Sunderland),* 1–39.

Ananhiadou, K., & Claro, M. (2009). *21st century skills and competences for new millenium learners in OECD countries (No. 41).* Paris, France: OECD.

Ananny, M., & Winters, N. (2007). Designing for development: Understanding the one laptop per child in its historical context. In *Proceedings of the IEEE/ACM International Conference on Information and Communication Technologies and Development,* Bangalore, India (pp. 1-12).

Anderson, G. (1990). *Fundamentals of educational research.* London, UK: Falmer Press.

Anderson, T., & Elloumi, F. (2004). Introduction. In Anderson, T., & Elloumi, F. (Eds.), *Theory and practice of online learning* (pp. 1–11). Athabasca, AB, Canada: Athabasca University Press.

Andrews, P., & Rayner, A. (2008, October 1-10). Using mobile technology to enhance the problem-solving abilities of students in key transitional courses in engineering, mathematics and science. In *Proceedings of the mLearn Conference: The Bridge from Text to Context*, Shropshire, UK.

Aoki, P. M., Grinter, R. E., Hurst, A., Szymanski, M. H., Thornton, J. D., & Woodruff, A. (2002). Sotto voce: Exploring the interplay of conversation and mobile audio spaces. In *Proceedings of the SIGCHI Conference on Human Factors in Computing Systems*, Minneapolis, MN.

Arnedillo-Sánchez, I., Sharples, M., & Vavoula, G. (Eds.). (2007). *Beyond mobile learning workshop*. Dublin, Ireland: Trinity College Dublin Press.

Arvaja, M., Häkkinen, P., Eteläpelto, A., & Rasku-Puttonen, H. (2000). Collaborative processes during report writing of a science learning project: The nature of discourse as a function of task requirements. *European Journal of Psychology of Education, 15*, 455–466. doi:10.1007/BF03172987

Atkinson, L., Buntine, A., & McCrohan, R. (2007, September 4-6). Podcasting at RMIT University: Evaluating a faculty-based trial. In *Proceedings of the ALT 14th International Conference*, Nottingham, UK.

Attewell, J. (2005). *Mobile technologies and learning: A technology update and m-learning project summary*. Retrieved from http://www.m-learning.org/docs/The%20m-learning%20project%20-%20technology%20update%20and%20project%20summary.pdf

Attewell, J., & Savill-Smith, C. (2004). *Learning with mobile devices*. London, UK: LSN.

Attewell, J., Savill-Smith, C., Douch, R., & Parker, P. (2010). *Modernising education and training - mobilising technology for learning*. London, UK: LSN.

Attwell, G. (2007). The personal learning environments - the future of elearning? *eLearning Papers, 2*(1), 1-8.

Attwell, G., & Costa, C. (2008). *Integrating personal learning and working environments*. Retrieved from http://www.pontydysgu.org/wp-content/uploads/2008/11/workandlearning.pdf

Attwell, G. (2006). The Wales-Wide Web. *Personal Learning Environments, 2006*, 11.

Ausubel, D. P. (2000). *The acquisition and retention of knowledge: A cognitive view*. New York, NY: Springer.

Bachmair, B., Pachler, N., & Cook, J. (2009). Mobile phones as cultural resources for learning – an analysis of mobile expertise, structures and emerging cultural practices. *MedienPädagogik, 29*, 1–29.

Ballagas, R., & Walz, S. (2007). REXplorer: Using player-centered iterative design techniques for pervasive game development. In Magerkurth, C., & Röcker, C. (Eds.), *Pervasive gaming applications - A reader for pervasive gaming research*. Aachen, Germany: Shaker Verlag.

Bandura, A. (1977). *Social learning theory*. New York, NY: General Learning Press.

Barab, S., Evans, M. A., & Baek, E.-O. (2004). Activity theory as a lens for characterizing the participatory unit. In Jonassen, D. (Ed.), *Handbook for educational communications and technology* (pp. 199–214). Mahwah, NJ: Lawrence Erlbaum.

Barendregt, W., Bekker, M., & Baauw, E. (2008). Development and evaluation of the problem identification picture cards method. *Cognition Technology and Work, 10*(2), 95–105. doi:10.1007/s10111-007-0066-z

Barker, A., Krull, G., & Mallinson, B. (2005). *A proposed theoretical model for m-learning adoption in developing countries*. Paper presented at the mLearn Conference.

Baron, N. S. (2008). *Always On: Language in an Online and Mobile World*. Oxford, UK: Oxford University Press.

Barton, R. (2004). *Teaching secondary science with ICT*. Buckingham, UK: Open University Press.

Baskerville, R., & Myers, M. (2004). Special issue on action research in information systems: Making IS research relevant to practice. *Management Information Systems Quarterly, 28*(3), 329–335.

Bassey, M. (1999). *Case study research in educational settings: Doing qualitative research in educational settings*. Buckingham, UK: Open University Press.

Bates, A. W. (1995). *Technology, open learning and distance education: Routledge studies in distance education*. London, UK: Routledge.

Beddall-Hill, N., & Raper, J. (2010). Mobile devices as 'boundary objects' on field trips. *Journal of the Research Center for Educational Technology, 6*(1).

Bederson, B. B. (1995). Audio augmented reality: A prototype automated tour guide. In *Proceedings of the Conference on Human Factors in Computing Systems*, Denver, CO (pp. 210-211).

Beldarrain, Y. (2006). Distance education trends: Integrating new technologies to foster student interaction and collaboration. *Distance Education, 27*(2), 139–153. doi:10.1080/01587910600789498

Bell, T., Cockburn, A., Wingkvist, A., & Green, R. (2007). Podcasts as a supplement in tertiary education: An experiment with two computer science courses. In Parsons, D., & Ryu, H. (Eds.), *Proceedings of Mobile Learning Technologies and Applications* (pp. 70–77).

Benbasat, I. (1985). An analysis of research methodologies. In MacFarlan, F. (Ed.), *The Information System Research Challenge* (pp. 47–85). Boston, MA: Harvard Business School Press.

Benford, S., Anastasi, R., Flintham, M., Drozd, A., Crabtree, A., & Greenhalgh, C. (2003). Coping with uncertainty in a location-based game. *IEEE Pervasive Computing / IEEE Computer Society [and] IEEE Communications Society, 2*(3), 34–41. doi:10.1109/MPRV.2003.1228525

Bennett, S., Maton, K., & Kervin, L. (2008). The 'digital natives' debate: A critical review of the evidence. *British Journal of Educational Technology, 39*(5), 775–786. doi:10.1111/j.1467-8535.2007.00793.x

Benvenuto, M. (2002). Educational reform: Why the academy doesn't change. *Thought & Action, 18*, 63–74.

Berger, P., & Luckman, T. (2002). The social construction of reality. In Calhoun, C., Gerteis, J., Moody, J., Pfaff, S., & Virk, I. (Eds.), *Contemporary Sociological Theory* (pp. 42–50). London, UK: Blackwell Publishing.

Bertozzi, E., & Lee, S. (2007). Not just fun and games: Digital play, gender and attitudes towards technology. *Women's. Studies in Communications, 30*(2), 179–204.

Bhaskar, N., & Govindarajulu, P. (2010). Advanced and effective learning in context aware and adaptive mobile learning scenarios. *International Journal of Interactive Mobile Technologies, 4*(1), 9–13.

Bherer, L., Kramer, A. F., Peterson, M. S., Colcombe, S., Erickson, K., & Becic, E. (2005). Training effects on dual-task performance: Are there age-related differences in plasticity of attentional control? *Psychology and Aging, 20*, 695–709. doi:10.1037/0882-7974.20.4.695

Bliuc, A.-M., Goodyear, P., & Ellis, R. A. (2007). Research focus and methodological choices in studies into students' experiences of blended learning in higher education. *The Internet and Higher Education, 10*(4), 231–244. doi:10.1016/j.iheduc.2007.08.001

Bogost, I. (2007). *Persuasive games: The expressive power of videogames*. Cambridge, MA: MIT Press.

Botha, A., Vosloo, S., Kuner, J., & Berg, M. (2009). Improving cross-cultural awareness and communication through mobile technologies. *International Journal of Mobile and Blended Learning, 1*(2), 39–53. doi:10.4018/jmbl.2009040103

Bottentuit, J. B., Jr., & Coutinho, C. (2008). The use of mobile technologies in higher education in Portugal: An exploratory survey. In *Proceedings of the World Conference on E-Learning in Corporate, Government, Healthcare, and Higher Education* (pp. 2102-2107).

Boulos, M., Maramba, I., & Wheeler, S. (2006). Wikis, blogs and podcasts: A new generation of web-based tools for virtual collaborative clinical practice and education. *BMC Medical Education, 6*(41), 1–8.

Bourdieu, P. (1990). *The Logic of Practice*. Stanford, CA: Stanford University Press.

Bowles, M. S. (2004). *Relearning to E-Learn: Strategies for electronic learning and knowledge*. Melbourne, Australia: Melbourne University Publishing.

Boyle, A., & Wallace, R. (2008). The role of e-learning in 'holistic' approaches to VET in remote Australian Indigenous contexts. In *Proceedings of the 2008 AVETRA Conference*, Adelaide, Australia.

Bradford, K. T. (2010). *Mobile device users drive Wi-Fi hotspot proliferation.* Retrieved from http://blog.laptopmag.com/mobile-device-users-drive-wi-fi-hotspot-proliferation

Bradley, C., & Holley, D. (2010, September 7-9). An analysis of first-year business students' mobile phones and their use for learning. In *Proceedings of the 17th ALT-C Conference on Into Something Rich and Strange: Making Sense of the Sea-Change*, Nottingham, UK (pp. 89-98).

Bradley, C., Haynes, R., Cook, J., Boyle, T., & Smith, C. (2009). Design and development of multimedia learning objects for mobile phones. In M. Ally (Ed.), *Mobile learning: Transforming the delivery of education and training.* Washington, DC: AU Press.

Bradley, C., Smith, C., & Cook, J. (2010, December 1). Location and context sensitive mobile learning: The evaluation of an urban education tour. In *Proceedings of the MoLeNET Mobile Learning Conference*, London, UK.

Bradley, C., Weiss, M., Davies, C., & Holley, D. (2010, June 16-17). A little less conversation, a little more texting please - A blended learning model of using mobiles in the classroom. In *Proceedings of the 5th International Blended Learning Conference.*

Bradwell, P. (2009). *The edgeless university: Why higher education must embrace technology.* Retrieved from http://www.demos.co.uk/publications/the-edgeless-university

Brennan, R. (1996). Generalizability of performance assessments. In Phillips, G. (Ed.), *Technical issues in large-scale performance assessment* (pp. 19–58). Washington, DC: National Center of Education.

Brewster, S. (2002). Overcoming the lack of screen space on mobile computers. *Personal and Ubiquitous Computing, 6*(3), 188–205. doi:10.1007/s007790200019

Bristow, H. W., Baber, C., Cross, J., & Woolley, S. (2002). Evaluating contextual information for wearable computing. In *Proceedings of the 6th IEEE international Symposium on Wearable Computers*, Seattle, WA (pp. 179-185).

Brooke, J. (1996). SUS: A quick and dirty usability scale. In Jordan, P. W., Thomas, B., Weerdmeester, B. A., & McClelland, I. L. (Eds.), *Usability evaluation in industry* (pp. 189–194). Boca Raton, FL: Taylor & Francis.

Brown, E. (Ed.). (2010). Education in the wild: Contextual and location-based mobile learning in action. In F. Fischer, L. Hofmann, & S. Schulz (Eds.), *D3.1: A report from the STELLAR Alpine Rendez-Vous workshop series.* Nottingham, UK: University of Nottingham.

Brown, T. H. (2005). Beyond constructivism: Exploring future learning paradigms. *Education Today, 2.*

Brown, J. S., & Adler, R. P. (2008). Minds on fire: Open education, the long tail, and learning 2.0. *EDUCAUSE Review, 43*(1), 16.

Brown, J. S., Collins, A., & Duguid, S. (1989). Situated cognition and the culture of learning. *Educational Researcher, 18*(1), 32–42.

Bruns, A. (2005). *'Anyone can edit': Understanding the produser.* Retrieved from http://snurb.info/index.php?q=node/286

Bruns, A. (2007, March 21-23). *Beyond difference: Reconfiguring education for the user-led age.* Paper presented at the ICE3: Ideas in Cyberspace Education: Digital Difference, Loch Lomond, Scotland.

Brusilovsky, P., Schwarz, E., & Weber, G. (1996). ELM-ART: An intelligent tutoring system on World Wide Web. In C. Frasson, G. Gauthier, & A. Lesgold (Eds.), *Proceedings of the Third International Conference on Intelligent Tutoring Systems* (LNCS 1086, pp. 261-269).

Bryce, J., & Rutter, J. (2003). Gender dynamics and the social and spatial organization of computer gaming. *Leisure Studies, 22,* 1–15. doi:10.1080/02614360306571

Brynjolfsson, E., Hu, Y., & Smith, M. D. (2006). From niches to riches: Anatomy of the long tail. *Sloan Management Review, 47*(4).

Bryson, C., & Hand, L. (2007). The role of engagement in inspiring teaching and learning. *Innovations in Education and Teaching International, 44*(4), 349–362. doi:10.1080/14703290701602748

Buchman, D., & Funk, J. (1996). Video and computer games in the '90s: Children's time commitment and game preference. *Children Today, 24*(1), 12–31.

Bull, M. (2005). No dead air! The iPod and the culture of mobile learning. *Leisure Studies, 24*(4), 343–355. doi:10.1080/0261436052000330447

Bull, S., & McEvoy, A. T. (2003). An intelligent learning environment with an open learner model for the Desktop PC and Pocket PC. In Hoppe, U., Verdejo, F., & Kay, J. (Eds.), *Artificial intelligence in education* (pp. 389–391). Amsterdam, The Netherlands: IOS Press.

Burgess, R. G. (Ed.). (1989). *The ethics of educational research*. New York, NY: Falmer Press.

Burke, D. (2010). Using mobile devices to enhance fieldwork. In Law, P., & Wankel, C. (Eds.), *Streaming media in higher education*. London, UK: Streaming Media.

Burrill, D. A. (2010). Wii will become silhouettes. *Television & New Media*, *20*(10), 1–11.

Busa, D., Greenop, K., & Volsoo, S. (2008, October 7-10). Guerrilla learning – developing highly enjoyable, deeply engaging and professional looking educational games for the mobile phone. In *Proceedings of the mLearn Conference: The Bridge from Text to Context*, Shropshire, UK.

Buscher, M., & Urry, J. (2009). Mobile methods and the empirical. *European Journal of Social Theory*, *12*(1), 99–116. doi:10.1177/1368431008099642

Caftori, N., & Papryzcki, M. (1997). The design, evaluation and usage of educational software. *Technology and Teacher Education Manual*, *1*, 23–27.

Campbell, A., McNamara, O., & Gilroy, P. (2009). *Practitioner research and professional development in education*. London, UK: Sage.

Campbell, G. (2005). There's something in the air: Podcasting in education. *EDUCAUSE Review*, *40*(6), 32–47.

Caribexams. (2004). *Caribbean Examination Council (CXC) mathematics pass rates assembled from data published by CXC annual school reports.* Retrieved from http://www.caribexams.org/m_pass_rates

Carrier, L. M., Cheever, N. A., Rosen, L. D., Benitez, S., & Chang, J. (2009). Multitasking across generations: Multitasking choices and difficulty ratings in three generations of Americans. *Computers in Human Behavior*, *25*, 483–489. doi:10.1016/j.chb.2008.10.012

Carroll, J. M. (2000). Five reasons for scenario-based design. *Interacting with Computers*, *13*(1), 43–60. doi:10.1016/S0953-5438(00)00023-0

Carvalho, A. A., Aguiar, C., Santos, H., Oliveira, L., Marques, A., & Maciel, R. (2009). Podcasts in Higher Education: Students and Teachers Perspectives. In Tatnall, A., & Jones, A. (Eds.), *Education and Technology for a Better World* (pp. 417–426). Berlin, Germany: Springer. doi:10.1007/978-3-642-03115-1_44

Cavus, N., & Uzunboylu, H. (2009). Improving critical thinking skills in mobile learning. *Procedia Social and Behavioral Sciences*, *1*(1), 434–438. doi:10.1016/j.sbspro.2009.01.078

Cebeci, Z., & Tekdal, M. (2006). Using podcasts as audio learning objects. *Interdisciplinary Journal of Knowledge and Learning Objects*, *2*, 47–57.

Centraal Bureau voor de Statistiek. (2009). *De digitale economie 2009*. Retrieved from http://www.cbs.nl/NR/rdonlyres/E87BCAE8-8F0E-4F43-90FE-B44F3D513E8A/0/2009p34pub.pdf

Cerratto Pargman, T. (2003). Collaborating with writing tools: An instrumental perspective on the problem of computer support for collaborative activities. *Interacting with Computers: The Interdisciplinary Journal of Human-Computer Interaction*, *15*, 737–757.

Chan, A., Lee, M. J., & McLoughlin, C. (2006). *Everyone's learning with podcasting: A Charles Sturt University experience*. Paper presented at the ASCILITE Conference of Who's learning? Whose technology? Sydney, Australia.

Chee, Y. S., Gwee, S., & Tan, E. M. (2011). Learning to become citizens by enacting governorship in the *Statecraft* curriculum: An evaluation of learning outcomes. *International Journal of Gaming and Computer-Mediated Simulations*, *3*(1).

Chen, Y. S., Kao, T. C., Yu, G. J., & Sheu, J. P. (2004, March 23-25). A mobile butterfly-watching learning system for supporting independent learning. In *Proceedings of the 2nd IEEE international workshop on wireless and mobile technologies in education*, JungLi, Taiwan (pp. 11-18).

Chen, Y. S., Kao, T. C., & Sheu, J. P. (2003). A mobile learning system for scaffolding bird watching learning. *Journal of Computer Assisted Learning*, *19*, 347–359. doi:10.1046/j.0266-4909.2003.00036.x

Chen, Y. S., Kao, T. C., & Sheu, J. P. (2005). Realizing outdoor independent learning with a butterfly-watching mobile learning system. *Journal of Educational Computing Research*, *33*, 395–417. doi:10.2190/0PAB-HRN9-PJ9K-DY0C

Cherng, R., Liang, L., Hwang, I., & Chen, J. (2007). The effect of a concurrent task on the walking performance of preschool children. *Gait & Posture*, *26*, 231–237. doi:10.1016/j.gaitpost.2006.09.004

Chi, M., & Hausmann, R. (2003). Do radical discoveries require ontological shifts? In Shavinina, L., & Sternberg, R. (Eds.), *International handbook on innovation* (*Vol. 3*, pp. 430–444). New York, NY: Elsevier Science. doi:10.1016/B978-008044198-6/50030-9

Chou, C., & Tsai, M.-J. (2007). Gender differences in Taiwan high school students' computer game playing. *Computers in Human Behavior*, *23*(1), 812–824. doi:10.1016/j.chb.2004.11.011

Christakis, N., & Fowler, J. (2009). *Connected – The Amazing Power of Social Networks and How they Shape Our Lives*. London, UK: Harper Press.

Christie, M. (2004). *Aboriginal Knowledge on the Internet*. Retrieved from http://www.cdu.edu.au/centres/ik/pdf/AbKnowInternet.pdf

Christie, M. (2007). Fracturing the Skeleton of Principle: Australian Law, Aboriginal Law, and Digital Technology. *Learning Communities: International Journal of Learning in Social Contexts*.

Ciussi, M., Rosner, G., & Augier, M. (2009). Engaging students with mobile technologies to support their formal and informal learning. *International Journal of Mobile and Blended Learning*, *1*(4), 84–98. doi:10.4018/jmbl.2009090805

Clarebout, G., Coens, J., & Elen, J. (2008). The use of ipods in education: The case of multi-tasking. In Zumbach, J., Schwartz, N., Seufert, T., & Kester, L. (Eds.), *Beyond knowledge: The legacy of competence* (pp. 75–82). New York, NY: Springer. doi:10.1007/978-1-4020-8827-8_11

Cobcroft, R., Towers, S., Smith, J., & Bruns, A. (2006). Mobile learning in review: Opportunities and challenges for learners, teachers, and institutions. In *Proceedings of the Online Learning and Teaching (OLT) Conference 2006* (pp. 21-30).

Cochrane, T., Bateman, R., & Flitta, I. (2009, April 22-24). *Integrating mobile Web 2.0 within tertiary education*. Paper presented at the m-ICTE Conference, Lisbon, Portugal.

Cochrane, T., Bateman, R., Cliffin, P., Gardner, J., Henderson, I., & Holloway, S. (2009, July 6-8). *Mobilizing learning: Mobile Web 2.0 scenarios in tertiary education*. Paper presented at the EDULEARN International Conference on Education and New Learning Technologies, Barcelona, Spain.

Cochrane, T. (2006). Learning with wireless mobile devices and social software. In. *Proceedings of ASCILITE*, *06*, 143–146.

Cochrane, T. (2009). Mobilizing learning: Intentional disruption. Harnessing the potential of social software tools in higher education using wireless mobile devices. *International Journal of Mobile Learning and Organisation*, *3*(4), 399–419. doi:10.1504/IJMLO.2009.027456

Cochrane, T. (2010a). Beyond the yellow brick road: Mobile web 2.0 informing a new institutional elearning strategy. *ALT-J Research in Learning Technology*, *18*(3), 221–231. doi:10.1080/09687769.2010.529110

Cochrane, T. (2010b). Exploring mobile learning success factors. *ALT-J Research in Learning Technology*, *18*(2), 133–148. doi:10.1080/09687769.2010.494718

Coens, J., Clarebout, G., & Reynvoet, B. (2009a, May). *Mobile learning: een stand van zaken*. Poster presented at the Onderwijsresearchdagen, Leuven, Belgium.

Coens, J., Clarebout, G., & Reynvoet, B. (2009b, August). *Mobile learning viewed from the perspective of multitasking*. Poster presented at the Earli Biennal Conference, Amsterdam, The Netherlands.

Coens, J., Reynvoet, B., & Clarebout, G. (2011). Mobile learning. Can students really multitask? *Journal of Educational Multimedia and Hypermedia*, *20*(1), 5–20.

Cohen, L., Manion, L., & Morrison, K. (2000). *Research Methods in Education* (5th ed.). London, UK: Routledge-Falmer. doi:10.4324/9780203224342

Cohen, L., Manion, L., & Morrison, K. (2001). *Research methods in education* (5th ed.). London, UK: Routledge.

Cole, H., & Stanton, D. (2003). Designing mobile technologies to support co-present collaboration. *Personal and Ubiquitous Computing*, *7*(6), 365–371. doi:10.1007/s00779-003-0249-4

Collazos, C., Guerrero, L., Pino, J., & Ochoa, S. (2002). Evaluating collaborative learning processes. In J. M. Haake & J. A. Pino (Eds.), *Proceedings of the 8th International Workshop on Groupware*, La Serena, Chile (LNCS 2440, pp. 203-221).

Colwell, J., & Payne, J. (2000). Negative correlates of computer game play in adolescents. *The British Journal of Psychology*, *91*, 295–310. doi:10.1348/000712600161844

Comas-Quinn, A., Mardomingo, R., & Valentine, C. (2009). Mobile blogs in language learning: Making the most of informal and situated learning opportunities. *Re-CALL*, *21*(1), 96–112. doi:10.1017/S0958344009000032

Conole, G. (2007). Describing learning activities: Tools and resources to guide practice. In Beetham, H., & Sharpe, R. (Eds.), *Rethinking Pedagogy for a Digital Age: Designing and delivering e-learning* (pp. 81–91). London, UK: Routledge.

Conole, G., de Laat, M., Dillon, T., & Darby, J. (2008). Disruptive technologies, pedagogical innovation: What's new? Findings from an in-depth study of students' use and perception of technology. *Computers & Education*, *50*(2), 511–524. doi:10.1016/j.compedu.2007.09.009

Consalvo, M. (2007). *Cheating: Gaining advantage in videogames*. Cambridge, MA: MIT Press.

Continental Research. (2008). *Continental Research: The Autumn 2008 Mobile Phone Report*. Retrieved from http://www.iabeurope.eu/

Conway-Smith, E. (2010). *Teaching with cell phones*. Retrieved from http://www.globalpost.com/dispatch/education/100720/south-africa-teaching-cell-phones?page=0,0

Cook, J., Holley, D., Smith, C., Bradley, C., & Haynes, R. (2006, July 14-16). A blended m-learning design for supporting teamwork in formal and informal settings. In *Proceedings of the Conference on Mobile Learning*.

Cook, J. (2010). Mobile phones as mediating tools within augmented contexts for development. *International Journal of Mobile and Blended Learning*, *2*(3), 1–12. doi:10.4018/jmbl.2010070101

Cook, J., Bradley, C., Lance, J., Smith, C., & Haynes, R. (2007). Generating learning contexts with mobile devices. In Pachler, N. (Ed.), *Mobile learning: Towards a research agenda* (pp. 55–74). London, UK: WLE Centre.

Cooney, G. Learnosity, & Keogh, K. A. (2007). *Use of mobile phones for language learning and assessment for learning, a pilot project*. Paper presented at the mLearn Conference, Melbourne, Australia.

Copley, J. (2007). Audio and video podcasts of lectures for campus-based students: Production and evaluation of student use. *Innovations in Education and Teaching International*, *44*, 387–399. doi:10.1080/14703290701602805

Corbeil, J. R., & Valdes-Corbeil, M. E. (2007). Are You Ready for Mobile Learning? *EDUCAUSE Quarterly*, *30*(2), 51–58.

Cortez, C., Nussbaum, M., Woywood, G., & Aravena, R. (2009). Learning to collaborate by collaborating: A face-to-face collaborative activity for measuring and learning basics about teamwork. *Journal of Computer Assisted Learning*, *25*(2), 126–142. doi:10.1111/j.1365-2729.2008.00298.x

Council of Australian Governments. (2009). *National Indigenous Reform Agreement (Clo9sing the Gap)*. Retrieved from http://www.coag.gov.au/coag_meeting_outcomes/2009-07-02/docs/NIRA_closing_the_gap.pdf

Cresswell, J. W., & Plano-Clark, V. (2007). *Designing and conducting mixed methods research*. Thousand Oaks, CA: Sage.

Crossan, A., McGill, M., Brewster, S., & Murray-Smith, R. (2009). Head tilting for interaction in mobile contexts. In *Proceedings of the 11th International Conference on Human-Computer Interaction with Mobile Devices and Services* (p. 6).

Crossan, A., Williamson, J., Brewster, S., & Murray-Smith, R. (2008). Wrist rotation for interaction in mobile contexts. In *Proceedings of the 10th International Conference on Human Computer Interaction with Mobile Devices and Services* (pp. 435-438).

Cucu, C., Cristescu, M.-P., & Cristescu, C.-I. (2010). Contributions to using IT in education: An educational video player. *Informatica Economica, 14*(2), 108–119.

Da Silveira, G., Borenstein, D., & Fogliatto, F. S. (2001). Mass customization: Literature review and research directions. *International Journal of Production Economics, 72*(1), 1–13. doi:10.1016/S0925-5273(00)00079-7

Daher, W. (2010). Mathematics learning community flourishes in the cellular phone environment. *International Journal of Mobile and Blended Learning, 2*(2), 1–17. doi:10.4018/jmbl.2010040101

Dale, C. (2007). Strategies for using podcasting to support student learning. *Journal of Hospitality, Leisure, Sport and Tourism Education, 6*, 49–57. doi:10.3794/johlste.61.155

Davis, F. D. (1989). Perceived usefulness, perceived ease of use, and user acceptance of information technology. *Management Information Systems Quarterly, 13*(3), 319–340. doi:10.2307/249008

Davis, F. D., Bagozzi, R. P., & Warshaw, P. R. (1989). User acceptance of computer technology: A comparison of two theoretical models. *Management Science, 35*(8), 982–1003. doi:10.1287/mnsc.35.8.982

Davis, S. B., Moar, M., Jacobs, R., Watkins, M., Riddoch, C., & Cooke, K. (2006). Ere Be Dragons: Heartfelt gaming. *Digital Creativity, 17*(3), 157–162. doi:10.1080/14626260600882430

de Crom, E. P., & de Jager, A. (2005). The "ME"-learning experience: PDA technology and e-learning in ecotourism at the Tshwane University of Technology (TUT). In *Proceedings of the MLEARN Conference*, Cape Town, South Africa.

de Freitas, S., & Griffiths, M. (2008). The convergence of gaming practices with other media forms: What potential for learning? A review of the literature. *Learning, Media and Technology, 33*(1), 11–20. doi:10.1080/17439880701868796

De Jong, T., Specht, M., & Koper, R. (2008). Contextualized media for learning. *Journal of Educational Technology & Society, 11*(2), 41–53.

Dearnley, C. J., Haigh, J., & Fairhall, J. (2008). Using mobile technologies for assessment and learning in practice settings: A case study. *Nurse Education in Practice, 8*(3), 197–204. doi:10.1016/j.nepr.2007.07.003

Denscombe, M. (1998). *The good research guide for small scale social research projects* (1st ed.). Buckingham, UK: Open University Press.

Design-Based-Research-Collective. (2003). Design-based research: An emerging paradigm for educational inquiry. *Educational Researcher, 32*(1), 5–8. doi:10.3102/0013189X032001005

Dewson, S., Eccles, J., Tackey, N. D., & Jackson, A. (2002). *Measuring soft outcomes and distance travelled: A review of current practice*. London, UK: Department for Business Innovation & Skills.

Dillenbourg, P. (1999). What do you mean by collaborative learning? In Dillenbourg, P. (Ed.), *Collaborative-learning: Cognitive and computational approaches* (pp. 1–19). Oxford, UK: Elsevier.

Dillenbourg, P., Järvelä, S., & Fischer, F. (2009). The evolution of research in computer-supported collaborative learning: From design to orchestration. In Balacheff, N., Ludvigsen, S., de Jong, T., Lazonder, A., & Barnes, S. (Eds.), *Technology-enhanced learning*. New York, NY: Springer. doi:10.1007/978-1-4020-9827-7_1

Dillenbourg, P., & Schneider, D. (1995). Mediating the mechanisms which make collaborative learning sometimes effective. *International Journal of Educational Telecommunications, 1*(2-3), 131–146.

Dix, A., Rodden, T., Davies, N., Trevor, J., Friday, A., & Palfreyman, K. (2000). Exploiting space and location as a design framework for interactive mobile systems. *ACM Transactions on Computer-Human Interaction, 7*(3), 285–321. doi:10.1145/355324.355325

Donnan, P. A. (2007). *Conducting assessment online: Educational developers perspectives*. New South Wales, Australia: University of Wollongong.

Doolittle, P. E., Lusk, D., Byrd, C., & Mariano, G. (2009). iPods as mobile multimedia learning environments: Individual differences and instructional design. In H. Ryu & D. Parsons (Eds.) *Innovative mobile learning: Techniques and technologies*. Hershey, PA: IGI Global.

Doolittle, P. E., & Mariano, G. J. (2008). Working memory capacity and mobile multimedia learning environments: Individual differences in learning while mobile. *Journal of Educational Multimedia and Hypermedia, 17*, 511–530.

Draper, S. W., & Brown, M. I. (2004). Increasing interactivity in lectures using an electronic voting system. *Journal of Computer Assisted Learning, 20*(2), 81–94. doi:10.1111/j.1365-2729.2004.00074.x

Drewes, T. M., Mynatt, E. D., & Gandy, M. (2000). Sleuth: An audio experience. In *Proceedings of the International Conference on Auditory Display*, Atlanta, GA (pp. 1-6).

Druin, A. (1999). Cooperative inquiry: Developing new technologies for children with children. In *Proceedings of the ACM CHI Human Factors in Computing Systems Conference*, Pittsburgh, PA (pp. 592-599).

Duncan-Howell, J., & Lee, K. T. (2007, December 2-5). M-learning: Finding a place for mobile technologies within tertiary educational settings. In *Proceedings of the Ascilite ICT Conference on Providing Choices for Learners and Learning*, Singapore (pp. 223-232).

Durbridge, N. (1984). Media in course design, No. 9, audio cassettes. In Bates, A. W. (Ed.), *The role of technology in distance education* (pp. 99–108). Kent, UK: Croom Helm.

Dye, A., Jones, B., & Kismihók, G. (2006). *Mobile Learning: The Next Generation of Learning-Exploring Online Services in a Mobile Environment*. Paper presented at the EDEN Annual Conference 2006.

Dyson, L. E., Raban, R., Litchfield, A., & Lawrence, E. (2009). Addressing the cost barriers to mobile learning in higher education. *International Journal of Mobile Learning and Organization, 3*(4), 381–398. doi:10.1504/IJMLO.2009.027455

Eaton, B. C., & Schmitt, N. (1994). Flexible manufacturing and market structure. *The American Economic Review, 84*(4), 875–888.

Eliasson, J., Nouri, J., Ramberg, R., & Cerratto Pargman, T. (2010). *Design heuristics for balancing visual focus on devices in formal mobile learning activities*. Paper presented at the 9th International Conference on Mobile Learning.

Eliasson, J., Spikol, D., Pargman, T., & Ramberg, R. (2010). Get the bees away from the hive: Balancing visual focus on devices in mobile learning. In *Proceedings of the IADIS International Conference on Mobile Learning* (pp. 77-84).

Eliasson, J., Pargman, T., Nouri, J., Spikol, D., & Ramberg, R. (2011). Mobile devices as support rather than distraction for mobile learners – Evaluating guidelines for design. *International Journal of Mobile and Blended Learning, 3*(2), 1–15.

Ellis, R. A., Goodyear, P., Prosser, M., & O'Hara, A. (2006). How and what university students learn through online and face-to-face discussion: conceptions, intentions and approaches. *Journal of Computer Assisted Learning, 22*(4), 244–256. doi:10.1111/j.1365-2729.2006.00173.x

Engeström, Y. (1991). Non scolae sed vitae discimus: Toward overcoming the encapsulation of school learning. *Learning and Instruction, 1*, 243–259. doi:10.1016/0959-4752(91)90006-T

Engeström, Y. (2009). Wildfire activities: New patterns of mobility and learning. *International Journal of Mobile and Blended Learning, 1*(2). doi:10.4018/jmbl.2009040101

Epstein, M., & Vergani, S. (2006). *History unwired: Mobile narrative in historic cities*. Paper presented at the Working Conference on Advanced Visual Interfaces, Venezia, Italy.

European Union. (2003). *Decision No 2318/EC of the European Parliament and of the Council, December 2003 adopting a multiannual programme (2004-2006) for the effective integration of information and communication technologies (ICT) in education and training systems in Europe (eLearning Programme)*. Retrieved from http://europa.eu/eur-lex/pri/en/oj/dat/2003/1_345/1_3452003 1231en00090016.pdf

Evans, C. (2008). The effectiveness of m-learning in the form of podcast revision lectures in higher education. *Computers & Education, 50*(2), 491–498. doi:10.1016/j.compedu.2007.09.016

Evans, C. (2008). The effectiveness of m-learning in the form of podcast revision lectures in higher education. *Computers & Education, 50,* 491–498. doi:10.1016/j.compedu.2007.09.016

Eysenck, M. W., & Keane, M. T. (2005). *Cognitive psychology: A student's handbook.* Hove, UK: Psychology Press.

Facer, K., Joiner, R., Stanton, D., Reidt, J., Hull, R., & Kirk, D. (2004). Savannah: Mobile gaming and learning? *Journal of Computer Assisted Learning, 20,* 399–409. doi:10.1111/j.1365-2729.2004.00105.x

Faulkner, X. (2000). *Usability engineering.* London, UK: Palgrave.

Faux, F., McFarlane, A., Roche, N., & Facer, K. (2006). *Learning with handheld technologies: A handbook from Futurelab.* Bristol, UK: Futurelab.

Federale Overheidsdienst Economie. (2009). *ICT-indicatoren bij huishoudens en individuen 2005-2009.* Retrieved from http://statbel.fgov.be/nl/modules/publications/statistiques/arbeidsmarkt_levensomstandigheden/ict_indicatoren_bij_huishoudens_individuen_2005_2009.jsp

Federation of American Scientists. (2006). *Harnessing the power of video games for learning.* Retrieved from http://agamerseducation.wordpress.com/2005/10/25/harnessing-the-power-of-video-games-for-learning/

Feenberg, A., & Bakardjieva, M. (2004). Consumers or citizens? The online community debate. In Feenberg, A., & Barney, D. D. (Eds.), *Community in the Digital Age: Philosophy and practice* (pp. 1–30). Lanham, MD: Rowman & Littlefield.

Fetaji, M. (2008). Literature review of m-learning issues, m-learning projects and technologies. In *Proceedings of the World Conference on E-Learning in Corporate, Government, Healthcare, and Higher Education* (pp. 348-353).

Field, J. (2005). *Social Capital and Lifelong Learning.* Bristol, UK: The Policy Press.

Foehr, U. G. (2006). *Media multitasking among American youth: Prevalence, predictors and pairings.* Menlo Park, CA: The Henry J. Kaiser Family Foundation.

Fowler, F. (2002). *Survey research methods* (3rd ed.). Thousand Oaks, CA: Sage.

Freytag, G. (1895). *Technique of the drama: An exposition of dramatic composition and art.* Chicago, IL: S. C. Griggs & Company.

Frohberg, D., Göth, C., & Schwabe, G. (2009). Mobile learning projects - a critical analysis of the state of the art: Original article. *Journal of Computer Assisted Learning, 25*(4), 307–331. doi:10.1111/j.1365-2729.2009.00315.x

Frydenberg, M. (2008). Principles and pedagogy: The two Ps of podcasting in the information technology classroom. *Information Systems Education Journal, 6*(6).

Füstös, L., Kovács, E., Meszéna, G., & Simonné Mosolygó, N. (2004). *Alakfelismerés.* Budapest, Hungary: Új Mandátum.

Gabriel, M. A. (2004). Learning together: Exploring group interactions online. *Journal of Distance Education, 19*(1), 54–72.

Garrison, D., & Vaughan, N. (2008). *Blended learning in higher education: Framework, principles, and guidelines.* New York, NY: John Wiley & Sons.

Gartner. (2010). *Gartner Says Worldwide Mobile Phone Sales Grew 17 Per Cent in First Quarter 2010.* Retrieved from http://www.gartner.com/it/page.jsp?id=1372013

Gaver, W., Beaver, J., & Benford, S. (2003). Ambiguity as a resource for design. In *Proceedings of the SIGCHI conference on Human Factors in Computing Systems,* Ft. Lauderdale, FL (pp. 233-240).

Gayeski, D. (2002). *Learning unplugged - using mobile technologies for organizational and performance improvement.* New York, NY: American Management Association.

Gee, J. P. (2003). *What Video Games Have To Teach Us About Learning and Literacy.* New York, NY: Palgrave Macmillan.

Genette, G. (1997). *Paratexts: Thresholds of interpretation.* Cambridge, UK: Cambridge University Press. doi:10.1017/CBO9780511549373

Germain-Rutherford, A., & Kerr, B. (2008). An inclusive approach to online learning environments: Models and resources. *Turkish Online Journal of Distance Education, 9*(2), 64–85.

Gibson, J. J. (1977). The theory of affordances. In Shaw, R., & Bransford, J. (Eds.), *Perceiving, acting and knowing*. Mahwah, NJ: Lawrence Erlbaum.

Gil, D., & Pettersson, O. (2010). Providing flexibility in learning activities systems by the use of multi-role mobile devices. In *Proceedings of the 6th IEEE International Conference on Wireless, Mobile, and Ubiquitous Technologies in Education* (pp. 166-170).

Giles, J. (2009). *Physios recommend a healthy dose of gaming*. Retrieved from http://www.newscientist.com/article/mg20227145.700-physios-recommend-a-healthy-dose-of-gaming.html

Gilmore, J. H., & Pine, B. J. (1997). The four faces of mass customization. *Harvard Business Review, 75*(1), 91.

Gore, J. M. (2001). Disciplining Bodies: On the Continuity of Power Relations in Pedagogy. In Paechter, R. E. C., Harrison, R., & Twining, P. (Eds.), *Learning, Space and Identity*. London, UK: Paul Chapman Publishing.

Gorra, A., Sheridan-Ross, J., & Finlay, J. (2009, April 22-24). Podcasting - an evaluation of two case studies from the UK. In *Proceedings of the 5th International Conference on Multimedia and Information and Communication Technologies in Education*, Lisbon, Portugal.

Göth, C., & Schwabe, G. (2010). Navigation support for mobile learning. In *Proceedings of the 43rd Hawaii International Conference on System Sciences* (pp. 1-10).

Göth, C., Frohberg, D., & Schwabe, G. (2006). The focus problem in mobile learning. In *Proceedings of the Fourth IEEE International Workshop on Wireless, Mobile and Ubiquitous Technology in Education* (pp. 153-160).

Greenfield, A. (2006). *Everyware: The dawning age of ubiquitous computing*. Berkeley, CA: New Riders.

Green, M. E., & McNeese, M. N. (2008). Factors that predict digital play. *The Howard Journal of Communications, 19*(3), 258–272. doi:10.1080/10646170802218321

Grenman, K. (2010). *The future of printed school books*. Espoo, Finland: VTT Technical Research Centre of Finland.

Guenther, S., Winkler, T., Ilgner, K., & Herczeg, M. (2008). Mobile learning with moles: A case study for enriching cognitive learning by collaborative learning in real world contexts. In *Proceedings of the World Conference on Educational Multimedia, Hypermedia and Telecommunications* (pp. 374-380).

Gustafsson, A., Bichard, J., Brunnberg, L., Juhlin, O., & Combetto, M. (2006). Believable environments: Generating interactive storytelling in vast location-based pervasive games. In *Proceedings of the ACM SIGCHI International Conference on Advances in Computer Entertainment Technology*, Hollywood, CA.

Guthrie, C. (2010). Towards greater learner control: Web supported project-based learning. *Journal of Information Systems Education, 21*(1), 121–130.

Guy, R. (Ed.). (2009). *The evolution of mobile teaching and learning*. Santa Rosa, CA: Informing Science Press.

Gwee, S., Chee, Y. S., & Tan, E. M. (2010). Assessment of student outcomes of mobile game-base learning. In *Proceedings of the 18th International Conference on Computers in Education*, Putrajaya, Malaysia (pp. 412-416).

Hameed, K., & Shah, H. (2009, February 26-28). *Mobile learning in higher education: Adoption and discussion criteria*. Paper presented at the IADIS International Conference on Mobile Learning, Barcelona, Spain.

Hård, Y. (2002). *Use and Adaptation of Written Language to the Conditions of Computer-Mediated Communication*. Retrieved from http://www.ling.gu.se/~ylvah/dokument/eng_diss_abstract.pdf

Hart, C. (1999). *Doing a literature review: Releasing the social science research imagination*. London, UK: Sage.

Hartnell-Young, E. (2007). *Making the connections: theory and practice of mobile learning in schools*. Paper presented at the mLearn Conference, Melbourne, Australia.

Hartnell-Young, E., & Heym, N. (2008). *How mobile phones help learning in secondary schools*. Nottingham, UK: Learning Sciences Research Institute.

Hazra, T. K. (2002). Building enterprise portals: Principles to practice. In. *Proceedings of ICSE, 02*, 623–633.

Head, G., & Dakers, J. (2005). Verillon's Trio and Wenger's Community: Learning in technology education. *International Journal of Technology and Design Education, 15*, 33–46. doi:10.1007/s10798-004-6194-3

Heeks, R. (2008). ICT4D 2.0: The next phase of applying ICT for international development. *Computer, 41*(6), 26–33. doi:10.1109/MC.2008.192

Herman, T., & Banister, S. (2007). Face-to-Face versus Online Coursework: A Comparison of Learning Outcomes and Costs. *Contemporary Issues in Technology & Teacher Education, 7*(4), 318–326.

Herrington, A., & Herrington, J. (2007). Authentic mobile learning in higher education. In *Proceedings of the AARE International Educational Research Conference*, Fremantle, Australia (pp. 1-9).

Herrington, J., Herrington, A., Mantei, J., Olney, I. W., & Ferry, B. (2009). *New technologies, new pedagogies: Mobile learning in higher education.* Retrieved from http://ro.uow.edu.au/edupapers/91

Herrington, A., Herrington, J., & Mantei, J. (2009). Design principles for mobile learning. In Herrington, J., Herrington, A., Mantei, J., Olney, I., & Ferry, B. (Eds.), *New technologies, new pedagogies: Mobile learning in higher education* (pp. 129–138). New South Wales, Australia: University of Wollongong.

Herrington, J., Herrington, A., Mantei, J., Olney, I., & Ferry, B. (Eds.). (2009). *New technologies, new pedagogies: Mobile learning in higher education.* Wollongong, NSW, Australia: University of Wollongong.

Herrington, J., & Oliver, R. (2000). An instructional design framework for authentic learning environments. *Educational Technology Research and Development, 48*(3), 23–48. doi:10.1007/BF02319856

Higginbotham, D. (2006). An assessment of undergraduate student's mobility skills and needs in curriculum delivery. In *Proceedings of the 29ᵗʰ Annual Conference of the AECT*, Dallas, TX (pp. 98-115).

Hilmy, A. H., & Loke, S. K. (2009). *Design document for Statecraft X.* Unpublished manuscript, Singapore.

Hine, N., Rentoul, R., & Spechty, M. (2004). Collaboration and roles in remote field trips. In Attewell, J., & Saville-Smith, C. (Eds.), *Learning with mobile devices: A book of papers* (pp. 69–72). London, UK: Learning and Skills Development Agency.

Hirsjärvi, S., & Hurme, H. (2000). *Tutkimushaastattelu: Teemahaastattelun teoria ja käytäntö.* Helsinki, Finland: Yliopistopaino.

Hirsjärvi, S., Remes, P., & Sajavaara, P. (2007). *Tutki ja kirjoita.* Helsinki, Finland: Kustannusosakeyhtiö Tammi.

Hoadley, C. M. (2004). Methodological alignment in design-based research. *Educational Psychologist, 39*(4), 203–212. doi:10.1207/s15326985ep3904_2

Hoggan, E., Anwar, S., & Brewster, S. (2007). Mobile multi-actuator tactile displays. In I. Oakley & S. Brewster (Eds.), *Proceedings of the Second International Conference on Haptic and Audio Interaction Design* (LNCS 4813, pp. 22-33).

Holmes, B., & Gardner, J. (2006). *e-Learning: Concepts and practice* (pp. 35-42). London, UK: Sage.

Holzinger, A., Nischelwitzer, A., & Meisenberger, M. (2005) Mobile phones as a challenge for mlearning. In *Proceedings of the IEEE International Conference on Pervasive Computing and Communications* (pp. 307-311).

Höysniemi, J., Hämäläinen, P., & Turkki, L. (2004). Wizard of Oz prototyping of computer vision based action games for children. In *Proceedings of the International Conference on Interaction Design and Children* (pp. 27-34).

Höysniemi, J. (2005). Käytettävyystestaus lasten kanssa. In Ovaska, S., Aula, A., & Majaranta, P. (Eds.), *Käytettävyystutkimuksen menetelmät* (pp. 259–282). Tampere, Finland: Tampere University Press.

Hsu, H., Wang, S., & Comac, L. (2008). Using audioblogs to assist English-language learning: an investigation into student perception. *Computer Assisted Language Learning, 21*(2), 181–198. doi:10.1080/09588220801943775

Huang, J.-H., Lin, Y.-R., & Chuang, S.-T. (2007). Elucidating user behavior of mobile learning: A perspective of the extended technology acceptance model. *The Electronic Library, 25*(5), 586–599. doi:10.1108/02640470710829569

Huang, J., Lin, Y., & Chuang, S. (2007). Elucidating user behavior of mobile learning: A perspective of the extended technology acceptance model. *The Electronic Library, 25*(5), 586–599. doi:10.1108/02640470710829569

Huizenga, J., Admiraal, W., Akkerman, S., & Dam, G. (2009). Mobile game-based learning in secondary education: Engagement, motivation and learning in a mobile city game. *Journal of Computer Assisted Learning, 25*(4), 332–344. doi:10.1111/j.1365-2729.2009.00316.x

Hunton, J., & Rose, J. M. (2005). Cellular telephones and driving performance: The effects of attentional demands on motor vehicle crash risks. *Risk Analysis, 25*, 855–866. doi:10.1111/j.1539-6924.2005.00637.x

Impagliazzo, J., Cassel, L. N., & Knox, D. L. (2002). Using Citidel as a portal for CS education. *Journal of Computing Sciences in Colleges, 17*(6), 161–163.

International Organization for Standardization. (2010). *ISO 9241-210:2010: Ergonomics of human-system interaction – Part 210: Human-centred design for interactive systems*. Retrieved from http://www.iso.org/iso/catalogue_detail.htm?csnumber=52075

ITU. (2009). *Measuring the Information Society: ICT Development Index. 2009 edition*. Retrieved from http://www.itu.int/ITU-D/ict/publications/idi/2009/index.html

Jackson, N. J. (2008). *The life-wide curriculum concept: A means of developing a more complete educational experience?* Retrieved from http://lifewidecurriculum.pbwiki.com/A-more-complete-education

Järvälä, S., Laru, J., & Näykki, P. (2007). How people collaborate to learn in different contexts scaffolded by the mobile tools. In *Proceedings of the Beyond Mobile Learning Workshop*.

Järvenpää, E., & Kosonen, K. (1999). *Johdatus tutkimusmenetelmiin ja tutkimuksen tekemiseen*. Espoo, Finland: Helsinki University of Technology.

Järvinen, P. (2004). *On research methods*. Tampere, Finland: Juvenes-Print.

Jensen, J., & Skov, M. (2005). A review of research methods in children's technology design. In *Proceedings of the 2005 Conference on Interaction Design and Children* (pp. 80-87).

Jeong, S., & Fishbein, M. (2007). Predictors of multitasking with media: Media factors and audience factors. *Media Psychology, 10*, 364–384. doi:10.1080/15213260701532948

JISC. (2005). *Innovative practice with e-learning: A good practice guide to embedding mobile and wireless technologies into everyday practice*. Bristol, UK: Joint Information Services Committee.

JISC. (2009). *Effective Practice in a Digital Age: A guide to technology-enhanced learning and teaching*. Retrieved from http://www.jisc.ac.uk/publications/programmerelated/2009/effectivepracticedigitalage.aspx

JISC. (2009). *Higher education in a Web 2.0 world*. Retrieved from http://www.jisc.ac.uk/publications/documents/heweb2.aspx

JISC. (2009). *Learning literacies in a digital age*. Retrieved from http://www.jisc.ac.uk/media/documents/publications/bpllidav1.pdf

Johnson, R. B., Onwuegbuzie, A. J., & Turner, L. A. (2007). Towards a definition of mixed methods research. *Journal of Mixed Methods Research, 1*, 112. doi:10.1177/1558689806298224doi:10.1177/1558689806298224

Johnson, D. W., & Johnson, R. T. (1985). The internal dynamics of cooperative learning groups. In Slavin, R., Sharan, S., Kagan, S., Hertz-Lazarowitz, R., Webb, C., & Schmuck, R. (Eds.), *Learning to cooperate, cooperating to learn* (pp. 103–124). New York, NY: Plenum.

Johnson, D. W., & Johnson, R. T. (1991). *Learning together and alone: Cooperative, competitive, and individualistic* (3rd ed.). Upper Saddle River, NJ: Prentice Hall.

Johnson, D. W., & Johnson, R. T. (2009). An educational psychology success story: Social interdependence theory and cooperative learning. *Educational Researcher, 38*, 365–379. doi:10.3102/0013189X09339057

Johnson, L., Levine, A., Smith, R., & Stone, S. (2011). *The 2011 Horizon Report*. Austin, TX: The New Media Consortium.

Johnson, R. L., Penny, J., Gordon, B., Shumate, S. R., & Fisher, S. P. (2005). Resolving score differences in the rating of writing samples: Does discussion improve the accuracy of scores? *Language Assessment Quarterly, 2*(2), 117–146. doi:10.1207/s15434311laq0202_2

Johnson, S. D., Aragon, S. R., Shaik, N., & Palma-Rivas, N. (2000). Comparative analysis of learner satisfaction and learning outcomes in online and face-to-face learning environments. *Journal of Interactive Learning Research, 11*, 29–49.

Jones, A., Issroff, K., Scanlon, E., Clough, G., & McAndrew, P. (2006, July 14-16). Using mobile devices for learning in informal settings: Is it motivating? In *Proceedings of the IADIS International Conference on Mobile Learning*, Dublin, Ireland (pp. 251-255).

Jones, A., Issroff, K., Scanlon, E., Clough, G., & McAndrew, P. (2006, July 14-16). Using mobile devices for learnings in Informal Settings: is it Motivating? In *Proceedings of IADIS International Conference on Mobile Learning*, Dublin, Ireland.

Jones, A., Issroff, K., & Scanlon, E. (2007). Affective factors in learning with mobile devices. In Sharples, M. (Ed.), *Big issues in mobile learning* (pp. 17–22). Nottingham, UK: University of Nottingham.

Jones, C. R., Ramanau, R., Cross, S., & Healing, G. (2010). Net generation or Digital Natives: Is there a distinct new generation entering university? *Computers & Education, 54*(3), 722–732. doi:10.1016/j.compedu.2009.09.022

Jonker, V., & Wijers, M. (2008, June 23-28). Thinklets for mathematics education, re-using computer games characteristics in educational software. In *Proceedings of the 8th International Conference for the Learning Sciences*, Utrecht, The Netherlands (pp. 406-413).

Jordan, B., & Henderson, A. (1995). Interaction analysis: Foundations and practice. *Journal of the Learning Sciences, 4*(1), 39–103. doi:10.1207/s15327809jls0401_2

Kafai, Y. B. (1994). *Minds in play: Computer design as a context for children's learning*. Mahwah, NJ: Lawrence Erlbaum.

Kahneman, D. (1973). *Attention and effort*. Upper Saddle River, NJ: Prentice Hall.

Kalloo, V., & Mohan, P. (2011, July 6-8). Correlation between student performance and use of an mLearning application for high school mathematics. In *Proceedings of the Eleventh IEEE International Conference on Advanced Learning Technologies*, Athens, GA.

Kane, S. K., Wobbrock, J. O., & Smith, I. E. (2008). Getting off the treadmill: Evaluating walking user interfaces for mobile devices in public spaces. In *Proceedings of the 10th International Conference on Human Computer Interaction with Mobile Devices and Services* (pp. 109-118).

Kaptelinin, V., & Nardi, B. (2006). *Acting with technology: Activity theory and interaction design*. Cambridge, MA: MIT Press.

Kaptelinin, V., & Nardi, B. A. (2006). *Acting with technology: Activity theory and interaction design*. Cambridge, MA: MIT Press.

Karpova, E., Correia, A.-P., & Baran, E. (2009). Learn to use and use to learn: Technology in virtual collaboration experience. *The Internet and Higher Education, 12*, 45–52. doi:10.1016/j.iheduc.2008.10.006

Kato, P. M., Cole, S. W., Bradlyn, A. S., & Pollock, B. H. (2008). A video game improves behavioral outcomes in adolescents and young adults with cancer: A randomized trial. *Pediatrics, 122*(2), 305–317. doi:10.1542/peds.2007-3134

Katz, E., Blumler, J. G., & Gurevitch, M. (1973). Uses and gratifications research. *Public Opinion Quarterly, 37*(4), 509–523. doi:10.1086/268109

Katz, J. E., & Aakhus, M. (2002). *Perpetual Contact: Mobile Communication, Private Talk, Public Performance*. Cambridge, UK: Cambridge University Press. doi:10.1017/CBO9780511489471

Kebritchi, M., & Hirumi, A. (2008). Examining the pedagogical foundations of modern educational computer games. *Computers & Education, 5*(4), 1729–1743. doi:10.1016/j.compedu.2008.05.004

Keegan, D. (2005). The incorporation of mobile learning into mainstream education and training. In *Proceedings of mLearn 2005: 4th World Conference on Mobile Learning*.

Kennedy, G. E., Judd, T. S., Churchward, A., Gray, K., & Krause, K.-L. (2008). First Year Students' Experiences with Technology: Are they really Digital Natives? *Australasian Journal of Educational Technology, 24*(1), 108–122.

Kenyon, S. (2008). Internet use and time use: The importance of multitasking. *Time & Society, 17*, 283–318. doi:10.1177/0961463X08093426

Kim, P. H. (2009). Action research approach on mobile learning design for the underserved. *Educational Technology Research and Development, 57,* 415–435. doi:10.1007/s11423-008-9109-2

Kirschner, P. A., & Karpinski, A. C. (2010). Facebook® and academic performance. *Computers in Human Behavior, 26*(6), 1237–1245. doi:10.1016/j.chb.2010.03.024

Kirschner, P., Sweller, J., & Clark, R. (2006). Why minimal guidance during instruction does not work: An analysis of the failure of constructivist, discovery, problem-based, experiential, and inquiry-based teaching. *Educational Psychologist, 4*(2), 75–86. doi:10.1207/s15326985ep4102_1

Kismihók, G. (2007). *Mobile Learning in Higher Education: The Corvinus case.* Paper presented at the Online Educa Berlin 2007 Conference, Berlin, Germany.

Kismihók, G., & Vas, R. (2009). Mobile Learning Research at the Corvinus University of Budapest. In A. Szűcs (Ed.), *Book of Abstracts: LOGOS Conference on Strengthening the Integration of ICT Research Effort.* Budapest, Hungary: EDEN.

Kjeldskov, J., & Graham, C. (2003). A review of mobile HCI research methods. In *Proceedings of Mobile HCI 2003: 5th International Symposium on Mobile Human-Computer Interaction.*

Klein, H., & Myers, M. (1999). A set of principles for conducting and evaluating interpretive field studies in information systems. *Management Information Systems Quarterly, 23*(1), 67–93. doi:10.2307/249410

Klopfer, E., Perry, J., Squire, K., & Jan, M.-F. (2005). Collaborative learning through augmented reality role playing. In *Proceedings of Computer Supported Collaborative Learning,* Taipei, Taiwan (pp. 316-320).

Klopfer, E., & Squire, K. (2007). Environmental detectives - the development of an augmented reality platform for environmental simulations. *Educational Technology Research and Development, 56*(2), 203–228. doi:10.1007/s11423-007-9037-6

Kneebone, R., & Brenton, H. (2005). Training perioperative specialist practitioners. In Kukulska-Hulme, A., & Traxler, J. (Eds.), *Mobile learning: A handbook for educators and trainers.* London, UK: Routledge.

Koh, K., & Luke, A. (2009). Authentic and conventional assessment in Singapore schools: An empirical study of teacher assignments and student work. *Assessment in Education, 16*(3), 291–318. doi:10.1080/09695940903319703

Kolb, D. A. (1984). *Experiential learning: Experience as the source of learning and development.* Upper Saddle River, NJ: Prentice Hall.

Kozma, R. B. (2003). Technology and Classroom Practices: An International Study. *Journal of Research on Technology in Education, 36*(1), 1–14.

Krämer, B. J. (2007). *Data Analysis Report on the Impact of Technology on Learning in Open Universities and Distance Education.* Retrieved November 23, 2008, from http://deposit.fernuni-hagen.de/62/

Kratz, S., & Rohs, M. (2009). HoverFlow: Expanding the design space of around-device interaction. In *Proceedings of the 11th International Conference on Human-Computer Interaction with Mobile Devices and Services* (p. 4).

Kress, G., & Pachler, N. (2007). Thinking about the 'm' in m-learning. In Pachler, N. (Ed.), *Mobile learning: towards a research agenda.* London, UK: WLE Centre, IoE.

Kristoffersen, S., & Ljundberg, F. (1999). "Making place" to make IT work: Empirical explorations of HCI for mobile CSCW. In *Proceedings of the International ACM SIGGROUP Conference on Supporting Group Work* (pp. 276-285).

Kukulska-Hulme, A., & Pettit, J. (2006, October 23-25). Practitioners as innovators: emergent practice in personal mobile teaching, learning, work and leisure. In *Proceedings of Mlearn '06: Mobile Learning Conference,* Banff, AB, Canada.

Kukulska-Hulme, A., & Traxler, J. (2005, April). Making the case for personalization through mobile learning. In *Proceedings of CAL,* Bristol, UK.

Kukulska-Hulme, A., Sharples, M., Milrad, M., Arnedillo-Sánchez, I., & Vavoula, G. (2009). Innovation in mobile learning: A European perspective. *International Journal of Mobile and Blended Learning, 1*(1), 13–35. doi:10.4018/jmbl.2009010102doi:10.4018/jmbl.2009010102

Kukulska-Hulme, A. (2005). Introduction. In Kukulska-Hulme, A., & Traxler, J. (Eds.), *Mobile learning: A handbook for educators and trainers* (1st ed., pp. 1–6). London, UK: Routledge.

Kukulska-Hulme, A., & Pettit, J. (2008). Semi-formal learning communities for professional development in mobile learning. *Journal of Computing in Higher Education, 20*(2), 35–47. doi:10.1007/s12528-008-9006-z

Kukulska-Hulme, A., & Pettit, J. (2009). Practitioners as innovators: Emergent practice in personal mobile teaching, learning, work and leisure. In Ally, M. (Ed.), *Mobile Learning: transforming the delivery of education and training* (pp. 135–155). Athabasca, AB, Canada: Athabasca University Press.

Kukulska-Hulme, A., Sharples, M., & Milrad, M., Arnedillo- Sánchez, I., & Vavoula, G. (2009). Innovation in mobile learning: A European perspective. *International Journal of Mobile and Blended Learning, 1*(1), 13–35. doi:10.4018/jmbl.2009010102

Kukulska-Hulme, A., Sharples, M., Milrad, M., Arnedillo-Sánchez, I., & Vavoula, G. (2009). Innovation in mobile learning: An European perspective. *International Journal of Mobile and Blended Learning, 1*(1), 12–35.

Kukulska-Hulme, A., & Traxler, J. (2005). *Mobile learning: A handbook for educators and trainers.* Boca Raton, FL: Taylor & Francis.

Kukulska-Hulme, A., & Traxler, J. (2005). Mobile teaching and learning. In Kukulska-Hulme, A., & Traxler, J. (Eds.), *Mobile Learning: A handbook for educators and trainers* (pp. 25–44). London, UK: Routledge.

Kukulska-Hulme, A., Traxler, J., & Pettit, J. (2007). Designed and user-generated activity in the mobile age. *Journal of Learning Design, 2*(1), 52–65.

Kumar, R. (2011). *Research methodology.* London, UK: Sage.

Kurti, A., Spikol, D., & Milrad, M. (2008). Bridging outdoors and indoors educational activities in schools with the support of mobile and positioning technologies. *International Journal of Mobile Learning and Organization, 2*(2).

Kuula, T., Vihavainen, S., & Seisto, A. (2009, October). *Playful learning with hybrid school books.* Poster presented at the MindTrek Conference, Tampere, Finland.

Kuutti, W. (2003). *Käytettävyys, suunnittelu ja arviointi.* Helsinki, Finland: Talentum Media Oy.

Laister, J., & Koubek, A. (2001, September 26-28). 3rd generation learning platforms requirements and motivation for collaborative learning. In *Proceedings of the 4th International Workshop on Interactive Computer Aided Learning.*

Lally, V., Sharples, M., Bertram, N., Masters, S., Norton, B., & Tracy, F. (2010). *Researching the ethical dimensions of mobile, ubiquitous, and immersive technology enhanced learning (MUITEL) in informal settings: A thematic review and dialogue.* London, UK: University of Glasgow.

Lambert, N., & McCombs, B. (2000). Introduction: Learner-centered schools and classrooms as a direction for school reform. In Lambert, N., & McCombs, B. (Eds.), *How students learn* (pp. 1–15). Washington, DC: American Psychological Association.

Land, R., Cousin, G., Meyer, J., & Davies, P. (2005). Threshold concepts and troublesome knowledge (3)*: Implications for course design and evaluation. In Rust, C. (Ed.), *Improving student learning diversity and inclusivity* (pp. 53–64). Oxford, UK: Oxford Centre for Staff and Learning Development.

Lane, C. (2006). *UW podcasting: Evaluation of year one.* Seattle, WA: University of Washington. Retrieved from http://www.washington.edu/lst/research_development/papers/2006/podcasting_year1.pdf

Langelier, L. (2005). *Working, learning and collaborating in a network: Guide to the implementation and leadership of intentional communities of practice.* Quebec City, QC, Canada: CEFIRO (Recherche et Études de cas collection).

Laurillard, D. (2007). Pedagogical forms of mobile learning: Framing research questions. In N. Pachler (Ed.), *Mobile learning: Towards a research agenda* (Vol. 1, pp. 33–54). London, UK: WLE Centre, Institute of Education.

Laurillard, D. (2002). *Rethinking university teaching: A framework for the effective use of learning technologies* (2nd ed.). London, UK: Routledge. doi:10.4324/9780203304846

Lave, J. (1988). *Cognition in practice: Mind, mathematics, and culture in everyday life*. Cambridge, UK: Cambridge University Press. doi:10.1017/CBO9780511609268

Lave, J., & Wenger, E. (1991). *Situated Learning: Legitimate peripheral participation*. Cambridge, UK: Cambridge University Press.

Learn Out Loud. (2005). *Dead time learning*. Retrieved from http://www.learnoutloud.com/content/blog/archives/2005/09/dead_time_learn.html

Lee, A. S., & Baskerville, R. L. (2003). Generalizing generalizability in information systems research. *Information Systems Research, 14*(3), 221–243. doi:10.1287/isre.14.3.221.16560

Lee, M., & Chan, A. (2007). Pervasive, lifestyle-integrated mobile learning for distance learners: An analysis and unexpected results from a podcasting study. *Journal of Open and Distance Learning, 22*(3), 201–218.

Lehtinen, E. (2003). Computer supported collaborative learning: An approach to powerful learning environments. In De Corte, E., Verschaffel, L., Entwistle, N., & van Merriëboer, J. (Eds.), *Basic components and dimensions of powerful learning environments*. New York, NY: Pergamon Press.

Leichtenstern, K., & André, E. (2009). Studying multi-user settings for pervasive games. In *Proceedings of the 11th International Conference on Human-Computer Interaction with Mobile Devices and Services* (p. 25).

Leino, M., Turunen, H., Ahonen, M., & Levonen, J. (2002). Mobiililaitteet oppimisen ja opetuksen tukena. In P. Seppälä (Ed.), *Mobiili opiskelu: Joustavasti liikkeessä* (pp. 47-58). Helsinki, Finland: Helsingin yliopisto, Opetusteknologiakeskus.

Liebenberg, J. (2008, October 7-10). Mobile mathematics – lessons learnt. In *Proceedings of the mLearn Conference: The Bridge From Text To Context*, Shropshire, UK (p. 346).

Lien, M., Ruthruff, E., & Johnston, J. C. (2006). Attentional limitations in doing two tasks at once. *Current Directions in Psychological Science, 15*, 89–93. doi:10.1111/j.0963-7214.2006.00413.x

Lim, M. Y., & Aylett, R. (2007). Narrative construction in a mobile tour guide. In M. Cavazza & S. Donikian (Eds.), *Proceedings of the 4th International Conference on Virtual Storytelling: Using Virtual Reality Technologies for Storytelling*, Saint-Malo, France (LNCS 4871, pp. 51-62).

Lin, Y. (2007, November 23-25). Integrating scenarios of video games into classroom instruction. In *Proceedings of the First IEEE International Symposium on Information Technologies and Applications in Education*, Kunming, China (pp. 593-596).

Lindstrom, L. (1953). *Cargo cult: Strange stories of desire from Melanesia and beyond*. Honolulu, HI: University of Hawaii Press.

Lipshitz, A. R., & Parsons, S. P. (Eds.). (2008). *E-learning: 21st century issues and challenges*. New York, NY: Nova Science.

Litchfield, A., Dyson, L. E., Lawrence, E., & Zmijewska, A. (2007). Directions for m-learning research to enhance active learning. In *Proceedings of ASCILITE 2007*, Singapore (pp. 587-596).

Litchfield, A., Dyson, L. E., Wright, M., Pradhan, S., & Courtille, B. (2010, July 5-7). Student produced vodcasts as active meta-cognitive learning. In *Proceedings of the 10th IEEE International Conference on Advanced Learning Technologies*, Sousse, Tunisia (pp. 560-564).

Llewellyn-Jones, C. (2007). The value of location-based games for learning [Electronic Version]. In *Proceedings of the IAS Workshop Three: What do Mobile Technologies do Best?* Retrieved from http://www.bristol.ac.uk/education/research/networks/mobile/events/iaswshop3notes/gamesforlearning.pdf

Locomatrix. (2010). *Locomatrix homepage*. Retrieved from http://locomatrix.com

Lonsdale, P., Barber, C., Sharples, M., Byrne, W., Arvanitis, T., Brundell, P., et al. (2004). Context awareness for mobilearn: Creating an engaging learning experience in an art museum. In *Proceedings of the World Conference on Mobile Learning*, Rome, Italy.

Lorist, M. M., Kernell, D., Meijman, T. F., & Zijdewind, I. (2002). Motor fatigue and cognitive task performance in humans. *The Journal of Physiology*, 313–319. doi:10.1113/jphysiol.2002.027938

Lucas, K., & Sherry, J. L. (2004). Sex differences in video game play: A communication-based explanation. *Communication Research*, *31*(5), 499–523. doi:10.1177/0093650204267930

Luckin, R., Clark, W., Garnett, F., Whitworth, A., Akass, J., & Cook, J. (2010). Learner-generated contexts: A framework to support the effective use of technology for learning. In Lee, M., & McLoughlin, C. (Eds.), *Web 2.0-based e-learning: Applying social informatics for tertiary teaching* (pp. 70–84). Hershey, PA: IGI Global. doi:10.4018/978-1-60566-294-7.ch004

Luckin, R., du Boulay, B., Smith, H., Underwood, J., Fitzpatrick, G., & Holmberg, J. (2005). Using mobile technology to create flexible learning contexts. *Journal of Interactive Media in Education*, (22): 1–21.

Luminiţa, Ş. (2010). Internet - a new way of training: Designing an e-learning platforms. *Young Economists Journal / Revista Tinerilor Economisti, 8*(14), 151-158.

Lumsden, J., Kondratova, I., & Langton, N. (2006). Bringing a construction site into the lab: A context-relevant lab based evaluation of a multimodal mobile application. In *Proceedings of the 1st International Workshop on Multimodal and Pervasive Services* (pp. 62-68).

Lund, A. (2003). *The teacher as interface. Teachers of EFL in ICT-rich environments: Beliefs, practices, appropriation*. Unpublished doctoral dissertation, University of Oslo, Norway.

Luria, R., & Meiran, N. (2005). Increased control demand results in serial processing. Evidence from dual-task performance. *Psychological Science*, *16*, 833–840. doi:10.1111/j.1467-9280.2005.01622.x

Lyons, K., Gandy, M., & Starner, T. (2000). Guided by voices: An audio augmented reality system. In *Proceedings of the International Conference on Auditory Display*, Atlanta, GA (pp. 57-62).

Maag, M. (2006). iPod, uPod? An emerging mobile learning tool in nursing education and students' satisfaction. In *Proceedings of the 23rd Annual Conference of the Australasian Society for Computers in Learning in Tertiary Education Who's Learning? Whose Technology?* Sydney, Australia (pp. 483-492).

MacCallum, K., & Kinshuk, K. (2006). *Mobile technology in facilitating learning goals.* Paper presented at the mLearn Conference, Banff, AB, Canada.

Malan, D. J. (2007). Podcasting computer science E-1. In *Proceedings of the 38th SIGCSE Technical Symposium on Computer Science Education*, Covington, KY (pp. 389-393).

Malone, T. W. (1980). What makes things fun to learn? Heuristics for designing instructional computer games. In *Proceedings of the 3rd ACM SIGSMALL Symposium and the First SIGPC Symposium on Small Systems* (pp.162-169).

Maniar, N. (2007). M-learning to teach university students. In *Proceedings of the World Conference on Educational Multimedia, Hypermedia and Telecommunications* (pp. 881-887).

Marković, F., Petrovic, O., Kitti, C., & Edegger, B. (2007). Pervasive learning games: A comparative study. *New Review of Hypermedia and Multimedia*, *13*(2), 93–116. doi:10.1080/13614560701712873

Marriott, M. (2005, July 4). Use this phone to find a date. Or see video. Or even talk. *New York Times*.

Marschalek, I., Unterfrauner, E., & Fabian, C. M. (2009). Mobile learning activities to reach out for young marginalised people. In Metcalf, D., Hamilton, A., & Graffeo, C. (Eds.), *Proceedings of mLearn 2009* (p. 222). Orlando, FL: University of Central Florida.

Marsh, J. (2010). New literacies, old identities: Young girls' experiences of digital literacy at home and school. In C. Jackson, C. Paechter, & E. Renold (Eds.), *Girls and education 3-16: Continuing concerns, new agendas* (pp. 197-209). New York, NY: Open University Press.

Marshall, J. (2009). I seek the nerves under your skin. In *Proceedings of the Seventh ACM Conference on Creativity and Cognition*, Berkeley, CA (pp. 477-478).

Marshall, P., Fleck, R., & Harris, A. Rick, J., Hornecker, E., Rogers, Y. et al. (2009). Fighting for control: Children's embodied interactions when using physical and digital representations. In *Proceedings of the 27ᵗʰ International Conference on Human Factors in Computing Systems: Enhancing Reality* (pp. 2149-2152).

Martin, E., & Webb, D. (2001). Is e-learning good learning? In Brook, B., & Gilding, A. (Eds.), *The ethics and equity of e-learning in higher education* (pp. 49–60). Melbourne, VIC, Australia: Victoria University.

Mayes, T., & de Freitas, S. (2004). *Stage 2: Review of e-learning theories, frameworks and models.* Retrieved from http://www.jisc.ac.uk/uploaded_documents/Stage%20 2%20Learning%20Models%20(Version%201).pdf

Mayo, E. (1933). *The human problems of an industrial civilization.* New York, NY: Macmillan.

McConatha, D., Praul, M., & Lynch, M. J. (2008). Mobile learning in higher education: An empirical assessment of a new educational tool. *Educational Technology, 7*(3), 15–21.

McConnell, D., & Sharples, M. (1983). Distance teaching by CYCLOPS: An educational evaluation of the Open University's telewriting system. *British Journal of Educational Technology, 14*(2), 109–126. doi:10.1111/j.1467-8535.1983.tb00454.x

McDonough, T. F. (1994). Situationist space. October, *67*, 59-77.

McFarlane, A., Roche, N., & Triggs, P. (2007). *Mobile learning: Research findings.* Retrieved from http://dera.ioe.ac.uk/1470/

McGarr, O. (2009). A review of podcasting in higher education. *Australian Journal of Educational Technology, 25*(3), 309–321.

McKinney, D., Dyck, J. L., & Luber, E. S. (2009). iTunes University and the classroom: Can podcasts replace professors? *Computers & Education, 52*(3), 617–623. doi:10.1016/j.compedu.2008.11.004

McLoughlin, C., & Lee, M. (2007). Social software and participatory learning: Pedagogical choices with technology affordances in the Web 2.0 era. In *Proceedings of the ASCILITE ICT Conference: Providing Choices for Learners and Learning* (pp. 664-675).

McLoughlin, C., & Lee, M. (2008b). Mapping the digital terrain: New media and social software as catalysts for pedagogical change. In *Proceedings of the ASCILITE Conference*, Melbourne, Australia (pp. 641-652).

McLoughlin, C., & Lee, M. (2008a). Future learning landscapes: Transforming pedagogy through social software. *Innovate: Journal of Online Education, 4*(5), 7.

McLoughlin, C., & Lee, M. (2010). Pedagogy 2.0: Critical challenges and responses to Web 2.0 and social software in tertiary teaching. In Lee, M., & McLoughlin, C. (Eds.), *Web 2.0-based e-learning: Applying social informatics for tertiary teaching* (pp. 46–69). Hershey, PA: IGI Global.

McLuhan, M. (1962). *The Gutenberg galaxy: The making of typographic man.* London, UK: Routledge & Kegan Paul.

McLuhan, M., & Fiore, Q. (1967). *The medium is the massage.* London, UK: Penguin Books.

Meng, P. (2005). *Podcasting & vodcasting: A white paper. Definitions, discussions & implications.* Columbia, MO: University of Missouri.

Merriam, S. B. (1998). *Qualitative research and case study application in education.* San Francisco, CA: Jossey-Bass.

Merriam, S. B. (2002). Assessing and evaluating qualitative research. In Merriam, S. (Ed.), *Qualitative research in practice: Examples for discussion and analysis.* San Francisco, CA: Jossey-Bass.

Merriam, S. B. (2002). Introduction to qualitative research. In Merriam, S. (Ed.), *Qualitative research in practice: Examples for discussion and analysis.* San Francisco, CA: Jossey-Bass.

Metcalf, D. S. (2006). *mLearning: Mobile learning and performance in the palm of your hand.* Amherst, MA: HRD Press.

Metcalf, S. J., & Tinker, R. F. (2004). Probeware and handhelds in elementary and middle school science. *Journal of Science Education and Technology, 13*(1), 43–49. doi:10.1023/B:JOST.0000019637.22473.02

Mevarech, Z. R., & Kramarski, B. (2003). The effects of metacognitive training versus worked-out examples on students' mathematical reasoning. *The British Journal of Educational Psychology, 73*, 449–471. doi:10.1348/000709903322591181

Middleton, A. (2009). Beyond podcasting: Creative approaches to designing educational audio. *Journal of Research in Learning Technology, 17*(2), 143–155. doi:10.1080/09687760903033082

Miles, M. B., & Huberman, A. M. (1984). *Qualitative data analysis*. Newbury Park, CA: Sage.

Miller, L., Chaika, M., & Groppe, L. (1996). Girls' preferences in software design: Insights from a focus group. *Technology and Electronic Journal the 21ˢᵗ Century, 4*(2), 1-6.

Miller, C. (2008). *Digital storytelling: A creator's guide to interactive entertainment*. Berkeley, CA: New Riders.

Milrad, M. (2006). How should learning activities using mobile technologies be designed to support innovative educational practices? In Sharples, M. (Ed.), *Big issues in mobile learning*. Nottingham, UK: Kaleidoscope Network of Excellence Mobile Learning Initiative.

Minocha, S., & Booth, N. M. (2008). Podcasting and learning experience: User-centred requirements gathering. In *Proceedings of the mLearn Conference on the Bridge from Text to Context*, Wolverhampton, UK.

MobiThinking. (2011). *Global mobile statistics: All quality mobile marketing research, mobile Web stats, subscribers, ad revenue, usage, trends*. Retrieved from http://mobithinking.com/mobile-marketing-tools/latest-mobile-stats

MoMath. (2010). *Mobile learning for mathematics: Nokia project in South Africa*. Retrieved from http://www.symbiantweet.com/mobile-learning-for-mathematics-in-south-africa

Morganteen, J. (2006). *Casting around*. Museums Journal.

Morrison, A., Oulasvirta, A., Peltonen, P., Lemmelä, S., Jacucci, G., Reitmayr, G., et al. (2009). Like bees around the hive: A comparative study of a mobile augmented reality map. In *Proceedings of the International Conference on Human Factors in Computing Systems: Enhancing Reality* (pp. 1889-1898).

Motiwalla, L. F. (2007). Mobile learning: A framework and evaluation. *Journal of Computer Assisted Learning, 49*, 581–596.

Mwanza, D., & Engeström, Y. (2003, November 7-11). Pedagogical adeptness in the design of e-learning environments: Experiences from the Lab@Future project. In *Proceedings of the World Conference on E-Learning in Corporate, Government, Healthcare, and Higher Education*, Phoenix, AZ.

My Sports Pulse. (2007). *My sports pulse game mechanics*. Retrieved from http://www.mysportspulse.com/index.php?option=com_content&task=view&id=80&Itemid=56

Naismith, L., & Corlett, D. (2006, October 22-25). Reflections on success: A retrospective of the mLearn conference series 2002-2005. In *Proceedings of the mLearn Conference*, Banff, AB, Canada.

Naismith, L., Sharples, M., & Ting, J. (2005). Evaluation of CAERUS: A context aware mobile guide. In *Proceedings of the 4th World Conference on mLearning*, Cape Town, South Africa.

Naismith, L., Lonsdale, P., Vavoula, G., & Sharples, M. (2004). *Literature review in mobile technologies and learning*. London, UK: NESTA Futurelab Series.

Najimi, A., & Lee, J. (2009). Why and how mobile learning can make a difference in the K-16 classroom? In *Proceedings of the Society for Information Technology & Teacher Education International Conference* (pp. 2903-2910).

Nataatmadja, I., & Dyson, L. E. (2008). The role of podcasts in students' learning. *International Journal of Interactive Mobile Technologies, 2*(3), 17–21.

Nathan, P., & Chan, A. (2007). Engaging undergraduates with podcasting in a business project. In *Proceedings of the ASCILITE ICT Conference: Providing Choices for Learners and Learning*.

Navon, D., & Gopher, D. (1979). On the economy of the human information processing system. *Psychological Review, 86*, 214–255. doi:10.1037/0033-295X.86.3.214

Needham, G., & Ally, M. (Eds.). (2008). *M-libraries: Libraries on the move to provide virtual access*. London, UK: Facet Books.

Nezamirad, K., Higgins, P., & Dunstall, S. (2005). Cognitive analysis of collaboration as an activity. In *Proceedings of the Annual Conference of the European Association of Cognitive Ergonomics* (pp. 131-38).

Ng'ambi, D. (2005). Mobile dynamic frequently asked questions (DFAQ) for student and learning support. In *Proceedings of the 4th World Conference on mLearning (mLearn 2005)*, South Africa, Cape Town (pp. 1-8).

Nichols, J. D. (1996). The effects of cooperative learning on student achievement and motivation in a high school geometry class. *Contemporary Educational Psychology, 21*, 467–476. doi:10.1006/ceps.1996.0031

Nikoi, S. (2007). *Literature review on work-based mobile learning*. Retrieved from http://wolf.lec.ac.uk/file.php/1/Literature_Reviews/LITERATURE_REVIEW_ON_WORKBASED_MOBIL_LEARNING_1.pdf

Norman, A., & Pearce, J. (Eds.). (2007). Making the Connections. In *Proceedings of mLearn 2007: 6th World Conference on Mobile Learning*, Melbourne, VIC, Australia.

Norris, C., & Soloway, E. (2009). Leadership + Mobile technologies = Educational benefits: Cell phones in K12 are inevitable. *District Administration, 28*.

Nortcliffe, A., & Middleton, A. (2009a, September 8-10). *Audio, autonomy and authenticity: Constructive comments and conversations captured by the learner*. Paper presented at the ALT Conference of In Dreams Begins Responsibility: Choice, Evidence, and Change, Manchester, UK.

Nortcliffe, A., & Middleton, A. (2009b, December 18). iGather: Learners as responsible audio collectors of tutor, peer and self-reflection. In *Proceedings of the National Conference of A Word in Your Ear*, Sheffield, UK.

Nouri, J., Eliasson, J., Rutz, F., & Ramberg, R. (2010). Exploring mediums of pedagogical support in an across contexts mobile learning activity. In M. Wolpers, P. Kirschner, M. Scheffel, S. Lindstaedt, & V. Dimitrova (Eds.), *Proceedings of the International Conference Sustaining TEL: From Innovation to Learning and Practice* (LNCS 6383, pp. 414-419).

O'Malley, C., Vavoula, G., Glew, J. P., Taylor, J., Sharples, M., & Lefrere, P. (2005). *Pedagogical methodologies and paradigms: Guidelines for learning/ teaching/ tutoring in a mobile environment*. Bristol, UK: Futurelab Series.

Obama, B., & Biden, J. (2007). *Reforming and strengthening America's schools for the 21st century*. Retrieved from http://www.timeandlearning.org/Obama%20Campaign%20Education%20Proposal.pdf

Oblinger, D. G., & Oblinger, J. L. (2005). *Educating the Net Generation*. Retrieved from http://www.educause.edu/educatingthenetgen

Oblinger, D. G., & Oblinger, J. L. (2005). *Educating the net generation*. Washington, DC: EDUCAUSE.

OFTA. (2009). *Key Telecommunications Statistics*. Hong Kong: Office of the Telecommunications Authority of Hong Kong. Retrieved from http://www.ofta.gov.hk/en/datastat/key_stat.html

O'Hara, K., Kindberg, T., Glancy, M., Baptista, L., Sukumaran, B., Kahana, G., & Rowbotham, J. (2007). Collecting and sharing location-based content on mobile phones in a zoo visitor experience. *Computer Supported Cooperative Work, 16*, 11–44. doi:10.1007/s10606-007-9039-2

O'Neil, K., Singh, G., & O'Donoghue, J. (2004). Implementing eLearning programs for higher education: A review of literature. *Journal of Information Technology Education, 3*(1), 313–323.

O'Reilly, T. (2005). *What is Web 2.0: Design patterns and business models for the next generation of software*. Retrieved from http://www.oreillynet.com/pub/a/oreilly/tim/news/2005/09/30/what-is-web-20.html

Oulasvirta, A., Tamminen, S., & Roto, V. (2005). Interaction in 4-second bursts: The fragmented nature of attentional resources in mobile HCI. In *Proceedings of the SIGCHI Conference on Human Factors in Computing Systems* (pp. 919-928).

Paavilainen, J., Saarenpää, H., Seisto, A., & Federley, M. (2009). Creating a design framework for educational language games utilizing hybrid media. In *Proceedings of CGAMES USA 14th International Conference on Computer Games*, Wolverhampton, UK (pp. 81-89).

Paay, J., Kjeldskov, J., Christensen, A., Ibsen, A., Jensen, D., Nielsen, G., & Vutborg, R. (2008). Location-based storytelling in the urban environment. In *Proceedings of the 20th Australasian Conference on Computer-Human Interaction on Designing for Habitus and Habitat*, Cairns, Australia (pp. 122-129).

Pachler, N., & Seipold, J. (2009). Harnessing mobile devices to connect learning in formal and informal settings: the role of digital narratives and discontinuous text production for narratives and discontinuous text production for meaning making. In *Proceedings of the 8th World Conference on Mobile and Contextual Learning*, Orlando, FL.

Pachler, N., Bachmair, B., & Cook, J. (2010). *Mobile learning: Structures, agency, practices*. New York, NY: Springer.

Pachler, N. (2010). The socio-cultural ecological approach to mobile learning: An overview. In Bachmair, B. (Ed.), *Medienbildung in neuen Kulturräumen: Die deutschsprachige und britische Diskussion* (pp. 155–169). Wiesbaden, Germany: VS Verlag für Sozialwissenschaften.

Pachler, N., Bachmair, B., Cook, J., & Kress, G. (2010). *Mobile learning: Structure, agency, practices*. New York, NY: Springer.

Papachristos, D., Alafodimos, N., Arvanitis, K., Vassilakis, K., Kalogiannakis, M., & Kikilias, P. (2010). An educational model for asynchronous e-learning: A case study in higher technology education. *International Journal of Advanced Corporate Learning*, *3*(1), 32–36.

Papasterigou, M. (2009). Digital game-based learning in high school computer science education: Impact on educational effectiveness and student motivation. *Computers & Education*, *52*(2), 1–12. doi:10.1016/j.compedu.2008.06.004

Parkinson, J. (2004). *Improving secondary science teaching*. London, UK: Routledge. doi:10.4324/9780203464328

Parkinson, J. (2005). *Reflective teaching of science* (pp. 11–18). New York, NY: Continuum.

Parsons, D., Ryu, H., & Cranshaw, M. (2007). A design requirements framework for mobile learning environments. *Journal of Computers*, *2*(4), 1–8. doi:10.4304/jcp.2.4.1-8

Parsons, V., Reddy, P., Wood, J., & Senior, C. (2009). Educating an iPod generation: Undergraduate attitudes, experiences and understanding of vodcast and podcast use. *Learning, Media and Technology*, *34*(3), 215–228. doi:10.1080/17439880903141497

Pascoe, J., Ryan, N., & Morse, D. (2000). Using while moving: HCI issues in fieldwork environments. *ACM Transactions on Computer-Human Interaction*, *7*, 417–437. doi:10.1145/355324.355329

Pashler, H. (1984). Processing stages in overlapping tasks: Evidence for a central bottleneck. *Journal of Experimental Psychology. Human Perception and Performance*, *10*, 358–377. doi:10.1037/0096-1523.10.3.358

Pashler, H. (1994). Dual-task interference in simple tasks: Data and theory. *Psychological Bulletin*, *116*, 220–244. doi:10.1037/0033-2909.116.2.220

Pashler, H. (1998). *The psychology of attention*. Cambridge, MA: MIT Press.

Paterson, N., Naliuka, K., Jensen, S. K., Carrigy, T., Haahr, M., & Conway, F. (2010). Design, implementation and evaluation of audio for a location aware augmented reality game. In *Proceedings of the 3rd International Conference on Fun and Games*, Leuven, Belgium (pp. 149-156).

Peng, H., Tsai, C., & Wu, Y. (2006). University students' self-efficacy and their attitudes toward the Internet: the role of students' perceptions of the Internet. *Educational Studies*, *32*(1), 73–86. doi:10.1080/03055690500416025

Penny, J. (2003). My life as a reader. *Assessing Writing*, *8*(3), 192–215. doi:10.1016/j.asw.2003.08.001

Penuel, W. R., Roschelle, J., & Shechtman, N. (2007). Designing formative assessment software with teachers: An analysis of the co-design process. *Research and Practice in Technology Enhanced Learning*, *2*(1), 51–74. doi:10.1142/S1793206807000300

Perry, D. (2003). *Handheld computers (PDAs) in schools*. Retrieved from http://www.tes.co.uk/teaching-resource/Handheld-computers-PDAs-in-schools-6072726/

Peters, O., & Keegan, D. (1994). *Otto Peters on distance education: The industrialization of teaching and learning*. London, UK: Routledge.

Petrova, K., & Li, C. (2009). Evaluating mobile learning artefacts. In *Proceedings of the Ascilite Conference Same Places, Different Spaces*, Auckland, New Zealand (pp. 768-772).

Petticrew, M., & Roberts, H. (2006). *Systematic reviews in the social sciences: A practical guide*. Oxford, UK: Blackwell. doi:10.1002/9780470754887

Pettit, J., & Kukulska-Hulme, A. (2007). Going with the grain: mobile devices in practice. *Australasian Journal of Educational Technology, 23*(1), 17–33.

Pew, R. W., & Mavor, A. S. (1998). *Modeling human and organizational behavior: Application to military simulations*. Washington, DC: National Academy Press.

Pfeiffer, V. D. I., Gemballa, S., Jarodzka, H., Scheiter, K., & Gerjets, P. (2009). Situated learning in the mobile age: Mobile devices on a field trip to the sea. *International Journal of Research in Learning Technology, 17*(3), 187–199. doi:10.1080/09687760903247666

Phelps, K. (1998). *Story shapes for digital media*. Retrieved from http://www.glasswings.com.au/modern/shapes

PhoneBook. (2010). *PhoneBook at mobile art lab*. Retrieved from http://www.mobileart.jp/phonebook_en.html

Piaget, J. (1928). *Judgment and reasoning in the child*. London, UK: Routledge & Kegan Paul. doi:10.4324/9780203207260

Pléty, R. (1996). *Cooperative learning*. Lyon, France: Presses Universitaires de Lyon.

Pontefract, C., & Hardman, F. (2005). The discourse of classroom interaction in Kenyan primary schools. *Comparative Education, 41*(1), 87–106. doi:10.1080/03050060500073264

Pool, M. M., van der Voort, T. H. A., Beentjes, J. W. J., & Koolstra, C. M. (1999). De invloed van achtergrondtelevisie op de uitvoering van gemakkelijke en moeilijke huiswerktaken. *Pedagogische Studiën, 76*, 350–360.

Potts, C. (1995). Using schematic scenarios to understand user needs. In *Proceedings of the ACM Symposium on Designing Interactive Systems*, Ann Arbor, MI (pp. 247-256).

Power, T., & Thomas, R. (2006, September 6-9). *mLearning: The classroom in your pocket?* Paper presented at the BERA, Warwick.

Pratchett, R. (2005). *Gamers in the UK: Digital play, digital lifestyles*. Retrieved from http://open.bbc.co.uk/newmediaresearch/files/BBC_UK_Games_Research_2005.pdf

Prensky, M. (2005). *If we share, we're halfway there*. Retrieved September 20, 2010, from http://www.marcprensky.com/writing/Prensky-If_We_Share.pdf

Prensky, M. (2009). H. Sapiens Digital: From Digital Immigrants and Digital Natives to Digital Wisdom. *Innovate, 5*(3).

Prensky, M. (2001). Digital natives, digital immigrants. *Horizon, 9*(5), 1–6. doi:10.1108/10748120110424816

Price, K., Lin, M., Feng, J., Goldman, R., Sears, A., & Jacko, J. (2004). Data entry on the move: An examination of nomadic speech-based text entry. In C. Stary & C. Stephanidis (Eds.), *Proceedings of the 8th ERCIM Workshop on User Interfaces for All* (LNCS 3196, pp. 460-471).

Priestnall, G., Brown, E., Sharples, M., & Polmear, G. (2009). A student-led comparison of techniques for augmenting the field experience. In *Proceedings of the mLearn Conference*, Orlando, FL (pp. 195-198).

Project, K. -Nect. (2008). *Project K-Next homepage*. Retrieved from http://www.projectknect.org/Project%20K-Nect/Home.html

PTS. (2009). *The Swedish Telecommunication Market – First half year 2009 – PTS –ER-2009: 29*. Retrieved from http://www.pts.se/en-gb/Documents/Reports/Telephony/2009/Svensk-telemarknad-forsta-halvaret-2009---PTS-ER-200929/

Pulman, A. (2008). *Mobile assistance – the Nintendo DS Lite as an assistive tool for health and social care students*. Retrieved from http://www.swap.ac.uk/docs/casestudies/pulman.pdf Rainger, P. (2005). Accessibility and mobile learning. In A. Kukulska-Hulme & J. Traxler (Eds.), *Mobile learning: A handbook for educators and trainers*. London, UK: Routledge.

Punch, K. F. (2009). *Introduction to research methods in education*. London, UK: Sage.

Ragus, M., Meredith, S., Dacey, D., Richter, C., Paterson, A., & Hayes, A. (2005). The Australian mobile learning network: Australian innovations. In *Proceedings of mLearn 2005* (pp. 1-21). Retrieved September 20, 2010, from http://www.mlearn.org.za/papers-full.html

Ramsden, A. (2005). Evaluating a PDA for delivering VLE functionality. In Kukulska-Hulme, A., & Traxler, J. (Eds.), *Mobile learning: A handbook for educators and trainers*. London, UK: Routledge.

Reid, J., Hull, R., Cater, K., & Clayton, B. (2005). Riot! 1831: The design of a location based audio drama. In *Proceedings of the 3rd UK-UbiNet Workshop*, Bath, UK.

Richardson, J., & Lenarcic, J. (2007, June 4-6). E-inclusion through text messaging: The emergence of an administrative ecology within an university student population via the use of a mobile academic information delivery system. In *Proceedings of the 20th Bled eConference*, Bled, Slovenia (pp. 1-9).

Roberts, G. (2002, March 26-28). Complexity, uncertainty and autonomy: The politics of networked learning. In *Proceedings of the 3rd International Conference on Networked Learning*, Sheffield, UK.

Robey, D., Khoo, H. M., & Powers, C. (2000). Situated learning in cross-functional virtual teams. *IEEE Transactions on Professional Communication: Technical Communication, 43*(1), 51–66. doi:10.1109/47.826416

Robson, C. (2002). *Real world research* (2nd ed.). Oxford, UK: Blackwell.

Robson, C. (2007). *Real World Research: A Resource for Social Scientists and Practitioner-Researchers*. Oxford, UK: Blackwell Publishing.

Roden, T. E., Parberry, I., & Ducrest, D. (2007). Toward mobile entertainment: A paradigm for narrative-based audio only games. *Science of Computer Programming, 67*(1), 76–90. doi:10.1016/j.scico.2006.07.004

Rogalski, J. (1994). Formation aux activites collectives. *Le Travail Humain, 54*(4), 425–443.

Rogers, Y. (2006). Moving on from Weiser's vision of calm computing: Engaging UbiComp experiences. In P. Dourish & A. Friday (Eds.), *Proceedings of the 8th International Conference on Ubiquitous Computing* (LNCS 4209, pp. 404-421).

Rogers, Y., Price, S., Fitzpatrick, G., Fleck, R., Harris, E., Smith, H., et al. (2004). Ambient wood: Designing new forms of digital augmentation for learning outdoors. In *Proceedings of the Conference on Interaction Design and Children: Building a Community*, Baltimore, MD (pp. 3-10).

Rogers, E. (2003). *Diffusion of Innovations* (5th ed.). New York, NY: Free Press.

Rogers, E. M. (1962). *Diffusion of innovations*. New York, NY: Free Press.

Rogers, E. M. (1995). *Diffusion of innovations* (4th ed.). New York, NY: Free Press.

Rogers, Y., Connelly, K., Hazlewood, W., & Tedesco, L. (2010). Enhancing learning: A study of how mobile devices can facilitate sensemaking. *Personal and Ubiquitous Computing, 14*(2), 111–124. doi:10.1007/s00779-009-0250-7

Rogers, Y., & Price, S. (2009). How mobile technologies are changing the way children learn. In Druin, A. (Ed.), *Mobile technology for children* (pp. 3–22). San Francisco, CA: Morgan Kaufmann. doi:10.1016/B978-0-12-374900-0.00001-6

Rogoff, B. (1982). Integrating context and cognitive development. In Lamb, M. E., & Brown, A. L. (Eds.), *Advances in developmental psychology* (*Vol. 2*). Mahwah, NJ: Lawrence Erlbaum.

Roschelle, J. (2000). Choosing and using video equipment for data collection. In Lesh, R. (Ed.), *Handbook of research data design in mathematics and science education*. Mahwah, NJ: Lawrence Erlbaum.

Roschelle, J., Rafanan, K., Estrella, G., Nussbaum, M., & Claro, S. (2010). From handheld collaborative tool to effective classroom module: Embedding CSCL in a broader design framework. *Computers & Education, 55*, 1018–1026. doi:10.1016/j.compedu.2010.04.012

Roschelle, J., & Teasley, S. D. (1989). The construction of shared knowledge in collaborative problem solving. *Knowledge Creation Diffusion Utilization, 128*(3), 69–97.

Roseth, C. J., Johnson, D. W., & Johnson, R. T. (2008). Promoting early adolescents' achievement and peer relationships: The effects of cooperative, competitive, and individualistic goal structures. *Psychological Bulletin, 134*, 223–246. doi:10.1037/0033-2909.134.2.223

Rothwell, L. (2008). Podcasts and collaborative learning. In Salmon, G., & Edirisingha, P. (Eds.), *Podcasting for learning in universities* (pp. 121–131). Buckingham, UK: Open University Press.

Rowland, D., Flintham, M., Oppermann, L., Marshall, J., Chamberlain, A., Koleva, B., et al. (2009). Ubikequitous computing: Designing interactive experiences for cyclists. In *Proceedings of the 11th International Conference on Human-Computer Interaction with Mobile Devices and Services*, Bonn, Germany (p. 21).

Rozier, J., Karahalios, K., & Donath, J. (2000). Hear & there: An augmented reality system of linked audio. In *Proceedings of the International Conference on Auditory Display*, Atlanta, GA (pp. 63-67).

Rudman, P. D., Sharples, M., Vavoula, G. N., Lonsdale, P., & Meek, J. (2008). Cross-context learning. In Tallon, L., & Walker, K. (Eds.), *Digital technologies and the museum experience: Handheld guides and other media* (pp. 147–166). Lanham, MD: Alta Mira Press.

Russo, A., Watkins, J., Kelly, L., & Chan, S. (2006). How will social media affect museum communication? In *Proceedings of NODEM* (pp. 1-8).

Ryan, M.-L. (2001). *Narrative as virtual reality: Immersion and interactivity in literature and electronic media*. Baltimore, MD: Johns Hopkins University Press.

Säljö, R. (1999). Learning as the use of tools: A sociocultural perspective on the human-technology link. In Littleton, K., & Light, P. (Eds.), *Learning with computers: Analysing productive interaction*. London, UK: Routledge.

Säljö, R. (2000). *Lärande i praktiken: Ett sociokulturellt perspektiv*. Stockholm, Sweden: Prisma.

Salmon, G., & Nie, M. (2008). Doubling the life of iPods. In Salmon, G., & Edirisingha, P. (Eds.), *Podcasting for learning in universities* (pp. 1–11). Buckingham, UK: Open University Press.

Salmon, G., Nie, M., & Edirisingha, P. (2007). *Informal Mobile Podcasting and Learning Adaptation (IMPALA)*. Leicester, UK: Beyond Distance Research Alliance, University of Leicester.

Salvucci, D. D., & Taatgen, N. A. (2008). Threaded cognition: An integrated theory of concurrent multitasking. *Psychological Review, 115*, 101–130. doi:10.1037/0033-295X.115.1.101

Samarajiva, R. (2008). *Mobile penetration in Sri Lanka*. Retrieved from http://www.lirneasia.net/wp-content/uploads/2007/09/telecenternationalalliance101.ppt

Sanchez, J., Mendoza, C., & Salinas, A. (2009). Mobile serious games for collaborative problem solving. *Studies in Health Technology and Informatics, 144*, 193–197.

Sargeant, J., Curran, V., Jarvis-Selinger, S., Ferrier, S., Allen, M., Kirby, F., & Ho, K. (2004). Interactive on-line continuing medical education: Physicians' perceptions and experiences. *The Journal of Continuing Education in the Health Professions, 24*(4), 227–236. doi:10.1002/chp.1340240406

Satyanarayanan, M. (1996). Fundamental challenges in mobile computing. In *Proceedings of the Fifteenth Annual ACM Symposium on Principles of Distributed Computing* (pp. 1-7).

Scanlon, E., Jones, A., & Waycott, J. (2005). Mobile technologies: Prospects for their use in learning in informal science settings. *Journal of Interactive Media in Education, 25*.

Schaefer, S., Krampe, R. T., Lindenberger, U., & Baltes, P. B. (2008). Age differences between children and young adults in the dynamics of dual-task prioritization: Body (balance) versus mind (memory). *Developmental Psychology, 44*(3), 747–757. doi:10.1037/0012-1649.44.3.747

Schaffers, H., Cordoba, M. G., Hongisto, P., Kallai, T., Merz, C., & van Rensburg, J. (2007). Exploring business models for open innovation in rural living labs. In *Proceedings of the 13th International Conference on Concurrent Enterprising* (pp. 49-56).

Schell, J. (2008). *The art of game design*. San Francisco, CA: Morgan Kaufmann.

Schnädelbach, H., Egglestone, S. R., Reeves, S., Benford, S., Walker, B., & Wright, M. (2008). Performing thrill: Designing telemetry systems and spectator interfaces for amusement rides. In *Proceedings of the Twenty-Sixth Annual SIGCHI Conference on Human Factors in Computing Systems*, Florence, Italy (pp. 1167-1176).

Schuck, S., Aubusson, P., Kearney, M., & Burden, K. (2010). Mobagogy – Mobile learning for a higher education community. In *Proceedings of the IADIS Mobile Learning Conference*.

Schwabe, G., & Goth, C. (2005). Mobile learning with a mobile game: Design and motivational effects. *Journal of Computer Assisted Learning, 21*(3), 204–216. doi:10.1111/j.1365-2729.2005.00128.x

Seisto, A., Federley, M., Aarnisalo, S., & Oittinen, P. (2009). Hybrid media application for language studies in elementary school. In *Proceedings of IADIS International Conference on Mobile Learning*, Barcelona, Spain.

Seppälä, P., & Alamäki, H. (2003). Mobile learning in teacher training. *Journal of Computer Assisted Learning, 19*(3), 330–335. doi:10.1046/j.0266-4909.2003.00034.x

Seppala, P., & Alamaki, H. (2003). Mobile learning in teacher training. *Journal of Computer Assisted Learning, 19*, 330–335. doi:10.1046/j.0266-4909.2003.00034.x

Sharples, M. (2005). Learning as conversation: Transforming education in the mobile age. In *Proceedings of the Conference on Seeing, Understanding, Learning in the Mobile Age*, Budapest, Hungary (pp. 147-152).

Sharples, M. (2006). *Big issues in mobile learning: Report of a workshop by the Kaleidoscope Network of Excellence Mobile Learning Initiative*. Retrieved from http://www.lsri.nottingham.ac.uk/msh/Papers/BIG_IS-SUES_REPORT_PUBLISHED.pdf

Sharples, M., Lonsdale, P., Meek, J., Rudman, P., & Vavoula, G. (2007). *An evaluation of myartspace: A mobile learning service for school museum trips*. Paper presented at the mLearn Conference, Melbourne, Australia.

Sharples, M., Taylor, J., & Vavoula, G. (2005). Towards a theory of mobile learning. In *Proceedings of the mLearn 4th World Conference on mLearning*, Cape Town, South Africa.

Sharples, M. (1993). A study of breakdowns and repairs in a computer-mediated communication system. *Interacting with Computers, 5*(1), 61–77. doi:10.1016/0953-5438(93)90025-O

Sharples, M. (2000). The design of personal mobile technologies for lifelong learning. *Computers & Education, 34*(3-4), 177–193. doi:10.1016/S0360-1315(99)00044-5

Sharples, M. (2001). Disruptive devices: Mobile technology for conversational learning. *International Journal of Continuing Education and Lifelong Learning, 12*(5-6), 504–520.

Sharples, M. (2002). Disruptive devices: Mobile technology for conversational learning. *International Journal of Continuing Engineering Education and Lifelong Learning, 12*(5-6), 504–520. doi:10.1504/IJCEELL.2002.002148

Sharples, M. (2003). Disruptive devices: Mobile technology for conversational learning. *International Journal of Continuing Engineering Education and Lifelong Learning, 12*(5-6), 504–520.

Sharples, M. (2006). *Big issues in mobile learning*. Nottingham, UK: Kaleidoscope Research.

Sharples, M. (2009). Methods for evaluating mobile learning. In Vavoula, G., Pachler, N., & Kukulska-Hulme, A. (Eds.), *Researching mobile learning* (pp. 17–39). Bern, Switzerland: Peter Lang.

Sharples, M. (Ed.). (2006). *Big issues in mobile learning: Report of a workshop by the Kaleidoscope Network of Excellence Mobile Learning Initiative*. Nottingham, UK: LSRI, University of Nottingham.

Sharples, M. (Ed.). (2006). *Issues in Mobile Learning: Report of a workshop by the Kaleidoscope Network of Excellence Mobile Learning Initiative*. Nottingham, UK: Learning Sciences Research Institute, University of Nottingham.

Sharples, M., Corlett, D., & Westmancott, O. (2002). The design and implementation of a mobile learning resource. *Personal and Ubiquitous Computing, 6*(3), 220–234. doi:10.1007/s007790200021

Sharples, M., Crook, C., Jones, I., Kay, D., Chowcat, I., & Balmer, K. (2009). *CAPITAL year one final report*. Nottingham, UK: University of Nottingham.

Sharples, M., Milrad, M., Arnedillo-Sánchez, I., & Vavoula, G. (2008). Mobile learning: Small devices, big issues. In Balacheff, N., Ludvigsen, S., de Jong, T., Lazonder, A., Barnes, S., & Montandon, L. (Eds.), *Technology Enhanced Learning: Principles and Products*. Berlin, Germany: Springer.

Sharples, M., Taylor, J., & Vavoula, G. (2007). A theory of learning for the mobile age. In Andrews, R., & Haythornthwaite, C. A. (Eds.), *The Sage handbook of e-learning research*. Thousand Oaks, CA: Sage.

Shih, K., Chen, H., Chang, C., & Kao, T. (2010). The development and implementation of scaffolding-based self-regulated learning system for e/m-learning. *Journal of Educational Technology & Society, 13*(1), 80–93.

Shin, N., Norris, C., & Soloway, E. (2006, June 27-July 1). Effects of handheld games on students learning in mathematics. In *Proceedings of the 7th International Conference on Learning Sciences*, Bloomington, IN (pp. 702-708).

Shulman, L. (1987). Knowledge and teaching. *Harvard Educational Review, 57*, 1–22.

Sims, K. (2003). *Paul Ricoeur*. London, UK: Routledge.

Sinanan, J. (2008, December 8-12). Social tools and social capital: Reading mobile phone usage in rural Indigenous communities. In *Proceedings of OzCHI* (pp. 267-270).

Slavin, R. E. (1990). Point-counterpoint: Ability grouping, cooperative learning and the gifted. *Journal for the Education of the Gifted, 14*(3), 3–8.

Slavin, R. E. (1996). Research on cooperative learning and achievement: What we know, what we need to know. *Contemporary Educational Psychology, 21*, 43–69. doi:10.1006/ceps.1996.0004

Slyper, R., & Hodgins, J. (2008). Action capture with accelerometers. In *Proceedings of the ACM SIGGRAPH/Eurographics Symposium on Computer Animation*, Dublin, Ireland (pp. 193-199).

Smith, C. (2009). *The unit of construction + the multiple point of view = the evolution of form: Electronic visualisation and the arts*. London, UK: British Computer Society.

Smith, G., & Ferguson, D. (2002). Teaching over the Web verses in the classroom: Differences in the instructor experience. *International Journal of Instructional Media, 29*(1), 61–67.

Smyth, J., Hattam, R., & Cannon, J. (2004). *Dropping Out, Drifting Off, Being Excluded: Becoming someone without school*. New York, NY: Peter Lang.

Snyder, I., & Prinsloo, M. (Eds.). (2007). The digital literacy practices of young people in marginal contexts. *Language & Education: An International Journal, 21*(3), 171-270.

Solimeno, A., Mebane, M. E., Tomai, M., & Francescato, D. (2008). The influence of students and teachers characteristics on the efficacy of face-to-face and computer supported collaborative learning. *Computers & Education, 51*(1), 109–128. doi:10.1016/j.compedu.2007.04.003

Solomonidou, C., & Mitsaki, A. (2009). Boys' and girls' computer activities and learning in internet café. *International Journal of Learning, 16*(11), 169–177.

Spikol, D., & Eliasson, J. (2010). Lessons from designing geometry learning activities that combine mobile and 3D tools. In *Proceedings of the 6th IEEE International Conference on Wireless, Mobile, and Ubiquitous Technologies in Education* (pp. 137-141).

SPIRE. (2007). *Results and analysis of the Web 2.0 services survey undertaken by the SPIRE project*. Retrieved from http://www.jisc.ac.uk/media/documents/programmes/digitalrepositories/spiresurvey.pdf

Spiro, R. J., Coulson, R. L., Feltovich, P. J., & Anderson, D. (1988). Cognitive flexibility theory: Advanced knowledge acquisition in ill-structured domains. In *Proceedings of the 10th Annual Conference of the Cognitive Science Society* (pp. 375-383).

Sprake, J. (2006). Accidental tours and illegal tour guides: Taking the textbook out of the tour. In Naripea, E., Sarapik, V., & Tomberg, J. (Eds.), *Place and location: Studies in environmental aesthetics and semiotics* (pp. 195–214). Tallinn, Estonia: Estonian Academy of Arts.

Squire, K., & Jan, M.-F. (2007). Mad city mystery: Developing scientific argumentation skills with a place-based augmented reality game on handheld computers. *Journal of Science Education and Technology, 16*(1), 5–29. doi:10.1007/s10956-006-9037-z

Squire, K., & Klopfer, E. (2007). Augmented reality simulations on handheld computers. *Journal of the Learning Sciences, 16*(3), 371–413. doi:10.1080/10508400701413435

Srivastava, L. (2008). The mobile makes its mark. In Katz, J. E. (Ed.), *Handbook of mobile communication studies* (pp. 15–27). Cambridge, MA: MIT Press.

St Mary's. (2008). *St. Mary's City schools mobile learning technology.* Retrieved from http://www.smriders.net/Mobile_Learning/

Stake, R. E. (1995). *The art of case study research.* Thousand Oaks, CA: Sage.

Stake, R. E. (2000). Case studies. In Denzin, N. K., & Lincoln, Y. S. (Eds.), *Handbook of qualitative research* (2nd ed.). Thousand Oaks, CA: Sage.

Stanton, D., & Neale, H. (2002). *Designing mobile technologies to support collaboration.* Retrieved from http://www.techkwondo.com/external/pdf/reports/2002-stanton-2.pdf

Stead, G. (2005). Moving mobile into the mainstream. In *Proceedings of mLearn 2005* (pp. 1-9). Retrieved September 20, 2010, from http://www.mlearn.org.za/papers-full.html

Stead, G. (2006). Mobile technologies: Transforming the future of learning. In Pinder, A. (Ed.), *Emerging technologies for learning* (*Vol. 2006*, pp. 6–15). Coventry, UK: British Educational Communications and Technology Agency.

Stenton, S. P., Hull, R., Goddi, P. M., Reid, J. E., Clayton, B. J., Melamed, T. J., & Wee, S. (2007). Mediascapes: Context-aware multimedia experiences. *IEEE MultiMedia, 14*, 98–105. doi:10.1109/MMUL.2007.52

Stockwell, G. (2008). Investigating learner preparedness for and usage patterns of mobile learning. *ReCALL, 20*(3), 253–270. doi:10.1017/S0958344008000232

Straub, E. (2009). Understanding Technology Adoption: Theory and Future Directions for Informal Learning. *Review of Educational Research, 79*, 625–649. doi:10.3102/0034654308325896

Strauss, A., & Corbin, J. (1998). *Basics of qualitative research: Techniques and procedures for developing grounded theory.* Thousand Oaks, CA: Sage.

Strayer, D. L., & Johnston, W. A. (2001). Driven to distraction: Dual-task studies of simulated driving and conversing on a cellular telephone. *Psychological Science, 12*, 462–466. doi:10.1111/1467-9280.00386

Stuart, M. (2009). *Student diversity, extra curricular activities and perceptions of graduate outcomes.* Retrieved from http://www.heacademy.ac.uk/resources/detail/publications/Stuart_Final

Styles, E. A. (2006). *The psychology of attention.* Hove, UK: Psychology Press.

Suthers, D. D. (2005). Technology affordances for intersubjective learning: A thematic agenda for CSCL. In *Proceedings of the Conference on Computer Support for Collaborative Learning: Learning 2005: The Next 10 Years!* Taipei, Taiwan.

Sutton-Brady, C., Scott, K. M., Taylor, L., Carabetta, G., & Clark, S. (2009). The value of using short-format podcasts to enhance learning and teaching. *Journal of Research in Learning Technology, 17*(3), 219–232. doi:10.1080/09687760903247609

Switalla, L. (n.d.). *Does the use of a podcast facilitate feedback/reflection to improve the pronunciation of Maori language.* Retrieved September 20, 2010, from http://www.scribd.com/doc/22622018/Maori-Language-Podcasting

Taber, K. S. (2005). Conceptual development. In Alsop, S., Bencze, L., & Pedretti, E. (Eds.), *Analysing exemplary science teaching* (pp. 127–136). Buckingham, UK: Open University Press.

Tamin, R. M., Bernard, R. M., Borokhovski, E., Abrami, P. C., & Schmid, R. F. (2011). What forty years of research says about the impact of technology on learning: A second-order meta-analysis and validation study. *Review of Educational Research, 81*(1), 4–28. doi:10.3102/0034654310393361

Tangentyere Council & Central Land Council. (2007). *Ingerrekenhe antirrkweme: Mobile phone use among low income Aboriginal people, a Central Australian snapshot.* Alice Springs, NT, Australia: Author.

Tapscott, D. (1998). *Growing up digital: The Rise of the Net Generation.* New York, NY: McGraw Hill.

Tapscott, D. (2008). *Grown Up Digital: How the Net Generation is Changing Your World.* New York, NY: McGraw Hill.

Taylor, J., Sharples, M., O'Malley, C., Vavoula, G., & Waycott, J. (2006). Towards a task model for mobile learning a dialectical approach. *International Journal of Learning Technology, 2*(2-3), 138–158. doi:10.1504/IJLT.2006.010616

Te Puni Kokiri (Ministry of Maori Development). (2010). *Te reo paho: Use of broadcasting and e-media, Maori language and culture.* Retrieved September 20, 2010, from http://indigenouspeoplesissues.com/attachments/4722_Maori-Media-Factsheet2010.pdf

Te Riele, K. (2003). *An Inclusive Learning Culture: Post-compulsory Education for a "Second Chance" Enriching Learning Cultures.* Paper presented at the 11th International Conference on Post-Compulsory Education and Training.

Teichler, U. (1999). Massification: A challenge for institutions of higher education. *Tertiary Education and Management, 4*(1).

Telecoms, S. L. (2009). *Sri Lanka - telecoms, mobile, broadband and forecasts.* Retrieved from http://www.marketresearch.com/product/display.asp?productid=2508373&g=1

Titrade, C., El Baaboua, F., Sion, B., & Mihalcescu, C. (2009). E-learning. *Annals of the University of Oradea: Economic Science, 4*(1), 1066–1069.

Tolvanen, J., Rossi, M., & Liu, H. (1996). Method engineering: Current research directions and implications for future research. In S. Brinkkemper, K. Lyytinen, & R. Welke (Eds.) *Proceedings of IFIP TC8, WG8.1/8.2: Working Conference on Method Engineering.* London, UK: Chapman & Hall.

Tosey, P. (2006). Interfering with interference. In Jackson, N., Oliver, M., Shaw, M., & Wisdom, J. (Eds.), *Developing creativity in higher education: An imaginative curriculum* (pp. 29–42). London, UK: Routledge.

Tozzi, V. (2000). Past reality and multiple interpretations in historical investigation. *Studies of Social Political Thought, 2*, 41–57.

Traxler, J. (2007). Flux within change. In *Proceedings of mLearn 2007: 6th World Conference on Mobile Learning.*

Traxler, J. (2008) Mobility, modernity, development. In *Proceedings of the 1st International Conference on M4D Mobile Communication for Development*, Karlstadt, Germany.

Traxler, J. (2008). From Text to Context. In *Proceedings of the mLearn 2008 Conference: The Bridge from Text to Context.*

Traxler, J. (2008). Modernity, mobility and the digital divides. In *Proceedings of the International Conference on Research in Learning Technology.*

Traxler, J. (2009). Learning in a mobile age. *International Journal of Mobile and Blended Learning, 1*(1), 1–12. doi:10.4018/jmbl.2009010101 doi:10.4018/jmbl.2009010101

Traxler, J. (2010). Students and mobile devices. *ALT-J. Research in Learning Technology, 18*(2), 149–160. doi:10.1080/09687769.2010.492847 doi:10.1080/09687769.2010.492847

Traxler, J. (2010, June 21-22). Mobile people, mobile societies, mobile cultures not just mobile learning. In *Proceedings of the ICA Mobiles Preconference*, Singapore.

Traxler, J., & Bridges, N. (2004, June). Mobile learning—the ethical and legal challenges. In *Proceedings of the MLEARN Conference on Mobile Learning Anytime Everywhere*, Bracciano, Italy (pp. 203-208).

Traxler, J., & Griffiths, L. (2009). IWB4D – interactive whiteboards for development. In *Proceedings of the International Conference on Information and Communication Technologies and Development*, Doha, Qatar (p. 488).

Traxler, J., & Kukulska-Hulme, A. (2005) Evaluating mobile learning: Reflections on current practice. In *Proceedings of mLearn 2005: 4th World Conference on Mobile Learning.*

Traxler, J., & Kukulska-Hulme, A. (2005). *Mobile learning in developing countries.* Vancouver, BC, Canada: Commonwealth of Learning. Retrieved September 20, 2010, from http://www.col.org/SiteCollectionDocuments/KS2005_mlearn.pdf

Traxler, J., & Kukulska-Hulme, A. (2006). The evaluation of next generation learning technologies: The case of mobile learning. In *Proceedings of the International Conference on Research in Learning Technology*, Oxford, UK.

Traxler, J., & Riordan, B. (2004). Using PDAs to support computing students. In *Proceedings of the Annual ICS Subject Centre Conference*, Belfast, UK.

Traxler, J., Riordan, B., & Dennett, C. (2008). The bridge from text to context. In *Proceedings of the MLEARN Conference*, Wolverhampton, UK.

Traxler, J., Riordan, B., & Dennett, C. (Eds.). (2008). The Bridge from Text to Context. In *Proceedings of mLearn 2008: 7th World Conference on Mobile Learning.*

Traxler, J. (2007). Defining, Discussing, and Evaluating Mobile Learning: The moving finger writes and having writ.... *International Review of Research in Open and Distance Learning, 8*(2).

Traxler, J. (2007a). Defining, discussing and evaluating mobile education. *International Review of Research in Open and Distance Learning, 8*(2).

Traxler, J. (2007b). IS4DEV – IS development & development issues. In Barry, C., Lang, M., Wojtkowski, W., Wojtkowski, G., Wrycza, S., & Zupancic, J. (Eds.), *The inter-networked world: ISD theory, practice, and education.* New York, NY: Springer.

Traxler, J. (2009). Learning in a mobile age. *International Journal of Mobile and Blended Learning, 1*(1), 1–12. doi:10.4018/jmbl.2009010101

Traxler, J. (2009). Mobile learning evaluation: The challenge of mobile societies. In Vavoula, G., Pachler, N., & Kukulska-Hulme, A. (Eds.), *Researching mobile learning: Frameworks, methods and research designs* (pp. 151–165). London, UK: Peter Lang.

Traxler, J. (2010). *Education and the impact of mobiles and mobility an introduction to mobiles in our societies.* Berlin, Germany: Springer-Verlag. van't Hooft, M., & Swan, K. (2007). *Ubiquitous computing in education: Invisible technology, visible impact.* Mahwah, NJ: Lawrence Erlbaum.

Traxler, J. (2010). Sustaining mobile learning and its institutions. *International Journal of Mobile and Blended Learning, 2*(4), 129–138. doi:10.4018/jmbl.2010100105

Traxler, J., Smith, T. F., & Waterman, M. S. (2007). Defining, discussing and evaluating mobile learning: The moving finger writes and having writ. *International Review of Research in Open and Distance Learning, 8*(2).

Trinder, K., Guiller, J., Margaryan, A., Littlejohn, A., & Nicol, D. (2008). *Learning from digital natives: bridging formal and informal learning.* Retrieved from http://www.heacademy.ac.uk/assets/York/documents/LDN%20Final%20Report.pdf

Trinder, J. (2005). Mobile technologies and systems. In Kukulska-Hulme, A., & Traxler, J. (Eds.), *Mobile learning: A handbook for educators and trainers* (pp. 7–24). London, UK: Routledge.

Tuomi, J., & Sarajärvi, A. (2002). *Laadullinen tutkimus ja sisällönanalyysi.* Helsinki, Finland: Kustannusosakeyhtiö Tammi.

Turnock, C., & Gibson, V. (2001). Validity in action research: A discussion on theoretical and practice issues encountered whilst using observation to collect data. *Journal of Advanced Nursing, 36*(3), 471–477. doi:10.1046/j.1365-2648.2001.01995.x

Tutty, J., & Klein, J. (2008). Computer-mediated instruction: A comparison of online and face-to-face collaboration. *Educational Technology Research and Development, 56*, 101–124. doi:10.1007/s11423-007-9050-9

U.S. Department of Education, Institute of Education Sciences. (2003). *Identifying and implementing educational practices supported by rigorous evidence: A user friendly guide.* Washington, DC: Author. Retrieved from http://www.excelgov.org/evidence

Uden, L. (2007). Activity theory for designing mobile learning. *International Journal of Mobile Learning and Organisation*, *1*(1), 81–102. doi:10.1504/IJMLO.2007.011190

Unterfrauner, E., Marschalek, I., & Fabian, C. (2010). Mobile learning with marginalized young people. In *Proceedings of the IADIS International Conference on Mobile Learning* (pp. 28-35).

Vahey, P., Tatar, D., & Roschelle, J. (2004, June 22-26). Leveraging handhelds to increase student learning: Engaging middle school students with the mathematics of change. In *Proceedings of the Sixth International Conference of the Learning Sciences on Embracing Diversity in Learning Science* (pp. 553-560).

Valenta, A., Therriault, D., Dieter, M., & Mrtek, R. (2001). Identifying Student Attitudes and Learning Styles in Distance Education. *JALN*, *5*(2), 111–127.

Valk, J.-H., Rashid, A. T., & Elder, L. (2010). using mobile phones to improve educational outcomes: An analysis of evidence from Asia. *International Review of Research in Open and Distance Learning*, *11*(1).

van der Merwe, H., & Brown, T. (Eds.). (2005). Mobile Technology: The Future of Learning in Your Hands. In *Proceedings of mLearn 2005: 4th World Conference on Mobile Learning*.

Van Selst, M., Ruthruff, E., & Johnston, J. C. (1999). Can practice eliminate the psychological refractory period effect? *Journal of Experimental Psychology. Human Perception and Performance*, *25*, 1268–1283. doi:10.1037/0096-1523.25.5.1268

van't Hooft, M., Swan, K., & Bennett, J. (2009, March 27). Learning math while mobile: Creating opportunities for elementary math learning. In *Proceedings of the 3rd WLE Mobile Learning Symposium: Mobile Learning Cultures across Education, Work, and Leisure*, London, UK (pp. 65-68).

Vandierendonck, A. (2006). *Aandacht & geheugen*. Gent, Belgium: Academia Press.

Vas, R., Kismihók, G., Kő, A., Szabó, I., & Bíró, M. (2007). Hungarian Experiences of Using an Ontology-based Adaptive Knowledge Evaluation Approach in Teaching Business Informatics in a Mobile Learning Environment. In *Proceedings of the Workshop on Cross-Media and Personalized Learning Applications on top of Digital Libraries*, Budapest, Hungary (pp. 47-64).

Vas, R., Kovács, B., & Kismihók, G. (2009). Ontology-based mobile learning and knowledge testing. *International Journal of Mobile Learning and Organisation*, *3*(2), 128–147. doi:10.1504/IJMLO.2009.024423

Vavoula, G. (2007). *Learning bridges: A role for mobile technologies in education*. Paper presented at the M-Learning Symposium, London, UK.

Vavoula, G. N., Lefrere, P., O'Malley, C., Sharples, M., & Taylor, J. (2004). Producing guidelines for learning, teaching and tutoring in a mobile environment. In *Proceedings of the 2nd IEEE International Workshop on Wireless and Mobile Technologies in Education* (pp. 173-176).

Vavoula, G., Pachler, N., & Kukulska-Hulme, A. (Eds.). (2009). *Researching mobile learning*. Bern, Switzerland: Peter Lang.

Vavoula, G., & Sharples, M. (2009). Meeting the challenges in evaluating mobile learning: A 3-level evaluation framework. *International Journal of Mobile and Blended Learning*, *1*(2), 54–75. doi:10.4018/jmbl.2009040104

Vavoula, G., Sharples, M., Rudman, P., Meek, J., & Lonsdale, P. (2009). Myartspace: Design and evaluation of support for learning with multimedia phones between classrooms and museums. *Computers & Education*, *53*(2), 286–299. doi:10.1016/j.compedu.2009.02.007

Veen, W. (2009). *Homo Zappiens. Opgroeien, leven en werken in een nieuw tijdperk*. Amsterdam, The Netherlands: Pearson Education.

Verghese, J., Kuslansky, G., Holtzer, R., Katz, M., Xue, X., Buschke, H., & Pahor, M. (2007). Walking while talking: Effect of task prioritization in the elderly. *Archives of Physical Medicine and Rehabilitation*, *88*, 50–53. doi:10.1016/j.apmr.2006.10.007

Verhaeghen, P., Steitz, D. W., Sliwinski, M. J., & Cerella, J. (2003). Aging and dual-task performance: A meta-analysis. *Psychology and Aging*, *18*, 443–460. doi:10.1037/0882-7974.18.3.443

Vihavainen, S., Kuula, T., & Federley, M. (2010). Cross-use of smart phones and printed books in primary school education. In *Proceedings of the 12th International Conference on Human Computer Interaction with Mobile Devices and Services*, Lisbon, Portugal (pp. 279-282).

Voelcker-Rehage, C., Stronge, A. J., & Alberts, J. L. (2006). Age-related differences in working memory and force control under dual-task conditions. *Aging. Neuropsychology and Cognition, 13*, 366–384. doi:10.1080/138255890969339

Vogel, B., Spikol, D., Kurti, A., & Milrad, M. (2010). Integrating mobile, web and sensory technologies to support inquiry-based science learning. In *Proceedings of the 6th IEEE International Conference on Wireless, Mobile, and Ubiquitous Technologies in Education* (pp. 65-72).

Vosloo, S., Walton, M., & Deumert, A. (2009). m4Lit: A teen m-novel project in South Africa. In D. Metcalf, A. Hamilton & C. Graffeo (Eds.), *Proceedings of mLearn 2009* (pp. 207-211). Orlando, FL: University of Central Florida.

Vygotsky, L. S. (1978). *Mind in society.* Cambridge, MA: Harvard University Press.

Wadsworth, Y. (1998). *What is participatory action research?* Retrieved from http://www.scu.edu.au/schools/gcm/ar/ari/p-ywadsworth98.html

Wagner, E. D. (2005). Enabling mobile learning. *EDUCAUSE Review, 40*(3), 40–53.

Wagner, T. (2010). *Change leadership: A practical guide to transforming our schools.* New York, NY: Basic Books.

Wali, E., Winters, N., & Oliver, M. (2008). Maintaining, changing and crossing contexts: An activity theoretic reinterpretation of mobile learning. *Journal of Research in Learning Technology, 16*(1), 41–57. doi:10.1080/09687760701850190

Walker, A. (2009). Confessions of a Reluctant Podcaster. In V. King, C. Broughan, L. Clouder, F. Deepwell, & A. Turner (Eds.), *Academic Futures* (pp. 209-222). Newcastle-upon-Tyne, UK: Cambridge Scholars Publishing.

Walker, K. (2004). Learning on location with cinematic narratives. In *Proceedings of the 1st ACM Workshop on Story Representation, Mechanism and Context,* New York, NY (pp. 55-58).

Wallace, R. (2009). Empowered learner identity through m-learning: Representations of disenfranchised students' perspectives. In Metcalf, D., Hamilton, A., & Graffeo, C. (Eds.), *Proceedings of mLearn 2009* (pp. 13–17). Orlando, FL: University of Central Florida.

Walls, S. M., Kucsera, J. V., Walker, J. D., Acee, T. W., McVaugh, N. K., & Robinson, D. H. (2010). Podcasting in education: Are students as ready and eager as we think they are? *Computers & Education, 54*(2), 371–378. doi:10.1016/j.compedu.2009.08.018

Walsh, C. (2010). Systems-based literacy practices: Digital games research, gameplay and design. *Australian Journal of Language and Literacy, 33*(1), 24–30.

Wang, M., Shen, R., Novak, D., & Pan, X. (2009). The impact of mobile learning on students' learning behaviours and performance: Report from a large blended classroom. *British Journal of Educational Technology, 40*(4), 673–695. doi:10.1111/j.1467-8535.2008.00846.x

Webb, M., & Cox, M. (2004). A review of pedagogy related to information and communications technology. *Technology, Pedagogy and Education, 13*(3), 235–286. doi:10.1080/14759390400200183

Wellington, J. (2004). Multimedia in science teaching. In Barton, R. (Ed.), *Teaching secondary science with ICT* (pp. 87–102). Buckingham, UK: Open University Press.

Wenger, E. (2010). SIKM community presentation online. Theme: Rethinking Ourselves (KM People) as Technology Stewards. Retrieved from.http://technologyforcommunities.com/

Wenger, E., White, N., & Smith, J. (2009). *Digital habitats: Stewarding technology for communities.* Portland, OR: CPsquare.

Wenger, E., White, N., Smith, J., & Rowe, K. (2005). Technology for communities. In Langelier, L. (Ed.), *Working, learning and collaborating in a network: Guide to the implementation and leadership of intentional communities of practice* (pp. 71–94). Quebec City, QC, Canada: CEFIRO.

Wenger, L., McDermott, R., & Synder, W. M. (2002). *Cultivating communities of practice.* Cambridge, MA: Harvard Business School Press.

Wertsch, J. V. (1991). *Voices of the mind: A sociocultural approach to mediated action.* Cambridge, MA: Harvard University Press.

Wickens, C. D. (1980). The structure of attentional resources. In Nickerson, R. (Ed.), *Attention and performance VIII* (pp. 239–257). Mahwah, NJ: Lawrence Erlbaum.

Wickens, C. D. (2002). Multiple resources and performance prediction. *Theoretical Issues in Ergonomics Science, 3*(2), 159–177. doi:10.1080/14639220210123806

Wiesner, K., Foth, M., & Bilandzic, M. (2009). Unleashing creative writers: Situated engagement with mobile narratives. In *Proceedings of the 21st Annual Conference of the Australian Computer-Human Interaction Special Interest Group: Design: Open 24/7*, Melbourne, Australia (pp. 373-376).

Wijers, M., Jonker, V., & Drijvers, P. (2010). MobileMath: Exploring mathematics outside the classroom. *ZDM*, 1-11.

Williams, B., & Bearman, M. (2008). Podcasting lectures: The next silver bullet? *Journal of Emergency Primary Health Care, 6*(3), 1–14.

Willmott, H. (1995). Managing the academics: Commodification and control in the development of university education in the UK. *Human Relations, 48*(9), 993–1028. doi:10.1177/001872679504800902

Wilson, D., Andrews, B., & Dale, C. (2009). Choreo:pod: Dance and the iPod towards blended learning. *International Journal of Mobile and Blended Learning, 1*(1), 49–60. doi:10.4018/jmbl.2009010104

Wingkvist, A., & Ericsson, M. (2009). Addressing sustainability for research initiatives in mobile learning through scalability. In *Proceedings of the IASTED International Conference, Web-based Education (WBE 2009)*.

Winn, J., & Heeter, C. (2009). Gaming, gender, and time: Who makes time to play. *Sex Roles, 61*(1), 1–13. doi:10.1007/s11199-009-9595-7

Winter, M., & Pemberton, L. (2010). *Unearthing invisible buildings: Device focus and device sharing in a collaborative mobile learning activity*. Paper presented at the 9th International Conference on Mobile Learning.

Winters, N., & Price, S. (2005). Mobile HCI and the learning context: An exploration. In *Proceedings of the International Workshop on Context in Mobile HCI*, Salzburg, Germany.

Wishart, J. (2007). *The seven 'c's - no, eight - no nine 'c's of m-learning*. Paper presented at the Kaleidoscope Alpine Rendez-Vous, Villars, Switzerland.

Wobbrock, J. (2006). The future of mobile device research in HCI. In *Proceedings of the Workshop on Next Generation of Human-Computer Interaction* (pp. 131-134).

Worsley, P. (1957). *The trumpet shall sound: A study of "cargo" cults in Melanesia*. London, UK: MacGibbon & Kee.

Wyatt, T. H., Krauskopf, P. B., Gaylord, N. M., Ward, A., Huffstutler-Hawkins, S., & Goodwin, L. (2010). Cooperative m-learning with nurse practitioner students. *Nursing Education Perspectives, 31*(2), 109–112.

Wynekoop, J., & Conger, S. (1990). A review of computer aided software engineering research methods. In *Proceedings of IFIP TC8, WG 8.2: Working Conference on The Information Systems Research Arena of The 90's*, Copenhagen, Denmark.

Yatigammana Ekanayake, T. M. S. (2009). *Mobile phones for teaching and learning science*. Retrieved from http://www.schoolnet.lk/research/mobile_phones_for_teaching_learning_science/

Yau, J., & Joy, M. (2006). Context-aware and adaptive learning schedule for mobile learning. In *Proceedings of the International Workshop on Mobile and Ubiquitous Learning and the International Conference on Computers in Education* (p. 31).

Yiannoutsou, N., & Avouris, N. (2010). Reflections on use of location-based playful narratives for learning. In *Proceedings of the IADIS International Conference on Mobile Learning*, Porto, Portugal (pp. 149-156).

Yin, R. K. (2003). *Case study research: Design and methods* (3rd ed., *Vol. 5*). Thousand Oaks, CA: Sage.

Yordanova, K. (2007). Mobile learning and integration of advanced technologies in education. In *Proceedings of the International Conference on Computer Systems and Technologies* (pp. 1-5).

Zijdewind, I., van Duinen, H., Zielman, R., & Lorist, M. M. (2006). Interaction between force production and cognitive performance in humans. *Clinical Neurophysiology, 117*, 660–667. doi:10.1016/j.clinph.2005.11.016

Zurita, G., & Nussbaum, M. (2004). A constructivist mobile learning environment supported by a wireless handheld network. *Journal of Computer Assisted Learning, 20*(4). doi:10.1111/j.1365-2729.2004.00089.x

About the Contributors

David Parsons is Associate Professor of Information Technology at Massey University, Auckland, New Zealand. He has a PhD in Information Technology from Nottingham Trent University (UK) and a Master's degree in Computer Science from the University of Southampton (UK), and has wide experience in both academia and the IT industry. He is the founding editor in chief of the International Journal of Mobile and Blended Learning (IJMBL) and author of a number of texts on computer programming, web application development and mobile learning. His work has been published in many international journals, including Computers & Education, IEEE Transactions on Learning Technologies and Software Practice and Experience. He chaired the Conference on Mobile Learning Technologies and Applications in 2007 and was co-editor of 'Innovative Mobile Learning: Techniques and Technologies' (Information Science Reference, 2009). He also edits the annual compilations of papers from IJMBL that are published as a regular series of books. He is a member of the International Association for Mobile Learning and a professional member of the British Computer Society.

* * *

John Traxler is Professor of Mobile Learning, probably the world's first, and Director of the Learning Lab at the University of Wolverhampton. He is a Founding Director of the International Association for Mobile Learning, Associate Editor of the *International Journal of Mobile and Blended Learning* and of *Interactive Learning Environments*. He is on the Editorial Board of *Research in Learning Technology* and *IT in International Development*. He was Conference Chair of *mLearn2008*, the world's biggest and oldest mobile learning research conference. He has guest edited three special editions of peer-reviewed journals devoted to mobile learning including *Distance Education*. He is now editing an African edition of the *International Journal of Mobile and Blended Learning*. John has co-written a guide to mobile learning in developing countries and is co-editor of the definitive book, *Mobile Learning: A Handbook for Educators and Trainers*, with Professor Agnes Kukulska-Hulme. They are working a second book together on contextual mobile learning. He has written more than 16 book chapters on mobile learning, and talks and writes frequently on the consequences of connectedness and mobility on learning, knowledge and societies.

Anna Wingkvist earned her PhD in Computer Science in 2009 from Växjö University, Växjö, Sweden. Currently, she is an Assistant Professor at the School of Computer Science, Physics and Mathematics, Linnaeus University, Växjö, Sweden. Her scientific interests and publications are mainly in the mobile learning domain with a focal point from an information systems development perspective, methodological and research methods reasoning, and project management. She has also been involved in utilizing podcasts in higher education as a learning tool.

Morgan Ericsson received his Ph.D. in Computer Science in 2008 from Växjö University, Växjö, Sweden. He is currently a Post-doctoral Fellow at the Department of Information Technology, Uppsala University, Sweden. His research interests are on how to best use technology to enhance learning and education, with a special focus on connected, mobile devices and personal learning. Software plays a major part in this research, and he has been involved in the creation of programming models and software development frameworks to aid developers working with Internet services and mobile devices.

Pamela Pollara is a Doctoral Candidate in Educational Technology at Louisiana State University. Her focus of study is on mobile learning and the formal and informal uses of mobile devices in the classroom. Ms. Pollara received her Bachelor of Arts degree in Journalism (summa cum laude) from Duquesne University in 2004 and her Master of Science degree in Secondary English/Language Arts Education from Duquesne University in 2007.

Kelly Broussard is a Highly Qualified Social Studies Teacher. Mrs. Broussard received her Bachelors of Education in Secondary Social Studies from Louisiana State University in 2003 and is currently pursuing a Masters degree in Educational Technology from Louisiana State University. Mrs. Broussard has 7 years of teaching experience teaching Honors and regular sections of World History and American History.

Marcus Winter is a Research Fellow in the Interactive Technologies Research Group at the University of Brighton. He has a background in computing, where he focused on the development of animation authoring tools. His experience in setting up and running an online animation community for children sparked a more general interest in the use of technology for creative purposes and how this can be leveraged to support formal and informal learning. As a researcher he has worked on several TEL projects, funded by JISC, the Technology Strategy Board and the European Commission, exploring augmented reality and ubiquitous computing technologies in educational contexts. His most recent work focuses on mobile content generation and sharing for situated language learning.

Lyn Pemberton is a Reader in Human Computer Interaction in the University of Brighton's School of Computing, Engineering and Maths. She has worked on many learning technology projects, mostly concerned with aspects of communication, writing and language learning, reflecting her background in language, AI and HCI. Most recently she has been involved in projects involving interactive television for learning, augmented reality and in particular mobile learning. The Technology Strategy Board-funded project Invisible Buildings used context-aware mobiles to encourage schoolchildren to play an archaeology-themed game based on the Time Team concept. Through two recent JISC- funded projects, she has been exploring mobile techniques for integrating material captured in everyday life into classroom teaching. This continues in her current EU-funded Lifelong Learning project SIMOLA, which provides situated support for language learners across six European countries plus Japan.

Elizabeth FitzGerald is an Associate Research Fellow at the Learning Sciences Research Institute at the University of Nottingham. She has a BSc in Environmental Life Science and a PhD in Computer Science, both from the University of Nottingham and has previously worked as a secondary school teacher. Her work combines ubiquitous computing, usability and interaction design with education and pedagogy. Her current research focuses on geolocated user-generated content for informal learning and she is also investigating the use of audio narratives for effective visitor experiences.

Mike Sharples is Professor of Learning Sciences and Director of the Learning Sciences Research Institute at the University of Nottingham. He has an international reputation for research in mobile learning and the design of learning technologies. He inaugurated the mLearn conference series and was founding President of the International Association for Mobile Learning. He is author of over 200 publications in the areas of educational technology, interactive systems design and artificial intelligence.

Robert Jones is a PhD student at the Horizon Doctoral Training Centre/Learning Sciences Research Institute at the University of Nottingham in 2009. With a background in linguistics and theatre studies, his research focuses on exploring the literary and emotional effects of interactive fiction. Bringing together findings from psychology, language studies and critical theories of game and play, he is working to form a cognition-based model of how interactivity affects our processing of narrative and conceptions of literary effect within such works.

Gary Priestnall is an Associate Professor within the School of Geography at the University of Nottingham. He has a BSc in Geography from Durham University and a PhD in Computer Science from the University of Nottingham. His research interests are focused in the area of geographic representation and visualisation. This includes landscape visualisation; technologies for augmenting reality; GPS-enabled mobile computing and locative media; Digital Heritage applications; geospatial models; and Geo-Art collaborations.

Andrew Middleton is an educational developer based in the Learning and Teaching Institute at Sheffield Hallam University. He teaches Creativity in various disciplines, researches academic innovation and literacy, and is an active member of the Media-Enhanced Learning Special Interest Group. He runs workshops on how Digital Voice techniques, like media-enhanced feedback, are being used in higher and further education.

Joke Coens is a doctoral student at the Katholieke Universiteit Leuven Kulak and member of the Center for Instructional Psychology and Technology. Her research focuses on the use of mobile technologies in higher education and more in particular on the multitasking aspect of it. Geraldine Clarebout and Bert Reynvoet are the supervisors of her research project.

Ellen Degryse was a masters student at the Katholieke Universiteit Leuven. She was involved in a research project on mobile learning, podcasting an multitasking within the scope of her masters thesis.

Marie-Paul Senecaut is a clinical psychologist who is presently engaged in the MAPLE-project (Mobile, Adaptive & Personalized Learning Experience) of the Interdisciplinary Research on Technology, Education and Communication Center. She is also involved in research on multitasking in mobile learning. She combines this with a private practice as a therapist.

Jorge Cottyn is a lecturer in Physical Education Teacher Training at the Katholieke Hogeschool Zuid-West-Vlaanderen, Department of Education RENO. His research interests are mobile learning, observational learning, video feedback and motivational processes.

Geraldine Clarebout is assistant professor at the Katholieke Universiteit Leuven and member of the Center for Instructional Psychology and Technology and the Interdisciplinary Research on Technology, Education and Communication group. Her research focuses on the design of learning environments and the use of technology in education. She teaches basic courses in learning and instruction, and more advanced courses on educational technology.

Laurel Evelyn Dyson is a Senior Lecturer in Information Technology at the University of Technology Sydney. Her research focuses on mobile learning and the use of mobile technologies by Indigenous people. She has over 20 years experience teaching in the university and adult education sector where she seeks to create innovative ways of engaging all students in their learning, including student-generated mLearning, mobile-supported fieldwork and interactive classroom systems. She is President and founder of anzMLearn, the Australian and New Zealand Mobile Learning Group.

Andrew Litchfield is a Senior Lecturer in the Faculty of Engineering and Information Technology (FEIT) at the University of Technology, Sydney, and co-ordinates the Faculty's Technology and Education Design and Development (TEDD) Research Group. He has extensive professional experience in media production and the design and management of successful innovative educational projects through his production company Positive Image Ltd. He is an award-winning producer and director of many large-scale video projects. His current research interests include active experiential mobile learning, the diffusion of innovations, work-ready curriculum renewal, self and peer assessment and the design of mixed-media and online educational resources.

Anu Seisto (PhD) has a Doctoral Degree in Pulping Technology from Helsinki University of Technology (1998). She is currently the Team Manager of User Centric Media Concepts at VTT. She started her career by looking at the possibilities of utilizing organic solvents for producing paper for publishing and packaging purposes. In 2001 she started a new group at KCL, the research institute for the Finnish forest industry, to study the future use of paper based materials. The group concentrated on consumer studies and utilized methodology to study consumer perception and human technology interaction. In 2009 the whole group moved to VTT, the Technical Research Institute in Finland and continued consumer studies in the field of Media Technology. The main focus in the studies of the group is still in reading products and packages, but recent studies have also been made in the field of hybrid media combining print and digital media. Since 2001 the group has produced 9 MSc Theses works, 1 PhD, 20 conference papers and several confidential reports for the Finnish forest industry.

Maija Federley, M.Sc. (Tech.), is a research scientist at VTT Technical Research Centre of Finland. After graduation from Helsinki University of Technology she worked in the field of process modeling and analysis at KCL, the research institute for the Finnish forest industry. In 2005 she joined the research group studying the future use of paper based materials. Since that, she has been involved in projects that are focused on user-centric development of new product concepts for media, packaging and technology enhanced learning, particularly mobile learning. Her other areas of interest are human-technology interaction and applications of printed intelligence.

Timo Kuula (M.Ed.) graduated from University of Helsinki. He has a degree in adult education, including studies in media education and social psychology. Since his Master's Thesis, he has been interested in media use and media technologies. Currently Timo works as a research scientist at VTT Technical Research Centre of Finland. His main area of research is pedagogical and user-centric design of ICT-based learning solutions. Timo's other areas of interest include mobile learning, development of learning materials, social media and reading habits.

Janne Paavilainen is a project manager at the Game Research Lab, University of Tampere, Finland. He has been involved in several games research projects focusing on casual, mobile, educational and social games, and he has published several articles on these domains. Janne's interests in games research are in design and evaluation methods, especially in heuristics. Currently Janne is working in the SoPlay project studying games and play in social media. His current task is to develop design and evaluation heuristics for Facebook social games. Janne holds a master's degree in economics and is currently planning his Ph.D. studies focusing on usability, playability and user experience in first-person shooter games.

Sami Vihavainen, M.Sc., is a researcher at Helsinki Institute for Information Technology HIIT where he is a member of Self Made Media research group. He is also a doctoral student at the Department of Human Centered Technology in Tampere University of Technology. During 2007-2008 Vihavainen acted as a Visiting research scholar at University of California Berkeley's School of Information for 1,5 year. Sami's research interests consist of understanding people's use of media in their everyday lives and use that understanding for designing new media services. His doctoral thesis (in progress) concentrates on studying user's interaction with automation in everyday social applications. He has several publications on the implications of media technology to people's everyday social interaction.

Jalal Nouri is following the postgraduate program in Human-Machine Interaction at the Department of Computer and System Sciences, Stockholm University, Sweden, and taking part in the Swedish National Research School in Cognitive Science. Before starting his PhD studies he did a MSc in Mathematics and a MSc in Education. His research interest has a strong focus on pedagogical design aspects of technology enhanced learning in general and of mobile learning in particular.

Teresa Cerratto-Pargman is associate professor of Human-Computer Interaction (HCI) at the department of Computer and Systems Sciences (DSV)at Stockholm University (SU). She works with a particular focus on design, adoption and use of technologies for reflective and collaborative purposes. Teresa has published over 70 articles in international journals, refereed conferences, books and technical reports. She has also been presenting and giving lectures about her work in Sweden and abroad. During the last years she has been serving as a program committee member in a number of international scientific conferences. At the present, Teresa is the scientific responsible for the research network Nordic LEAF (Learning ecosystems and activities of the future) funded by NordForsk.http://nordicleaf.info/.

Johan Eliasson is following the postgraduate program in Human-Machine Interaction at the Department of Computer and System Sciences, Stockholm University, Sweden, and taking part in the Swedish National Research School in Cognitive Science. Before starting his PhD studies he did a MSc in Computer Science: Human-Computer Interaction and MA in Computer and Systems Science: Cognitive Science. His current research has a focus on interaction design for location-based and contextual learning activities supported by mobile devices.

Robert Ramberg got his PhD in cognitive psychology at the department of psychology, Stockholm University and now holds a position as professor at the department of computer- and systems sciences at Stockholm University (SU). At the department he is the research director of K2-lab (the Knowledge and Communication Laboratory). He has published numerous articles in journals and refereed conferences. He has served as program committee and editorial board member for several international conferences as well as acted as reviewer for several international journals within the field of technology enhanced learning.

Susan Gwee is a Ph.D. candidate at the National Institute of Education, Nanyang Technological University in Singapore. Her research interests include mobile learning, literacies, and assessment.

Yam San Chee is an Associate Professor in the Learning Sciences & Technologies Academic Group and the Learning Sciences Lab at the National Institute of Education, Nanyang Technological University, Singapore. His research focuses on new literacies and new media in education, with a special emphasis on game-based learning. Recent games developed for research include *Space Station Leonis* and *Escape from Centauri 7*. Current games developed through National Research Foundation funding are *Legends of Alkhimia* and *Statecraft X*. Chee was the founding executive editor of *Research and Practice in Technology Enhanced Learning*, the journal of the Asia-Pacific Society for Computers in Education. He is currently an Associate Editor of the *International Journal of Gaming and Computer-Mediated Simulations* and an Advisory Board Member of *Journal of Educational Technology and Society*.

Ek Ming Tan is a trained schoolteacher on secondment to the Learning Sciences Lab, National Institute of Education, Singapore, as a Lecturer (Research). He obtained his BArts from the National University of Singapore and a Masters in education from the University of Western Australia. Prior to his current position, he was a level head in a Singapore Secondary School and acting head of Department for English Language and Literature.

Lisa Soon is a lecturer in Central Queensland University, Mackay, Australia. She holds a Bachelor of Information Technology from Queensland University of Technology, Australia, and Master of Arts (International Studies) as well as Doctor of Philosophy from Griffith University, Australia. She has considerable industrial as well as academic experience. She is a member of the Institute of Electrical and Electronics Engineers, Association for Computing Machinery, Australian Computer Society and Australian Institute of Export. Her main research interests include knowledge management, knowledge and technology, and knowledge in online learning.

Vani Kalloo is currently pursuing an M.Phil. in Computer Science at the University of the West Indies, St. Augustine, Trinidad and Tobago. She is currently doing research work in mobile learning for mathematics with secondary school students, game-based learning and personalization. She was a secondary school teacher for four years and is currently a Teaching Assistant at the University of the West Indies.

Permanand Mohan is a Senior Lecturer in Computer Science in the Department of Computing and Information Technology at the University of the West Indies, St. Augustine Campus in Trinidad and Tobago. He has a Ph.D. in Computer Science. Dr. Mohan was a Fulbright Visiting Scholar to the School of Information Sciences at the University of Pittsburgh. He was the principal investigator of a Microsoft Research funded mobile health project for diabetic patients. He is currently working on several research projects investigating the use of mobile technology to provide on-going education to diabetic patients and to support the learning of mathematics at the secondary level. He presently supervises several post-graduate students in the areas of mobile health, mobile learning, e-learning, and games for learning. Dr. Mohan is also the Chief Examiner of the Caribbean's CXC CAPE Examinations in Computer Science.

Claire Bradley (MA) is a Research Fellow at the Learning Technology Research Institute. For the past 14 years she has worked on a number of UK and European research projects involved in mLearning, eLearning, online communities, multimedia and the general application and evaluation of digital technologies in teaching and learning. She has co-authored a number of journal articles and papers in these areas. Her current interests are in looking at the potential to harness students' own mobile devices for mobile learning and looking at current student mLearning practice.

Debbie Holley (PhD MSc FCILT MCIPS FHEA FRSA) is a Principal Lecturer in the Faculty of Education at Anglia Ruskin University. Debbie uses a range of innovative technologies to engage her students both inside and outside the classroom. She is interested on digital literacies for students, and is part of the JISC funded Anytime Learning Literacies Environment (ALLE) project. Her research interests include second life for educational purposes, web 2.0 technologies for communication and collaboration and the creative curriculum initiative.

Index